Morocco

Fodor's Morocco

Editor: Andrew E. Beresky
Contributors: Penny Gibbins, Peter Hiett, Carolyn Price
Art Director: Fabrizio La Rocca
Cartographer: Swanston Graphics, Raymond Xhardez
Illustrator: W. Rondas, Beryl Sanders
Cover Photograph: Boisberranger/Viesti Associates

Design: Vignelli Associates

Special Sales

Fodor's Travel Publications are available at special discounts for bulk purchases
(100 copies or more) for sales promotions or premiums. Special editions,
including personalized covers, excerpts of existing guides, and corporate
imprints, can be created in large quantities for special needs. For more
information write to Special Marketing, Fodor's Travel Publications, 201 East
50th St., New York, NY 10022. Inquiries from the United Kingdom should be
sent to Fodor's Travel Publications, 20 Vauxhall Bridge Rd., London, England
SW1V 2SA.

Fodor's

ELEVENTH EDITION
11th

MOROCCO

Previously published as *Fodor's North Africa*

FODOR'S TRAVEL PUBLICATIONS, INC.
New York & London

CONTENTS

CONTENTS

FOREWORD

Wrapped around the northwest corner of Africa, fronting the Atlantic and the Mediterranean, lie three countries—Morocco, Algeria and Tunisia (we have placed them geographically in this book, from west to east). Between them they encompass hundreds of miles of beaches, shelving into peacock-blue water; cities, oases and caverns that hold in their hearts historical mysteries reaching back into the dawn of time; mountain ranges so toweringly impressive that they take their name from a Titan who was compelled to hold up the sky; vast stretches of desert, apparently dead, but actually teeming with strange life; a bewildering variety of tribes and races—and everywhere color, diversity and fascination.

This is the nearest Islamic region to both Western Europe and the eastern coast of the States, the easiest point to reach from both, where mosque and minaret, Roman arch and souk provide the background for a vacation to remember.

With no geographical north-south boundaries, these three countries have shared a common fate, especially during their formative periods. Now, their constitutions vary radically, one a multi-party constitutional monarchy, one a People's republic with a socialist economy, and the third a parliamentary republic with a free-enterprise system. Yet, in spite of their widely divergent politics, they share bonds of race, language, and—above all—religion. They also share a privileged climate—throughout the year the sunworshipper can bask somewhere, the mountaineer and skier can enjoy the pleasures of high places, the intrepid traveler can visit romantically out-of-the-way spots.

Morocco and Tunisia have invested huge sums in developing their tourist attractions and have a fairly sophisticated tourism infrastructure as a result. Algeria has concentrated on industry rather than tourism, so that its hotels and restaurants often lack international polish. Yet Algeria's inherently interesting milieu makes the excitement of a trip to this unusual destination worthwhile.

*

We owe a debt of gratitude to the many friends who have helped us with the preparation of this edition of our guide to North Africa. Among the officials of the three countries who have extended their kindness and interest during our work we would like to thank especially—Taieb Hachaichi, head of marketing, Hatem Aouij, head of public relations, Mme. Bardak, and Mohammed Essayem at the Tunisia National Tourist Office, Tunis; Saf Houssine, Information Ministry. Mohammed Amedjahdi, Mohammed Arron, and Mme. Souad Benazzou at the Tourism Ministry, Morocco; Abdellah Jmamou and Abderramane Ouakim at the National Tourist Office, Morocco; and Boukhelifa, sales director at O.N.A.T. (Office National Algérien de Tourisme) and British embassy staff in Algeria.

*

All prices quoted in this guide are based on those supplied to us in mid 1990. Given the volatility of exchange rates and market forces, it is inevitable that changes will have taken place by the time this book becomes available. We hope, therefore, that you will take such prices as indicators only and be sure to double-check on the latest figures.

*

While every care has been taken to assure the accuracy of the information in this guide, the passage of time will always bring change, and consequently the publisher cannot accept responsibility for errors that may occur.

All prices and opening times quoted in this guide are based on information supplied to us at press time. Hours and admission fees may change, however, and the prudent traveler will avoid inconvenience by calling ahead.

Fodor's wants to hear about your travel experiences, both pleasant and unpleasant. When a hotel or restaurant fails to live up to its billing, let us know and we will investigate the complaint and revise our entries where the facts warrant it.

Send your letters to the editors of Fodor's Travel Publications, 201 E. 50th Street, New York, NY 10022.

PLANNING YOUR TRIP

WHAT IT WILL COST. Much will depend on how you travel and what kind of amusement you take in, whether you are on a package tour (particularly suited for North Africa) or a pay-as-you-go, go-where-you-please traveler. We suggest in each country section how much it will cost to visit and travel on four price levels: luxury, expensive, moderate and inexpensive.

Luxury (L) means staying in the top-grade hotels, eating in the best restaurants, traveling by plane, by chauffeur-driven car or your own, and devoting several evenings to nightclub entertainment.

Expensive (E) means staying in first-class hotels, having a room with a bath, but not at the highest levels, eating in good restaurants, traveling first class by train, in a privately-owned or rented car without chauffeur, and taking in various evening entertainments.

Moderate (M) means staying in second-class hotels, eating in decent quality restaurants that are often jammed because their moderate prices attract numerous customers, traveling by bus or train, and taking your evening entertainment modestly, or in a café over a glass of wine.

Inexpensive (I) means staying in the cheapest of the classified hotels, which may be just as clean (or dirty) as the next place, but will probably also be used by the locals. Most importantly it will probably mean eating out, and relying on excursions and your own sense of adventure for entertainment (the low-life recorded by the French Romantics Delacroix and Flaubert in their journals may give you a few clues).

EXCHANGE RATES. Because of constantly changing exchange rates, prices are given only in local currency. Even so, inflationary trends make accurate budgeting long in advance an impossibility. Prices mentioned throughout this title are indicative only of costs at time of going to press. Check with your travel agent near the time of your trip.

We give the rates of exchange of each of the three currencies at time of going to press, in the *Facts at your Fingertips* for each country.

WHEN TO GO. In the Maghreb the tourist season lasts the whole year round—but not in the same regions. January and February are the peak months for the desert and the inland south. Their season begins in November or late October, and lasts until May. Spring (March–May) is a lovely time for seeing the spring flowers in the mountain regions and much of the inland area. Summer (late May to September) is the best period for the seaside, both the Atlantic and Mediterranean coasts, though winters are mild along the Med. shore and at Agadir, on the far southern Atlantic coast.

October and early November, often the year's driest period, can be the best season for touring by road. From December to April good skiing may be enjoyed on the Moroccan and Algerian mountains.

Don't believe that the Maghreb is always hot. No matter what the time of year, part of it will be at least pleasantly cool. The Algerian High Plateaux are icy cold in winter, and unless you are flying to the oases, snow may block the mountain passes in Algeria as well as in Morocco. One road to the oases goes through Ifrane, where Morocco's lowest ever temperature was recorded, while the skiing and desert seasons were both at their peak. The thermometer, in fact, sank to −13°F, and anyone who was following the often-given advice to take only tropical clothes must have been in a decidedly poor way.

Similarly, get the idea that the Maghreb is dry out of your mind. It isn't. July and August may be the driest months, but that doesn't mean that rain stops completely, even in the south. A torrential thundery downpour can produce a flash flood capable of folding up a reinforced concrete bridge like a bit of waste paper. Rain doesn't last long in summer, but it can be fierce for an hour or two. It is usually heaviest in December to February, and flooding is not uncommon. In spring it can be wet for days at a time.

For farmers in the Maghreb, too much rain too often falls too quickly at the wrong time. But at least, for the tourist, that leaves plenty of time for the sun. There are about 3,000 to 3,250 hours of sunshine a year in most spots.

Important Note. The month of Ramadan is strictly observed in Morocco and Algeria, slightly less noticeably in Tunisia. Public services, banks, offices, shops, and even transport move at half speed. Tourists isolated in vacation complexes in Moroccan or Tunisian beach resorts will feel little inconvenience, as hotels and restaurants are tuned to their needs. Any reluctance to consume food and drink in view of the fasting population is most laudable, but most eating places in the popular quarters are closed anyway from sunrise to sundown. In Algeria, which is less tourist-oriented, most restaurants and even some provincial hotels may be closed. A careful check should be made before setting out.

HOW TO COORDINATE THE CALENDARS. If you are a folklore enthusiast, and particularly interested in Moslem traditions, you may wish to go to the Maghreb at the time of a religious festival. However, the average tourist is more likely to avoid Ramadan, when for one month life practically comes to a standstill during the day, while nights are given over to noisy festivities. Exact dates are hard to determine, as not only is the Moslem year shorter than the Gregorian year (354 days, or 355 days in leap years), but their calendar starts with the date of the emigration of the Prophet from Mecca to Medina, on Friday, July 16, A.D. 622 (the *Hegira* or *Hijra,* abbreviated to A.H. for Anno Hegirae).

It is advisable therefore to check the dates of various religious festivals at any of the Maghreb National Tourist Offices.

Months of the Mohammedan Year

Muharram	Jumada I	Ramadan
Safar	Jumada II	Shawwal
Rabia I	Rajab	Zu'lkadah
Rabia II	Shaban	Zu'lhijjah

Whether a month has 29 or 30 days depends on the moon, or rather when it is sighted. On the 29th of each lunar month, the *ulema* in each Moslem country, watch for the new moon from a high place at sunset. If the moon is not visible when the sun has gone down, the month will have 30 days. Two 29-day or two 30-day months might thus occur in succession, but not necessarily in all the Moslem countries. This calendar is used to determine religious festivals only, while for everyday life the western calendar is observed, even in Algeria, where the weekly holiday is Friday, while it is Sunday in the two other countries.

The variable religious holidays are the same throughout the Maghreb. Here are the most important ones: Ras el Am, New Year's Day; Ashoura, Memorial Day; Mouloud, anniversary of the birth of Mohammed; Aid-es-Seghir, the end of Ramadan; Aid-el-Kebir, celebrated in spiritual communion with the pilgrims to Mecca, commemorating Abraham's willingness to sacrifice his son.

Ras el Am, Mouloud, Aid-es-Seghir and Aid-el-Kebir are public holidays. Ceremonies at Kairouan take place on Mouloud. Non-Moslems are welcome. Aid-es-

Seghir and Aid-el-Kebir are more family holidays. At the time of Aid-es-Seghir, candy and toys are distributed to the children. Aid-el-Kebir is marked by the sacrifice of a sheep.

TRAVEL AGENTS. Once you decide where you want to go, your next step is to consult a good travel agent. The American Society of Travel Agents, Box 23992, Washington, DC 20026–3992; or the Association of British Travel Agents, 55–57 Newman Street, London W1, will advise you. The *American Automobile Association,* World Wide Travel Division, 8111 Gatehouse Road, Falls Church, VA 22042, can also help you plan overseas travel.

If you wish your agent to book you on a package tour, reserve your transportation and even your first overnight hotel accommodation, his services should cost you nothing. Most carriers and tour operators grant him a fixed commission for saving them the expense of having to open individual offices in every town and city. If, on the other hand, you wish him to plan for you an individual itinerary and make all arrangements down to hotel reservations and transfers to and from rail and air terminals, he will make a service charge on the total cost of your planned itinerary. This charge may amount to 10 or 15%, but it will more likely *save* you money on balance.

There are many opportunities on offer for Morocco and Tunisia and far fewer for Algeria. This reflects the state of tourist development in each country, but does not reflect necessarily the interest that the particular country can hold for the visitor. We list a few of the available programs, but suggest that you contact your travel agent for a fuller exploration of what can be found. You might find that to cross the Atlantic on a cheap fare and pick up a tour from Britain would be advantageous, but of course this will mean booking the tour in advance, as they are very popular.

From the U.S. Of the many tours available, some cover Morocco exclusively while others link Morocco with, for example, Spain and Portugal, or Egypt, or Greece. Prices listed below are accurate as of this writing (May 1990) but are intended for reference purposes only. Unless otherwise noted, roundtrip airfare from your point of departure must be added.

Maupintour, Box 807, Lawrence, KS 66044 (tel. 800–255–6162) has a 16-day *Moroccan Treasures* package (about $2,598) that adds Tetuan, Chauen, Fez, Meknès, Erfoud, Ouarzazate, and Marrakesh to the main sights of Tangier, Rabat, and Casablanca.

Le Soleil Tours, 25 W. 39th St., Suite 902, New York, NY 10018 (212–869–1040), run by Moroccan Azzeddine (Alan) Bennouna, has a 10-day tour, *Thousand Kingdoms* ($780), which includes half-board, a car, 4-star hotels, tax, and insurance.

Persepolis Travel, 501 Fifth Ave., Rm. 1414, New York, NY 10017 (212–972–1333), has two 8-day deluxe tours, *Desert Song* and *Imperial Cities,* both featuring transport by air-conditioned, chauffeured limousine (from $565). The 12-day *Pyramids and Kasbahs* tour combines Egypt with Morocco (from $2,215). Marsans International, 19 W. 34th St., Suite 3302, New York, NY 10001 (212–239–3880), begins (and ends) its tours of North Africa from Spain. Trips run from four to fourteen days and cost from $343 to $1239.

For the more adventurous, Forum Travel International, 91 Gregory Lane, Ste. 21, Pleasant Hill, CA 94523 (415–671–2900), and Turtle Tours, Box 1147, 9446 Quail Trail, Carefree, AZ 85377 (800–283–2334 or 602–488–3688) specialize in hiking, trekking, and what are called "overland" tours (in which you travel in a 4-wheel drive vehicle over the sort of terrain that a tour motorcoach won't normally attempt). These tours tend to be more expensive (around $1,000 to $3,000) and take smaller groups (4–10 people).

From the U.K. The major Moroccan specialist in Britain is Morocco Bound Travel, Suite 603, Triumph House, 189 Regent St., London W1R 7WB (071–734 5307). A wide variety of tours is on offer. *Discovery of Morocco* lasts 15 days, and visits a great deal of the country by bus. Prices are £756–£894, full board, twin sharing. *Great South and Casbah Tour* lasts 9 nights and costs £473–£530 per person. The tour includes visits to Marrakesh, Segora, El Kelaa, Des, and M'Gouna. There's an option of going to Mohammedia (this costs extra). The *Imperial Cities Tour* is an 8-day bus trip that takes in the imperial sites. Prices are £478–£1,215 full board.

Swan Hellenic Art Treasures Tours, 77 New Oxford St., London WC1A 1PP (tel. 071–831 1616) have an excellent 13-day tour of Tunisia accompanied by an expert in Tunisian art and history. The tour takes in all the major sites of historic and artistic interest—Tunis, Maktar, Sfax, Sousse and Carthage among them—and costs £1,065.

For bird watchers there is a very special trip arranged by Sunbird, P.O. Box 76, Sandy, Bedfordshire SG19 1DF (tel. 0767 682969). Every November they organize a tour to Agadir, to watch a magnificent variety of birds on the Sous estuary—greater flamingos, terns, bulbuls, redstarts, crested larks, the bald ibis, marbled ducks, pallid swifts . . . the exotic list is seemingly endless. One week in Agadir costs £715.

WHAT TO TAKE. The first principle is to travel light. Do not take more than you can carry yourself; it's a lifesaver if you go to places where porters are hard to find. It's a good idea to pack the bulk of your things in one large bag and put everything you need for overnight, or for two or three nights, in another. Motorists should limit luggage to what can be locked into the trunk when making stops.

Clothing. In summer, pack plenty of light clothes, plus a sweater and perhaps warm slacks for a cool evening or a trip through mountain forests, which can be distinctly cold even in summer: the desert too gets very cold at night. In spring and autumn, add at least a light waterproof. Sunglasses and protective headgear are musts in summer and be sure to cover up in the sun. The long robes you see everyone wearing for just that purpose are called *fokia* if they are made of cotton and *caftan* if they are made of silk. *Jellabas*, which are often wool, are worn over the robe against the cold and they nearly always have a hood. Winter skiing needs normal gear. Warm clothing is also needed in winter on the northern part of Morocco's Atlantic coast, where misguided tourists often shiver in inappropriately light clothing.

Hotels used by business visitors, such as the Hyatt Regency and El Mansour at Casablanca, the Rabat Hyatt Regency, the Tunis Hilton, the Aurassi at Algiers, tend to be rather formal. The resort hotels are far more casual.

Medicines and toiletries. Take all the medicines, cosmetics and toiletries you think you may need. Most French brands are available throughout Morocco and Tunis, though American and English brands are rare. In Algeria it is mainly local products, so take your favorite brand of suntan lotion with you. Insect repellants will be useful, but toilet paper and Kleenex can be purchased anywhere.

TRAVEL DOCUMENTS. Americans: Major post offices and many county courthouses process passport applications, as do U.S. Passport Agency offices in various cities. If you still have your latest passport (issued within the last twelve years), you may use this to apply by mail. In addition to the completed application (Form DSP-11), new applicants will need:

1—proof of citizenship. An old passport, issued in your name, is acceptable, as is a birth certificate, though it must give your name, date, and place of birth, and show clearly the seal and signature of the registrar of births. Hospital and baptismal certificates are *not* acceptable;

2—two, recent, photos 2 inches square, full face, black and white or color, on nonglossy paper;

3—$35 for the passport itself plus a $7 processing fee (no fee when renewing your passport by mail) for those 18 and older; those under 18 pay $20, plus the $7 in-person processing fee;

4—proof of identity that includes a current photo and signature, such as a driver's license or government ID card. A previous passport is also acceptable.

When you get your passport, write down its number, date and place of issue. If it's lost or stolen, get in touch with the nearest American Consul, or the Passport Office, Department of State, 1425 K St. NW, Washington DC 20524.

British Subjects must apply for passports on special forms obtainable from the nearest head post office or your travel agent. The application must be countersigned by your bank manager or by a solicitor, barrister, doctor, clergyman or Justice of the Peace who knows you personally. You will need two photos and birth certificate. Fee—£15. Applications must be returned to the passport office dealing with the area where you live. These are listed on the application form. Allow at least five weeks for processing.

Canadians. Canadian citizens apply in person to regional passport offices or post offices, or by mail to the Bureau of Passports, External Affairs, Ottawa, Ontario, K1A OG3. A $25 fee, two photographs, a guarantor, and evidence of citizenship are required. Canadian passports are valid for five years; you must reapply for a new one.

Visas. Morocco and Tunisia do not require visas for nationals of the United States, United Kingdom, or most other countries. To visitors on a cruise the port-commissioner can issue a 72-hour landing permit if no passport can be produced. Algeria demands visas from holders of U.S., British, and Canadian passports.

Health Certificates. Not required for entry to any of the countries. Check what your own country demands when you return from any of the countries. In normal times the U.K. does not require special measures. But this may change in case of any outbreak not only in the Maghreb but also in neighboring countries. Canada and the U.S.A. do not require smallpox vaccination for returning residents.

Staying in North Africa

CUSTOMS. As frequently happens all over the world, customs officers are usually easy on package tours, perhaps because of the large numbers to be checked, but they are unpredictable with individual travelers, especially when they are unconventionally dressed. The search of luggage may be more thorough at land entry points, where there is much less traffic, than at airports and ports.

The usual international regulations on imports are applied: personal jewelry up to 500 grams, 1 bottle of spirits, 1 bottle of wine, 200 cigarettes or 50 cigars or 250 grams of tobacco. Tunisia generously doubles the tobacco ration.

MONEY. The exchange rates of the Moroccan Dirham (DH) as well as of the Algerian (DA) and Tunisian (DT) Dinars are fixed daily by the respective Central Bank. The Moroccan and Tunisian currencies are realistically adjusted, but the DA is maintained at an artificially high rate, four times its value outside Algeria and even more on the local black market. It is forbidden to import or to export any of the local currencies. Foreign currencies above the value of 5,000 DH or DA, and 500 DT, have to be declared on arrival for re-export. On exchanging at banks, exchange bureaus, travel agencies or authorized hotels (but not at shops), retain the receipts so as to convert excess money back for up to 30% of total currency exchanged. Better still, arrange to have no surplus on departure. Whatever the theoretical arrangements, it may in fact prove impossible to change it back at the last moment as the banks at airports and ports are rarely open at departure time, while on the land borders the customs authorities offer a decidedly one-way exchange into the local currency, but not from any of the other two countries, at least not officially, as this is illegal.

Banknotes are denominated in Arabic and French, but coins indicate their value only in Arabic. These are not difficult to understand: a thick vertical line is a one; a small square, zero; a kind of large comma, two; a heart, five.

We give further information about money in the individual *Facts at Your Fingertips* for each country.

CREDIT CARDS. Accepted in Luxury and most Expensive hotels, but in the latter rather capriciously, so that it would be rash to make any definite statement. Only a very few restaurants are willing to undertake the paper work—and lose the percentage. Except at the official craft cooperatives, it is not advisable to use credit cards at shops (see *Shopping*).

TIME. Maghreb time is the same as Greenwich Mean Time and five hours ahead of Eastern Standard Time. Summer time varies from country to country annually, as the clocks are put forward one or two hours. Morocco is usually one hour behind the other two countries. If Ramadan falls in summer, clocks may be put back to winter time, to make the day seem shorter.

LANGUAGE. To refer to Arabic as an intricate language is to indulge in the understatement of all time. It is a language, especially when written, of a complexity and convolution that will almost certainly defeat any vain attempt to master more than a few basic words. Moreover, the porter, waiter and similar victims of the earnest tourist are most unlikely to comprehend his well meant efforts and almost certainly speak very adequate French. The *Vocabulary* at the end of this volume is, therefore, given in French, with the strong recommendation to keep to it, with the possible exception of an occasional *salam* (greeting). There is, however, a glossary of Arab and Berber geographical as well as architectural terms and names, which have been adopted into French and, to a lesser degree, English. Being untranslatable, at least in one word, these terms have been employed throughout the text, especially the very special vocabulary of the Sahara, but always accompanied by an initial explanation.

The only rule of pronunciation is that there is none, or, if you prefer, so many and contradictory that it amounts to the same thing. Arabic is written in a Semitic script from right to left, which lends itself artistically to calligraphy as a major form of sacred decoration, but is almost impossible to render in English by transliteration. This is one reason for the bewildering inconsistency of spelling Arab words, which mixes Mohammed with Mohamed, Abd-el-Kader with Abdelkader, Oqba ibn-Nafi with Okba Ibn Nafaa. Bad editing? Perish the thought, the former is simply the official spelling in Morocco, the latter in Algeria, and in Tunisia it might be either. A new variation has recently been added by Morocco and Tunisia replacing time-honored dj by j. Just to simplify matters the following vowel might also be dropped in the process. Thus Fes Djedid is now printed on official handouts Jdid, and Djerba has become Jerba. But in Algeria a djebel (mountain) has not become a jebel, nor a jbel as on Moroccan maps. There is no way to escape this confusing tangle, once a fashion has become a practice and has proved its regional staying power.

Another complication, another but by no means the last, is the recent English fashion—tit for tat—of substituting u for ou in names, thus Abu instead of Abou. We have adopted this version in the text, but have necessarily retained the French spelling for places, as it appears on all maps, signboards, and street signs. So be prepared for plenty of fancy spellings. The question of capital or small initials is better left untouched.

As if this wasn't enough, here is a morsel of technical information that you will, of course, easily digest. Though the position of the thirty-one consonants, bilabial, labiodental, apical, palatal, velar, uvular, glottal and pharyngeal, with voiceless and voiced fricatives not to mention flap trills, is fixed, that of the six vowels is not; the a and e, o and u are freely interchangeable or might even be left out, at the speaker's choice, besides the fascinating gamut of elisions and inversions. As for diphthongs . . . Don't worry, all those you are likely to come into contact with are bilingual or speak at least adequate French.

HOTELS. Nearly all the hotels listed in Morocco and Tunisia and about one half of those in Algeria have been built or brought up to date during the last 35 years. However, the hotel building spree is over, at least for the present, as the tourist industry has been stagnating for the last couple of years in Morocco and Tunisia, and has never taken off in Algeria. Maintenance is frequently neglected, and modern amenities, especially airconditioning, are remarkable mainly for the number of times they fail to function. Plumbing is another weak point; hot water is not always available and cockroaches are common in the bathrooms. Lights are sufficient for dressing, but not for reading or writing. The international chains, represented by the French Club Méditerranée, Meridien, PLM and Sofitel, and the American Hilton, Hyatt and Sheraton, maintain their standards, but elsewhere comfort, service and, in rare cases, even cleanliness vary unpredictably in the occasional ups and more frequent downs of management changes. The ever larger holiday complexes face increasing difficulties in recruiting and retaining trained staff.

All classified hotels which are listed, as any selection, however carefully researched, would be necessarily arbitrary with such rapid changes in standards. Comments are therefore restricted, as they may be out of date before printing, thus giving rise to readers' complaints. The few exceptions to the rule that have proved their staying power over a number of years will gladly be pointed out in the *Practical Information* of the relevant chapters. Classification is based on price and potential facilities which remain constant among unpredictable performances. However, North African standards should not be compared, or confused with American standards. The weekly folkloric performances in the package-tour establishments are tailored to the supposed taste of the tourists—most will sample, few will become addicted!

Our customary rating coincides more or less with the star system of the three countries:

Rising from one star Morocco tops at five stars L, Algeria at five stars, and Tunisia at four stars L. As the distinguishing L is only very sparingly given, we have included a few of those without in our *Luxury* (L) grading—i.e. our (L) and the official L may not always coincide.

Expensive (E) comprises the remaining five and four stars, with an occasional 3 stars in Tunisia; within this price category the formula of Club des Vacances, increasingly adopted, consists more often than not of an ageing, mediocre hotel relying on self-service, with basic sporting facilities, plus an entertainment organizer. The glossy brochures' claim that everything is included proves a highly elastic concept. This point should be cleared with the booking agent, preferably in writing, as should the hotel's construction date, which is in general more important than the number of stars, because of poor maintenance.

Moderate (M) 3 and 2 stars.

Inexpensive (I) 1 star.

All (L) are airconditioned, as are (E) hotels in towns, but in beach resorts only where indicated; (M) and (I) at least with showers unless otherwise stated, in a few old hotels in Algeria and Tunisia. As single rooms hardly exist, we quote hotel prices for double rooms only; single occupancy is usually charged at 80% of the full price. Breakfast and service charges are included, and we quote high season prices. The numerous small, unclassified hotels in all towns may be clean and friendly, but they are too unreliable to warrant inclusion. They might be considered after an on-the-spot check.

Except for a very few luxury hotels, all the larger establishments are package-tour oriented; that is, they serve the basic needs of mass tourism and little else. The independent traveler often gets the worst of both worlds; he pays much more but is treated like one of the herd. Smaller hostelries frequently offer a more flexible alternative and may even reply to booking requests. Prices are strictly controlled, for rooms as well as meals, but food and service in hotel restaurants are notoriously unpredictable, and are usually just adequate. Although personnel are, on the whole, helpful, receptionists are almost universally discourteous and incompetent.

VACATION VILLAGES. These self-contained holiday communities offer a full range of entertainment and activities—swimming and sunbathing, sailing, riding, water skiing, tennis, windsurfing, scuba diving, even judo. Excursions are available to many points of interest.

The largest concern operating vacation villages is Club Méditerranée, with headquarters in Paris (place de la Bourse, Paris 75088, Cedex 02) and offices in London (106–108 Old Brompton Rd., London SW3) and New York (3 East 54th St., New York, NY 10022).

CAMPING AND CARAVANNING. Only recommended in organized camps, however inviting an isolated site may appear. Most camps are adequate, though a few off the tourist track are a bit primitive but ALL have piped water, toilets, showers, and a grocery store on the site within 500 yards. Generally, they are enclosed with "guards" on duty day and night. At the small seasonal grounds the cost of a night's stay is variable, but in the larger towns, where they remain open all year, there is a fixed tariff. The atmosphere and attitudes vary greatly from camp to camp even within each country.

MEDICAL SERVICES. The International Association for Medical Assistance to Travelers, Inc. (IAMAT), 417 Center St., Lewiston, NY 14092, or 188 Nicklin Rd., Guelph, Ontario N1H 7L5, makes available a free list of English-speaking doctors who have agreed to a fixed-fee schedule (office visit $20; house or hotel call, $30; night and holiday call, $40).

Travel Assistance International, the American arm of Europ Assistance, offers a comprehensive program providing immediate, on-the-spot medical, personal and financial help. Trip protection ranges from $35 for an individual for up to eight days to $220 for an entire family for a year. Full details from travel agents or insurance brokers, or from Europ Assistance Worldwide Services, Inc., 1333 F St., NW, Washington, DC 20004 (800–821–2828). In the U.K., contact Europ Assistance Ltd., 252 High St., Croydon, Surrey (01–680 1234).

Health Warning. Most rivers and lakes, even some rock pools of seemingly clear blue water, may contain bilharzia-bearing snails.

DRINKS. Tap-water is bacteriologically pure throughout the Maghreb, and therefore theoretically fit to drink. But it may vary a good deal from what you've been used to and so is better avoided. Instead, you can drink the local bottled mineral waters, with a choice of gassy or flat. Bottled imported French mineral waters, such as Vittel and Vichy are also often available, though considerably more expensive. At a wayside cafe, it is advisable to order something out of a sealed bottle. Hotels serve excellent fresh orange juice.

You should also try at least once the strongly sweetened, delightfully aromatic mint tea that the Maghrebis drink after their meals. The Maghreb produces many good table wines at reasonable prices. Imported French wines and all other imported alcoholic drinks are expensive, and bar prices for spirits at least double American prices. The sale of alcohol to Moslems is, theoretically at least, illegal, and you should be careful to whom you offer drinks.

TIPPING. A service charge of 10–15 per cent is usually added to a restaurant bill, and is virtually universal in hotels, which makes tipping no less expected. At the end of a week's stay, give 50 to 100DH, somewhat less in DA and one-tenth in DT, to the chamber maid or room boy or their Algerian or Tunisian equivalents and 100 to 200DH to the head-waiter, the same to the hotel porter, according to his service, and depending on the hotel. Leave 3DH in the cloakroom of a café-restaurant, 2 to 5DH to festival and movie ushers, and 10 to 15DH to luggage porters, etc. Porters seem insatiable in all three countries and the official rates regularly cause shouts of protest but should be the basis of tips. Taxi drivers usually try to overcharge you so there is no reason to give them anything over the agreed price. If you do find one of the rare honest ones—especially in a *petit taxi*—then a small additional payment is not out of order.

One tips the official parking attendants (those with badges) 1DH and the unofficial *gardiens* rather less. Tip hairdressers 20 per cent.

MUSEUMS AND ARCHEOLOGICAL SITES. Most are open daily except Monday in Tunisia, Monday or Tuesday in Algeria, Tuesday in Morocco, from 9 A.M. to 5 P.M.; some minor sites close between 12 and 2. All times are liable to change, thus opening hours will be given only when admission is restricted to a few days or hours.

MOSQUES. Open to non-Moslems in Algeria and Tunisia, but not in Morocco. Admission is, however, increasingly restricted—usually only in the morning, sometimes not to the prayer room, never during prayers, and occasionally not at all during Ramadan.

SHOPPING. For those who are accustomed to fixed prices, a word of advice: shopping in the Maghreb requires a good bargaining sense. A rough and ready rule is to offer one third of the price asked and eventually split the difference. But no matter how much you may be drawn to something that's on sale, feign indifference. Walking out of the shop for a look next door not only weakens the shopkeeper's resolve, but also gives you a better idea of the variety to be had and the prices in other shops. Some of the shopkeepers know enough English to do business with you.

Warning: Alterations on credit card vouchers are as common as charging sea or air freight, then sending the goods airmail, "*collect,*" or, increasingly, not at all. With the possible exception of the official cooperative or state-approved shops, our advice in the few shops listed for their renown is to pay cash and take all goods with you. The shops to which your guide will inevitably take you pay him, of course, a hefty commission, which is included in the price.

THEFT. The old-established and highly efficient pickpockets of the souks have spawned bag-snatchers on motor scooters. So far they are limited to larger towns and even there they are less in number than in many a European country.

Needless to say, all money and valuables left in the hotel room should be locked up; larger amounts should be deposited at reception. It is not advisable to leave your belongings unattended on a beach: ask a nearby family to keep an eye on them, but not an individual, who might consider it an invitation to help himself to useful moveables.

PHOTOGRAPHY. Its picturesque quality and beautiful countryside make the Maghreb a dream country for the amateur photographer. Some country people are still a little frightened by the camera, and you will succeed better by making friends with them than by trying to catch them unawares. Don't forget that you are in Islamic territory, where discretion should be used when filming or photographing women. Some characters, such as the watersellers in and around the Jamaa-el-Fna in Marrakesh and the performers in the free circus, demand payment if you photograph them: at least 3DH for an uncomplicated shot. All types of film are available in the large cities, but at relatively high prices.

Traveling by Car in North Africa

IMPORTING VERSUS RENTAL. Renting a car is expensive in all three countries, but so are the ferry fares. The choice depends on the length of stay and the amount of traveling; for shorter periods it is more economical to hire a car. The international car hire firms are well-represented in Morocco and Tunisia; in Algeria cars are hired from the O.N.A.T. offices and various garages.

On production of the registration certificate of an imported vehicle and an international driving licence, a tourist card in French is issued by the customs authorities—often ungraciously and slowly—valid for three months, with the possibility of extension. Most green cards include Morocco and Tunisia, but in both countries a cheap third party insurance is available at the ports of entry. The address of the foreign company's local correspondents should be ascertained, because it is often surprisingly difficult to obtain when most needed. No green card is valid in Algeria, where it is obligatory to purchase a temporary insurance at the customs, like the other local insurances valid for periods from 3 days to 3 months, but, unlike the others, expensive, more so at the land borders than at the ports. Other considerations aside, however, the appalling quality of North African driving makes renting infinitely preferable to driving your own car.

ROAD CONDITIONS. Well-surfaced but undulating highways on which you can travel comfortably enough at 80 k.p.h. (50 m.p.h.) are the norm. But during the rainy season roads and tracks may become impassable through flooding, while from November to April mountain roads are frequently blocked by snowfalls. Little stone pyramids on a road may indicate that a sizeable chunk of road is missing. By the fall the damage has usually been repaired, and many new miles of road built elsewhere. In each country there is only one motorway, starting in the respective capital city. Many roads are only just wide enough for two cars, though they have fairly broad dirt verges. If you see a vehicle hurtling head-on at you on one of these roads, sidestep to the right onto the gravel shoulder; better be safe than sorry.

In the deep south especially, asphalt eventually gives way to gravel and then to tracks, called *pistes*. On these, conditions vary from easy to impossible, with every degree of bumpiness in between. You'd be well advised to enquire first from hotel porters and National Tourist Offices.

USEFUL HINTS. Spare Parts. No problem in Morocco and Tunisia, but difficult to find in Algeria, for which it is recommended to bring a spare-part kit, which can usually be returned to the dealer. For mechanical repairs, one can find garages in all the large and small towns. Most European car manufacturers have agents in the larger cities.

Rules of the Road. Occasionally one wonders if there are any, but theoretically vehicles keep to the right-hand side of the road and overtake on the left. At road junctions, traffic traveling from the right has absolute priority, even when this traffic is entering a main road. At certain places, however, road signs indicate special main road priority. Military convoys, funeral processions, ambulances and police vehicles have priority at all times.

Road Signs. The international Road System is used on main roads in the Maghreb, although certain signs have slight variations in the coloring and outline of the symbols.

Border Crossings. The manners of customs and passport officials range from friendly to outright unpleasant. The latter is especially true on the Moroccan-Algerian border, depending on the state of relations between the two countries, as well as the moods of the officials. This border may be closed for trains, but open for foreigners in their own cars, though not in local buses. Double check before setting out.

Leaving North Africa

CUSTOMS ON RETURNING HOME. U.S. residents may bring in $400 worth of foreign merchandise as gifts or for personal use without having to pay duty, provided they have been out of the country more than 48 hours and provided they have not claimed a similar exemption within the previous 30 days. Every member of a family is entitled to the same exemption, regardless of age, and the exemptions can be pooled.For the next $1,000 worth of goods a flat 10% rate is assessed.

The $400 figure is based on the fair retail value of the goods in the country where acquired. Included for travelers over the age of 21 are one liter of alcohol, 100 cigars (non-Cuban) and 200 cigarettes. Any amount in excess of those limits will be taxed at the port of entry, and may additionally be taxed in the traveler's home state. Only one bottle of perfume trademarked in the U.S. may be brought in. However, there is no duty on antiques or art over 100 years old—though you may be called upon to provide verification of the item's age. Unlimited amounts of goods from Morocco and Tunisia may also be brought in duty-free as they are designated "developing" countries; check with the U.S. Customs Service, 1301 Constitution Ave., NW, Washington, DC 20044 as to whether this is applicable for any of the North African countries. You may not bring home meats, fruits, plants, soil or other agricultural items.

Gifts valued at under $50 may be mailed to friends or relatives at home, but not more than one per day (of receipt) to any one addressee. These gifts must not include perfumes costing more than $5, tobacco, or liquor.

If you are traveling with such foreign-made articles as cameras, watches or binoculars that were purchased at home, it is best either to carry the receipt for them with you or to register them with U.S. Customs prior to departing.

British subjects, except those under the age of 17 years, may bring home *duty-free* from *any* country, 200 cigarettes or 100 cigarillos or 50 cigars or 250 grams of tobacco; 1 liter of alcoholic drink over 22% volume or 2 liters of alcoholic drink under 22% volume, and 2 liters of still table wine. Also 60 milliliters of perfume, ¼ liter of toilet water and £32 worth of other dutiable goods.

Returning to Britain from any European Community (EC) country you may, *instead* of the above exemptions, bring in the following, provided you can prove they were not bought in a duty-free shop: 300 cigarettes or 150 cigarillos or 75 cigars or 400 grams of tobacco; 1½ liters of alcoholic drink over 22% or 3 liters under 22% volume, plus 5 liters of still table wine; 90 millileters of perfume and 0.375 liter of toilet water and £250 worth of other normally dutiable goods.

You can import free of duty the following: antiques (made before 1870), original paintings and other original works of art, including prints not mass-produced, and unset gems.

Canadian residents may, after 7 days out of the country, and upon written declaration, claim an exemption of $300 a year plus an allowance of 40 ounces of liquor, 50 cigars, 200 cigarettes and 2.2 lbs. of tobacco. Personal gifts should be mailed as "Unsolicited Gift—Value Under $40."

INTRODUCTION TO
NORTH AFRICA

by
PETER SHELDON

*Peter Sheldon, who lives and works in Athens, has written many books
on Greece and other Mediterranean countries.*

The Maghreb, as Morocco, Algeria, and Tunis, are collectively known,
really is different. The faithful reader of Fodor's Guides will be forgiven
a distinct feeling that he has come across this perhaps not entirely original
statement somewhere before, but there are truisms which impose themselves so overwhelmingly that they cannot be avoided, even at the risk of
losing the gloss that sophisticated travel writers love to give their advice
to travelers.

The three Maghreb states are different not only in comparison with
other countries but internally, from region to region, from town to town,
geographically, ethnographically, architecturally, and politically. Not perhaps in the culinary arts, which are basically similar throughout—though,
of course, at very distinctive levels—but certainly different in flora and
fauna, and above all, in their way of life. Not just different, but totally
unrelated. Yet in a splendidly oriental paradox this very variety is repeated
on all the diverse planes. No less a paradox is the derivation of the name
Maghreb, from *gharib,* to go to the unknown, which in the case of the

Arab conquerors meant the west—however decidedly it remained part of the Moslem east.

Mere geographical and climatic variations can indeed be expected—are even demanded by the jaded modern traveler—in so large a slice of the African continent, stretching from the Atlantic halfway across the width of the Mediterranean against a superb backdrop of rugged peaks and cliffs unequaled on this scale, before gradually flattening to the long sweeps of fine sandy beaches hemming a deep blue sea on the eastern Tunisian coast.

South of the Atlas, the Sahara stretches for a thousand miles, hardly less formidable a barrier than the ocean to the west, north and east, sealing the Maghreb off so effectively that no southern invader ever prevailed over its emptiness. To draw the border some hundreds of miles further north or south is, therefore, determined by the play of politics rather than geography, without any transgression of the limits set by nature. The French colonial administration transferred a large slice of the Sahara from the Protectorate of Morocco to the Metropolitan Department of Oran in Algeria, but during the brief honeymoon interlude of 1972 in the habitually strained relations between the two independent states, this arbitrarily imposed borderline was accepted by the Agreement of Ifrane. When the former colony of Spanish Sahara became part of the kingdom of Morocco in 1976 and 1979—in an annexation unrecognized by the rest of the world—a thousand miles of straight-line borders were added in the western sector of the endless sands, now marked by a great wall to keep out the Polisario guerrillas operating from Algerian bases.

Shattered Illusions

The popular picture of a burning land, of scattered palm groves in oases peopled by fierce tribes and assorted actors in highly inappropriate clothes or—climatically even less suitable—without any, is not quite up to date. These oases exist indeed, poignantly romantic with the strange architecture of the *ksour* (the fortified villages of the Berber) and the *kasbahs* (the castles of their notables) giving the Sahara region a unique quality of agelessness. But on the coastal regions and high plateaux, where the overwhelming majority of the population is concentrated and where all the important towns are situated, the soil is as fertile and the methods of cultivation as varied as anywhere round the Mediterranean. The Maghreb's salient features, however, are the mighty mountain ranges of the Atlas, as different from one another as geology and imagination allow. Rivers irrigate plentiful and varied crops in large and small plains. Despite the impressive storage dams these rivers are often too much of a good thing, especially when this regular water supply is swollen by persistent torrential rains. Floods are so frequent that unless at least a dozen people are drowned little attention is paid.

After the rains, snow! Roads to the pre-Sahara have to be kept open by snow plows for months on end. Skiing is possible in Morocco and Algeria into May, while eternal snow crowns Djebel Ayachi, a peak in the eastern High Atlas. Floods and blocked roads feature rarely among major tourist attractions, but they are the cause of an abundance of vegetation unparalleled in these latitudes, not only in the lower regions, but on the mountains themselves. In spring, between February and June, depending on the altitude, the slopes and pastures are carpeted with wild flowers. Afforestation is continuing on a large scale, with due regard to the distinctive indigenous vegetation of the ever higher ranges.

One last illusion to be demolished: North Africa is too hot by far for summer tourism. Not quite unexpectedly, it can become unpleasantly hot in the pre-Sahara, let alone the Sahara itself, though apparently not deterring the group tours filling the oases to capacity, summer and winter alike, largely because airconditioning is now so general in the hotels that the few real scorchers are bearable. The climate on the Mediterranean is remarkably uniform along its entire coast, to the delight of millions of sun worshippers; on the Atlantic it has been known to be too windy to bathe at Tangier, too rainy at Rabat and too foggy at Agadir, at the height of the summer season.

Morocco derives from Mauretania, the Roman province to which the present kingdom roughly corresponds—though what is now Mauritania, the Islamic Republic, lies hundreds of miles to the south of the Roman border. The Greek *Mauri* (Black) has, with the course of time, assumed a bewildering gamut of meanings. Western Moslems, the Moors of Spain as opposed to eastern Moslems or Saracens; inhabitants of Mauretania; or simply Black Man, as in Shakespeare's Moor of Venice—take your choice. Moorish as applied in art, especially architecture, is yet another matter, ranging from the Alhambra in Granada to Hindustani in India.

Abandoning this Moorish confusion, the inhabitants of Morocco not unnaturally prefer to be known as Moroccans, (regardless of their origin and mother tongue), as opposed to Algerians or Tunisians despite the similar Moorish racial mixture and background. The absence of friction between Arabs and Berbers, ruled by dynasties sometimes belonging to the one, then to the other race, for over a thousand years, is mainly due to the unifying influence of Islam, which hospitably embraced on an equal footing the descendants of negro soldiers and slaves from West Africa.

The Great Unifier

Though the saying "There are no Arabs in North Africa, only Berbers who have in varying degrees become Arabs" is an obvious exaggeration, the deep divergences have indeed been overlaid by Arab culture and men of different origins have been united by Islam.

Islam means submission to the will of God (Allah), and is the name of the Moslem religion which has been revealed by God to the Prophet Mohammed. Moses as well as Christ are recognized as prophets, charged with the guidance of humanity in their times, but their precepts were superseded by those of Mohammed.

The Koran is the sacred scripture of the Moslems, a recapitulation of the records of the ancient evangelists as revealed to the Prophet Mohammed, which sets its adherents a stern moral code by which to live and to bring out what is best in the human race. From it derives the code of jurisprudence of the Moslems, as well as their political and social traditions.

Just as with Christianity, there are in Islam "heretic" groups following doctrines diverging from those of the supreme office of the *khalifa,* and forming various sects. The Moroccans are mainstream Sunnites, following the *sunna* or *ahadith,* sayings of Mohammed. This is a collection of commentaries laid down by the companions of the Prophet and the four orthodox caliphs. The Sunnites date back to the first serious crisis that split Islam in A.D. 656 when the third caliph was murdered and the Prophet's son-in-law, Ali, claimed the succession. Sunnites maintain that the first caliphs were the true upholders of orthodox Islam. They constitute a majority in the Moslem world.

This orthodoxy itself is expressed by four different rites: Malikite, Hanafite, Shafite and Hanbalite. The Malikite rite, one of the strictest, has been practiced in the Maghreb since the days of the Almoravids in the 11th century and is the official form of worship. Its founder, Malik Ben Anas (713–95), forbade any interpretation of the Koran and enjoined the enforcement of the letter of the the Law. Some descendants of the Turkish administrators of Algeria and Tunisia observe the more lenient Hanafite rite, while the Kharijite sect, Islam's puritans, is represented by communities in the M'Zab in Algeria and on the island of Jerba in Tunisia.

An Absence of Priests

The essence of Islam lies in a single sentence: "There is no God but God and Mohammed is his Prophet." This declaration of faith is enough to illuminate the believer's entire religious life. At anytime, he can enter into communication with God through prayer. He needs neither sacrament nor priest.

In Christianity, priests and clergymen contrast with the "laymen" who form the ranks of their flocks. But there are no Moslem laymen because there is no clergy. Religion and daily life are inseparable. In a way, the believer acts as his own priest.

Yet even Islam recognizes certain religious officials, headed by the *alem* (plural: *ulema*), the teacher of Moslem law and dogma. The council of ulema is still influential in Morocco and Algeria.

The *khatib* preaches the Friday sermon in the mosque, while the *imam* acts as the leader of prayers; the *muekkit* sets the exact time for prayers and ceremonies; the *muezzin* calls the faithful to prayer with his singsong chant from the top of the minaret; and the *hezzab* specializes in reciting the Koran. All these religious officials are paid by the government which also maintains the mosque. A government ministry takes care of these matters and administers religious property, the *habbous* willed to the Moslem community by pious persons when they die.

Considerable religious influence is also wielded by men who have displayed unusual holiness and whose deeds and words lead people to practice their religion more perfectly. These *marabouts* often found a *zaouia* which begins as a study group of disciples who meet with their master to hear him preach and to follow his teachings. Later, it becomes a religious brotherhood which assumes the task of perpetuating the influence wielded by its founder during his lifetime.

Members of a zaouia have a number of duties. They must follow to the letter the customs and practices laid down by their holy man, they must come to meetings of the brotherhood and they must render assistance to other members. Some of the numerous zaouias have adopted spectacular rites, like the wild dances of the Aissawas who commemorate every year at Meknès the memory of Sidi Mohammed ben Aissa. But there are many others whose members come from the highest classes of society and who therefore are extremely influential.

It can also be said that the zaouias play a preponderant religious role because, since they continually seek perfection, they prevent Islam from remaining static.

The Berbers have always shown a predilection for their own local marabouts. After his death, a *koubba* (dome) is erected to the holy man's memory. These immaculate white square buildings, crowned by a dome, are scattered over the countryside, sometimes forming the center of a village, more often located on the outskirts. Holy places have succeeded in perpetuating their position by adapting a pagan divinity or Christian saint to Moslem practices. Though always respected there are some whose occupants have been forgotten. This happens when a holy man does not continue his career for posterity. But, most of the time, the koubba is the objective of a *moussem*—that is, an annual pilgrimage.

This can be a strictly local affair bringing people from two or three surrounding villages to a koubba. But it can also be a large assembly of believers on the scale of a province or even the entire nation. In aspect and atmosphere, a moussem is not unlike a Christian fair. The first part is devoted to group prayer and to the celebration of the holy man's virtues while the second part is given over to popular rejoicing.

Children Should Be Seen but Not Heard

This maxim somehow goes wrong when a considerable number of far from angelic children surrounds the luckless tourist when he emerges from his hotel, eats at open-air cafés or restaurants, or at his most defenceless, sunbathes on the beach. Their aim is lucre and loot, demanded by gesture rather than sound, yet unmistakable. Sometimes, however, they just stare with a persistency that would do credit to a bird watcher. These little ones are a pest, at least to the foreigner, because their elders seem to find no fault with them and up to a certain age spoil them outrageously.

The children are attractive enough, but then the young Maghrebis, men and women alike, are good-looking in all their racial variety, ranging from the red-haired, white-skinned, blue-eyed descendants of the Germanic Vandals, via the basic ingredients of Arabs and Berbers to the blacks, who are more often than not endowed with Semitic rather than negroid features. Needless to say, all possible interracial mixtures have been tried out with a remarkable degree of success. Though a Berber or Arab may be proud of his racial heritage, he is completely free of any color prejudice; equality of all the races is a totally natural fact of life, not something to be laboriously imposed by legislation.

But the children still lay siege to the tourist. The simplest way to get rid of them is to give them some coins, which, however, may only lead to a changing of the guard, since children seem as numerous as the sands of the Sahara.

Of Touts and Beggars

A more serious nuisance are the touts who badger you to buy all sorts of decidedly unwanted goodies or offer to act as guides to places of fame and ill-fame. This is a protection racket in full swing, made no more palatable by the fact that due to the Maghreb population explosion, almost sixty per cent are under twenty years old and cannot find employment, but have to earn their living somehow. Official guides provide some defence; on your own, a firm rejection of the services offered is about all you can do. Shouting will only lead to unpleasantness. A show of indifference, however difficult, has been known to work in the long run. Mostly, it is the victim that gives up. Policemen provide at best temporary relief.

Beggars are, if anything, even more ubiquitous. Our readers occasionally complain that in restaurants listed in this guide, beggars are allowed to expose the guests to a kind of moral blackmail. But the Moslem does not see things in this light. He follows the precepts of charity enjoined by his religion more readily than most Christians, whose squeamishness, moreover, he rather despises.

The medical revolution is still under way—the hygienic one could hurry up a little. Disease and mutilation are part of daily life and it would be sinful to be repelled by what Allah might send you on the morrow. So out comes the moneybag again and far from ruining you, it should add to your other enjoyments the glow of having helped a fellow human being. And above all, don't take on a high and mighty moral attitude and try to reform people who have not the slightest desire to adopt a conduct of life that seems to them in no way superior to their own.

A Western Part of the Arab World

Inevitably, the guileless tourist is taken for a ride by itinerant vendor, shopkeeper, hotels and restaurants alike. But this is no more so than in many other Mediterranean and most oriental countries. Though geographically in the west, the Maghreb is part of the Arab world and the orient. Taken for a ride usually means overcharged, mainly because of insufficient or inexpert bargaining. It is no good saying you don't like bargaining when this is the accepted way of doing a deal. And if you really are so gullible as to believe that the unknown youth loitering in front of your hotel will lead you to the best and cheapest shop, restaurant or nightclub, you have it coming to you. Moreover, there are shops with fixed—fairly high—prices in the modern quarters of the big cities, so if you aren't up to it, don't shop in the *souks*.

More justified is the complaint about overcharging or bad service in hotels, even those, perish the thought, mentioned in this guide. But doesn't this happen in all countries with a tourist boom, and in several without? There is nothing more annoying than finding after a long and tiring journey that your accommodation and mod. cons. are very different from what your travel bureau had led you to expect, or after you have settled in that breakfast is not served in your room, that food is indifferent, that the walls are so thin that you know a surprising amount about the intimate secrets of the couple next door. Similar information can be gleaned involuntarily all over the world, when there simply are not sufficient managerial or other staff to maintain the standard briefly achieved at the opening of a new hotel. If you demand in a reasonable manner what is due to you, Allah will look after you. As for overcharging on your bill, a no-nonsense attitude is advised. Prices are strictly controlled by the respective National Tourist Offices, and the threat that you will contact the local agency should smooth over any differences.

Yet the very same hotel manager, shopkeeper or other miscreant who has made your life a misery will turn on the full blast of oriental hospitality should you ever get to know him well enough to be asked to his home. It is easy to make friends in these easygoing countries. There is an old Berber saying: "When you come to our house, it is we who are your guests for this is your home," but this applies now more to the country than the towns, where the social life consists mainly of visits among the huge families—veritable clans—and some neighbors. Sitting around and doing nothing seems an entertainment in itself, elevated to ritual status. Relatives call on each other simply to sit endlessly over sticky sweet refreshments, while innumerable children play around, making more noise than you would think humanly possible.

Talk is desultory rather than sustained, but then, as everyone knows, words do not necessarily bear any relation to reality or logic, at least not to the Western concept of either. Manners—or more accurately set norms—are paramount. To refuse a request outright amounts to an inconceivable breach of etiquette, while promises can be made in a tone of voice that leaves scant hope that they will ever be fulfilled. Vagueness is preferable to precision, verisimilitude to verity. Polite phrases are a sign of the good breeding on which Arabs pride themselves. Formulas assuring that everything is for the best in the best of all worlds have to be exchanged, before settling down to a recital of disasters that sounds like the plot of a horror film.

The Higher the Wall . . .

There is little chance of escaping the prying eyes of neighbors in the popular quarters, let alone in the narrow alleys of the medinas, where occupancy rates must be among the world's highest. But oriental elites have, since time immemorial, adopted the simple yet effective device of surrounding their houses and gardens with high walls. This continues in the socialist as well as in the monarchical states, in a rare equal disregard of outward appearances.

A wooden door, braced with iron, opens on an often dark corridor that ends in a bright patio. The various rooms of the house are grouped around this open-air square generally decorated by a flowerbed or a fountain. First, there is the room where guests are received. In most cases, its walls are whitewashed and a long bench upholstered in gaily colored material and covered with cushions runs along one wall. The floor is covered with warm, colorful rugs. This reception room is also used as a dining room. At mealtimes, very low round wooden tables, actually metal trays placed on wooden legs, are brought before the master of the house and his guests. Dishes are placed on them and then, once the feasting is over, the tables are removed. The other rooms are used for everyday living—the family's bedrooms and the kitchen. In a fairly opulent house, there is more than one patio. A door leads to a second patio or to a small garden around which are grouped the bedrooms of the women and the innumerable children.

This traditional house of the prosperous few has been compressed by the rising middle class of higher government employees, officers, technocrats, and businessmen into gleaming white concrete cubes, which, despite their ominously narrow conception, maintain the old basic design.

The traditional approach is likewise used in workers' settlements in the towns of all three countries and the socialist villages of Algeria. Architects have succeeded through skill and ingenuity in reproducing in an unbelievably small space the old patio and the rooms leading on to it. And they have surrounded the result with walls so that a family's sacrosanct private life is respected even in a block of two or three hundred low-cost homes. For that matter, even in the shanty towns—no sooner replaced by permanent buildings than springing up again on the remoter urban fringes—tarpaper, galvanized iron and junk are combined into pathetic replicas of typical houses. Needless to say, out in the *bled* (the countryside) farmers still build their farmhouses the old way.

Pictures are rarely used as decoration. A few family photographs on a low table, a portrait of the king or the president . . . and that's all. On the other hand, ceilings and the upper parts of walls are readily decorated. In the oldest houses, floors are covered with mosaics, walls with ornamental tiles and ceilings with a combination of carved wood and stucco. Old ways disappear and so do the old craftsmen who executed such marvelous work, yet some beautiful things are still being made today.

The Legend of the Harem

Ever since the first crusaders returned to Europe, lurid stories of the mysterious orgies in an Arabian Nights setting have been associated with the harem. Polygamy holds great fascination for the average Westerner and he always associates it with a world of forbidden pleasures. Yet polygamy was originally practiced by most populations in hot countries where child mortality rates were terrifying and where the very survival of the race was at stake. Brigham Young and his Mormons were certainly not rakes and libertines but they turned to polygamy during the last century because they faced the problem of populating Utah.

The nomadic Moslem of the past was polygamous, his urban descendent is predominantly monogamous. For purely economic reasons, the Maghrebi of today has generally one wife and feels that one is quite enough. This does not mean that there is only one woman living in his family, he is probably also responsible for his widowed mother and, sometimes, his mother-in-law. Naturally, he has one or more daughters and he thinks it quite natural to take in one or two aunts, if need be, while his sisters live with him until they marry. Except for prostitutes, hardly any woman lives alone and it is almost unheard of to find an old woman dying in lonely poverty, as is all too often the case in industrialized countries.

Along with these women born or married into the family, there may be one or two servants among the well-to-do in all three countries, regardless of the social system. A servant becomes an integral part of the family, often with her own children as well. Her problems are settled in the same way as those of all the other women in the household and she often has her say in her employer's affairs.

According to another widely-held misconception, women are relegated to an inferior status in Islam, with dominant men reigning over an obedient world of cloistered creatures. This is no longer true, and perhaps never was. The Maghrebi woman is now perfectly aware of her role in the family and society—and even in the nation, while her personal property is protected by law. Though in some houses and particularly in the countryside, male visitors will not meet the lady of the house, company is becoming increasingly mixed. The young can, on the whole, associate as freely as anywhere in the world, with the greatest objection coming from their own contemporaries, especially from fundamentalist students.

The *Arabian Nights* depict a higher proportion of headstrong, domineering women a thousand years ago than were to be found in medieval Europe. History seems to bear this out, as it was upon the advice of a woman, his grandmother Kenza, that Mohammed, the successor of Idriss II, divided his kingdom among his brothers. And it was thanks to the shrewd advice of Zeineb, his wife, that Yusuf ibn-Tashfin became the leader of the Almoravid movement and the most powerful ruler in Maghreb history. More respected than the wife is the mother to whom men turn long after reaching manhood, for consolation and advice.

The status of women has undergone a revolution since they received the active and passive vote, but women, veiled or not, are still a minority at the polling booths; much more in the representative assemblies. A Moroccan, Nawal Moutawakil, won the first gold medal ever by an African or Arab woman, running in the 400-meter hurdles at the 1984 Olympics.

To Thee I Wed

The marriage festivities are an outstanding event, especially for the bride who leaves her family to enter a new one according to the Koranic law. As in all traditional societies, marriage is not only a union between individuals, but also a link between two families.

In town, it is no longer the young man's mother who chooses the bride, as the young people have increasing opportunities for meeting and getting to know one another themselves. But the negotiations leading to the marriage contract are still the prerogative of the parents. The complex ceremonial varies greatly from region to region; in the Atlas mountains, for instance, pre-Islamic practices have survived, but in a town, the engagement is celebrated by prayers in the mosque. During the engagement, which lasts from six months to two years, the groom sends his intended lengths of cloth, gowns or perfume on feast days. The dowry, paid before a notary, is spent on the bride's trousseau as well as on the purchase of furniture.

Five days before the wedding night, mattress, blankets and other necessities are carried to the nuptial chamber. After a bath in the *hammam*, regulated to the last detail, the bride is placed behind a curtain, symbolizing the transition to a new way of life. The following evening, the heavily made-up and veiled bride, sitting on a round table, is carried on the shoulders of professional female wedding-attendants, the *negaffa*, in a cacophony of songs and shouts to the bridal alcove, but only to rest, because there is still a lot of singing, fetching and carrying before the couple is at last left to its own devices. Festivities continue for another seven days, till the young wife takes a second ritual bath—high time one would think—and the negaffa leave the house.

Attention to the minutest details of this demanding ritual is deemed essential for the strength and vigor of the new branch of the family tree, though the effete Westerner would rather suspect a dampening of the passions and desires.

A Stern Test

Moslems renounce all daytime food and drink during the great fast of Ramadan. The month of Ramadan is a time of great physical trial for all the adults in the family. Between the rising and the setting of the sun, they abstain from eating, smoking and drinking. Because the Moslem calendar is based on the lunar year, the month of Ramadan makes the rounds of all four seasons over a period of thirty years. When it falls in winter, it is not that much of a hardship. But in summer it really represents a very great sacrifice offered to God. During hot days that are often torrid, people must go from five in the morning to eight in the evening without eating or drinking. Many even deprive themselves of a dip in the sea, for fear that a drop of water might pass their lips. Nerves are frayed and tempers are ruffled till the time comes to break the day's fasting.

In cities, the muekkit tells an artillery battery to fire a salvo just as the sun goes down. For a good fifteen minutes, ever since the first shadows invaded the house, the *harira* has been on the table, wisps of steam rising from the tureen. This is a thick soup composed of eggs, chunks of meat and chick-peas and everyone sits around it, spoons at the ready, to await those cannon shots. As soon as the guns go off, the family sighs with satisfaction and starts to eat. In the previous quarter of an hour the streets have emptied, traffic has stopped, and everyone has gone home to gulp his harira.

In villages the signal comes from the muezzin on top of his minaret. If it is only a small hamlet or a remote farm, the decision can be taken by the *mokkadem* (the government agent) or simply by the head of the family. In the latter case, he keeps an eye on the setting sun and decides when "he can no longer distinguish a black from a white thread."

Modern life has made the hardships of Ramadan even more difficult to bear because the country must still function. Government, administration, and industry continue—but only up to a point. Working hours are changed and shortened; this is definitely not the time for serious business, when lack of sleep is added to fasting. Small children are exempted, but dispensations are exceptional—they may be granted because of illness or travel—and must be made up during the year.

Eating and feasting at night compensate for the deprivations suffered during the day. The atmosphere changes from morose languor to feverish liveliness after the meal-break, when even the poorest have partaken of the *harira,* as Ramadan is the month of charity and nobody remains hungry. Music starts up on public squares at midnight, a mixed blessing for tourists whose hotels are within earshot. Quiet returns only with the *sohour,* the second meal, shortly before dawn.

The Five Big Days

Apart from the five daily prayers which are increasingly neglected in towns, and the month of Ramadan, there are also five big days in the Moslem calendar.

The first month of the year is Muharram. On the tenth day of Muharram, *Ashura* is celebrated and this marks the beginning of the Moslem year. It is a day both of joy and sadness. It marks the beginning of the new year but also the passing of time. Although joyful bonfires may be kindled in certain regions, all Moslems give alms on this day and go to their cemeteries.

The third month of the year is known as Rabia al Awal. Its twelfth day is *Mulud,* the anniversary of the birth of the Prophet. Needless to say, this is a joyful day and children are its heroes. Pupils from Koranic schools bear greetings from house to house. The luckier ones receive presents but all of them manage to shoot off at least one firecracker. Compulsory on each Mulud menu: every possible variety of dried fruit.

Ramadan, the month of fasting, is the ninth month of the year. Everyone is glad to see it go and the first day of the tenth month, Shawwal, is called *Aid es Seghir,* the little day, the little feast day. The night before, everyone has whitewashed his house and repainted his shutters. On the feast day, people put on their best clothes to visit their friends and trade presents of pastry.

Dhul Hijja is the twelfth month of the Hegiran year. On its tenth day, the biggest holiday in Islam is celebrated, *Aid el Kebir* (the big day). In all of Islam and at the same moment as in Mecca—for this is the high point of the pilgrimage—the head of every family sacrifices a sheep and calls for the blessing of God upon his neighbor and himself. Part of this sheep is set aside for the poor, for everyone must feast on this day.

In addition to this family ritual, the same observance is carried out officially by the *cadi* in each tribe, by the highest official in each city, by the governor in each provincial capital and by the head of state in the respective capitals. Particularly colorful is the ceremony in the M'kalla of Rabat, a place for public prayer outside the walls of the city where, decked out in ribbons, a superb ram peacefully enjoys the last moments of its existence.

The Moroccan sovereign arrives in a carriage preceded by the band of the Royal Guard while trumpets are sounded on the city walls. Under the leadership of the *imam,* prayer immediately begins and lasts for half an hour punctuated by kneeling and prostration. Then the ram is brought in and the king slits its throat with a slashing stroke.

In the old days, the animal was thrown across the saddle of a horse whose rider then set off at full gallop for the house of the cadi in town. According to tradition, the following year would be a happy one for the country if the animal was still alive when it reached its destination. Today, there is a slight tendency to cheat. The game with destiny is played under 20th-century rules: the sheep is thrown into the back seat of a jeep which then races off at top speed behind an escort of motorcycle policemen, their sirens screaming. The ram really does not have much of a chance to die on the way. And, in every Moroccan city at the same time, sacrificed rams are rushed down main avenues at 60 miles per hour. Meanwhile, in homes, a sheep is cut up and roasted while everyone joyfully gets ready for a family feast.

In poor families, the purchase of a sheep is no small matter. It takes skilful juggling of budgets and even loans. Farsighted families prepare for the event well in advance because, needless to say, prices rise in the souks when Aid el Kebir draws near.

Religion determines the daily existence. In addition to the community ceremonies and obligations that fall to every Moslem, there are also family events: births, the choice of a name for the baby a few days later, circumcision, marriage and death.

The greatest event in a Moslem's life is the fifth of his main obligations: the pilgrimage to Mecca. In the past the pilgrimage was an expedition for Moslems from the "far west," traveling on foot or by camel for months or even years at enormous risks. Bandits swarmed on the way and wars ravaged huge regions, so that many a pilgrim ended as a slave. Today the pilgrimage is well organized, mostly by chartered planes, while special national representatives to the Holy Places look after the pilgrims.

It is still a great honor for a family to have a *hadj* who prays for all his relatives at the Kaaba. While he is away, his family will not only think of him but his meal will be served every evening and given to a poor man. There is great joy upon his return with the honored title of hadj preceding his name.

Dress and Generosity

Though European suits predominate in towns, the jellabas have not been abandoned by men and are readily worn over the suit in the street. This is not affected worship of tradition, but commonsense as it would be impossible to find a more practical garment in the western wardrobe. The jellaba is loose, it does not hinder any movement and it protects the suit from rain and dust alike. Jellabas are made of all materials, particularly of gabardine, but connoisseurs insist that the best come from cloth woven by hand in some mountain village.

Shoes are taken off on entering a house and replaced by babouches, popular with tourists for slippers at home. But walking in the street in babouches is another matter . . . for they're easy to slip out of, too. Men's babouches, usually white or light-colored, are very simple, but women's are decorated with gold or silver embroidery and the result is delightful.

Veils, though rarely worn by young urban women, are in evidence: the rather fetching variously-colored long concealment below the eyes in Morocco; the decidedly unbecoming black or white pad over the lower face only in Algeria; or the headveil often—and somewhat unhygienically—held together between the teeth in Tunisia. Topless female tourists are confined to segregated hotel beaches, but the few who have wandered away have outraged Moslem fundamentalists. As a political protest, the reaction was strongest among the young, and university students have forced some of their female colleagues into the anonymity of *chadors* that would pass unnoticed even in Iran.

Country people often still dress in the old traditional style: the *serwal*, trousers very loose around the hips for comfort but with tapering legs that hug the calves. Above the serwal is worn a simple shirt. Women likewise wear a finely-embroidered serwal and a delicate blouse covered by a *caftan*. This is a loose robe buttoned in front and going all the way down to the feet. While caftans are nearly always of the same cut, the variations on this theme are infinite. The caftan can be extremely simple or it can be the world's most sumptuous garment in brocade, satin, lamé or embroidery. And the acme of elegance and taste consists of softening the beauty of the caftan by covering it, in turn, with a *mansouriah*, a sort of "outer caftan" consisting of a light veil that enhances rather than hides the heavy jewels.

One last serious word of warning. Don't express your admiration for the necklace worn by the mistress of the house or the little object decorating the top of the old family chest. If you do, you'll walk out with it as a sample of Maghreb generosity.

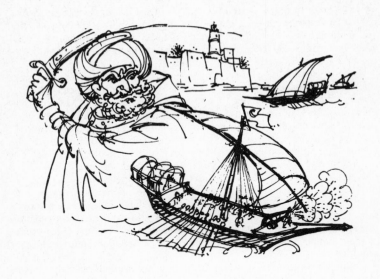

A BRIEF HISTORY OF
NORTH AFRICA

From Homo Atlanticus to Homo Turisticus

No need to dwell on the stone tools used by Homo Habilis in Morocco some two million years ago, or even on the Algiers Bardo Museum's jawbone of Homo Atlanticus, the local variant of Homo Erectus, who lived some 500,000 years ago at Ternifine, near modern Oran. From 50,000 B.C. onwards a better substantiated species obligingly left entire skulls, but the comparatively recent Late Paleolithic Age will do nicely for a beginning, when olive-skinned, dark-haired people, who had arrived in about 10,000 B.C. were using flint tools and weapons. But these hunters were all too discreet and left few traces, even in the Capsian Period (the name comes from Capsa, the ancient name of Gafsa) in the 7th millennium B.C., when major developments seem to have occurred.

Less down-to-earth are the remarkable rock engravings and painting of the Hoggar and the Tassili N'Ajjer in the South Sahara, which provide a uniquely exhaustive illustration of the way of life of the negroid inhabitants as well as of their white conquerors in the changing flora and fauna from 6000 B.C. to the time of Christ. For much of that period the climate of the Sahara was more propitious to human survival than the harsher coastal regions, which explains why cave art has been mainly discovered in the pre-Sahara and Atlas ranges.

However, a large number of dolmen from the Neolithic Period are scattered over North Africa, with diminishing frequency from east to west, though some cromlechs have been found in northwestern Morocco facing the Iberian Peninsula. In Tunisia these megalithic monuments were used as tombs during the Bronze Age, of which curiously little is known, though there is plenty of copper in the Atlas Mountains. The Bronze Age seems to have bypassed western North Africa, because man overlooked the wealth at his feet, while in the eastern parts bronze was introduced by blond-haired, blue-eyed invaders of vague antecedents. Perhaps they were Cretans fleeing after the fall of the Minoan Empire, but these Sea People soon interbred with the native population and the resulting mixture gradually spread westwards under the name of Libyans.

The Romans called them *Barbari,* not in any pejorative sense, as all races outside the Greek and Roman civilization were designated as Barbarians. The "Berber" derivation of the word was indiscriminately interchanged with Numidian, Getulian and Mauritanian.

In the Beginning Were the Berbers

No matter what gaps may still remain in the story of these men who lived during the dawn of time, one thing is certain: at the beginning of the historical era, North Africa's inhabitants were Berbers. Scholars have long wondered about the Berbers' origin, but their language is linked to the ancient Libyan language. Today, it is mainly a spoken language, but the Touaregs of the Sahara still write it. On the basis of their alphabet, ancient Libyan inscriptions have been deciphered.The Berber culture and language are now undergoing a renaissance centered around the Algerian town of Tizi-Ouzou.

What there was of Berber architecture survives in villages clinging to mountainsides or scattered throughout pre-Sahara oases. Some experts think this architecture was derived from the Egypt of the Pharaohs, believed to have spread from the Nile Valley. Berber art was translated into designs clearly distinct from those inspired by Islam. The lozenges and chevrons found so frequently on rugs reflect motifs similar to those of early peoples of Asia or of southern Europe. Pottery is similarly linked to other Mediterranean areas.

Then there were the gods. The Berbers certainly practiced a form of agrarian animism. Some of their divinities may have been imported into Italy by the Romans, always great assimilators of gods, after their African campaigns.

Though the problem of the Berbers' origin has not yet been solved, they and their civilization belong basically to the peoples of the Mediterranean basin for whom this sea forms a common denominator. Yet the character of the Berbers has kept them to a large extent free of external influences. While Islam wrought great changes in their world, this only came about because the Berbers freely accepted the religion of the Prophet. Previously, the civilizations of antiquity had not affected them. And this is why the first study of the Berber world—and still the most complete one—was made by an Arab historian, ibn-Khaldun (1332–1406).

The dawn of history saw the Berbers divided among three great tribes, the Masmoudas, the Sanhajas and the Zenatas.

The Masmoudas were settled in the region of the Rif, along the Atlantic, in the High Atlas and the Anti-Atlas, as farmers deeply attached to their land.

The Sanhajas were more adventurous and historians believe that this was the tribe that set out to conquer the Sahara in about the 3rd century.

They are the camel-riding nomads who inspired so much romantic litera-ture. They are the Veiled Men who at one time dominated Morocco, who conquered the south of the Sahara and the negro kingdoms of Senegal and Sudan for Islam.

The Zenatas were centered on the steppes and high plateaux of Algeria, where they had come from southern Tunisia and Tripolitania before spreading over all of North Africa. They claimed Arab origin, but ibn-Khaldun believed that they had been in North Africa as long as the other Berbers. While the Sanhajas are camel-riding nomads, the Zenatas once were Nomad horsemen. In their day, they played the same role in North Africa as the Mongols in Asia. They were the most feared cavalrymen in the armies of western Islam.

For centuries, tribes belonging to three great Berber families struggled for political supremacy. Clan loyalties, the basis of all social organization, submerged national spirit. Early writers describe them as living in mud huts, raising horses and oxen, harvesting with a sickle, eating principally wheat semolina rolled by hand, dressed in tunics and hooded cloaks and with a liking for primitive jewelry. This description is still valid despite two profound changes: the first, in the 8th century, turned them into Mos-lems; the second, in the 10th century, added nationalism. Even before the arrival of the Arabs, the Berbers had been converted to Judaism, possibly by Jews who fled in the Great Dispersion following the destruction of the Temple in A.D. 70. But the Berbers have remained basically the same and the old virtues of their race are still intact. In the Rif, the Atlas, Kabylia and the oases, the villagers have much in common with the Berbers whom the Phoenicians met on the shores of North Africa when they arrived to colonize Carthage.

Carthage

According to the Roman historian Velleius Paterculus, Barbary made its first appearance in recorded history in 1101 B.C., when Phoenician sail-ors from Tyre and Sidon in the Eastern Mediterranean landed at the mouth of the Medjerda river in Tunisia. There they founded Utica, which later served them as a port of call on the maritime route from Tyre to Andalusia. Soon they had established other trading posts along the coast, westwards at Hippo (Bay) Diarrhytus (Bizerte), another Hippo (Annaba), Rus Cicar (Skikda), Chullu (Collo), Igilgili (Jijel), Saldae (Bejaia), Eikoci (Algiers), Tipasa, Iol (Cherchell), Kartene (Tenes), Siga (Rachgoun), Ta-muda (Tetouan), Tingi (Tangier); and southwards at Hadrumetum (Sousse). The rural Berbers lived side by side with luxury-loving Phoeni-cians dressed in purple and covered with heavy gold jewelry, but their daily lives remained unaffected by the presence of the Phoenicians until the foundation of Carthage in 814 B.C.

Queen Elyssa, better known as Dido, the Wanderer, was expelled from Tyre by her brother Pygmalion. At Cyprus she collected eighty virgins for the oldest, most lucrative and highly respectable profession: sacred prostitution. Landing on a promontory not far from Utica, she concluded the shrewdest land deal in history—until the purchase of what was to be-come New York—with a local chief, modestly asking for what could be covered by the hide of a bull. The hide of the largest bull was then cut into the thinnest strips and stretched round the Hill of Byrsa (Greek for hide), where she founded Quart Hadasht (new city) which Roman pronunciation deformed into Carthago. This was not just another port of call. A compact colony of Phoenicians settled on the shores of Africa and founded a new metropolis. A thousand years of Semitic civilization thus took root along the coastline and on the fertile plains of the interior.

The Carthaginians brought the vine and the olive tree to North Africa. The Semitic city dwellers, and especially the farmers, lived in close touch with the Berbers, who gradually assimilated their techniques and ideas. The Berber princes emulated the Semitic life-style, which to them represented civilization. Carthage was a trading republic governed by a senate, while the executive power was exercized by a civilian governor, the Suffete. As the parent cities of Phoenicia declined, Carthage grew in power and wealth, gradually imposing its rule on the older trading posts and establishing new ones along the silver route to Spain; on the Balearic Islands, Malta, Sardinia, Sicily; along the tin route to Cornwall; and on the Atlantic, Thrinké and Melitta (near Larache), Thymiaterion at the mouth of the Oued Sebou, and Sala (Salé) at the mouth of the Bou Regreg; on the road to the gold deposits of Rio de Oro. Explorers, enticed by hopes of profit, were constantly extending Carthage's tentacles. One of them, Himilco, went beyond the Mediterranean to Brittany and may even have reached Ireland. Hanno sailed down the coast of Africa as far as Guinea and left an account of the journey, *The Periplous of Hanno*.

Hanno, of course, put in at all Carthaginian settlements on the way to Sala. Then, according to the normal method of primitive sailing vessels, he hugged the coast as he pushed southward. His expedition is supposed to have taken place between 475 and 450 B.C. It was obviously more than just one trip and Hanno must have back-tracked many times.

It is said that the temple of Tanit in Carthage was decorated with pygmy skins. The name of the goddess Tanit evokes a hideous memory—the sacrifice of first-born children by fire and by branding. Recent archeological digs in the Carthaginian sanctuaries have confirmed texts dating from antiquity which say that young children were offered to Baal, the most powerful of the gods, and to the goddess Tanit.

But the Carthaginians were traders, not conquerors, who sought trade agreements and treaties of friendship with local leaders. Besides, they never tried to extend their influence beyond coastal regions. The nomadic shepherds, now called by the Greek name Numidian, remained aloof in their mountains.

Enter the Romans

In the 5th century B.C. Carthaginian war galleys and merchant ships plowed up and down the Mediterranean and along the Atlantic coast. Gold and precious metals flowed into Carthage and the soil of Africa produced wheat and oil for the city to export. Riches piled up inside the palaces of the senators and in the temples of the gods.

The first difficulties occurred in Sicily, which, though very close, was well defended by Greek settlers. In 480 a Carthaginian general was defeated at Chimera by Gelon, the Greek tyrant of Syracuse. Another Syracusan tyrant, Dionysius, sacked Carthage's possessions in Sicily. The Carthaginians were realists; they signed a peace treaty and withdrew from the island which had brought them nothing but disappointment. The Greeks of Sicily then went on the offensive, landed in Africa and carried out a profitable raid before being beaten by mercenaries in the pay of Carthage. Eventually things settled down and each side devoted itself once again to its commercial interests.

The rich Carthaginian merchants, however, had not abandoned Sicily. Also the need to keep watch on the maritime routes made it necessary to station garrisons at strategic points. In 270 a handful of Carthaginians settled at Messina to guard the straits. On the mainland shore the Romans, pursuing their southerly conquests, settled at Regium (Reggio). The situation became explosive and the confrontation took place over the inhabitants of Mamers, Sicilians allied to Rome on whom the Carthaginians wished to impose their rule. The struggle was to extend over three major wars between the years 264 and 146 B.C., and it ended with the death of Carthage.

First Punic War (264–241 B.C.)

Due to their long maritime experience, the Carthaginians considered themselves to be masters of the sea. The Romans undertook to prove the contrary, equipping their ships with grappling hooks and ramming devices to pierce the Carthaginian hulls and thus immobilize the boats, which the Romans then boarded and seized.

The Roman general Regulus landed in Africa with 330 ships and 40,000 soldiers. Carthage spent a fortune hiring mercenaries of all nationalities— Greeks, Gauls, Iberians, Libyans. Regulus was defeated and captured. The Carthaginian senate sent him to Rome as an emissary after making him give his word of honor that he would return and give himself up. Regulus went to Rome, advised his countrymen to continue the struggle and, faithful to his promise, returned to Carthage. Finally, in 241, having lost its navy and gold reserves, Carthage laid down its arms, abandoned first Sicily, then Sardinia and Corsica, and agreed to pay tribute to the Romans.

Carthage was ruined and unable to pay her soldiers their back pay. The soldiers revolted, inciting the Berbers of the African countryside to fight along with them. Another Hanno was appointed to restore order, but was massacred. Then Carthage called back from Sicily her most able general, Hamilcar, hired other mercenaries, and bought new elephants. An early victory forced the foe to retreat toward the south. By a series of clever maneuvers, Hamilcar succeeded in trapping the rebels in a rocky pass, known as the Defile of the Axe, south of the present-day Zaghouan, where they starved to death. This was the revolt that inspired Flaubert's colorful novel *Salammbô*.

Second Punic War (219–201 B.C.)

As Carthage no longer ruled the waves, it attempted to consolidate its possessions in Africa, thus coming into conflict with the Numidian tribes who had federated into two kingdoms, of the Masaesyls in the west, and of the Massyls from Kabylia to Carthaginian territory. Along the Atlantic coast lived the Mauritanians (Phoenician *mahour,* men of the west).

Hamilcar's popularity was resented by the Carthaginian senators, who sent him off to Spain. Accompanied by the most valiant of the Berbers, he conquered very nearly the entire country in nine years, before dying on the battlefield. His son-in-law, Asdrubal, succeeded him, but was later assassinated.

Then this nation of merchants produced one of the greatest military geniuses of all time—Hannibal, son of Hamilcar. In 219 B.C. Hannibal was

23 years old. Carthage no longer ruled the waves. Hannibal set out for Italy via the overland route, with 50,000 infantrymen, 9,000 horsemen, and 370 combat elephants following him. He crossed the Pyrenees, the Rhône, and the Alps and finally reached Italy. The huge animals depicted in innumerable historical paintings are very different indeed from the small African elephants actually used to crush the Roman legions. Rome seemed to be at the mercy of Hannibal, but, bypassing the city, he continued down into Campania. In a last-ditch stand the Romans sent in a new army, which was beaten at Cannae. In Rome panic broke out, even though Hannibal was not at its walls, no doubt because he did not have the necessary equipment for a siege. The Carthaginian army sank deeper and deeper into the proverbial delights of Capua while awaiting reinforcements which never came, but for ten years Rome lived in dread of the elephants.

Rome's counter-move was slow in coming but devastating when it arrived. She reconquered Spain and the Carthaginian reinforcements were repelled. Scipio Africanus, the shrewd and energetic Roman leader, took the war to the African continent, where he allied himself to Massinissa, who ruled the Massyls for 56 years, had a son at 86 and died at 90, after having settled his semi-nomadic subjects round his capital, Cirta (Constantine). It was now Carthage's turn to tremble. Hannibal was recalled to Africa. In 202, at Zama, in what is known today as the Plain of Sers, between Le Kef and Maktar, a tired and disheartened Hannibal faced Scipio's army. The Romans pierced the stomachs of the elephants in the spot where the skin is thinnest. Carthage sued for peace, paid an enormous tribute, scuttled her fleet, and disbanded her army. Hannibal escaped to the Orient to avoid being handed over to the Romans by the Carthaginian senate. Pursued by Rome's hatred right into his sanctuary at the court of the King of Bithynia, he poisoned himself in 184 to "deliver the Romans from terror which an old man inspires in them—an old man whose death they dare not await."

Third Punic War (149–146 B.C.)

Carthage had been reduced to no more than its outskirts and was held in bondage by Rome. Rome, fearing the rebirth of a Numidian Carthage under Massinissa, sent Cato to Africa to investigate the situation. He visited Carthage and returned impressed with the way the city was recovering. *Ceterum censeo Carthaginem esse delendam* "Besides, I think that Carthage must be destroyed" became the theme of all his speeches. Eventually his warning was heeded.

In 149 the Roman army landed at Utica. Rome demanded hostages; Carthage handed over 300 young aristocrats. Rome demanded the delivery of war material; Carthage turned over 2,000 catapults. Rome demanded the fleet; it surrendered. The Romans demanded that the inhabitants abandon the city, and then and only then did the people, driven by despair, resolve to fight. They tore down their palaces and used the cedar beams to build ships and catapults; the women cut off their hair to make rope; gold dinner services were melted into ingots; night and day smoke from the sacrifices of children rose above the sanctuaries. The siege lasted three years.

The gods were unrelenting. Another Scipio, Scipio Aemilianus, grandson of the earlier Scipio, attacked in 146. The final curtain of this tragedy fell on thousands of desperate people flinging themselves into a huge fire.

Nothing remained of Punic Carthage but a memory and a vast field of ruins which the Roman priests sprinkled with salt, declaring it damned forever.

Roman Africa

A Roman governor took up residence in Utica, the capital of *Africa Vetus* (Old Africa), as Rome proceeded cautiously, contenting itself at first with a few coastal cities and the countryside around Carthage. Through dismantling Massinissa's kingdom after his death in 148, the interior was left in the hands of the Numidian princes. Massinissa's grandson, Jugurtha (154–104 B.C.), had his rivals assassinated, not sparing his cousin Adherbal, Rome's ally, who had sought refuge at Cirta, and created a powerful state. Alarmed, Rome sent a commission to investigate. Jugurtha bribed all its members. He was summoned to Rome, where he played on uneasy consciences and insulted the Senate before returning to Africa by calling Rome a "venal city." He resisted the army of the Consul Metellus, and even the famous Marius, though occupying all towns, had to resort to treason to dislodge him from his impregnable positions in the mountains. Jugurtha was betrayed by his father-in-law Bocchus I, King of Mauretania, in 105 and died in prison.

Rome was not yet prepared to go all the way in Africa, being above all concerned with the regular supply of wheat, olive oil and livestock. Bocchus was rewarded with west and central Numidia, the east was divided between two princes, but reunited under King Hiempsal (80–60 B.C.), who was succeeded by his son Juba I, all allies of Rome, but not of the same Roman rivals. Bocchus II opted for Caesar, Juba for Pompey who was beaten in 46 at Tapsus (modern Ras Dimasse, between Monastir and Mahdia).

Caesar incorporated eastern Numidia into the proconsular province of *Africa Nova,* which covered about the same area as present-day Tunisia. Roman colonists, mostly veterans, were given land divided into squares of 50 hectares (125 acres), which were called centuries. In 44, six thousand colonists settled in Carthage and this cursed land, where only thistles grew, began to thrive once more. Increasingly luxurious cities sprang up all over the country. Hydraulic works opened up new areas to cultivation, and nomadism became less common. Some of the Berber shepherds followed the example of the Romans and became farmers. Even the Punic gods were Romanized—Baal became Saturn, Tanit became Caelestis. The province of Africa produced a third of Rome's wheat supplies.

Bocchus II was rewarded with western Numidia; this Mauretanian kingdom was given in 25 B.C. to Juba I's son, Juba II, who had been brought up in Rome. Juba II, enamored of Hellenism, was one of the great scholars of his day. And he was doubly an aristocrat: by birth, for this Berber was a king's son; and then by marriage, for he had wed Cleopatra Selene, the daughter of Antony and Cleopatra. Under such a brilliant scepter, Mauretania was to experience its brightest and happiest years. Juba II, more Roman than any Roman, transformed his kingdom into a truly Roman region. During the forty-eight years of his reign, Mauretania enjoyed peace as Rome's faithful ally, except for the revolt of the Getulians of the Aurès under Tacfarinas, bloodily suppressed between A.D. 17 and 24.

But Rome still feared Cleopatra—and her descendants. In A.D. 40, Caligula had Juba's successor, Ptolemy, murdered at Lugdunum (Lyon).

Mauretania came directly under Roman rule, and in 42 Claudius divided the kingdom into two provinces: Mauretania Caesariensis, which ran from the mouth of the Ampsaga (the Rhumel) in the Constantine area to the mouth of the Moulouva in eastern Morocco; and Mauretania Tingitana which stretched to the Atlantic with Tingis (Tangier) as its capital and Volubilis as the largest inland city. A few miles south of Rabat, on the road to Casablanca, are the remains of the *limes* marking the boundary of the empire.

During the first two centuries of the Christian era Roman Africa flourished despite several insurrections, one sufficiently critical to necessitate the intervention of the Emperor Hadrian and the foundation of Lambesis (Tazoult) in the Aurès. Many Latinized Berbers became Roman citizens and one of them, Septimus Severus, became emperor. The African army, the *Tertia Legio Augusta,* recruited Berbers into its ranks. After 20 years of service, they were given the title of veteran and a plot of land, just like the Roman soldiers.

The splendid cities, the majestic temples and the sumptuous villas were a heavy burden for an agricultural country with an unpredictable climate, and the *Tertia Legio Augusta* was forced to intervene increasingly to put down small revolts.

Christianity readily found followers, and martyrs. St. Cyprian's episcopate of Carthage (248–58) made the African church famous. When Christianity became the state religion in the 4th century, the two provinces were divided into ten dioceses. The Church condemned Donatus, the schismatic bishop of Carthage, at the Council of Arles (314). St. Augustine (354–430), Bishop of Hippo Regius (Annaba), fought against Donatus's followers and defended religious orthodoxy.

The End of a World

During Rome's protracted decline, Africa, thanks to its geographical position, was long spared invasion. But when the conquerors finally came, they contributed more than any of the Germanic settlers elsewhere to the change from Roman money to the medieval food-and-service-based economy, due to the dominance of the Vandal fleet in the Mediterranean.

The Vandals and the Alans crossed the Pyrenees into Spain in 409, were defeated by the Visigoths, and continued south to the Mediterranean coast, turning to piracy. In 428 Gaiseric, stunted, lame and ruthless, became their king. He sailed across the straits and in a single terrible year, 429–30, occupied the land from Tangier to Carthage. That *vandalism* is still used throughout Europe to denote barbaric depredations reflects the scale of havoc wrought by the 50,000 Vandals.

Only a few walled towns held out for some years. In 435 the Emperor Valentinian recognized Vandal occupation of Mauretania Tingitana; after the fall of Carthage, which Gaiseric made his capital in 439, the Emperor ceded the entire diocese of Africa. The Vandals swept the Mediterranean unopposed, plundered Sicily, Sardinia and Corsica and in 455 landed at Ostia, the port of Rome. Due to the intervention of Pope Leo, Gaiseric consented not to sack the city, but stripped it of gold, silver and even the bronze roof of Capitoline Jupiter's temple. Less burdensome was the widowed Empress Eudoxia, whom he forced to marry his son, Huneric. When Gaiseric extended his raids to Alexandria, the Romans sent unsuccessful expeditions against him.

After his death in 477, his successors continued to enjoy life in an ever-shrinking area around Carthage, till Belisarius reconquered Africa for his master Justinian, Emperor of Byzantium. In 534 Belisarius reached Carthage, but the imperial administration hardly extended beyond the coast and some isolated cities in the interior.

The Arab Conquest

The Byzantines considered themselves heirs to the Romans and Justinian attempted to rebuild the empire. The great Byzantine Governor Salomon advanced as far as Tolga, Timgad and Tigis, but after his death in battle in 544 his successors followed the retrenchment process of the Vandals, withdrawing to the eastern parts, though clinging to a few western outposts like Ceuta. Byzantine decadence, interrupted by brief upsurges, lasted until the seventh century. The Byzantines were reduced to taking stones from Roman monuments to build fortresses against Berber uprisings, military rebellions, heretics and the *rezzas* (raiding parties) launched by the Libyan Bedouins.

The Arabs put an end to these death throes in three phases. In 647, in the year 26 of the Hegira, Abdullah ben Bou Saad launched 10,000 cavalrymen and 10,000 infantrymen across what he called Ifriqiya. The Byzantine patrician Gregory was killed at Sufetula (Sbeitla) and the Arabs left laden with booty. They came back in 660–3 to collect what they had left behind the first time. In 670 they returned once again but this time for good. Kairouan (Kairwan), the city of the steppe, replaced Carthage, the maritime city. The country turned its back on the sea and served as a base for the conquest of the Maghreb and Spain. In 683, Oqba ibn-Nafi, the founder of Kairouan, led his Arab horsemen across Maghreb to the Atlantic, thus making good his claim to advance Islam to the end of the world, but fell in battle at Biskra, on his return.

The Berbers, faithful to their traditions, resisted the newcomers. A Christian prince, Kosaïla, led the guerrilla movement and the Arabs were unable to eliminate him until 688. The people then found a heroine in a Berber princess, perhaps of the Jewish faith, called Kahena, the prophetess. She harassed the Arabs, who had just sacked Carthage (695), and drove them back into Libya. They returned in force and she fled before them, using scorched earth tactics. The story goes that after taking refuge in the enormous Roman amphitheater of Thysdrus (El Jem) she continued to fight to the death. Berber resistance split up and finally evaporated.

The Arab conquest soon became a victory over souls as well, and the Berbers adopted the Moslem religion. Latin and Christianity disappeared, together with the fertility of Rome's granary. The flocks of goats accompanying the conquerors greatly contributed to the desiccation caused by the northward shift of the rain-bearing winds. The province of Africa had been an extension of Italy; Ifriqiya was a step in Islam's march. Islamicized Berbers, under Arab leadership, set out from here to conquer the Maghreb and Spain.

The pacification of the Maghreb lasted 25 years even though the Moslems held two high cards. The first was their dynamic, monotheistic religion. It certainly appealed to the population of a country that had known Christianity. The second was the conquest of Spain that was to begin in 709 and into which the Arabs enlisted many Berbers. Harsh demands and political mistakes by governors sent by the Ommiad did not slow the spread of Islam. When the Berber world revolted in 740 against its masters, it was in the name of religion: the Berbers joined the revolt of the puritan Kharijites (Those Who Have Left), which was rocking Islam at the time.

Unity and Dissension

When the Abbasids succeeded the fourteen Ommiad caliphs the center of gravity of the Moslem world shifted toward Baghdad. The West, sometimes united but more often rent by fierce dynastic struggles, gradually split from eastern Islam, not only in the political but even in the religious sphere. Kairouan and Cordoba became the two lighthouses of Arab culture, soon to be followed by a third, Fez.

Out of the anarchy of revolt emerged three kingdoms: of the Idrissids of Fez, who ruled Morocco including Tlemcen; of the Aghlabids of Kairouan, who held sway over Tunisia and the region of Constantine; and as an uneasy buffer between its mightier neighbors, the Kingdom of Tahert, capital of the puritan Kharijite followers of the Persian Abd Er Rahman Ben Rostem.

Idriss, a *sherif*—a supposed descendant of the Prophet—from Arabia, had joined a revolt against the Abbasid caliph in 786. After it failed, Idriss escaped to North Africa and eventually reached the city of Oulili (Volubilis) where he asked the Aoureba Berbers for protection. They showered honors upon the descendant of the Prophet, proclaimed Idriss their *imam* and swore loyalty to him. At their head he set out to convert to Islam all tribes that had not yet adopted his faith, thus spreading Islam throughout Morocco.

But the Caliph of Baghdad envied the glory of Idriss I and dispatched a traitor to his court. Disguised as a refugee this man gained Idriss' confidence, then poisoned him. This was in 792 and the Caliph's name was Harun al-Rashid.

The kingdom by then was already islamized. It still had to be arabized. Idriss' son, Idriss II, set out to accomplish this . . . and also to find a site for a capital. For he dreamt of a vast city and Oulili was too small to house it. He chose the site of Fez. Since his reign and for more than a thousand years thereafter, the religious, intellectual and artistic glory of Fez has shone not merely over the Moslem West but over all of Islam.

When Idriss II died, his eldest son Mohammed divided the kingdom among his seven brothers, reserving for himself only Fez and its surrounding region. He also maintained a certain degree of suzerainty over the other princes. This move may have been disastrous for the unity of the kingdom but it was the best possible solution as far as the country's future was concerned. These Idrissid principalities became so many focal points of islamization and arabization in Morocco. Idriss II not only set up a *maghzen*—an Arab government—but Fez was strengthened from its very start by an influx of 800 families from Cordoba and 300 from Kairouan.

This new structure certainly enabled Morocco to survive a power vacuum that lasted 140 years following the fall of the Idrissid dynasty in 920. There is no doubt that the country went through a century-and-a-half of confusion, but it seemed to be gathering its strength for the leap that was to take it to the top of the Moslem West.

To contain Idriss II, the Caliph of Baghdad appointed Ibrahim ben Aghlab Governor of Ifriqiya in 800. He ruled wisely, acting as a virtually independent leader, and his dynasty lasted until 909. He built the Great Mosque of Kairouan (or Quairawan) and the fortified monasteries at Sousse and Monastir.

Anxious to find an outlet for their restless army, the Aghlabids conquered Sicily, but they gradually lost their ebullience, and their will-power flagged as a result of their luxurious and debauched way of life. Intellectual energy degenerated into religious disputes between the Malikites, who believed in a strict interpretation of the Koran, and the Hanafites, who favored a more liberal interpretation.

The Berbers threw themselves into politico-religious argument. They were Shi'ites (members of the Shi'ite sect) and recognized only the authority of the descendants of Ali and his heirs, the 12 imams. The twelfth imam had disappeared, and his return was to be announced by a precursor, the Mahdi. Then lo and behold, he suddenly appeared! His name was Obeid Allah. His followers, who had come down from Kabylia, defeated the Aghlabid troops and settled at Kairouan.

The Fatimids

Obeid Allah was a realist. He had the leaders of his followers assassinated so as to avoid having to show his gratitude to them. He founded the Fatimid dynasty, named after Fatima, daughter of Mohammed and wife of Ali, from whom he claimed descent. In 911 he conquered and destroyed Tahert, and drove the heretical Kharijites into the desert. Continuing his triumphal progress westwards, he occupied Fez and put an end to the Idrissid principalities. Turning his ambitions toward the Eastern Mediterranean he founded his capital on a small headland on the coast and named it Mahdia. His aim was to replace the caliphs of Baghdad and become Caliph of Islam. But the Maghreb was not a good enough springboard for his ambitions so he embarked on the conquest of Egypt. He did not succeed, for his fleet was sunk and Sousse was sacked by the Sicilian Moslems. To get his revenge he razed Palermo to the ground. Obeid Allah departed for a better world in 934.

His son had to ward off an uprising led by a preacher from Jerib called Abou-Yazib (and nicknamed "the man with a donkey"), whose followers, burdened with huge taxes and sickened by the authoritarian rule of the Fatimids, almost succeeded in capturing Mahdia but were hacked to pieces in front of the city's walls.

Emir al-Mu'izz succeeded in bringing the Fatimid dream to fruition when his generals conquered Egypt. He founded Cairo and proclaimed himself caliph in 973.

Hammadids and Zirids

Before leaving Ifriqiya for Cairo al-Mu'izz entrusted its rule to the Zirid family. In 935 Bologuin, a chief of the Sanhaja Federation, established El Djezaïr (Algiers) on the remains of Phoenician Eikoci. His son, Emir Hammad, founded in 1007 a very different town in the Hodna Mountains, Kalaâ des Beni Hammad, a flourishing political and spiritual center, abandoned in 1090 by the Hammadids for Bejaïa on the sea, because in the meantime a catastrophe surpassing the Vandals had befallen the Maghreb.

In 1048 the Zirids had openly declared their independence by having prayers said in the name of the Caliph of Baghdad, rival of the Fatimids of Cairo. The Fatimids had little money and no army but they did possess a ruthless strategy and a subtle sense of vengeance. Two years after being repudiated by the Zirids, waves of plundering tribes from Upper Egypt, the Beni Hilal and the Beni Sulaim, poured into Ifriqiya, bringing with them their women, their children and their flocks. They uprooted trees, destroyed irrigation channels and left behind utter desolation. Ibn-Khaldun likens the invasion to a devastating cyclone and the Beni Hilal to an army of locusts. With the destruction of Kairouan in 1057 the operation was over. The efforts of 1,500 years had been reduced to nothing and Tunisia was once again arid steppe. The country never completely recovered.

The Beni Hilal and the Beni Sulaim tribes settled their personal differences. Hammadids and Zirids still held a few coastal cities and were careful, though it was a little late in the day, to have prayers said in the name of the Fatimid caliph, which did not prevent the Genoese from sinking their fleet and freeing the Christian galley slaves. The last of the Zirids implored the Spanish Moslems to come to their aid, but Roger II, the Norman King of Sicily, arrived instead. Landing on the island of Jerba in 1148, he conquered Mahdia, Sousse and Sfax. He became King of Africa, reestablished the see of Carthage and died in 1154.

A King Rises from the Sands

While the great Sanhaja Federation was thus sorely tried in the East, the long-awaited purifier of the faith and unifier of the Maghreb arose in one of its western tribes. For centuries the Lemtunas had waged a constant struggle on the borders of the Sahara with negroes from Senegal and the Sudan. This tribe had long adopted Islam, and the great Almoravid adventure began when its emir, Yahya ibn-Ibrahim, decided to make the pilgrimage to Mecca.

Mecca was a revelation to him. When he returned, he asked a sage in the kingdom of Sijilmassa (now part of Tafilalet) to enlighten the religion of the Lemtunas. Abdallah ibn-Yasin had his work cut out for him when he decided to reform the morals of the Veiled Men of the desert who showed little more than token obedience to Islam's strict recommendations. Perhaps he went too far or perhaps virtue bored the Sanhajas . . . in any case, they drove out their missionary. But pious Yahya ibn-Ibrahim, disgusted by the attitude of his brethren, decided to follow Abdallah. So did his brother, Abu Bekr. All three withdrew to a *ribat* to meditate on the ingratitude of mankind.

Historians are unable to agree on the site of this ribat, an institution which really has no equivalent in the western world. It was a monastery because it was devoted to religion but it was also a fortress because its inhabitants were warriors. The fateful star of the Almoravids began to rise here among the "people of the ribat" (*al morabitin*). For the three men did not remain three for long. Soon, they were joined by many other repentant Sanhajas. When their number reached a thousand, Abdallah ibn-Yasin decided that it was time to go into action and to hammer all the tribes of the desert into his mold of orthodoxy.

The men of the ribat took the leadership of a federation of three tribes: the Lemtunas, the Goddalas and the Messufas. Their first step was to take Sijilmassa, their second to conquer the oases and then the Sous. The Emir was their right arm and Abdallah ibn-Yasin their brain. Reigning princes put up a stiff fight but the Almoravids gained the upper hand everywhere and immediately abolished taxes prohibited by their religion, which won the people over; they also restored virtue and orthodoxy, which won the *fquihs* (men of religion) to their side as well. During this violent campaign, two Lemtuna emirs died in battle and so did Abdallah ibn-Yasin himself. In 1060, the Almoravids were fighting on the Atlantic plains and their leader was now Yusuf ibn-Tashfin (Youssef ben Tachfin), one of the great figures of Maghreb history. He was over 50 when he became emir, yet he was to reign for another half century.

He was a Veiled Man of great virtue and stern morals. He also had the vision of a statesman. In 1062, he took the vitally important step of founding Marrakesh. It was from this region, similar in many ways to the desert from whence the Lemtunas had sprung, that he was to conquer not only all of Morocco but all of western Algeria, where he founded Tlemcen, up to Algiers. Nor did he overlook that ancestral combat in the south of the Sahara: in 1086, the Almoravid empire stretched all the way to Senegal. That was also the year when the Veiled Men crossed the Strait on their conquest of Andalusia.

By the end of the Ommiad caliphate in Spain, the kingdom had been chopped into a number of small principalities bearing up badly under pressure from the Reconquista campaign that was being waged by the Christians from the north of the peninsula. This pressure became so strong that, as early as 1069, the Moslems in Spain thought of turning for help to the Almoravids, whose prowess had already become legendary. In 1085, Toledo fell to Alphonso VI, and the Almoravid army, under the command of Yusuf ibn-Tashfin himself, marched into Spain.

After his early victories against the Christians, the Veiled Men's emir soon felt that he was being betrayed by the petty little decadent kings of Andalusia. Reasoning with the harsh logic he had learned in the Sahara, he decided to bring some order to this comfortable chaos, the only way to resist the Christian onslaught against Moorish Andalusia.

When ibn-Tashfin died in 1106—aged nearly 100—his son, Ali ibn-Yusuf, reigned at the start of the 12th century over an empire that stretched from the Atlantic to Algiers and from Saragossa and the Balearic Islands to Senegal.

The Almohads—Conquerors and Builders

For 50 years the Almoravids had spent themselves wildly on countless battlefields. Peace and prosperity were now reigning everywhere. Moslem civilization in the West attained its peak but the delights of Andalusia were undermining the asceticism of the Sahara. It might have been a long decline if another reformer had not arisen in the Atlas Mountains.

Mohammed ibn-Tumart, a pious young man, quickly learned all that his native land could teach him about Islam. So he decided to study in the East and it was there that he worked out his doctrine of the Unity of God, the Almohad doctrine (*al muhadin,* those of unity).

Back in Marrakesh, this reformer soon made his presence felt with his agitation. Ali ibn-Yusuf, the Almoravid sovereign, did not know he was signing his empire's death warrant when he allowed him to slip away into the mountains. For the Mahdi (Allah's envoy) settled at Tin-Mal in the Atlas. There, on a well-protected height, Ibn-Tumart began to rally supporters as he preached revolt against the Almoravids whose principles had slackened since their own pure beginnings. Under his iron hand, a new political and religious entity was born, an entity whose influence would spread under the command of his disciple, Abd al-Mumin (Abd el Moumen).

First, he set out to conquer the mountains, the Atlas, the Anti-Atlas, the Middle Atlas and even the Rif. When he took the offensive in 1145, the days of the Almoravids were numbered. After the fall of Fez and then of Meknès, the last of the dynasty's rulers died in the final attack against Marrakesh in 1147.

The new ruler first pacified Morocco, the heart of his empire. Then he found himself up against the same problems faced by his predecessors: Spain and Ifriqiya. Christian pressure was increasing on the peninsula and the other flank of the Arab West was also teetering. Bedouin were growing bolder in their invasions and the Norman King of Sicily, Roger II, had gained a foothold on the Tunisian coast. Perhaps it was this second Christian threat that guided the efforts of Abd al-Mumin. He pushed the boundaries of his empire east to the border of Libya and united the Maghreb for almost a hundred years. But though the Normans had been driven from Ifriqiya, the Almohads could not personally control the outlying provinces of their vast empire. They appointed one of the clan as governor, Abu Hafs, who was succeeded by his son Zakariya.

In Spain he was much less successful. While he had to intervene there as Yusuf ibn-Tashfin had done, he used relatively limited forces and he was not able to drive back the Christians or to secure full control over the emirs of Andalusia. When he died in 1163, after having assumed the title of caliph, he left a considerable but fragile heritage.

His successor, Abu Yakub Yusuf, was able to preserve his father's realm by energetically carrying on the struggle against foreign foes. The third Almohad ruler, Yakub al-Mansur (the Victorious), had a more troublesome reign. An Almoravid uprising had begun in the Balearic Islands and brought war to Ifriqiya. In Spain, his reign was marked by a great victory over Christian troops at Alarcos in 1195. But history remembers Yakub mainly for his monumental buildings. It was he who completed the great mosque in Seville with its minaret, the famed Giralda. At Marrakesh, he built an imperial city. His mosque's tower, the Koutoubia, can still be seen. Even though Marrakesh was his capital, he still wanted to build the city of his dreams. It was on the site of Rabat that he laid the foundations of the biggest mosque in the Moslem West, but his death in 1199 prevented him from completing it. Overlooking the forest of broken columns is the Hassan Tower, strikingly similar in design to the Giralda and the Koutoubia.

Mohammed al-Nasser took up the torch, but the end of his reign was darkened by a severe defeat at Las Navas in Spain at the hands of the Catholic kings. After his death in 1213, decadence set in. The sultans who followed him on the throne until 1276 were unable to reverse the tide. The last of the Almohads died at Tin-Mal where their greatness had begun, under successive blows by insurgents tempted into revolt by their decline.

Hafsids, Zianids and Merinids

The break-up of the Almohad Maghreb was started by Abu Zakariya, Governor of Ifriqiya, who proclaimed himself emir in 1230. A few years later he ordered prayers to be said in his name, thus founding the Hafsid dynasty; he then renamed the country after his new capital, Tunisia.

Abu Zakariya and his son El Mostansir extended their authority as far as Fez. For 50 years prosperity reigned in the coastal regions thanks to skilful Hispano-Moorish immigrants who transformed the coastal plains into orchards.

During El Mostansir's reign, Saint Louis, Louis IX of France, diverted the last crusade to Tunis to collect the tribute due to his brother, King Charles of Sicily. Saint Louis thought that he could convert the Hafsid monarch and obtain his help in conquering the Holy Land. For six months a fruitless dialogue took place at the gates of Carthage. Saint Louis died of the plague in Carthage on August 25, 1270, laid out on a bed of ashes as a sign of penitence.

The Hafsids succeeded in upholding their authority relatively peacefully until 1433, when anarchy broke out once more. At the beginning of the 16th century, Ifriqiya had become a mere pawn in the game played by the two great powers—Spain and Turkey—who were fighting for control of the Mediterranean.

The Hafsid example was followed by Yaghmoracen, Governor of Tlemcen, a Zianid Zenata who established an independent kingdom in 1236. Last, but most decidedly not least, were the Merinids, nomad Zenatas from the Sahara to whom the Almohads, exhausted by warfare, had turned for help. During the second half of the 13th century, their rulers led them on to yet another conquest of Morocco. Like their predecessors, they patiently restored the cycle of Moroccan authority in the Middle Ages—first Fez and its surrounding region under Abu Yahia (1248–58); under Abu Yusuf Yakub (1258–86) the entire south and the beginning of the conflict with the Zianids of Tlemcen, which was going to dominate the history of the 14th century. The same inexorable process took them to Spain and then, under Abu Yakub (1286–1307) to the conquest of Algeria.

Now the Merinids were at their zenith. Their army was feared throughout North Africa, their fleet was powerful. The 14th century marked the peak of Granada towards which the eyes of the Merinids were often turned. Many corsairs were based on Merinid Barbary ports. Their exploits on the Atlantic and Mediterranean coasts along trade routes sailed by European merchantmen were the talk of all Christian kingdoms.

This financial prosperity was naturally echoed by the country's artistic and intellectual growth. The 14th century was the great era of Moorish Andalusia and also of the Maghreb. The Merinid sultans and particularly Abu Inan (1349–58) left a precious heritage. Abu Yusuf al Yakub founded in 1276 a new Fez (Fès Jedid) next to the old city and built his palace there. But the Merinid empire neglected none of its cities. Taza and Tlemcen were given new mosques and Salé an arsenal. Most important of all, new *medersas* were founded in all cities of any size so that great teachers could attract students from the most remote corners of the Maghreb.

Looking at these medersas it is easy to realize why they were particularly fit places for the polishing of minds, confronted by their elegant and harmonious decoration. In those days, too, artists paved the way for intellectuals—but under rather unique conditions. The skilled craftsman or the talented sculptor was the darling of the regime. He had his place in the court of his king who dressed him royally. It is said that, during this golden age, decorators of Merinid monuments worked to the sound of orchestras brought up to inspire them. And it is also said that they were paid not by the hour nor by piecework like the vulgar artist of today, but by a weight of gold dust equal to the weight of the plaster or the sawdust that fell from their chisels. Nothing was too beautiful nor too expensive for the Merinids who had understood that gold takes on value only when it is transformed into a thing of beauty.

A Historian Making History

The career of ibn-Khaldun, the greatest Arab historian, illustrates the complicated interrelation among the rival Arab dynasties in a brilliant complement to his *Kitab al-Ibar* (History of the World).

Born and educated in Tunis, he quickly gained the confidence of his sovereign and was appointed Master of the Signature in his early twenties. But ibn-Khaldun became alarmed at the Hafsid decline and tried his luck at Fez. First suspected for his Hafsid background, he soon took an active part in the power game of sultans becoming figureheads controlled by their ministers, rulers asserting themselves over the bodies of fallen favorites, struggles between and within the dynasties, which he later described in his work.

In 1363, when the Merinid government passed through a particularly unstable period, ibn-Khaldun shifted his allegiance to the last Moslem state in Spain, Granada, where he was entrusted with a mission to Pedro the Cruel of Castile. Though the Christian king was so attracted by the young ambassador that he offered to restore the family property confiscated after the fall of Seville, ibn-Khaldun returned to Granada. His growing influence aroused the prime minister's jealousy so that ibn-Khaldun had to flee to the Maghreb, to become in his turn prime minister of two Hammadid emirs of Bejaia. Falling out of favor with the second, ibn-Khaldun tried the court of Tlemcen, working first for the Zianid sultan and then against the same sultan for the Merinids.

In 1375 ibn-Khaldun retired to a castle near Frenda in central Algeria where, under the protection of a powerful local chieftain, he finished the *Muqaddimah,* somewhat pompously but not inappropriately translated under the title of *Prolegomenoi* to stress the influence of ancient Greek thought. Ibn-Khaldun's 20th-century counterpart, Professor Arnold Toynbee, called this *Introduction to History* "undoubtedly the greatest work of its kind." Needing access to a library for the main body of his work, he obtained permission from Abu al-Abbas to teach and study at Tunis. But the Hafsid ruler insisted on being accompanied on his frequent military expeditions, which the middle-aged historian found taxing. He therefore accepted a professorship at al-Ahzar University in Cairo, lecturing on Moslem law and his *Muqaddimah.* Appointed Chief Malikite Judge of Egypt by Sultan Barquq, he adroitly passed through coups and counter-coups, accompanied the Sultan's heir to Damascus, interviewed the Mongol conqueror Tamerlane, and died shortly after his fourth reappointment as Chief Judge in 1406.

Desert Gold

One hundred and fifty years was a ripe old age for a dynasty in those days. By the end of the 14th century, the Merinids were completely decadent and were replaced by the Wattasids, likewise of Zenata stock, who carried out a dangerous policy by setting up Christian trading posts at Azemmour, El Jadida, Safi, Essaouira and Agadir. The inevitable result quickly followed: not only did Moroccan Moslems lose confidence in these temporary rulers, but the presence of Christians on their soil touched off a religious reaction that had its roots once more in the country's poorest and toughest regions. The curtain had risen on the Saadians.

They came from the Dra Valley, occupied the Sous in 1510, Marrakesh in 1520 and Fez in 1548. But Marrakesh remained their capital and their tomb. The rallying cry of the Saadians was a holy war against the Spanish and Portuguese to whom the Wattasids had opened Morocco's gates and who were clinging to their strongly-fortified footholds on the coast. First Agadir, then Safi and Azemmour were reconquered. But while the Merinids rivalled Granada in elegance, the Saadians were to rival the Ottoman Turks in wealth.

Starting his reign with the conquest of El Jadida in 1578, Ahmed al-Mansur covered his kingdom with gold by leading a military expedition into the eastern Sahara, to Timbuctoo in 1591. From then on, desert caravans began to bring the precious metal into Marrakesh. The city was beautified with mosques and palaces, but the Saadian sultans did not build their empire's prosperity on gold alone. Their era was also one of large-scale agricultural growth.

History tells us that few dynasties can survive happiness and prosperity. While Marrakesh glittered and wealth poured through the fingers of its kings, other descendants of the Prophet were living in poverty, modesty and virtue at Sijilmassa in the Tafilalet, for the wheel of history was ready to turn once more. The austerity of the Almoravids and the mysticism of the Almohads appeared in the reaction of Moulay Rashid, the first Alaouit ruler, who captured northern Morocco in the middle of the 17th century. The Saadian sultans, gone soft in their splendor at Marrakesh, were no longer able to strike back. The Alaouit dynasty that still reigns today in Morocco had been established.

The Turkish Conquest

Taking advantage of the decline of Hafsid power, the coastal cities declared themselves independent. Their chief means of subsistence was a series of pirate raids on the Christians. But once Granada had fallen, united Christian Spain counter-attacked and, emulating the Portuguese occupation along the Atlantic, took possession of the Maghreb's Mediterranean ports, beginning in 1509 with Oran, which was to be held till 1794. The Algerians called to their help the notorious pirate Arroudj, a Greek converted to Islam, who was killed in 1518 and succeeded by his equally ruthless brother Khair al-Din. Both featured flaming red beards and were known as the Barbarossa brothers. Khair al-Din Barbarossa landed at Tunis and Algiers with 4,000 janissaries as the Sultan of Constantinople, an ally of France, was at the same time being threatened by the German Emperor Charles V, who was also King of Spain.

Spain reacted and Tunis was recaptured the following year by Charles V. The Hafsid sovereign, al-Hassan (Moulay Hassan), was restored as a vassal of Spain. Before Algiers, however, the Emperor was defeated and barely escaped with his life. Algiers became the capital of Khair al-Din Barbarossa, who was confirmed as Beylerbey (Governor) and appointed Grand Admiral of the Turkish fleet. Moreover, the Tunisian Moslems objected to a king backed by the Christians and Kairouan, Tunis's old rival, seceded. Al-Hassan wavered and the Turks counter-attacked. The Turkish pirate Dragut settled on Jerba and brought the people of Kairouan, who had become much too independent, to heel. A Calabrian, Ali the Renegade, captured Tunis for the Turks in 1569, but Don John of Austria chased him out the next year. While the last of the Hafsid emirs, Hamid (Moulay Hamida), wandered on the steppe bewailing his lost throne, the Turks once again counter-attacked and Tunisia became an Ottoman province in 1574.

Beylerbeys, Pashas, Deys and Beys

By a subtle graduation of hierarchy the Turkish Sultan tried to keep control of the two pashalics of Algeria and Tunisia. The *pasha* was appointed by Constantinople, and under him a *dey,* the administrative chief, who in turn was assisted by a *bey,* in charge of the army, and a *captan,* in charge of the navy. In practice, the bey in Tunisia and the dey in Algeria, who throughout the 17th century was usually elected by the Turkish janissaries, imposed their authority, and as their skill at collecting taxes increased they became the real rulers and founded dynasties.

For a time, Turkish rule extended into the interior. Tlemcen was occupied in 1555, but no further advance westwards into Morocco was attempted, as much because of the Spanish garrisons at Oran and Melilla as because of the strength of the Saadians. The salient feature of the Turkish Maghreb was the constant naval warfare with the Christian powers, which is just a polite name for Barbary piracy, a lucrative enterprise for some 250 years but a dying industry in the 18th century.

In 1671 the last Turkish-appointed dey of Algeria was murdered, his successors were locally elected, either by the whole military establishment or the higher officers, but the nominal sovereignty of the sultans was recognized till 1710 and Turkish janissaries kept guard till the end. How far the dey's writ ran outside his capital depended on his personality and the cooperation of his *Divan* (Council). Kabylia was never subjugated, and recalcitrant provincial beys were often assassinated, as for instance Salah Bey of Constantine in 1792. Some beys waged private wars of their own, as the formidable beys of Mascara with the Spanish garrison of Oran, which obliged Charles VI of Spain to cede the port to the dey of Algeria rather than withstand the costly attacks. But by then France had replaced Spain as the principal enemy of the Barbary states.

In 1612 Murad Bey, a Corsican turncoat, took over in Tunisia and Constantinople hastened to ratify his usurpation. Murad II (1659–75) imposed his own beys, but after his death, no one knew exactly who was in charge. Finally, the *agha* of the janissaries, Ibrahim, proclaimed himself simultaneously pasha, dey and bey. He had all his rivals assassinated and was eventually assassinated himself by the janissaries.

Husain ben Ali, a Greek turncoat from Crete, was luckier; he had himself nominated bey by the janissaries, whom he rewarded royally. Thus the last of the dynasties was founded: the Husainids (1705–1957). The throne of Tunis proved to be an uneasy one. The Ottoman Turks, the Algerian deys and the European powers stirred up the tribes and the beys rarely died in their beds. On the credit side, nomadism receded making it easier to rule a sedentary people and to wring money out of them. Long columns of soldiers criss-crossed the interior of the country, acting as an armed escort for the tax inspectors and collectors. Disgusted, the nomads went down to the extreme south; the olive tree timidly reappeared along the coast.

Foreign influence came from two sources: on the one hand, the beys brought Andalusian, French and Italian architects, engineers and artisans; on the other, Christian captives, sold in Tunis by privateers, renounced their faith if the Lazarist priests did not ransom them quickly enough, and put their skills and technical know-how at the service of their masters.

From Versailles to Meknès

Fate came to the aid of the Alaouits during their early years with a set of favorable circumstances. Not only were the Turks in Algeria occupied with preserving the last shreds of their dominion, but the dynasty's second king was a tireless and far-sighted man who reigned fifty-five years from 1672 to 1727.

Moulay Ismail succeeded to the throne when English, Spanish and Portuguese invaders were at the gates of his kingdom after having captured a number of towns on the coast. First, he brought order to the country by raising an army of 40,000 negroes to put down tribal rebellions. Soldiers of fortune also served in this campaign and one of them, a Welshman named Thomas Pellow from Penrhyn, wrote the story of his adventures.

After the successful completion of the Reconquista, Spain was expelling the last Moslems to North Africa, while in France, a reign not dissimilar to that of Moulay Ismail had begun: indeed, Louis XIV was to remain on his throne from 1643 to 1712.

Perhaps it is too tempting to compare the two rulers and Moulay Ismail's Meknès to Louis XIV's Versailles, but the parallels are striking. The Moroccan Sultan worked tirelessly to pacify his kingdom completely and to spread his rule even into the most remote mountain fastnesses. He protected his eastern border against the Turks in Algeria, evicted the Portuguese from their Atlantic ports, wrested Tangier from the English, drove the Spaniards from Larache and Mehdia and finally reduced their two last holdings, Ceuta and Melilla, to their tiny dimensions of today.

These would have been impressive achievements for any normal ruler, but Moulay Ismail was not content to rest on them. He realized that he was living in an age of international relations and that Morocco had to enter this age. In his capital at Meknès, where he built enthusiastically and gigantically, he received the ambassadors of many countries. He sent out his own, particularly to the King of France. Contemporary chronicles tell us of the mutual esteem of the two sovereigns: when the Moroccan ambassador gave Louis XIV a letter from the Sultan in 1699, the Sun King affectionately kissed him three times after taking off his hat. Only then did he open the letter.

After a steep decline under his weak son Moulay Abdallah, order was restored by his grandson Sidi Mohammed ben-Abdallah (1757–90), who founded Essaouira and finally drove the Portuguese from El Jadida. Moulay Sliman (1792–1822) further consolidated his hold over the tribes, but while these rulers were able to preserve the great king's achievements despite internal quarrels, they did not have the vision that would have enabled Morocco to modernize and carry out the necessary evolution into the 19th century. In 1830, Morocco was stupefied by the French capture of Algiers, an event whose repercussions could be compared to those of the fall of Toledo in 1085. But the days of Yusuf ibn-Tashfin were long dead. Sultan Moulay Abd al-Rahman (1822–59) tried unsuccessfully to annex Tlemcen, joined forces with Emir Abdelkader and the battle of Isly was fought in 1844. Facing the French army of Marshal Bugeaud were Moroccan troops under the command of Moulay Mohammed, the Sultan's son.

Moulay Mohammed outnumbered his adversary but Bugeaud had artillery and the Prince de Joinville was shelling Tangier. Less than a month after this battle, fought on August 14, the treaty of Tangier, supplemented by a convention signed in March 1845, at Lalla Marnia in western Algeria, defined relations between Morocco and France. In particular Morocco was forced to abandon Abdelkader who surrendered to General Lamoricière two years later. The conquest of Algeria had entered its final phase.

The French Presence

When the dey of Algeria struck the French ambassador with his fly swatter he provided Charles X of France with an opportunity to shore up his teetering throne with popular colonial conquest. Yet the French landing at Sidi Fredj on June 14, 1830 did not prevent the July Revolution in Paris. The Bourbon fell, but Louis Philippe continued the expansionist policy, in which his son, the Prince de Joinville, played a leading part. The French quickly deposed the dey, but it took 17 years of fighting under the command of Marshal Bugeaud to overcome the resistance of Emir Abdelkader; Kabylia was only pacified in 1871. By then France had become involved to the east and west.

From the 16th century onwards, consuls and merchants of Marseilles held a dominant position in Tunis. On several occasions the French fleet had come to the help of the beys when they were threatened from outside. But Italy was entering the colonial scramble and France was forced to increase her pressure. England, too, poked her oar in.

Louis Philippe and Napoleon III received the beys in Paris, for Tunisia was undergoing a succession of economic and social crises. As security for her loans, France obtained telegraph and railway concessions from them, and Tunisia was even docile enough to send an expeditionary force to be massacred in the Crimea.

No matter what the cost, the beys decided to "modernize" the country; plans for a constitution, lay courts and audit offices emerged from the viziers' green portfolios, but the populace would have none of it and revolted. European appetites were whetted; the Italian, English and French consuls all proffered their good offices and fought each other tooth and nail behind the scenes. But the Italian consul was too greedy and alarmed his English counterpart, who agreed in 1878 to French intervention which occurred three years later.

The Chamber of Deputies voted a sum of five million francs for Jules Ferry to finance an expedition against the Kroumir tribes of Tunisia and secure the Algerian frontier. From then on French interference increased and the Convention of La Marsa (1883) established the protectorate. The bey was now subject to the Resident, and French officials duplicated the Tunisian ministers. Well-organized efforts in all fields resulted within fifty years in a considerable improvement in Tunisian living standards.

The country attracted saints and soldiers, grasping foreigners, aesthetes and artists. Of the 9 million hectares (22 million acres) of arable land 4 (9.9) million were under cultivation; of the latter 50,000 (125.000) were owned by the Société Franco-Africaine, 30,000 (75,000) by the Société des Phosphates and 30,000 (75,000) by l'Omnium Immobilier Tunisien.

The world-wide economic depression hit Tunisia hard and Tunisian nationalism gained ground. Between 1920 and 1934 the Constitutional Party, or *Destour,* demanded internal autonomy, but in 1934 the party split—the "Old Turbans" were supplanted by the *Neo-Destour* Party, which commanded greater popular support. One of its youthful leaders was Habib Bourguiba.

A Panther in Agadir

Hardly had peace between France and Morocco been restored, when Sidi Mohammed (1859–73) was involved in a war with Spain, which obtained concessions by the Peace of Tetouan. Moulay Hassan (1873–94) tried to maintain the unity of his country and to reorganize it. But co-existence with a French-administered Algeria was difficult. It became even more difficult under the reign of the next sultan, Moulay Abd al-Aziz (1894–1908), who was 14 years old when he acceded to the throne.

Inside Morocco, agitation increased along with the intrigue of various foreign groups. On the border between Algeria and Morocco, the situation became confused; General Lyautey occupied Béchar in 1903 and Berguent in 1904. Not at all eager to see her European rival move into Morocco, Germany reacted in 1906 at the Conference of Algeciras in Spain, attended by the representatives of ten major European powers and the U.S.A. The independence and integrity of Morocco were guaranteed, but a mandate was granted France and Spain to maintain order in Morocco. These two countries were chosen because of their specific interests in this part of the world. Obviously, this situation was a step along the road to a protectorate.

On the economic level, the "open door" status was intended to prevent any of the signatories from carving out economic privileges in Morocco. Despite the Algeciras agreement unrest continued and incidents cropped up regularly. This led French troops first to occupy the Oujda region and then to land at Casablanca. Sultan Moulay Abd al-Aziz was dethroned in 1908 and replaced by his brother, Moulay Abd al-Hafiz, who had proclaimed himself sultan in Marrakesh in 1907 but failed to establish his authority throughout the country. The situation boiled over into a crisis when the French army entered Fez in 1911 to relieve the besieged Sultan.

In Berlin tension was at a high pitch. To the Germans, France was obviously taking over Morocco. Germany decided to thwart her neighbor by sending a cruiser, the *Panther,* into the bay of Agadir. This move led to a Franco-German crisis that nearly touched off the powder keg of the world war that was to explode three years later. But diplomats were negotiating and bargaining. On November 30, 1911 an agreement was reached. France granted Germany rights in the Congo. In return, Germany gave France a free hand in Morocco.

It was under these conditions that, on March 30, 1912, the French minister in Tangier, Regnault, signed with Sultan Abd al-Hafiz a treaty affirming the sovereign's authority and setting up a protectorate headed by a French resident commissioner-general. At the same time, the Spaniards led an expedition to Ksar-el-Kebir and strengthened their positions. An agreement settled the border of the Spanish zone of the protectorate.

Once the agreement had been signed, it then had to be translated into reality: that is, Morocco had to be conquered. The two protecting powers actually had control only over accessible areas on the plains. The mountains were not yet "protected."

A Favorable Balance Sheet

General Louis Lyautey was appointed first French resident-general in Morocco on April 28, 1912. He arrived in Fez on May 24, effectively inaugurating the protectorate that was to last forty-four years; its balance sheet is far from unfavorable.

Lyautey took on the military task of pacification but he did not overlook the human task of organization. This great soldier had a deep love for the country at whose head he had been placed. True, he loved it with a protective love, but this aristocrat was a monarchist at heart and he felt great esteem for the Sherifian monarchy. A devout Catholic, he scrupulously respected the religion of Islam. His attitude brought results. When the Great War broke out in Europe in 1914, Lyautey was forced to interrupt his pacification and send most of his troops to France. And yet, the task he had begun was not compromised. On the contrary, Moroccan units fought on the French front, creating a brotherhood of arms whose memory could never fade.

When pacification began again after 1918, it was accompanied by a big public works program. This meant the expansion of Casablanca, the construction of its harbor and rules of town planning imposed upon its builders. It meant the expansion of Kenitra, a harbor given the name of Port Lyautey. It also meant the building of new areas in Fez, Meknès and Marrakesh while these cities were being linked by railways and roads.

In the mountains the fighting was bitter as the Berber tribes held out for years. In 1920, it was only the death of the old chieftain, Moha ou Hammou, that led the Zaïans of the Middle Atlas to submit, bringing about the surrender of the Taza region and the pacification of Upper Moulay. But a great warrior appeared in the Rif in 1921. He was Abd-el-Krim who, after inflicting a serious defeat upon the Spaniards, was threatening Fez. It took the French and Spaniards six years to get the upper hand of this fierce foe. Against his 20,000 fighting men, the French had an occupation army of 325,000 troops and auxiliaries and the Spaniards an army of 100,000. After his defeat, Abd-el-Krim was deported to Reunion Island and the French were able to turn to the south. Yet seven more years were needed before French troops were through in the Anti-Atlas and ready to march on Tindouf in 1934.

In 1927 a young man ascended the throne in Rabat. His name was Sidi Mohammed ben-Yusuf and his reign was to be of capital importance. After the pacification, Morocco enjoyed a period of economic growth in agriculture and mining, accompanied by large-scale public works of high quality. Many Frenchmen settled in Morocco, introducing contemporary administration, education and commerce.

The French Twilight

When France was submerged by the tidal wave of Germany's armies in 1940, the French administration and army in North Africa opted for the Vichy government, while the native rulers in Morocco and Tunisia as well as the population remained loyal to France. But during the two years preceding the Allied landings in North Africa and while Jews were being persecuted throughout occupied Europe, Sidi Mohammed ben-Yusuf protected not only his own Jewish subjects but also others who came to his country seeking refuge.

When the Allies landed in 1942, Admiral Darlan, Marshal Pétain's presumptive heir, was appointed Governor General of French North Africa and Commander-in-Chief of the armed forces. His assassination the same year relieved the Allies of dealing with a new adherent, who had only recently opposed them, and whose refusal to hand over or even neutralize the fleet had led to the unfortunate naval engagement of Mers El Kebir in 1940. After the effacement of his successor, General Giraud, in 1943, General de Gaulle was recognized by the Allies and throughout North Africa.

But the colonial power had been crushed by Germany; the myth of French invincibility was shattered for ever: liberation came from British-American forces and Marshal Rommel's German Africa Corps had withdrawn before Marshal Montgomery's British VIII Army entered into Tunisia, where from November 1942 to May 1943, the 'Tunisian Campaign' laid waste the country. Heavy fighting took place in the south, the British forces finally breaking through the Mareth Line and in the area of the Dorsal the Americans attacking from Algeria. The Free French Forces, who had come up from the desert, and the French Army of North Africa, which had at last resumed fighting, contributed to the victory. Tunis and Bizerta fell on May 7, 1943. North African troops, especially Moroccans, took part in the invasion of Italy.

Independence: The Easy Way

After the war Bourguiba's influence increased and France's Tunisian policy became more and more hesitant. Incidents multiplied and armed resistance developed, ending in a period of serious tension in 1953–4. The state of siege paralyzed the country. On July 31, 1954 Pierre Mendès-France, the French Premier, recognized Tunisia's autonomy in a ceremony at the Bardo Palace. On June 1, 1955 Habib Bourguiba, the "supreme fighter," returned from exile and was welcomed by enthusiastic crowds. He negotiated Tunisia's independence which was recognized by France on March 20, 1956.

From 1890 to 1956, the population of Tunisia had doubled. France's contribution in the fields of public health and agricultural and industrial equipment had been considerable, but probably her greatest contribution lay in having trained men capable of administering and developing the country.

When, on July 25, 1957, Habib Bourguiba deposed the bey and had himself declared President of the Republic, the economic and social state of the country was alarming. French settlers, who at independence numbered 181,000, were leaving *en masse*. Bourguiba, a realist, undertook the task of picking up the pieces. Progress was sometimes a question of trial and error, but at least something was being done. In the field of foreign policy, the Tunisian President quickly became an outstanding statesman. Disliking any form of rigid formula, he let it be known that although Tunisia was linked to the Arab community by her traditions, she was also part of the western world because of her geographical position and way of thinking.

Relations between emerging Tunisia and France have not always been sunny, especially in 1961, when at least one thousand Tunisians were killed by French troops who opened fire on a crowd of demonstrators invading the still-French naval base at Bizerta (July 18), an act which eventually forced the French government to hand over the base to Tunisian control. Furthermore, in 1964, French-owned lands were expropriated and France stopped her economic aid. In 1967 collectivization of all agricultural land was attempted, resulting in a dramatic fall in output. The pragmatic President disgraced the minister in charge, who was sentenced to ten years' imprisonment but escaped abroad. Private ownership was largely restored, though cooperatives were retained on a much reduced scale, mainly in the central areas. Cooperation with France, America and Britain, which contributed to assistance programs, was resumed.

Despite occasional student and labor unrest, the very real economic advance, accompanied by a high degree of female emancipation, seems to have laid a stable basis for peaceful development. Opposition parties have been allowed to form, but they abstained from the 1986 election, so that only the National Front is represented in the single-chamber parliament. In the fall of 1987 Bourguiba was overthrown in a bloodless palace coup because of his advanced age. He was succeeded by the recently appointed prime minister, Zine El Abidine Ben Ali, who is maintaining Tunisia's pro-Western stance while also bringing about a reconciliation with Libya.

Ben Ali was elected president unopposed in April 1989. Parliamentary elections held at the same time resulted in all seats going to the newly renamed RCD, to general dismay both inside and outside the government. However, the elections revealed that the unofficial political party of the Islamic fundamentalists was easily the second force in the country.

Royal Independence

In Morocco, the Sultan headed the movement for independence, expressing the increasing demand for the end of the protectorate—not through tribal revolts and the scattered uprisings of the past but through a national unity that Morocco had never known before.

The first revelation of this movement was the *Istiqlal* (Independence) manifesto in 1947. The Sultan backed it unequivocally in a speech he made two years later during an official trip to Tangier. Since Tangier was an international zone (and therefore not under the authority of the protectorate), he was able to take a stand there. This led to a test of strength that reached its climax on August 20, 1953, when General Guillaume, the French resident-general, exiled Sidi Mohammed ben-Yusuf to Madagascar and, with the help of El Glaoui, the Pasha of Marrakesh, placed Moulay Arafa, an obscure member of the Alaouit family, on the throne.

The next two years cemented Moroccan unity and polarized a new-style patriotism around the exiled Sultan. Revolt was stirring but France luckily reversed her decision before it was too late and, above all, before relations between the two countries and the peoples could suffer irreparable harm. After a conference held at Aix-les-Bains with representatives of various political tendencies in the Moroccan independence movement, the Sultan returned triumphantly to Rabat on November 18, 1955, the twenty-eighth anniversary of his reign.

From then on, negotiations for independence were carried out actively. On March 3, 1956, an agreement was reached with the French government. On April 7, Mohammed V signed in Madrid the treaty granting independence to the northern zone; the Sultan's subsequent visit to the Spanish cities of the Almoravids and Almohads was the first of a reigning Moroccan monarch for over seven hundred years. On October 29, the international status of Tangier was abrogated. Sidi Mohammed al-Mokri, who had been Grand Vizir throughout the entire forty-four years of the protectorate, died in office at the age of 105.

In the end, independence had come quicker than expected, a prolonged struggle with the resulting bitterness had been avoided, but once this independence had been acquired, it still had to be built. In 1957, Mohammed V changed his title to king, thus indicating a more contemporary style of government. A National Consultative Assembly was appointed to supervise the ministers, but the intransigence of a breakaway faction of the Istiqlal party led the King to assume the premiership, pending the promulgation of a constitution. By the end of the year, elections for municipal and provincial councils had been held to represent new administrative areas which were based on economic instead of tribal criteria. But Mohammed V barely had the opportunity to start on this new road before he died of heart failure on February 26, 1961. He was the only hereditary Moslem ruler to put his trust in his people rather than in the protecting power, but he was never blinded by shortsighted chauvinism to reject the beneficial innovations of the protectorate.

Mohammed V had relied increasingly on his eldest son, who accompanied his father into exile. In 1957, after taking the advice of the ulemas, Mohammed V promulgated a *dahir* (law) making Prince Moulay Hassan heir to the throne; in 1960, he entered the government as vice premier.

A New Era

The new King was educated at the College for the Sons of Notables in Rabat, and received a degree in law from Bordeaux University, but is fully conscious of being heir to a dynasty which even Lord Palmerston, no great respector of foreign potentates, called imperial. He has thus never felt compelled to make sensational gestures, popular if destructive, like dismissing all French administrators, teachers, doctors and other experts essential to Morocco's orderly progress.

On succeeding to the throne, Hassan II retained the premiership until after the election of the first parliament in 1963 according to the constitution adopted by a referendum the previous year. But though Moroccan ministers had taken over from the French heads of departments as smoothly as, on the lower level, Moroccan *caids* had replaced their French and Spanish counterparts, the advance to the parliamentary system granting all citizens, male and female, equal political rights, had been too rapid. Small but vociferous radical groups provoked a latent crisis, with attempts on the King's life, and he was forced to suspend the constitution and rule by decree. In 1972 another referendum approved a new constitution, under which one third of the 264 deputies in the single chamber are elected by provincial councils and professional associations, two thirds by direct vote.

The acquisition of the northern half of the phosphate and iron-rich former Spanish Sahara in 1976 greatly increased the King's prestige, though nearly leading to war with Algeria, which allows the Polisario guerrillas to operate from its territory. At the end of that year, the Independents, the King's supporters, gained an overwhelming victory in the municipal and provincial elections as well as early in the following year in the elections to the professional bodies representing commerce, industry and the crafts. On Throne Day 1977, the King appointed the leaders of the main opposition parties ministers of state, a preliminary step to the parliamentary elections in which the Independents won an absolute majority. In 1979 the divided leftist opposition declared its full support for the incorporation of the Sahara evacuated by Mauritania. Choosing as usual his ministers for their abilities rather than their affiliations, the King named a government supported by four center-right parties that won 215 out of the 306 seats in the enlarged parliament elected in 1984.

Morocco has continued a policy of moderation as a member of the Arab League, but left the Organization of African Unity in protest against the recognition of the Polisario. Except for Egypt the only Arab ruler sufficiently courageous to receive an Israeli prime minister, the King abrogated in 1986 a vague unity treaty with Libya. Special relations have been maintained with France, without impeding cooperation with the U.S.A. Application to join the European Community (EC) has stalled.

Independence: The Hard Way

1945 was a terrible year for Algeria. The cereal ration was 300 grams per day for Europeans, 250 for Arabs, the black market flourished and the villagers were eating grass. In May, the revolt began in the High Plateaux of the Constantine Region, the mob killing some 30 Europeans at Sétif. Violence spread to the countryside, where over a hundred Europeans were massacred, many more wounded. The repression was ruthless: bombardments from cruisers and planes, countermassacres by the Foreign Legion and Senegalese troops as well as German and Italian prisoners of war armed for the occasion; 1,500 dead, according to official estimates. Then a few years of deceptive peace.

The first shots in the Algerian Revolution were fired near Biskra on November 1, 1954. In December, Mohamed Boukharouba, who had assumed the name of Houari Boumedienne in honor of Tlemcen's patron saint, successfully accomplished his first mission by seizing the yacht of King Hussein of Jordan at Alexandria in Egypt and sailing it with a cargo of arms to Nador in Morocco, by then independent and like Tunisia assisting the insurgents. The terrible civil war, which was to last seven years and cost one million lives, had started. A civil war and not a colonial freedom movement as in the other two Maghreb countries, because Algeria was not a protectorate but part of metropolitan France, inhabited by three million homogeneous French settlers against seven million Moslems of great diversity.

In May 1958, the army and the French settlers of the three Algerian departments swept de Gaulle back into power under the slogan of French Algeria, but despite the military successes of General Challe, culminating in the abortive Revolt of the Generals in Algeria in April 1961, President de Gaulle considered the drain too great and by the agreement of Evian in March 1962 Algerian independence was recognized; the safeguards for the French settlers were quickly disregarded, and three million returned to France, abandoning what they and their fathers had created, in one of the biggest population movements in history. Only some 40,000 remained, including a large number of by now fairly old ladies. At the same time the number of Algerians in France grew to over 80,000 as, ironically, the great influx of Maghrebi workers reached its peak only after obtaining independence from the country they had fought so passionately and to which they now, equally passionately, wish to emigrate.

Boumedienne had become Chief of Staff of the F.L.N. (National Liberation Force) and while increasingly radical political leaders succeeded one another, he kept the all-important Ministry of Defence. In June 1965, Boumedienne together with 25 fellow officers—of which only eight are still in power as the Council of the Revolution, forming the nucleus of the 17-member Polit Bureau—overthrew President Ben Bella, who had followed a ruinous policy of support to all liberation movements throughout the world.

Boumedienne tried to reconcile the irreconcilable: Islam, socialism and Algerian nationalism, all the more difficult in the economic and administrative chaos caused by the departure of the French officials. The first two Four-Year Plans of the development program to 1977, made possible by the large petrol and natural gas revenues, allocated 70 per cent of investments to rapid industrialization, and a mere 15 per cent to agriculture. The Agrarian Revolution, launched in 1971, failed to stop the exodus from the country to the big urban centers and led to a decline in production, so that Algeria, only recently a big exporter of agricultural products, has become increasingly dependent on food imports. The Algerian fellah, like every peasant the world over, hates the concepts of collectivization and neglects the soil, trees and beasts that do not belong to him. This was finally recognized in the more pragmatic mood of the '80s, when the huge state farms were broken up and agriculture was returned to the private sector.

Falling into a coma on November 19, 1978, President Boumedienne was attended by a large number of famous physicians from a greater number of countries than any head of state up to then. He died, however, without regaining consciousness, from a rare blood disease on December 27.

The 3,290 delegates, of which 600 were officers, designated Colonel Chadli Bendjedid unique candidate for the presidency, at the F.L.N. congress held at the Olympic complex of Ben Aknoun on the heights of Algiers on January 31, 1979. At 50, the oldest member of the Council of the Revolution, with the highest military rank, commander of the region of Oran where most of the army is concentrated near the Moroccan border, Chadli—the name was adopted during the war—was duly elected President on February 7 with a customary 94.23 per cent of votes. In his acceptance speech he stressed the continuity of Boumedienne's policies, but faced by formidable economic and social problems, despite the huge revenues from hydrocarbon exports, Chadli has changed course. Riots in October 1988 accelerated his reforms, and the hard-line F.L.N. old guard in the government has largely been replaced by Western-minded technocrats. Opposition parties have mushroomed, and fundamental economic reforms are under way, reversing the trend of nearly thirty years of centralized socialism. But the political and economic reforms ar vigorously opposed, both by old-style F.L.N. leaders and the increasingly important Islamic fundamentalists—even stronger in Algeria than in Tunisia.

The Problem in Common

In spite of the very real political, social and economic differences, the three countries partake of a common Berber, Arab-Islamic and French heritage. Though various Berber dialects are spoken by scattered minorities, French has remained the second official language, especially in the expanding sphere of higher education. Moslem fundamentalists present another common danger, which led to the founding of the Emir Abdelkader University of Islamic Sciences in Constantine, Algeria, in 1984 to preserve spiritual equilibrium and avoid deviations.

One problem, so far only partially tackled, provides the strongest common denominator: the exceptionally high birthrate, a true population explosion, whereby 45 per cent of the population is under 14 years of age, almost 60 per cent under 21. None of the countries has been able to deal effectively with the ever-increasing unemployment, especially since the traditional safety valve, migration to France, has been closed. Some of the 2 million Maghreb workers in Europe have already returned, which has decreased the remittances from emigrants, an important item in the payment balances of the three countries, which are heavily indebted abroad. The very magnitude of the problem might bring about a common policy and thus overcome temporary misunderstandings and hostilities. After Tunisia, where family planning has long been a priority in successive National Development Plans, Morocco has recently likewise reduced population growth below the terrifying average 3 percent in most Arab countries. In the deeply conservative countryside the proudly ironical saying still stands—each family its own football team.

Algeria and Morocco are, therefore, threatened by the same insoluble problem: how to find work and feed 35–40 million inhabitants each by the year 2000 if present population trends continue. However different the forms of government, both try to overcome religious and traditional opposition to family planning in an unfavorable medical and social climate. A glimmer of hope resulted from the better education of women, some of whom have ceased to consider the regulation dozen offspring as Allah's greatest blessing.

A brighter glimmer came in February 1989, when Tunisia, Morocco, and Algeria—along with Libya and Mauretania—signed a treaty setting up the Arab Maghreb Union, a regional association which they hope will act something like the twelve-member European Community. Although the five countries have widely divergent political systems and outlooks—for example, King Hassan sitting at the same table as Colonel Qaddafi—the prospects for economic cooperation are reasonable. And as the rest of the world splits up into trading blocs, the Maghreb, too, needs the clout that can only come from speaking with one voice.

MOORISH CUISINE

Fruits of the Sun

One chapter for three countries on so important a subject might appear audacious. But where the Maghreb is concerned this is not so, or in any case less than for one country like France, where regional variety is infinitely greater. In North Africa the difference is more often etymological than gastronomical, and even the wines never differ as much as, for instance, a Bordeaux from a Burgundy. Yet Morocco is generally conceded pride of place, with seasoning largely responsible for the high standing. Every souk spice merchant concocts his own *ras el hanout,* a mixture which might include 24 different spices. Some are pungent, some piquant, some perfumed, while some are included for their alleged aphrodisiac properties. Cumin is usually a main constituent and the chief flavoring item. It is often put on the table together with salt in a two-bowl cruet instead of pepper. Next in prominence are fresh coriander, garlic, ginger, and onions. Subtlety more than compensates for lack of variety. Geography is the determining factor, as in most parts, especially in the south, it is too arid to graze cattle, while pigs are forbidden by Islam. Except at the coast, where seafood is plentiful, chickens, goats, pigeons, rabbits and sheep, occasionally camel, but above all eggs, are the basic foodstuffs.

Tunisia comes a close second in the culinary hierarchy, mainly because of more than 60 varieties of *couscous,* the national dish. It also produces the most delicious *brik à l'oeuf,* the most exotic of condiments, rose-petal powder, and the hottest of sauces, the ubiquitous fiery red pepper paste *harissa.* Time and labor are of no consequence in Maghreb cooking, as the preparation of certain dishes takes more than a day.

52

At its best, Moorish cuisine is tasty, savory, and rich, but somewhat defective in raw vegetables and salads. Indulging in a whole *diffa,* a ceremonial banquet, means a stomach strained if not surfeited. In private however, the average family diet is less exuberant and even tends to be rather frugal. Salads and refreshing dishes are then served which accord well with the climate, but festivities demand the grand cuisine of international reputation.

Recipes Galore

There are virtually no outstanding restaurants in the Maghreb. The better foreign-owned establishments, mainly French but also Italian, Spanish, Vietnamese and Chinese, have long closed in Algeria, are disappearing in Tunisia, and are thinning out in Morocco. The elderly expatriates are rarely replaced, while the numerous European-style eating places are on the whole second-hand imitations of the real thing. Fast food has made a tentative appearance, though why anyone should prefer a hamburger to *kefta,* the tasty local minced meat served in a variety of preparations, would be hard to say.

The expensive Arab restaurants in the larger towns and tourist centers rarely justify their prices, but the moderate and even the inexpensive local eating places are usually preferable to hotel dining rooms, even though they mostly include one Maghreb specialty in their menus. The all-too-few praiseworthy exceptions are singled out in the regional chapters. The setting of the restaurant will dictate the charges more often than the quality of the food. On the whole, the seafood restaurants are the best bet, especially along the Atlantic coast. Service, though not always very efficient, is usually willing.

Perhaps it may once again be wise to exercise a certain restraint before attempting all the 250 recipes listed in the standard *short* cook books. Luckily, the temptation is not all that great—though the dishes sound and sometimes actually are delicious—simply because the bill of fare in most restaurants is limited to the popular stand-bys. As for bread, it is nearly always a thin white loaf, the typically French *baguette,* the staple diet of Algerian and Tunisian homes, while in Morocco the unleavened round Arab bread is still common, as it is so much handier to wipe up the sauces.

Among the soups the *harira* is queen, an ideal dish to restore one's strength. Consumed mainly in winter and more especially for the breaking of the fast on evenings during Ramadan, it is best enjoyed in the little native restaurants in the medinas where contact with local life sharpens the pleasure of the fare. The harira is a three-stage preparation of numerous alternatives within some guiding essentials: first, cook for two hours or more portions of chicken offal, diced mutton, chick-peas, parsley, ginger, onion and saffron; when boiling add a large piece of butter. Second: prepare a platter of rice duly seasoned with the required spices depending on the cook's imagination. Thirdly: mix coriander, tomatoes and bread yeast. When each dish is fully cooked all three are mixed into one delicious whole which is sometimes improved with the addition of eggs. One or two bowls of harira are sufficient to make an evening meal.

The *chorba beïda,* a favorite in Algiers, is a chicken soup containing the bird plus onions, chick-peas, vermicelli, pepper, cinnamon and parsley bound with egg yolk. The Constantine *chorba beïda bel kefta* replaces the chicken with meat balls and the vermicelli with almonds and saffron. The *chorba loubia* is a simpler bean soup, and the Tunisian *lebabli* chick-pea soup spiced with garlic and cumin, to which one adds lemon juice and a dash of *harissa,* a mixture of red pepper, salt and garlic softened in oil, which is always on the table to burn the mouth of the unwary.

The most popular entrée is the *bourak* in its various shapes, pasties filled with ground meat, chopped hard-boiled eggs, cheese or vegetables and baked in the oven. A succulent variation is *brik,* which contains an egg inside the dough, fried without breaking the yolk. It's as difficult to eat as to prepare; try biting into it without letting the yolk slide out. *Melfouf* is sheep's belly stuffed with little squares of meat, liver, heart and kidney grilled on charcoal. *Merguez* is heavily spiced lamb sausage.

The Glory of Bstila

The *bstila* is the sum total of Moroccan gastronomy, albeit a comparatively rare one, as it is so complicated to prepare. Several cooks are called in, under the orders of a chief cook who will slave throughout the day. Her masterpiece will only be ready for a late evening meal, as the shopping list for this operation, for twelve persons, reads as follows: three pounds of butter, thirty eggs, four pounds of flour, six pigeons, twelve ounces of sugar, one pound of almonds, a seasoning of cinnamon, ginger, pimentoes, onions, saffron and coriander.

The cook will devote all her talent, all her art to the preparation of the dough: the bstila presents itself as an enormous, stuffed, flaky pastry. The pastry itself is baked by throwing small pellets of dough on a large metal griddle heated to the appropriate temperature. This little game goes on until the whole griddle is covered with a thin film of crust. This is dexterously removed from the plate before it has had time to brown. The layer of baked pastry is placed on one side and the next one is baked in a similar way. *One hundred and four* of these layers, as thin as tissue paper, are needed to make a bstila for twelve.

The finely chopped meat of the pigeons goes into the stuffing together with scrambled eggs, sugar and such variety of spices as the cook decides to choose. The stuffing is also cooked on the griddle previously used for pastry. When ready, the finishing touches are added and it is decorated with a mosaic of cinnamon and powdered sugar. The successful bstila is as exquisite a dish as can be found anywhere but its complexity bans it from the recipe books of the do-it-yourself school of cooks which flourish in the pages of the brighter ladies' magazines. The bstila is certainly not a cheap item in restaurants, but something will be missing from your program if you don't stretch your budget to take in the experience.

For Your Pleasure: A Hundred Touajen

Tajin (plural *touajen*) figures on the menu of every self-respecting eating place. Used by itself the word tajin means stew; it is only a very general description without precise definition. The tajin is left to simmer for hours on a slow heat. Any number of recipes can be aptly described as touajen, always provided they are left to stew, very slowly, on low heat. Naturally, dishes of this sort leave an open door to the cook's imagination as to what ingredients they should include. There are touajen for all seasons, every climate and mood. Fez, reputedly the gourmet capital, even produces a fruit tajin, but the best is probably *jej emshmel,* chicken with olives and brine-preserved lemons, sometimes topped with a poached egg. The toua-jen's traditional constituents are chicken, pigeon, mutton and beef, but they are not restricted to these classics: camel meat, turkey, fish or game will do just as well.

The secret of a good tajin is in the liquid in which the meat has been left to cook for hours on end. Again, time is of no consequence and what counts is the excellence of the end product, of which there are two: the 'bouillon' or soup, and the meat. The soup itself is finally reduced to a concentrated stock: during the cooking those twin requisites, butter and olive oil, have been added as well as spices according to the cook's discretion. After all these manipulations, what remains of the original soup is not so much a concentrated stock as a fragrant sauce, or gravy. The prolonged cooking leaves the meat absolutely melting, offering no resistance to the fingers with which the tajin is meant to be eaten.

If beef or mutton are used, they are usually diced before cooking but poultry or game are left whole. The main point is that there should be an abundance of everything on the table. The tajin is served in a vessel of glazed earthenware.

There should be no inhibition regarding seasoning: audacity is the password and in consequence these dishes have a character difficult to describe in cold print. One must have tasted them to realize how well sweetening and sugar go with spices and what excellent company prunes and raisins keep with tomatoes, peppers and pimentoes, and even with garlic. These may be unlikely allies but you must entrust yourself to the knowing hands.

Lemon Chicken

Another set-piece of ingenuity is olive and lemon chicken. It is served with a sauce which has a slightly sour taste and its composition may intrigue you. Once trussed and ready for the pot, the chicken is put to bed on a cushion of aromatic spices: onion, garlic, coriander, saffron, pepper. It is then half covered with water. To this is added a ladle of olive oil. The whole is left to simmer on a very low heat to reduce the stock. When this is done another long slow simmering session begins but this time, of prepared olives and lemons. They are repeatedly moistened with the meat-stock until they are ready for serving.

Chicken and poultry are the *pièces de résistance* of many unrecorded family recipes not served in restaurants: in these heirloom formulae passed from mother to daughter, chickens can be stuffed with endless ingredients, with almonds, semolina, raisins, honey and rice. One can eat chicken repeatedly but never cooked twice in the same way.

A Noble Tradition

Mutton is the staple meat of the Maghrebi's table and the mainstay of the *mechoui*. To enjoy it fully you will need perhaps a modicum of luck, because the roast meat of some sheep tastes better than that of others which smell of suet. So choose a young sheep, but not too big. Praise Allah, plunge the knife into the carotid and let the blood spurt out to the last drop. Make a hole with the point of the knife above the knee joint of one of the back legs, put a stick in the hole and loosen the skin. Through this opening blow till the air gets to the fore legs and make them stick up. The sheep will then swell and stiffen.

Cut the skin between the legs and skin the sheep, put aside the liver and heart, scrape and rinse the tripe, singe and clean the head and trotters. Dig a hole of appropriate size, place at each end two forked sticks and light a good fire in the hole. When the fire is covered with light ashes, impale the sheep from tail to throat on a stick long enough to rest on the two forks. Cook slowly, throwing a little earth on the fire when too hot or add charcoal when more heat is needed.

Two pounds four ounces of butter or an equivalent of olive oil are required for constant basting. Five hours are necessary for the skin to become crackly while the flesh remains juicy. The choicest morsels to pick out, at the risk of burning the fingers, are the kidneys and the meat on the shoulders. Place the sheep on a deep copper tray, the four legs tucked underneath, the head raised, the grilled liver and heart stuck into the back. Serve with salt, powdered cumin and red pepper.

At ceremonial banquets where bstila, tajin and mechoui are served, the feast is wound up with *couscous*. By the time the latter is placed in front of you, you may have exhausted your potential, a regrettable consequence of excessive bravado during the early stages of the meal; it is probable that you will be unable to face up to the pleasure of the couscous. In less formal circumstances, either at a restaurant or at the home of friends, you may be offered the couscous as a single course and you will then appreciate its lightness and delicacy.

Couscous is simply semolina, cooked in innumerable ways, allowing a free hand to display imagination and sense of occasion by selecting the meat constituents, usually chicken or mutton, and is eaten with two sauces or gravies: one to moisten the semolina and the other to spice the dish. A respectful approach to the latter is advisable: it is spiced with red peppers and unless used cautiously it is apt to set the palate on fire. Included in recipes are turnips, courgettes, raisins, chick-peas and onions. These vegetables are cooked and cooked again until they are reduced to a sort of chutney. The sweetened couscous for dessert is mixed with cinnamon, honey, and almonds.

Fish and Kebabs

All three countries have long coastlines, but only Morocco enjoys the added advantage of Atlantic seafood, at its best in the fishing ports and some beaches. Bouillabaisse, fish soup, mussels, clams, oysters, a choice selection of fish according to the locality, prawns, crayfish and (occasionally) lobster, boiled, fried, grilled, *au gratin, meunière,* with a galaxy of sauces and mayonnaises in the grand French tradition contribute at least one course to the menu of all the better restaurants, but to hardly any hotel menu.

The shad is an Atlantic deep sea fish which swims upstream in the coastal rivers where it is caught, and cooked with stuffed dates, while the sar, also an Atlantic fish, is fried with fennel. Sardines are exported to the whole world from Safi, but grilled they make a very recommendable beach snack. Along the Mediterranean there is a choice of bass, perch, red mullet and sole, while the tunny is mainly fished around Cap Zebib and Sidi Daoud in Tunisia. Octopus should be tried, at least once. Tunisia's large continental shelf harbors almost all Mediterranean sea species: blue fish, bream, grouper, mackerel, and many others.

And lastly, if you wish to enjoy the full flavor of local life and habit, a meal of *kebabs* is a must. Kebabs are the regular fare in the medina, where no alcoholic drinks are served, or on the terrace of a café in the popular quarter of any modern city. Whatever the setting, the kebabs remain the same: on three skewers are impaled different sorts of meat: mutton, liver, kidney and minute beef sausages. They are roasted on a fire of charcoal embers. After cooking, each skewer is placed on an open *kesrah* (a flattish bread roll, soft and round) and withdrawn, discharging its savory bits. A generous helping of gravy (pimentoes and cumin) is poured upon the open roll and its contents, and capped with the top half of the kesrah. The taste, fragrance and the ritual of the kebabs are particularly enjoyable on a warm evening. Somehow the combination of aroma and ambience is completely relaxed and yet invigorating. The cook's only tool is a humble piece of cardboard with which he fans the fire. The real secret of perfect kebabs is not so much in the cooking as in the spices of the marinade in which the meat has been left to pickle for hours to absorb the succulent juices of tomatoes, onions, garlic and exotic herbs.

The Sweets of Life

Desserts are numerous; besides the sweet couscous, rice and sorghum flour are cooked in milk and garnished with ground hazelnut, pistachio or walnut. Pastries are of the very sweet oriental variety, where nuts, almonds and sugar seem to be mixed in equal proportions, often sticky with syrup, as the *baklava, khtayef, makrout* and *sasma,* as well as pancakes and doughnuts (not the American kind, with a hole in the middle, but the European one). The choice confectionery is known as *kab el ghzal* (gazelle's horn), and is delicious when eaten with mint tea. It is a sort of croissant stuffed with crushed almonds and rolled in powdered sugar.

Yogurt, usually flavored with vanilla or fruit, is served everywhere. The genuine Maghreb cheeses are made from ewe's and goat's milk and can be very savory, occasionally too much so, while the pasteurized, boxed, cream squares produced by the big dairies taste the same all over the world.

Fruit is excellent and extremely varied, but strangely enough not in hotel restaurants, where the choice is often very limited. In the markets, however, mountains of every imaginable fruit will please the eye and the appetite of the most demanding, though in Algeria there may be sudden shortages. Outstanding are the cantaloupes and nectarines in Morocco, the apricots in Algeria, cherries and strawberries in Tunisia. In late summer the prickly pear, or Barbary Fig, originally from the New World, ripens in masses on every cactus hedge and is sold on road sides; it is very cheap, difficult to eat, and pleases only the hardy.

Le Vin

The years of French influence in the Maghreb have left a deep though diminishing mark on eating and drinking habits. In Morocco and Tunisia a few French gourmet haunts remain, dependent on the survival of their fast-fading owners, but there are plenty of adequate restaurants of medium price and quality. In most places your meals will go down pleasantly accompanied by one of the local vintages. As a matter of course, the sun-drenched Maghreb vineyards produce heady wines with a high alcoholic content. Much of the wine is exported to France and used for blendings, though it ages well.

Though greatly reduced in extent since independence, the vineyards still cover vast areas in all three countries. In Morocco, particularly between Fez and Rabat, with Meknès as the center, numerous foreign plantings had taken root most successfully. The main brands like *Saint Maxime, Valpierre* and *Vieux Pape,* carefully select vintages, no longer maintain their once uniformly high standard.

All these wines are red, with a minimum alcoholic content of 12 degrees. They go very well with meat but are apt to become overwhelming if taken in hot weather. *Chaudsoleil,* the very uneven *Oustalet, Valgrave* and *Val Saint Jean* come in red, white and rosé; the white *Semillant, Blanc de Blanc,* and the *Coquillage,* a Chablis-type best with seafood as its name indicates, are rightly appreciated by connoisseurs. In a class of their own are the rosé wines from vineyards south of Casablanca, on the slopes of Oum-er-Rebia, over which broods the fortified Kasbah of Boulaouane. Among these, *Gris de Boulaouane* and the *Gris de Gris* deserve special notice. The *Beni Snassen* muscatel is preferable to the cloyingly sweet liqueurs for dessert.

As for Algerian wines, production has fallen to less than a third of what it once was. White wines are sometimes difficult to obtain except in the leading establishments. A lot is exported to the Eastern Block states. Perhaps to retain a politically balanced wine policy, the vineyards of El Harach still furnish the liturgical wine for mass in many countries. The high prices of alcoholic drinks in Algeria—about twice as much as in the two neighbors—are part of the Moslem-socialist austerity.

In Algeria, a thinning belt of vineyards stretches from Tlemcen via Mascara to Médéa. Similar climate, soil, provenance and cultivation have produced the same results as in Morocco, with the *Cuvée du Président,* a blend of the best red Mascaras, definitely holding pride of place. Not that the ordinary red *Mascara* is to be despised and the *Aïn Bessem, Côteaux de Tlemcen, Côteaux du Zaccar, Dahra, Médéa, Mont du Tessalah* are all tasty but heady.

The same names for the rosé wines, with the addition of the outstanding *Alicante,* with 13.50 degrees the strongest of all. Among whites, the *Blanc de Blanc* is only 12 degrees, the others, reverting to a respectable 13, are named after the main winegrowing towns. The aperitifs are *El Bordj, Anisette Cristal* and *Ricard;* for the dessert *Domaine de la Trappe* or *Staouelli Blanc.*

In Tunisia, the grapevine thrives in the Cap Bon area and in the Thibar region, in the middle of the Beja plain. Production is controlled and guaranteed to be at least one year old. Most widely served are *Vieux Thibar, Haut Mornag* and *Koudiat,* all red, white and rosé. *Gris de Tunisie* is a pleasant light rosé. Also recommendable is *Côteaux de Carthage,* while the introduction of the Cabernet strain from Bordeaux has been largely successful, once again headed by the *Cuvée du Président.* The best red, and certainly the most expensive, is *Tyna.* Here, as in Algeria and Morocco, champagne is strictly for those who like it sweet, otherwise the *Cordon Vert* will only turn you green, not least because of the price. To accompany fish, *De Messe* is a palatable dry white, while the *Sidi Raïs* from the Korbous region is a fruity white or rosé.

In the oases an exotic note is provided by the *lagmi,* the wine from pollarded palm trees which must be drunk within twenty-four hours. The muscatels make excellent dessert wines, ranging from the white muscatel of *Kelibia* to the ones from *Radès* and *Thibar. Boukha,* an excellent *eau de vie,* is equally enjoyable as an aperitif and a digestif. *Thibarine* brandy is not bad at all with coffee, and the fig liqueur might also be sampled.

The beers are all of the very light French lager type: *Flag* and *Stork* in Morocco; *Bière Algérienne* (Export); *Celtia* and *Stella* in Tunis. The Danish beers made locally under license seem well worth the higher price. The mineral waters are adequate: *Oulmès,* pleasantly sparkling, a good soda substitute in long drinks, *Sidi Ali* and *Sidi Harazem,* still, in Morocco; *Benharoun,* sparkling, *Saïda,* still, in Algeria; *Aïn Garci, Safia,* sparkling, *Aïn Oktor,* flattish, and *Melliti,* still, in Tunisia.

There is no lack of soft drinks: *Coca* and *Pepsi Colas,* fizzy *Fanta* (orange, lemon, etc.), are very sweet; better try the fruit juices, fresh or bottled, among which the apricot juice in Algeria is particularly recommended. White *orgeat,* green *menthe,* and red *grenadine* are sweet aromatic fruit drinks. Coffee (*kaoua*) comes French, Nes and Turkish style.

Tastes of Paradise

Few Moslems drink wine or alcoholic beverages, which are forbidden by their faith. What, then, do they drink at meal-times? The answer to that is rather drastic: at meals they do not drink at all. They say that liquid of any kind would cause the couscous to swell in the stomach . . . therefore they follow the saying that abstinence is the father of safety. If drink must be taken during the meal it is usually only a sip of water, though two non-alcoholic drinks are worthy of notice: one is orange juice perfumed with orange blossom extract which gives it a most exquisite aroma. The other, only rarely met with nowadays, except perhaps in the wealthiest homes, is almond milk. You are most unlikely to find it in a restaurant, but should you be lucky enough to be offered it and wonder how it is prepared, here is the recipe: take one pound of fresh almonds, and crush them very finely into a paste (this operation takes a very long time). Prepare some sugared water, using seven ounces of sugar for two pints of water, with a few dashes of orange blossom extract for exotic relief. Now, mix the almond paste with the water, strain, and then serve iced. It is well worth the trouble as this delightful beverage is highly refreshing.

When the meal at home is finished, the table is removed; basin and ewer are passed to pour warm water over the greasy fingers; rose water is sprinkled from silver bottles to refresh face and neck; incense is placed on the burner.

And then begins the tea ceremony, a blessed, albeit surprisingly recent, relief. In 1854, during the Crimean War, British merchants, unable to sell in the Baltic, unloaded their stocks at Tangier, whence tea gradually replaced the traditional sage infusion with mint throughout the whole Maghreb.

The mixture of tea, mint, and sugar is highly individualistic and may not appeal to everyone. There are no proportions, no rules, for the scented mint to bring the full fresh flavor to the bitterness of tea, which is all-too-often spoilt by an overdose of sugar. Verbena, sweet basil or marjoram may be substituted for mint.

MOROCCO

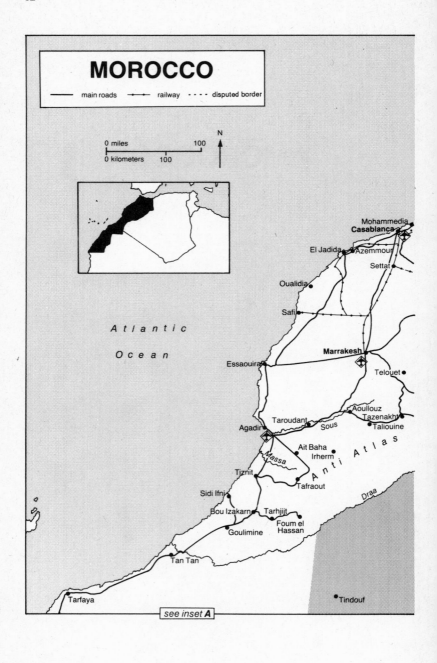

MOROCCO

—— main roads ·—·— railway - - - - disputed border

0 miles   100
0 kilometers   100

N

A t l a n t i c

O c e a n

Mohammedia
Casablanca
El Jadida · Azemmour
Settat
Oualidia
Safi
Marrakesh
Telouet
Essaouira
Aoullouz
Tazenakht
Taroudant · Sous · Taliouine
Agadir
Ait Baha
Massa · Irherm
A n t i A t l a s
Tiznit
Tafraout
Sidi Ifni · Draa
Bou Izakarn · Tarhjijt
Goulimine · Foum el Hassan
Tan Tan
Tarfaya
Tindouf

see inset **A**

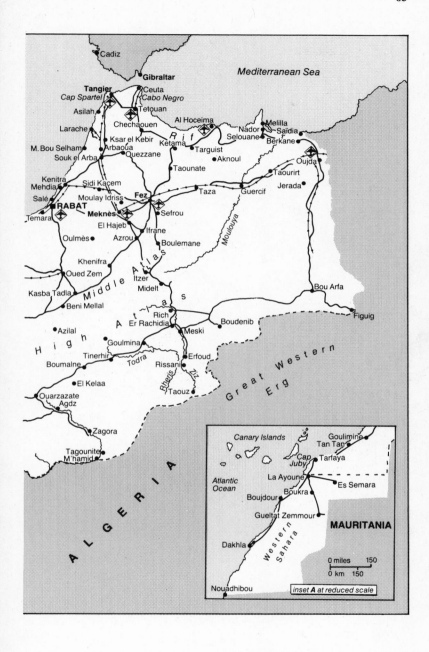

Mediterranean Sea

Cadiz

Gibraltar

Tangier
Cap Spartel
Ceuta
Cabo Negro

Asilah
Tetouan

Larache
Chechaouen
Al Hoceima
Melilla
Nador
Saïdia

R i f
Selouane
Berkane

Ksar el Kebir
Ketama

M. Bou Selham
Arbaoua
Targuist

Souk el Arba
Quezzane
Taourirt

Aknoul
Oujda

Taounate
Taourirt
Jerada

Kenitra
Sidi Kacem

Mehdia
Taza
Guercif

Salé
RABAT
Moulay Idriss
Fez

Temara
Meknès
Sefrou

El Hajeb
Oulmès
Ifrane

Azrou
Boulemane

Khenifra

Oued Zem
Itzer

M i d d l e
Midelt

Kasba Tadla

Beni Mellal
A t l a s

Bou Arfa

Azilal
Rich

A Er Rachidia
l
Boudenib

Figuig

Goulmina
Meski

Boumalne
Tinerhir
Erfoud

Todra
Rissani

El Kelaa
Ghéris
Ziz

H i g h
Taouz

Ouarzazate
Agdz

G r e a t   W e s t e r n

Zagora
E r g

Tagounite
M'hamid

A   L   G   E   R   I   A

Canary Islands
Goulimine
Tan Tan

Cap Juby
Tarfaya

Atlantic Ocean
La Ayoune
Es Semara

Boujdour
Boukra

Gueltat Zemmour
MAURITANIA

Dakhla
Western Sahara

0 miles   150
0 km   150

Nouadhibou

*inset **A** at reduced scale*

PRELUDE TO MOROCCO

The only Arab state bordering on the Atlantic as well as the Mediterranean, Morocco's 174,000 square miles fill the west of the Maghreb. The limits are clearly defined in the north by the two hundred and ninety miles of Mediterranean coast from the Straits of Gibraltar to the Algerian border, though the narrowness of the Straits, a mere nine miles to Tarifa in Spain, has imposed close relations on the two countries every since antiquity. Sometimes hostile, sometimes friendly, for most of recorded history some land in Africa has been in possession of the government ruling in Europe, not necessarily to the political liking of the temporarily subjected, but always to the cultural advantage of both. Northern Morocco and the southern part of the Iberian peninsula form thus a distinct intermediate region, containing European as well as African elements.

The western confines are even more decisively marked by the Atlantic Ocean, all the 800 miles from the Straits to the border of Mauritania. The lack of natural harbors forced traffic with West Africa into crossing the forbidding desert rather than attempting the stormy immensity of the ocean. Rabat and Salé briefly gained notoriety as pirate bases in the 17th century, but operations were directed north against European shipping. It was only in the 20th century during the French protectorate that the construction of artificial ports, especially Casablanca, endowed Morocco with windows to the west, of ever-increasing commercial importance. The artificial harbor of Jorf El Asfar, just south of Cap Blanc, is gradually assuming its role as Africa's biggest, though for the time being concentrating on the export of phosphate. To the south, the Sahara equally effectively limits all life and settlement, but the sands allow easy shifts of borderlines drawn by men in ephemeral treaties.

Only in the east has nature failed to provide a clearly recognizable break
in the ranges of low mountains and valleys near the Mediterranean coast,
and the vast empty plain stretching south, gradually changing from partial
to genuine desert. The similarity of the geological structure, the climate,
fauna and flora, on both sides of the border with Algeria, is equaled by
the human factor: the same Berber tribes speaking the same language, following the same religion and customs. Naturally, this non-frontier has
been the usual approach route of invaders, as the only serious obstacle
further east, the Taza corridor between the Middle Atlas and the Rif
mountains, is not all that easily defensible.

The Lay of the Land

Geographically Morocco is divided into seven distinct regions: the
plains and plateaux of western Morocco; the Rif mountains, separated
from the Atlas ranges by the Sebou and Innaouen plains; the Atlas systems, High, Middle and Anti-Atlas; the pre-Sahara region; and the "High
Plateau" of eastern Morocco. The country is rich in phosphates, minerals
and coal, and about 20 million acres are cultivated for the production of
barley, wheat, citrus fruits and wine grapes. The main rivers, the Sebou,
Bou Regreg and Oum-er-Rbia empty into the Atlantic; only the longest
but equally not navigable Moulouya empties into the Mediterranean. Of
the three mountain chains, dividing the country from west to east, the
most northerly, the isolated Rif, follows the Mediterranean coast from Tetouan past Al Hoceima before turning inland to face the Middle Atlas
across the Taza corridor. The woodlands of the latter mountain chain offer
a splendid variety of holm oak, pine and majestic cedars set round open
meadows and lakes several thousand feet above sea level. East of Marrakesh the Middle Atlas joins the utterly different High Atlas, three hundred
miles of awesome peaks, Mount Tubkal rising to 13,671 feet in the west,
Mount Bouiblan to 10,958 feet in the east, effectively separating the prosperous, cultivated, modernized and even partly industrialized north from
the unchanging palm groves of the south.

Yet even there, the scattered oases are most delightfully complemented
by long ribbon-like valleys, through which rivers fed by the snows of the
High Atlas stretch right into the desert. The Dadès and the Todra are
shaded in their upper reaches by mulberry and walnut trees, in their lower
by date palms; while the Wadi Zis and Wadi Gheris create the miracle
of the Tafilalet before being swallowed up by the sands.

The High Atlas is especially double faced, fir trees in the best Alpine
tradition on the north face, dramatically barren red sandstone on the
south, where desert winds have seared away all traces of vegetation.
Branching off near Mount Tubkal, the granite rocks of the Anti-Atlas
frame the orange- and olive-groves of the Sous in a wide crescent to
Goulimin near the Atlantic. Jebel Sarrho with its many-hued strata and
faults is a geologist's dream come true, while further south the colors of
the rocks and boulders change from hour to hour, comprising all gradations between palest pink and deepest purple.

Where Tolerance Is Practised but Not Preached

About one third of the present Moroccan population of over 26 million
speaks one or other of the numerous Berber dialects, but thanks to a school

system which now reaches into the most remote mountain villages, the younger generation is also taught Arabic and French. Numerically speaking, the Arab population was insignificant in Morocco until the influx of Moors from Spain between the 12th and 16th centuries. Arab descendants are said to inhabit the big cities and the Berbers the rural regions, but it is difficult to define any ethnic frontiers; there has been too much intermingling of the two races through the centuries. There is also a very ancient Jewish community. The first Jews to arrive followed the Carthaginians in the 3rd century B.C. and converted some Berbers to Judaism. More arrived after the destruction of the Temple in Jerusalem in A.D. 70 but the biggest influx were the refugees from the Spanish persecutions of the 15th century. Reduced from 250,000 in 1950 to some 20,000 after mass emigration to Israel, a few are returning after the invitation by the King in 1977 in a show of tolerance equaled only by Egypt two years later. Slave traffic and the recruitment of negro soldiers in the Sudan and Mauritania by Moulay Ismail in the 17th century added yet another layer to the Moroccan population.

Nor are there any insurmountable social barriers, as the upper strata of society have never been closed to arrivals from the lower. Slaves became viziers, and since independence some ministers have risen from the working or peasant class. Moroccans are justifiably annoyed when western democracies, preaching the theory of equality but often failing in its practice, set themselves up as models. Even more regrettable seems to them the western lack of refinement of manners, a dignified yet never servile politeness, which is universal throughout the country, from the nomad on the remotest hillside to the sophisticated member of Rabat society.

A Triumph of Personalities

Morocco is one of the rare African and Arab countries—the wealth of the oil sheikdoms makes them a case to themselves—that achieved transition from the Middle Ages to full participation in the 20th century within fifty years without violent revolution but by relatively peaceful evolution, thanks to one of the outstanding colonial administrators in history, Marshal Lyautey, and to two enlightened monarchs, Mohammed V and Hassan II.

At the beginning of this century Morocco was the most backward and isolated country on the Mediterranean. In 1903 the heads of forty rebels replaced those of earlier traitors over the battlements of Bab Mahruk at Fez, while in 1908 a pretender was exhibited to the populace in an iron cage before being executed. Until 1912 the gates of the walled cities were still closed at night, sometimes one quarter of a town was shut off from another. These places were visited, at the risk of their lives, by a handful of adventurous foreigners, whose tales still make thrilling reading.

Lyautey had the vision to build the new while preserving the old; his artistic sense, rarely equaled in a career officer, led him to create new towns some distance from the walls of the old, yet preserving the distinctive styles of the white northern towns (an extension of Andalusia across the Straits), and the red towns of the South (so unmistakably African). Only at Casablanca, where the existing medina was too insignificant, was a neo-Moroccan style developed, with some of the drawbacks of all neo-architecture, but preferable to most fancy 19th- and 20th-century adaptations.

This happy blend was extended to government and administration, and continued after independence. King Hassan II has elaborated an essential dualism of western and Moroccan methods and values. This is most strikingly illustrated in comparing the king's appearance at an official function in army uniform or European costume to his white robes as religious leader when attending Friday prayers.

Moroccanization has been gradual and orderly; the French, still the most important foreign factor, have been joined by American banks and hotel chains, European Community (EC) assembly plants and factories. Industrialization has been assisted by the country's mineral wealth, above all phosphate, exploited by a state monopoly.

Morocco is the third-largest producer of phosphate in the world, but the largest exporter. However, a pricing dispute in 1989 with its main customer, India, provoked balance of payments problems which have had serious repercussions on the economy elsewhere.The petrol extracted near Souk el Arba is insufficient to provide an economic base as in luckier North African neighbors. Hydroelectricity is, therefore, a priority. Despite austerity measures, 15 large new dams are due to increase the total capacity of the artificial lakes to 10 billion cubic meters of water, producing 1,500Mv and irrigating one million hectares, one-seventh of all arable land. Products of Moroccan light industry fill the souks to the detriment of local craftsmen.

And, of course, there are the sardines, of which Morocco has now become the biggest shipper. Centered on Safi, this, like all the other industries, has created a new working class, mostly first-generation landless farmers. Successful efforts are being made to improve living conditions in the shanty towns, especially around Casablanca, by constructing huge basic housing estates, although the problem is too big to be solved quickly. One part of the government's 'clean-up' policy is to expel people not born in the area. Squatters are sent back to their original homes in the countryside. Agriculture, which still employs two-thirds of the population and through fruits and vegetables contributes about one-fourth of the export receipts, has made the country self-sufficient in most foods.

A spectacular advance has taken place in the tourist industry, which not only is a main employer but has also put Morocco on the itinerary of the luxury as well as the package traveler. The varied attractions of beaches, cities and oases provide for a continuous flow of foreign visitors throughout the year, and are marred only by the leech-like and even abusive touts who pester tourists at all sites. Stable tourist revenues have recently overtaken declining remittances from Moroccan workers in the EC, half a million in France alone. Some 800,000 artisans make an important contribution to the economy and their products hold sixth place in exports.

Severe austerity measures continue to reduce a heavy trade deficit, at the risk of social and political unrest. Morocco's foreign debt of some 21 billion dollars puts it in 11th place on the list of third world debtors. But, as the first candidate outside Latin America or the Far East to benefit from the Brady plan, it has recently rescheduled its private debt and is rescheduling its public debt as well. Wages of the unskilled workers are low, but the higher-skilled can afford scooters; veiled figures clinging to their devil-may-care husbands—who else?—are a common sight.

While in most countries that have undergone radical changes, draconian measures regulating the way of life even down to what clothing can be worn have been enforced by dictatorial revolutionaries, Morocco, like Tunisia, has never interfered in the privacy of its citizens and thus achieved a delightful variety and informality.

FACTS AT YOUR FINGERTIPS

WHAT IT WILL COST. The average daily cost per person for each of our standard categories, including transportation within the country, entertainment and extras, is, in the Luxury category, about 1500DH; Expensive, 900DH; Moderate, 600DH; Inexpensive, 250DH.

For hotel and restaurant costs, see below under *Staying in Morocco.*

Among some other costs you may encounter are—a cup of Turkish coffee will cost from 5 to 15DH; a beer from 10 to 25DH for a small bottle; wine from 45 to 130DH in a restaurant, half the price in a shop. No alcoholic beverages are served in the medina restaurants. Cigarettes from 3 for *Casa Sport* to 12 for *Marlboro, Kent* and *Winston,* made locally under licence.

Men pay from 25 to 70DH for a haircut; women from 50 to 150DH for a shampoo and set. A hotel laundry will charge about 20DH per shirt; dry cleaning of a dress comes to about 40DH, and a man's suit about 50DH.

Festival tickets range from 40 to 75DH; movie seats go from 10 to 20DH. The most casual stop at a cabaret costs at least 80DH, no matter how mediocre the show and the drinks. At a good spot the minimum will be somewhere between 150 and 220DH.

WHEN TO GO. In Morocco the tourist season lasts the whole year round—but not in any one spot. January and February are the peak months for the desert and the inland south, including Marrakesh. Their season begins in November or late October, and lasts until May. Spring (March–May) is a lovely time for seeing the flowers in the mountain regions and much of the inland area. Summer (late May to September) is the best period for the seaside, both the Atlantic and Mediterranean coasts, though winters are mild along the Med. shore and at Agadir, on the far southern Atlantic coast. October and early November, often the year's driest period, can be the best season for touring by road. From December to April the snow on the Rif, Middle Atlas, and High Atlas is at its best, and you may be able to enjoy good skiing.

Don't believe that Morocco is always hot. No matter what the time of year, part of it will be at least pleasantly cool. But that may not be the part you're going to. And it may not be the part you've got to go through to get there. Similarly, get the idea that Morocco is a dry country out of your mind. It isn't. July and August may be the driest months. But that doesn't mean that rain stops completely, even in the south. A torrential thundery downpour can produce a flash flood capable of folding up a reinforced concrete bridge like a bit of waste paper. Rain doesn't last long in summer. But it can be fierce for an hour or two or drizzle for a day or two anywhere along the Atlantic coast. It is usually heaviest in December to February, and flooding in the fertile Rharb is regular. In spring, it can be wet for days at a time.

For the farmers in Morocco, too much rain too often falls too quickly at the wrong time. But at least, for the tourist, that leaves plenty of time for the sun. There are about 3,000 to 3,250 hours of sunshine a year in most spots.

Average afternoon temperatures:

	Jan.	Feb.	Mar.	Apr.	May	June	July	Aug.	Sep.	Oct.	Nov.	Dec.
Marrakesh												
F°	65	68	74	79	84	92	101	100	92	83	73	66
C°	18	20	23	26	29	33	38	38	33	28	23	19

Tangier

F°	60	61	63	65	71	76	80	82	78	72	65	61
C°	16	16	17	18	22	24	27	28	26	22	18	16

SPECIAL EVENTS. Except for the Marrakesh Festival of Popular Arts, one week in the middle of June, the so-called cultural and folkloric events, especially the Touristic Week or Fortnight organized by the local tourist offices in most coastal resorts, are largely for the benefit of tourists. The traditional regional events are much more genuine, and are often little more than joyful harvest festivals. The *moussems* are pilgrimages, much like fiestas in honor of a patron saint, lasting up to ten days. The most interesting festivals are:

mid-February	Almond Festival, Tafraout.
March	Cotton Festival, Beni Mellal.
	From March 2, all Morocco celebrates the Fête du Trône for three days, the anniversary of the present king's accession. The celebrations, which include *fantasias* in all the towns and sizable villages, are in no way aimed at tourists.
April	Wax Lantern Festival, Sale; Al Moggar, Festival of African Popular Arts, Agadir.
late April/May	Casablanca International Fair (biennial).
May	Clementine Festival, Berkane, near Oujda; Rose Festival, El Kelaa des M'gouna, near Ouarzazate.
May or October	Festival of Traditional Arts, Fez.
July	Sea Festival, Al Hoceima; Week of Popular Mediterranean Arts, Tangier; Honey festival, Immouzer des Ida Outanane. Orange Festival, Agadir.
August	Cultural Festival, Asilah; Apple and Pear Festival, Immouzer du Kandar.
September	Arab Theater Festival, Rabat; Horse Festival, Tissa, near Fez.
early October	Date Festival, Erfoud.
mid-December	Olive Festival, Rafai, near Fez.

Regional Fairs. Fez and Meknès, May/June; Oujda, May; Taza and Tetouan, July/August; Marrakesh, November.

International Sport Competitions. Golf Championship, early April; Golf Grand Prix, early December; Dar es Salam, Rabat. Moroccan Auto Rally, early April; Plane Rally, mid-May. Mohammed V Soccer Tournament, Casablanca, late August. The dates of the Show Jumping, Rabat, Regatta Grand Prix, and Auto Grand Prix vary.

Principal Moussems. Based on the lunar year, the dates of the main *moussems,* listed province by province in alphabetical order, are only approximate.

Province of Agadir. Sidi Bou Moussa, Ouled Taima, June; Sidi Bihi, Biougra, August.

Province of El Jadida. Moulay Abdellah, six miles from El Jadida, August, one of the largest; Sidi Beni Dghough, Sidi Bennour, September.

Province of Er Rachidia. Engagement Festival at Imilchil, in the High Atlas, attracts 30,000 tribesmen, three days in September; Moulay Ali Cherif, 13 miles south of Erfoud, September.

Province of Essaouira. Zaouira El Kettania, May; Sidi Maghdoul, June; both Essaouira.

Province of Fez. Moulay Idriss Alamayin, Fez, local craftsmen sacrifice cattle in a rather bloody spectacle in honor of the city's founder and patron saint, the greatest urban moussem, mid-September; Sidi Lahcen Lyoussi, Sefrou, August.

Province of Goulimine. Camel Market moussem, large number of dromedaries, popular with tourists because of the guedra dancing, Asrir, early June.

Province of Kénitra. Sidi Ahmed Ben Mansour, Moulay Bouselham, May; Sidi Boughaba, Ain El Aouda, August; Sidi Kacem, at that village, September.

Province of Marrakesh. Setti Fatna, Ourika, 34 miles from Marrakesh, three days of celebration in August. Moulay Ibrahim, 32 miles from Marrakesh on the road to Asni, June; Sidi Abdelkader Ben Yassine, Marrakesh, September; El Aouina, 12 miles from Marrakesh, fantasia with many horsemen.

Province of Meknès. Moulay Idriss, Idriss Zerhoun, in the holy city and the most important religious festival, August.

Province of Nador. Zaouia Kadiria, Driouch, July.

Province of Ouarzazate. Moulay Abdelmalek, Ait Yahya, February; Sidi Ahmed Ou Driss, Tazenakt, August.

Province of Oujda. Sidi Ali Ben Salah, Ouled Amran, September.

Province of Rabat. Dar Zhirou, Rabat; Sidi Lahcen, Temara; both August.

Province of Safi. Sidi Muallahbad, Ras El Ain, August.

Province of Settat. Sidi Bouknifa, August; Sidi Loghlimi, September; both Settat; Sidi Moussa, at the village, September.

Province of Tangier. Dar Zhirou, Tangier, September.

Province of Tan Tan. Sidi Mohammed M'a El Ainin, great gathering of the Blue People of the neighboring tribes, July; Sidi Mohammed Laghdal, October; both Tan Tan.

Province of Taza. Sidi Ahmed Zerrouk, on the road to Bab El Mrouj, early September.

Province of Tetouan. Moulay Ali Ben Rashid (patron of the city of Chechaouen). After the Mouloud festival, two days of festivity. Moulay Abdelkader Jilali, Larache, June.

Province of Tiznit. Sidi Ahmed Ou Moussa, Tiznit, late August.

WHAT TO SEE. The four imperial cities, Rabat, Meknès, Fez, and Marrakesh are—despite their distinctive attractions—of equal interest, but only if sufficient time is available should all four be attempted at a first visit. Second in importance to them would be a trip to the Deep South.

Antiquity seekers will want to stop and investigate the Roman city of Volubilis and other ancient sites. The four major main mountain regions—the Rif, Middle Atlas, High Atlas and Anti-Atlas ranges—the pre-Saharan desert area in the south and accessible parts of the Mediterranean coast provide magnificent scenery. For winter sports go to Ifrane or Oukaimeden. For summer bathing to Tangier, Al Hoceima, Mohammedia, Restinga-Smir, M'Diq or Agadir.

In any case, Morocco is a country that requires a good deal of time to see it thoroughly and to get really acquainted with it. To see the most in the least time we suggest the following itinerary for two weeks by car:

Day

1 Leave Casablanca early for Rabat and visit the city.
2 Leave for Tangier, with stops at Larache and Asilah.
3 Visit Tangier, leave for Chechaouen.
4 Visit Chechaouen, leave for Meknès.
5 Visit Meknès.
6 Leave for Fez via Volubilis and Moulay Idriss.
7 Visit Fez.
8 Leave early for Erfoud.
9 Leave for Tinerhir and an excursion to the gorges of the Todra.
10 Leave for Ouarzazate with a detour to the gorges of the Dadès.
11 Leave for Marrakesh.
12 Visit Marrakesh.
13 Leave for Essaouira, go for a swim and visit the city.
14 Return to Casablanca by way of El Jadida, for a swim and visit to the city.

MOROCCAN NATIONAL TOURIST OFFICES. In the U.S.: 20 E. 46th St., Suite 1201, New York, NY 10017. **In Canada:** 2001 Rue Université, Ste. 1460, Montréal, PQ H3A 2A6. **In the U.K.:** 174 Regent St., London W1R 6HB (tel. 01–437 0073).

There are National Tourist Offices (O.N.M.T.) and Syndicats d'Initiative (local information offices) in all major towns and touristic centers within Morocco. See *Practical Information* sections for regional chapters.

Getting to Morocco

FROM NORTH AMERICA

By Plane. Royal Air Maroc, 680 Fifth Ave., New York, NY 10019, operates a direct service to Morocco with several flights weekly, depending on the season. All go to Casablanca, mostly direct but occasionally via Tangier. Alternatively, you can fly across the Atlantic to Paris, Madrid or Lisbon from where there are direct flights to Morocco. From Paris Royal Air Maroc offers services to Tangier, Casablanca, Fez, Agadir, Oujda, and Marrakesh. From Madrid flights go direct to Tangier and Casablanca.

Air Fares. On the direct route from New York to Casablanca the roundtrip air fares are: first class, $4,084; business, $2,188; economy, $1,416; Apex, $766. Apex tickets are good for stays of 1 week to 2 months and must be purchased at least 7 days in advance of departure.

By Boat. There are no direct sailings by passenger ships from North America to Morocco. For sailings by passenger-carrying freighters see *Practical Information for Casablanca* below. For sailings from Europe see section *From the Continent* below.

FROM BRITAIN

By Plane. Royal Air Maroc operates several flights weekly to Casablanca from London Heathrow airport. Some go direct, others via Tangier. British Airways and Gibair now run a joint operation—GB Airways, which runs flights to Casablanca from London Gatwick twice a week and to Tangier once a week. The flying time is a little over three hours. These are all scheduled services.

However, there are also charter flights mainly in connection with inclusive holidays from a number of U.K. provincial airports. A limited number of seats can be obtained on these for independent travelers. For example, there are flights from Luton to Tangier, Marrakesh and Agadir; from Manchester and Birmingham to both Tangier and Agadir. The frequency varies and you should check with a travel agent if seats are available as the rules about these are subject to change.

Air Fares. The London to Casablanca air fare for '91 will range from £580 roundtrip business class to about £180 Apex roundtrip. But remember that a full package holiday including flight can be bought for as little as £100.

By Train. Strictly for the rail enthusiast or those holding the Inter-Rail Card (valid for travel within Morocco). The route from London would be via Madrid to Algeciras for the short crossing by ferry to Tangier and Ceuta, or fast hydrofoil to Tangier. By this route the journey from London occupies the best part of three days. There is also a ferry service from Sète (France) to Tangier. Sète has a good rail service from Paris.

By Bus. Currently there is one bus service from the U.K. which can be used to reach Morocco. National Express-Eurolines runs a twice weekly service from London Victoria Coach Station to Tangier, Rabat, Casablanca, Marrakesh, Agadir, and Tiznit via Paris. The coach run to Tangier takes three days, and four to Rabat onwards. Fare around £200 roundtrip. There is also a twice weekly service to Algeciras via Madrid. Details from National Express-Eurolines, The Coach Travel Center, 13 Lower Regent St., London SW1Y 4LR (tel. 01–730 0202), or from Eurolines, 52 Grosvenor Gdns., London SW1W 0AU (tel. 01–730 8235/for credit card bookings).

By Car. Considerably shortening the long drive, Brittany Ferries operates a twice-weekly service from Plymouth to Santander in northern Spain. That leaves you about 850 miles to Algeciras or Málaga, where you board another ferry for Morocco.

When driving the whole way, it makes surprisingly little difference which of the Channel ports you start from. Algeciras and Málaga are only 100 miles or so further from Calais than from Cherbourg—and this extra distance may be more than compensated by the mileage you do inside Britain trying to save miles on the Continent. In any case, the quickest way through France is not the shortest. It is the *autoroute sud* and the nearest ports to it are between Ostend and Dieppe. So, choose the car-ferry crossing most suited to your starting-point.

The London AA or RAC can supply information to members about routes, and also make ferry reservations. So can the Caravan Club. Ordinary travel agents will look after ferry reservations once you've chosen your route.

Whichever way you go, you'll have to cross the water again between the European Continent and Morocco (see *By Boat* section below).

FROM THE CONTINENT

By Plane. Royal Air Maroc or the appropriate national carrier operate direct services to Casablanca from most European, African and Middle Eastern capitals, as well as from most major French cities. In addition there are less frequent services to Tangier, Fez, Agadir, Marrakesh and Rabat.

In addition GB Airways operates one flight a day, Mon. to Fri. from Gibraltar to Tangier. There are flights also from Málaga to both Tangier and Fez by Royal Air Inter, the domestic division of Royal Air Maroc.

By Boat. The most convenient ways by sea are by the ferries across the Straits of Gibraltar and the western Mediterranean to Tangier and also to Ceuta and Melilla (Spanish enclaves which, however, give direct access to Morocco and from which there are bus services into that country). Ferry routes from Algeciras in southern Spain go to Tangier, Ceuta and Melilla; from Gibraltar to Tangier (also a hydrofoil service on this route, weather permitting); Málaga to Tangier; Sète in southern France to Tangier, 38 hours, every 4th day, July through October, otherwise once weekly. There is also a hydrofoil service from Tarifa in southern Spain to Tangier— again weather permitting. If you bring your car, it is best to avoid the four weeks between mid-July and mid-August, when returning expatriate Moroccans for summer holidays can cause delays of up to 24 hours at the ferry terminals of Ceuta and Algerciras. Tangier is not as bad, but the crossing is more expensive.

Many cruise liners call at Tangier and/or Casablanca with excursions inland as part of their programs.

By Train. The most convenient route is through 2nd class *couchette* from Paris (Gare d'Austerlitz), leaving there in the evening around 10:15 P.M. and traveling via Irún, Madrid and Cordoba; arrives in Algeciras some 36 hours later. Ferry connections from there to Tangier etc. Alternative, and more comfortable, method is to travel by the overnight TALGO sleeper express from Paris to Madrid and change trains there going on to Algeciras. This way you can travel either by 1st or 2nd class and use a sleeper for the overnight sections.

Staying in Morocco

MONEY. Current exchange rates are about 8DH to the US dollar, and 14DH to the pound sterling—subject to change!

The dirham is divided into 100 centimes. There are coins of 5, 10, 20 and 50 centimes, of 1 and 5 dirhams, and bills of 5, 10, 50 and 100 dirhams.

The Moroccan Bank of Foreign Commerce (Banque Marocaine de Commerce Extérieur) in theory opens its exchange booths at the time of each arrival and departure by boat or plane in Casablanca, and by boat in Tangier or Ceuta (Sebta). Exchange facilities are available on boats from Spain bound for Morocco, but don't rely too much on quayside, early morning or Sunday facilities.

HOTELS. The prices we quote are high season rates for double rooms with bath or shower and include breakfast and service charges. Luxury 900DH and up; Expensive 400–900DH; Moderate 200–400DH; Inexpensive 100–200DH.

In all sizable centers there is a wide choice. The most reliable hotels in the top categories are the international and Moroccan chains. The Hyatts at Casablanca and Rabat, the Meridien at Mohammedia, the Sheraton, part of the Es Saada hotel chain, and Holiday Inn at Casablanca, and the Safir at Rabat are all in the Deluxe (L) class. Similarly P.L.M. manages Expensive (E) hotels in many locations throughout the country. The Moroccan chains range from the Safir (L) and (E) to Kasbah Tours, Maroc Tourist, O.N.C.F. (Moroccan State Railways), and Salam (E). Nearly all are in the new towns, sometimes quite a distance from the main sites. To reserve it is best to phone the hotels directly or go through one of the numerous travel agencies.

In larger towns and tourist centers, hotels graded Moderate (M) are generally adequate, though in smaller towns standards drop. Inexpensive (I) hotels everywhere are at best quaint. See also the Hotel section in *Planning Your Trip*, page 6 for the warning about the unpredictable and rapid changes in standards.

Moroccan hotels are bookable in the U.K. through Moroccan Hotel Associates, 304 Old Brompton Rd., London SW5 (tel. 01–373 4411).

YOUTH HOSTELS. The Moroccan Youth Hostel Association, the Union Marocaine des Auberges de Jeunesse, 6 Place Admiral Phillibert, Casablanca, is a member of the International Federation of Youth Hostels. Members of similarly affiliated associations can use Moroccan hostels in the normal way on production of their membership card. Not many hostels are of the standard expected in most European countries, but they provide obvious advantages for younger travelers who do not know the country.

Hostels exist at the moment at Asni, Azrou, Beni Mellal, El Jadida, Casablanca, Essaouira, Fez, Ifrane, Marrakesh, Meknès, Ouarzazate, Oujda, Rabat, Safi, Taza, and Tetouan. Additions and closures, however, are always possible. Ask for the latest information from: YHA, 14 Southampton Street, London, WC2, or American Youth Hostels Inc., Box 37613, Washington, DC 20013.

RESTAURANTS. Eating places cover as wide a spectrum as hotels, with equally varying values at every level. Hardly any are outstanding, though a few specializing in Moroccan cuisine are worth the rather stiff prices. Seafood is best along the Atlantic coast.

In the smaller towns, keep to the hotel restaurants, where the food is acceptable but by no means *haute cuisine*. Village eating houses are better avoided. The more adventurous should try the "brochette"—kebab—places, where you can get quick service; you just order the number of kebabs you want (about four is an average first serving) and add up the total at the end; each one costs from 3–5DH, depending on the place. Wayside eating-spots can provide very tasty food, but vary a good deal in hygiene: best look them over before you go in.

Meals are from 150 to 250DH per head in an Expensive restaurant; 90–150DH in a Moderate one, with the uniformly uninteresting fixed hotel menus at the lower end; and 40–90DH at restaurants frequented by the locals. Even less at some unpretentious eating places not serving alcoholic beverages. A 17% service charge may be added to the bill, but this and the 7.5% tax are frequently included in the basic price.

GUIDES. It is advisable to have a guide when you go into the larger medinas, especially the one in Fez, where you might get hopelessly lost without one. Official guides usually wear a *jellaba* and a red tarbosh, or other oriental headgear; they also show their authorization. Self-appointed guides are usually in western dress, and have a more forward approach. They should ask for one third to half the official rate. If you choose one of these unofficial guides you must be prepared to accept the consequences of your character judgment; some of them are informative and amusing while others are just out for a quick profit (but then unfortunately so are some of the official guides who get a percentage from any purchases you may make in stores they take you to).

Rates for official guides—some of whom are knowledgeable, while others were appointed because they speak English—vary from one city to another. They will, for example, be higher in Rabat, slightly less in Marrakesh, Fez and Meknès. Remember if you want to be rid of the overly-opportunistic hassling you'll be sure to encounter in any street or market, firmly and loudly say "No thank you" once and thereafter ignore any further attempts at conversation. It sometimes requires the help of a policeman to get rid of the abusive rejects, the worst pursuing their victims on bikes.

To find an official guide, call at the local National Tourist Office or City Information and Promotion Bureau (Syndicat d'Initiative) whose addresses are quoted in each regional chapter. The bigger hotels and the travel agencies can also arrange guides.

MAIL. Postcards—(airmail) to the U.S. and Canada, 2.50DH, Europe 2DH. Letters—to the U.S. and Canada, 3.50DH, Europe 3DH, both up to 20 grams. Within the country—1DH for a letter, 0.80DH for a postcard. Prices are liable to change, so check before mailing.

TELEPHONES, TELEGRAMS. As in France and in most other European countries, all communications, telephone and telegraph services operate through the post offices. Urban calls from public call-boxes cost 1DH. Long-distance calls between the larger Moroccan cities are automatic. A 3-minute call to England costs about 40DH. Telegrams entrusted to the hotel porter are not necessarily despatched; better take them to the post office. The Moroccan telephone system is being updated, but it is still cumbersome. It can be complicated making long distance calls but top hotels provide a good service, and save walks to the main telephone centers where large lines gather from 5 p.m. to late at night.

SHOPPING. The cooperative shops of Moroccan craftsmen, Copartim, which operate under state control, sell local handicrafts at fixed prices in all main towns and tourist centers. Addresses are given in the regional chapters. Receipts or a certificate of origin may be required by customs.

Market (Souk) Days. Certain agricultural centers in the country carry the name of the day when the weekly market is held; Souk-el-Khemis, Souk-el-Arba, etc. Remember that the days of the week, in Arabic, are numbered. Sunday: *el had* (number 1); Monday: *et tnine;* Tuesday: *et tleta:* Wednesday: *el arba;* Thursday: *el khemis;* Saturday: *es sebt.* The only exception (and not a market day) is Friday: *el jmaa* (the assembly).

PUBLIC HOLIDAYS. The national holidays are—March 3, accession of the king; May 23 and Jan. 11, national holidays; July 9, the very popular Youth Festival; Aug. 14, Oued Eddahab Allegiance day; Aug. 20, the anniversary of the Revolution; Nov. 6, anniversary of the Green March; Nov. 18, Independence Day. Sunday is the weekly rest day. For the moveable religious holidays see page 2.

Opening Hours. Stores usually open 8:30–12 and 2:30–7. Shops in the souks close on Sunday, but a few close on Friday, the Moslem day of rest. Banks are mostly open 8:15–2:15, Monday to Friday; during Ramadan 9:30–2:30. Post Offices are open 8:30–6:30 in the large towns; elsewhere they usually close between noon and 3.

NEWSPAPERS. Paris newspapers and the *International Herald Tribune* arrive in the main towns on day of publication, generally early in the afternoon, and British and other papers the day after. The main French-language morning papers are *L'Opinion* and *Le Matin du Sahara,* evening *Maroc Soir.* Casablanca's weekly *7 Jours à Casa* is useful for local information.

HASHISH (or *kif*) is fairly common in Morocco. Remember that though you may encounter Moroccans smoking it quite openly, it is strictly forbidden to tourists and you risk arrest. On return to Europe, cars are very thoroughly searched, especially in the Spanish ports, and it may take hours to be cleared through customs. We suggest that you give hashish the widest possible berth, for every conceivable reason.

BEACHES. The two sea coasts which border Morocco are very different: the Mediterranean coast is essentially rocky; the Atlantic coast, almost flat, has many fine sand beaches. The magnificent sweep of sand extending along the Mediterranean from Martil to Restinga has been taken over by huge holiday villages filled with package tourists. But further east, on the Rif coast around Al Hoceima, there are many solitary beaches of sand or pebbles, and steep cliffs plunging into the sea. Plans for extensive touristic developments have been drawn up as the calm waters of the bays are ideal for water-skiing and for underwater fishing. Both coasts are fairly unpolluted though tar can occasionally cover miles of beach. The Atlantic can be surprisingly cold, even in summer.

At Tangier high winds, even in mid-summer, can unpleasantly whip up the fine sand on the beach. Rabat and Casablanca have a series of popular bathing beaches: the Plage des Nations, Temara, Sehl Dheb, Sables d'Or, and Skhirat for Rabat; and the resort of Ain Diab, including Anfa Plages, Sables d'Or, Tahiti, Acapulco, Miami and Sun Beach for Casablanca. Between these two cities, Mohammedia, with its beach and camping, is also an important bathing resort. Toward the south, there are the traditional resorts: El Jadida, Oualidia, Safi, Essaouira, and largest of all, Agadir.

Mehdia and Asilah, between Rabat and Tangier, are becoming popular. The deserted Atlantic beaches often have superb surf but beware of strong currents. Surfing is good here. Larger beach hotels provide facilities for nautical sports, but sailing is, of course, more hazardous on the Atlantic than on the Mediterranean coast.

FISHING is possible in trout streams, trout lakes, pike lakes and the sea. Permits for the first three are issued by the Waters and Forests Department or by local clubs. Trout angling starts the last Sunday in March and generally closes the first Sunday in October; days and hours within this period are closely observed. Only one rod can be used at any one time for light casting, fly fishing and so on.

The main trout streams are the Arhbal, Guigou and Almiss Guigou in the easily accessible Azrou area, the most difficult Amengouss of Bekrit above Timhadit and the wild Ouaoumana and Chbouka in the Khenifra area. The trout lakes, created by damming up streams, are in the Azrou, El Hajeb, Ifrane and Immouzer areas. The pike lakes in the Immouzer, Khenifra, Beni Mellal and Midelt areas contain black bass, carp, perch, rudd, tench, sun fish and others of respectable sizes.

Permits and Licenses (subject to change). The annual fishing permit for streams and lakes costs around 150DH, the daily permit about 10DH, and the club permits for fishing in certain lakes around 100DH annually, between 5DH and 10DH daily. Fishing in the sea is free. The address of the *Fishing Club du Moyen-Atlas* is 4 rue Richard in Fez.

Underwater Fishing. The countless inlets of the rocky Mediterranean coast teem with many varieties of fish. The much longer but flatter Atlantic coast presents climatic diversities. The waters, which are warmer at the surface, move and roll around the colder mass according to current and location, the result being that zones such as those of Safi or Essaouira are colder in summer than in winter. Other regions such as Cap Rhir near Agadir, or the coastal waters between Rabat and Casablanca, are characteristically tropical. This remarkable anomaly explains why there is such an uncommon mixture of tropical and cold water fish along the Moroccan coast.

In the region of Rabat, the longest catch (30 to 70 inches, and up to 90 lbs) is the tarpon. In the south one can find pretty big skate; elsewhere there are umbrine (up to 4 lbs), sea perch (up to 8 lbs), mullet (up to 5 lbs), and conger-eels of a respectable size.

Of the whole Mediterranean region, the Moroccan coast is one of the least frequented, and consequently rich in underwater fauna including small sharks, but the large fish encountered most frequently is the grouper (certain groupers weigh up to 60 lbs): on the Atlantic coast it's the tarpon. An ideal spot of underwater fishing on the Atlantic coast is Moulay Bousselham.

There are highly active spear-fishing clubs in Rabat, Casablanca, Tetouan, Kenitra, and Agadir. Here is a list of the best places along the Mediterranean coast, going from east to west: Melilla and vicinity; especially recommended, the Cap des Trois Fourches; Cap Ras Tarf; Al Hoceima and vicinity; Peñon de Velez; Pointe des Pêcheurs; Oued Laou, Tabernoust; and finally Cabo Negro, before reaching the Straits.

Compressed air sales points can be found in all major towns.

For all additional information, write to Fédération Royale Marocaine d'Etudes et Sports Sous-Marines, B.P. 368 in Rabat.

SKIING AND MOUNTAINEERING. Of the country's four main mountain ranges, three—the Rif, Middle Atlas, and High Atlas—have sufficient snow for fair, if unpredictable, skiing. Only the areas near Ifrane in the Middle Atlas and Oukaimeden in the High Atlas are, however, "developed" in any way, and if you go elsewhere you must fend for yourself with uphill walking, meals, etc. The most popular areas for this "expedition-type" skiing are Mount Tidiquin (or Tidighine) in the Ketma district, within easy driving distance of the Hotel Tidighine; and the slopes of Jebel Bou Iblane, the Middle Atlas's highest peak, at the range's eastern end. Like all Moroccan skiing areas they suffer from inability to guarantee the condition of the snow at any given period.

Mountaineering and speleology are relatively little practiced in Morocco, though mountain expeditions on muleback are popular, particularly in the Jebel Toubkal area south of Marrakesh, where a certain amount of climbing is also practised. The Speleology Club of Taza organizes visits to the tremendous caves of Chiker and Friouato. Other groups are: Alpine Club, 13 Blvd. de la Résistance, Rabat, and Blvd. Brahim Roudani, Casablanca; Mountain and Ski Federation, 53, Rue Allal Ben Abdellah, Casablanca; Club De Ski, Meknès, Azrou, Oukaimeden; and Centre de Ski, Oukaimeden.

GOLF. Very popular in Morocco and with good reason. Though riding carts are not available the turf is delightfully smooth and springy for walking. The greens are usually superbly manicured and, especially at Marrakesh, the surrounding scenery superb. Courses are not crowded and service, caddies and pros, excellent.

The Dar-es-Salam Club in Rabat is Morocco's outstanding offering to golfers, laid out by Robert Trent Jones on flat land thickly covered with cork trees. A sumptuous clubhouse provides all the necessary facilities, as well as a first-rate restaurant and bar, swimming pool, and landscaped garden with palms, pools and cool trickling streams. There are two 18-hole courses, one 9-hole, par 73. Green fees and caddies are reasonable.

Only a grand taxi can drive to the clubhouse outside the Rabat boundary, unless you have your own car. The charge should not exceed 50DH each way for up to four passengers, but you must argue sometimes to see that this is stuck to.

The Mohammedia course, designed for championship golf, lies about half a mile from the resort, and is open to all golfers. It has 18 holes, and par is 73. The fairway is 6,369 yards long, and is partly on the sea shore. Clubs, balls and carts are available for rent. Patrons of the Miramar Hotel pay no green fee, other visitors 70DH per day, 300DH per week. Many international tournaments are held here every year.

Tangier Country Club is two miles out, next to a polo ground. It has 18 holes and the greens are well cared for all the year. There are clubs for rent, but no golf-carts.

Casablanca's Royal Golf Anfa is less than 15 minutes' drive from the center of the city. This is only a 9-hole course, but is used for 18 holes, par 67. The fairway is 4,770 yards long. Clubs and carts are available for rent. Green fees: 70DH per day, 300DH per week.

The course in Marrakesh is set in desert scenery which makes sharp contrast with its greens. It is near the Ouarzazate road, about 5 km. (3 miles) out. This 18-hole course, 5,255 yards long, has a par of 71. It is open all the year, but is busiest during the tourist season (November to May). Green fees: 70DH on weekdays, 100DH at weekends; caddies 50DH, clubs 35DH, no carts. Several tournaments are held here, mainly during Christmas and Easter.

The 9-hole course at Ketama is mainly for the guests of the Hotel Tidighine.

The 9-hole course at Agadir is between Inezgane and Aït Melloul. For further information contact the Royal Moroccan Golf Federation, 2 Rue Moulay Slimane, Rabat.

HORSEBACK RIDING. There are equestrian clubs with facilities for non-members in all major towns, notably at Casablanca where there are three clubs (L'Etrier, C.A.F.C. Section St. Georges, and Club Equestre Bayard), at Rabat, Tangier, Marrakesh, Agadir and Fez. Several clubs organize horseback treks in the Middle Atlas. Horses and camels are provided by all bigger hotels.

Traveling in Morocco

BY PLANE. Royal Air Inter's domestic air services make touring Morocco by plane easy, connecting Casablanca to Agadir, Marrakesh, Ouarzazate and Tan Tan in the south; Al Hoceima, Fez, Meknès, Oujda, Rabat, Tangier and Tetouan in the north.

BY TRAIN. The partly electrified railway system connects Tangier with Marrakesh via Casablanca, and Casablanca with Oujda via Fez. A few branchlines are rather uncomfortable.

Rail travel is cheap and overnight services carry both sleeping cars and couchettes. Unless you are roughing it, we suggest 1st class travel other than on the air-conditioned expresses from Tangier to Casablanca. You can use the *Inter-Rail* card in Morocco.

BY BUS. There is an extensive long distance bus service network in the country linking the main cities and towns. It is cheap but always very crowded. On certain trunk routes e.g. Agadir to Marrakesh, Rabat to Fez the coaches are airconditioned.

BY TAXI. *Petits taxis* operate only inside city boundaries, and are cheap—at the most 5DH per trip for up to three passengers plus luggage, including tip. However, for foreigners this is rather a myth. Meters, if any, are purely decorative, and to avoid arguments it is advisable to fix the price in advance. The same holds good for *grands taxis,* whose rates are double, but which can go anywhere. Prices for long trips must definitely be arranged in advance. If you do not feel capable of doing this, ask a local travel agent's or your hall porter's help: there are recognized prices for more popular runs, and he will know them. A third possibility is the *service taxi,* a *grand taxi* operating to a fixed destination and not leaving until the vehicle is full—sometimes very full. The rates on these routes are often surprisingly low. You must not, however, expect comfort.

BY CAR. As there were no roads to speak of until 1910, no old trails had to be followed, so that the highway network offers direct and easy routes. Where the country is relatively flat, the roads are straight, especially in the desert areas, but narrow. Mountain roads are well graded. The 9,700 km. (6,000 miles) of paved roads are classified and numbered; P for the principal and S for the secondary roads, marked in Arabic and French on signposts and kilometer stones; alternate stones may show distances to different towns, which is useful for checking a turning has not been missed. Street signs are likewise bilingual, but *Avenue* and *Rue* have occasionally been replaced by *Charia* and *Zankat,* especially in Rabat. The 22,500 km. (14,000 miles) of dirt tracks (pistes) present no particular difficulties, except rarely after heavy rains.

Principal Routes. The maps in the hand-outs of the National Tourist Office are quite adequate for the tourist driver, but omit the road numbers, though indicating the classifications by thick purple lines for P, thinner yellow for S, and even thinner white for the pistes. The P network is as follows:

From Tangier roads radiate along the Rif range (P38, P28, and P39) via Tetouan, Chechaouen and Ketama to Al Hoceima and Nador, and continue as the P27 to Berkane and Oujda on the Algerian frontier: to Fez via Chechaouen and Ouezzane (P38, P28, P26), or via the breathtaking P39 to Ketama and from there the scenic and highly recommended S302 passing through the Rif range and unspoilt Berber villages; to Meknès via Ouezzane (P28) or Souk el Arba (P2, P6); and to Rabat (P2). Morocco's only motorway leads south from Rabat to El Jadida via Casablanca.

From Rabat the P1 sweeps east to the Algerian frontier via Meknès, Fez, Taza, and Oujda; the P22 runs due south to Oued Zem and the Fez-Marrakesh road, with a branch (P13) from Oued Zem to Kasba Tadla. Beside the motorway, there is a coastal road to Casablanca.

Fez's two main roads apart from those already mentioned, are the P24 to Marrakesh via Azrou, Khenifra, Kasba Tadla, Beni Mellal, and El Kelaa des Srarhna; and the P20–P21 to Erfoud and Rissani in the pre-Sahara via Sefrou, Midelt, Rich, and Er Rachidia.

Meknès's special contribution is the P21, which passes through Azrou, joins the P20 near the village of Boulojoul, and then continues to Rissani.

The route from Casablanca to Marrakesh. Leaving by the Mediouna road and passing through this center with its 16th-century kasbah, the main road P7 leads to Berrechid (though this large agricultural center can also be reached by S109 passing through Nouasser and Bouskoura, in a pleasant forest). From Berrechid the P7 runs to Settat, a main provincial town and important cereal center where a large camel market is held, then through small rural centers—Khemisset des Ouled Bouziri and Mechra-Ben-Abbou (exactly halfway)—crossing the imposing Oum-er-Rbia river, meaning "mother of greenness," a well-justified name as it irrigates the plain to Benguerir.

After crossing the Tensift river over a 300-year-old bridge, built by Portuguese slaves, the road passes the celebrated palm groves, and enters Marrakesh either by Gueliz or by Bab Doukkala.

From Casablanca the P7 runs SSW to Marrakesh; and the P8 down the coast to Agadir via El Jadida, Safi, and Essaouira, continuing as the P30 to Bou Izakarn, and as the S512 to Goulimine, Tan Tan, and Tarfaya.

Roads numbered P9, P12, and P11 link Marrakesh with El Jadida (final section runs on the P8), Safi, and Essaouira, and from Marrakesh the P31 crosses the High Atlas via the Tizi N'Tichka pass to Ouarzazate and Zagora.

The P32 is in some ways the most interesting of all the country's fascinating main routes. It runs from Agadir on the Atlantic coast all the way eastward through the pre-Saharan region to the remote oasis of Figuif, via Taroudant, Ouarzazate, Tinerhir, Er Rachidia, Boudenib and Bou Arfa. From the last P19 runs parallel to the railway north to Oujda.

Motor Fuel. The price of gasoline (petrol) is about 5.85DH per liter for normal (2 star), 6.05DH per liter for super, with local variations, highest in the south. There are Esso, Agip, Total, Mobil, Shell and other filling stations in most main towns and at strategic points along major roads. Keeping the tank full is no problem at all here. BP has an information center near Tangier harbor, in the Avenue d'Espagne.

Car Hire. Cars can be hired in all main towns. Rental rates start from about 170DH per day plus 80DH per km. for small French or Italian cars, rising to 380DH per day plus 3.50DH for larger makes. For a week with unlimited mileage rates are 2,200DH and 5,600DH respectively. Minimum deposit 3,000DH. All prices are liable to increase. No caravans for hire. Though you can haggle over rates at local agencies, it is safer to stick to Avis, Hertz, or Europcar.

For further information see *Traveling by Car in North Africa* in *Planning Your Trip,* above.

RABAT AND CASABLANCA

A Tale of Two Cities

For 1,000 years the capital of Morocco seesawed between Fez and Marrakesh, with Meknès enjoying a brief period of fame as the center of government selected for his rule by the great Moulay Ismail, founder of the present Alaouit dynasty. Rabat, on the other hand, was only a small town at the mouth of the Bou Regreg river till the early years of the 20th century. History had passed it by, apart from one brief fling 700 years ago, when the Almohad sultans Abd al-Mumin, his son Yusuf, and grandson Yakub al-Mansur made it their military base for the Moorish invasion of Spain. As for Casablanca, though inhabited for at least seven centuries, it has never been more than a tiny trading post, where first Portuguese and later Spaniards were allowed to exchange their wares for the carpets and silver, metalware and leather produced in its hinterland. Today, however, Morocco's political and commercial activities have their chief centers in these two settlements. They, and the 97 km. (60 miles) separating them, contain a high proportion of the country's total population.

When Moulay Yusuf succeeded to the sultanate in August 1913, he and his French advisers decided on an early move of the capital away from Fez, a city riddled with plots and intrigue. Morocco needed a fresh start politically and commercially. Rabat, with its imperial past, was an excellent choice for the capital, but Kenitra-Port Lyautey, 32 km. (20 miles) north at the mouth of the Sebou river, was soon overshadowed by Casablanca, whose hinterland included not only Marrakesh, gathering-point for the major part of southern Morocco's products, but also the rich phosphate deposits of Khouribga, barely 129 km. (80 miles) away. As the modern port took shape, it was to "Casa" that the major commercial, financial, and industrial headquarters gravitated, and the city soon became the country's undisputed economic capital.

Both towns are fine examples of modern planning. Both are genuinely modern while yet contriving to preserve their Moroccan heritage and atmosphere. Both enjoy a profusion of parks, flowers and trees that enable the inhabitants to breathe fresh air. Both contain fine examples of buildings erected since French rule ended, including excellent housing for the poor. The slums of Casa, the *bidonvilles*—the shanty towns—around the outskirts, are constantly replaced by large utilitarian housing complexes. But in a country where poverty is still rampant and the drift to the towns is running at flood level, it is impossible to prevent new ones rising overnight.

Exploring Rabat

Rabat, Morocco's fourth-largest city, now has over a million inhabitants. Designed for the operation of government, far from Casablanca's commercial bustle, it is the seat of the King's main residence, of the government and foreign embassies, in a stately and dignified setting.

When the capital was transferred here in 1913, the area inside the 12th-century pink ramparts, originally ten miles long and mostly still standing, was empty. Today the city has not only filled the girdle of ramparts, but overflowed far out to the south and southwest. The main artery, the Avenue Mohammed V, runs two miles through the center from north to south. The most northerly section, nearest the sea, is a narrow straight road cutting through the ancient medina. Further south, it widens and becomes a fine boulevard with palms planted down the center.

A *Ribat* (a fortified monastic stronghold, the word from which the name Rabat is derived) was built on the present site of the Kasbah of the Oudaias in the 10th century as a base for expeditions against unruly tribes in the area. Commanding the mouth of the Bou Regreg estuary, this headland has been the key to Rabat's history until the transference there of the capital from Fez by the French in 1913. The Almoravids reconstructed the Ribat around 1140, but it was not until after its capture by the Almohads in 1146 that the place assumed an important role in Moroccan history. Abd al-Mumin, the first Almohad sultan, used the Ribat as a rallying point for the tribes in his *jihad* (holy war) against the Christians in Spain, and it was his grandson, Yakub al-Mansur, who began the building of the city under the name Ribat al Fath—Ribat of Victory. He built the great walls, constructed a palace adjoining the Ribat, of which only the magnificent gate remains, and began construction of the enormous mosque and minaret, the Tour Hassan, which was never completed. With his death the city reverted to a village, and the neighboring town of Salé became pre-eminent.

A Pirate Stronghold

The Merinids fortified the inland Roman settlement of Sala and constructed a necropolis and place of religious retreat there; but it remained a backwater until the 17th century when the Saadian sultan, Al Zaydan (1603–1628) settled refugees from Moslem Spain in the area below the Ribat which is now the medina. These immigrants, whose numbers in-

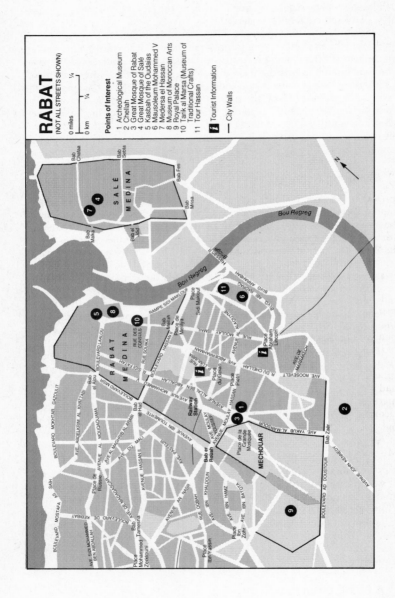

creased with subsequent expulsions from their homeland, were much more sophisticated than the local population and lived apart; it was they who constructed what is known as the Andalusian Wall which forms the limits of the present-day medina. They called their city 'new Salé' to differentiate it from the "old Salé" across the estuary, and their main purpose was the harassment of Spanish shipping, if not the recapture of the Iberian peninsula—thus their name, the "Salé rovers." With the decline of Saadian power, they established an independent state, the Republic of Bou Regreg, which lived off piracy and was used as a pawn by England and Spain in their battle for control of the sea routes to the New World. Finally, in 1666, Moulay Ismail, the first Alaouit, put an end to their independence and incorporated both "old and new Salé" into his new Moroccan empire.

His successors settled on the site of the old Ribat members of the Oudaia tribe—an Arab tribe which Moulay Ismail had enlisted as mercenaries and which had subsequently rebelled—in order to contain the surrounding Zaer Berbers and force their submission to the Alaouit sultan. Thus the present name, Kasbah of the Oudaias, which dates from that period, having used the former Almohad palace (of which only the gate remains) as building material. Yet the site remained insignificant—except as a base for piracy from which the sultan now prospered—and was outshone by its neighbor Salé until this century.

Buildings of Rabat

But despite its troubled history, Rabat possesses some Islamic monuments which rival those of Fez and Marrakesh. From the upper end of the Avenue Mohammed V, the Avenue Moulay Hassan leads to the Almohad Walls and the Bab er Rouah (Gate of the Winds), the most splendid of the five surviving city gates; notice especially the concentric arches surrounding the doorway and the marvelous bluish hue of the pink sandstone (photography is best in the afternoon). On this side of the town, the Almohad Walls run in an unbroken line for two miles. The Avenue Ibn Toumerte to the right follows the ramparts and the public gardens filled with jacarandas, bougainvillea, hibiscus and other tropical trees and plants laid out beside them.

After taking the Avenue Ibn Toumerte and its continuation, Boulevard Misr, turn right into Boulevard Laalou to the Kasbah of the Oudaias. Its great fortified gateway is one of the masterpieces of Almohad architecture and can be compared to the famous Bab Agnaou in Marrakesh. Constructed in dark red sandstone with bands of floriated Kufic decoration, it was the ceremonial entrance of the audience hall of the palace which has since disappeared. Below is the entrance to the kasbah which leads into a delightful Andalusian garden in which is the Museum of Moroccan Arts, housed in a building constructed by Moulay Ismail around 1680. It contains an interesting collection of old Berber jewelry, fabrics and brocades, manuscripts, and musical instruments. It is pleasant to stop for a drink in the adjoining Café Maure with a fine view over the estuary and the white houses of Salé.

From the Kasbah of the Oudaias follow the road that flanks the medina's eastern (riverside) edge, the Rampe de la Douane, and then fork right into the Rue des Consuls (so called because foreign consuls at one time were obliged to live in it), lined with shops selling arts and crafts products, especially carpets of the unique design for which Rabat is famous. Before buying, take a look at the Museum of Traditional Crafts, Tarik al Marsa. The whole medina has to be explored on foot.

The Rampe Sidi Maklouf leads upstream to the square of the same name. Above rises Rabat's landmark, the Tour Hassan. The Tower is 53 feet square, 144 high, and has walls eight feet thick. It was built between the years 1195 and 1199 by Yakub al-Mansur, part of a never-completed enormous great mosque—big enough to contain the entire army for prayers, the largest in the Maghreb.

The ramp to the top, designed to allow pack animals to carry stones up during its construction, has long been closed for repairs, but according to local gossip, to stop suicides. In the core of the minaret are six rooms, one on top of the other, with vaulted and domed ceilings and rich decoration. Facing the tower, the mausoleum and mosque of Mohammed V rise from a white marble terrace beyond the 200 broken columns of the ancient mosque. The sunken sarcophagus, watched over by four members of the Royal Guard, was obviously inspired by Napoleon's tomb, but impeccably adapted to the timeless Islamic architecture. The effectiveness of this outstanding contemporary sacred building is greatly enhanced by floodlighting.

Returning to the main crossroads at the top of Avenue Mohammed V, near the modern Great Mosque in the Zankat al Brihi is the small Archeological Museum which contains a fine collection of antique bronzes, mainly from Volubilis and the neighboring sites of the Roman province of Mauretania Tingitana. Noteworthy are the guard-dog (2nd cent. A.D.), a Roman copy of the Greek youth by Praxiteles, and a Hellenistic fisherman from Alexandria (1st cent. A.D.). The *Head of a young man with his hair bound by a fillet* may be a much idealized portrait of the Numidian King Juba II, or a Hellenistic work of the 1st century A.D.

By following Avenue Yakub al-Mansur from the Place de la Grande Mosquée, you reach the Bab Zaër, one of the original Almohad gates, very simply decorated. To the left within the walls are the gardens which contain the French Embassy, the former villa of the Residents-General, and the Mausoleum of Marshal Lyautey, whose remains were returned to France after independence.

Outside the ramparts, descending from a small elevation to the Bou Regreg, is the 14th-century Merinid Necropolis of Chellah, surrounded by fortifications and entered through a crenellated gateway of monumental proportions flanked by two towers. Within, the ground slopes steeply through beautiful gardens, and at the bottom are the ruins of a mosque and royal tombs, among which is that of Abu el Hassan, the Black Sultan, with its stalactite roofed portico. Only traces of the tiles, stucco decoration and horseshoe arches of the mosque remain but it is the legends surrounding the place which imbue it with an atmosphere of piety and retreat. The well-restored large hammam, an outstanding example of a Merinid bath, indicates that a town once surrounded the necropolis. Excavations have revealed the foundations of Roman Sala Colonia.

Royal Pageantry

Inside the Bab Zaër, the Royal Palace, a splendid replica of the greatest Islamic architecture, extends along one side of the Mechouar. When the King is in residence, he attends the Friday prayers in the Great Mosque at the opposite end of this vast, impressive square. This is a spectacular ceremony and crowds start gathering well before 10 A.M., when the Royal Guard are parading in their brilliant scarlet uniforms in front of the palace. Service in the Guard is still hereditary and the members of this hand-picked, highly-disciplined force, though today all of course free men, are mainly descendants of the West African slaves whom the Sultan Moulay Ismail collected for his personal bodyguard 300 years ago.

After the initial parade, infantrymen take up positions along the road the King follows, and the detachment which march beside him on his return station themselves near the mosque. Then the mounted band and a cavalry detachment move over to the mosque. Finally, the King, dressed entirely in white, riding in a magnificently carved and gilded coach drawn by four horses and accompanied by the main body of scarlet-clad troops, crosses the compound while the crowd applauds with rather shrill cries which, in Islamic countries, indicate approval.

Prayers are relayed to the crowds outside the mosque by loudspeaker, and when the time for the King's return is approaching, a number of superb horses are led over to the mosque. Each horse is a different color and each has a blanket, or *hanbel,* woven from brilliantly-dyed wools, thrown across the saddle. Then the doctors of Koranic law, who have been praying with the King and who are dressed like him entirely in white, leave the mosque and form up for the return procession. The troops and the now empty coach move into place. Finally, the King emerges and mounts a white horse. With a large scarlet parasol held high above his head, he and the whole procession move slowly back to the palace, while the crowd again applauds.

Sale

Salé is joined to Rabat by the Hassan II bridge, and for the incurably romantic, by small and smelly boats from below the Rampe Sidi Maklouf across the Bou Regreg. Its history is bound closely with that of Rabat, but, while Rabat was primarily a military camp, Salé was the chief port and mercantile center of medieval Morocco. The site has been inhabited since the time of the Romans when it was the port of ancient Sala, and by the beginning of the 12th century it was already a prosperous town. Salé resisted Almohad conquest, and as a result Abd al-Mumin demolished the walls. They were rebuilt in the 14th century by the Merinids, who preferred it to Rabat and consequently embellished the town with several rich buildings. Its prosperity made it a frequent target for invasion.

From the early 17th century, Salé received Andalusian refugees, but it remained a commercial center visited by many European traders. Most of the piracy often so wrongly associated with its name was carried out from "new Salé," based on the Kasbah of the Oudaias and the adjoining Andalusian medina. It will be remembered that Robinson Crusoe's adventures began with his capture by "Salee rovers." Its migrant Spanish Moslems forced the reluctant Arab inhabitants to join the ill-fated Bou Regreg Republic. After capture by the Alaouits in 1666, Salé never regained its former power and glory and is today no more than a suburb of the capital.

Merinid walls surround the town, and of the several original gates, the Bab Mrisa just to the left of the road coming from Rabat, is the most interesting. Completed before 1270 by Abu Yusuf al Yakub (1258–1286), it was originally a water-gate connected to the sea by a canal through which ships sailed or were drawn to be anchored in safety within the walls. The area of the inner harbor and the dry docks has long since been drained and is now covered in part by the mellah and also by arsenals and barracks in a ruined state from the time of Moulay Ismail.

Salé, with its narrow white-washed streets lined with windowless houses, often having elaborately carved doors, presents a vivid contrast to its modern neighbor and has retained the atmosphere of another era, recalling the Andalusia of Cordoba. The twisting arcaded streets are full of charm, but can be confusing. Better keep to the circular road inside the ramparts, and near the beach, turn left (on foot only) towards the Great Mosque which can be identified by its high minaret. On the way you will pass the white marabout of the patron saint of Salé and its boatmen. From here, on the eve of Maloud, the birthday of the Prophet, there is a candlelight procession through the streets of the old town. Preceded by boatmen in traditional costume, the candles—many molded with elaborate motifs and decorated with iridescent colors—are carried on frames mounted on the tops of poles in a ceremony which is certainly unique in Morocco, more reminiscent of Ottoman Turkey. The Great Mosque was founded by the second Almohad, Abu Yakub Yusuf (1163–1184) and retains much of the purity of the original design.

Opposite the main entrance of the Mosque is the outstanding Medersa el Hassan founded in 1341 by the same Black Sultan, Abu el Hassan who is buried at Chellah and whose name it bears. Brilliantly restored, it is entered by a horseshoe arched doorway surmounted by an elaborately carved porch of cedarwood, the roof of which is in green tiles. Beyond the vestibule is the courtyard surrounded on all sides by arcades decorated with faience mosaic, with a fountain in the center; the thin columns recall the pavilions in the Patio de los Leones in the Alhambra which also date from the mid-14th century. The effect is achieved by the use of color and the contrast of the deeply carved cedarwood pediment with the white stucco walls and the mosaic tiles below. In the prayer hall—which can be visited—there is a mihrab of elegantly carved stucco, and again, a ceiling of cedar on which traces of painted decoration survive. Above are two floors of small student cells—for this was a religious college—and from the roof is an excellent vista over the courtyard to the white walls and green tiles of Salé to the estuary, the Kasbah of the Oudaias and the ocean beyond. The Medersa of Salé ranks with those of Fez and Meknès among the highest achievements of Moorish architecture in the Maghreb.

Along the Coast to Casablanca

The 97 km. (60 miles) motorway from Rabat via Temara to Casablanca is the country's most traveled route. Less heavy traffic is encountered on the far more scenic coast road with branches to a series of beaches: El Harhoura and Temara Beach—a major entertainment center with many discos and some Saudi palaces—closely followed by Sehl Dheb, Ech Chiahna, Skhirat with its royal palace, Bouznika, and finally, Mohammedia. Most of the beaches, though equipped with facilities like changing cabins, bars and restaurants, are small by Moroccan standards, even Mohammedia, which holds a special place in Moroccans' affections.

This little seaside town is half industrial, half tourist. Canning plants, and a big oil refinery to the south, compete with one of Morocco's few casinos, a well-rated golf course, a luxury hotel set in seven acres of its own gardens, and a harbor where pleasure craft are plentiful. To Morocco's jet-set, Mohammedia represents the height of comfort, good living and relaxation, but it is unlikely to become an international resort.

Casablanca

Morocco's biggest city enfolds the small seaside Medina, close to the port, as much a historical relic as a living part of the town. It appears as Anfa for the first time in the 12th century, but this name now applies to the elegant western suburb on a hill overlooking the sea. Destroyed by the Portuguese in 1468 because of its piratical tendencies, the small port became known as Casa Branca during a second Portuguese occupation from 1515 to 1755, when a severe earthquake laid it open to conquest by neighboring tribes. For a time called Dar el Beida, it reverted to the similar name of Casa Blanca (White House) when Spanish merchants obtained trading privileges, soon shared with French and English competitors for the vast hinterland which stretched to Fez and equidistant Marrakesh.

By the beginning of this century the population had grown to 27,000 from a mere 600 in 1830, but it needed the impetus of industrialization after World War II to attract ever-increasing numbers of villagers into sprawling shanty towns. Under the personal supervision of the King these have largely been cleaned up; popular housing estates with gardens increasingly line the wide new arteries. The city's inhabitants, numbering over three million, depend on industry and on the artificial harbor, with its long jetties extending far out to sea to shelter Morocco's largest and busiest port from the Atlantic rollers. Only the shipments of phosphates, from the Khouribga mining center near Oued Zem, are gradually being transferred to Jorf El Asfar, 110 km. (68 miles) south, which will eventually become the world's biggest phosphate port. This will result in a much-needed decongestion of the overworked communication system and add to rather than detract from Casablanca's commercial pre-eminence.

Exploring Casablanca

The sights can easily be covered in a morning, which is the time allowed by the travel agents' conducted tours. The well-planned, westernized new town is crossed by wide palm-lined avenues radiating from vast central squares; the Rabat-El Jadida motorway cuts through the inland suburbs. The city centers on the huge Place des Nations Unies, whose lovely garden sets off a fountain throwing multi-colored jets high in the air to the slightly incongruous sound of Strauss waltzes. Around are a number of fine buildings in pleasing neo-Moroccan style: the head-office of the Banque du Maroc, the Town Hall—whose 50-meter (165-foot) high tower affords a fine view over the whole vast agglomeration—the Law Courts and Central Post Office, as well as the Moroccan Automobile Club. The Law Courts are particularly interesting for their elaborate and colorful traditional-style decorations.

Further inland, the spacious Parc de la Ligue Arabe contains a small stadium at the entrance from Ave. Hassan II. At the side facing the Rue Alger rise the twin towers, from which the crosses have been removed, of the deconsecrated Catholic Cathedral; the peeling walls of the sacristy house some of the city's health services. Casablanca's largest green space extends across Boulevard Moulay Youssef, whose rows of tall palms continue through an elegant residential quarter to meet the sea stylishly at

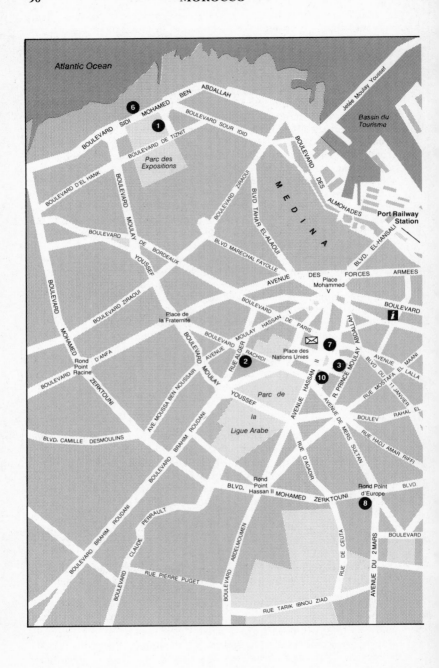

Atlantic Ocean

Jetée Moulay Youssef

Bassin du Tourisme

BOULEVARD SIDI MOHAMED BEN ABDALLAH

BOULEVARD SOUR IDID

BOULEVARD DE TIZNIT

Parc des Expositions

BOULEVARD D'EL HANK

BOULEVARD ZIRAOUI

BLVD TAHAR EL-ALAOUI

M E D I N A

BOULEVARD DES ALMOHADES

Port Railway Station

BOULEVARD MOULAY DE BORDEAUX

BOULEVARD

BLVD MARECHAL FAYOLLE

BLVD. EL-HANSALI

BOULEVARD

YOUSSEF

AVENUE DES FORCES ARMEES

Place Mohammed V

BOULEVARD

BOULEVARD ZIRAOUI

D'ANFA

Place de la Fraternité

BOULEVARD DE PARIS

BOULEVARD HASSAN I

i

BOULEVARD MOHAMED

Rond Point Racine

BOULEVARD MOULAY

AVENUE

RUE ALGER RACHIDI

Place des Nations Unies

7

AVENUE EL MAANI

ZERKTOUNI

AVE. MOUSSA BEN NOUSSAIR

BRAHIM ROUDANI

MOULAY

2

3

10

R. PRINCE MOULAY ABDALLAH

BLVD. DU 11 JANVIER

RUE MOSTAFA EL LALLA

YOUSSEF

Parc de

AVENUE HASSAN II

RAHAL EL

BLVD. CAMILLE DESMOULINS

la

Ligue Arabe

AVENUE DE MERS SULTAN

BOULEV

RUE HADJ AMAR RIFFI

BOULEVARD

RUE D'AGADIR

Rond Point Hassan II

BLVD.

MOHAMED ZERKTOUNI

Rond Point d'Europe

BLVD

8

BOULEVARD BRAHIM ROUDANI

CLAUDE PERRAULT

BOULEVARD ABDELMOUMEN

RUE DE CEUTA

AVENUE DU 2 MARS

BOULEVARD

BOULEVARD ROUDANI

RUE PIERRE PUGET

RUE TARIK IBNOU ZIAD

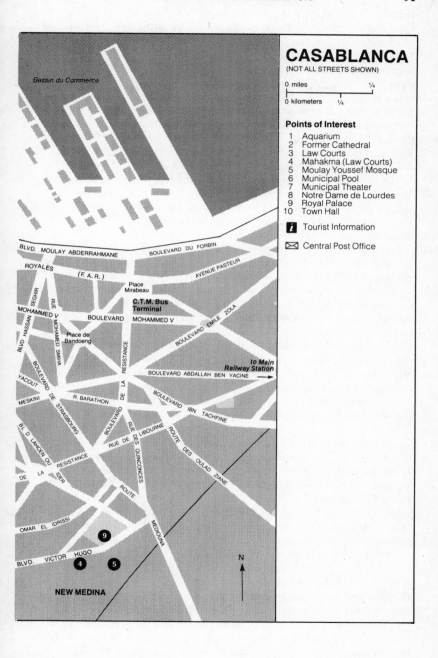

CASABLANCA
(NOT ALL STREETS SHOWN)

0 miles   ¼

0 kilometers   ¼

Points of Interest

1   Aquarium
2   Former Cathedral
3   Law Courts
4   Mahakma (Law Courts)
5   Moulay Youssef Mosque
6   Municipal Pool
7   Municipal Theater
8   Notre Dame de Lourdes
9   Royal Palace
10   Town Hall

i   Tourist Information

✉   Central Post Office

the Municipal Pool, one of Africa's largest. To the left, Boulevard de la Corniche passes the El-Hank lighthouse on the attractive drive to Aïn Diab and the hill of Anfa, where Churchill and Roosevelt made plans in 1943 for post-war Europe. Hotels, restaurants and nightspots alternate with swimming-pools on Morocco's most sophisticated waterfront. On the right, Boulevard Sidi Mohamed Ben Abdallah skirts the interesting aquarium which backs onto the fairground and becomes Boulevard des Almohades, dividing the Medina from the busy port.

Among the mosques inside the ramparts are the Jamaou el-Kebir, built by the 18th-century Sultan Sidi Mohamed Ben Abdallah, the Jama ech-Chleuh and the Sanctuary of Sidi Ali el-Kairouani, an early patron. Narrow twisting lanes of white-washed houses lead to a sort of souk, strong on plastic wares. Better buys are available in the crafts shops on Boulevard El-Hansali which begins at the Port Railway Station and the Centre 2000 shopping mall with restaurants and fastfood bars, a favorite hangout of westernized hookers, of whom Sidi Beyliout, buried in a nearby marabout, could hardly have approved.

Boulevard Moulay Abderrahmane continues along the seafront to the popular Aïn Sebaa suburb on the shortest route to Mohammedia, while el-Hansali branches right to Place Mohammed V, the vast downtown center traversed by underground passages topped by a rather mysterious colored cupola in the middle. Avenue des Forces Armées Royales (usually called "des F.A.R." or simply "de l'Armée Royale" according to the variations existing in all major towns) is lined with hotels, cafes and travel agencies. The parallel Boulevard Mohammed V is the business center with the city Tourist Office (Syndicat d'Initiative). The pedestrian zone round Rue Prince Moulay Abdallah accommodates the most elegant shops, but the shopping district extends along Boulevard Tahar el-Alaoui which fringes the Medina in the opposite direction. Vibrantly alive throughout the day, this large modern section becomes uncannily deserted at sundown.

Avenue Hassan II, the main inland artery, crosses Place des Nations Unies to carry on along Parc de la Ligue Arabe to Rond Point Hassan II on the inner ring-road. Boulevard Mohamed Zerktouni leads right to Boulevard de la Corniche, left past the gardens of the hospitals to Rond-Point d'Europe, where Notre Dame de Lourdes presents a creditable example of modern European architecture, using stained-glass decoration to provide not only the windows, but the whole walls of the church, in striking contrast to so much based on Moroccan inspiration.

The church is passed up Avenue du 2 Mars, as large a thoroughfare as the second turn to the left, Boulevard Victor Hugo, which divides the Royal Palace, smaller than in the four imperial cities, from the Mahakma, the local law courts, where judges and lawyers wear the traditional green and black robes. Behind rises the minaret of the Jamaa Moulay Youssef, one of contemporary Morocco's largest and finest, at the entrance to the arcaded streets of a vast, clean but unremarkable souk. Beyond stretch the ever-increasing quarters of the New Medina, swarming with what seems to most a surfeit of humanity.

PRACTICAL INFORMATION FOR RABAT

WHEN TO GO. Summer (June to end of September) is the best time. Temperatures are rarely excessive and cooling sea breezes temper the sun; sea mists, frequent at night, may extend well into the day. May, October and November can also be sunny and very pleasant. But overcast, slightly muggy days are also possible. In winter (December to April) these may continue for quite long periods, with dampness making the temperature seem lower than it really is. Rain is possible throughout the year, though most frequent in January and February; summer showers are mostly short and sharp but evenings often cloud over at that time of year.

GETTING THERE. By Train. The quickest train, the Al Beida Express, takes 54 min. from Casablanca and 4½ hrs from Tangier. The Al Quaraouyine Express takes 4 hrs 40 min from Fez, but it is a long 9 hrs from Oujda.

By Car. Tangier is 272 km. (169 miles) away, Marrakesh 320 (199), Agadir 663 (412), Fez just over 161 (100). Good coach services to these towns and other destinations.

By Plane. The Rabat-Salé airport is connected to most major Moroccan towns.

HOTELS. There are insufficient accommodations for the heavy summer season, when package tour parties may fill the (E) and (M) hotels. Only some (E) are air-conditioned; none has pools. Book in advance.
Area code 07.

Deluxe

Hotel Safir, Pl. Sidi Maklouf (tel. 731091-4). 190 rooms, 8 suites. Near the Mausoleum Mohammed V. 3 restaurants, one at panorama pool on 5th floor.
Rabat Hyatt Regency, Aviation Souissi (tel. 771 234 or 800–233–1234 in U.S.). 259 rooms, 9 suites. In the diplomatic quarter outside the ramparts. Two restaurants; fine gardens with pool, cabanas and 5 tennis courts; convention facilities and shopping arcades. This was formerly the Hilton. Golf at the 18-hole Royal Dar Es Salam course 10 minutes away. Popular Justine's Restaurant

Expensive

Belere, 33 Ave. Moulay Youssef (tel. 769 901). 90 small rooms. No parking area.
Chellah, 2 Rue d'Ifni (tel. 764 052). 100 airconditioned rooms Chellah is by far the best in this section. It is modern, clean, and has helpful staff and efficient service. Two restaurants—one outstanding and the winner of several trophies for its cordon bleu cuisine. Across from the Antiquities Museum.
Les Oudayas, 4 Rue Tobrouk (768 235). Slightly cheaper than Chellah, but much more basic, this old hotel is in need of some renovation, but there are a friendly and helpful staff and comfortable beds. 35 rooms.
Tour Hassan, 34 Ave. Abderrahman Annegaï (tel. 733 814). 150 airconditioned rooms. Fine patio in a quiet central position; it is luxurious architecturally and in price. Part of the Kasbah Tour chain. Outstanding Moroccan restaurant, though the international dining room is not so good. *El Farrah* nightclub.

Moderate

Balima, Rue Jakarta (tel.767 755/768 255). Café terrace on Ave. Mohammed V; good to watch the world go by.
Bou Regreg, Rue Nador (tel. 734 002). 31 rooms.
Hotel D'Orsay, 11, Ave., My Youssef (tel. 761 319). 30 rooms. Clean and comfortable but no restaurant.

Grand, Rue Patrice Lumumba (tel. 727 285). 52 rooms.

Hotel de la Paix, 2, Rue De Ghazzah (tel. 722 926). 52 rooms, 38 with shower or bath. No restaurant.

Hotel Royal I, Rue Ammam (tel. 721 171). 67 rooms, 15 with bath and 30 with shower. No restaurant.

Luxeor, Rue Abdelmoumen (tel. 722 916/64). 26 modern rooms; no restaurant.

Shéhérazade, Rue de Tunis (tel. 722 226). 36 rooms. Long established; best in grade.

Splendid, Rue Ghazza (tel. 723 283). 40 rooms, 17 showers; no restaurant.

Velleda, Ave. Allal Ben Abdallah (tel. 769 531). 28 rooms, 17 showers; no restaurant.

Rabat Environs

Kasbah (E), at Ech Chiahna (tel. 416 33). 40 rooms. Beach hotel with pool.

Amphritrite (M), adjoining the royal summer residence at Skhirat (tel. 422 36). 36 rooms; beach, pool.

La Felouque (M), at Temara Plage (tel. 443 88). 20 rooms. Beach hotel with pool.

The **Sun Dance Village** on the Salé bank of the Bou Regreg estuary provides the best camping.

RESTAURANTS

Expensive

Diffa Room, the Moroccan restaurant of the Tour Hassan Hotel has good local specialties.

Le Gouland, 9, Rue Moulay Ali Cherif. Very good seafood dishes are served here.

Les Delices D'Asie, 17, Rue Ogbah, Agdal. Try this place for some fine Oriental cuisine.

Oasis, 7 Zankat Al-Os-Gofia. More relaxed than the Diffa Room, also has local dishes.

Palais Kabbaj, Rue Mokhtar Soussi. Local specialties.

Moderate

Au Crépuscule, 10 Rue de Toulouse. Pleasantly French.

Hong Kong, Ave. Mohammed V. Chinese food.

Kanoun Grill, in the Chellah Hotel, 2 Rue d'Ifni.

Koutoubia, Zankat El Brihi. Moroccan specialties at a lower rate.

La Mamma, Rue Tanta. Good for Italian cooking.

Pagode, Rue Baghdad. Chinese dishes.

Pizza Roma, Pl. de l'Unité Africaine. Italian food at a reasonable price.

Inexpensive

Café de la Paix, opposite the railroad station. A good stop for budgeteers.

Le Capri, Pl. des Alaouites. Boasts long menus and short prices.

Chatham, 7 Rue Allal Ben Abdallah. Pronounced shatt-am, it serves cheap meals and snacks.

La Fouquine, Ave. Mohammed V. French food at reasonable prices.

La Fritta, Ave. Abdelkrim El Khattabi. Good fries as expected.

Hacienda, 7, Tabrou St. This centrally located restaurant offers simple local specialties, but the portions may be small for the price.

Jour et Nuit, Place Melilya. Café, restaurant and disco all in one. It is really open 24 hours a day.

Beach Fare

On all beaches near Rabat is at least one moderate restaurant, usually serving French food. At **Temara,** 16 km. (10 miles) south, the *Provençal* is a pleasant auberge in the village; *La Baraka* and *La Khaïma* are disco-restaurants on the beach. The *Sables d'Or* on the coast road bears the same name as the beach below, where the *Felouque* restaurant has a disco attached.

The *Auberge des Martinets* is in the Zaërs forest past the golf club, but by far the best restaurant is to the north, the *Auberge Savoyarde* (E). See under Sidi Bouknadel, p. 105.

NIGHTSPOTS. Besides the nightclubs in the Hyatt, Balima and Belere hotels, there are the discos: *Jefferson*, 3 Rue Patrice Lumumba, *La Biba* and *L'Entonnoir*, both Place Mellilia. *5th Avenue*, 4, Rue Bin El Windane, Agdal.

SPORTS. Sailing: Fath Union Sport, Olympic Morocain, Sailing Club of l'Aviron de Rabat, and Yacht Club of Rabat, all at Quai de la Tour Hassan. **Horseback riding:** Club Equestre de Dar Es Salam. **Golf:** Royal Dar Es Salam Golf Club, one 9-hole, two 18-hole courses in the Zaërs forest 10 km. (6 miles) from town. **Tennis:** Stadium, Ave. Haroun Rachid.

SHOPPING. All the traditional items of Moroccan craftsmanship may be found at Coopartim, corner of Rue Renard and Rue Jabarti. Quality guaranteed and fixed prices assured by state control.

Also: Exposition Vente Permanente, 45 Rue Allal Ben Abdallah. Elegant caftans and antique tribal jewelry are available at Farah, Zankat Tihama opposite the entrance of the Balima Hotel. The boutique of Francesco Smalto, the King's tailor, is at 2 Zankat Gabass. American Bookstore, 137 Charia Allal Ben Abdallah.

USEFUL ADDRESSES. Tourist information at O.N.M.T. (Office National Marocain du Tourisme), 22 Ave. d'Alger (tel. 772 252); Syndicat d'Initiative (City Information Bureau), corner of Rue Lumumba (tel. 723 272); Delegation of Tourism, Aguelmane Sidi Mane St., Immeuble B, Agdal (tel. 773 644).

Consulates. American, 2, Charil Marakesh B.P.O. 120 (tel. 752 265); 17, Blvd. de la Tour Hassan (tel. 720 905).

Travel Agencies. Wagons Lits/Cooks, 1 Ave. Al Amir Moulay Abdallah. Afric Voyages, 28 Ave. Allal Ben Abdallah; Maroc-Tourisme, 289 Ave. Mohammed V.

Airlines. Royal Air Maroc, 289 Ave. Mohammed V; Air France, 281 Ave. Mohammed V; Pan American, 10 Pl. des Alaouites.

Transportation. C.T.M. Bus Terminal, Route de Casablanca. Frequent services to Casablanca (1½ hrs.), Meknès (2½ hrs.), Fez (3½ hrs.), Tangier (5 hrs.) and other destinations.

English-speaking Guides. From Syndicat d'Initiative (tel. 723 272), or through larger hotels' concierges. The official rates for guides (from 2–10 persons) is 70DH for half a day, and 120DH for a full day.

Car Hire. Arrow Car, 1, Patrice Lumumba (tel. 734 895; Avis, 7, Rue Abou Faris El Marini (tel. 767 503 or 767 959); Budget Car, Railway Station ONCF (tel. 767 689); Europcar, Hyatt Regency Hotel (tel. 770 218); Fly Drive, 2, Ave. Prince Moulay Abdella (tel. 731 650); Inter Rent, 25, Bis Patrice Lumumba St. (tel. 722 321); Matei Express, 9, Rue Benzerte (tel. 761 249); North Car, 1, Tabaya St. (tel. 724 810); Olympia Car, 4, Kahira St. (tel. 769 004); Pacific Car, 11, Baghdad St. (tel. 765 565); Royal Rent Car, Abou Faris El Marini St. (tel. 769 804).

Helpful for motorists is Touring Club de Maroc, 45 Rue Lumumba (tel. 275 48).

Taxis. If the petit taxi's meter is not functioning, it is advisable to fix the fare before setting out; between 5 and 10DH in-city. Avoid the big limousines hovering in front of the hotels which will charge you at least 50DH per ride.

PRACTICAL INFORMATION FOR MOHAMMEDIA

HOTELS. (Area code 32.) **Miramar-Meridien** (L), Rue de Fès (tel. 20 21). 183 rooms; surrounded by extensive grounds with an 18-hole golf course; deserves its luxury classification.

Samir (E), Blvd. Moulay Youssef (tel. 20 05). 146 rooms. Looks onto the beach and offers tennis, horse riding, nightclub, pool and convention facilities.

RESTAURANTS. The Sunday poolside buffet at the Samir Hotel is specially recommended, though crowded in August (E).

Auberge des Grands Zenata (E). On Coast Road, 15 km from Casablanca (tel. 352 102). Delicious seafood dishes served here.

SPORTS. Golf: The 18-hole course on the Mohammedia coast has been considered the best in Morocco before the opening of the course in Dar Es Salaam. **Horseback riding:** Club Equestre at Blvd. Moulay Youassef. **Tennis:** Club de Mohammedia. **Watersports:** On the coast there is swimming and other watersports. Regattas are held every Sunday between May and Oct. 30 at the Yacht Club of Mohammedia.

ENTERTAINMENT. The Casino de Fédala is a major gathering-point for Casa's socialites. You can dance here as well as play roulette, boule and baccarat. Day admission tickets are available for tourists. Swimming in the pool May-Sept. Also Le Sphinx, cabaret, bar and dancing.

PRACTICAL INFORMATION FOR CASABLANCA

GETTING THERE. By Plane. Casablanca's Mohammed V International Airport is the hub of Morocco's air communications. Domestic flights from all provincial centers by Royal Air Inter. Bus service to the CTM Terminal in town, fare 20DH. A taxi to town will cost about 100DH.

By Train. Most trains arrive at the port railway station. From Marrakesh 3–4 hrs.; from Fez 5½–6 hrs.; from Tangier 6 hrs. The Al Maghreb Al Arabi Express from Oujda has sleeping cars for the 10 hr. journey. Trains from Oued Zem via Khouribga take 2½–3 hrs. to Casa Voyageurs, the town railway station, Blvd. Ba-Hammad.

By Boat. Rashid Line, a comparatively new Egyptian shipping company, has fairly regular sailings from New York by passenger-carrying freighters. At press time, tickets are available only with an Alexandria destination. Includes various Mediterranean ports-of-call, as cargo designates.

By Car. Casa lies roughly 92 km. (57 miles) from Rabat; 241 km. (150 miles) from Marrakesh; 290 km. (180 miles) from Fez; 644 km. (400 miles) from Oujda near the Algerian border; 378 km. (235 miles) from Tangier; 241 km. (150 miles) from Safi; and 547 km. (340 miles) from Agadir. All these roads are fast (beware of children and donkeys). C.T.M. have coach services with reserved seats to main towns; overnight Pullmans to Agadir and Tangier. Buses to lesser destinations are uncomfortably overcrowded and slow.

HOTELS. It is advisable to book well in advance during the summer and during the annual Casablanca Trade Fair (end April to early May). Many hotels in Morocco have been reclassified recently because they fell below standards. In Casablanca, any hotel marked as a three-star and downward should be checked out beforehand, since the standards at these places become very variable. Many of the moderate and inexpensive hotels are old and management may be lacking, but some have been renovated.

Area code 0.

Deluxe

Casablanca Hyatt Regency, Pl. Mohammed V (tel. 224 167 or 800–233–1234 in U.S.). 300 large rooms. Most luxurious in town. Several restaurants include *Maison Blanche* for gourmet cuisine and *Dar Beida* for Moroccan specialties and entertainment. *Black House* nightclub; spacious pool, fitness center and conference facilities.

Hotel Holiday Inn, Rond Point Hassan II (tel. 268 713 or 800–465–4329 in U.S.). 200 rooms. Amenities here include swimming pool, sauna, gymnasium, steam bath, and Jacuzzis. There are also conference facilities, 3 restaurants, 2 bars, and a nightclub.

El Mansour, 27 Ave. des F.A.R. (tel. 31 30 11). 192 rooms. Completely renovated, this hotel now offers luxurious accommodations, with 3 restaurants, swimming pool, and nightclub. Business atmosphere but attentive service. Sauna.

Safir, 61 Ave. des F.A.R. (tel. 31 12 12). 300 rooms, 12 suites; three restaurants, heated pool. A good representative of this reliable chain.

Sheraton, 100 Ave. des F.A.R. (tel. 317 878 or 800–325–3535 in U.S.). Besides pleasant rooms, this chain hotel offers 4 restaurants—French, International, Oriental, and Japanese cuisines—as well as a swimming pool, gymnasium, sauna, Jacuzzi, squash court, nightclub, and conference facilities.

Expensive

Les Almohades, Ave. Moulay Hassan I (tel. 22 05 05). 138 airconditioned rooms; pool, boutiques, bank, restaurant, and piano bar.

Basma, 35 Ave. Hassan I (tel. 223 323). 177 rooms. Modern in appearance, the Basma features TV and video in all rooms; boutiques, bank, restaurant and bar.

Idou Anfa, 85 Blvd. d'Anfa (tel. 264 004). 222 rooms. Offering the same facilities as most deluxe hotels, this place features 3 restaurants, swimming pool, sauna, and conference facilities.

El Kandara, 44 Blvd. d'Anfa (tel. 261 560). 202 rooms. Featured here are three restaurants, including a Moroccan one with floor shows, tea lounge, bar, pool, sauna, and conference facilities.

Washington, 107 Blvd. Rahal El Meskini (tel. 279 717). This clean and comfortable hotel has been recently renovated and upgraded.

Moderate

Astoria, 53 Rue d'Azilal (tel. 305 701). 30 rooms.

Astrid, 12 Rue Ledru-Rollin (tel. 27 78 03). 22 rooms, all with bath; no restaurant.

Dades, 25 Rue Oudjar (tel. 276 018). 58 rooms, restaurant.

Metropole, 89 Rue Mohammed Smiha (tel. 30 12 13). 57 rooms.

Plaza, 18 Blvd. El Hansali (tel. 221 262). 25 rooms. The Plaza is considered one of the best hotels in its price range, with a fine restaurant and a bar.

Windsor, 93 Pl. Oued El Makhazine (tel. 27 88 74). 32 rooms, 20 with bath; no restaurant.

Inexpensive

Excelsior, 2 Rue Nolly (tel. 276 543). 54 rooms, 32 with bath.

De Paris, 2 Rue Branly (tel. 273 871). 34 rooms. This place has been recently renovated.

Sully, 284 Blvd. Rahal Meskini (tel. 305 491). 46 rooms, all with bath.

Trocadero, 88 Blvd. Lahcen Ider (tel. 314 701). 28 rooms, 18 with bath; restuarant and bar.

At Aïn Dab on the Boulevard de la Corniche

Riad Salam Le Meridien (L), tel. 36 35 35. 100 rooms, 50 bungalows; sports facilities. This outstanding place was recently taken over by Air France and upgraded. Facilities include five restaurants, a pool, tennis courts, nightclub, and conference room.

Anfa Plage (E), tel. 368 646. 126 rooms. Bungalows; seawater pools, tennis, private beach and nightclub.

Karam (E), tel. 36 73 14. 96 rooms. Pool.

Suisse (E), tel. 36 02 02. 192 airconditioned rooms; 5 restaurants, pool, sauna, nightclub. Newest on the sea.

Tarik (E), tel. 36 78 41. 58 rooms. Pool.

Tropicana (E), tel. 367 595. 66 rooms. Restaurant, 2 pools, car hire.

Bellerive (M), tel. 36 71 92. 35 rooms.

RESTAURANTS. Casablanca is not only Morocco's commercial, but also its gastronomic capital, especially as far as seafood is concerned. Fish, lobster, oysters and prawns are served on terraces over the rocks along Blvd. de la Corniche; the best are clustered round the El-Hank lighthouse. Telephone numbers are given where it is advisable to make reservations.

Expensive

Seafood

Le Cabestan, tel. 363 265. A mainstay, near the lighthouse.

La Cambuse, tel. 36 71 05. Farther along the coast; good for late suppers.

Le Clapotis, tel. 36 77 44. Wide choice.

Ma Bretagne, at the far end of Aïn Diab (tel. 36 21 12). Food justifies extra distance.

La Mer, tel. 36 33 15. Close to the lighthouse; excellent service. Closed Monday.

Au Petit Rocher, tel. 36 11 95. Near the lighthouse.

Les Pêcheurs, tel. 22 05 61. Closer to town; with a Spanish touch. Slightly less expensive than the others.

Porte de Pêche, tel. 318 561. In the fishing port.

Even closer to the station, the Centre 2000 concentrates a goodly mixture round trees in the courtyard. La Gondole, Italian; La Marée and Rétro 1900, French; Le Mekkong, Vietnamese; and La Tajine, Moroccan.

French

La Bavaroise, Blvd. Allal Ben Abdallah (tel. 31 17 60).

Le Buffet, Blvd. Mohammed V (tel. 31 23 44).

Le Cardinal, Blvd. Mohammed V (tel. 22 15 60).

Chateaubriand, Blvd. Rahal El Meskini (tel. 27 35 13).

Chez Milhet, Blvd. Allal Ben Abdallah. Also specializing in grills.

Le Neroli, 83 Blvd. d'Anfa (tel. 263 700). Both French and International cuisines are featured here.

Happy, Rue Pont à Mousson Mers Sultan (tel. 27 82 30).

La Reserve, Blvd. de la Corniche (tel. 367 110). You can dine while watching the waves at this restaurant that stretches out over the ocean.

Moroccan

Al Mounia, Rue Prince Moulay Abdallah (tel. 22 26 69). One of the best.

L'Etoile de Marrakech, Blvd. Mohammed V (tel. 27 12 59).

Romantic, Rue Farhat Hachad (tel. 26 41 76).

Sinilmassa, Blvd. Sidi Abderrahmane, Aïn Diab (tel. 36 73 04). The only one on the coast.

Asiatic

Le Hanoï, Rue de Terves (tel. 260 563).
La Pagode, Rue Ferhat Hachad (tel. 27 71 85).
La Tonkinoise, Ave. de la Cote Emeraude (tel. 363 187).

Spanish

La Corrida, Rue Gay Lussac (tel. 27 81 55). Guitars and flamenco.

Moderate

La Broche, Rue Gay Lussac. Charcoal grills.
Champoreau, Blvd. de Paris. Honest French cuisine.
Las Delicias, Blvd. Mohammed V. Reasonably Spanish.
Drugstore Majestic, Av. Lalla Yacout (tel. 31 09 51). A drugstore in the French rather than the American sense.
Ouarzazate, Rue Mohamed el Quorri. Moroccan specialties.
Oued-Zin, Rue Allal Ben Abdallah. Moroccan food.
Au Petit Poucet, Blvd. Mohammed V. For snacks as well as meals.
Saint James, Rue de Tours. Snacks and quick service.
La Taverne du Dauphin, 75 Blvd. Felix Hophouet, Boigny (tel. 22 12 00). Near the port railway station. Local fish served simply.

IN-TOWN TRANSPORT. Taxis. The meters of the petits taxis usually function, with 10DH as average fare. The 8 km. (5 miles) to Aïn Diab costs up to 25 DH. For sightseeing, you can hire a petit taxi by the hour, at 50 to 60DH an hour. Grands taxis are permitted outside the city limits, but visitors should make sure of the price of the journey before setting out. The meters never work, and tourists are always overcharged, a practice seemingly countenanced by the authorities. Night rates are 50% above day rates.

Buses and trolleys are the cheapest means of getting to the suburbs. Most lines start at Place Mohammed V, between the Pl. des Nations Unies and the port. Unfortunately, they stop at about 9 P.M., apart from a few night services.

PORTERS. They'll try to get as much as they can, although the official rate is 8DH per large piece of luggage and 5DH per small. It's cheaper, incidentally, to have a petit taxi take your luggage from the air terminal in the C.T.M. terminus to nearby hotels—even the El Mansour, 100 yards away—than to hire a porter.

NIGHTLIFE. For a city which much of the world imagines to be a great center of international vice and gaiety, Casa goes to bed horribly early. In town, except for the luxury hotels' nightclubs, there are the *Puerto del Sol* (E), 7 Ave. Hassan II, *La Cage* (M), 2000 Centre St., and *Le Rex* on Poincare Street. The *Arizona* (M), Rue Nolly, somewhat incongruously declares itself an Oriental cabaret. Don't even bother looking for a "Rick's Place." If you find one, it won't come near the trendy bars by that name in many U.S. cities emulating the cafe Humphrey Bogart operated in the movie *Casablanca*.

Out at Aïn Diab, popularity shifts from one disco-restaurant to another: contenders are *Balcon, Calypso, La Notte, Le Tangage, Tio Pépé, Topkapi,* and *Le Tube.* On weekends the scene moves to beaches further out.

Though not just a nightspot, the *Tiffany Drugstore,* 153 Blvd. de Paris, is worth visiting for its Moroccan and European restaurants and its shopping center.

SPORTS. Because of the dangerous currents, only the foolhardy **swim** in the sea at Casa, but there are many pools along the Aïn Diab coastline—the Tahiti, Acapulco, Miami, Plage, Palm Beach, Anfa and the large municipal pool closest to town.

Spectator sports include soccer, rugby and basketball matches at the Marcel Cerdan Stadium. Bicycle racing at the Vélodrome and horse racing at the Hippodrome near Anfa where there is also a fishing and sailing port.

Horse riding at the Club Bayard, 2 Rue Schumann at Anfa, at the Club de l'Etrier, Quartier des Stades. The club also treks through the middle Atlas mountains.

Tennis at the U.S.M.-Tennis Club, Parc de la Ligue Arabe.

Golf at the Royal Golf Club d'Anfa, 10 minutes from the town center; also at the Mohammedia Golf Club, 29 km. (18 miles) from town.

Aeronautics at the Parachute Club de Maroc, Aerodome Titmellil/Ain Harrouda.

SHOPPING. For traditional items and souvenirs, Coopartim, Ave. des F.A.R., across from the Hotel Safir, is under state control. Other shops are unreliable about forwarding goods after payment, at best shipping by seamail instead of airmail, occasionally not at all. Le Cadeau Marocain, 10 Place Mohammed V, has typical Moroccan gifts (ancient and modern carpets, inlaid small furniture, ceremonial daggers, leather Berber jewelry, etc.). Bazar Bel Bacha, 8 Ave. des F.A.R., sells the same type of merchandise as does Benkirane Rajae, Bijoux d'Orient, Dubac and La Minaudière, all in the Rue Prince Moulay Abdallah. Caftans and gowns at Kenz, El Mansour Hotel. But the best selection, including several models for men, is at the boutique of Fakhita Sebti, in the Hyatt Regency. Also high-fashion caftans at the Boutique Soraya, 6 Ave. des F.A.R. For men's shoes try any of the branches of Derby, at half the European price. Fine quality leather goods—ladies' and men's bags, belts, etc.—are readily available and at most reasonable prices.

USEFUL ADDRESSES. Tourist Information at the Syndicat d'Initiative (City Information Bureau), 98 Blvd. Mohammed V (tel. 22 15 24).

Travel Agencies and Airlines. Except for Royal Air Maroc, 44 Ave. des F.A.R. (tel. 31 11 22), there is no reason to single out any among the large number between the port railway station (tel. 223 011 or 271 837), and the C.T.M. bus terminal, Rue de Léon l'Africain, off Ave. des F.A.R. (tel. 268 061).

Consulates. American, 8 Blvd. Moulay Youssef (tel. 22 41 49); British, 60 Blvd. d'Anfa (tel. 261 440 or 221 853).

Car Hire. Avis, 19 Ave. des F.A.R. (tel. 314 451); Azur Rent, 138 Blvd. Rahal Mekini (tel. 316 537); Budget, 71 Ave. des F.A.R. (tel. 314 027); Car Loc, 95 Rue Allal Ben Abdellah (tel. 317 896); Europcar, 144 Ave. des F.A.R. (tel. 367 973); Express, 245 Blvd. Mohammed V (tel. 307 847); Hertz, 25 Rue de Foucauld (tel. 312 223); Inter Rent, 44 Ave. des F.A.R. (tel. 313 737); Safloc, 77 Moulay Hassan I (tel. 278 355).

Motoring Information. Touring Club du Maroc, 3 Ave. des F.A.R. (tel. 27 13 04); Royal Automobile Club, 3 Rue Lemercier (tel. 25 05 62).

Places of Worship. Catholic: Notre Dame de Lourdes, Rond Point d'Europe; St. Francois d'Assise, Rue d'Azilal. Protestant: Rue d'Azilal. Synagogue: E.M. Habanim, Rue de Lusitanie.

TANGIER

And the Road from Rabat

The road north from Rabat to Tangier has recently been widened to accommodate the heavy traffic and is scenically rather dull. The best views are those in the rolling hill country just south of Tangier, with the first glimpses of the mighty Rif range further east.

In the narrow triangle of land between Rabat, Meknès and Tangier several highlights of Moroccan history were contributed by Europe, the Mediterranean, the Near East and Africa. Phoenicians and later Carthaginians planted their peaceful trading centers along these northern shores, occupied then, as largely now, by Berbers. When Carthage was destroyed, the Romans moved in and founded here their main cities which outlasted the ephemeral Vandal kingdom into the Byzantine revival.

Then Arab invaders took possession, but from the fifteenth century on, Spain and Portugal made repeated attempts to gain footholds on the coast. Spain was at different times successful and still maintains an enclave at Ceuta. Portuguese hopes were extinguished at the "Battle of the Three Kings," fought in 1578 near Ksar el Kebir, one of the towns on our route. The Portuguese King, Sebastian, assisted by the former Sultan el Motawakil, opposed the reigning Sultan Abd el Malik in this battle, and all were killed. The Portuguese lost 20,000 troops and were so weakened that their country came under the power of Spain.

By this date combined Arab and Berber armies had, on more than one occasion, marched northward into Spain while, no less often, Moorish refugees—and Jews—had flooded back into this territory from Andalusia's rich towns.

All this has left traces on the ground and in the people's lives and character. You can visit the remains of Phoenician and Carthaginian trading stations and Roman towns, as well as of Portuguese and Spanish buildings. Tangier embodies this rich cultural mixture. To generations of cinemagoers and readers of romantic novels and thrillers it is still a "mysterious" oriental city of charm and intrigue. Package tourists may even feel that the wondrous orient has been revealed. Escapists of all ages hope for a lessening of the pressures of Western life. Neither are right and neither wrong; Tangier is quite simply itself.

It is probably the oldest continuously inhabited town in Morocco. Phoenicians settled there even before they founded Carthage. The Romans took it in 82 B.C. and made Tingis the capital of the province of Mauretania Tingitana in A.D. 42. The Arabs occupied it in A.D. 705, and in 788 Idriss I began in Tangier the moves which resulted in the separate kingdom of Morocco. The Portuguese captured it in 1471 and in 1661 it became English, having been given to Catherine of Braganza as part of her dowry when she married Charles II. The English held it for 23 years against attacks by the great Moulay Ismail. But Parliament decided that the cost was not worth the advantages and despatched Samuel Pepys, the diarist, to carry out the withdrawal in 1684.

So many U.S. ships called at Tangier that Congress sought recognition from Morocco, which was granted in 1777, making Morocco the first country to recognize the United States. A treaty of friendship signed in 1786 by Thomas Jefferson is the longest existing treaty in U.S. history. Sultan Moulay Ismail did not want Christian ambassadors intriguing at his court in Meknès so he made them stay in Tangier, despite the distance. As more and more foreigners settled in Tangier the ambassadors acquired the right to settle lawsuits between their own nationals according to their own laws. In 1912 the Franco-Moroccan and Franco-Spanish treaties under which the protectorates were established both recognized Tangier's "special character" which was embodied in the 1923 Statute of Tangier.

Under this agreement 140 square miles covering Tangier and its surroundings were set aside as international territory. It was administered by a Council consisting of six Moroccan Moslems, six Moroccan Jews, and the representatives of France, Spain, Britain, Italy, Holland, Belgium and Portugal. Though the Sultan's authority was recognized, the courts were under international control, and the Sultan himself was represented only by a "Mendoub" or agent. When Morocco became independent in 1956 the European powers agreed to surrender their rights in Tangier. The international territory became part of Morocco and for a time Tangier suffered an economic decline which, thanks to a quarter of a million tourists annually, has now been reversed.

The only signs of Tangier's past as hideout of the jet and almost any other set are the cosmopolitan street names, the Mendoubia, the residence of the Sultan's former Agent-General, and a broken-down, deserted frontier post which marks the limit of Tangier's former International Zone.

The Rabat–Tangier Road

Leaving Rabat by the bridge over the Oued Bou Regreg, the wide but very crowded road divides at the landgate of Salé into P1 inland to Meknès and Fez, and P2 to Tangier. The latter passes a private botanical garden to the left, the Jardins Exotiques, famous for their collection of trees and plants. Sidi Bouknadel and the turning on the left to the Plage des Nations are almost next door. Here many of Rabat's better-off citizens and foreign residents come to swim and sun-bathe.

Kenitra, the first town, seems fixed in the 1920 mold, when, as Port Lyautey, it was groomed as Morocco's main port. A new town was laid out and a harbor built near the mouth of the Oued Sebou. The newly-built railway connected it to the towns of Meknès and Fez and, via the junction at Sidi Kacem, to the rich lands of the Gharb and to Tangier.

However, planners' schemes are often damned from the outset. It was, instead, Casablanca's artificial harbor which became Morocco's foremost port. Port Lyautey, now known again by its original name of Kenitra, despite over one million inhabitants, plays only a secondary role, shipping out large quantities of wine, canned food and cork.

Mehdia Plage is a convenient beach for Kenitra's inhabitants, but not equipped to receive tourists. It is the probable site of Thymaterium, a Carthaginian colony founded in the fifth or sixth century B.C. by Hanno during his voyage of exploration down the coast. A little under 64 km. (40 miles) from Kenitra you can turn right at Souk el Tleta du Rharb, cross the Sebou, and visit the rather sparse remains of Banasa, a Roman settlement.

Souk el Arba du Gharb, some 19 km. (12 miles) further on, is the next main port of call. The metaphor isn't wholly inapposite, for this can be a watery stretch of road. In the first three months of the year the Sebou has an unpleasant habit of overflowing its banks, flooding the fertile fields and drowning a number of local inhabitants. Even desert oueds may occasionally flood the surrounding countryside, but along the Atlantic coast this is quite common, especially on the roads just south of Souk el Arba—on the P2 and the P6, leading to Sidi Kacem and Meknès.

The narrow road to the left leads over flat farmland to Moulay Bou Selham between a 20,000-acre lake and a beach flanked by two small headlands. In spring the lake is aglow with the colors of migrating water birds, including flamingos. In summer underwater swimmers come to train in the sea that the lake empties into. In winter (Oct.–March) Moulay Bou Selham is popular for shooting.

Pheasant, mallard, quail, hare, rabbit, wild boar—the game is varied and plentiful. But its greatest pride is snipe. Three migration routes converge on the marshy land between Souk el Arba, Moulay Bou Selham, Arbaoua and Larache. The marshland to the north, grazed in summer by light cattle, makes a particularly good feeding ground for these birds. Local folk claim that the world's best snipe-shooting is to be had in the 86,000 acres of the Arbaoua reserve, one third of which is set aside for tourists.

A road branches right, six miles north of Souk el Arba for Ouezzane, Chechaouen and Tetouan—an alternative route to the Rif. Beyond the village of Arbaoua, road and railway cross the Oued Lekkous to Ksar el Kebir, some 40 km. (25 miles) inland, was known to the Romans as Oppidum Novum. But it was the Almohad Sultan Yakub al-Mansur, responsible for much building in Rabat, among other places, who re-fortified it and gave it importance as another of his military bases in the 12th century. Ksar el Kebir, no longer a fortress-town, has become a prosperous small commercial center for surrounding farmers.

Skirting the Lekkous marshes, P2 heads seaward towards Larache, a pleasant white town, where modern Spanish and traditional Moorish architecture blend harmoniously, thanks to their common ancestry. Larache was held by Spaniards till driven out by Moulay Ismail in the seventeenth century, and occupied again in 1911, just before the establishment of the protectorate.

The Spanish circular plaza extends just outside the main gate into the old town. The long rectangular square beyond, the main market place, was also laid out by the Spaniards. Two ancient fortification towers overlook the medina and the little harbor—the Kebitat Tower and the Stork Kasbah. Jean Genet, the French writer who lived here for the last years of his life, is buried here.

Forty kilometers (25 miles) of wooded terrain separate Larache from Asilah, which justifies its name, the Authentic, by the Artistic Festival in August. By gaining an African reputation, the mayor was made Minister of Culture. Asilah is Africa's first pedestrian town. You enter through the two gates in its fortified walls.

In the not-so-distant past, however, it achieved a certain distinction as the home-base of an extraordinary adventurer named Sharif Moulay Ahmad ar-Raisuni, usually referred to as Raissuli by Europeans. Formerly the Sultan's Governor of the Atlantic Province, he was piqued at not being appointed Viceroy for the Spanish Zone and decided to go it alone. He managed this very successfully for a time, helped partly by the disruption of World War I. Kidnapping was one of his specialties. His victims included the Greek-American citizen Ion Perdicaris whose abduction prompted President Theodore Roosevelt's cable to the Sultan: "Perdicaris alive or Raissuli dead."

In Asilah he built himself a sumptuous palace which can still be visited. But Raissuli himself faded from history's page in an unhappy way. In 1924, his power mostly gone, he was captured by Abd-el-Krim, whose own rebellion in the Rif to the east was in full swing, and left to rot in poverty and madness in the Rif town of Targuist.

Tangier

The last 48 km. (30 miles) to Tangier run mainly through undulating green hills, but hug the sea for a few miles. If pushed for time take the left-hand turning a little past the airport to the Caves of Hercules (Grottes d'Hercule). This leads you to the spectacular Robinson Beach, the ancient caves where Stone Age millstones seem to have been manufactured. Swimming from this vast expanse of sand with the Atlantic breakers rushing in is very dangerous.

After the Caves, the road ascends Cap Spartel, with a lighthouse where the Atlantic joins the Mediterranean. You may climb the lighthouse for an even better version of the view.

Past the lighthouse the road continues to a plush residential area, the famous Mountain (Montagne). The most sumptuous residences are two royal palaces, one still used by the king. The views from this high point can be superb, but from the Belvédère de Sidi Amar—the holy man's tomb lies a little below the summit—all you can see are the tops of the neighboring pines and the gardens of Hollywood-style villas. At last the road drops down to Tangier through pleasant woods.

Mark Twain described Tangier as "clear out of this world," while Edith Wharton, in 1917, called it "frowzy." Between the two world wars Walter Harris, the famous correspondent of the *London Times,* built himself a villa on the bay of Malabata; he is buried, under a Moorish green-tiled

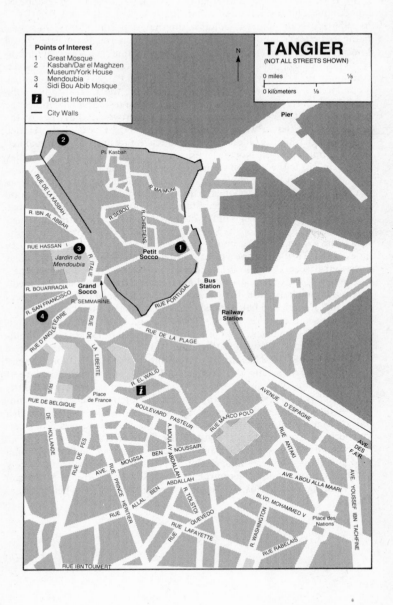

Points of Interest

1 Great Mosque
2 Kasbah/Dar el Maghzen
   Museum/York House
3 Mendoubia
4 Sidi Bou Abib Mosque

i Tourist Information

— City Walls

TANGIER
(NOT ALL STREETS SHOWN)

N

0 miles   ⅛
0 kilometers   ⅛

roof, in the cemetery of the fine Anglican church at the opposite end of town. It was between the wars that the town rapidly expanded to 300,000 inhabitants. The cosmopolitan expatriates whose haunt it was from 1923 to 1956 are gone, and the colorful international community that once numbered 60,000 has dwindled to about 800 Spaniards, fewer French and some 150 Americans and Britons. The white medina on a steep promontory slopes down to the small but sheltered natural harbor. The Kasbah, containing the Dar el Maghzen, the former Royal Palace (now a museum), York House, the 17th-century fortress built for the English governors, some 19th-century mansions as well as a first-rate restaurant, occupies the hill's summit. On Rue d'Amerique, amid the crowded alleyways of the old Jewish quarter, a white villa displays the Great Seal of the United States, designating the oldest U.S.-owned real estate and only national historic landmark not on North American soil. A gift from Sultan Moulay Sliman in 1821, the 30-room building served as the U.S. consulate and later the legation till the diplomats moved to Rabat. Restored as a museum, the collection of engravings, paintings and books testifies to the bond of friendship between the United States and Morocco for more than two centuries. The crooked lanes of the medina descend to the Petit Socco near the port. The ramparts of the kasbah afford a fine view across the Straits which have seen so much coming and going across the less than thirty miles of sea. Tarifa, Europe's most southerly point, looks so close on clear days that it seems easy to bridge the gulf between Europe and Africa.

The new town's main streets radiate from the square outside the medina's main landward gate, the Grand Socco or Main Market, whose very name, half French and half Spanish, indicates Tangier's international past. The Rue de la Liberté rises to the Place de France, the town's true center, well provided with cafés. A large number of hotels, restaurants and nightspots crowd the slope down to the flatter land immediately behind the fine sandy beach that stretches eastward from the harbor right around Tangier Bay. The sea promenade, the Avenue des F.A.R., is lined with the largest hotels, with many pools, as the sea's temperature is definitely Atlantic, while fierce gales often whip up the sand, emptying the beach, even in summer. A little inland stands the deserted bull-ring, while another Spanish relic, the cathedral in the southwestern residential districts, is now overtopped by a large mosque, the gift of the Emir of Kuwait.

Nowhere in Morocco is there such a choice of national and international food as well as of entertainment. But nowhere else is the tourist so likely to be taken for a ride in his purchase of local handicrafts, as Moroccan dealers bring these items to Tangier because they can get better prices there.

PRACTICAL INFORMATION FOR
THE RABAT–TANGIER ROAD

HOTELS AND RESTAURANTS. Because of the relatively heavy traffic on this road there are, besides the hotels listed, numerous simple places for a meal, a snack or a soft drink.

Arbaoua *Route de France* (M), 11 km. (7 miles) south of Ksar el Kehir (tel. 090 2669). 13 rooms. A reasonably-priced French-style hostelry catering for shooting folk.

Asilah. *El Khaima* (M), Route de Tanger (tel. 091 7230/74). 58 rooms; no shower facilities. *Oued El Makhasine* (M), tel. 091 7090. 29 airconditioned rooms; no showers *Oasis* (I), tel. 091 7186. 12 rooms, 3 showers. In town center.
Restaurants. *La Alcazba* (M). Seafood in a pleasant garden below the ramparts. The *Asilah* has a bar-restaurant (M). *El Oceano* (I), budget seafood.

Kenitra. *Hotel Assam* (E), Ave. Hassan II (tel. 016 2924). 60 rooms; pool, tennis, nightclub. *Safir* (E), Pl. Administrative (tel. 016 5600). 93 airconditioned rooms; pool, sauna, nightclub. *Ambassy* (M), Ave. Hassan II (tel. 016 2925). 27 rooms. *Mamora* (M), Ave. Hassan II (tel. 016 5006). 72 rooms; restaurant, pool, nightclub. *La Rotonde* (M), Ave. Diouri (tel. 016 2943). 42 rooms.

Larache. *Riad* (M), tel. 26 26. 26 rooms. The former residence of the Duchesse de Guise, mother of the Pretender to the French throne. It combines Moroccan décor with sound food and cheerful service. Kasbah Tours chain. *España* (I), tel. 31 95. 47 rooms, 8 showers. Known chiefly for its restaurant.

Mehdia. *Atlantique* (M), Some fairly simple bungalows and a pleasant restaurant round an exceptionally large swimming pool; excellent sandy beach.

Moulay Bou Selham. *Le Lagon* (M), tel. 090 28. Fine view; French and Moroccan cuisine. Facilities for riding, shooting, underwater fishing; 30 rooms with air conditioning, pool.

Sidi Bouknadel Beach (Plage des Nations). *Firdaous* (E), tel. 07 80407. 17 rooms. The fairly luxurious bathing complex, which includes this hotel, has heated swimming pool.
Restaurant. *Auberge Savoyarde* (E), just before leaving the main road for the beach. Serves the best French food in the region.

Souk El Arba. *Gharb* (M), tel. 090 2203. 36 rooms.

PRACTICAL INFORMATION FOR TANGIER

WHEN TO GO. Tangier, despite some misty days in winter, is pleasant to visit the whole year through. Bathing is limited to the summer season. However, even in winter, the temperature never falls below 17°C (62°F); while on land you can count on warm winters (from 14° to 20°C, 57° to 69°F) and summers which are warm without excessive heat (temperatures between 24° and 29°C, 75° and 84°F)

GETTING THERE. By Air. Direct flights from London, Paris, Madrid and other European cities. Internal flights from Casablanca, Rabat, Marrakesh and Agadir by Royal Air Inter, as well as to Málaga and Gibraltar.

By Train and Ferry would take 38 hours from Paris, 5 from Rabat, 6½ from Fez with a change at Sidi Slimane. By C.T.M. bus Tangier is 6 hours from Casablanca.

Car ferry services by Transmediterránea and by Limadet from Algeciras and Gibraltar. Weather permitting, daily hydrofoil from Tarifa, Spain's southernmost point, and Gibraltar (passengers only).

By Car. The narrow P2 from Rabat to Tangier takes about 3 hours for the 280 km. (175 miles). A possible variation is the coastal route north from Kenitra to Moulay Bou Selham, rejoining the main road at Souk el Arba. The alternative inland road, which branches off about 24 km. (15 miles) north of Larache, is nearly as fast to Tangier via Ouezzane, Chechaouen and Tetouan.

GETTING AROUND BY TAXI. The meter may register or not, but in a large taxi (5 or 6 passengers) the trip from the airport to the hotel will cost about 90DH. There is not always a bus service to the airport, so you are at their mercy and, especially on arrival, drivers try to extort whatever they can from tourists. To make short trips outside town, discuss the price beforehand; longer excursions are on a basis of kilometers covered, and you must settle on the price per km. before setting out. Petits taxis operate only inside city boundaries. Tip only if the driver has been helpful (and that is not often).

HOTELS. The great variety of modern hotels in Tangier, ranging from the deluxe category to the smaller city hotels, not usually found in a holiday center, have deteriorated, especially the reception. Deluxe and Expensive are mostly airconditioned and have pools.

Area code 09.

Deluxe

Almohades, Ave. des F.A.R. (tel. 403 30). 150 rooms. Nightclub, 3 restaurants; near beach, heated pool. Popular with tours; in Africa Palace chain.

El Minzah, Rue de la Liberté (tel. 358 85). 100 rooms and 10 suites. Moorish décor, tiled central patio and lovely garden with pool where buffet lunch is served. *El Erz* restaurant with Moroccan and international specialties. Ask for a room with a view over the bay. Maintains tradition despite package tours.

Intercontinental, Parc Brooks (tel. 360 53). Not to be confused with the American chain. 130 rooms; pool. Quiet location in a residential district. The distance from the town and the beach makes it more suitable perhaps for business visitors than for the holiday maker.

Expensive

Africa, Ave. Moussa Ben Noussair (tel. 355 11). 86 rooms. Airconditioning that works.

Ahlen Village, 5 km. (3 miles) inland on the Route de Rabat (tel. 430 00). 111 rooms; pool.

El Oumnia, Ave. Beethoven (tel. 403 66). 100 rooms. Faces the beach.

Pasadena, Route de Tetouan (tel. 363 47). 150 rooms. Quite a walk from the beach, but has tennis courts, pool. Package guests have their own, simpler rooms and dining room.

Rembrandt, Blvd. Mohammed V (tel. 378 70). 80 rooms. In the center of town; pool.

Rif, Ave. d'Espagne (tel. 359 08). 130 rooms. The restaurant is disappointing and there is no airconditioning, but the pool and terrace are agreeable.

Shéhérazade, Ave. des F.A.R. (tel. 405 00). 146 rooms.

Tanjar Flandria, Blvd. Mohammed V (tel. 330 00). 175 good rooms. In town; tiny roof pool.

Tarik, Route de Malabata (tel. 409 44). 154 rooms. A little far out, but the only one directly on the beach.

Villa de France, Rue de Hollande (tel. 314 75). 60 rooms. Outstanding; maintains a long-established standard at reasonable prices. Quiet situation.

Moderate

Anjou, Rue Ibn Al Banna (tel. 343 44). 24 rooms; no restaurant.

Atlas, Rue Moussa Ben Noussair (tel. 364 35). 36 rooms.

Chellah, Rue Allal Ben Abdallah (tel. 383 88). 173 rooms. Airconditioning that usually doesn't work. The restaurant is popular with resident foreigners.

Charf, Rue Dante (tel. 344 93). 19 rooms.

El Jenina, 8 Rue Grotins (tel. 347 59). 21 rooms.

Mamora, Rue de la Poste (tel. 341 05). 30 rooms; no restaurant.

Miramar, Ave. des F.A.R. (tel. 389 48). 40 rooms.

Tanger, Rue Delacroix (tel. 355 64). 112 rooms. One of the best in this category.

Inexpensive

The numerous inexpensive establishments in Tangier are not really cheap enough to justify their lack of comfort.

Out of Town

On the Bay of Tangier, 13 km. (8 miles) along the Cap Malabata road, *Safir Malabata* (tel. 406 40). 300 rooms. Safir chain. The only deluxe hotel on the beach; heated swimming pool.

On the same bay is the large holiday complex of the *Mar-Bel Résidence* (E). 135 rooms; restaurants, nightclub, tennis, pool, on private beach.

Also in the same area is the *Club Méditerranée Malabata* (E), tel. 405 88. It is built around the famous Walter Harris villa. 800 bungalows in a 13-acre park. All outdoor activities. Open May–Oct. only.

On the other side of town, 16 km. (10 miles) west, on a rather dangerous Atlantic beach, *Les Grottes d'Hercule* (M), tel. 387 65. 116 bungalows, pool.

RESTAURANTS. Tangier does justice to its reputation as an international city in the wide variety of cooking it offers to the adventurous traveler. There are several traditional Moroccan restaurants, as well as a cross-section of many other cuisines.

Expensive

Chez Larbi Dolce Vita, Rue Samuel Pepys (tel. 396 78). A bit of everything.
Le Claridge, Blvd. Pasteur. International cuisine.
Coeur de Tanger, 1 Anoual St., 1st Floor. Newest and most luxurious.

Le Detroit, Riad Sultan, Kasbah. Pleasant décor, good Moroccan food and a beautiful view.

Le Grillon, Blvd. Mohammed V. Noted for its seafood.

Hamadi, Rue de la Kasbah. Unassuming décor, but excellent Moroccan food.

Mamounia Palace, Rue Semmarine. Fine local dishes and music.

Rubis Grill, Rue Henri Regnault (tel. 394 95). Excellent meat.

Moderate

Les Ambassadeurs, Ave. Prince Moulay Abdallah. Italian specialties.

Damascus, Ave. Prince Moulay Abdallah. Moroccan dishes.

La Eucalyptus, La Montagne. Good Moroccan cuisine.

La Grenouille, Rue El Jabha Elouatania. Fine French cuisine.

Guitta's, 110 Pl. Koweit. Charming, old-fashioned garden for summer dining; excellent fish.

Al Mabrouk, Rue Ahmed Chaouki. Moroccan dishes.

Nautilus, Rue Khalid Ibn Oualid; and **Nautilus Plage,** on the beach.

La Pagode, 3 El Boussairi St. Vietnamese cuisine.

Le Paname, Blvd. Pasteur. Grill room and snack bar.

Le Provençal, Rue Fernando de Portugal. What the name promises.

Raïhani, Rue Ahmed Chaouki. One of the best; local cuisine.

Romero, Ave. Prince Moulay Abdallah.

San Remo, Rue Ahmed Chaouki. Italian cuisine.

Zagora, Blvd. Pasteur. Mainly French despite the name.

CAFÉS. The best are the *Café de Paris* and the *Café de France* in the Place de France; the meeting places of Tangier where it's fun to watch the world go by.

La Banquise on the Rue Quevedo is a pleasant salon de thé, with excellent pastries; as is *Porte,* Rue Prince Moulay Abdallah.

NIGHTLIFE. The nightclubs and bars of Tangier are seedy at best and dangerous at worst. Forget your illusions about a city of international intrigue and watch your wallet. Prices are exorbitant, drinks are watered, and touts and pimps abound, so you go at your own peril. However, there are still a few exceptions:

The Moorish-style *Koutoubia* (E), Rue El Mountanabi, and the *Morocco Palais* (E), Ave. Prince Moulay Abdallah, offer oriental dancing.

Discos include *Churchill's* (M), *Gospel* (M) and *Scott's* (M), Rue El Mountanabi; *El Piano* (M), Rue Amerique du Sud; *Boga Boga* (M), Ave. Prince Moulay Abdallah. More incongruous, *Trudy's Viennese* (M), Ave. Prince Héritier, has piano music. The roof-top *Up 2000* (M) disco at the Almohades Hotel offers a splendid view.

SPORTS. Tangier's privileged position on the Straits, yet in a sheltered harbor, makes it an ideal base for all **watersports,** especially sailing. From spring to fall there is a regatta every week with local boats racing each other, while Sailing Week in summer is devoted to international races. The Tangier Yacht Club, Port (tel. 385 75), is not only for boating enthusiasts but also has a private beach and organizes deep-sea fishing parties.

Tennis is another year-round sport; several of the hotels have their own courts, and you can take out temporary membership at the Emsallah Club, Ave. Hassan II and the Tennis Club Municipal, Rue Raimonde Lulic.

The Country Club at Boubanah, the gathering place for Tangier's international society, has a Bridge Club, an 18-hole **golf** course and a **polo** field. The Club de l'Etrier (Stirrup Club), also at Boubanah, has **riding** rings.

SHOPPING. Go shopping by yourself rather than with a guide. The Chameau Blanc, 4 Rue Kadanie, and Dar Al Kasbah, Pl. de la Kasbah, have attractive merchandise, but you'll have to bargain: offer 25% of the asking price and you'll get 50% discount. No haggling at Moroccan Arts and Crafts, 24 Blvd. Pasteur.

Art objects, antiques, jewelry and elegant caftans at Velasco, 26 Blvd. Mohammed V. Art objects at Arditti, and Chez Mansour, 87 Rue de la Liberté, or Boutique Majid, 66 Rue des Chrétiens and Bazar Sebou, 18 Rue Sebou. Jewelry at Clarice, 20 Ave. Prince Moulay Abdallah, and Mounya, 99 Rue de la Liberté. Optique Photo Ravassard, 84 Rue de la Liberté, also stock prescription eyeglasses and sunglasses.

USEFUL ADDRESSES. Tourist Information. O.N.M.T. (National Tourist Office, 29 Blvd. Pasteur (tel. 382 39); Syndicat d'Initiative (City Information Office), 11 Rue Khalid Ibn Oualid (tel. 354 86); Chamber of Commerce, 31 Blvd. Pasteur (tel. 325 35).

Travel Agencies. Wagons-Lits Tourisme, 86 Rue de la Liberté (tel. 316 40). Numerous others in the streets round Place de France.

Airlines. Royal Air Maroc, Pl. de France; Air Inter, same place; British Airways at Gibair, 22 Blvd. Mohammed V; Air France, 20 Blvd. Pasteur; Iberia, 35 Blvd. Pasteur.

Shipping Lines. Bland Line (Tangier-Gibraltar), 22 Blvd. Mohammed V; Transmediterránea, 31 Rue Quevedo; Limadet Ferry, 13 Rue Prince Moulay Abdullah; Comanav, 43 Ave. Abbou Aalla El Maari.

Consulates. American, Rue El Achouak (tel. 359 04); British, Rue d'Angleterre (tel. 358 95).

Motoring Information. Royal Automobile Club du Maroc, 8 Ave. Prince Héritier.

Car Hire. Avis, 54 Blvd. Pasteur (tel. 330 31); Hertz, 36 Ave. Mohammed V (tel. 333 22); Europcar, Hotel Rembrandt (tel. 331 13). Alanbar, 24 Regnault St. (tel. 338 70); Avis, 54 Blvd. Pasteur (tel. 330 31); Best Cars, 128 Ave. D'Espagne (tel. 430 98); Cadi, 3 Alla Ben Abdallah (tel. 341 51); Danny's Cars, 10 7 Mousse Ibn Noussair (tel. 317 78); Eurocar, Hotel Rembrandt (tel. 331 13); Inter Rent, 87 Blvd. Mohammed V (tel. 382 71); Moroccan Holidays, 23 Rue Rembrandt (tel. 338 27); Tangier Rates Cars, 10 Omar Ibn Alhass St. (tel. 430 98); Tourist Cars, 84 Blvd. Mohammed V (tel. 354 93).

FEZ, MEKNÈS AND AREA

Where Morocco Was Born

Fez and Meknès are two historic towns less than 64 km. (40 miles) apart. Both in their time have been Morocco's capital and occupy picturesque sites where vital north-south arteries cross the centuries-old road, and now the railway from the Atlantic to the Fifth Imperial city, Tlemcen in Algeria. Both lie close to two even older capitals, Moulay Idriss and Volubilis. Yet in spirit and history, they are extraordinarily different.

Fez (spelled Fès in French and on signs) was founded as the country's first real political capital in 809 by Moulay Idriss II, son of the Abbasid prince who established Morocco's first Moslem dynasty. The abundant springs of fresh water made the site particularly attractive. Since then, though the political capital has been moved to other towns, Fez has scarcely ever ceased to be Morocco's most important intellectual, cultural and religious center, and is the second largest town. Its university is the oldest in the world, its handicrafts the finest and its monuments second to none.

Meknès, on the other hand, was established by a Berber tribe, the Meknassa, some generations later. Only after many vicissitudes was it selected as capital in 1673 by the great Alaouit sultan Moulay Ismail. Its most impressive structures are Moulay Ismail's gigantic palace, storerooms, stables and barracks, now almost all in ruins. Though much smaller, Meknès yet possesses some unique sites.

The two towns are inevitably rivals, even as touring centers. Each can easily be visited from the other, and many excursions in the region are common to both. Those who rely on public transport however, may find Meknès more conveniently sited.

Fez

Fez occupies a position of outstanding beauty, surrounded on every side by hills. The oldest part of the medina, Fès el Bali (Old Fez)—not to be confused with the small township of the same name 89 km. (55 miles) to the north—slopes down westward from Bab Ftouh and Bab el Khoukha to the Oued Fez. On the far bank, Fès Jedid (New Fez) was new in 1276 when it spread southwest towards the plateau on which the Ville Nouvelle (New Town) has been built. When in 1980 U.N.E.S.C.O. proclaimed the medina a World Patrimony, it contained an incredible 290,000 inhabitants within an unbroken line of ramparts, since completely restored. The resettlement outside the walls of at least one third of this multitude was given top priority and has been surprisingly successful in reducing Medina dwellers to a just manageable 200,000. The population explosion was threatening to destroy one of the last living medieval cities in the world, the most remarkable among some 30 medinas lived in by around three million people. The Committee for the Salvation of Fez worked out a 41-point program—perhaps the world's most ambitious reconstruction project—of which 12 have already been completed. The cost will be well over half a billion dollars: it is hoped to divide this evenly between the Kingdom and international contributions.

The panoramic ringroad provides wonderful views of its rooftops, towers, and winding alleys spread against a backdrop of hills that are sometimes bright green with spring growth, sometimes yellow and brown with autumn drought, fading to infinite gradations of purple, blue and mauve in the distance.

Fez was founded in 809 by Idriss II, on a site chosen but not developed by his father, Idriss ibn-Abdullah. As Idriss II was the real builder of the Idrissid state, Fez and the new realm grew together. After a rebellion in Cordoba in 818, a number of Arab refugees from Spain settled in the capital on the bank of the Oued Fez, which has come to be known as Adwat al-Andalus, the Andalusian Bank. As a result of the turmoil which followed the establishment of Aghlabid rule in Qairawan, Arabs from Tunisia took refuge in the city and established a settlement on the other bank of the Oued Fez, Adwat al-Qarawiyin, the Qairawan bank; Berbers and Jews soon joined the expanding settlement. When Idriss II died in 828, the state stretched from the Shaliff River in Algeria to the High Atlas in the south of Morocco. The Arabization of Morocco had begun, with the district of Fez becoming predominantly Arabic speaking.

Under Idriss's successors, Fez was transformed into a flourishing Arab capital and with the founding of the Qarawiyin Mosque in 859, and the Mosque of al-Andalus in 861, began to emerge as an important religious center. Whereas the al-Andalus has never been of more than local importance, the Qarawiyin became a center of learning and education attended in the following centuries not only by Moslems from the whole Islamic world, but also by Christian scholars, and it attained a prestige and influence in North Africa only rivaled by the al-Azhar in Cairo (founded in 972).

Apart from religious studies, which have always been of primary importance, the courses offered included mathematics, astronomy, law, philosophy, music and medicine. With so famous a center of learning and so many men of taste and discernment in its midst, the town, perhaps inevitably, became the focal point for fine craftsmanship of every sort. In pottery, metalwork, jewelry, leatherwork and textiles its products are the equal or superior of any in Morocco.

Fez's Background

With the decline of Idrissid power in the second half of the 10th century, Fez was fought over by the Ommiad caliphs of Cordoba and the Fatimid governors of Tunisia. It was then that a much stronger circuit of ramparts was built, and bridges were constructed over the Oued Fez, although walls in the river bed still separated the two quarters. The city changed hands several times and each victor, in his turn, added new fortifications.

The fate of Fez was bound up with events in Moslem Spain. In 1031 the collapse of the Ommiad caliphate of Cordoba removed all opposition to the weak Fatimid-controlled governor of Fez and created a power vacuum in the northern Maghreb, which was soon filled by the Almoravids, a zealous war-like religious community of Zanata Berbers from the Sahara. Their leader, Yusuf ibn Tashfin, captured Fez in 1063 and though Marrakesh remained the religious and administrative center of the Almoravid movement, Fez prospered in this new era of stability. The walls separating the two banks of the Oued Fez were dismantled and the city began to assume a new urban character. By the time of Tashfin's death in 1106, all Andalusia was under Almoravid rule. The Orthodox leaders of the movement in Marrakesh did not welcome the Spanish Moslems, whom they considered corrupt and decadent, and it was to Fez that Andalusian craftsmen migrated, thus enhancing the city's prosperity and increasing its importance as a trading center in the Maghreb.

The reign of Tashfin's successor, Ali ibn-Yusuf (1107–43), saw not only the peak, but also the decline, of Almoravid power. A rival religious sect, the Almohads, was emerging in the south. In 1146, Fez was captured by the first Almohad sultan, Abd al-Mumin, and the walls destroyed, not to be rebuilt until after the capture of Marrakesh and other remaining centers of resistance in the following year. The northern section of the wall around Fès-el-Bali (Old Fez) dates from the Almohad reconstruction. Although Marrakesh remained the capital, and Rabat prospered as the country's chief military base, Fez continued to enjoy considerable prosperity as intermediary between the Maghreb and Moslem Spain.

With the Merinid capture of Fez in 1250, the city entered its most brilliant period. Abu Yusuf el Yakub (1258–86), the second Merinid sultan, made it his capital and in 1276 inaugurated Fès Jedid (or Jdid), a virtually self-contained new city overlooking the older town. Fès Jedid became the country's administrative center, a capital within a capital, and a fortified stronghold of Merinid rule—a bastion against the inhabitants of the old city. The Merinids, while being great patrons of the arts, still felt uneasy with the sophisticated Arabs from Andalusia who made up the intelligentsia and set the taste of their empire. In contrast to their predecessors, their interest in Spain was mainly as a buffer state to contain a possible Christian invasion of the Maghreb, and they focused their attentions on Morocco, rather than Andalusia. Fez reached its golden age during the reigns of Abu al-Rabi (1308–10) and Abu Said Othman (1310–31) when medersas, the highpoint of Hispano-Moorish architecture, were constructed around the Qarawiyin and Andalus mosques to receive foreign students. The opulence of 14th-century Fez was only rivaled in the Islamic world by the Cairo of the Mamelukes. As the Christian conquest of the Iberian peninsula gained momentum, Fez received further refugees, and after the fall of Granada, the last of the Moslem kingdoms, in 1492, Fez was left heir to almost 800 years of Andalusian culture.

But by then the Merinids had been replaced by the Wattasids (Ouatta-sids), who ruled rather unsuccessfully for less than a hundred years. In 1554, the last Wattasid sovereign, Bou Hassan, surrendered Fez to the Saadians, who moved the capital to Marrakesh. The first great Alaouit ruler, Moulay Ismail, favored Meknès, and it was only under his son, Moulay Abdallah, that Fez resumed its imperial role, after a siege and the destruction of the main gates in 1730. He and his successors rebuilt mosques, medersas and palaces, especially Moulay al-Hassan, who con-structed the Boujeloud Palace and enlarged the Dar el Makhzen at the end of the last century.

His sons, Abd al-Aziz and Moulay Hafiz, added further extensions, but most of their limited energies was taken up with fighting one another. Be-sieged in his own capital by rebellious Berber tribes, Sultan Moulay Hafiz requested French aid and in May 1911 French troops under General Moi-nier entered Fez. After the establishment of the French Protectorate the capital was transferred yet once again, this time to Rabat, but the Ville Nouvelle outside the ramparts is constantly spreading among the timeless hills above the town.

Exploring Fez

Arriving in Fez by car from the west (Meknès, Sidi Kacem or the Col du Zegotta) or south (Azrou or Sefrou), follow the signs to Fès N.V. (Nou-velle Ville) as far as the Place de Florence, the large square in the middle of Avenue Hassan II, separated by broad beds of flowers and tall palm trees. Even arriving from the north or east (from Ketama, Oujda, etc.), it is advisable to take the ringroad which circles the medina to the New Town's most prominent artery, near which most hotels and restaurants are situated.

The tourist office on Place de la Resistance at the lower end of Avenue Hassan II is a useful orientation point. Start sightseeing with a drive along the circular road round the ramparts. A taxi should be hired on a time basis, but though the distance is only about 16 km. (10 miles), one hour is a minimum time to allow for the necessary stops, two hours to enjoy the magnificent view, especially at sunset, from the terrace of the Hotel Merinides.

From Place de la Resistance descend Avenue de la Liberté, planted with palms and other tropical plants, then turn right into Route Principale 1 (P1) along the Oued ez Zitoun for the anti-clockwise drive. After crossing the Oued Bou Fekrane, P1 climbs towards Bab Ftouh, keeping close to the ramparts, affording fine views into and across the crowded medina to-ward the great green bulk of Jebel Zalagh. From certain angles, Zalagh's silhouette looks like the profile of a recumbent woman and is referred to locally as Lalla (Lady) Fatima.

Beyond Bab Ftouh, always crowded and busy, right forks to Taza, Oujda and Algeria (P1) and to Taounate and Ketama (S302) follow in quick succession. After swinging round to Bab Khoukha, the road de-scends into the Oued Sebou's valley away from the ramparts till another fork, signposted for Ouezzane (P26). The first few miles of this road, climbing the flank of Jebel Zalagh through orchards and olive groves toward a 610-m. (2,000 feet) pass, provide the best view of the whole of Fez.

Past Bab Guissa and a cemetery, the circular road enters the area where tombs of the Merinid dynasty are scattered over the hillside. Among them, the Hotel Merinides commands a splendid view over Morocco's largest medina. The tightly packed houses are white or fawn, topped by colored tiles and decorations on the mosque's square towers. To the south, the hills, snowcapped in winter, climb to over 1,524 m. (5,000 feet), while to the southwest gleam the new town's tall buildings on their plateau. The Sebou's flat, well-watered valley shines with the multi-colored gloss of fertile land in the south east. And beyond the river the long ridge of Jebel Bou Iblane, highest part of the Middle Atlas (1,807 m., 10,500 feet), glows blue in the distance, its snow-fields sparkling bright.

The Borj Nord, a well-preserved medieval fortress, contains an interesting arms museum. After circling the 17th-century Kasbah des Cherarda and the cattle market, the Boulevard des Saadiens turns at right angles to the railway station, near the starting point on Place de la Resistance.

Toward the Medina

If you want to get lost, the medina offers the chance of a lifetime. Though you can drive right through the walled town by taking Avenue de la Liberté to Place de l'Istiqlal, then Rue Ed Douh and Rue Talaa Kebira to Bab Guissa, stopping or parking is almost impossible. Sightseeing in Fès Jedid and Fès el Bali has to be done on foot. Starting again from Place de la Resistance, the only concession is the short drive on Boulevard Moulay Youssef to Place des Alaouites, a vast square before the present entrance to the Dar el Makhzen, the Royal Palace. Rue Bou Ksissat crosses the Mellah with its Jewish goldsmiths to the many-vaulted Bab Smarine, beyond which the Grande Rue passes the mosque of al-Azhar built by the Merinid sultan Abu Inan in 1357. Through the arches of the stone gateway, with a carved screen across it—which tradition says was brought from Andalusia—you can see the brilliantly white walls and horseshoe arches of the mosque with a wooden porch covered in green tiles over the entrance.

The Grande Rue ends at the Petit Mechouar, a small square in front of the monumental Bab Dekaken, the former gateway into the Dar el Makhzen, closed to tourists like all the royal palaces. This vast complex covers over 200 acres of gardens, courtyards, barracks, mosques, bathhouses and a harem to house a thousand women. The palace, begun by Abu Yusuf Yakub when Fez Jedid was built, was decorated by his Merinid successors with splendid plasterwork reflected in pools according to the Hispano-Moorish style, inspired by the Alhambra of Granada. Subsequent rulers added pavilions and audience halls, constructed of clay and lime by Christian slaves, who were occasionally incorporated into the mixture to give it more body.

Between the Bab Dekaken and the fortified Bab Segma lies the Vieux (Old) Mechouar, a vast esplanade surrounded by high, crenellated walls, where the sultans reviewed the troops and received foreign ambassadors, but now crowded with jugglers, storytellers, dancers and their audiences. Above the Bab Segma rises the Kasbah des Cherarda, extending almost to the Bab el Mahrouk, the Gate of the Burned, erected by Mohammed al Nasser.

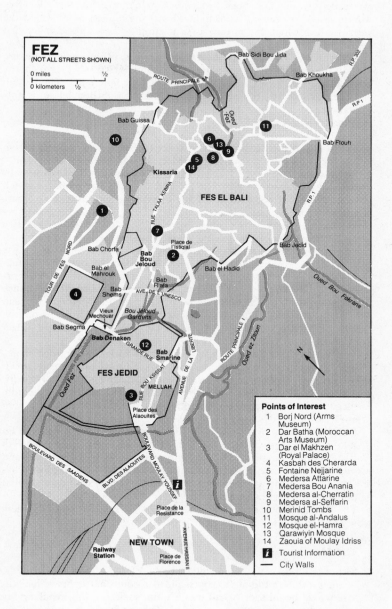

FEZ
(NOT ALL STREETS SHOWN)

0 miles ½
0 kilometers ½

Bab Sidi Bou Jida

ROUTE PRINCIPALE

Bab Khoukha

R.P. 302

Bab Guissa

R.P 1

10

Oued Fez

11

Bab Ftouh

6 13
5 9
14 8

Kissaria

FES EL BALI

RP 1

1

RUE TALAA KEBIRA

TOUR DE FES NORD

7

Bab Chorfa

Place de l'Istiqlal

2

Bab Jedid

Bab Bou Jeloud

Bab el Hadid

Oued Bou Fekrane

Bab el Mahrouk

Bab Riafa

AVE. DE L'UNESCO

4

Bab Shems

Vieux Mechouar

Bou Jeloud Gardens

Bab Segma

Oued ez Zitoun

N

Bab Denaken

12

GRANDE RUE

Bab Smarine

Oued Fez

FES JEDID

RUE BOU KSISSAT

MELLAH

AVENUE DE LA LIBERTE

ROUTE PRINCIPALE 1

3

Place des Alaouites

BOULEVARD DES SAADIENS

BOULEVARD MOULAY YOUSSEF

BLVD. DES ALAOUITES

i

Place de la Resistance

NEW TOWN

AVENUE HASSAN II

Railway Station

Place de Florence

Points of Interest

1 Borj Nord (Arms Museum)
2 Dar Batha (Moroccan Arts Museum)
3 Dar el Makhzen (Royal Palace)
4 Kasbah des Cherarda
5 Fontaine Nejjarine
6 Medersa Attarine
7 Medersa Bou Anania
8 Medersa al-Cherratin
9 Medersa al-Seffarin
10 Merinid Tombs
11 Mosque al-Andalus
12 Mosque el-Hamra
13 Qarawiyin Mosque
14 Zaouia of Moulay Idriss
i Tourist Information
— City Walls

At the side of the Bab Dekaken are the pleasant Bou Jeloud gardens, while beyond the Bab Shems extends the square before the Bab Bou Jeloud, the entrance to Fès el Bali. This is the highest point round the depression in which the medina is situated and has always commanded its defenses.

On the site of the dismantled Almoravid castle, Mohammed al-Nasser, the fourth Almohad sultan (1199–1213) built a kasbah in which the Merinids resided while Fès el Jedid was being constructed. The kasbah has been replaced by ordinary houses, while the Bab Bou Jeloud is now actually two gates, the fortified Merinid structure to the left and a tiled entrance dating from 1913 to the right through which one enters the medina.

The Rue Talaa Kebira, the main street of Fès el Bali, descends from the Bab Bou Jeloud. On the right, the Medersa Bou Anania was constructed by Abu Inan between 1350 and 1357. This largest of the Merinid religious colleges in Fez is entered under an elaborately carved porch which extends over the street, a feature of many medersas and a way of recognizing them in the surrounding maze of lanes. The great wooden door, covered with engraved bronze plaques, leads to the sumptuous vestibule, two stories in height and surmounted by a stalactite-type ceiling of cedarwood. Beyond is the courtyard, a striking blend of onyx, and the pink and white marble of the pavement, the arabesque and geometric designs on the stucco walls, the deeply carved cedarwood of the window frames and the enormous corbelling and pediment topped with green tiles. Before the entrance of the prayer hall is a channel of flowing water used for ablutions instead of the usual fountain. Student cells are on the upper floors, and from the first landing of the vestibule there is a good view of the magnificent stalactite ceiling.

The winding Rue Talaa Kebira is lined with little open-fronted shops, covered in places with trellis-work or matting to provide shade and crowded with people, donkeys and mules from before dawn until dusk. The curious row of bowls high up on your right, just past the Bou Inania's porch, is alleged to be part of an ancient clock, constructed in 1357 by a craftsman from Tlemcen.

Instead of returning through Bab Bou Jeloud, turn left down Rue Ed Douh, past the Post Office to the Dar Batha, the 19th-century palace of Sultan Moulay Hassan. It now houses the Museum of Moroccan Arts and Crafts which has an interesting display of woodwork rescued from decaying medersas, elaborate costumes, a fine collection of carpets and what is probably the best collection of weapons in the country.

The Rue Ed Douh ends in the ever-crowded Place de l'Istiqlal, where you will find it easy to pick up a "petit taxi."

The Medina

Morocco's most confusing medina is best explored with an official guide, who knows which buildings are open and also points out sights which otherwise would be missed. A half day is quite sufficient, but avoid Friday morning when the medersas are closed. The troublesome and persistent touts offering their dubious services know little else than which shopkeeper will pay them the largest commission. The worst are those on motorcycles, but even the eight-year-olds at "small size, small price" can be obnoxious. The itinerary usually begins at Bab Bou Jeloud and descends the Rue

Talaa Kebira past the Bou Inania Medersa for about a mile. The streets become narrower and narrower, fountains with tiled basins are at almost every corner, and the houses have white walls—and large cedarwood doors with green tiled porticos. This is the Kissaria, the commercial center mainly given over to textiles. It retains a genuine oriental atmosphere—living evidence of an age-old tradition.

Beyond the Souk al-Attarine, reserved for the grocers and redolent of spices, is the famous Attarine Medersa, perhaps the most beautiful religious building in Fez, which is open to visitors. Built by the sultan Abu Said between 1323 and 1325, it is smaller than the Bou Inania, and the decoration is more delicate. Again, cedarwood is used to great advantage, especially in the window grilles of the student cells above; there was room for 60 students. The profusion of detail is staggering—bands of brilliant tiles alternating with the finest examples of deeply carved Arabic calligraphy achieve a contrast of light and shade. In the center of the court is a fountain. The prayer hall, entered by an arch of stalactites in stucco, contains a 14th-century chandelier of excellent workmanship. From the roof, now closed for restoration, one should soon be able to see again into the great courtyard of the Qarawiyin Mosque just opposite, at the far ends of which are two kiosks, added by the Saadians in the 16th century and modeled on the pavilions in the Patio de los Leones in the Alhambra. So, before you is the summation of Hispano-Moorish artistic achievement—the secular inspiration of the Alhambra on one side and its sacred counterpart, the elegant medersa, on the other.

The Qarawiyin Mosque

The Qarawiyin (Quaraouiyin) is the largest mosque in Morocco. Founded in 859, it was enlarged by the Fatimids in 933. The caliph Abd al-Rahman III of Cordoba added the minaret in 956, but its present form dates from the Almoravid sultan Ali ibn-Yusuf in 1135. The basically austere design is enhanced rather than contradicted by innumerable architectural details such as the sumptuous plasterwork and woodcarving. Only two of the 14 original doors survive, one, covered with splendidly engraved bronze plaques, being opposite the entrance of the Palais du Fès restaurant.

It is possible to look through the various doorways into the courtyard and even to photograph if you are discreet. The marble ablutions basin in the center is from the time of the Almohads (1202), and, again, you can catch glimpses of the fanciful Saadian pavilions with their colonnades and green-tiled roofs at each end. Unfortunately the main entrance of the prayer hall has been gaudily painted, but even so its contrast with the stark simplicity of the white horseshoe arches on each side is effective. In the interior, which contains a forest of 270 pillars, the central aisle and the mihrab constitute what is the most important ensemble of Maghrebian art of the first half of the 12th century and form the link between the 9th-century buildings of Cordoba and Qairawan and the subsequent Almohad and Merinid styles. A note of austerity is re-introduced as the seemingly endless floor is covered by reed mats rather than colorful carpets. This is the center of the Qarawiyin University of Fez which, for over 1,100 years has remained the leading exponent of Moslem orthodoxy, only rivaled by Cairo's Al Azhar (less venerable by 100 years). Students still come from all over the Islamic world to pursue courses in classical Arabic grammar and literature, as well as in Islamic jurisprudence and theology. Its library houses one of the finest collections of Islamic manuscripts extant today, and since the Middle Ages the Qarawiyin has enjoyed an enviable reputation for the quality of its scholarship. The exterior is almost as difficult to view, as the building is surrounded by alleyways six to ten feet wide. It takes surprisingly long to walk around, jostled within the densely packed flow of humanity and pack animals. These camels and donkeys, when aged and sick, find a refuge in the American Animal Hospital.

In addition to the Attarine Medersa, there were three more religious colleges attached to the mosque. Very near is the Medersa al-Misbahiya built by Abu el Hassan, the Black Sultan, in 1346. Behind the elaborately carved door frame and the portico opens the court with a large white marble basin brought from Andalusia. Situated near the river is the Medersa al-Seffarin which is the oldest of the religious colleges in Morocco, founded by Abu Yusuf al Yakub in 1280. The actual form of the Merinid medersa was largely modelled on the early Mameluke religious colleges in Cairo, but, whereas in the Mameluke counterpart there were four liwans (or arched recesses), one on each side of the courtyard, and each representing one of the four schools of Islamic jurisprudence, in Morocco only the Malakite school has been recognized since the time of the Almoravids, and so there is only one liwan, which also serves as the prayer hall; arcades fill the other three sides. The last medersa attached to the Qarawiyin is the much later al-Cherratin which was constructed by the Alaouit sultan Moulay al-Rashid in 1670, where unadorned plaster walls are used with great effect to set off the elaborately carved stucco friezes and the massive wood corbelling.

Within a few minutes' walk you reach the Fondouk Nejjarine (Caravanserai of the Carpenters), no longer used as stables for pack animals, but housing poor students. In front of the monumental gateway with 18th-century corbelling, a finely carved wooden canopy tops the much photographed Fountain. Still in use as a warehouse is the nearby Fondouk Tetouine, constructed in the 14th century for merchants from Tetouan. The carved balconies on the floors above are worthy of notice, and its atmosphere recalls the important commercial role Fez has played for more than 1,000 years. More narrow streets, sometimes stepped, lead to the Zaouia of Moulay Idriss the founder of the city. This is the principal shrine of Fez and of all Morocco and is still a place of pilgrimage. The present building, with its green peaked roof of tiles, which is perhaps the only outstanding city landmark when viewed from the surrounding hills, dates largely from the 18th century. It has a rather rococo air about it, with its many chandeliers.

Crossing the Oued Fez, skins are often seen drying on the banks, and the stench indicates that the tannery quarter and dyeing vats are nearby. Commanding the Adwat al-Andalus is the great mosque of the same name founded in 861 and reconstructed by Mohammed al-Nasser in the early 13th century. The tall gateway with its by now familiar ornamentation dates from that period. Of the many medersas once attached to the mosque, only two remain. The al-Sahrij was established in 1321 by Abu Hassan Ali while he was still crown prince. The decoration is simpler than in the richer establishments near the Qarawiyin, the long reflecting basin in the courtyard giving it the air of a pleasure pavilion rather than a religious institution. Attached to it is the al-Sebayin Medersa dating from the same period; its name is derived from the Arabic word for seven (sabbah), and it was here that the seven styles of recitation of the Koran were taught.

This completes the most important sights in Fez and from here the Palais Jamai Hotel can be reached through an incomprehensible maze of streets. A cooling drink by the pool might be welcome. Taxis are available near the Bab Guissa, just in front of the hotel's entrance.

The Merinid Tombs

In the late afternoon go up to the heights above the old city—either to the Hotel Les Merinides, whose terrace commands a fine view, or, for more atmosphere in considerably less comfort, to the Tombs of the Merinids on the hill near the hotel. From here, amongst the ruined memorials of that dynasty which endowed Fez with so many of its riches, unfold 12 centuries of a great intellectual and religious capital's history, a conglomeration of medieval fondouks, fountains, hammams, medersas, mosques, palaces, souks, and a few gardens. The view has probably changed little since the time of the Merinids buried here. Built of mud and stone, the apparently solid town is constantly crumbling away, cracking, being shored up, and endlessly restored. In the spring, when the ground is covered with red and orange wild flowers, the almost ochre walls and the myriad white roofs take on a pinkish glow in the light of the setting sun; only the many minarets and the green-tiled roof of the tomb of the city's founder, Idriss II, challenge the prevailing hue.

During Ramadan deep silence descends over the whole city as the last light fades and the fast is broken; there is only the distant sound of rushing water from the hundreds of underground streams which feed the Oued Fez. Then, gradually, as if rising from the earth itself, come the sounds of music—singing and blowing of trumpets and conch shells with the cries of the muezzins floating above all. For that instant you may experience the sensual essence of a great Moorish metropolis, a way of life that has hardly changed since the 14th century.

Meknès

The contrast between Fez and Meknès is striking. Though set in rich farmlands, the latter has not really developed or prospered greatly since independence—its new town was one of the chief centers of French colonization. Seen from a distance, the medina, separated from the modern suburbs by the deep gorge of the Oued Boufekrane, seems pleasant enough with its many minarets and tiled roofs, but without much real identity. Within the old town there is a rather tumbledown and dingy atmosphere. But what one notices above all are the walls, enormous and decayed, stretching for more than 15 miles and dwarfing the adjacent medina. It is within these walls that the uniqueness of Meknès lies—the Dar al-Kabira, the great imperial "city-within-a-city" of Moulay Ismail. By comparison, the Merinid palace and administrative center in Fez Jedid seems insignificant. This enormous complex, now a ruin, was once the largest palace in the world, and the history of Meknès, the Imperial City, is the history of its building and its subsequent rapid decay; for Meknès, in contrast to Fez and Marrakesh and even Rabat, was the capital of only one sultan of one dynasty, and it is only seen through his life that the city and its monuments assume any coherent meaning.

Meknès owes its foundation to the Berber tribe, the Meknassa, who made the present site their commercial center not long before Idriss II established Morocco's first capital at Fez. However, it was little more than a group of ksours—fortified strongholds which served both as storehouses for the produce of the rich surrounding farmlands and places of retreat during raids by neighboring tribes—until it was taken by the Almoravid ibn-Tashfin in 1069. Both under the Almoravids and their successors, the Almohads, it had little role to play in the country's history. During the long struggle for power between the Almohads and the Merinids, the town was constantly devastated and it was not until its final occupation by the Merinids that it began to settle and grow. Abu Yusuf al Yakub ordered its rebuilding in 1276. Never rivaling its neighbor, Fez, Meknès was, however, embellished with a medersa begun by Abu el Hassan and completed by his successor Abu Inan in the mid-fourteenth century. During the latter decades of Merinid rule, it became a base for rebellion by pretenders claiming the throne in Fez, and was the scene of revolts against the central government, which only further decreased its prosperity. It was taken by the Saadians in 1547, before Fez, and with the transfer of the capital to Marrakesh in the south, it slipped back into insignificance.

Moulay Ismail's Military Base

When Moulay Ismail in 1672 succeeded his half-brother Moulay al-Rashid, the founder of the Alaouit dynasty, his first aim was to establish a stable military base for his authority, and he chose Meknès, of which he had been governor. The decision was one inspired by considerations of political security. To settle in Fez or Marrakesh would identify him with the interests of one group of the country's established élite and their dependent tribal areas to the exclusion of the other. Meknès had no such association. It was in a more central position on the route from the Algerian frontier to the ports of Rabat and Salé on the Atlantic; and it was the ideal situation for the concentration of his military forces. Indeed, the French followed his example 250 years later when they made Meknès their military headquarters. In order to establish his rule over the loosely-held domains of his half-brother, it was necessary for Moulay Ismail to strengthen not only his military position, but also the political and religious foundations of his authority. The methods he used and their inevitable results were to change the face and fabric of Moroccan society.

Moulay al-Rashid had used the loyalty of certain tribes to seize power, but, as a result, he had become the victim of their whims and was overthrown. Moulay Ismail, while having fomented the tribal unrest which put him on the throne, realized that their loyalty could only be relied upon so long as they were allowed to form an exclusive and privileged segment of the populace. He sought to solve the problem by the creation of a personal negro army from the descendants of slaves who had been brought to Morocco since the time of the Almohads. Moulay Ismail was, himself, half negro, his mother having been a slave girl. Negro slaves (Abid) were bought (or taken) from their owners and enlisted, together with free-born negroes, in special black regiments. By means of their fanatic loyalty he established a solid basis for his autocratic rule and achieved the pacification of the country. By the end of his reign, the Abid regiments totalled more than 40,000 men—or *bouakhars* as they were called. Their role in Moroccan affairs was to be decisive for centuries to come.

The isolation of Morocco from the rest of the Islamic world can be seen as the direct consequence of Moulay Ismail's religious and social policies. The Alaouit Sherifs, of whom he was the greatest, founded their power on their claims of blood-relationship with the Prophet and the resulting divine inspiration, which is summed up in the word *baraka,* a mystic spiritual power. This was not a new phenomenon in Morocco—both the Almoravids and the Almohads had risen through the support of religious movements, but as champions of orthodoxy, and had consolidated their positions by creating pious foundations and advocating current trends in Islamic thought.

Moulay Ismail did no such thing; by exaggerating his quasi-religious status he was able to solidify his rule to an extent never before accomplished by his predecessors. But the inevitable result was that Morocco separated itself from the rest of the Moslem world. Moulay Ismail demanded complete obedience and severed all connection with the Turkish caliphate, thus breaking the unity of Sunni Islam.

This isolation was compounded by Moulay Ismail's disastrous relations with Europe. More than any other sultan since the first Almoravids in the 11th century, he distrusted Christians and considered them the enemies of his country and of Islam. But he needed European manufactured goods and so had to allow Christian merchants into Morocco to trade. Unable to retrieve the European footholds on his coasts without European help, he went so far as to try to conclude a military pact with Louis XIV, a project which came to nothing, and to ask for the hand of Marie Anne de Bourbon, Princess de Conti, in marriage. He signed a treaty in 1682 with France regarding piracy, but piracy was a state enterprise, the sultan himself owning over half the vessels and taking 60% of the pirates' gains. This, combined with his continual harassment and persecution of Europeans, served to diminish trade and increase European suspicions, so cutting off any exchange of ideas with the Christian world.

A Tyrant's Power

Moulay Ismail is one of the great tyrants of history, with a maniacal combination of building fever and sadism. The enormous palace complex at Meknès was built by an army of slaves, many of whom were Christians, using materials pillaged from Volubilis and the great Saadian palace of al-Badi at Marrakesh, the sultan himself whipping the workers if there was a delay; slackers were built into the nearest section of somber wall. Guides try to spare the feelings of their modern Western charges by insisting that it was entirely a question of blacks with an occasional brigand of unspecified race thrown in. In fact, Moslem corsairs at Salé maintained a supply of Christian captives as constant as fresh fish.

In the Dar al-Kebira tens of thousands of slaves and officials were housed so that the sultan could keep all under surveillance and detect any sign of revolt. In this respect it might have been similar to Versailles and the great Russian palaces of the era, but there the similarity stops. John Windus, an English traveler in the early 18th century, left a vivid account of the court of Moulay Ismail in his *A Journey to Mequinez.* Yellow was his "killing color," and he killed often and indiscriminately; his favorite means of execution was for the victim to be sawn in half from the head down until the body fell in two pieces.

When Moulay Ismail died in 1727 after a reign of 45 years, he left Morocco with no stable or responsible bureaucracy nor with any religious or political body to ensure continuity. His was a negative legacy—which implied that the existence of effective government depended on the next sultan's ability to develop new means of having his authority obeyed; his autocracy had lasted so long that there was no one to fill his place. He left more than 500 male heirs, and, by Alaouit tradition, each had equal baraka and each was as eligible to rule as the other. In the ensuing chaos, the Abid regiments stepped into the power vacuum and took on the role of kingmakers. Whether the capital was at Fez or Marrakesh, the new sultan had to come to Meknès to be confirmed in office—only to be discarded at their will. The Alaouit sultan's position vis à vis the bouakhars was comparable to that of the contemporary Ottoman sultan's control by the janissaries; both had been slave guards recruited to impose the sultan's power and both became the governing power themselves for two centuries.

Exploring Meknès

A tour of Meknès usually begins at the Place al-Hedim, the large open space—once the rival of Marrakesh's Jemaa el-Fna—before the great walls of the palace enclosure and the borders of the medina. A guide is not absolutely necessary, but very helpful if you want to penetrate far into the medina. The palace complex can be explored on foot, but, with the walls stretching for more than 24 km. (15 miles), and the ruins being very confusing, a car and a knowledgeable driver are helpful.

The Imperial City, Dar al-Kebira, is entered by the Bab Mansour, a rather squat horseshoe arch of massive proportions flanked by two ornamental bastions decorated in green ceramic tiles, rather reminiscent of a cinema version of the Baghdad of the Arabian Nights. Beside is the small but graceful Bab Jamai en-Nouar. Both lead into the Place Lalla Aouda, the former mechouar, which is now a garden of sorts. On the far end, the Bab Filela is the entrance to the palace proper.

This is more a city than a palace, as understood in the west. On all sides are high walls in a ruinous state, with only the roofs and gates of some structures being visible; and, indeed, most of the palace has been a ruin for more than 200 years, the result of an earthquake in 1755. What remains is only an evocation of the past. In a grassed square within the Bab Filela and adjoining a largely underground prison built especially for Christian captives, is a smallish (or at least, small in comparison with the enormity of the surroundings) pavilion, the Qoubbet al-Khiyatin, where Moulay Ismail received foreign ambassadors and which has been restored. Opposite is the Mausoleum of Moulay Ismail, whose mosque can be entered by non-Moslems. To the right, at the end of the court, a small road descends through an opening in the walls to what was the vast garden of the sultanas with its ancient trees, and is now the Royal Golf Club. It is strange to think that till the 1950s this was the domain of aged princesses and black eunuchs from the court of Moulay al-Hassan (1873–1894). It is only now that you can begin to appreciate the great scale of the Imperial City—walls as far as you can see, and behind them, more walls, and here just *one* of the gardens, and it is large enough to contain an 18-hole golf course! But it should be remembered that, at the beginning of the 18th century, at least 50,000 slaves, servants and eunuchs, along with the bouakhars, the court, and the imperial family of some 500 wives and 1,500 children were housed here.

Beyond the grass esplanade, a road lined with high walls stretches for more than a mile. About halfway, it passes under the Bab al-Rih, the Gate

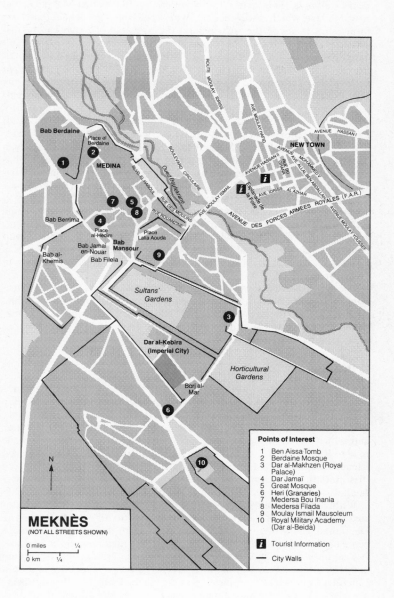

Bab Berdaine

Place el
Berdaine

2

1

MEDINA

ROUTE MOULAY IDRISS

AVE MOULAY HAFID

AVENUE HASSAN I

NEW TOWN

AVENUE MOHAMED V

BOULEVARD CIRCULAIRE

Oued Boufekrane

AVENUE HASSAN II

RUE DE FÈS

RUE EL MEHDI

BLVD EL HADDAD

AVE MOULAY ISMAIL

AVE IDRISS   AL AZHAR

Esplanade de
la Foire

Bab Berrima

7   **5**

RUE DES MOULINS

8

RUE BOUAMOINE

AVENUE DES FORCES ARMEES ROYALES (F.A.R.)

AVENUE MOULAY YOUSSEF

4

Place
al-Hedim

Place
Lalla Aouda

Bab Jamaï
en-Nouar

**Bab
Mansour**

Bab al-
Khemis

Bab Filela

9

*Sultans'
Gardens*

3

**Dar al-Kebira
(Imperial City)**

*Horticultural
Gardens*

Borj al-
Mar

6

10

N

MEKNÈS
(NOT ALL STREETS SHOWN)

0 miles	¼
0 km	¼

Points of Interest

1 Ben Aissa Tomb
2 Berdaine Mosque
3 Dar al-Makhzen (Royal
   Palace)
4 Dar Jamaï
5 Great Mosque
6 Heri (Granaries)
7 Medersa Bou Inania
8 Medersa Filada
9 Moulay Ismail Mausoleum
10 Royal Military Academy
   (Dar al-Beida)

i   Tourist Information

——   City Walls

of the Wind, a long vaulted corridor, with a series of arches standing on heavy columns. This marks the beginning of the Dar al-Makhzen, the Royal Palace, which is still occupied when the King is in Meknès (entrance forbidden). It lies to the right behind the walls, and all that can be discerned is a perspective of courts and green tiled roofs seen through dilapidated doorways. Finally the long road bears to the right and under the Borj al-Mar (Water Bastion) to enter another immense mechouar wherein is the present entrance to the palace. From here, under another gate, the Bab al-Nouara, you pass the ruins of barracks, more gardens (botanical) and reservoirs and arrive at the Heri, the enormous silos and granaries which fed the palace. Then come more crumbling walls, the military academy which occupies an 18th-century palace, and finally the Jbabra Quarter and the Roua—stables with room for 12,000 horses, each with its own stall, divided by high arcades. On the great platform above (which has now disappeared) were the harems of Moulay Ismail, consisting of 24 pavilions. No doubt it was on this terrace that contemporary travelers saw the sultan and his favorite women being drawn in a kind of chariot by a team of negro eunuchs. Beyond are a few survivors of those days—some ostriches in a park set up by Moulay Abdallah in the mid 18th century, and several poor villages where some descendants of the once proud bouakhars remain. Beyond here, the landscape becomes open prairie, with mysterious walls and ruins, never satisfactorily explained, stretching in every direction.

The architecture is mediocre, but the buildings impress by the immensity of their scale. Everything is decayed—except for the Royal Golf Club. In the end, the structures become more and more inexplicable. The granaries look like the stables, and both like ruins designed by Piranesi, but of greater barbaric splendor.

The Medina

After the wonders of Moulay Ismail, the medina of Meknès is an anticlimax. There are two further gates from the imperial period—the Bab Berdaine (Gate of the Saddlers) at the north end of the medina—a tall, slender structure, whose doorway frames the mosque of the same name, and which makes a good photograph—and the Bab al-Khemis, on the road to Rabat, a little lighter than its counterparts and decorated in glazed faience mosaic with a frieze of black cursive calligraphy framed in green tiles. Both these gates are best visited by car; they formed part of the outer ramparts of Moulay Ismail's city, most of which have disappeared.

Within the medina itself, two buildings deserve attention. Both are situated at the far end of the Place al-Hedim, opposite the Bab Mansour. The Dar Jamai, the Museum of Moroccan Art, lies to the right, the entrance being on the small street which ascends into the medina under an arcade. It was the Moorish-style palace of the same late 19th-century vizier who built the original Palais Jamai in Fez. The garden of cypresses and bougainvillea is an especially pleasant place to rest on a hot day. Beyond, bearing left at the Great Mosque which was begun by the Almohads and rebuilt by Abu Yusuf al Yakub in 1276, is the Medersa Bou Inania lying at the center of a T-junction with its bridge-building or portico covering the street at the top of the T, which is the main souk of the medina (small tip to the custodian). Begun by Abu el Hassan and completed by Abu Inan about 1350, it is smaller than its namesake in Fez, and of the same rich and tasteful decoration so typical of the Merinids and so lacking in 18th-century Meknès. The medersa, which has been restored, is entered by a gate covered with bronze plaques, the courtyard lying to the right at the end of a corridor two stories high. Paved in tiles with an ornamental reflecting pool in the center, the court is exceptionally lofty, as is the richly carved cedarwood ceiling of the prayer hall. From the roof one can see the ruined Filada Medersa which was built by Moulay Ismail in the late 17th century and, compared with its Merinid counterpart, is rather clumsy in detail and decoration.

To explore the souks—which are often roofed with trailing vines and lined with painted shop fronts and shutters—a guide is useful. There are many picturesque angles and perspectives; deep in the medina is the evocative tomb of Ben Aissa, founder of the Aissaouia sect of mystics. Supported and encouraged by Moulay Ismail, and one of the most powerful instruments of Alaouit power, the movement spread across the Maghreb. On feast days, the members devoured live sheep and goats, ate fragments of broken glass and lacerated their chests in dances of wild ecstasy. After the last war these barbarous habits gave way to the annual Festival of the Fantasia with the participation of some thousand horsemen, occurring in September.

Moulay Idriss and Volubilis

Moulay Idriss, the holy city, and the ruins of Volubilis, lie close to each other, the former on the lower slopes and the latter at the foot of Jebel Zerhoun, nearer to Meknès than Fez.

16 km. (10 miles) north on P6 to Sidi Kacem, turn right on to the P28A. After about 5 km. (3 miles), you have a choice of route, either keeping straight on or following a turning on the right that is not signposted for Volubilis but for Merhasiyne. This steep and narrow road over the Zerhoun provides a wonderful 27-km. (17-mile) drive over this gaunt, forbidding, flat-topped mountain, past the tomb of Sidi Ali ben Hamdouch, founder of the Hamadcha Brotherhood (still active in the region), and through miles of olive groves. On the way up, you look miles and miles across the Saïs Plain to Meknès and beyond. The steep descent on the other side allows magnificent views down on to Moulay Idriss and the even more distant plain in which Volubilis lies. The easier main road crosses the Mlali Pass and gives impressive glimpses of Moulay Idriss towering up above.

If you approach by this last road, drive through the gate (Bab Jedid) and continue up through the main market, bearing left when you have a choice, until you clear the town and can park. The Zerhoun road, described above, runs vertiginously down the mountainside into a gorge and after crossing the river brings you out at a crossroads in a large dusty open space, where you turn left and park *before* entering the town.

The town of Moulay Idriss occupies two conical hills on the western flank of Jebel Zerhoun and takes its name from the father of Fez's founder, Moulay Idriss I, who established Morocco's first dynasty. He lies buried in the mausoleum, whose green-tiled roof you can see on the saddle between the two hills, and every year, usually in September, a pilgrimage is held in his honor in the dusty open space just mentioned. Because the town is still held sacred, modernization has made relatively very few inroads.

Two views are particularly worth seeing. One is from the terrace of the Sidi Abdullah al-Hajim mosque on the lower of the two hills, and the other from the top of the higher cone. You reach the mosque by a street that runs off to the right beside Bab Jedid, and the higher summit by a steep road just inside the upper gate beyond which we suggested you should park your car. It is actually possible to drive a short way up this road, which takes the edge off a strenuous but not specially long climb. The route cannot be described: you must just try likely turnings and if they end in blind alleys turn back and start again. When you get to the top, however, you have a magnificent view down on to the town's other hill and the surrounding countryside.

On the few miles from Moulay Idriss to Volubilis magnificent views open across the valley, with the green-folded sides and cliff-sprinkled summit of Jebel Zerhoun in the background.

The admission charge includes the services of a uniformed guide, who pilots you on a detailed tour of the ruins, lecturing lengthily the while in French. But it seems more in tune with the severe isolation of the ruins to wander off on one's own trying to imagine the past splendor of this great Roman outpost.

Though the capital of King Juba II, whose admirable bronze head is in the Rabat Museum, and then of Mauretania Tingitana, Volubilis is less impressive than other Roman sites in North Africa. The surprisingly small town, much damaged by an earthquake in 1755, was built on a polygonal plan. Peculiar to the houses are two completely asymmetrical doors on the street frontage, the smaller one being perhaps the original tradesman's entrance. Only fragments remain of the Punic ramparts, but the Roman enclosure was 2,300 m. (7,700 feet) long with almost 40 towers protecting seven gates. A magnificent colonnaded main shopping street led from the Tangier Gate to the not-so-magnificent triumphal arch built by the Emperor Caracalla in A.D. 217. Most houses have been named after statues and other objects found in them.

The forum, a biggish paved square, was flanked by lavishly decorated porticoes, a rectangular tribune and a large basilica, where the courts sat. By far the largest building is the Governor's Palace, entered by the characteristic two doors leading to a fine vestibule, which opens on to a triple bay. The rectangular peristyle is surrounded by columns. Among the mosaics, well preserved in situ, are the Labors of Hercules, the Four Seasons and the Dolphins in the House of Venus. There are remains of a bakery and several oil presses.

More striking than the ruins is the intense peace of the site, and its location in an unprotected plain. The ramparts, still visible in places, were not constructed until the second century A.D., but then safeguarded Volubilis till the arrival of the first Arab invaders in A.D. 683. A small museum near the entrance contains some of the finds—a marble young Bacchus with a panther, and a Satyr with waterskin—but most of the bronze statues are in the Rabat Archeological Museum.

To avoid backtracking, continue north from Volubilis along a mountainside covered with olive groves, joining P3 at the Zegotta Pass, and turn right for Fez.

Traveling in the reverse direction has the advantage of arriving at Moulay Idriss when the light is best for photographing from the higher summit.

Oulmès

The spa of Oulmès is a pleasant day excursion from Meknès via Khemisset or from Rabat via Tiflet. The road from Khenifra is very narrow though surfaced. Because Oulmès lies well off main routes, it has remained unspoilt, though the water from the Lalla Haya spring has been bottled and sold in Morocco for generations.

The higher village of Oulmès proper and the lower one of Oulmès-les-Thermes or Tarmilate both stand in an extraordinary forest of over 100,000 acres, where wild boar and other game abound. The forest itself spreads over mountainsides whose slopes rise to well above 1,200 m. (4,000 feet). Oulmès in fact is located at about this height in this lovely upland area which tempers the frenzy of the summer sun.

PRACTICAL INFORMATION FOR FEZ

WHEN TO GO. Each May, the spiritual capital of the realm brings its past to glowing life in a Sound and Light spectacle. From the top of El Kolla hill, the spotlights pick out one by one the monuments that portray better than any narration the glorious history of Fez. September is another good month because of the great moussem at Moulay Idriss with its charges of Arab horsemen—but any time is good for visiting Fez, since even in summer the dryness of the climate makes the heat entirely bearable. The Fête du Trône celebrations, March 3, are also specially fine in Fez.

GETTING THERE. By Plane. Three times weekly service from Paris by Royal Air Maroc, one continuing to Marrakesh and the other to Casablanca. Royal Air Inter has services to Casablanca via Rabat and also to Oujda, continuing to Oran in Algeria.

By Train. Tangier–Fez via Sidi Slimane and Meknès, 6 hrs.; from Rabat, 4 hrs.; from Oujda, 5 hrs.

By Bus. CTM buses link all the principal cities of Morocco with Fez.

By Car. Some distances: Rabat–Fez 201 km. (125 miles); Casablanca–Fez 296 km. (184 miles); Meknès–Fez 61 km. (38 miles); Marrakesh–Fez 515 km. (320 miles); Tangier–Fez 312 km. (194 miles).

HOTELS. All (L) and (E) hotels are airconditioned and have pools. Area code 06.

Deluxe

De Fès, Ave. des F.A.R. (tel. 250 02). 295 rooms, 5 suites; tennis in large garden; 4 restaurants, heated pool, conference facilities. On the fringe of the Ville Nouvelle.

Des Merinides, Borjes Nord (tel. 452 25). 79 rooms. Part of the Kasbah Tours chain; above the old city and commanding the best views of Fez. But here, too, only half the rooms have the view, the others look onto the parking lot. Magnificent panoramic terrace, and the situation of the pool is breathtaking. The location is rather isolated for those without a car.

Palais Jamaï, (tel. 230 56). 20 suites in a pleasure pavilion built in 1880. 100 rooms and apartments in a new wing. Probably Morocco's most luxurious. Inside

Bab Guissa, at the entrance to the medina, over which half of the rooms have a magnificent view; pool, nightclub, conference room.

Expensive

Sofia, Rue du Pakistan (tel. 242 60). 102 spacious rooms, 4 suites. Newest in town center; pool, nightclub.

Volubilis, Rue Allal Ben Abdellah (tel. 211 25). In the P.L.M. chain. 120 rooms. Noisy, pleasant garden.

Zalagh, Rue Mohammed Diouri (tel. 228 10). 64 rooms. In the Salam chain. Less expensive and with unusual décor and package tour dining room; on hillside near new town; pool.

Moderate

Amor, Zankat Pologne (tel. 233 04). 35 airconditioned rooms.

Grand, Blvd. Chefchaouni (tel. 255 11). 98 rooms. Living on prewar glory; good position near Place Mohammed V. Its praised French restaurant, *Le Normandy,* seems overrated.

Lamdaghri, 10 Kabbour El Mangad (tel. 203 10). 20 rooms.

Mounia, 60 Rue Azilah (tel. 248 38). Probably the most comfortable hotel in this category, the Mounia has 94 airconditioned rooms.

Moussafir, Rue Les Almohades, Gare ONCF (tel. 519 02/03). This new 50-room hotel has both comfort and a pleasant decor.

Olympic, Ave. Mohammed V (tel. 245 29). 35 rooms.

De la Paix, Ave. Hassan II (tel. 250 72). 35 rooms.

RESTAURANTS. Characteristic of Fez cuisine, reputedly Morocco's best, are meat and fruit combinations, best sampled in the superb **Al Fassia** of the Palais Jamaï. Less original in food, though not in décor, are the converted old mansions in the Medina, where the ceremoniously served dishes seem secondary to the arts and crafts on sale.

Expensive

Dar Mnebhi, 15 Zankat ben Safi (tel. 338 83). The palace of a 19th-century vizier.

Dar Saada, 21 Rue Attarine (tel. 333 43). Near the Atterine Medersa.

Dar Tajine, Palais Hadj Omar Labbar, 15 Ross Rhi (tel. 341 43).

La Fassia, Batha Sala (tel. 346 24). Outstanding Moroccan food is served here.

Al Firdaous, 10 Rue Jenfour, Bab Guissa (tel. 343 43). The newest, most serious about food and entertainment.

Palais de Fès, 16 Rue Boutouil (tel. 347 07). Opposite the Qaraniyin Mosque. The tourist restaurant in Fez.

Pavillon L'Anmbra, 47 Route d'Imouzzer (tel. 416 87). At the edge of the new town.

Moderate

La Creperie, Ave. Mohammed V (tel. 223 77). French dishes with a touch of Moroccan flavor are served here.

La Medina, 13 bis Derb el Hamam Guerniz (tel. 334 08). Hidden in the medina, this is a real find for excellent local cooking, and authentic atmosphere.

Du Voyageur, Blvd. Mohammed V. The most popular of the international establishments that line this avenue.

SPORTS. Swimming at the Ain Chkeff and Municipal pools. **Fishing.** The Fishing Club du Moyen Atlas (biggest group of its kind in the country) organizes a competition every year in May open to tourists as well as members.

Ski. The Ski Club of Fez also has its prize day, the Grand Prix de Fès run on the slopes of Bou Iblane (8,000 ft. altitude)—the date varies.

Horseback riding. Club Equestre de Fez, Rue Moulay El Kamel.

Racing. Horse races with the extra-added-attraction of tribal races at the Grand Prix de la Ville de Fès.

SHOPPING. Fez is famous for its carpets (the neighboring tribes are prolific and expert weavers) and also for its wall hangings, hand-woven fabrics and embroideries. You'll find a selection of all of these at the Maison Moulay Rachid, 23 Ras Cherratine or 11 Rue Attarine, Kissaria, in the medina. The Dar Saada, 21 Rue Attarine, has a first-rate stock, as well as a good restaurant. Restaurant Palais de Fès, 16 Rue Boutouil, also sells lovely but very expensive Moroccan crafts. Anywhere in the medina, bargaining is part of the game. The straw workers' stalls are at the junction of Boulevard Arrahbeh and Route 14. The pottery factories with their salesrooms a bit further out on Route 14. For oriental confectionery, etc., Pleux, 120 Blvd. Mohammed V. Bear in mind that guides get commissions on your purchases from the shops they take you to. The Palais du Caftan, Derb El Gebas Batha, makes jellabas to order.

USEFUL ADDRESSES. Tourist Information and Guides at the O.N.M.T. (National Tourist Office), Place de la Resistance (tel. 234–60) or at the Syndicat d'Initiative (City Information Bureau), Pl. Mohammed V. (tel. 247–69).

Travel: Wagons-Lits Tourisme, Rue de la Liberté; Bab Agnaou Tours, 2 Blvd. Chefchaouni; Automobile Club, 52 Ave. Hassan II (tel. 226–66), Royal Air Maroc and Royal Air Inter, Ave. Hassan II.

Car Hire: Avis, 50 Chefchaouni (tel. 267 46); Budget, Rue Bahrein (tel. 209 19); Gold Car, 6 Abdelkrim Khattabi (tel. 204 95); Hertz, Hotel de Fez (tel. 228 12); Inter Rent, Ave. Hassan II (tel. 228 12).

PRACTICAL INFORMATION FOR MEKNÈS

GETTING THERE. By Train. The same as to Fez (only an hour away). Likewise the C.T.M. buses: several daily departures in both directions on the Casablanca–Fez route. Casa to Meknès takes 4 hrs.; Rabat–Meknès, 2½ hrs. Meknès is also the start of the oases tour: Azrou–Midelt–Er Rachidia–Erfoud–Rissani, a good alternative to the route via Marrakesh, 10½ hrs.

By Car. A few distances by road: Casablanca–Meknès via Rabat and Khemisset, 230 km. (143 miles); Tangier–Meknès via Rabat and Khemisset, 230 km. (143 miles); Tangier–Meknès via Ksar-el-Kebir and Sidi Kacem, 266 km. (165 miles); Marrakesh–Meknès via Kasbah Tadla, 475 km. (295 miles); Er Rachidia–Meknès via Azrou, 335 km. (208 miles).

HOTELS
(Area code 05)

Deluxe

Transatlantique, Rue El Meriniyine (tel. 250 50/55), at the edge of the new town. 120 rooms and suites. In the O.N.C.F. chain. Beautifully situated in a garden with view over the old town. Two swimming pools, poolside bar and restaurant. New unobtrusive block, but rooms in older part are better. The small first-floor restaurant gets hectic when hotel is full.

Expensive

Rif, Zankat Accra (tel. 225 91). 124 rooms. Well placed for both the old and new town and convenient for buses and taxis. Rooms comfortable, but somewhat rundown, poor lighting and not really good value for the price.

Zaki, Blvd. Massira (tel. 209 90). 163 rooms. Restaurant, pool, nightclub.

Moderate

The following are the best of a poor selection:

Bab Monsour, Rue Amin Abdelkadar (tel. 252 39). This new hotel has 65 modern, airconditioned rooms and a pleasant restaurant.

Nice, Zankat Accra (tel. 201 02). 30 rooms. Owned by the Rif and the guests use the Rif's restaurant.

Palace, Zankat Ghana (tel. 223 88). 30 rooms.

Volubilis, Ave. des F.A.R. (tel. 201 02). 34 rooms, 27 showers.

OULMÈS. *Les Thermes* (tel. 055 2353). 50 rooms, 32 with bath or shower. Somewhat old-fashioned thermal establishment.

RESTAURANTS

Expensive

Bellevue, Quartier Belle Vue (tel. 208 26). Fine French cuisine is served here.

La Coupole, Ave. Hassan II (tel. 224 38). French and Moroccan fare.

Hacienda, less than 3 km. (2 miles) along the Fez road and in a little wood to the left—follow the signposts (tel. 210 98). One of the better French restaurants, with a bar and dance floor, outdoor dining terrace and a swimming pool.

Zaitoune, 44 Jamai Zitoune (tel. 302 81). Traditional Moroccan food served in heaping portions.

Moderate

Dauphine, Ave. de Paris. Reliably French.

Pizzeria, Zankat Atlas, off Blvd. Mohammed V. Popular for Italian cuisine.

Inexpensive

Inexpensive cafes include the **Roi de la Bière** on Ave. Mohammed V and the **Metropole** facing the central market.

The simple **Refuge de Zerhoun** is in an olive grove near the campsite between Moulay Idriss and Volubilis.

SHOPPING. Permanent display of Moroccan wares with price tags at the Coopartim, Place Lalla Ouda. Souk (bazaar) days are held in Meknès each Wednesday.

SPORTS. Municipal **Swimming** Pool (Piscine Municipale), Lahboul; **Tennis** Club, Lahboul; **riding** at the Club Equestre, Le Haras Marocain Stables, Imperial City. **Golf** at the Royal Golf Club, Sultan's Garden.

USEFUL ADDRESSES. Tourist Information and Guides at the National Tourist Office (tel. 244 26), Place Administrative, or the Syndicat d'Initiative (tel. 201 91), Esplanade de la Foire, between the new and the old towns.

Travel. Wagons-Lits Tourisme, Rue du Ghana. Automobile Club, 17 Rue Allal ben Abdullah. C.T.M. Bus Station, 43 Ave. Mohammed V. Royal Air Maroc and Royal Air Inter, 7 Blvd. Mohammed V. The Mezerques airport is only for military planes.

Car Hire. Stop Car, Rue Essaouira (tel. 250 61); Zeit, 4 Rue Antissade (tel 259 18).

ACROSS THE RIF AND
THROUGH THE TAZA GAP

From Tangier to the Algerian Border

The wild beauty of barren, sun-scorched mountains, bathed in the light
of the Mediterranean is traversed by an east-west highway cut by north-
south secondary roads. The Rif has become accessible without losing either its mystery or its beauty, but invaders have found it a difficult area
to conquer. Two hundred and twenty miles of parallel mountain chains
bar the way to all unwanted visitors. The Romans never gained a foothold
in the Rif, while Arab or Berber chieftains were only able to subdue it
armed with the Word not the sword. The already legendary figure of Emir
Abd-el-Krim resisted the French and Spanish armies for many years until
he was finally obliged to surrender in 1926. The harshness of existence
on the barren mountains has made the Berbers of the Rif distinctive in
tradition, dress and even language.

At each of its extremities, the Rif slopes down to the sea, at towns that
still belong to Spain—Ceuta to the west and Melilla in the east. Between
them are a few islets, one bearing the fortress of Al Hoceima; however
the coast is too steep and craggy for any significant settlements.

Exploring the Rif

The coastal road from Tangier via Ksar es Serhir to Ceuta is scenic but
potholed, but the 55 km. (34 miles) over the Fondak Ridge from Tangier

to Tetouan are easy going. Though with 250,000 inhabitants slightly smaller than Tangier, Tetouan is the administrative capital of the Rif. Founded by the Merinid sultan Abou Thabit in 1306 near the ruins of Roman Tamuda on the slopes of Jebel Dersa, Tetouan was destroyed by Henry III of Castile in 1399 and repopulated only at the beginning of the 16th century by Jews and Moslems from Andalusia. These refugees introduced the still prevailing Moorish architecture. In 1862 Spain occupied Tetouan for a year, but evacuated under British pressure. In 1913 Spain regained her foothold and made Tetouan the capital of the Spanish protectorate in Northern Morocco.

The Martil river, which flows into the sea nearby, long contributed to Tetouan's prosperity, due to the trade it brought, and often the pirates it sheltered. During the Rif War Emir Abd-el-Krim established a base on Jebel Dersa.

From a distance Tetouan resembles a Cubist painting, to which the minarets of seventeen mosques have been added. Closer inspection can be disappointing, but the view over the fertile Martil valley to the hills beyond is attractive. The center of the modern town is Mohammed V Square, dominated by the former residence of the Spanish governor, now a uniquely sumptuous consulate, more imposing than the nearby palace of the Khalifa, the King's representative. The Mosque of the Pasha is in the town center, near the Archeological Museum, which houses pottery and statues from Roman Lixus and Tamuda, with a surfeit of funerary monuments from various periods. The Folklore Museum at Bab el Ogla conveys a picture of regional crafts. The souks are richly stocked with plastics, while the narrow, crowded lanes of the medina within the ramparts are claustrophobic rather than picturesque. For the very energetic, the steep ascent to the kasbah is rewarded with a fine view over the town. 11 km. (seven miles) or so east the Martil river empties into the sea at a sandy beach, very popular with the locals.

A Stopover in Andalusia

No need to cross the Straits, as the architecture of the white town on Africa's northernmost promontory is as unmistakably Spanish as the 67,000 residents including the 20,000 Moslems who were granted Spanish citizenship in 1986. The thousands of Moroccan workers, who trudge daily across the border, are a very distinctive element. "A thousand times accursed"—because from here started the Arab-Berber invasion of the Iberian Peninsular in 710. Ceuta was occupied by the Portuguese in 1415 and became Spanish in 1580 when Philip II temporarily united the two crowns. It has remained like Melilla a *presidio* ever since—and as such an integral part of Spain—so that the 20 square km. (eight square miles) never formed part of the protectorate. But to Moroccans the decolonization will only have been completed with the incorporation of these last foreign enclaves.

On the point of the peninsula Mount Hacho rises abruptly 183 m. (600 feet) from the sea, sufficiently impressive to have featured as one of the Pillars of Hercules, forming with Gibraltar the monumental gateway to the classical world of the Mediterranean.

Arriving in Ceuta involves crossing a border, which can take a very long time because of the endless streams of cars. Also be prepared for the banks on the Moroccan side to be low on pesetas, while those in Ceuta might not accept dirhams which are illegal to export. A circular road passes the main points of interest, the 14th-century Merinid walls which the Portuguese strengthened with a moat, the Hermitage of San Antonio, the church of San Ildefonso and the Monument of Llano Amarillo which commemorates the rising of General Franco at Ketama, and was reerected in Ceuta after Morocco became independent. Ceuta's heart is the very Andalusian Plaza de Africa, with a 15th-century cathedral, the white 18th-century church, Our Lady of Africa, and the Palacio Municipal opposite. The mortal remains of King Sebastian of Portugal, killed in the Battle of the Three Kings at Ksar el Kebir, supposedly lie in the church of San Francisco, on the Plaza Capitán Ramos.

From the fortress on top of Mount Hacho a stunning view extends over the Straits—in good weather the houses of Gibraltar are visible. It's only 24 km. (15 miles) across at this point—a mere one-and-a-half hours by ferry—but only a fraction of the 2–3 million passengers a year ever go on to Morocco, for Ceuta's main attraction is its free port status, which has led to a proliferation of shops stocked mainly with Far Eastern products. But this lucrative trade has been reduced by the opening of Spain's frontier with Gibraltar.

Through Cedar Forests

The longest stretch of road along the Moroccan shore of the Mediterranean is east of Tetouan to the mouth of the Oued Laou, whose beautiful valley is carpeted with pink oleanders in late spring. The quality of the scenery remains high, but that of the road gradually deteriorates along the beaches of Points des Pêcheurs above El Jebha, after which it improves, turning inland to El Khemis near Ketama.

P28 south of Tetouan to Meknès bypasses picturesque Chechaouen, but the three-mile detour to the delightful little town on the slopes of Jebel ech Chaou (Mountain of the Horns) is strongly recommended. Founded by a local chieftain, Moulay Ben Rachid, in 1471, Moorish refugees and the Spanish influence combine to create a very Andalusian atmosphere among luxuriant gardens and bubbling springs. The central Place el Maghzen is particularly attractive, with a small mosque and the medieval dungeon in which Abd-el-Krim was briefly imprisoned at the end of the Rif War.

From the junction below the town, P28 continues southwest (right) through the pleasant valley of the Lekkous to Ouezzane and on to Meknès with a branch to Fez. P39 turns east (left) through the entire length of the Rif, peak-to-peak 209 km. (130 miles), to Al Hoceima and then on to Nador. After the village of Bab Taza the road straddles the spine of the Rif, each of its hairpin turns revealing bare summits from 1,500 to 2,500 meters (5,000 to 8,000 feet) high, while far below are wild valleys, blue lakes, or sometimes a hollow cultivated as it can only be in a land where farmland is scarce.

Forests of cedar and pine trees surround Ketama, named after the Berber tribe that occupies the heart of the Rif. Pleasantly cool in summer, with a 9-hole golf course, popular for hunting wild boar and other game, the only accommodation for skiing on 2,342-m. (7,680-feet) Jebel Tidighine (Tidhirine), Ketama is also the center of kif (hashish) cultivation. Aggressive vendors, mostly children, stand in the middle of the road to sell the home-grown product to passing cars. They can become exceedingly unpleasant, so it is best to maintain an even, reasonable speed (and temper), and keep the windows closed.

The road south to Fez crosses the Oued Ouargha at Taounate, where the El M'Jara dam, Morocco's largest, is under construction, planned to form a lake of 35km. (22 miles) length. P39 twists and turns east past El Khemis on a high ridge before straightening in the fields round the little town of Targuist. If it happens to be Saturday, don't miss the busy market when the Rifan women come in from miles around in their implausible huge straw hats covered with ribbons, pompons, and mirrors!

Near Targuist another road goes north to a beautiful and nearly undiscovered beach, Kala Iris, which can also be reached by a better if longer branch further along the remaining 64 km. (40 miles) to Al Hoceima.

Glimpses of the Mediterranean

The little port of Al Hoceima is slowly growing into a beach resort. The government, properly sensing the irresistible temptation to speculators and land-grabbers, has declared the whole coastal region state domain and grants building permits only to those whose constructions will not mar the site. Al Hoceima lies on the west end of a bay, where the tiny port is sheltered by a rocky point, but is deep enough to harbor a fleet of fishing vessels and pleasure craft. The boats haul in several tons of fish every day, which are either shipped out fresh or stocked in refrigeration plants. Don't miss the daily morning scene of the lamparo fishermen returning from the sea. The lamparo is a big acetylene lantern mounted on the boats which attracts the fish at night and dazzles them so that the men have only to scoop them from the clear water.

Not quite 160 km. (100 miles) lie between Al Hoceima and Nador. P39 stays nearly at sea level for about 32 km. (20 miles). The government is giving every aid and comfort to farmers willing to turn this coastal plain into the rich farmland it ought to be. But there are still mountains enough ahead, then a road to the right southward towards Taza via Aknoul.

After more mountains P39 descends again and passes through the hamlets of Midar, Driouch and Tiztounine. Just before Selouane, S605 branches south across the Oued Moulouya to P1 near El Aïoun. Several pistes lead south as the topography of the Rif grows less forbidding. At Selouane, P27 continues east to Berkane, Oujda and Algeria, while P39 widens to the Mediterranean.

Nador is an unprepossessing provincial capital lying on the banks of a small lagoon the Spaniards call "Mar Chico" or Little Sea. Already endowed with a cement factory all too close to the university campus, Morocco's largest industrial plant will use the iron reserves of the Rif and the Tafilalet with the coal from Jerada to feed an iron and steel foundry. This project will create a great many jobs for Rifans who up to now have often been forced to seek work beyond their own frontiers.

P39 ends north at Melilla which was known as Rusadir to the Phoenicians who first colonized it. It is possible to drive to the Cape of Three Forks (Cap des Trois Fourches), a wild and rocky point which juts 40 km. (25 miles) out into the sea. The Cape rises over 427 m. (1,400 feet) above the sea and offers a remarkable view of the Mediterranean.

Conquered in 1497, Melilla has remained Spanish through countless wars and sieges, and the 60,000 inhabitants of the *presidio* are administered from Málaga. Ramparts encircle the tip of the promontory; from the highest point, El Pueblo, the view extends over the new town climbing the gentle slopes of Monte Gurugú and the Cape of Three Forks. A short tunnel leads past a Gothic chapel to the stately Puerta de Santiago; a drawbridge crosses the moat beyond the Plaza de Armas. The 17th-century Franciscan Church of La Purísima Concepción, with a fine carving of Our Lady of Victory, backs on to the Municipal Museum, whose exhibits span 3,000 years. The Indian shopkeepers in the Mantelet district beyond the moat form a noteworthy bazaar. The luxuriant Parque de Hernández is a lovely extension of the huge Plaza de España above the port.

From the Selouane road junction P27 continues east across the Oued Moulouya, the largest Moroccan river emptying into the Mediterranean. Due to the large dam of Mechra Kelila the entire valley has been irrigated down to the sea. Flattish green country extends round Berkane to Ahfir on the Algerian border, where the road divides north of Saïdia on the Mediterranean, and south to Oujda.

Though the Rif is emerging from its age-long isolation with giant dams, model farms, steel plants and modern hotels, folklore has retained its special flavor, and solitude can be found not only in the remote mountains but, uniquely, on many Mediterranean beaches.

Road of the Invaders

Fez, the heart of Morocco, communicates with the east by a wide swath cut between the Rif range to the north and the middle Atlas to the south: the Taza Gap. Beyond this gateway, the wide open spaces begin—so much so that there is no real geographical border between eastern Morocco and western Algeria. Small wonder that this should be the glory road for conquerors. Through this wide path the first Arab conquerors came to overwhelm the Berber tribes; the Almoravids and the Almohads left by the same way to extend their empire throughout Algeria; Merinid armies marched to capture Tlemcen. But tourists tend to neglect this part of eastern Morocco, as beyond Taza the region holds little interest.

The scenery along the 116 km. (72 miles) between Fez and Taza is unexciting but not unpleasing. One mile right of P1, beyond a small wood, lies Morocco's best-equipped spa, Sidi Harazem. Further on, the Sebou has been dammed into the huge artificial Lake Idriss I. For most of the journey, the mountains are sufficiently removed from the gently undulating hills to disguise the strategic importance of the area, which is, however, dramatically revealed when the road ascends the Touahar Pass (about 518m., 1,700 feet).

The Taza Gap

Some geologists maintain that the Taza Gap is the true frontier between Europe and Africa, as the Straits of Gibraltar are an accident caused by the collapse of land into the sea and not a "structural" feature of the earth at all. Thus the Rif mountains become a prolongation of the Spanish Sierra Nevada, and in the totally unpolitical view of the geologists are European mountains. Some startling evidence backs up this theory—somewhat akin to the rare experience of seeing it rain on one side of the street and not the other. A few miles before the Touahar Pass you can see for yourself: to the left is the north and the Rif; here the earth is nearly white—while to the south and right it is reddish, the color of the Middle Atlas; the space between is not more than 18m. (60 feet).

Before the pass, S311 branches right at Sidi Abdallah for the Jebel Tazzeka Circuit, through the restful green of the Alpine landscape south of PI. It is possible to drive close to the 1,971 m. (6,500 feet) high summit of Jebel Tazekka, from which the view extends from Fez to Guercif. An easier road leads through splendid cedars to the bracing air of the holiday camp of Bab Bou Idir, at a height of 1,450 m. (4,756 feet). Then come the deep gorges and the caves of Chiker, and especially the cavern of Friouato reached after a comparatively easy descent. The impression of depth at the foot of the cyclopean walls is overwhelming, and an eerie twilight adds to the striking effect. The Friouato is the deepest cave in North Africa, and one of the world's five deepest (245 m., 803 feet). The Speleology Club of Taza has mapped out and even added some amenities to the enormous chambers beneath the earth.

Along the final miles of P1 are remains of prehistoric villages and of course Roman garrisons were once stationed there. The succeeding Islamic dynasties all recognized the importance of Taza; the Almohad Sultan Abd al-Mumin gave it its walls and its great mosque; and the Merinid Abu Yakub not only strengthened its ramparts and defenses but added beautiful monuments. The founder of the present dynasty, the Alaouit Moulay Rashid, made it his first capital before repeating history by going on from Taza to conquer Fez and then the rest of the country.

Taza thus holds attractive memories of the past, like the medina with the Andalusian mosque topped by a 13th-century minaret, the early 14th-century Merinid medersa, and the great mosque. Better than the monuments is the location itself, for Taza is a cliff-hanger town, whose ramparts are often built just above the sheer drop. A walk around these fortifications which circle the medina affords fine views over the new town in the fertile plain below, framed by the vast screen of the Rif which extends as far as the Mediterranean to the north. To the south stretch olive groves and orchards, watered by little streams.

You can reach the Mediterranean at Al Hoceima from Taza via Aknoul by crossing the eastern end of the Rif.

The Road to the Border

Communication with the north is getting easier on approaching the Algerian border as the Rif recedes. But the first branch to Nador is only a piste from Guercif, in the center of Morocco's sheep-raising country and a halt on the steppes which go on almost uninterrupted into Algeria. In ancient times it was known as Galafa and has served as a battlefield since Ptolemy's time. When the Saharans came up from their oasis in the Tafilalet, they joined battle with the northern forces on this plain, won, and eventually gained control of the country.

At Guercif we cross the Oued Moulouya, Morocco's longest river, before venturing into the desert steppes. Taourirt, 48 km. (30 miles) northeast, also served more than once as a battlefield, as the Kasbah of Moulay Ismail (to the left of the road) testifies. From Taourirt S605 branches north to the artificial lake Mohammed V (Mechra Kelila) and soon afterwards S412 crosses the Moulouya at the Mechra Hommadi dam, through flat country to Nador, since the Rif has at last subsided.

There is only one more village before Oujda—El Aioune. The road is like an endless ribbon with the lifeless plain stretching to the distant hills on either side. This infinite flatness is no place to be at noon on a summer day.

Oujda is the capital of eastern Morocco. During the Middle Ages Oujda was the capital of the eastern kingdom established by the Zenata tribe, but it was the Almoravids who built fortifications before setting out to conquer western Algeria in the early 11th century. Unfortunately for Oujda, its location made it always someone's military rear or advance position throughout six hundred years; and it was only in the beginning of the 19th century that Moulay Slimane brought it under Moroccan control for good.

Contrary to the pattern in the rest of the kingdom, the medina and the modern town intermingled without any outstanding landmarks along the broad flowered avenues. The most pleasant feature is the Laila Aicha Park. Oujda's present importance stems from its proximity to the Algerian frontier on the east-west trade route, intersected by the north-south axis, to the splendid beach of Saïda on the Mediterranean, connected through the Rif with Tangier, and due south to Figuig at the edge of the Sahara.

PRACTICAL INFORMATION FOR THE REGION

GETTING THERE. The Rif: By Bus. Six times daily between Tangier and Tetouan (departure from the Avenue des F.A.R.). There is also a less regular direct bus service for Restinga-Smir, Ketama and Al Hoceima. Tetouan is the starting point for buses to all destinations on the Rif, also for the seven-hour haul to Casablanca, daily service. A few distances by road: Tangier–Al Hoceima 330 km. (205 miles); Tangier–Melilla 515 km. (320 miles); Chechaouen-Ceuta 105 km. (65 miles); Al Hoceima–Melilla 183 km. (114 miles); Fez–Ketama 161 km. (100 miles); Rabat–Chechaouen via Ouezzane 241 km. (150 miles).

Direct buses link most major cities of Morocco with both Taza and Oujda. There is one bus a day from Meknès and Fez. From Oujda there are direct buses to the beach at Saïdia: an hour and a half, or two hours Berkane.

By Plane. Several services a week from Paris and other French cities to Oujda by Royal Air Maroc and Air France, one via Al Hoceima and some going on to Casablanca. Some charter flights from Germany. Daily flights to Casablanca, less frequent to other Moroccan towns.

Several flights per week between Al Hoceima, Tetouan, Oujda and Casablanca. Four flights daily from Málaga to Melilla, once daily from Almería.

By Ferry. At least five ferries daily from Algeciras to Ceuta, double in summer. Daily ferries from Almería and Málaga to Ceuta and Melilla.

By Train: East of Fez. Rabat–Taza at least 6½ hours, Oujda 3 hours more. There is a sleeping car service on the night train which has an immediate connection to Algeria when the border is open. 2 hours to Tlemcen; 5 hours to Oran, and about 11 hours to Algiers with a change at Oran.

By Car. An adequate west-east axis links Tangier via Tetouan, Chechaouen, Ketama, Al Hoceima, Nador, Berkane to Oujda on the Algerian border. This is paralleled further south by the faster, less mountainous P1 from Rabat via Meknès, Fez, Taza, Taourirt, El Aïoun to Oujda. The best north-south connections between the two are at the extremes, Tetouan to Meknès or Fez, Saïda to Oujda. Ketama via Taounate to Fez and Talamagait via Aknoul to Taza, as well as the west-east Taounate over the Col du Nador to Aknoul are difficult in rain or snow, but not the shorter link from the Selouane junction over the Oued Moulouya to east of Taourirt.

Beside the roads from Tetouane to Ceuta, and from Ceuta to El Jebha along the Mediterranean, there are branch roads to the major beaches.

Distances By Car. Fez–Taza 121 km. (75 miles); Taza–Oujda 225 km. (140 miles); Casablanca–Oujda 636 km. (395 miles); Tangier–Oujda 660 km. (410 miles); Oujda–Saïdia via Ahfir 61 km. (38 miles), or via Taforalt and Berkane 100 km. (62 miles); Oujda–Tlemcen 87 km. (54 miles); Oujda–Oran 275 km. (171 miles); Oujda–Algiers 623 km. (387 miles).

HOTELS AND RESTAURANTS

Al Hoceima. (Area Code 098) Insufficient accommodations for such a good beach. *El Maghreb El Jadid* (M), tel. 25 04; 40 rooms. *Karim* (M), tel. 21 84; 51 rooms. *Mohammed V* (M), tel. 22 33; 34 rooms, pool, tennis. *Quemado* (M), tel. 23 71; 102 rooms, pool. Part of the Maroc-Tourist chain. This is a clean place with good service. *National* (I), tel. 24 31; 16 rooms, no restaurant. Three small (I)s not recommended.

About 16 km. (10 miles) east, the *Club Méditerranée* (M), tel. 20 20, has its largest establishment in Morocco with 1200 beds in simple thatched huts. Facilities include excellent swimming pool, water sports, fishing, hunting, tennis, riding, sailing, etc. Open May–Oct.

Berkane. *Laetizia* (I); 13 rooms.

Cabo Negro. (Area Code 091). *Petit Merou* (M), tel. 781 15; 23 rooms. Trying so hard to look like a Rif village that hardly two rooms are on the same floor. The Club Méditerranée's *Yasmina* (M), tel. 780 95/99, is their most elegant establishment in the north of Morocco; 300 rooms, waterskiing, fishing, hunting, tennis, riding, sailing, excellent pool, etc. Open May–Oct.

Chechaouen. (Area Code 098). *Chaouen* (E), tel. 61 36; 37 rooms, pool. Part of Maroc-Tourist chain. *Magou* (M), tel. 62 75; 27 rooms. *Rif* (I), tel. 62 07; 20 rooms.

On the main road below, the *Asma* (M), tel. 60 02; 94 rooms, pool. Part of Kasbah Tours chain.

Guercif. *Des Voyageurs* (I). In an emergency.

Ketama. *Tidighine* (M), tel. 16 10; at the junction of the Route du Rif (P39) and the S302 leading to Fez. 70 rooms. Pool, golf course, tennis. Maroc-Tourist.

M'Diq. (Area Code 091). Between Restinga-Smir and Cabo Negro. *Golden Beach* (E), tel. 750 77; 81 rooms, beach, pool, disco. *Kabila* (E), tel. 750 71; 64 rooms, beach, pool. Book well in advance. *Playa* (I), tel. 75 66; 21 rooms.

Two (M) complexes: the *Holiday Club,* tel. 85 45, and *Parc Hotel Méditerranée,* tel. 85 24; each with 300 bungalows. Reservations cannot normally be made locally, but only as part of package tours. Try the new *Club M'Diq* (M), Route de Sebta, tel. 750 55; 300 rooms, restaurant, nightclub, and tennis courts.

Nador. (Area Code 060). *Mansour Ed-Dahab* (M), tel. 65 85; 54 rooms. *Rif* (M), tel. 65 35; 64 rooms, pool, tennis and better-than-average restaurant. Maroc-Tourist.

Oujda. (Area code 068.) *El Massira* (E), Blvd. Maghreb Al Arabi (tel. 53 01/03). 180 airconditioned rooms; quiet, pool. *Terminus* (E), Place de l'Unité Africaine (tel. 32 11), near the railway station. 177 rooms, airconditioned wing, tiny pool.

Lutetia (M), Blvd. Hassan Loukili (tel. 33 65), near the station. 40 rooms; good value, no pretensions, but no restaurant either.

Restaurants. *Coupole* (M), off Blvd. Mohammed V. *De France* (M), Blvd. Mohammed V. Good food and service in attractive surroundings; better-than-average.

Restinga-Smir. (Area Code 09). North of M'Diq, on the same magnificent, long, sandy beach. Maroc-Tourist's holiday complex with a capacity of 500 beds comprises *Karabo* (E), tel. 77070; 24 rooms, and *Boustane* (E), tel. 770 02; 91 rooms, marina, nightclub, tennis courts and pool.

The Club Méditerranée's *Smir* (M), tel. 770 36 or 771 46; consists of two hotels and small family chalets with a capacity of 750 beds. Facilities include almost everything—sailing, scuba diving, tennis, volleyball, pool, judo, nightclub, excursions. Is especially comfortable for families with children. Open June–Oct.

Saïdia. (Area code 061). *Hannour* (M), tel. 51 15; 9 rooms. *Al Kalaa* (M), tel. 51 23; 33 rooms. *Front de Mer* (I), tel. 51 55; 52 rooms in holiday village on beach. *Select* (I), tel. 51 10; 18 rooms.

Selouane. Restaurant. *Brabe* (M), European cooking. Near junction of P39 and P27.

Sidi Harazem. (Area Code 06). *Sidi Harazem* (M), tel. 455 25; 64 rooms. In the P.L.M. chain. Close to spa.

Taza. (Area Code 067). *Friouato* (M), tel. 25 93; 58 rooms, pool. A Salam hotel on the outskirts of the new town. *Dauphiné* (M), tel. 35 67; 35 rooms, 15 baths. Central.

Restaurant. The *Brasserie* (I) is possible for simple meals.

Tetouan. (Area code 096.) *Safir* (E), Ave. Kennedy, below the town (tel. 70 177). 98 rooms; pool, tennis. *Paris* (M), Rue Chakib Arsalan (tel. 67 50), 41 rooms.

Restaurants. The Nacional's restaurant, *Zerhoun* (M), is adequate. *Italiano* (I) and *Samy* (I) in the same street. *Bricha Palace* at Bab el Okba for Moroccan food. *Economique* (I) and *Familiale* (I) in Mohammed V.

In Spanish Territory

Ceuta (Sebta). *Gran Hotel Ulises* (E), Camoens (tel. 51 45 40). 124 rooms, nightclub, pool. *La Muralla* (E), Plaza de Africa (tel. 51 49 40). 83 airconditioned rooms, nightclub. *Africa* (M), in the port (tel. 51 41 40); 39 rooms. *Miramar* (M), tel. 51 41 46; 22 rooms. *Skol* (M), tel. 51 41 48; 16 rooms.

Two very simple pensions: *Málaga* (I), tel. 51 18 50, 7 rooms; and the *Oriente* (I), tel. 51 11 15, 6 rooms.

Restaurants. *Muralla* (E) is the best restaurant. *La Campaña* (M), José Antonio. *Casa Fernando* (M), at Playa de Benitez, towards the top of the price category. *Delfín Verde* (M), in the port, also at the top of the (M) range. *Mesón de Serafín* (M) and *Oasis* (M) are on Monte Hacho. *Vicente* (M), José Antonio.

The leading cafeteria is *Milord,* Plaza de Africa and best nightclub *El Candelaro,* Puente del Cristo.

Melilla (Mlilya to Moroccans). The *Parador Don Pedro de Estopinan* (E), tel. 68 49 40; 27 rooms, is outstanding.

Among a half dozen (M) hotels the better ones are *Anfona,* tel. 68 33 40, 147 rooms; *Avenida,* tel. 68 49 49, 78 rooms; and *Rusadir San Miguel,* tel. 68 12 40, 27 rooms.

Restaurants. The leading restaurants include *La Choza Barbacón, Estación, Granada Salazoner, Marítima, Nápoli* and *Las Palmeras.*

SPORTS. Excellent underwater **fishing** all along Mediterranean coast. Best bases are at Ksar es Serhir, Restinga, Pointe des Pêcheurs (El Jebha), Peñón de Velez, Al Hoceima. **Swimming** at Martil, M'Diq, Oued Laou, Cabo Negro and Restinga, all near Tetouan, and at Al Hoceima where rocky escarpments overlook the beaches named Esfeha, Souani, Boussikir and El Quemado.

USEFUL ADDRESSES. Tourist Information: O.N.M.T. (National Tourist Office), 30 Ave. Mohammed V, **Tetouan;** Place 16 Aout, **Oujda.** At **Taza,** Syndicat d'Initiative at the Chamber of Commerce. At **Tetouan,** Royal Air Maroc and Air Inter, 5 Ave. Mohammed V, at **Oujda,** Blvd. Mohammed V, as also is Wagons-Lits Tourisme (for reservations on the overnight train to Casablanca).

THE MIDDLE ATLAS

Land of Murmuring Springs

The itinerary below starts from Fez, though as the Middle Atlas is dead center in Morocco, it would be just as easy to explore by starting out from Rabat (via Meknès), from Casablanca (via Oued Zem and Kasbah-Tadla), or even from the south coming from Marrakesh.

The Berber tribes of the Middle Atlas bear musical names like Guerouane, Beni Mtir, Zaïans, Beni Mguild—to mention only the most important ones. Their main occupation, like that of countless generations before them, is sheep raising. They live in a beautiful setting of mountains whose slopes are thick with cedar, oak or pine forests; where rocky springs bubble over to feed silvery trout streams, and lakes and ponds are blue against the red earth—but their life is far from idyllic. In this Moroccan Arcadia snowfalls are frequent, and though you may think of the kingdom as a place where the sun never stops shining, there are villages which can remain snowbound and isolated for weeks on end. In January and February, seven feet of snow is common, but fortunately the Berbers need not suffer all the rigors they once did, for helicopters are now sent to drop supplies.

History here is not a recital of wars and dynasties and empire building as in other parts of the realm. The Berber character and also their language have kept them aloof to some degree from the rest of the country. They speak a dialect called Tamazight, although Arabic and French are understood and used officially. The Middle Atlas has always been a trouble spot for anyone who hoped to control the whole of Morocco. These mountain people have been prompt to revolt against any form of oppression, and were always the last to give in—even the French protectorate spent 20

143

years before it could call the Middle Atlas its own. These proud people bow only before the guest, and hospitality is a sacred duty which they fulfill in style. In fact, the Berbers and their landscape—robust and bracing yet welcoming too—seem made for each other.

The Tadla, the foothills and plain in the southwest, is dominated by Kasba Tadla built by Moulay Ismail, on the Oued-Oum-er-Rbia.

Following the Flock

Heading south from Fez, Imouzzer du Kandar is the first of several towns up in the mountain greenery—very refreshing indeed after the Sais Plain we have just crossed. This is already Berber country; the special domain of the Ait Seghrouchene tribe, though the fishermen and seekers of summer coolness hardly notice them and head instead for the Dayet Aoua, the little lake to the left of the road. Underground water reservoirs feed numerous streams and lakes which give the area a pleasant aspect with orchards, meadows and woodlands.

From here on, thickets, woods and forests are constant companions until we reach Ifrane, the most popular mountain resort in Morocco, at the edge of a river bearing its name. The royal family gave the final accolade to Ifrane by building a princely chalet.

In summer, the 1,655 m. (5,431-foot) altitude ensures coolness for trout-fishing in the Oued Tizguit, for hikes into the woods, and for longer expeditions on horseback; while, as soon as the first snows have fallen, the ski crowd foregathers for the winter sports season. Snowfields like the Michlifen close by or the Jebel Hebri and Jebel Abri farther on (also accessible from Azrou) attract sports enthusiasts; and since this is not ski country where you need three sweaters and a parka, sunbaths and exercise are wholly compatible. These three slopes all have ski lifts and refuges. If you see someone in uniform go flashing by, it's sure to be a member of the Royal Moroccan Army's élite ski corps. If necessary they help out in case of accident or other emergency.

The secondary road from Ifrane to Boulemane will take you even higher, to the Tizi N'Tretten plateau (nearly 1,934 m., 6,345 ft.), which has a wild beauty quite different from that of Ifrane, and also the best view of this part of the Middle Atlas. Since the sheep is one of the most important elements in the life of every Moslem farmer, it is not surprising that a religious feast in which each family sacrifices a sheep (its head turned in the direction of Mecca) should be an important celebration each year. This is the Aid el Kebir, commemorating Abraham's willingness to sacrifice his son, Isaac. The ceremony is often performed communally on the plateau of Tizi N'Tretten, where innumerable sheep that will later be slaughtered are raised. With the shepherd wrapped in his brown striped jellaba and his dog at the head of the procession, the vast bleating herd stumbles down the mountainside towards the tender spring grass of the valley.

This valley of the Oued Guigou, in the heart of the rocky wooded country, makes it evident why the Middle Atlas has always been next to impossible to conquer and hold. The tallest peaks of the range are in this neighborhood, like the summit of Lalla Oum el Bent (just as you pass the forest house at Tihrboula) which rises to a height of over 2,800 m. (9,186 feet).

The road itself follows the gorges of Recifa, heads upwards again over the Souiguer Pass (1,952 m., 6,404 ft.) crossing the great divide which marks the separation between the waters which flow into the Mediterranean or into the Atlantic, and finally decides to return to the plain; at least until it joins the main road from Azrou to Midelt just a few miles from Itzer.

Itzer is a big Berber kasbah, before another uphill drive towards the Zad Pass (2,087 m., 6,845 ft.), where evergreen oaks and cedars grow thick. Here we make a very short detour to the right in order to see the aguelmane (mountain lake) of Sidi Ali; the biggest in the Middle Atlas. Since this lake lies in the crater of a volcano, it is very deep and also full of fish, particularly the succulent grayling, a variety of trout.

P21 heads north to Azrou, the Rock, which rises—though not very high—in the center of a typical Berber town built like an amphitheater on the mountainside. It would be profitable for both you and the Berbers to visit the House of Craftsmanship (Maison de l'Artisanat), where woodcarvings and carpets are on show. The Benj Mguild tribe has plenty of time to lavish on weaving and carving—those snowy winter evenings can be long indeed—and the result is at the same time naive and elegant.

From Azrou to Meknès P21 crosses a bleak plateau culminating in the strange moonscape you can see from Ito. From El Hajeb, on the cliff that overlooks the Meknès plain, a few hairpin turns descend to the plain, and after witnessing the hard life of the mountain folk, it's quite a shock to see all those rich fields and vineyards and white-washed farms again.

But we rejoin P24 at Azrou on its southwesterly course, to branch off to the left for Ain Leuh, past Tioumliline, which was the only Benedictine monastery in Morocco. During the years of Morocco's struggle for separation from France it served as a bridge between the two peoples. After independence the Benedictines left, and the monastery buildings now house a technical school.

Monkey and Other Business

Ain Leuh lies in the heart of a forest where the pines and green oaks are dwarfed by the centuries-old cedars which here reach a height of 100 to 130 ft. An enormous tribe of practical-joking and extremely touchy monkeys live in this forest. They do not like to be approached and are very good at launching a variety of guided missiles at those who hope to get a closer look at them.

The next lonely 35 km. (23 miles) of track, to the south of Ain Leuh, lead to the source of the Oum-er-Rbia, one of the country's most important waterways. Many other streams have their birthplace at this point: there are numerous springs—the most spectacular among them leaps over a sheer cliff to become a waterfall before deciding to be a more prosaic river. The other springs seem bent on imitating it and form brooklets swarming with trout.

After Mrirt, P24 follows the Oum-er-Rbia to pleasantly shady Khenifra, headquarters of the Zaïan tribe. The Zaïans are formidable horsemen who love to compete on the local racetrack. Near Zaouia Ech-Cheikh another huge dam is under construction.

P24 descends into the plain; the first turn-off left (south) leads back into the mountains to El Ksiba, a little summer resort where the tents sprout like mushrooms when vacation time comes, but the rest of the year there are far more monkeys than humans in the environs—the woods seem alive with their screams and trapeze-artist antics. El Ksiba is also the gateway to the lake plateau: if you have time you should take the 113-km. (70-mile) track which snakes slowly southward across the mountains. Here it's really back to nature: outside of an occasional Berber hamlet or a small caravan of donkeys clip-clopping towards Arhbala or Bou Mia, there is nothing to trouble your contemplation of a landscape of jagged rocks, oak groves and pine woods. As the track heads south, it also heads upward until, in the neighborhood of Imilchil, it reaches the lake plateau.

Somber purple mountains serve as a backdrop to the plateau, 1,980 m., (6,500 feet) high, where life is hard and vegetation sparse. The people of the remote villages are an impenetrable and incomprehensible race. Here and there the deep blue stillness of a lake dots the landscape. Two of these lakes, the largest, are lovers, betrothed since the dawn of memory. Her name is Tislit, his is Isli—and they must long for each other eternally for they cannot join together. And yet, each year they witness the betrothal and marriage of dozens of their protegés of the Ait Addidou tribe. Each year in September this Berber clan gathers at Imilchil for a moussem which is rapidly growing from a huge family fête into a tourist attraction since the Ait Addidou's moussem is doubled by a sort of marriage mart.

The families are there to watch over the proceedings—they have set up their big chieftains' tents, and the shop-keepers are sure of selling some wedding presents. Soon the beat of tambourines is heard in the center of the crowd, and the dancing begins. But the young man of marriageable age is too nervous to dance. He is wandering around in his white jellaba with a shining silver ornamental dagger. The young lady is no less decked out in a long brown striped robe which covers her body but leaves no mystery as to her face. She wears as much jewelry as her family's station permits—but always a bandeau of coins across her forehead. When two kindred souls meet, they walk hand-in-hand among the crowd now and then looking at the acrobats, but mostly looking timidly at each other. Though the young people are free to choose each other, the families move in en masse when it's time to discuss the marriage contract. An *adoul* (public notary) registers all the contracts, and that evening a new couple joins the dance of the Ait Addidou.

From the lake plateau you can take the Agoudal track still farther to the south towards the gorges of the Todra and Tinerhir. There is some fiercely rough driving, but the country is practically uninhabited and savagely beautiful.

Water Galore

In the plain, at the junction of P24 to Marrakesh and P13 to Casablanca lies Kasba Tadla. Moulay Ismail built the stern kasbah on the rocks above the Oum-er-Rbia towards the end of the 17th century as an army post for keeping an eye, and possibly an iron hand, on the Berber people of the Tadla. The fortress is a handsome example of military architecture and encloses two mosques within its walls. The best overall view of the site is from the left bank of the Oum-er-Rbia.

32 km. (20 miles) south, Beni Mellal is attractively situated between the plain of the Beni Amir and the Tadla hills, fringed with gardens and olive groves. After a few miles along P24, S508 branches left (south) to Ouaouizarht, whose weekly market is quite a sight when the mountain tribes come down with their "shopping lists."

S508 skirts the vast lake created by the dam at Bin-el-Ouidane, an enormous piece of masonry which took seven years to complete (1948–55) and changed the face of the entire region. The first of the huge dams that are still being constructed all over Morocco. French engineers built concrete walls over 128 m. (420 feet) high which flooded the valley upstream under 1,3000,000,000 cubic meters of water. At the foot of the dam is an electrical generating plant, but after the water has passed through its turbines it is channeled towards a second, smaller dam, then sent through the heart of the mountain in a tunnel seven and a half miles long. A forced conduit sends the water hurtling over the edge of the cliff to the plain below, where a second generating plant at Afourar takes over. Then the water of the Oued-el-Abid is channeled into two enormous concrete canals which are the basis of an irrigation system covering 325,000 acres, on which the semi-nomadic Beni Amir and Beni Moussa tribes have been transformed into modern farmers.

Ascending from Bin-el-Ouidane to the mountain top which rises above Afourar, on the return loop of S508 northward to P24, the two long concrete life-lines on the vast plain below are very clear.

A spectacular alternative is to continue on the S508 to Azilal, a typical village of the Tadla above a peaceful plain. From Azilal there is another worthwhile excursion, to the rock cathedral and the fascinating and austere zaouia of Ahansal. Still further south, S508 provides also the easiest approach to the Ouzoud Falls of the Oued el Abid. A steep path descends towards a canyon whose vertical sides are nearly 107 m. (350 feet) tall and completely covered with ivy and climbing green plants. The water rushes over the brink of the cliff and falls into a natural basin, then separates into two streams before dropping into the river bed below. Here thousands of years of erosion have created stone bathing pools of different shapes and sizes and the water jumps playfully from one to another before hurrying into the rapids downstream. As if the scene were not romantic enough, turtle doves nest and coo in the ivy behind the cascades of water.

The piste continues fairly comfortably north via Aït Attab to P24, but returning to S508 offers the quaint town of Tanant and the fine view on the surrounding high plateau and jebel, while just south of Demnate, at an altitude of over 915 m. (3,000 feet), is Imi N'Ifri where the little river has carved out a sort of tunnel inhabited by hundreds of crows. These black birds seemed like evil omens to the hill folk who tell fearful legends of how they came to roost there. The natural bridge of Imi N'Ifri is the site of an annual moussem whose traditions are more rooted in ancient superstition than in monotheistic religion.

Double back 10 km. (6 miles) to S508 which continues west across the Oued Tessaout to rejoin P24 near Tamlelt in the Haouz Plain northeast of Marrakesh.

PRACTICAL INFORMATION FOR
THE MIDDLE ATLAS

WHEN TO GO. Imouzzer du Kandar, 36 km. (22 miles) from Fez, lies at an altitude of 1,280 m. (4,200 ft.) at the edge of a plateau, itself at the edge of the Middle Atlas. A pleasant place when the heat gets you down—but the smart place is Ifrane where the King has a palatial chalet. Ifrane was created as a resort during the nineteen thirties and has an ideal climate and altitude (1,650 m., 5,413 ft.). In the summer, the plain dwellers (or at least the wealthiest among them) head for the cool, restful vistas of Ifrane, and need only return to the cities for a change of clothes before coming back for the skiing season.

Average temperatures during the winter range from 37° to 50°F., and the sun almost always smiles on the ski slopes. But beware! The lowest temperature in Ifrane was minus 15 degrees Fahrenheit, or 47 degrees below freezing! Azrou, which means 'the Rock' in Berber is lower (1,250 m., 4,101 ft.), amidst cedars and oak forests, and more temperate in climate.

GETTING THERE. By C.T.M. Buses. Casablanca–Ifrane–Azrou via Meknès takes 6 hours; Meknès to Midelt via Azrou 4½ hours.

By Car. The main roads in the Middle Atlas are practicable in all seasons. To get into the "backwoods" country there is an intricate system of dirt roads (pistes) which take the traveler right to the heart of the cedar and oak forests. If you don't try to get about in an actual blizzard, we can assure you that the way will be cleared within a short time after even the heavy snowfalls, since the region has motorized snowplows and sanding equipment. The third-rate roads are best left unlooked-at during winter, but are perfectly negotiable from April to November. You would be well advised not to try the more adventurous roads in a vehicle with low clearance.

The picturesque circuit from Beni Mellal climbs up to the R'Nim Pass, goes on to Ouaouizarkt and the backwater of the Bin-el-Ouidane dam, heads into the Middle Atlas as far as Azilal, and leaves a choice as to the return road: on paved roads via the Ait Ouarda dam and Afourar, or by the Ouzoud waterfalls on C1811, a very rough 27 km. (17 miles). Coming from Marrakesh, good secondary roads take you to Demnate and to the natural bridge of Imi N'Ifri. Secondary road 1901 south of El Ksiba is worth the short detour.

Some distances—Rabat–Ifrane via Meknès 209 km. (130 miles); Meknès–Azrou 68 km. (42 miles); Fez–Ifrane via Imouzzer 60 km. (37 miles); Ifrane–Khenifra 100km. (62 miles).

HOTELS AND RESTAURANTS

Ait Isshaq. *Transatlas* (M), via Khenifra, tel. 30. 25 airconditioned rooms, pool. For mountain holidays.

Azrou. *Panorama* (M), tel. 20 10. 39 rooms, 12 showers. In the new town a little off the main road; fine view, as the name suggests. *Azrou* (I), tel. 21 16. 10 rooms, 5 showers.

Beni Mellal. *Chems* (E), Route de Marrakech, tel. 34 60. 77 airconditioned rooms; pool in large garden. *Ouzoud* (E), Route de Marrakech (tel. 37 52). 60 rooms, airconditioning, pool. Best in the region and part of the P.L.M. chain.

De Paris (I), tel. 22 45. 9 rooms, all with showers. *Gharnatta* (I), tel. 34 82. 14 rooms, 6 showers. *Vieux Moulin* (I), Route de Kasba Tadla (tel. 27 88). 10 rooms; best food of the (I) hotels.

Bin-el-Ouidane. *Du Lac* (I). 42 rooms, no private baths but good restaurant.

Dayet Aoua. *Chalet du Lac* (M). 26 rooms, 20 with showers; lavatory at end of hall. Most rooms overlook the lake and delightful scenery. Traditional French cooking. Fishing and boating.

El Hajeb. *Les Peupliers* (I), Ave. Mohammed V. 30 rooms, half with bath. *Les Rochers* (I). 16 rooms. Rudimentary.

El Kelaa Des Sraghna (on Beni Mellai route to Marrakesh). *Capa Club* (E), tel. 334 29 or 332 96. There are 150 comfortable rooms in this new luxury holiday village; restaurants, heated pool, sports facilities.

El Ksiba. *Hostellerie Henri IV* (M), tel. 2. 18 rooms, 4 showers. Pool.

Ifrane. Insufficient accommodations for both summer and winter seasons. *Michlifen* (L), tel. 66 07 or 66 21. 95 rooms, some with TV. This is the main hotel in the area for skiers. Stands on hill in its own grounds; pool.
Grand (M), tel. 64 07. 30 rooms; recently refurbished. *Perce Neige* (M), tel. 63 50. 30 rooms. *Les Tilleuls,* Unclassified hotels include *Au Coin de France* and *des Chasseurs.*
Restaurants. Most are closed from Oct. 1 to Dec. 1. *Altitude 1,600* (M) is a (nearly) mountain top restaurant open during the season.

Imouzzer du Kandar. *Royal* (M), tel. 630 80. 42 rooms, 35 showers; a clean, simple hotel with a friendly staff. *des Truites* (M), tel. 630 02. 20 rooms, 8 showers. *De Repos* and *Kandar* not classified.
Restaurant. Meals or snacks at the *Brasserie Royale* (M).

Khenifra. *Hamou Azzayani* (E), tel. 60 20. 60 airconditioned rooms. Pool. In Salam chain.

Chouribga. *Safir* (E), tel. 20 13. 76 airconditioned rooms. Pool.

Oued Zem. *Au Petit Chez Soi* (I). A decent enough restaurant. Some rooms.

Sefrou. *Sidi Lahcen Lyoussi* (M), tel. 604 97. 22 rooms, pool.

Settat. *M'zamza* (M), tel. 23 66. 32 rooms. Adequate for anyone wishing to spend a night in so unlikely a place.

SPORTS. Fishermen will find lively trout in the Aïn Leuh, Ifrane, Tigriga Oueds and their tributaries. Foreign imports which have thrived in the Middle Atlas streams include pike, perch and American black bass. Around Imouzzer the various lakes (known as aguelmanes or daiets) will also send you home with a full creel.
The Michlifen, 16 km. (10 miles) from Ifrane, was a volcanic crater a few million years back, but is now one of Morocco's best **skiing** areas, equipped with a jump and lifts. Near Azrou, the Tizi Hebri and the Jebel Hebri are dotted with ski slopes and furnished with lifts or tows. You'll find a welcoming lodge with restaurant at these places. The Middle Atlas is also a fascinating and adventurous place for longer skiing trips.

FROM CASABLANCA
TO AGADIR

The Atlantic Seaboard

The commercial capital in the center and the biggest beach resort in the south are joined by a road 523 km. (325 miles) long. This is Morocco's doorway to the Atlantic, but the outside world has never had an easy time passing through that door: navigation is treacherous and ports are few. The people of the coast have never been seamen, and frequently they cannot even be fishermen. There are long stretches where the fine sandy beaches remain deserted, as the undertow can be murderous. However, towards Agadir, the rock and sand bars disappear, little fishing communities nestle by the sea, and their boats make the beach more welcoming.

The inhospitality of both coasts provided a natural protection against invasion from the sea as only the bravest mariners could get a foothold there; the first were the Carthaginians under the leadership of Hanno, the first to chart the coastline. It was fifteen hundred years before another nation of navigators, the Portuguese, managed to invade this natural stronghold.

There is almost no vestige of the Carthaginians, but the Portuguese left their stamp on many of the cities of the seaboard, building citadels at El Jadida, Safi, Essaouria and Agadir whose histories are full of blood and thunder; yet, strangely, these European fortifications look perfectly natural in their North African setting. Yet it was through the towns of this coast that Morocco became known in Europe—and a Frenchman,

Auguste Broussonet, wrote the ancestor of this and other guides in 1797 which he called *On the Usefulness of a Voyage of Discovery into the Interior of Morocco.*

All along the coast sand dunes, pebbly hillocks and stunted bushes face up to the sea winds. But these same winds make the climate as healthy as you're likely to find in this world—constant sun with temperatures between 15° and 30° C. (60° and 85°F.).

The White Capital of the Doukkalas

The Doukkala plain along the coast southwest of Casablanca, as well as the Chaouia plain to the south, provide easy access, and the relative fertility to feed the dense population. The road towards Agadir crosses the Doukkala, flat and dull perhaps compared to some of Morocco's spectacular scenery, but affluent. Whether you take inland P8 or the narrow coast road (usually cut off from the sea by sand dunes) you'll see the farms that produce Morocco's tiny and delicious spring vegetables, its brilliant tomatoes which are exported all over Europe; and farther on the grain and fodder crops. The latter go to feed the livestock which also flourishes on the Doukkala plain and which ranges from the chicken to the bull!

These 80 flat km. (50 miles) finally ascend a tiny hill, then suddenly we see the mouth of the Oum-er-Rbia and, on top of an ocher cliff, the whole city of Azemmour. Nowhere more than here does the history of this coast come alive. The Carthaginians came first and called their new stronghold Azama. When their civilization waned, the town remained protected for centuries by the almost intractable Atlantic. But this peace came to an end at the close of the 15th century when the Portuguese arrived, established a trading post, and forced the city to pay tribute. Fifty years later, the Portuguese hoped to extend their influence in Morocco and sailed to the gates of Azemmour with a formidable Armada of 500 ships, but were compelled to evacuate the town less than forty years later.

Later Azemmour became the capital of the Doukkala plain, but history and economics stripped her of this title in favor of El Jadida. Lying like the Sleeping Beauty behind rundown walls, Azemmour is still worth an hour's visit and some color film.

After Azemmour you cross a eucalyptus forest, but more attractive is the narrow coastal road above the magnificent golden sands stretching the 11 km. (7 miles) from Haouzia, Azemmour's beach, to El Jadida on the huge bay's southern promontory.

The Portuguese occupied El Jadida in 1502 and, thanks to their powerful fortifications, were not evicted until 1769, by Sultan Sidi Mohammed ben Abdallah. The old Portuguese town, surrounded by 16th-century walls with four bastions called Angel, St. Sebastian, St. Anthony and Holy Spirit, is entered by the Governor's Gate, above which is the coat of arms of Luis de Loureiro, the Portuguese governor from 1541 to 1551. The tour of the ramparts is combined with a visit to the huge underground cistern (open daily 8–12; 2–6), a nearly square (33 by 34 meters; 107 by 110 ft.) Gothic hall whose multiple arches are supported by 25 pillars. The hall is paved in brick and lighted by a circular opening nearly 12 ft. across. Before the conquerors were really sure of themselves it served as their armory, but when the colony grew, it was transformed into a cistern. The Portuguese port is no longer deep enough to harbor ships. Notice the old water gate which was the town's only access during the long sieges by tribes from the interior. The same sandflow which has made the port impracticable has made the beautiful beach of El Jadida one of the safest on the Atlantic coast.

A Fortress Through Rose-Colored Glasses

A detour of about 48 km. (30 miles) will take you to the Kasbah of Boulaouane, a lonely and impressive fortress which stands brooding above the broad curves of the Oum-er-Rbia crowning an admirable landscape. The inscription on the lintel above the monumental gate reminds us that the castle was completed in 1710 by that great soldier Moulay Ismail, the builder of Meknès. It was intended to serve as a royal palace with a mosque and great storerooms.

The terrorized subjects of Boulaouane had nothing to offer their ruler when he honored their town with his presence, so in lieu of gifts, they presented him with the most beautiful young girl of the neighborhood. Apparently it was a good choice, for the next morning Moulay Ismail presented the girl with all the land the eye could see from the Kasbah's topmost tower. The Kasbah's other claim to fame besides its magnificent site and massive, forbidding architecture is the delicious rosé wine known as *Gris de Boulaouane.*

Greatly preferable to the dull inland P8 between El Jadida and Safi is the coastal S121, hugging the Atlantic. It passes the lovely beach of Sidi Bousid and the huge shrine of Moulay Abdellah, where, during the Saint's Moussem in August, an enormous tent town of pilgrims recalls the Middle Ages down to the utter lack of sanitation. A few miles beyond, Jorf El Asfar, Africa's biggest artificial port, is nearing completion; the world's largest phosphate fertilizer plant, with an annual capacity of 16 million tons, will open at the same time. At Oualidia, situated on a pretty lagoon, the late King Mohammed V had an attractive villa. A decaying kasbah slowly adds quaintness and color to the Air Lagoon below. From Cape Bedouza on, the road is a real cliffhanger, and there are fine views of Safi.

His Majesty, King Sardine

During the Middle Ages, Safi was already one of Morocco's chief ports. The Portuguese took it over, like El Jadida and Azemmour, in the late 15th century and remained until 1541. The town achieved diplomatic importance when the first French consul arrived in the 16th century and when, 100 years later, the first Franco-Moroccan treaties were signed there. But Safi never expected its present world record: 70 to 80,000 tons of sardines leave its docks each year.

Early in the morning the night's catch is auctioned off at the fish market, but despite the all-pervading smell of sardines, Safi also ships out a good deal of the country's production of phosphate. Even after the completion of Jorf El Asfar, a large chemical complex producing sulfuric acid, triple superphosphates, and ammonium phosphate assures an industrial future to the detriment of tourism.

Yet Safi has a fascinating medina, full of color with its great mosque, its *kissaria*—market street, which is just what the name implies—and the Portuguese chapel dating from 1519, which was once the choir of the cathedral with its vaulted Gothic ceiling bearing the arms of Manuel II surrounded by those of the Order of Christ, the Holy See and the Bishop of

Safi. (Open daily 8–12; 3–7. Follow the main street of the medina, the Rue du Marché, and the signs marked "circuit touristique" on the left. The entrance is signposted on the right.) The same era saw the building of the restored Dar-el-Bahar (Castle of the Sea), once a fortress and probably also the palace of the Portuguese governor (open daily 8–12; 3–7). The Moroccan fortress called the Kechla is a four-angled citadel flanked by crenellated towers and encloses a mechouar (square). Dwellings dating from the 18th century are laid out around a patio in the northern corner. From the western platform there is a good view overlooking the medina.

The artisans in the potters' quarter keep up the traditions of an ancient trade. They knead the clay, then shape, decorate, varnish and bake the great variety of earthenware objects, some sticking to tried models, others displaying imagination and a sense of humor in what they turn out.

Carthaginians and Portuguese

The coastal road continues south to the cliffs of Jorf El Yhoudi, then ends after a ruined Portuguese fort at the 18th-century Hamidouch Kasbah, on the mouth of the Oued Chichaoua. P8 turns inland, through progressively hillier country from Tleta Sidi Bouguedra to Ounara, both junctions with roads to Marrakesh. Heading back to the sea, the road passes first through a forest of rare argan trees, which gradually give way to a fairyland of mimosas. These flowering shrubs were planted to anchor the shifting sand dunes, but their effect is to create a triumphal entry into Essaouira, once known as Mogador.

Hannibal may have crossed the Alps, but the exploits of an earlier Carthaginian, Hanno, were almost as spectacular. He was explorer, general, journalist in one and Essaouira was one of the places where he founded a colony, as described in a short account of his travels, roughly translatable as *Hanno's Voyage.* Juba II, King of Mauretania, later took an interest in Essaouira—for sound business reasons. A strong purple dye could be extracted from certain mollusks living in the waters near the town, so Juba set up a dye factory which was soon to supply the robes of Roman patricians; hence the expression "born to the purple."

The Portuguese, when their turn came, fortified the city, which they called Mogador (probably derived from the Berber word *amogdul,* meaning safe anchorage), but Essaouira's really prosperous era began with the 18th century. Sultan Sidi Mohammed ben Abdallah, and his prisoner the French architect Cornut saw its possibilities as a port, and proceeded to construct one, plus the fortifications to protect it. Instead of fighting off foreigners, the Sultan welcomed them, handing out all sorts of trade concessions which made Essaouira richer as the years passed. In 1884, France declared war on Morocco because of some border incidents involving Algeria—and one of the first acts of the conflict was the shelling of Essaouira. A French force under the Prince de Joinville occupied the island across from the city until the following year when the Lalla Marnia treaty was signed.

A cool breeze, sometimes becoming a strong wind, usually sweeps across the attractive beach. Behind rises the white town, accented by deep blue shutters and doors in the Portuguese style. Inside the town walls the inlayers are hard at work on their small furniture pieces which they encrust with wood and mother of pearl. The best view of the port and fortifications is from the two *scalas,* the defense platforms. Some of the cannons, made in Seville in the 18th century, are of the finest workmanship, ornamented with the crowns of the kings of Spain, Philip V and Charles III, together with the arms of the Bourbons and the Order of the Golden Fleece. Near the Marine Gate is the fish market, morning or afternoon depending on the tides, where sardines are grilled over charcoal fires. Two worthwhile excursions are north to a couple of belvederes commanding splendid views, and south to Diabet where sand dunes have almost hidden the lonely ruins of a sultan's palace.

The scenery improves along the remaining 171 km. (106 miles) to Agadir. After 14 km. (nine miles) a piste branches right towards the sea through a wood of arbor vitae trees to the marabout of Sidi Kaouki above a lovely beach; this track skirts the sea for about 16 km. (ten miles) before rejoining P8. At Smimou a branch climbs inland through groves of arbor vitae and argan trees to Thine Imintlit and up Jebel Amsittene. The whole region can be viewed from a watchtower before returning on a rough track to Tamanar on P8, which has been rising steadily through the Atlas foothills coming ever closer to the sea. No need to risk any further pistes to the sea, which P8 rejoins at Tamri. The last 48 km. (30 miles) wind between the deep blue sea and the purple mountains, sometimes at the base of a cliff, sometimes on a miniature plain scooped out from the mountains, sometimes hard by the sandy beach. Here the Atlantic consents to be safe, the water is clear, and lots of strange sea creatures are waiting to be caught by underwater hunters among the rocks. But swimmers should not trust their luck too much on days when the wind blows and the sea swells. Eleven miles beyond Tamri a picturesque road branches left into the mainland foothills, following a palm-lined river to the waterfalls of Imouzzer des Ida Outanane.

Agadir

The main road leads past Tarazout's beach to the martyred city of Agadir. Though nothing but a miserable little town for hundreds of years, history seemed bent on reducing it to rubble time after time. Its situation on the bay at the mouth of the Oued Sous made it a natural breach in the Atlantic defenses—and yet, in spite of a threatening gesture by the Germans in 1911, it seemed destined at last for a little peace and quiet. The back country was producing plenty of citrus fruit and vegetables, the ocean was generous with its fish, hotels mushroomed and a port was built against enormous odds at the foot of Founti hill.

Then, on February 29, 1960, Leap Year Day brought no declarations of love, but an earthquake which killed 15,000 people in 15 seconds. With generous foreign help, a new town rose around the port, leaving the old site on the hill as a cemetery and memorial to the dead. Seismologists agree that it is unlikely that another earthquake should occur, but Agadir has still taken the precaution to build everything to earthquake-proof specifications. Some of the modern architecture is pleasing, the post office being especially interesting. Agadir is Morocco's outstanding tourist center, but bigger, though not necessarily better, developments are planned to provide 50,000 beds in 5 sites on the huge bay between Cap Chir in the north and Oued Massa in the south. Due attention is to be given to the preservation of the coast, at least in the plans.

Once you have finished basking in the sun and swimming in the beautiful bay, you can visit what was once the kasbah or the Founti quarter.

The road following the Oued Sous to Taroudant lies through the villages of Inezgane and Oulad Teima; deliciously perfumed in spring from the orange groves which line its path.

PRACTICAL INFORMATION FOR
THE ATLANTIC SEABOARD

WHEN TO GO. Best in winter, as the season is in full swing from December to March, extending through May. July and August are surprisingly cool thanks to the Atlantic, especially at Agadir, where the sky remains frequently overcast till the afternoon, when the sun appears for a few hours to entice bathers on to the magnificent beach. Warm clothes essential for the evening. A few statistics on this remarkable weather: Average temperature at Agadir in January 55°F.; in August 75°F.; at El Jadida 52°F. and 79°F. respectively; seven hours of sun daily at Essaouira in December; eight in Agadir in February. Monthly rainfall in the Safi–Agadir stretch from December to February: less than 2 inches.

GETTING THERE. By Bus. Very crowded C.T.M. buses twice daily Casablanca–El Jadida, almost 2 hours; equally crowded Casa–Essaouira, 6 hours; Essaouira–Agadir another 3 hours. The comfortable Greyhound type Pullman du Sud makes these trips during the night. However, local bus services, often infrequent, slow and uncomfortable, must be depended on south of El Jadida, as the through C.T.M. coaches from Casa are usually fully booked. All coastal towns have direct bus links with Marrakesh.

By Plane. The only airport is at Agadir, well served by direct charter flights. Scheduled flights from Europe usually call first at Casablanca or Tangier. Connections to most Moroccan towns, especially Casablanca.

By Train. Safi is connected to Casablanca and Marrakesh via the Benguerir junction.

By Car. P8 over the Azemmour bypass is the quickest connection between Casablanca and El Jadida; S130, closer to the sea, offers glimpses of several pretty little beaches, before passing through Azemmour. From Azemmour beach a dangerously narrow coastal road leaves the brilliant yellow of broom on one hand and the paler gold of a vast beach on the other for the 11 km. (7 miles) to El Jadida. Inland P8 to Safi is monotonously dull; S121 via Oualidia offers far more inspiring sights along the rocky, wave-beaten coast.

We recommend S-120 which joins the main road once more at Tnine Riat. There are some sites like the Kasbah Hamidouch and the Chicht Belevedere which are worth a visit but are reached only via dirt roads. From Essaouira to Agadir, the road is uniformly attractive.

Some distances—Casablanca–El Jadida inland 97 km. (60 miles), along the coast 109 km. (68 miles); El Jadida–Safi 142 km. (88 miles) along the coast, or 156 km. (97 miles) on P8; Safi–Essaouira 132 km. (82 miles); Marrakesh–Essaouira 172 km. (107 miles); Marrakesh–Agadir via Asni and Taroudant 303 km. (188 miles).

AGADIR

Hotels. Most of the larger hotels are built like boxes or as clusters of all-too-many bungalows set in all-too-small bits of green. This is very much package-tour territory, so the individual traveler tends to be rather neglected. Moreover, owing to the meteoric development of tourism, staffing problems are severe and service can be unsatisfactory; complaints about dining rooms are frequent. The (L) hotels are airconditioned and the top two categories have fairly large pools.

Area code 08.

Deluxe

Safir Europa, Blvd. du 20 Août (tel. 212 12). 240 rooms. Tall, well-designed building close to beach. Choice of restaurants, nightclub, shopping center.

Sahara, Blvd. Mohammed V (tel. 406 60). 300 rooms, apartments and bungalows. Four restaurants, disco.

Expensive—Clubs

These are all holiday villages with all sports facilities, almost entirely taken up by package tours:

Les Dunes d'Or, Secteur Touristique (tel. 401 50). 450 bungalows. P.L.M.

La Kasbah, Blvd. du 20 Août (tel. 401 36). 200 bungalows.

Salam, Blvd. Mohammed V (tel. 408 40 or 401 20). 150 rooms, 60 bungalows.

Sangho, Ave. Mohammed V (tel 403 42), 210 new bungalows.

Tamlelt, Quartier des Dunes (tel. 400 73). 250 bungalows.

Club Méditerranée, Secteur Touristique (tel. 407 40). The often copied but never equalled grand-daddy of holiday clubs. An excellent 300-room village among palm groves on the beach; best hotel food and all sports facilities.

Expensive—Hotels

Adrar, Blvd. Mohammed V (tel. 40873). 171 airconditioned rooms. 2 restaurants, 3 pools.

Ali Baba, Blvd. Mohammed V (tel. 233 26). 105 rooms.

Les Almohades, Quartier des Dunes (tel. 402 33), close to the beach. 300 rooms round a central court and pool area, sauna. Three restaurants, *Tan Tan* nightclub, grill room. In the Africa Palace chain.

Anezi, Blvd. Mohammed V (tel. 409 40). 90 rooms. Recently built, the Anezi has a modern decor and a fine restaurant; pool.

Atlas, Blvd. Mohammed V (tel. 232 32). 156 rooms, 50 bungalows. Elementary service and regimented meals for disciplined package tours.

Kamal, Blvd. Hassan II (tel. 239 40). 84 rooms. Well suited to the individual traveler; in town center, but adequate pool and terrace with coffee shop.

Marhaba, Blvd. Mohammed V (tel. 406 70). On a slight eminence, so all the 75 rooms have a sea view; quiet in large garden.

Omayades, Blvd. du 20 Aout (tel. 407 22). 144 rooms. Part of the PLM chain, this holiday village is considered one of the finest hotels in this category.

El Oumnia, Secteur Touristique (tel. 403 52). 180 rooms directly on the beach.

Tafoukt, Blvd. du 20 Aout (tel. 407 24). 90 rooms. Totally refurbished, the Tafoukt has a good restaurant, two bars, and a pool.

Tagadirt, Blvd. du 20 Août (tel. 406 30). 45 rooms. Near the beach.

Among the large number of *Résidences* (furnished apartments), all with restaurants and pools are:

Igoudart, Quartier des Dunes (tel. 203 99). 167 rooms.

Nejma, Ave. des F.A.R. (tel. 201 06). 62 rooms.

Soraya, Rue de la Foire (tel. 214 25). 54 rooms.

Tagadirt, Blvd. du 20 Août (tel. 406 30). 146 rooms; connected with the homonymous hotel.

Yasmina, Rue de la Jeunesse (tel. 200 60). 75 rooms.

Moderate

Atlantic, Ave. Hassan II (tel. 236 61). 54 rooms. No restaurant.

Royal, Blvd. Mohammed V (tel. 406 75), 98 rooms; seaview from rooftop bar.

Sindibad, Quartier Talborjt (tel. 234 77). 49 rooms. Rather far out.

Talborjt, Rue de l'Entraide (tel. 206 71). 46 rooms, 13 studios. Central.

Inexpensive

Only **Bahia, de Paris** and **Excelsior** have a few showers.

If Agadir is full, try **Inezgane,** near the airport, 10 km. (6 miles) from town: **Club Hacienda** (E), tel. 301 76. 50 bungalows in pleasant garden; usual sports facilities plus riding. P.L.M. chain. **La Pergola** (M), tel. 308 41; 23 rooms. **Provençal** (M), tel. 312 08; 41 rooms. **Pyramides** (M), tel. 307 05; 25 rooms. **Essafen** (I), tel. 304 13; 14 rooms.

Restaurants

Expensive

Chez Mania, Ave. General Kettani. Mediocre Moroccan cooking.
Kasbah de Tafraout, Ave. des F.A.R. Outrageously priced Moroccan cooking.
Marin Heim, Blvd. Mohammed V. Good for seafood.
Du Port, in the port. Maintains the best French traditions. Excellent fish, lobster and bouillabaisse.

Moderate

Chez Rachid, Ave. Hassan II.
Chez Tournevis, Ave. des F.A.R., near the great mosque. Best in class.
Crêpe d'Or, Ave. Prince Héritier Sidi Mohammed.
Dom, Ave. Hassan II.
Founty, Ave. Hassan II.
Guedra, Ave. Prince Héritier Sidi Mohammed.
Jour et Nuit. Snack bar on the beach.
Le Miramar, Blvd. Mohammed V. Good value.
Pampa, Ave. Prince Héritier Sidi Mohammed.
Panier, Ave. Prince Héritier Sidi Mohammed.
Pizzeria, Ave. Hassan II.
Tafoukt, Pl. du Prince Héritier Sidi Mohammed.

Nightlife

Agadir's nightlife is at best conventional. Besides the nightclubs of the (L) hotels and the discos in all the larger (E)s, King Beard is a moderately priced disco for those who want more of the same.

HOTELS AND RESTAURANTS FOR THE REST OF THE ATLANTIC SEABOARD

El Jadida. (Area code 034.) *Doukkala* (E), tel. 37 37. 81 rooms. Faces ocean across the beach promenade; pool, tennis. In the Salam chain. *Palais Andalous* (E), tel. 39 06. 36 rooms. This exquisite Andalusian replica was constructed by a local pasha; no pool.
Closed at present, despite the only direct access to the lovely beach, *Asfar* (M), tel. 26 39. 200 bungalows listed for the sake of completeness. By far the best buy is the English-owned *Provence* (I), tel. 23 47. Restaurant in small garden; above average comfort in an oasis of tranquility. Private transport from Casablanca airport on request.
Restaurants. *Tit* (E), next to the post office; barely justifies the price. *Le Dauphin* (I), near the Provence; is erratically adequate. Only *La Broche* deserves to be mentioned among the (I) establishments in the main street.

El Jadida–Safi Coast Road. 13 km. (8 miles) along S121, beyond the negligible restaurants of the Sidi Bousid beach, the *Beau Séjour* (M), is good for seafood. At 26 km. (16 miles), *Relais* (I), 7 rooms, excellent food.

Essaouira. *Des Iles* (E), Blvd. Mohammed V (tel. 23 29). 37 rooms, 40 bungalows round the pool; very humid because facing the sea. O.N.C.F. chain. Likewise, on the beach, but no pool, *Tafoukt* (M), tel. 25 04.
In town, *Mechouar* (I), Rue Oqba Ibn-Nafi (tel. 20 18). 24 rooms. *Des Remparts* (I), tel. 22 82. 27 rooms, most with bath. Its gloom accentuated by canned music. *Sahara* (I), Rue Oqba Ibn-Nafi (I), tel. 22 92. 70 rooms, 50 with bath; no restaurant.
Restaurants. Try the sardines straight from the sea, grilled by vendors in the port. *Chalet de la Plage* (M), not much in appearance but excellent fish and cheerful service. Same *Chez Sam* (M) in the port.

Imouzzer Des Ida Outanane. *Auberge des Cascades* (M), tel. 16. 14 simple rooms, 5 with showers; pool, tennis. Dining terrace overlooking waterfalls.

Oualidia. *Hippocampe* (M), tel. 111. 20 chalets; small pool. On the beach, worth the detour but avoid the crowded Sunday lunch. Famous for its oysters and shellfish, especially the local lobster. *La Lagune* (I), tel. 105. 10 rooms, on the clifftop, offers good seafood at very reasonable prices.

Safi. *Atlantide* (E), tel. 21 60. 50 rooms. View of the city, lovely gardens but no pool. *Safir* (E), Ave. Zerktouni, tel. 42 99. 90 rooms. Considered the finest hotel in town, the Safir has a heated swimming pool, a popular nightclub, and tennis courts. *Anis* (M), Rue de Rabat, tel. 30 78. 32 rooms, 28 with shower or bath. TV in rooms; restaurant. *Les Mimosas* (M), tel. 32 08. 26 rooms, all with shower or bath.
Restaurants. The best is *Refuge* (M), high above the town at Sidi Bouzid. Downtown, two small restaurants, *Chez Gégène* (I) and *Safi* (I).

SHOPPING. Safi is as famous for its pottery as Fez is for its ceramics. Essaouira is best known for its inlay work and its jewelry. The artisans of this town use thuya wood, a local variety of juniper with a pleasant aroma and interesting color and grain, for small boxes and tables, then inlay it with lemonwood, ebony and mother of pearl for stunning effects. The gold or silver jewelry is either hammered and chiseled or drawn out in fine threads. For the inlay work, the best bet is the Société Coopérative des Marqueteurs d'Essaouira, 6 Rue Alibert; also the many carpenters' workshops below the Square de la Casbah. Try the jewelry souk on Rue Syaghine for gold and silver (hard to bargain for gold). For embroidery try Artisanat, opposite the Provence Hotel in El Jadida.

USEFUL ADDRESSES. Tourist Information. National Tourist Office and Syndicat d'Initiative: **Agadir:** Ave. du Prince Héritier and Blvd. Mohammed V. **El Jadida:** Ave. Ibn Khaldoun (tel. 27 04). **Essaouira:** Sahat Moulay Abdellah. **Safi:** Place Rabat.
In Agadir: Wagons Lits Tours, 26 Ave. des F.A.R.; Sahara Tours, Ave. General Kettani; Transport T. Corail, 24 Ave. des F.A.R.; Royal Air Maroc, Ave. General Kettani (tel. 220 061); British Airways, Ave. Hassan II.
Car Hire. Afric Car, Ave. Mohammed V, tel. 40 750; Avis, Ave. Hassan II, tel. 40 695; Budget, Ave. Mohammed V, tel 40 762; Hertz, Blvd. Mohammed V, tel. 40 345. All in Agadir.
Taxis at Agadir are usually available in front of the larger hotels, but the meters rarely work and the drivers charge extortionate prices for the shortest distance. About 40DH to the airport.

TOWARDS THE ANTI-ATLAS

Wandering Berbers and Blue Men

An exotic way of life versus business as usual; in the Anti-Atlas these two seemingly incompatible worlds meet. The taste for the exotic will take us to the edge of the immense desert wastes where even the starry night sky is higher, wider, and handsomer than elsewhere. At Goulimine we will meet the Blue Men who possess nothing but their tents, their camels, and the freedom to live as they please on the world's largest camping ground—the Sahara. At Tafraout, the more mundane world takes over, for here we see a highly original and effective banking system in action. The main occupation in Tafraout is counting money—all the dirhams that went for beans and bacon in a thousand Chleuh grocery shops in a dozen cities of the north. The Anti-Atlas range comprises these totally alien societies. Ethnologically, however, the people who make them up are not so different. The R'Guibat Touaregs of the Western Sahara and the Chleuhs of the Anti-Atlas valleys both belong to the oldest Berber strains of North Africa. But there is no meeting of the minds!

Even in the age of the jet, it seems too abrupt to go directly from the lushness of the countryside around Agadir to the Sahara Desert. P30 south from Agadir complies with this need for gradual transition as it leads gently to the wide open spaces. Until the road fork at Ait Melloul, the Sous plain extends its rich farmlands, but farther south the landscape conforms to the traditional desert image.

The crossing of the Oued Massa brings to mind Oqba ibn Nafi, the Islamic conqueror of Morocco, who, at its mouth, spurred his horse into the waves of the Atlantic to show Allah there was no more land to be conquered in the Maghreb.

Tiznit is a good introduction to pre-Saharan architecture, ramparts with square towers and six gates to enter the fortifications which protect the handsome turn-of-the-century Dar el Maghzen Palace, the Great Mosque and the souks selling silver Berber jewelry. The whole is framed by extensive palm groves. The large map showing distances and routes at the crossroads outside the town indicates only about 245 km. (152 miles) to Tindouf in the Algerian Sahara, by courtesy of the Polisario guerrillas; and to Dakar in Senegal about 1,709 km. (1,062 miles).

Mood Indigo: A Meeting with the Blue Men

After Tiznit the road ascends the low Tizi Mighert Pass (975m., 3,200 ft.) where the argan trees grow thick. The argan tree is exclusive to the Anti-Atlas, though its cousin, the carob, is fairly common. The argan is friend to man and beast: the goats disregard its thorns as they climb up among its branches to get at the juicy leaves. Men harvest its yellow fruit to extract the oil used for cooking and as salad dressing. The carob seeds in long black pods long served as jeweler's weights and thus as measurements for gold and jewels—and they still do in the sense that the word "carat" comes from carob or "karab" in Arabic.

When P30 leaves the argans behind, all life seems to vanish as it heads south to Bou Izakarn, where the road left (southeast) leads through desolate landscape to the large oasis of Tarhjijt, very picturesque with its old white minaret and fortified mud villages, below the Agadir of Iznaguer, a fortress dating from the 12th century, commanding the valley. From here it is Land Rovers only; via Foum el Hassan to the Algerian frontier and Tindouf it is only 153 km. (95 miles). At the only crossroads head left across a rocky plain dotted with small oases with dark red mountains in the background to the remarkable valley of Amtoudi (about 16 miles from Tarhjijt).

At the village mules can be hired (70DH) to ascend to the great ksar which commands the whole plain and the narrow gorge which is one of the gates of the desert. Before the pacification of the Anti-Atlas by the French in 1934, these ksars commanded the track routes from the inner Sahara to the Sous. Always built at strategic positions, they held the passes, and caravans could not pass without paying tribute for safe passage. The ksar of Amtoudi is one of the few which is easily accessible, as well as being well preserved (most are now falling into decay). Crowning the summit of an enormous natural rock formation and surrounded by walls and crenellated towers, its antiquity could not be hazarded as for centuries the neighboring Berbers have been reconstructing it and carrying out repairs. Entered through three defensive doorways, it is an incredible maze of passages, tunnels, cisterns and granaries for each village with storage "slots" where the grain was carefully weighed and kept. From the terraces, there is a magnificent view across the plains to Tarhjijt and the desert. Beyond the ksar is the long gorge of the Oued Amtoudi with sheer rock cliffs on each side. A veritable garden cultivated with date palms, almond and fig trees, wheat and corn, it is irrigated by an elaborate network of ditches and dykes. A lovely walk of about a half mile from the village brings you to another ksar which crowns a seemingly inaccessible cliff, and several fresh pools and waterfalls make a wonderful spot for a swim and a picnic.

Returning to the main road, Goulimine is reached after 43 km. (27 miles). Here the last bald hillocks of the Anti-Atlas have petered out and the plain stretches into infinity; but two fairly large palm groves, both some 13 km. (8 miles) from the walls which completely encircle the town, break this limitless waste. At Abainou, warm thermal springs gush from the earth and are chaneled into two swimming pools, while at the oasis proper, some nomads have usually pitched their tents, to which Goulimine's self-appointed boy guides are overeager to direct you for an absurd 30DH. Better ask the way at the hotel.

Behind the imposing, though not especially solid, walls, each house is built like a miniature square kasbah out of the simplest of materials—reddish sun-dried mud. Since Goulimine (Guelmim) became the capital of the Western Sahara province in 1985, officials among the 50,000 inhabitants have outnumbered the artisans who make the heavy, primitive-looking jewelry and the curious sugar hammers the Moroccans use to break up their rock-like sugar loaves.

The main square, surrounded by arcades over the shops, is busy even on the hottest day, but Goulimine is at its picturesque best for the great annual camel market, held in July. The heat fails to prevent the influx of tourists, and every Saturday morning coaches outnumber the small caravans crossing the desert towards the market town; the camels are pale beige, almost white, the men riding or walking beside the animals blue. They have deep blue floating robes over their jellabas, indigo blue twisted turbans, and even blue-tinted skin where the dye has rubbed off. You can hardly accuse the Blue Men of being capricious or of following a whim—blue has been in fashion with them for four centuries. An enterprising English cloth merchant named Thomas Windham visited Agadir several times in the middle of the fifteen hundreds and introduced calico dyed indigo blue. The customers have been coming back for more ever since. The men are usually tall and have handsome angular profiles often ending in a pointed goatee.

Some of the camels rock along with a sort of sedan chair made of braided and colored wicker. This is the "litter" in which women or girls of high Saharan society ride. But most of the women walk, also draped in blue veils, their foreheads and chins tattooed in blue designs, their throats circled by a heavy amber necklace.

All these groups may have been on the march for days before arriving in Goulimine. "Home" for them is the wide sweep of desert occupied by the R'Guibat tribe whose capital Tarfaya is four days march south. They have come to sell the baby camels they have raised, animal skins and wool. The Chleuhs, sharp businessmen from the north, are shorter and wear white, but they dominate the souk, while the hobbled camels bellow stridently and men call out to one another. The men of the R'Guibat will soon return to months of solitude in the desert, but in the meantime they plan to enjoy the guedra for which Goulimine used to be famous. But like the market this erotic dance has degenerated into a tourist spectacle, to be put on at any time for a fee, though the setting among the tents is more inspiring than the "Moroccan Evenings" in the sterile atmosphere of Agadir's hotel dining rooms.

The Spanish Inheritance

From Goulimine, it is 80 km. (50 miles) through semi-desert to Tan Tan in what was, until 1958, the little enclave of Spanish Morocco governed from Rio de Oro, the Spanish Sahara. Tan Tan, surrounded by a vast expanse of emptiness, is rather unappealing, but replacing tourist-ridden Goulimine as the emporium of the Blue Men.

At the beginning of May a great moussem is held to honor Sidi Loghdof, one of the most revered of the desert "saints." All the tribes from the south attend, with some of them coming from Mauritania, Tindouf and as far as Senegal. It is a unique spectacle; thousands of Blue Men, camel-racing, and hundreds of black tents pitched in the desert outside the town. At night there are guedra dances, the real thing, by the best performers in the western Sahara.

About 16 km. (ten miles) west is Tan Tan Plage, where the surf of the Atlantic pounds against vast deserted beaches and high cliffs, with the fog rolling in from the ocean.

The road more or less follows the coast southwest for about 161 km. (100 miles) to Tarfaya, crossing vast oueds—like deep fjords extending from the Atlantic into the desert. The Oued Chebeïka is crossed by a causeway; along the Oued El Amra flamingos are often seen; at the Oued Fatami erosion has resulted in amazing rock formations and wonderful colors in the cliffs. Shifting dunes often cover the road to Tarfaya, but if you bear right you reach one of the most fascinating places in the south of Morocco, the magnificent Sabkhat (Lagoon) Knifis.

A tidal salt sea extending far into the desert, the lagoon is the only indentation deep enough for safe anchorage along the coast between the Oued Draa to the north of Tan Tan and Cap Juby to the south. In the 15th and 16th centuries, this was the site of the principal Spanish colonial trading center with the Saharan tribes. The ruins of a fortified tower, where the merchants could retreat in time of attack, are now surrounded by water at high tide. They date from around 1500, the exact date being disputed. It is only about 113 km. (70 miles) from here to Lanzarote in the Canary Islands, and this small coastal settlement was strategic to the Spanish conquest of the islands and vital to their security. The road continues past vast salt lakes beyond Tarfaya to La Ayoune (El Aïoun, Layoun), capital of the former Spanish Sahara, now Western Sahara and protected by a three-meter-high wall across 2,519 km. (1,565 miles) of desert. No longer the administrative capital, La Ayoune is now a modern town of 100,000 inhabitants.

The Atlantic foray necessitates retracing one's steps to Goulimine, for a visit to a luckily undisputed part. 32 km. (20 miles) through green and fertile hills lead north to the former enclave of Sidi Ifni 80 km. (50 miles) long and 21 km. (13 miles) wide. The sadly neglected town with decaying Spanish squares and gardens is situated on a cliff above the sea. The artificial port with pylons extending out to sea to the closest safe anchorage and the international airport lie abandoned. The splendid beach is a perfect spot for a peaceful holiday. From Sidi Ifni, it is a pleasant alternative to rejoin Tiznit directly, by a scenic coast road as far as Mirleft and then through green and hilly countryside with valleys of large flowering cacti (about 48 km., 30 miles).

Land of the Chleuhs

Having followed the men of the R'Guibat to their homeland, we shall do likewise with the Chleuh merchants who have probably made a number of good deals at Goulimine. Turn right at the Tiznit crossroads, and head for Tafraout, east into the mountains. After crossing the Oued Massa valley, bright with pink oleanders, the road ascends the 1,097 m. (3,600 feet) to the Kerdous Pass, and still has another 48 km. (30 miles) of mountains to negotiate. These natural obstacles explain why Tafraout has so often been successfully defended. The landscape seems a crazy assemblage of mammoth boulders stacked precariously on each other and reaching so high into the sky that an avalanche always seems imminent. But since the rose-colored granite never seems to tumble down, the Chleuhs have chosen to live in this incredible and impressive setting, where they have made the reputation of being the country's best exterior decorators.

The pink kasbahs of Tafraout perch on spurs of rock, hide beneath boulders, or cling tenaciously to the walls of the cliff and their façades are often painted with strange designs in white or ocher. Palm trees push up between them, while down in the valley are fields of grain with the brilliant accents of color provided by a great variety of fruit trees. Among granite blocks, olive, lemon, orange, almond, argan and carob trees share their place in the sun with the palms. In springtime, Tafraout is a feast for the eyes when all the trees are in flower and their perfume wafts across the valley. The Hôtel les Amandiers is oriented so that the village and most of the valley are visible from its terrace.

The excellent road from Tafraout to Taroudant, via Ait Baha, opens up the multiple facets of the Anti-Atlas valleys; but only a Land Rover will take you via Irherm, where the Idaou Kensou tribe continues the fashioning and decoration of rifles encrusted with precious metals, and carved daggers.

The Pearl of the Sous

Taroudant is usually reached from Agadir by P32 through the wonderfully fertile Sous Valley. The town's origins are uncertain, but it did have twenty years of glory as the Saadian capital when that dynasty first reigned. Even when the rulers moved to more strategic Marrakesh, they did not forget Taroudant and returned frequently on long pleasure trips.

It's easy to understand the sovereign's desire to return when you see Taroudant—a medieval town entirely surrounded by dark, red-brown crenellated walls twenty feet high. From the outside, these lowering bastions seem to guard some mighty and cruel fortress, but on the other side of the walls are orchards and gardens—unfortunately often hidden behind other walls, but sometimes flowering in the open. During the time of Taroudant's greatest prosperity, the red earth of the Sous brought forth all the crops the people needed, plus enough to make highly profitable exports to the Sudan in the form of rice, indigo, sugar cane and cotton, plus all the tropical fruits. On Thursday and Saturday, the tribes of the High and Anti-Atlas that the Qued Sous separates, come into town for the souk; particularly interesting are the iron workers and sculptors. If you wish to see the local color at full strength, try to make the tour of the ramparts by moonlight: we say try advisedly, since the condition of these walls is very precarious. Perhaps you would be wiser to take in the view in daytime, as is standard procedure.

Two interesting kasbahs are respectively at Freija, 8 km. (five miles), and Tiout, 19 km. (12 miles) further, off the Marrakesh road, which follows the Oued Sous upstream till the fork after Ouled Berrehil village. The left branch climbs in hairpin bends the Tizi N'Test Pass in the High

Atlas, the right is part of the main axis from Agadir through the pre-Sahara oases to Er Rachidia. The only stopping places on the section to Ouarzazate are Taliouine and Tazanakht, both picturesque desert villages. The detour on piste 6801, branching left at Aoullouz and returning at Anzel offers some startling scenery but likewise some fairly startling driving.

PRACTICAL INFORMATION FOR THE REGION

WHEN TO GO. Information under this heading in the chapter *The Deep South* also applies to the Anti-Atlas, i.e. don't venture into this neighborhood in the middle of summer if you're not of the "Some Like It Hot" class.

GETTING THERE. By Plane. Regular flights from some Moroccan towns to La Ayoune and Tan Tan.

By C.T.M. Buses. Casablanca–Agadir–Tiznit 10 hrs.; the 'Southern Pullman', Casa–Agadir takes 8 hrs.; Agadir–Tiznit–Goulimine, 5 hrs.; Agadir–Taroudant 2½ hrs.; Agadir–Ouarzazate 10 hrs.; Marrakesh–Tazenakht–Foum Zguid (once a week) 12 hrs.

By Car. P30 south from Agadir via Tiznit (branch east to Tafraout), Bou Izakarn (branch southeast to Tarhjijt and Foum El Hassan), Goulimine (branch north to Ifni), Tan Tan rejoins the coast at Tan Tan Plage and continues close to the ocean to Tarfaya, inland among the lakes to Al Youne, returning to the Atlantic once again at La Ayoune Plage. S509 makes a semicircle from Agadir via Ait Baha and Tafraout to Tiznit. Ait Baha is also connected to Taroudant by a scenic route par excellence. The road from Taroudant to Irherm, which leads directly to the Tiout Kasbah and its view of the Sous Valley, is well-surfaced, so that you might be tempted to continue to Tafraout; *don't* unless your vehicle is a Land Rover.

P32 east from Agadir via Taroudant and Tazenakht joins P31 north of Ouarzazate. From Tazanakht S510 crosses the desert 69 km. (43 miles) due east to Agdz, much farther south on the P31. After Ouled Berrehil the Marrakesh road forks left from P32 and climbs to 2,120 m. (6,956 feet) at the Tizi N'Test Pass, spectacular but only recommended for those used to mountain driving; keep away in winter, when snow and ice make it so dangerous that it is often closed. The fast road from Agadir to Marrakesh, 266 km. (165 miles), via Imi N'Tanout and Chichaoua is always open but less interesting.

For the really ambitious itineraries like Bou Izakarn-Foum Zguid via Foum el Hassan-Akka-Tata you need a fearless automobile which thrives on punishment, plus a driver of tough rally caliber. Ask the advice of one of Morocco's two automobile clubs before planning these trips.

To sum up: main roads are well maintained but narrow, secondary roads are somewhat unpredictable, pistes are much more adventurous than further north because of the long distances involved, and should only be attempted in Land Rovers.

Some distances—Marrakesh–Taroudant 222km. (138 miles); Agadir–Taroudant 82 km. (51 miles); Tiznit–Tafraout 124 km. (77 miles); Taroudant–Tafraout (via Ait Baha) 167 km. (104 miles); Agadir–Tafraout (via Ait Baha) 156 km. (97 miles); Agadir–Tiznit–Goulimine 201 km. (125 miles).

HOTELS AND RESTAURANTS. All the larger hotels in the south are built in the kasbah style in keeping with the architectural tradition. Only establishments in the (L) and (E) categories provide satisfactory accommodations and service.

Bou Izakarn. *Anti-Atlas* (M), tel. 41 34. 10 rooms, 5 baths.

Goulimine. *Salam* (M), tel. 20 57. 27 rooms, 6 showers. Near the camel market; Salam chain. At the *Pension Ere Nouvelle,* 12 rooms, the food is said to be better. **Restaurant.** You can get a simple meal at the *Rendez-vous des Hommes Bleus.* They dance the guedra on Saturday or Sunday nights, or at any other time if you are willing to pay.

La Ayoune. *Al Massira* (L), tel. 31 60. 75 airconditioned rooms. Pool, tennis. *Parador* (M), tel. 42 25. 31 airconditioned rooms, pool. *El Alia* (M), 22 31. 34 rooms, all with baths; no restaurant. tel 45 00. *Residencia* (M), tel. 38 29. 81 rooms, no private baths.

Sidi Ifni. *Ait-Baamran* (I), tel. 51 73; 20 rooms, is as squalid as the *Bellevue* (I), tel. 50 72; 16 rooms, 8 baths.

Tafraout. *Les Amandiers* (M), tel. 8. 60 airconditioned rooms, 51 showers. The water is not always flowing as there just isn't enough. Lovely terrace, small pool; only full December-January. **Restaurant.** *Mauretania* (M), in town, serves excellent couscous and kebabs.

Taliouine. *Ibn Toumert* (M), tel. 1. 106 airconditioned rooms; architecturally impressive, pool. P.L.M. chain.

Tan Tan. A hotel is planned on the magnificent beach. In town are *Royal* (I), tel. 71 86, 36 rooms appears run by army for the recreation of officers; good value, fast service and *Etoile du Sahara* (I), tel. 70 85; 34 rooms, 17 showers.

Taroudant. *Gazelle d'Or* (L), tel. 20 39. 23 rooms. One of North Africa's most famous. In a 20-acre park, ten pavilions of two apartments, plus a clubhouse with drawing rooms, games rooms, dining room and bar; the food is delicious; swimming, tennis, horse riding, falconry. As to the prices, it's as Lipton said about yachts—if you have to ask how much it costs, you can't afford it. Closed May–Oct. *Salam* (E), tel. 23 12. 74 rooms. In town, a former palace with a pretty garden, good pool. Food is superb and the staff is charming; beautiful, atmospheric surroundings. *Saadiens* (M), tel. 25 89. 57 rooms, 8 showers. *Taroudant* (I), tel. 24 16. 31 rooms, 18 showers.

Tiznit. *Tiznit* (M), tel. 24 11. 40 rooms round a patio, pool. Outside the walls on road junction, above a gas station. Good rooms and restaurant but poor service and a lack of hot water. *Mauritania* (I), tel. 20 72. 16 rooms, 10 showers.

SHOPPING. The silver here is cheaper than in the north, summarily refined on the spot, then fashioned into a great variety of *bijoux;* not everyone's cup of tea, but sensational on some clothes and on some women. This is Berber art—simple and direct like the people who make it. Clasps for the blue robes of the nomads, chains and pendants, heavy anklets, bracelets, clips with pompons, etc. Tiznit is the place for this, while Taroudant displays the pride of the Berber, carved silver daggers (also in copper), and also more heavy jewelry and gunpowder horns.

The *gandouras,* or blue smocks worn by the Tuareg camel drivers, are now chic, but often much overpriced for what they are and very poorly made. More exotic than a shotgun: the *moukkala* guns made at Irherm which have a long curved barrel. You lose everyone's respect if you're not a good bargainer—it's part of the fun for buyer and seller alike.

MARRAKESH

Where the Mountains and the Desert Marry

Marrakesh evokes dreams of palm trees and caravans, oriental markets and international espionage, merciless combats . . . or a perfect place for a honeymoon.

Historically Marrakesh has been stamped by two great influences: intimate connection with the desert and constant rivalry with Fez. Marrakesh is the magnet not only for the great Haouz Plain, but also for the Atlas beyond. It commands the southern part of the country, just as Fez the north. So if Fez served the Idrissids, the Merinids, and the Alaouits as capital, Marrakesh claimed first place under the Almoravids, the Almohads and the Saadians. Ever since 1913, when Rabat settled the question of capitals once and for all, Fez and Marrakesh have maintained a healthy rivalry in the economic field. As to population, Marrakesh is almost equal at the moment with 1,700,000 inhabitants.

Yet Fez and Marrakesh belong to different worlds; the former inclines to the orient and Andalusia, while the latter faces south towards the Sahara and Black Africa. The Almoravids understood this when they embarked upon their conquests at the end of the 11th century.

The Rise of Marrakesh

The actual date of the founding of Marrakesh and the identity of its founder are disputed, but certainly by 1062 the powerful Almoravid leader Abu Bakr had built a kasbah, the Qasr al-Hajar (Castle of Stone) near the present site of the Koutoubia Mosque, and there was a large tent encampment surrounding it. Abu Bakr was ousted by his cousin, Yusuf ibn-Tashfin, who, with the help of Christian and negro mercenaries, occupied the kasbah and around 1070 built a mosque either within its walls or adjoining it, of which no trace remains. This can be taken as the date for both the founding of the city and of the Almoravid dynasty. From Marrakesh, Tashfin set out on the conquest of Northern Morocco and by the time of his death in 1106 he had conquered most of the small Moslem principalities in Spain. The settlement derived great benefit from the rich spoils of victory, and was really opened for the first time to the civilized world of the Mediterranean as a result of the commercial relations established with the Iberian Peninsula.

Tashfin was succeeded by his son by a Spanish slave girl, Ali ibn-Yusuf (1107–43), and it was he rather than his father—who remained too much a nomad—who gave Marrakesh an urban character. It was he, too, who was responsible for the construction of the vast network of *khettara* (underground irrigation channels), which still provide water for the palmeries and the rich lands of the surrounding Haouz Plain. He built a new palace on the site of the Koutoubia Mosque, and a mosque in what is now the medina, of which only a pavilion, the Kouba al-Baroudiyin remains, as well as the great series of walls which still stand.

Under the first two Almoravid sultans, the city expanded, trade was carried on with all parts of the empire, and philosophers, physicians and poets from the whole Islamic world visited the city. However, the fanatic conservatism and orthodoxy of the Almoravid elders prevented any real flourishing of intellectual life and it was Fez which reaped the benefits from these new contacts.

Marrakesh was captured by the Almohad Abd al-Mumin in 1147 and most of the old Almoravid buildings were subsequently destroyed. On the site of the old Almoravid palace, kasbah and mosque, he built the first Koutoubia, which was replaced by the present building completed by his successor Abu Yakub Yusuf (1163–84), who also enlarged the city, extended the old walls and laid out a large garden which corresponds to the present Aguedal. His successor, Yakub al-Mansur (1184–99), who was responsible for the magnificent fortification and gates at Rabat, finished the great minaret in 1190 and added the domed cupola on the summit. He built a great kasbah containing twelve palaces with gardens, pavilions and ornamental lakes, of which only the Bab Agnaou, its monumental gateway, has survived.

The city prospered under the first three Almohads, but suffered in the civil wars during the declining years of the dynasty. Yakub al-Mansur's kasbah was destroyed in 1224, and the city pillaged in 1227, 1230, and 1232. It was finally captured by the Merinid Abu Yakub in 1269, and with the removal of the capital to Fez, Marrakesh became a backwater.

At the beginning of the 16th century, the Portuguese from the coast unsuccessfully attempted to take the city; it was subsequently occupied by the Saadians and made the capital of their empire in 1554. Abdullah al-Ghalib (1557–74) and Ahmed al-Mansur (1578–1603) restored some of the former grandeur; the great medersa of Ben Yusuf was completed in 1565; with the great wealth which came from the capture of Timbuctoo in 1591 a huge palace, the al-Badi, built of the most valuable marbles from Italy, and a royal necropolis, which is the last major example of the Hispano-Moorish style, were constructed. This was a golden era for Marrakesh, and the city prospered as it had not done since the 12th century.

However, the coming of the Alaouits signalled another period of decline. Moulay Ismail, in the late 17th century, destroyed the Badi palace and carried off the precious building materials to embellish his grandiose fantasies in Meknès. Marrakesh became a center for the slave trade from Black Africa, but little else. The center of power once more shifted to the north of the country, where it has remained since. During the French protectorate, a new city, the Guéliz, was built, and colonizers who had settled in the Haouz Plain brought back prosperity to the orchards and farmlands which had provided the region's wealth since Ali ibn-Yusuf planned the khettara in the 12th century.

Straddling the Mountain's Back

Coming from Taroudant, the exceptional panoramas from the Tizi N'Test Pass over the High Atlas range reveals towards the northwest the Atlantic catchment area—a crazy quilt of mountains and valleys stretching to the sea; to the southeast, the last summits before the Sahara.

The Roman geographer Pliny the Elder gave one of the most sweeping testimonies to the grandeur of this enormous range. "Such is the most fabulous mountain in all of Africa. Surrounded by sand, it lifts up towards heaven, rugged and barren on the side facing the Ocean to which it owes its name; but covered with thick shady forests and gushing streams on the side which faces Africa." The road clings to the side of the mountain and slowly follows its contours through the Atlas valleys. The kasbah of Tagoundaft is perched high on a mountain spur. The village of Talaat N'Yacoub with its little kasbah is set in the midst of gardens, close to the ruined mosque Tin-Mal, which crouches roofless on the mountain's flank. The Almohad dynasty was born in this mosque at the beginning of the 12th century. When ibn-Toumert was banished for "Revolutionary Activity" by the Almoravids, he took refuge at Tin-Mal and continued to preach his dangerous doctrine, namely, that the Almoravids were not only foreigners but idolators and immoral as well. Soon he had enough disciples to begin the warring crusade against his enemies and at the time of his death the tide had turned and the Mahdi (roughly "he who is sent by Allah to re-establish the true religion") could rest in peace. Twenty years later ibn-Toumert's successor, Abd al-Mumin, had brought the Almohad doctrine to all of North Africa and Spain and firmly established the dynasty the Mahdi founded. All that remains of the mystical revolution are the ramparts and the ruins of the mosque whose mihrab is still handsome.

Ijoujak is the cradle of the Goundafa tribe which has given its name to the nearby kasbah. The next 40 km. (25 miles) northwest follow mostly the Oued Nfiss, with ever-changing views of snow-covered Jebel Toubkal (4,164 m., 13,664 feet) to Asni. Here S6038 branches south to Imlil, the closest approach to Morocco's highest mountain. The descent along the Oued Ghehaïa (Reraya) passes an occasional mud-built flat-roofed village or a pattern of terraced fields. Strange superstitions survive here: to stop torrential rains that threaten harvests the mountain dwellers "plough" a corner of their small field with a cat and a dog harnessed to a stick. To make it rain when the season has been dry, young girls take a stroll among the meager crops singing in unison magic incantations.

The road winds tortuously through the Moulay Brahim gorge, named after yet another famous Berber holy man. After Tahanaout, where a livestock souk is held on Tuesdays on the bank of the Oued Gheghaïa, the plain takes over. This is the Haouz which rings Marrakesh for miles on all sides. In the distance rises the famous Koutoubia minaret above the palm grove, and finally the long red line of the ramparts is visible. This is a wonderful approach to the southern capital, strenuous but infinitely more rewarding than the shorter road from Agadir via Argana and Chichaoua.

Marrakesh—Its Focal Point

If you had, God forbid, only an hour to spend in Marrakesh—you would have to spend it where all the aspects of the southern capital converge—the enormous Jemaa-el-Fna square. It isn't really a square, but a huge rather vague triangle—named The Assembly of the Dead—a very macabre sobriquet for one of the liveliest and most colorful spots in Morocco. Once, however, the name was deserved as the week's collection of felons' severed heads was exposed here as a warning to potentially rebellious souls.

The mood of the Jemaa-el-Fna changes with the time of day. Dawn, first pale, then deep pink falls gently on the city roofs, then picks out the minarets one by one, setting them aflame like great candles. As day breaks in earnest the Jemaa-el-Fna comes to life. The shopkeepers take the heavy wooden shutters off, the cooks are seasoning their soups, and dozens of little charcoal stoves are lit and will keep burning all day to cook the couscous, the brochettes and to boil the water for mint tea. The stalls belong to traveling merchants who set out their trays of gimcrackery ranging from cheap but shiny jewelry to violently-colored portraits of the royal family.

Scribes write letters on blue-lined note-book pages; lower in the hierarchy are the sellers of chocolate, unwrapped and broken into morsels greatly appreciated by the flies; rows of dazzling white teeth are lined up on card tables. Itinerant vendors peddle daggers, fried fish, hashish pipes, Koranic texts, popcorn, and wooden spoons. Beggars pluck at the tourists' clothing, exhibiting their naked babies and mutilated limbs. Blind old men squat on the kerb, chanting their supplications in chorus. An occasional water carrier wanders about in his traditional costume, his bell tinkling, his copper cups shining. But he has no illusions: he makes more money posing for the tourists than by selling sips to the thirsty.

As the sun moves hotly towards noon, life on the Jemaa-el-Fna slows down and the crowd melts away to eat and sleep through the blazing hours of the day. This way everyone stores up enough energy for the hectic afternoons on the square when business largely gives way to fun and games. The Jemaa-el-Fna turns itself into the gigantic sideshow of the entertainers. The Atlas seems to be the breeding ground for the musicians and dancers who come down to captivate the people of the plain. The storyteller may act alone or with a couple of "straight men"—but however he may operate he is a very good mime and always has a fascinated circle around him.

In keeping with the tradition of local specialties, the acrobats of Amizmiz have the reputation of being the most spectacular. Many of them who start on the Jemaa-el-Fna end in the circuses of Europe. And what would an oriental sideshow be without a snake-charmer? He keeps his cobras in a wicker basket or an ordinary wooden box, and both snake and master think of their act in a blasé, all-in-the-day's-work fashion. The late afternoon is also host to mischievous monkeys and their trainers, while sword-

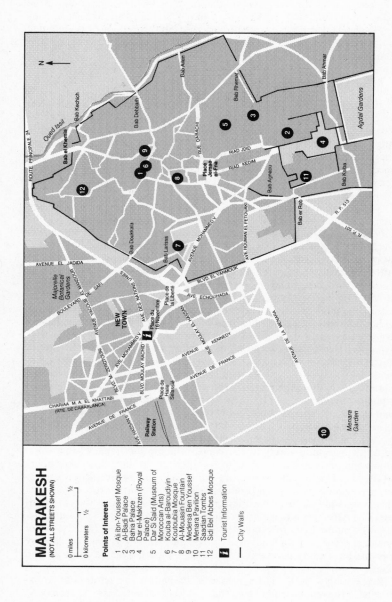

N ←

MARRAKESH
(NOT ALL STREETS SHOWN)

0 miles ½
0 kilometers ½

Points of Interest

1 Ali ibn-Youssef Mosque
2 Al-Badi Palace
3 Bahia Palace
4 Dar el-Makhzen (Royal Palace)
5 Dar Si Said (Museum of Moroccan Arts)
6 Kouba al-Baroudiyin
7 Koutoubia Mosque
8 Al-Mouasin Fountain
9 Medersa Ben Youssef
10 Menara Pavilion
11 Saadian Tombs
12 Sidi Bel Abbes Mosque

ℹ️ Tourist Information

— City Walls

swallowers and fire-eaters get their share of the attention. Musicians saw away on painted fiddles and rattle snare drums. Small boys whirl around at random. The tam-tam accompanying the dancers from Mauritania gives a rhythmic background to the general hubbub. There are several thousand spectators milling around this four-, five-, ten-ring circus, where neither tourists nor the dwellers of distant oases regret the coin thrown to reward the performers.

Evening on this square has another mood altogether, ushered in by the long wailing song of the muezzins calling the faithful to prayer. Many answer the call and leave the activity of the square for meditation in the mosque. The minarets are crowned with light as if to attract the eyes of all away from their mundane preoccupations towards the realm of heaven. Down on the square, the paler acetylene lights of the most obstinate merchants are flickering and will go out one by one as the last customers drift away. Soon no man-made light is seen and the moon shines over the deserted square until another dawn brings to the Jemaa-el-Fna the same pageant it has witnessed for centuries.

The Landmark of the South

The Jemaa-el-Fna, like the whole town, is dominated by the magnificent Koutoubia minaret, which is to Marrakesh what the Campanile of San Marco is to Venice. Its history mirrors that of the city, and it is probably the best known building in North Africa. The name Koutoubia is derived from the Arabic *Kutubbiyyin* meaning books or libraries, and the mosque has always had a notable library attached to it, its most famed possession having once been a copy of the Koran which the Merinid sultan Abd al-Mumin brought back from Córdoba; it had belonged to Uthman ibn-Affan, the third Orthodox caliph, and contained four prayers in his own script. This precious book was lost at sea in the 13th century. Throughout the Middle Ages, the mosque was surrounded by numerous booksellers and scribes.

Abd al-Mumin built the first mosque known as the Koutoubia, which was completed after 1158, and immediately after laid the foundation for an even larger structure which his successor, Abu Yusufal Yakub completed. Later, the older building was allowed to decay, but traces of its foundation have been excavated.

The interior of the Koutoubia (entrance forbidden) is starkly plain and consists of 112 columns of brick covered with a coating of white stucco. In its present state the mosque has been much altered, and little or none of the original decoration or doorways remain. The minbar is of carved cedarwood inlaid with mosaic panels and was made in Córdoba in the 12th century and brought to Marrakesh by the Almoravid Ali ibn-Yusuf.

The present minaret was begun by Abd al-Mumin around 1158 and completed by his grandson Yakub al-Mansur in 1190, who added the domed cupola on the top. It originally was contiguous to the earlier and later Koutoubia mosques until the former was dismantled. Measuring 203 ft. high and 40 ft. square, it is in the same style as the Hassan Tower in Rabat and the Giralda in Seville, but of much purer design—for the tower in Rabat was never completed, and the Giralda, incorporated into the Christian Cathedral, has been much altered from its original form. The exterior decoration of interlacing floral and geometric patterns is magnificent. In the interior, a ramp ascends to the summit, and there are six domed and vaulted chambers in the core, one on top of the other, the uppermost one with a feathered cupola in stucco and with stalactite squinches. Unfortunately it is impossible to climb the minaret, but the view from the top must be outstanding.

Through the Medina

To explore the vast medina which covers more than two square miles, a guide (who can be engaged at the National Tourist Office) is advisable. Your itinerary should include the Ali ibn-Youssef mosque with the Kouba al-Baroudiyin and the Medersa Ben Youssef. In 1030 Ali ibn-Youssef built a mosque which was probably similar to the Qarawiyin in Fez and the Great Mosque in Tlemcen which he founded five years later. The mosque escaped the Almohad destruction of the city, and al-Mutarda (1248–66), the last but one of the Almohad sultans, restored it. Falling into decay after the collapse of Saadian rule, it was completely rebuilt by the Alaouit sultan Moulay Suleiman about 1810 in neo-Merinid style, except the extraordinary Kouba al-Baroudiyin, a two-storied kiosk which must have been an annex to Ali's mosque. Only discovered in 1947 when the surroundings were cleared, the Kouba stands at least 10 feet lower, which illustrates vividly how often Marrakesh was destroyed and rebuilt on the rubble of previous structures.

The Kouba is important in the history of Islamic architecture in the Maghreb as the only Almoravid building preserved in its original form, the others having been much tampered with by subsequent rulers. On the ground level there are two horseshoe and two scalloped arches; on the next floor the number of arches is multiplied, the small horseshoe arches alternating with ones of a strange keyhole shape and others with scalloped edges. The whole is extremely sophisticated in concept, and its inspiration was most certainly Andalusian, although no precedents exist.

Nearby is the Ben Youssef Medersa founded in the 14th century by Abu el Hassan, the Black Sultan, who was responsible for so many fine Merinid buildings, and completely rebuilt by the Saadian Sultan Abdullah al-Ghalib in 1565. It is the largest medersa in the Maghreb and could accommodate more than 100 pupils in the cells above. Similar in plan to the Merinid medersas 300 years older, it is entered under a porch by a long, dark corridor which leads to the courtyard on the right. The contrast of the tile mosaics, elaborate plasterwork, and the gray patina of the old cedarwood screens and porticos is most effective. In the prayer hall is a magnificent marble ablutions basin from the original Almoravid mosque, made for a high official in the Court at Cordoba in the 10th century. Its decoration of heraldic beasts within a floral background shows the freedom of expression in Spanish Ommiad art.

The remaining important monuments lie in or near the location of the great kasbah built by Yakub al-Mansur between 1185 and 1190. Although it was destroyed less than 50 years later, the monumental gateway, the Bab Agnaou, remains. The horseshoe arch is surrounded by floral decoration with shell-shaped ornamentation and an inscription in a band of fine Kufic script. It is the best example of military architecture in Marrakesh. The original Almohad mosque in the kasbah was severely damaged in the 16th century and subsequently rebuilt several times; the Merinid medersa which adjoined it has completely disappeared.

The nearby necropolis of the Saadians warrants attention as the last flowering of architecture in the Maghreb. Constructed by the Sultan

Ahmed al-Mansur (1578–1603) as a burial place for the Saadian royal family, the entrance of the enclosure was walled up by the jealous Moulay Ismail around 1700 and only rediscovered in 1911 when Marshal Lyautey had an entrance made so access would be possible without going through the mosque. At the same time, much needed restorations were undertaken. Buried in the two pavilions are 62 sultans, their wives and their children, with more than 100 more in graves in the courtyard. The first pavilion to the left on entering is supported by twelve elegant but simple columns of honey-colored Carrara marble. The ceiling is of miraculous craftsmanship in inlaid cedarwood with honeycombed stalactite arches at the corners. Brilliant tiles cover the lower part of the walls and above are panels in stucco of astonishing variety. Of all the buildings in the Maghreb, the tombs of the Saadians, with their lovely garden and old trees, recall most vividly the Alhambra and its many courts, except for the two Saadian pavilions in the courtyard of the Qarawiyin in Fez which were directly copied from the Patio de los Leones.

Palaces, Souks and Gardens

In the same area as the site of the old kasbah are several palaces which include the Dar Si Said, housing the Museum of Moroccan Arts, and the rather ostentatious Bahia Palace. Both date from the late 19th century, while El Glaoui built two splendid residences in the 1920s, one reserved for visiting VIPs. The Dar el-Makhzen, the present Royal Palace, was begun by the Alaouit Sultan Sidi Mohammed ibn-Abdullah in 1747 and is closed to visitors.

The splendors of the Al Badi (Badii, El Bedi) Palace, extolled by poets are hard to recall among the sad ruins. Fit for a ruler whose domains extended from the Ebro in Spain to the Niger in Africa, the grandiose residence was still unfinished at the time of Ahmed al-Mansur's death in 1602. The choicest Italian marbles and other opulent building materials were used in the construction of this grandest of all Moroccan palaces and the summation in secular architecture of the Hispano-Moorish tradition. Whether it rivaled the Alhambra will never be known, as it was dismantled by Moulay Ismail in 1696; he used its precious stones and contents in his construction in Meknès. Today the ruins of the al-Badi form a magnificent and appropriate setting for the summer Festival of Popular Arts.

A walk through the souks is just as fascinating. From almonds to embroidered ribbons, from wickerwork to leatherwork, everything goes in the souks, and the cry "balek, balek" (make way!) sounds above the cacophony of screaming voices as everyone tries to get through the narrow streets at once. Save your film for the dyers' souk with brilliantly colored skeins and cloths hung out over the lanes to dry. But the fountains are the most evocative, though they are made for use, not for rest or coolness. The Al-Mouasin, dating from the 16th century, is so elaborate that it could be classed with the more important monuments of the city. The chief feature is a basin roofed with a beautiful porch of carved and painted woodwork. At the sides are three more tanks with domed roofs; they are for water for the animals. At the main tank the water carriers replenish their goatskin bags, gesticulating in the shadows on the brilliant geometric tiles.

In her love of gardens, Marrakesh is keeping up a noble tradition begun nearly a thousand years ago by the Almoravids planting palm groves all around. Thus gardens, like buildings, date from the 12th century as, for instance, the Agdal, a large grove of olive and other shady trees. Irrigation was, and still is, provided by a series of pools. The biggest of these in the Agdal measures 650 feet in length—not surprisingly, the sultans used to go pleasure-boating on its calm surface. From the terrace of a neighboring pavilion there is a marvelous view of the palm grove, the city, and in the background, the snowcapped peaks of the Atlas range. Smaller than the Agdal is the charming Menara Garden where the sultan used to meet his paramours in the elegant little pavilion framed by cypress trees. Occasionally the lady of the evening was thrown into the pool in the morning! From its terrace the view of the snow-covered Atlas is superb.

Both gardens were lovingly maintained by successive dynasties, surrounded by walls until the 19th century; a visit can be combined with a tour of the ramparts, preferably in a horse carriage. On this tour, continue to the palm groves beyond Guéliz, where over a hundred thousand trees spread out over some 32,000 acres.

It's interesting to see the city gates from the outside, not only for their architectural aspect but also for the scenes of local color, such as the "parking lot" at the foot of Bab Doukkala for everyone coming into town to sell his produce. All seems cheerful confusion: the rich farmers pull up their shiny new trucks next to the ancient carts, placid donkeys, illtempered mules and philosophical camels. And speaking of animals, another way to visit the palm grove is on horseback, or for the adventurous, camel back, especially early in the morning before it gets hot.

The entrance—badly indicated and easily overlooked—to the small but very pretty Majorelle Botanical Gardens (now called Bou Saf Saf) is from the Avenue Yakub al-Mansur in the Guéliz.

Defunct Headquarters and Ancestral Homes

Marrakesh is the hub of a wheel whose outer rim encircles the whole Haouz Plain, and whose spokes lead out in all directions, some into the Atlas range on excursions lasting from half to a full day. As spectacular in its own way as the road via Asni up to the Tizi N'Test Pass is the excursion to the narrow, well-wooded Ourika Valley and on to the ski resort of Oukaïmeden. After crossing the fertile plain, the road gradually rises along the Oued Ourika among the orchards and gardens, past the romantically wild setting of the Ighref Mosque on the right. From the narrowest point of the gorge, a mule track across the river climbs Jebel Yagour with its prehistoric rock carvings. The road follows the Oued at 900 m. (3,000 feet) to Setti Fatma, 63 km. (39 miles) from Marrakesh. At the Auberge Le Maquis, after 47 km. (29 miles), a branch climbs west to Oukaïmeden, a ski resort at 2,359 m. (7,740 feet) with Africa's highest chair lifts.

Close to the Ourika the Almoravids set up their first headquarters at Aghmat—more military garrison than capital. Shortly after, they headed for the plain and founded Marrakesh to serve as their capital.

S507 leads southwest, with a branch to Tameslouht, where the "Man of 366 Sciences" was credited with numerous miracles; several kasbahs of the Lords of the Atlas are in the vicinity. From the bridge over the Oued Nfiss at the Barrage Cavagnac there is a fine view over the four-mile long artificial lake which supplies most of the water that irrigates the Haouz Plain. Amizmiz, 58 km. (36 miles), is famous for its acrobats and pottery; market on Tuesday. The tracks beyond into the splendid mountain scenery should not be attempted after heavy rain or snow—and this applies to all Moroccan mountain tracks.

To the east are the kasbahs of El Glaoui and his cousin at Tazzerte, the dam and artificial lake of Ait Audel surrounded by red hills. Further east, beyond the Oued Tessaout, is Demnate, Morocco's oldest village, brilliantly white, carved into the rock below a strange kasbah, near the natural bridge of Imi N'Ifri (see page 145).

Having started this chapter at the Tizi N'Test Pass, it is fitting to end at the even higher Tizi N'Tichka Pass, at 2,260 m. (7,414 feet) Morocco's highest. P31 crosses the Haouz Plain through Ait Ourir, where a busy souk is held on Tuesday, to venture into the High Atlas. From Zerekten, below another kasbah of El Glaoui, the road follows a swift stream to Taddert and then rises in sharp turns amidst Aleppo pines, green oaks and pink oleanders to the Tizi N'Tichka, 105 km. (65 miles) from Marrakesh.

Shortly after the pass, a branch zigzags left 21 km. (13 miles) to Telouet, the fortress of the Lords of the Atlas, the Glaoua clan, whose last and most powerful chief was El Glaoui, Pasha of Marrakesh. He aided and abetted the French resident general, during the years of unrest preceding independence in 1956, in exiling Sultan Mohammed V to Madagascar and in placing an obscure member of the Alaouit family on the throne in his stead. But, as is often the case with "martyrs," popular sentiment for the exiled ruler and desire for independence favored by him crystallized round the person of the Sultan. Two years later, when the sovereign returned in triumph to his homeland, the disgraced Glaoui was very much out in the cold. Evoking the scene of the Emperor Henry IV kneeling in the snow at Canossa waiting for the Pope's pardon, El Glaoui made a public demonstration of repentance and humbly begged the *amam* (forgiveness) of his king. He died, broken and abandoned, at the age of 78, and was buried in Marrakesh in 1956.

Telouet, at 1,830 m. (6,000 feet) on the south slope of the High Atlas, though barely a hundred years old, is an outstanding piece of architecture; at once a palace for a great pasha and a medieval-looking citadel. But of the sumptuous interior of marbles, tiles, inlays, and an Arabian Nights profusion of precious furniture purchased mostly in France with complete disregard as to expense, only the naked crumbling walls remain. Restored to the Glaoui family, a caretaker shows visitors for a small tip through tumbledown rooms and staircases. The large ksar below is still inhabited, a reminder of the historic vocation of the Glaoui—to control an important communications route from an unconquerable position. Though a private car is ideal for all these excursions, they can also be made in organized day and half-day coach tours.

PRACTICAL INFORMATION FOR MARRAKESH

WHEN TO GO. Marrakesh is at its best December through April. The temperature averages 20°C (68°F), though of course some days are a great deal hotter. Rain, however, is far from unknown, especially in January and February. From May to the end of September the thermometer shows 30° to 41°C (85° to 105°F) in the shade. But it's a dry heat, and therefore tolerable with the aid of airconditioning and a pool. October to November is pleasant, though there may be the occasional shower.

Festivals. For folklore fans who enjoy even bigger crowds than usual in this city, a Festival of Popular Arts is held concurrent with a Week of the Artisanat (Handicrafts) in the middle of June. Almost 1,000 performers from all regions of the kingdom compete in traditional songs and dances nightly at 8:30 in the magnificent decor of the Al-Badi Palace. 500 riders are most impressive in the daily 4 P.M. Fantasia on Ave. Moulay Rachid.

HOTELS. Marrakesh is well-provided with hotels. In summer it is advisable to stay in the airconditioned (L) and, less reliably, (E) hotels with adequate pools, mainly in Guéliz. Package tours have led to a decline in service, except in the (I) hotels with restaurants.

Area code 04.

Deluxe

Es Saadi, Ave. El Qadissa (tel. 488 11). Almost as good as the Mamounia (see below), but much cheaper. Linked with the adjoining casino and set in lovely garden. Large pool and patio. Restaurant, bar, snack bar, nightclub.

Mamounia, Ave. Bab Jdid (tel. 489 81). 240 rooms, 20 suites. The most famous and the most expensive hotel in Morocco. Fine public rooms. The whole complex has been newly restored. A mainly one-armed-bandit casino, English managed, has been added. In the garden area tennis courts and large swimming pool. The rooms at the back, with verandahs on the upper floors, command fine views. The Churchill Suite is reverently preserved; the French and Moroccan restaurants are excellent; also the nightclub. O.N.C.F. chain.

Mansour Eddahbi, Ave. de France and Palais de Congres (tel. 482 22). 450 modernly appointed rooms in this new hotel.

Farah Safir, Ave. Kennedy (tel. 474 00). 300 soundproofed rooms; fine gardens. The chain's most prestigious.

Semiramis, Ave. de Casablanca (tel. 313 77). 185 spacious rooms in this addition to the Meridien group. There are indoor and outdoor restaurants, a heated pool in a palm grove, and tennis courts.

Expensive

Agdal, Ave. Mohammed Zerqtouni (tel. 336 70). 133 rooms. At the far end of Guéliz.

Les Almoravides, Arset Jenan Lakhdar (tel. 451 42). 100 rooms; opposite the Parc de la Koutoubia. In the Kasbah Tours chain.

Amine, Route de Casablanca (tel. 349 53). 146 rooms. Pleasant but a little far out.

El Andalous, (tel. 482 26). 195 rooms; newest, one of the best.

Chems, Ave. Houman El Fetouaki (tel. 488 13). 137 comfortable rooms, but small dining room; in palm grove near town center.

Club Méditerranée, (tel. 440 16). 190 rooms. Between the Koutoubia and the Jemaa-el-Fna Square; an excellent center. Swimming pool and arrangements for summer and winter sports. Occasional vacancies for non-members.

Ibn Batouta, Ave. Yacoub El Marini. (tel. 341 45). 52 rooms. Too small for package tours whose absence compensates for lack of pool.

Imilchil, Ave. Echouhada (tel. 341 50). 95 rooms. At the lower range.

Kenza, Ave. Yacoub El Mansour (tel. 487 43). 93 rooms. Tennis.

Le Marrakesh, Place de la Liberté (tel. 343 51). 367 rather small rooms; complaints about the food.

De la Ménara, Blvd. El Yarmouk (tel. 437 54). 100 rooms. Well situated but complaints about facilities.

Palais el Badia, Ave. De la Ménara (tel. 489 77). 300 rooms. The Moroccanized former Holiday Inn, pleasant décor; a little out of center. The least expensive in this category; comfortable, efficient and with a good restaurant.

P.L.M. N'Fis, Ave. de France (tel. 487 72), 125 rooms; and **P.L.M. Toubkal,** Place Haroun Errachid (tel. 488 72), 125 rooms. Both pleasant representatives of the French hotel chain.

Sahara Inn, Route de Casablanca (tel. 343 88). 167 rooms. Severely utilitarian.

Siaha Safir, (tel. 489 52). 207 rooms. The lesser in the chain, but likewise among the Ave. Kennedy gardens.

Smara, Blvd. Mohammed Zerqtouni (tel. 341 50). 49 rooms; no pool.

Tachfine, Blvd. Mohammed Zerqtouni (tel. 471 58). 50 rooms; no restaurant or pool.

Le Tafilalet, tel. 345 18. 84 rooms. In a palm grove 3 km. (2 miles) along the Route de Casablanca.

Tichka, Route de Casablanca (tel. 487 10). 140 rooms. Attractive pool and buffet; in palm grove.

Tropicana, Semlalia (tel. 470 50 or 339 13). 151 rooms. This new hotel, with a good restaurant and heated pool, is considered one of the best in this category.

Moderate

Chama, Rue Moulay Ali (tel. 475 17). 40 airconditioned rooms, pool.

Koutoubia, Rue Mansour ed Dehbi (tel. 309 21). 60 rooms.

Al Mouatamid, Ave. Mohammed V (tel. 488 55). 50 airconditioned rooms.

Du Pacha, Blvd. de la Liberté (tel. 313 26). 39 airconditioned rooms.

Renaissance, Ave. Mohammed V (tel. 479 98). 45 rooms, half airconditioned.

Inexpensive

C.T.M., Place Jemaa El Fna (tel. 423 25). 25 rooms, 15 showers. Noisy.

De Foucauld, Zenkat el Mouahidine, near Jemaa-el-Fna (tel. 454 99). 32 rooms.

Grand Hôtel Tazi, Zenkat Bab Agnaou (tel. 421 52). 61 rooms.

Oasis, Ave. Mohammed V (tel. 471 79). 33 rooms, 4 airconditioned.

Around Marrakesh

In the lovely **Ourika valley,** 42 km. (26 miles) along S513, the *Ourika* (E), tel. 04 Arbalou. 27 rooms, pool and nightclub. The pleasant *Le Maquis* and *La Chaumière* restaurants (M) are just past the fork to Oukaïmeden. 5 km. (3 miles) further on, the *Ramuntcho Auberge* (M), tel. 118 Arbalou. 12 rooms. Its restaurant is justly famous for both French and Moroccan specialties.

High up on the **Oukaïmeden plateau,** open only for the skiing season are: *Imlil* (M), (tel. 218 94). 33 rooms, but only 9 baths. *Ju Ju* (M), (tel. 590 05). 16 rooms, 7 showers; where you can hire skis and other equipment. The *Panoramique* and *Le Chouka* near the ski lift are basic; there is also a *Refuge* of the Alpine Club.

On the road to Taroudant is the *Hôtel du Toubkal* (M), tel. 3 par Marrakesh. At **Asni,** 48 km. (30 miles) from Marrakesh. There is a small pool and a wonderful view from the terrace to the majestic peak of Jebel Toubkal.

At **Ouirgane,** 13 km. (8 miles) further, *La Roseraie* (E), BP 769 Marrakesh (tel. 4 par Marrakesh), is for people who really want to coddle themselves and enjoy a quiet holiday away from everything. It has 12 rooms and 10 stone-built chalets with kitchen, bathroom, sitting room, etc., spread out among the trees and flowers. Outstanding restaurant, swimming pool, tennis courts, sauna. Less spacious, but with an excellent restaurant, is the *Au Sanglier Qui Fume* (M), tel. 09. 17 rooms, pool.

At **Ait Ourir,** by the bridge over the Oued Zat on the road to Ouarzazate, *L'Hermitage* (M), tel. 2. 28 rooms.

RESTAURANTS. European, mainly French, cooking is found in all large hotels, which also serve a selection of "touristic" Moroccan dishes.

Expensive

El Bahia, and also the poolside luncheon buffet in the Mamounia; outstanding for Moroccan food among the hotels and very likely the best in town. It is better to discuss the menu in advance rather than taking set dishes. Be on time, as there is nothing worse than a cold pastilla.

Dar es Salam, Riad Zitoun Kedim. Very touristy and bogus; offers folk dances and songs in a converted mansion.

Gharnatta, Riad Zitoun Jdid. In the medina.

Ksar el Hamra, 28 Zankat Goundafi. Rather like the Dar es Salam.

L'Hibiscus, 255 Rue de L'Hospital. French cuisine.

La Maison Arabe, 5 Derb El Ferran; in the medina. Probably the most famous restaurant in town, but very expensive and sadly declined from its days of glory. You'll almost certainly be urged to go there, but be ready for a great disappointment if you do. It has spurred some of the most pointed readers' letters we've had for some time. Best tackled in groups. Open Nov. to May only.

Palais Amabra Sidi Bouchouka, Arset Al Maarch. Traditional cuisine.

Le Riadh, Quartier Arset el Maach. Better for local color, in fine Moorish house.

Riadh el Bahia, Riad Zitoun Jdid. In the medina; local fare and entertainment.

Le Zagora, 9 km. (6 miles) along the Route de Casablanca, attempts a pre-Saharan atmosphere. 4 km. (2 miles) further, on the left turn after the bridge over Oued Tensift, **El Borge** offers Arabian Nights fancy attractions.

Moderate

Les Ambassadeurs, 6 Ave. Mohammed V. French-style restaurants cluster in this avenue, or in the side turnings just off it. This one is a little way from the main concentration, around the middle of the avenue.

La Bagatelle, Rue de Yougoslavie.

La Jacaranda, Place Abdelmoumen.

Le Petit Poucet, 56 Ave. Mohammed V. A pale shadow of its French heyday.

La Pizza, 63 Ave. Mohammed V. Italian specialties.

Rôtisserie de la Paix, 68 Rue de Yougoslavie. French and Moroccan cuisine.

Stylia, 34 Rue Ksour in the Medina, serves a variety of dishes.

La Trattoria, Rue Mohammed Beqal. Excellent Italian food.

Le 24/24, Ave. Mohammed V. Open most of the 24 hours.

Twi-Jin, Ave. Moulay Rachid.

Inexpensive

Ice Berg, Zankat el Mouahdine. In the medina.

Foucauld, Zankat el Mouahdine. The European restaurants in the medina are better value for money, and this is one of the good ones.

NIGHTLIFE. Except for the (L) hotel nightclubs, there are Fantasia shows at *Le Chaoia,* near the airport, *Zagora,* Route de Casablanca, and *Chez Ali,* Apres le Pont.

Discos on the Ave. Mohammed V: *L'Atlas, Le Flash,* nearby *La Rose des Sables,* Rue de Yougoslavie, and *Pub Laurent* in Rue ibn Aïcha.

SPORTS. Tennis at the Royal Tennis Club, Djenan El Hartsi; 18-hole **golf** course just outside Marrakesh on the road to Ouarzazate; **horse races** at various times at the racecourse; **riding** at the stables of the Club Equestre de l'Atlas, 54 Rue Abou Bakr Essadik.

Swimming at all the better hotels and the very crowded public pools—Koutoubia, Zagorah on the El Jadida road, and the large Municipal; **fishing** in the Oued Ourika about 32 km. (20 miles) from town; **skiing** 97 km. (60 miles) from Marrakesh in the Oukaïmeden range (see below).

WINTER SPORTS. Oukaïmeden is a winter sports resort in the Toubkal range of the High Atlas. 74 km. (46 miles) south of Marrakesh and 2,600 m. (8,530 ft.) up. Skiing can begin as early as December and end as late as June, but it is impossible to guarantee snow conditions even at the height of the winter season. Skis and boots can be hired. There are two ski-tows and two jumps. Even if no skiing is possible, you can still take the chairlift, Africa's highest, and enjoy the views from the top. Oukaïmeden closes in summer.

SHOPPING. Coopartim (under state control) for arts and crafts, in the National Tourist Office building, Abd el Moumen Square. Au Trésor Artisanal, 90–92 Ave. Mohammed V, fine selection of handicrafts, silverware, etc. Price tags, but a little haggling is not out of order. The boutiques in the luxury hotels feature the best selection of caftans, gowns and accessories at luxury prices. Slightly less exorbitant are the shops on Ave. Mohammed V for caftans, Berber jewelry and handicrafts.

USEFUL ADDRESSES. Tourist Information. The National Tourist Office (O.N.M.T.), Place Abd al-Mumin ben Ali, Guéliz (tel. 488 89). Syndicat d'Initiative, 176 Blvd. Mohammed V (tel. 320 97).

Travel Agencies and Transportation. Royal Air Maroc, 197 Ave. Mohammed V. Olive Branch Tours, Palais El Badia. Bland, 189 Ave. Mohammed V (also represent British Airways). Wagons-Lits Tourisme, 179 Ave. Mohammed V. Moroccan Adventure, 182 Ave. Mohammed V.

Car Hire. Avis, 137 Ave. Mohammed V and at airport; tel. 337 23. Azur Rent 221 Blvd. Mohammed V; tel. 310 95. Europcar, 63 Blvd. Zerktouni; tel. 312 28. Hertz, at the airport and 154 Ave. Mohammed V; tel. 346 80. Safloc, 221 Blvd. Mohammed V; tel. 463 58. Soumia Car, 37 Blvd. Mansour Eddahbi, tel. 492 64. Sud Car, 213 Ave. Mohammed V; tel. 327 80. Tourist Car, 65 Blvd. Zerktouni; tel. 484 52.

Garages. Auto Hall, Rue Yougoslavie. Renault, Ave. Mohammed V. Royal Automobile Club, Ave. El Maghzine (tel. 315 68).

THE DEEP SOUTH

The Ksour Royal Road

The Atlas cuts off the romantic land of the ksour and oases, so that in the pre-Sahara life is limited to that narrow band of land along the capricious *oueds* which have somehow managed to gain a foothold among sand and rock. One begins to understand why prophets have always gone into the desert to purify themselves—nothing matters here but the essentials!

Dadès, Draa, Todra and Ziz are the main oueds along which all the points of interest are concentrated. Between their valleys are trails across the desert which allow you to pass from one to the other, but beware: these pistes are not dangerous, but they merit a healthy respect—that is to say a rugged automobile in good shape and a sound knowledge of what is in store. The local automobile clubs, and usually the hotel managers too, have all the latest information on the pistes and can work out a precise itinerary. We are going to follow each valley in turn to give a complete picture of this strange and splendid region.

Though this stone desert may seem totally empty, the emptiness is peopled with groups of nomads whose existence is sustained by an occasional call at an oasis. There is consequently a whole chain of ksour (the plural of ksar). The ksar today has a sedentary population: its earlier role was to provide a place of contact and exchange. When the first nomads came this far, it was hundreds of years before they advanced any farther, but even then there was a contact with the outside world as the ruins of Sijilmassa witness.

All the ksour are built to a similar plan; a large enclosure with a single gateway surrounding a mosque, a collective storehouse and square houses with four brick corner pillars round a central patio. The building material is mostly adobe, decoratively used on the upper floors. Each ksar was built as a little fortress where the local population of small farmers could barricade itself against the nomads whose intentions were less than honorable, as often was the case in periods of over-population. Strange as it may seem, the vast Sahara has known many such periods when the number of mouths to feed was far greater than the resources at hand.

With peace, the ksour lost their reason for existence and prosperity departed. The inhabitants are gradually deserting their ancestral homes for greener pastures and, despite efforts to revive it, the Ksour Road may eventually cease to exist.

But everything the tourist has come for is still there: brilliant colors beneath a blazing sun, the call of the desert, and the mysterious life which somehow manages to survive in a setting of implacable wilderness.

The Crossroads of the Oasis

The High Atlas forms a great geographical divide. After the Tizi N'Tichka Pass the scenery changes totally; no more grass or green oaks, no more ash trees or pink oleander. A variety of two palm trees and a few sparse grain fields are its only vegetation.

The scenery is impressive in its own mineral way, and at Aguelmous, where the road branches to the kasbah of Telouet, manganese ore from the rich Imini mines is loaded into cable cars which haul it over the mountains to the Zat valley. At Amargane, P32 branches west (right) to Tazenakht, Taroudant and the Atlantic coast. P31 follows the Oued Imini southeast through the stony waste enlivened by a number of kasbahs, among which Tifoultout, to the right of the Ouarzazate bypass, is the most spectacular. Ouarzazate is a small provincial capital and important pre-Saharan crossroad, spreading along an oued which joins the Dadès in the large artificial Lake El Mansour Eddahbi, from which emerges the Draa. Ouarzazate is at the head of two valleys, but it gives a foretaste of the life of the oasis. On the streets, mixing with the local population, are members of the Ouzguita tribe who have come into town to sell their carpets famous for geometric designs in orange-red on black.

The attractions of a journey into the desert are notably increased by the certainty of a shower, a fairly good dinner and a comfortable bed at the end of the day at Ouarzazate, an excellent base for exploring the Draa Valley. Just outside town rise the massive walls and crenellated towers of the Taourirt Kasbah, built like so many others by El Glaoui.

The Birthplace of the Saadian Dynasty

Except for the first 69 km. (43 miles) to Agdz, high above the river, the road follows closely the Draa on the right bank. The thin ribbon of life rises from the water, first the meager grain crops, higher up almond and olive trees, bordered by towering date palms which like to "have their feet in the water and their heads in the fire," at the edge of the limitless, empty desert.

This is the landscape of the ksour which stand along the valley, protected by their red or yellow walls, the massive lines of their towers broken only by slit windows designed to let in air and keep out the heat. Life here is more than medieval—it is Old Testament. The women weave the cloth and make all the garments for the family. The men tan animal hides to make their saddles and their babouches (slippers) and also make pottery. The Draoua are a mixture of Berber and Arab tribes, with a sprinkling of Jews, Blue People and descendants of black slaves.

After 171 km. (106 miles), the best of the oasis hotels invites for a rest at Zagora, a hilltown dominated by a fortress. The excursion to Tamegroute across the Draa and a visit to the Dunes of Tinfou present no difficulty, but though the paved road continues as far as M'hamid, 282 km. (175 miles), it is open to traffic only by courtesy of the Polisario. Blue Men frequent the M'hamid souk on Monday.

The Jebel Bani, a gigantic desolate black rock, deflects river and road from their southern course to the west, through the Tagounite oasis to M'hamid where both give up. The river goes underground and only rarely emerges in the bed which continues across hundreds of miles as far as the Atlantic; but for exceptional heavy rains the Draa from M'hamid on is only a phantom river of sand. What little force the water has as it flows down the valley is diminished by draining off for irrigation, and there is nothing left in the lonely rocky plateau of the Hammada du Draa. As for the road, a sign says 65 days to Timbuctoo—by camel, as M'hamid, gateway to the Sahara, is still the point of departure for the caravans which traverse the desert.

From Zagora it is possible but by no means advisable to cut across to Rissani in the extreme south of the Tafilalet. It is so very much simpler to return to Ouarzazate and follow the Dadès upstream through the Valley of the 1,000 Kasbahs, visiting on the way the gorges of the Todra.

Morocco's Answer to the Grand Canyon

Heading northwest from Ouarzazate, P32 hugs the artificial Lake El Mansour Eddahbi, a surprisingly large if shallow sheet of water in this arid country. After playing hide and seek with the Dadès, P32 passes the photogenic palm grove of Skoura, where roses grow sufficiently profusely to provide the whole country with much appreciated rose water. Skoura looks like a fairyland when the roses are in bloom and the green palms form a background for a group of pretty kasbahs.

For the next 40 km. (25 miles) the Dadès Valley is a narrow band of cultivated land and handsome ksour. The most important of these fortresses are the picturesque Kelaa-des-M'Gouna, where a Feast of Roses is held every May, and Boumalne du Dadès at the issue of the gorges.

The road into the gorges of the Dadès affords some splendid views from high above the river, which can, however, be followed closely for some length on the piste at the bottom of the canyon. From its upper end the road cuts east across the mountains to the head of the Todra gorges.

If you like the Dadès, you'll rave about the Todra, whose walls rise well over a thousand feet. This incredible abyss separates the High Atlas range from the Jebel Sarro and is the same kind of geological accident (on a smaller scale) that produced the Grand Canyon.

Emerging from the gorges at the El Glaoui Kasbah and palm groves of Tinerhir, capital of the Tafilalet, you rejoin P32 for the dreariest stretch through a stone desert only occasionally relieved by small oases. From Tinejdad a surfaced road more or less follows an oued to its conflux with the Rheriss, and the latter southeast to Erfoud. P32 continues northeast via the large Goulmima oasis to Er Rachidia, and then through an endless stone desert to meet P19 and the railway at Bou Afra near the Algerian border. P21 extends south to Taouz and north via Midelt to Fez and Meknès.

The Country of King Hassan's Ancestors

Like the Draa Valley, the region between Erfound and Rissani marks the end of life and vegetation—but it's a spectacular end—a huge oval palm grove like a great ship run aground on the sands of the Sahara. 23 km. (14 miles) of road approximately follows the course of the Oued Ziz through the heart of this delightful oasis to Rissani, the final port of call before the dunes.

The ksar above the colorful souks and covered streets was built by the ubiquitous Sultan Moulay Ismail. Here you can also buy the heavy jewelry characteristic of the Sahara, made of barely refined silver smelted on the spot.

Very close to Rissani are the ruins of Sijilmassa—the Roman outpost of Sigillum Massae—which was of very considerable importance up to the Middle Ages. The town controlled one of the most important desert trade routes, and nothing went through her gates without leaving her richer. But in the 15th century the desert nomads got the better of the merchants, sacked the city and left only ruins which seem insignificant compared to the former glory.

Rissani is the homeland of the Alaouit dynasty, which has reigned for three hundred years. In the palm grove one can still see the "family seat" of the present king, and the splendid mausoleum of the founder. Both structures are in the care of "chorfa alaouits," meaning those who can boast a common ancestor with the king. The paved road continues south for 80 km. (50 miles) through several minor ksour and the sand dunes of Merzouga, the most easily accessible genuine Sahara scenery, to the Taouz oasis on the Oued Ziz.

North of Erfoud, P21 crosses for almost 64 km. (40 miles) a plateau with occasional glimpses of the trench-like valley of the Ziz. The scenery changes for the better at the Blue Spring of Meski, where water flows from a cleft rock, but the large pool, like the Ziz, is infected with bilharzia-bearing snails. Very shortly after the spring P32 branches east (right) via Boudenib and Bou Arfa to the easternmost point in Morocco, the oasis of Figuig, 426 km. (265 miles) of desert driving.

North of Er Rachidia, the administrative as well as the commercial center of the Tafilalet province, P21 crosses another 97 km. (60 miles) of ksour country to the north. Worth the short detour is the most impressive of these fortresses, the Kerrando ksar set above the steep banks of a Oued Ziz tributary on a branch road east (right) shortly after the Legionnaire's Tunnel, built in 1930. Other vestiges of the Foreign Legion's presence are the small look-out forts keeping a watchful eye on the valley and its once unmanageable inhabitants.

The only town of any importance after this is Rich, not all its name implies, but still administrative center of the upper Ziz. Then back into the mountains, never long absent from a tour in Morocco. The eastern spur of the High Atlas is crossed at "Camel Pass" (Tizi N'Talrhemt), the watershed for what rainfall there is, at 1,920 m. (6,300 feet).

Midelt, a town on the northern slopes, is a convenient starting point for an interesting excursion southwest, to a great natural amphitheater, the Cirque de Jaffar, below the eternal snows of Jebel Ayachi. After Midelt, one of the gateways to the desert and oasis world, P33 leads west to Kasba Tadla, while P21 runs north to Meknès or Fez via Azrou.

PRACTICAL INFORMATION FOR
THE DEEP SOUTH

WHEN TO GO. With the very definite exception of June-July-August-September the ksour country is very pleasant. Obviously, there is hardly ever any rain and you can expect blue skies at all times. In summer the mercury hits 107 degrees F. But the heat is dry.

GETTING THERE. By Plane. Direct flights Paris–Ouarzazate. Royal Air Inter flies to Ouarzazate from Casablanca, Marrakesh and Agadir.

By C.T.M. Bus. Casablanca–Zagora (5 trips weekly) 14 hours; Meknès–Rissani (daily service via Midelt–Er Rachidia–Erfoud) 10½ hours; Er Rachidia–Tinerhir 5½ hours.

By Car. Marrakesh is the usual starting point for the deep south, though P32 provides a direct link between Agadir via Taroudant, Taliounine, Taznakht, the Tizni N'Bachkoun Pass (1,701 m., 5,580 feet) and Ouarzazate. However, only Land Rovers should undertake the piste directly to the Gorges of the Todra and the Dadès Valley from El Ksiba via Lake Tislit–Agoudal–Tinerhir. Thus it is route P31, the most elevated in altitude in the Moroccan road system, which serves as the approach to the Draa Valley. The climb across the Atlas is relatively easy as far as Taddert, and then it becomes a steep haul up hairpin turns to the Tizi N'Tichka Pass at 2,260 m. (7,414 feet). The junction with P32 is in the Ouarzazate Valley, 26 km. (16 miles) before the town.

P31 continues southeast across the Tifernine Hills to Agdz, then follows the Draa through Zagora to M'hamid. P32 strikes northeast from Ouarzazate via Boumalne—branch north (left) up the Dadès gorge—Tinerhir—branch up the Todra gorge—to Er Rachidia and the intersection with P21.

P21, much frequented by tourists, provides access to the desert area from the east, Meknès or Fez via Midelt. This route crosses the eastern spur of the Atlas via the Tizi N'Talhremt Pass, 1,920 m. (6,300 feet), and more or less follows the Oued Ziz from the high valley to Taouz in the desert.

Some distances by road—Marrakesh–Zagora 370 km. (230 miles); Agadir–Ouarzazate 351 km. (218 miles); Ouarzazate–Er Rachidia 311 km. (193 miles); Fez–Erfoud (via Sefrou–Midelt–Ksar es Souk) 430 km. (267 miles).

During the winter months signposts just outside of Marrakesh indicate whether the Tizi N'Tichka and Tiai N'Test passes are open or not.

GETTING ABOUT BY C.T.M. BUS. Marrakesh to Ouarzazate (and return), 2 buses daily; Ouarzazate to Tinerhir (and return), 2 buses daily; Marrakesh to Tazenakht, departures Mon., Wed.; Tazenakht to Foum Z'Guild (and return), departures Mon., Thurs.; Zagora–Tagounit–M'hamid–Zagora, departures Mon., Thurs.; Zagora–Tagounit–Zagora, departures Wed., Fri., Sun.

From Er Rachidia twice daily for Goulmina and Tinejdad, once daily for Tinerhir (through Goulmina and Tinejdad) and return; twice weekly Mon., Thurs., for Bou Denib, Mengoub and Bou Arfa returning Tues., Fri.

HOTELS AND RESTAURANTS. The pre-Sahara is studded with airconditioned (E) hotels in the Kasbah Tours and P.L.M. chains. All of them are built in typical kasbah style, with pools, which blends in admirably with the landscape.

Boumalne du Dadès. *El Madayeq* (E), tel. 31. 100 rooms, but unheated pool at 1,550 m. (5,000 ft.) is a little chilly; otherwise in the best P.L.M. tradition.

Erfoud. *Salam* (E), tel. 66 65. Route de Rissani, 98 airconditioned rooms with TV. Built in a desert-style fortress, the Salam now has a heated pool and restaurants. *Tafilalet* (M), tel. 65 35. 20 airconditioned rooms and pool.
There are some simple restaurants in the main square.

Er Rachidia. *Rissani* (E), tel. 21 36 or 25 84. 60 rooms. Large and comfortable, with good service, friendly staff. Septic tank uncomfortably close to the pool. P.L.M. *Oasis* (M), tel. 25 26. 46 rooms.

Kelaa-des-M'Gouna. *Les Roses du Dadès* (E), tel. 18. 102 rooms; large pool. Kasbah Tours.

Midelt. *El Ayachi* (M), tel. 21 61. 28 rooms. Meals at the *Brasserie Excelsior. Meski,* (M) Ave. My Ali Cherif, tel. 20 65. 25 rooms and pool.

Ouarzazate. *Azghor* (E), tel. 20 58. 106 rooms. A one-night stopover for tours, resulting in unsatisfactory service. On a hill. *Bellere,* (E), tel. 28 03. 287 rooms. Restaurants, heated pool, tennis courts. *Club Karam,* Blvd. Prince Rachid, tel. 22 25. 143 airconditioned rooms. Sports facilities, restaurants, disco, even a movie theater. *Salam* (E), Rue Mohammed Diouri, tel. 22 06. 70 rooms, heated pool, tennis court. New. *Le Zat* (E), tel. 25 58. 60 rooms. Both P.L.M. *Tichka* (E), tel. 22 06. 113 rooms. Pleasant Moroccan setting on the main street.
La Gazelle (M), tel. 21 51. 30 rooms, pool. On the outskirts, good food and service. *Chez Dimitri* (I), provides decent meals and simple rooms.
Club Méditerranée, tel. 22 83. 60 rooms. First-rate cooking. In summer, it is used as an excursion stopover for groups from other centers and is available to casual users if not full. Regular holiday weeks operate in winter.

Tifoultout. At the end of a side road just before Ouarzazate, another *El Glaoui Kasbah* opens in winter as an (M) annex of the *Azghor* at Ouarzazate. Its 17 rooms have kept their authentic oriental décor and open onto the patio or gallery; most with shower.

Tinerhir. *Sargho* (E), tel. 01. 65 rooms, overlooking the oasis from a hill. Kasbah Tours. *Todgha* (M), tel. 09. 38 rooms. On the main square.

Zagora. *Reda,* (E), tel. 149. 155 rooms, restaurant, pool, tennis courts. *Tinsouline* (E), tel. 22. 90 rooms. Last stop before the open desert; heated pool. Kasbah Tours. *La Palmeraie* (I), tel. 08. 21 rooms, no private showers. *Vallée du Draa* (I), tel. 10. 14 rooms, 6 showers.

ALGERIA

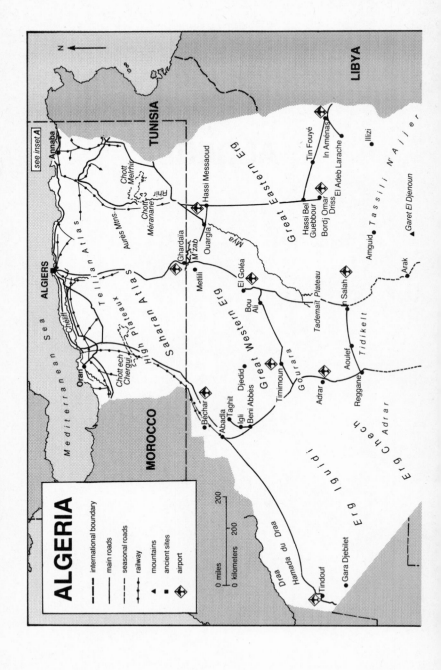

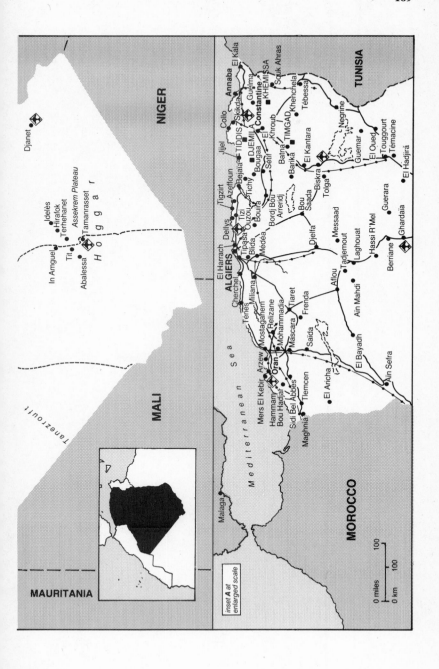

PRELUDE TO ALGERIA

With 2,381,740 square km. (919,681 square miles) the geographic giant of the Maghreb, Algeria's population is still slightly smaller than Morocco's, but increasing at an even more alarming 3.2% annually. Most of the 26 million live in the north, but the once unwanted sands of the immense Saharan south have been the mainstay of the national economy since independence, beside providing the touristically most original attractions. The recent decline in the gas and petrol revenues has turned the planners' attention once more to the potentialities of the splendid Mediterranean littoral, 1,223 km. (760 miles) of virgin coast awaiting the inevitable rape by package tours. In between can be found every conceivable Afro-Mediterranean landscape, from the window on the sea across the two enormous parallel chains of the Tellian and Saharan Atlas to the limitless sands of the Sahara.

Basic Geography

Except for the few resorts, mainly near Algiers and Oran, the innumerable beaches, large and small, remain fairly empty even in the height of summer. Their splendid isolation is due to a lack of accommodations within reasonable distance, while camping is definitely not recommended. Moreover, much of the littoral is difficult of access, high mountains sealing the sea from the hinterland, the Traras before Tlemcen, the Dahra before El Asnam and Miliana, the Sahel before Blida, Lower Kabylia before Tizi Ouzou, Lesser Kabylia before Sétif and Constantine, the Edough and the Medjerda before Souk Ahras.

Yet corniches have been cut out of the rocks above the sea and though narrow provide some of the most spectacular drives along the Mediterranean. Nearly all coastal towns and villages rise fairly steeply from the sea into the hills and cliffs, part of the attraction of Algiers, Bejaïa and Oran. The roads into the interior follow the gorges hollowed by the oueds on their way to the sea, thus making the valleys of the Chiffa, Isser, Kebir, Kedara, Rhumel and Tafna more familiar to tourists than the courses of the two main rivers, the Cheliff and the Soummam, flowing for the largest part parallel to the coast.

The Tellian Atlas, continuation of the Moroccan chain, traverses Algeria from west to east before descending into the sea at Cape Bon in Tunisia. Forests climb the slopes of the individual yet contiguous vast ranges, below barren peaks snow-covered for most of the year. The largest and touristically most interesting massif is the Ouarsenis in the center, extending northeast into the Atlas of Blida. Some of the summits have been classified as national parks, the Djebel Ouarsenis, Mount Kef Riga and the environs of the resort of Chréa, all accessible by road. Equally attractive is the Range of Djebel Djurdjura in Greater Kabylia, abutting on but not part of the Tellian Atlas, a position repeated by the Aurès Mountains in relation to the Saharan Atlas, which, some sixty miles south, presents a similar division into vast massifs progressing on a strictly parallel course; the Ksour Mountains round Aïn Sefra, Djebel Amour round Aflou, the Mountains of the Ouled Naïl centered on Djefa, the Zab Mountains between Bou Saada and Biskra.

The Miracle Plant

Between the two Atlases extends the immense depression of the High Plateaux, at 914 to 1,006 m. (3,000 to 3,300 ft.) not all that depressed, favored by glacial winds in winter and heat mirages in summer, an endless waste of small stones, except for the even worse salt desolation of the *chotts.* By rights no plant should have chosen so unpropitious a habitat, yet one of the riches of Algeria, the esparto grass locally known as alfa, grows in such profusion that in the western parts it successfully imitates a green sea. Thus the High Plateaux, however monotonous and dried up, are almost welcoming in comparison to the true desert.

The few dunes and 20,000 palm trees round Bou Saada do not make a Sahara, but good enough an attempt to satisfy the tourist in a hurry. The desert's real gates are at Béchar, Biskra and Laghouat, opening on the black fissured rocks of the Chebka, the white and cream waves of the Great Eastern Erg and the ocher and red of the Great Western Erg, the sterile dark plateau of the Reg, disintegrating to give a hold to the scarce salt bushes and wire-hard grasses of the Hammada.

The Democratic and Popular Republic of Algeria

The R.A.D.P. is divided into 48 *wilayate* (sing. *wilaya*), districts administered by a centrally-appointed *wali,* who is assisted by an *Assemblée Populaire de Wilaya* (A.P.W.). The *daïrate* (sing. *daïra*) are an administrative subdivision. Over 1,500 municipalities are managed by an Assemblée Populaire Communale and the mayor is called President of the A.P.C. The national gendarmerie is known as Darak el Watani, like the judicial organs of the caliphs of Baghdad and Córdoba.

In the approved socialist tradition, Algeria launched a gigantic industrialization program. Hundreds of factories have been built and their products supply most of the needs of the strictly disciplined and limited home market. This was achieved at the expense of the agricultural sector, to which only insignificant investments from the vast gas and oil export revenues were allocated. Even the hydraulic infra-structure was neglected and only one major dam, at Djorf Torba, was built in the first fifteen years of independence, totally insufficient for the additional industrial requirements, so that irrigation of over a hundred thousand acres of fertile farmland had to be stopped.

The construction of 16 large dams started in 1980. But agriculture is still fighting the encroachment of industrialization on the best farmland of the Mitidja. The green barrier of millions of drought-resistant pines on the High Plateaux and of date palms, planted at the confines of the Sahara to halt the advance of the sands, is considered by some experts a spectacular but costly prestige undertaking when the desert is gaining in the heart of cultivated zones.

The agricultural revolution has failed to stem the rural exodus, despite the distribution of land to some 130,000 families. Even the construction of over 200 of the planned 1,000 socialist villages—strictly functional but with all basic facilities—has not lessened the attraction of the towns where higher wages compensate for food and housing shortages. In fact, agricultural production has decreased as the population has grown.

Once a net food exporter, Algeria now imports almost 60 per cent of its food requirements, especially cereals, at a cost of $2–3 billion annually, using the greater part of the diminished export revenues. Though the best land that belonged to the French settlers has been given to cooperatives, it is the private sector that produces most of the food on the markets, better supplied since a more realistic price structure for staple foods has been adopted. A tree in a cooperative yields an average of 16 lb. of olives to 60 lb. in Tunisia, and 30 lb. of succulent *deglet nour* to a maximum of 160 lb. under free enterprise. The failure of socialist agriculture has led to a thorough restructuring, with the break up of the 2,000 self-managed state farms into several thousand smaller units, often returned to their former owners. A special bank assists private farmers, as pragmatism has replaced social rigidity.

Housing is an even more immediate problem. After the exodus of the French settlers, a large number of houses and flats became available. But since then construction has been totally inadequate and unable to keep abreast of the population explosion, aggravated by the migration from country into towns. Fifteen occupants for a three-room flat is common in the capital, where even cellars are let at fabulous rents. The Ministry of Construction plans, with the help of foreign firms, to build 100,000 housing units per year over the next decade. This extremely ambitious and costly objective will, however, at best only prevent a deterioration, as an equal number of new households is forming every year.

French into Arabic

As the three Algerian *départements* formed part of metropolitan France, administration and education were, till 1962, exclusively carried on in French, which a large segment of the population spoke better than Arabic. Arabization has been imposed since independence, but in 1985 President Chadli deplored before the High Council of the National Language the tardiness of its application. It is, moreover, strongly opposed in Kabylia, where the Berbers demand equal status for their language, which has been granted at the University of Tizi—Ouzou.

More than five million pupils attend primary schools, almost two million receive secondary or technical education, as 55 percent of the Algerians are under 18 years of age. Tidal waves of children converge six times a day on the insufficient numbers of school buildings, half of the pupils attending from 8 to 10 and 1 to 3, the other half from 10 to 12 and 3 to 5. The productivity of the educational machine is feeble, less than 20,000 high school graduates per year, as the standards of the French *baccalauréat* have not been forgotten, despite an over-ambitious reform on the American model. There are some 100,000 students at the four universities of Algiers, Annaba, Constantine and Oran, and the six university centers of the most important provincial towns.

Despite better education, women still face formidable obstacles in making their voices heard. In the 1984 elections to the Algerian local assemblies only a few hundred female candidates were elected to the 28,500 seats.

Life After Fossil Fuels

Algeria was, until recently, the only one of the three states to command a balance-of-trade surplus—entirely due to hydrocarbons—but the collapse of oil and gas prices halved the country's export income and led to stringent cuts in imports as well as in government expenditure and capital investment. A realistic projection of price uncertainties reduced the hydrocarbon contribution to only one quarter of the G.N.P. by the end of the Five Year Plan in 1989. Foreign indebtedness at $18 billion presents, so far, no problem, but heavy payments for food imports reduce the funds available for capital equipment. This has led to a shift in investment priorities from the nationalized heavy industries to the private sector, agriculture and housing in a distinct loosening up of the centralized socialist economy. In the economy as well as in politics, socialist ideology has given way to pragmatism as enshrined in the 1986 revision of the National Charter. Interestingly enough, while Algeria's origin is, for the first time, traced to Massinissa's Numidian kingdom, the predominance of Islam over foreign doctrines is stressed more strongly than ever. The tax basis has been broadened, but private entrepreneurs cannot be taxed beyond 50%. The 60 huge state corporations have been broken up into some 400 smaller enterprises and decentralization has raised factory utilization from a mere 40% to 75%. Joint ventures with foreign companies are now common and 15 years after expropriation, the international petrol companies were invited back for exploration, as at present only some 20 wells are drilled annually. But the need for austerity and self-reliance is undercutting the economic liberalization policy.

The silver lining is to be provided by tourism. Neglected amid the oil wealth of former years, tourists are sought after in today's deteriorating economy. Paradoxically, the impact of austerity is at present negative, as the reduction of the foreign exchange allowance for Algerian tourists has resulted in an even greater overcrowding of the few beach hotels. Projects abound, but the few actually under construction are mainly in the oases, as the Ministry of Culture and Tourism emphasizes the aspect with the least competition. The visitor had better concentrate on the sand and forget, at least for the time being, the sea. Though the enormous complex of the Ministry dominates the heights of Annassers, it has yet to establish Algerian travel offices abroad.

FACTS AT YOUR FINGERTIPS

WHAT IT WILL COST. An unrealistically high exchange rate makes Algeria the most expensive of the three countries in this book, especially when comparing the standards of accommodation and service in the five hotel categories. The average daily cost per person for each of our standard categories, including transportation within the country, entertainment and extras, is for Luxury about 1400DA; Expensive 800DA; Moderate 500DA; Inexpensive 220DA.

For hotel and restaurant costs, see below under *Staying in Algeria*.

A cup of coffee costs from 4 to 9DA; a beer from 6 to 10DA for a small bottle, wine from 40 to 70DA a half bottle, though often only large bottles are available, and then mostly red.

Men pay from 30 to 50DA for a haircut, women from 50 to 90DA for a shampoo and set. A hotel laundry charges about 12DA per shirt; dry-cleaning of a dress comes to 25DA, of a man's suit to about 30DA. Festival tickets range from 30 to 60DA, movie seats from 15 to 25DA. Nightclubs are disproportionately expensive, one drink from 60DA at the lowliest to 150DA at the still fairly unsophisticated top spot.

WHEN TO GO. May, June and October are the best months for traveling in the interior of this vast country, February, March extending into April the worst. The beach resorts, naturally, cater for summer visitors, the oases and the Hoggar and Tassili are preferred for winter tourism. The High Plateaux, at a fairly uniform altitude of over 900 m. (3,000 feet), are frankly unpleasant in winter, while nights in the Sahara are fresh even in the summer and downright cold in winter. The dry heat of the desert is much less debilitating than the lower but humid temperature of the coast. Day temperature on the coast in summer 27°–32°C (80°–90°F), rising when the Sirocco blows from the south. Day temperature in the Sahara in summer averages 43°C (109°F), falling to 10°C (50°F) or below at night.

Average afternoon temperatures

	Jan.	Feb.	Mar.	Apr.	May	June	July	Aug.	Sept.	Oct.	Nov.	Dec
Algiers												
F°	59	61	63	68	73	78	83	85	81	74	66	60
C°	15	16	17	20	23	26	28	29	27	23	19	16

SPECIAL EVENTS

March or **April**	Folkloric Spring Festivals at Biskra, Bou Saada, Djanet, Ghardaia, Laghouat, Timimoun, and Tizou.
March to **May**	Festivals with accent on a special product—Tomato Festival at Adrar, Orange Festival at Boufarik, Cherry Festivals at Miliana and Tlemcen, Carpet Festival at El Oued, Festival of Old Ksar at El Golea.
May	Sheep Festival at Sougueur; International Fair at Algiers.
June	Sheep Festival at Djelfa.
June through **August**	Cultural and Folklore Festivals in countryside; winners participate in the National Festival of Popular Arts in Algiers in **August.**
September	Horse Festival at Assihar.

25 December to **10 January**   Folklore performances at Tamanrasset.

ORGANIZED TOURS. The magnificent Roman ruins and the Saharan oases are certainly the most original attractions. The coastal resorts are nearly always booked out long in advance and the only chance of getting a room during the summer season is with a package tour. Organized tours are available, either from abroad or by O.N.A.T. (Office National Algérien de Tourisme), which offers the widest choice locally available. This is the recommended way to see the oases, because of judicious combination of air and bus travel, with guaranteed accommodation at Moderate hotels. More adventurous expeditions to the South Sahara, the Hoggar and the Tassili N'Ajjer, combine plane with dromedary rides, walking tours and sleeping in tents.

Except on a business trip, it is unlikely that a visit to Algeria would be limited to a day or two. However, Andalusian Tlemcen is just across the Moroccan border, and Roman Annaba is 63 miles from the Tunisian border, both very worthwhile one-day excursions. But on the whole, Algiers is the most likely place of arrival and though a pleasant town, one day is sufficient for sightseeing. Two- to four-day excursions can be made west along the coast via Roman Tipasa and Cherchell to Oran; east to Annaba, an equally attractive drive, combined with a visit to Greater and Lesser Kabylia, which can also be recommended on its own for a roundtrip. Three-day visits are possible to the Oases of Bou Saada, Biskra or Ghardaïa. The Roman sites, mainly concentrated in the east, can be seen in three or four days.

In one week, one might visit in the east, starting from Algiers along the coast, Tizi Ouzou in Kabylia, spending the first night at Bejaïa or if accommodation available at Tichi; second day along the coast to Annaba; third via Souk Ahras to Tebessa; fourth west via Khenchella and through the Aurès Mountains to Biskra; fifth north via Rhoufi to Timgad and return via Batna and El Kantara to Biskra; sixth west to Bou Saada; seventh north to Algiers. A very charged program, which had better be spaced over a longer period, while Constantine, Djemila and Sétif might be substituted for Biskra and Bou Saada.

In the west, likewise starting from Algiers along the coast, first night at Tipasa or Cherchell; second day to Oran; third via Beni Saf and Rachgoun to Tlemcen; fourth via Sidi Bel Abbès and Mascara to Tiaret; fifth via Aflou to Laghouat; sixth via Djelfa, with visitors to the rock engravings round Messaad to Bou Saada; seventh return to Algiers. This, too, is a very comprehensive tour, which should better be spaced out.

ALGERIAN NATIONAL TOURIST OFFICES. There are no Algerian tourist offices abroad, and thus travelers must rely on their own local travel agents and tour operators. Once in Algeria, the prime source of information is the O.N.A.T. (Office National Algérien de Tourisme), which also acts as travel agency. There are local O.N.A.T. offices in all major towns and tourist centers: see *Practical Information* sections for regional chapters.

Getting to Algeria

FROM NORTH AMERICA

By Plane. There are at present no direct flights from North America to Algiers. Fly to Paris (or London, Geneva, Zurich, Nice) and go on from there. See *From Britain* or *From the Continent* below.

By Boat. There are no direct passenger sailings from North America to Algeria. See *From the Continent* below.

FROM BRITAIN

British nationals will need visas to enter Algeria which should be applied for some 10 days before traveling. The new law became effective in April 1990.

By Plane. Air Algérie operate a several times weekly non-stop service from London (Heathrow) to Algiers with connecting services to other cities. Once a week to Oran.

FROM THE CONTINENT

By Plane. Air Algérie or the appropriate national carrier operate services from most European, African and Middle Eastern capitals, as well as from the main French towns and Barcelona and Palma de Majorca in Spain. In addition there are less frequent direct flights from the main French towns to Annaba, Constantine, Oran and Tlemcen. Twice weekly from Marseille to Tébessa.

By Boat. Regular car ferries by C.N.A.N. (Compagnie Nationale Algérienne de Navigation) from Marseille to Algiers, the crossing takes about 20 hours. There are also regular ferries from Marseille to Annaba, Bejaïa, and Skikida, as well as from Sète (southern France) and from Alicante (Spain) to Oran. But you should be warned that sailings can be infrequent and not always to a regular pattern, so it is essential to check the schedules well in advance. Full details of S.N.C.M. sailings from Continental Shipping & Travel, 179 Piccadilly, London W1V 9DB (tel. 01–491 4968). There are good rail services from Paris (Gare de Lyon) to both Marseilles and Sète. There are sailings from other ports during the high summer. Check with your travel agent for latest details.

FROM MOROCCO AND TUNISIA

By Train. There is a daily through train, the *Transmaghreb*, from Tunis to Algiers via Annaba. This takes just over 25 hours for the 1,000 km. (621 mile) run. There are through day carriages from Tunis to Algiers, but no couchettes or sleepers.

By Car. The main road from Morocco runs parallel to the railway line between Oujda and Maghnia, the only border crossing for foreigners in their own cars, but not in buses which are for local users only. The road between Figuig and Ben Ounif in the south is not always open even for private cars. From Tunisia there are several access roads, starting in the north from Tabarka to El Kala, from Ain Draham to El Aïoun, from Jendouba to Souk Ahras, from Kasserine to Tebessa, from Gafsa to El Oued. Even further south on the eastern border, pistes lead from Libya to In Aménas and Djanet. The pistes from Niger to Tamenghest or from Mali through the 740 km. (460 miles) of the Desert of Thirst are true expeditions.

Staying in Algeria

MONEY. Official exchange rates as we go to press are about 8DA to the U.S. dollar, about 12DA to the pound sterling, though these rates are changing all the time. The dinar is divided into 100 centimes. There are coins of 5, 10, 20 and 50 centimes, of 1, 2, 5, and 10 dinars, and bills of 20, 50, 100, and 500 dinars.

All foreign currencies and checks must be declared on a special form in duplicate, one copy being retained by the traveler, on which every exchange transaction at a bank or hotel must be entered. This form is handed back on departure and some difficult explaining might have to be done if insufficient sums have been changed, *after the obligatory 1000DA on arrival.* This is the minimum required even for a day excursion from Morocco or Tunisia. Changing the surplus back is always difficult and frequently impossible. A foreign currency black market flourishes: French francs are asked for quite openly in the streets of all towns near the border at four or five times the official rate. Algerian banknotes can be purchased at banks abroad at about the same rate, but importing them is strictly prohibited. The temptation is great, but so is the punishment and we would advise you not to succumb. The premium at Oujda in Morocco or the Tunisian border crossings is much smaller, but it may be necessary to purchase at least the legally permitted 50DA for import when arriving on a Friday, the official holiday.

HOTELS. The prices we quote are high season rates for double rooms with bath or shower and include breakfast and service charges. *Luxury* 700–950DA; *Expensive* 350–700DA; *Moderate* 200–350DA; *Inexpensive* 90–200DA.

The least tourist-oriented of the three countries in this book, Algeria has too few hotels, especially in the main towns and along the coast. They are fully booked during the summer season and service leaves much to be desired. In the comfortable oasis hotels—the best buys in Algeria, all with pools, but rather expensive—rooms are difficult to find during the winter season, unless you are traveling with O.N.A.T., the state tourist agency, which owns them. The privately-owned inexpensive establishments in the provincial capitals have had their day . . . at the beginning of the century. The non-classified hotels, especially in the smaller towns, never had their day.

See also the Hotel section in *Planning Your Trip,* at the beginning of this book.

VACATION VILLAGES. During the summer season these vacation settlements are fully booked up by Algerian holidaymakers, who find it more difficult to travel abroad than they once did.

CAMPING. Not advisable outside the 40 camps organized throughout the country. The best are the 8 of the Touring Club d'Algérie (T.C.A.), 3 Blvd. Zighout Youcef, Algiers (tel. 63 40 76).

RESTAURANTS. With the exodus of the French settlers, the European-style restaurants changed hands and standards. The recent encouragement of private initiative has brought about a welcome improvement in Arab and French cuisine, at least in the main towns. Noteworthy are the fairly expensive seafood restaurants in Algiers and Oran. The uninspired hotel menus can be varied by ordering *à la carte* which, however, might double the price.

Meals are from 120–220DA in an Expensive restaurant; 70–120DA in a Moderate establishment, with the uniformly uninteresting fixed hotel menus at the lower end; and 30–70DA at the Inexpensive places frequented by the locals, which only rarely serve alcoholic drinks. Prices are per person. Service charges and tax are usually included in the basic price.

In the regional chapters are listed some restaurants offering good food at reasonable prices, but beware of the fancy places with oriental decor, even if frequented by what seem to be truckdrivers and manual workers. That is exactly what they are, but to secure the services of European skilled laborers, the Algerian state enterprises have to pay such high wages that they can afford meals at 100DA and over per head, with drinks costing correspondingly.

SHOPPING. The local addresses of the Société National de l'Artisanat Traditionnel (S.N.A.T.) in the four main towns are given in the *Practical Information* section at the end of the regional chapters.

PUBLIC HOLIDAYS. The national holidays are: January 1, New Year; May 1, Labor Day; June 19, Commemoration Day; July 5, Day of Independence, of the F.L.N., and of Youth; November 1, Day of Revolution.

For the moveable religious holidays see page 2.

The weekly rest day has changed back from Sunday to Friday, which means that government offices are closed from Thursday midday to Saturday morning.

Opening Hours. Stores usually open 8–12 and 2:30–6. Foodshops stay open much longer. During Ramadan shops stay open at midday, but close earlier.

NEWSPAPERS. Paris newspapers and the *International Herald Tribune* arrive at Algiers and Oran the day of publication; British papers the day after. *El Moudjahid (The Combatant),* despite its name a French-language paper, is Algeria's largest.

SPORTS. Beaches, swimming pools, sailing and waterski clubs, skiing and mountaineering, Algeria's only golf course, horseback riding and camels for the inevitable snapshot are indicated in the relevant regional chapters.

MAIL. Postcards to the U.S. and Canada 2.20DA; to Europe 1.80DA. Letters to the U.S. and Canada 4DA; to Europe 2.40DA. Check carefully on current mail costs as they will certainly rise.

TELEPHONES, TELEGRAMS. Urban calls from public call boxes cost 0.50DA. Overseas calls and telegrams are relatively expensive; check latest prices.

Traveling in Algeria

BY PLANE. Compagnie Nationale Air Algérie's domestic air services extend to all major towns and oases. For the latter, flying is by far the most comfortable way of traveling, used by most organized tours, but very reasonable also for individual travelers.

BY TRAIN. 4,700 km. (3,000 miles) of railway connect all the major towns from Béchar in the southwest to Tébessa in the southeast. A west–east axis through the High Plateaux, Tiaret–Ain Ousséra–M'Sila–Ain Touta, is under construction. The railways *(Société Nationale des Transports Ferroviaires —*S.N.T.E.) offer first and second class, but both are crowded and far from clean. Trains are frequently late. There are couchettes on overnight routes, and airconditioned stock on main daytime trains.

BY BUS. The Entreprise Publique de Transport de Voyageurs (E.P.T.V.), organized into five regional enterprises, not only competes with the S.N.T.F. between all major destinations, cheaper and quicker except for very long distances, but goes to every inhabited spot a tourist might want to visit. The standard of comfort varies from comfortable to barely adequate.

BY TAXI. *Petits taxis'* meters start at 2.50DA and add 0.30 at every 100 meters. For *grands taxis* fix the price in advance, drivers are often surly. Sharing taxis for overland trips is less common than in Morocco.

BY CAR. About two-thirds of the 80,000 kilometers (50,000 miles) of roads are asphalted, but except for the *autoroute* (motorway) Blida–Algiers–Constantine are often narrow and occasionally badly maintained. All are classified and numbered, N (National) for the main, W (Wilayet) for the secondary arteries. The remaining third are pistes, dirt tracks, in the Sahara or communal roads to isolated villages.

Motor Fuel. As Algeria is one of the main O.P.E.C. countries, the price of gasoline (petrol) is relatively cheap, 2.80DA per liter for super, 2.40DA for normal, one liter of Naftilia Super Oil, the only available, 5.40DA. Smaller filling stations do not stock super and in any case are far spaced out, as under the state monopoly the customer is usually wrong, so why bother. Fill up in big towns, where the service may be less unwilling in expectation of a tip.

In order to be eligible to drive a car in Algeria you must have had a driving license for two years, be over 25 years, and, for some hire agencies, a returnable deposit.

Car Hire. Cars can be hired at O.N.A.T. agencies in all the main towns. Rental rates start at 375DA per day and 2,240DA per week, with unlimited mileage, for a small Italian car, rising to 500DA per day and 2,880DA per week, for a larger car. The deposit is 3,000DA. For a chauffeur-driven car the rates start at 740DA per day, including 200km., and 4,440DA per week, including 1,400km., with a km. supplement of 1.10DA; a Land Rover will cost 1,020DA per day and 7,140DA per week, with a km. supplement of 1.82DA.

For further information see *Traveling by Car in North Africa* in *Planning Your Trip.*

ALGIERS AND REGION

Romans, Redbeards and Cedar Forests

Unlike Morocco, where four imperial cities alternated as capitals, Algiers' supremacy has not been disputed for almost five hundred years, though the preceding 3,000 years had not been exactly easy.

Cretan sailors probably established a first trading post in the sheltered anchorage, where Phoenician merchants settled in about 1200 B.C. at Eiko-ci (Ikosim) which fell like all the African colonies to the most successful Phoenician foundation, Carthage. After the Roman conquest, Icosium prospered without great distinction for the centuries of the Pax Romana till the destruction by the Vandals in 430. But so fine a port could not be left unused for long and, when the Byzantines reconquered the African province almost exactly a hundred years later, a new though greatly diminished settlement had risen, which led the precarious existence of a Byzantine outpost among tribal Berber principalities till the coming of the Arabs.

In 935 Emir Bologuin Ibn Ziri, Chief of the Sanhaja Federation, refounded the town as El Djazaïr, named after the off-shore islets. Passing from Hammadite to Almohads and then to Zianids, El Djazaïr was also coveted by the Portuguese and Spaniards. The notorious Barbarossa brothers, Greek pirates converted to Islam, were called in to defend the town; the younger, with the redder beard, was confirmed as Beylerbey (Commander in Chief) by the Turkish Sultan, who also sent a garrison. Kair Eddin (Khair al-Din) Barbarossa repulsed a Spanish attack led by the Emperor Charles V in person and, for almost 300 years, piracy assured prosperity despite bombardments by Danes, Spaniards and the French.

The Turkish influence was strongest in the 16th and 17th centuries, both politically and architecturally. In 1830 French troops disembarked at Sidi Fredj and when the French occupation ended 132 years later, Algiers had been transformed into one of the loveliest Mediterranean towns. Conceived for 700,000, the population has grown to a very overcrowded 3,000,000.

Exploring Algiers (El Djazaïr)

Algiers, long a port before becoming a town, faces east on the wide bay which has brought prosperity from trade and piracy. At the western point, the Admiralty and Lighthouse rise from the original El Djazaïr islets, consolidated into the Ilot de la Marine; the connecting causeway shuts off the old Turkish harbor, now the Darse de l'Amirauté, reserved for the Algerian navy, fishing boats, and yachts.

The two-tier seafront extends as Quai #1 to #12 along the passenger port between the Gare Maritime (Passenger Embarkation) and the railway station; then assumes various street names along the cargo port until it widens in front of the main docks into the Route de l'A.L.N. (l'Armée de Libération Nationale) which follows the coast to the Hippodrome (Racecourse); becoming a motorway, it turns inland and crosses the Oued El Harrach towards the Bab Ez Zouar University and the Houari Boumelienne Airport.

Back at the Admiralty causeway, Boulevard Anatole France climbs to the northern city bus terminal on Place des Martyrs. This busy square is easily recognizable by two mosques, the Djemaâ El Kebir, founded by the Almoravid Youssef Ben Tachfin in the 11th century, facing the Turkish-style Djemaâ Ketchaoua, reconverted to Islam after an interval as a church. Close by, at the foot of the Kasbah, is the Dar Aziza, the 16th-century Palace of the Princesses, all that remains of the deys' residence. Below, on Quai #1, is the fish market.

From Place des Martyrs, the seafront's upper tier is Boulevard Che Guevara to Square Port Said with the National Theater; then continues as Boulevard Zighout Youcef, backed by the imposing Palais de Justice, Bank of Algiers, Town Hall, and Wilaya (Provincial Administration), which break the symmetry of the unmistakably French arcades lining the seafront as far as the intersection with the Boulevard Mohamed Khemisti. This palm tree-lined and flower-divided axis ascends in the city's center to the spacious Esplanade de l'Afrique with an enormous bas-relief memorial. In its lower part, in front of the neo-Moorish Post Office, the excavations for the first line of the subway have been slowed down by the austerity measures. Three lines totalling some 64 km. (40 miles) are planned.

The Flowering Heights

This is the town's center, from which roads climb the various hills that compose the spectacular amphitheater of Algiers. Center right, from the Palais du Gouvernement, the former French Gouvernement Général, on top of Boulevard Mohamed Khemisti, Avenue Docteur Frantz Fanon mounts past the National Library and the concrete pile of the Hotel Aurassi, which dominates the skyline from the heights of Les Tagarins, to the hill ringroad, here N36, descending to the right between the Ministry of National Defense and the Institute of Nuclear Studies to the Kas-

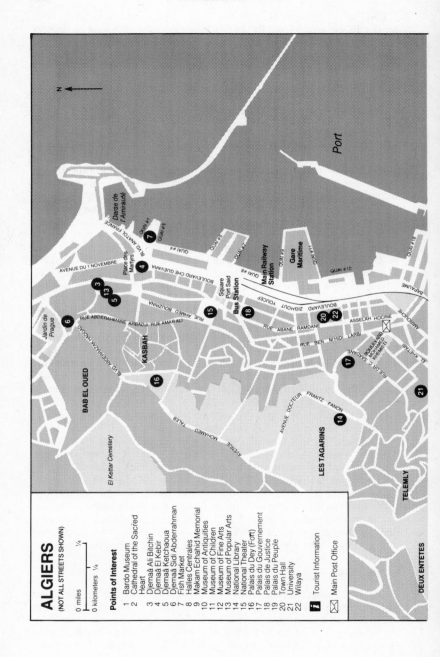

ALGIERS
(NOT ALL STREETS SHOWN)

0 miles ¼

0 kilometers ¼

Points of Interest

1 Bardo Museum
2 Cathedral of the Sacred Heart
3 Djemaâ Ali Bitchin
4 Djemaâ El Kebir
5 Djemaâ Ketchaoua
6 Djemaâ Sidi Abderrahman
7 Fish Market
8 Halles Centrales
9 Makam Echahid Memorial
10 Museum of Antiquities
11 Museum of Children
12 Museum of Fine Arts
13 Museum of Popular Arts
14 National Library
15 National Theater
16 Palais du Dey (Fort)
17 Palais du Gouvernement
18 Palais de Justice
19 Palais du Peuple
20 Town Hall
21 University
22 Wilaya

ℹ️ Tourist Information

✕ Main Post Office

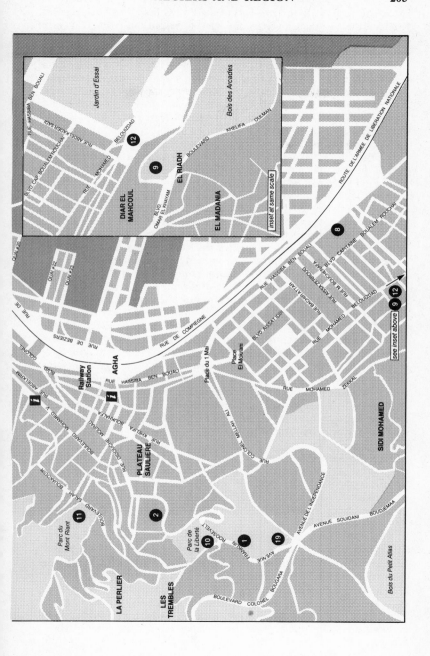

bah, to become N1 to the left. Left of the Post Office, Rue Abdelkrim El Khetabi rises past the University of Algiers to become busy Rue Didouche Mourad, lined with airline offices, boutiques, the S.N.A.T. shops, florists, candy stores, and the concrete Tent of God (according to St. John) of the Cathedral of the Sacred Heart. The portals of this very dated modernistic manifestation of Christianity's second coming to North Africa are barred. The tiny congregation, a score of old ladies, enter for the mass on Sunday, now an ordinary working day, by a backdoor and traverse the vast empty church before descending to a small crypt, rather like 4th-century Christians in the Roman catacombs.

Higher up the hill is the Museum of Antiquities, classical and Islamic, in the Parc de la Liberté, facing the Bardo Museum in an 18th-century villa of the deys. Here the exiled Bey Omar of Tunisia lived at the beginning of the 19th century, and some hundred years later the composer Saint Saens. In 1924 the enlarged villa became the Prehistoric and Ethnographic Museum, a mixture all the more unusual as some loosely termed African Collections have been added. Pride of the prehistoric part is the splendid horn, well over two meters long, of an homoiceras that became extinct in the Neolithic Age, as the conscientious labelling says. Ethnography is represented by lifesize dolls of odalisques in anything but seductive attitudes under tritely primitive wall paintings in the former harem. The serene tranquility of the patio is a delightful relief.

Quiet streets wind through the gardens of white villas to the other hills, revealing an ever-changing panorama of the town and bay. Boulevard Salah Bouakouir connects the Parc de la Liberté past the Parc du Mont Riant (Laughing Mountain), an appropriate name and setting for the Museum of Children, with the National Library. The Avenue Franklin Roosevelt ascends in the opposite direction past the luxuriant garden of the white marble Palais du Peuple (People's Palace)—as sumptuous as any royal residence, with the "people" having just as much chance of getting in. Avenue Souidani Boudjemaa continues past the British Council and the Anglican Church of the Holy Trinity to the Hotel Djazaïr before looping round the pleasant Bois (Grove) du Petit Atlas. Below are ministries embassies, and the Radio and Television Station.

All around are vast new popular quarters, one landward appropriately named Hydra, but seaward Diar El Mahçoul is architecturally the most interesting. Higher up, at El Riadh, the tremendous stylized cement palm of the Makam Echahid Memorial, inaugurated on the 20th anniversary of independence, rise 92 meters (302 feet), meeting above the cupola of the Musée du Djihad, of the Holy War that covers the period from 1830 to 1962, highlighted by souvenirs of Emir Abdelkader; closed Saturday. The view from the top, accessible by elevator, is staggering. A huge bronze statue of a *moudjahid* stands guard in this centerpiece of Riadh El Feth (Victory Park), the core of the new Algiers. The main part of the 146 hectares is taken up by the Bois des Arcades, which owes its name to the arcades surrounding an open square given over to a variety of performances. Grouped around this landmark are: an artists' village displaying handicrafts made in 26 workshops on two galleries; three reconditioned villas, a cafe, a restaurant, and a music room, all highly traditional; numerous other eating places are more up-to-date. Much bigger are the Socio Cultural Center, the Museum of the National Army, and a complex which will eventually house 161 boutiques and 26 restaurants, cafes and suchlike

Inland, across N5 here called Avenue Mohamed Belcacemi, extend the bare ocher hills on which African city planning has created the various Cités des Anassers, dominated by the vast Palais de la Culture, the seat of the Ministry of Culture and Tourism. Seaward, blue cable cars descend close to the Museum of Fine Arts, modern painting and sculpture, and the Pasteur Institute opposite the Jardin d'Essai (Botanical Gardens), which André Gide, perhaps slightly overenthusiastically, considered the world's loveliest.

Way beyond the Oued El Harrach, near the sea, the Palais des Expositions in the International Fair Grounds, housed in 1986 the first Algerian Tourist Exhibition, marking the conversion of Algeria to the possibilities of a hitherto neglected potential moneyspinner.

The Kasbah, Splendor and Decay

To the right of the Post Office, the largely pedestrian Rue Ben M'Hidi Larbi—its department stores, shops, and restaurants interrupted by a small square with the equestrian statue of Emir Abdelkader—is prolonged by less select streets leading towards the Place des Martyrs. Beyond, the tall modern buildings of the Avenue du 1er Novembre, the Fountain of the Sun Horses among flower beds, and the Overland Bus Terminal contrast sharply with the mosques and mansions of the Lower Kasbah. Among these are the Djemaâ Ali Bitchin constructed by an Italian pirate converted to Islam; the Medersa Taâlibia, also in Maghreb style, today a technical highschool for girls; at the limit of the Kasbah, the Djemaâ Sidi Abderrahman, constructed in 1696 over the tomb of a famous marabout, with lovely capitals as well as Persian and Rhodian tiles; the Turkish palace Khedaodj El Amia, first French town hall after the occupation and now the Museum of Popular Arts; one of Algiers' finest mansions, Dar Mustapha Pasha, constructed in 1799; Dar Ahmed, the deys' residence at the beginning of the last century.

The houses with overhanging upper floors supported by wooden beams in the maze of staircases, covered passages and crooked lanes above the wide Rue Amar Ali form a dying slum, where the sordid has long overwhelmed the picturesque. Adults are strangely scarce, only innumerable children play football with plastic bags wrapped around garbage. Here Algiers has turned its back on its past.

For those who can't bridle their curiosity, more or less official guides loiter near the Museum of Popular Arts, though they are by no means indispensable. It is much easier on your legs to drive up to the height of the very ruined Fort of the Kasbah, the citadel, and then descend through the Kasbah. There is little danger of getting lost, if you keep on a downward course, though you might miss the Cemetery of the Princesses, which is nothing more than the tombs of two daughters of Dey Hassan Pasha who died for love of the same warrior, a pretty story for very mediocre tombs; the Djemaâ Sidi Mohammed Chérif with an octagonal minaret; or the nearby 16th-century Djemaâ Safir which went octagonal in the 19th-century cupola. But, because of the depressing setting, these are all only marginally recommendable.

The Western Suburbs

The Rampe Areski Louni turns round the fine trees of the Jardin de Prague, site of a Roman necropolis. Across the Rue Bab El Oued, which leads to the quarter of that name constructed between 1880 and 1900, is the Dar El Hamra, and directly on the sea, at Bastion 23, the Turkish-Moorish Palais des Rais and some old houses.

A sinuous road ascends the hill to the Basilica of Our Lady of Africa, squat under a silvery cupola and onion domes. The church is closed, but the somewhat rusty statue of Cardinal Lavigerie, Algiers' first archbishop, looks out over the immense sea of concrete into which his modest see has grown. The heavy traffic on the coastal avenue passes the suburb of Bolo-ghine distinguished by some dolmens and a small forest. Farther on, the houses cling to the cliff overhanging the sea at Aïn Benian. N11 hugs the coast flanked by villas of indefinite styles but definite bad taste to the beach resorts of Sahel (Moretti) and Sidi Fredj, the latter on a pleasant promon-tory that can also be reached by a shorter inland road via Cheraga.

"Badly Worn"

Besides sand, sea and holiday villages, the coastal route also provides a fair choice of archeological sites. The first, 55 km. (34 miles) west of Algiers, near the Village of Brerard shaded by plane trees, is a Mausoleum of the Mauretanian Royal Family dating from the time of Christ. The huge tumulus of large blocks of stone in Berber tradition, but encircled by 60 columns with Ionic capitals, was empty when the masked entrance was at last discovered in 1865.

Tipasa is not only a large modern summer resort, but its extensive ruins are scattered over an idyllic setting. The Phoenician-Punic trading station became an important center of Greco-Roman culture under King Juba II and continued to prosper under the Romans. In the 4th century, Punic and Roman temples vied with Christian basilicas for devotees, till a Chris-tian girl named Salsa broke this tolerance and an idol at the same time. She was stoned and thrown into the sea which rose in protest until the body was fished out and given religious burial. The Basilica of Saint Salsa was built on the highest level of the eastern promontory when Christianity triumphed shortly afterwards. The faithful wanted to be buried near the saint and a vast necropolis extended all around by the time the Vandals took possession and imposed the Arian heresy. Those who clung to their Catholic faith had their tongues and hands cut off, others escaped to Spain. At the time of the Arab conquest the town was in such a state that it was called Tefassed, "Badly Worn."

Route N11 cuts through the ancient town, part of which is taken up by the modern village. On the eastern point of the small harbor is a large Punic tomb, on the west side is the attractive Museum, installed in a villa with a flowering patio; most interesting are the large mosaics, a marble sarcophagus and the lovely glassware.

Behind the Museum garden is the entrance to the Parc Archéologique. The Amphitheater is unique: it has a straight north side which has a mere six tiers to the thirty on the elliptical parts. Between the two adjoining temples ran the Decumanus, the town's main artery, which led past the fountains and colonnades of the Nympheum to the 4,000-seat Theater and the monumental Gate of Caesarea.

On the middle promontory are the remains of the Judicial Basilica and the Forum, with the Capitol and Curia. Villas lined the shore to the Public and Private Baths. The still impressive ruins of the vast 9-nave Great Christian Basilica rise on the summit of the western cliff. Beyond a Circular Mausoleum spreads the rather chaotic western necropolis to the Chapel of Bishop Alexander. Badly worn indeed, but the russet stones framed by the sea, asphodels, cypresses, eucalyptus and wild olive trees are poignantly romantic.

The Ancient Capital

The Romanized Berber King Juba II made Phoenician Iol co-capital of Mauretania with Volubilis. Renamed Caesarea in honor of the Emperor Augustus, whom Juba II loyally supported without becoming his vassal, the town became sole capital of Mauretania Caesariensis after the murder of Juba's son Ptolemy by order of the Emperor Caligula at Lugdunum (Lyon) in A.D. 40 and the division of the Mauretanian kingdom. Flourishing during the Pax Romana, destroyed by the Vandals and an earthquake in the 10th century, life gradually returned to Arab Cherchell under the rulers of Tlemcen.

On the square of the modern port is the Museum, containing mosaics and copies of Greek and Roman statues ordered by Juba II. Everywhere in and around the small town are scattered Roman vestiges, columns and walls of a Theater, Stadium, Nympheum, two large Baths, while much more is probably buried below fields and orchards.

In a less attractive setting but nearly as badly worn as Tipasa, it is difficult to recall the glory that was Caesarea. A group of buildings at the eastern entrance of Cherchell gives, however, a seductive picture of 17th-century Algeria. The Marabout of Sidi Brahim El Ghobrini consists of two pavilions connected by a colonnade opening on the sea, the tombs of the saint and of his family.

Of Sea . . .

For most of the 322 km. (200 miles) west to Arzew near Oran, N11 hugs the Turquoise Coast, which is at its scenic best as the Corniche des Dahra for the first 109 km. (68 miles) to Ténès, winding between the sea and the cliffs and forests of the Massif de Dahra. The Fountain of the Genie, a 33 ft-high monolith, stands at one of the innumerable creeks and beaches, of which Gouraya and the mouth of the Oued Bou Cheral offer the safest bathing. After Cap Lares, the gray- and fawn-colored rocks plunge straight into the sea, except at the Bays of Souhalia and Taranénia.

Westernmost port of the Algiers region, Ténès is derived from the usual Phoenician-Roman ancestry. 3 km. (2 miles) along N19, the best of the many connections between coastal and inland roads from Algiers to Oran, are the ruined ramparts, monumental gates, bridge and mosque of 10th-century Old Ténès.

. . . Mountains . . .

53 km. (33 miles) south, almost exactly halfway between Algiers (133 miles) and Oran (138 miles) among the heavy traffic of N4, Roman Castellum Tingitanum, refounded as Orléansville in the beginning of the French occupation, was destroyed by a terrible earthquake in 1954. Reconstructed and renamed El Asnam after independence, another earthquake shook the *wilaya* in 1980, leaving over 3,000 dead and half a million homeless. Foreign aid contributed to the speedy construction of six peripheral quarters around the ruined town that has remained the administrative and com-

mercial center, abandoned at night. Though small tremors continue, the survivors are gradually returning to what in the latest resurrection has now emerged as Ech Chlef. Reconstruction of the outlying villages was slower. N19 continues south into the thickly-wooded Massif de l'Ouarsenis, whose highest peak, 1,830 m. (6,000 feet)-high Djebel Ouarsenis, can be reached in less than an hour's drive through a National Park. Another branch road leads to the small Spa Hamman Sidi Sliman. At Tissemsilt, among the wheatfields of the Plateau du Sersou, N19 meets N14 which recrosses the Massif de l'Ouarsenis in a northeasterly direction via Teniet El Haad, from which the panoramic look-out Rond Point des Cèdres is easily accessible. Forest tracks negotiable by stout cars connect across the crests of the mountain chain with N19 and N4, but the main N14 is scenically just as exciting till Bordj Emir Khaled, whence it descends into the Valley of the Chélif to the crossroads of Khemis Miliana.

. . . Valleys and Plains . . .

N4 and the railway follow the Oued Chélif east through the irrigated orange orchards of this valley. W132 branches south (right) to the artificial lake created by the almost 300-ft.-high dam holding back the waters of the Oued Fodda.

From the crossroads of Khemis Miliana, W6 climbs to Miliana, which occupies a terrace on the slopes of Djebel Zaccar whose rocky peak dominates the town. Roman Succhabar was refounded as Miliana by Emir Bologuin Ibn Ziri in the 10th century, together with Algiers, and Médéa, passed to the Hammadites, Almohads, Hafsids of Tunis, Abd El Wadids of Tlemcen and Merinids of Fez. A stronghold of Emir Abdelkader, it resisted the French for ten years till its destruction in 1842, so that only the minaret of the 10th-century mosque in the main square and the 15th-century Sidi Ahmed Ben Youssef stand out in this typically colonial town of tree-lined avenues. But the luxuriant orchards of all Mediterranean fruits interspersed by vineyards are pleasing as the remainder of W6 to Cherchell crosses the eastern culmination of the Massif des Dahra, which separates the Valley of the Chélif from the coast; or the even more winding 29 km. (18 miles) on W9 amid pine- and oak-forests to the Spa Hammam Righa (Aquae Calidae of the Romans, who discovered the curative properties of the hot sulphur springs for rheumatic and intestinal disorders); W9 connects with N4 and N42 further east.

N4 provides the quickest link between Khemis Miliana and Algiers via Blida, but it is worthwhile to take N18 due east for a detour via Médéa, likewise surrounded by orchards and vineyards at almost 914 m. (3,000 feet) between Djebel Nador and the Ben Chikao Pass, both accessible by car for splendid panoramic views. Ever since the Romans founded Lambdia—the inhabitants still refer to themselves as Lambdani—and especially after the Merinids and Turks built strong fortifications used by Emir Abderkader after 1837, Médéa has been the key to the South. An interesting modern mosque with two minarets stands amidst the trees and flowers of the main square.

N1 leads south to Laghout, Gardaïa and El Goléa, north in 40 km. (25 miles) through the picturesque Gorges of the Chiffa to Blida, with over 100,000 inhabitants the main town of the fertile Mitidja plain, which stretches 101 km. (63 miles) from west to east. Founded by Sidi Yakoub Cherif, whose koubba (tomb) in the Sacred Wood is surrounded by centenarian cedars and olive trees, Blida has flourished since the 16th century, when Arab refugees from Andalusia harnessed the torrents of the Atlas of Blida into irrigation canals for the cultivation of the western part of the vast alluvial plain.

From the southern suburb, N37 zig-zags 18 km. (11 miles) up through the magnificent cedar forests of the Atlas of Blida, the eastern continuation of the Massif de l'Ouarsenis, to Chréa, at over 1,060 m. (3,500 feet) equally popular as summer and winter resort. Though the snow is variable, several ski-lifts make Chréa the favorite skiing center for nearby Algiers.

For the 50 km. (31 miles) to Algiers, N1 crosses the eastern part of the Mitidja, a malarial swamp drained by the French to be transformed into rice paddies round Boufarik, alternating with fields of flowers for the perfume industry, orange and lemon groves.

N8, the second access road to the South, leads via Sour El Ghozlane to Bou Saada, a mere 254 km. (158 miles) from Algiers the closest sample of an oasis.

Great Kabylia

Unlike N11 to the west, narrow N24 is repeatedly withdrawing from the coast east of Algiers, though touching the successive beaches of Bordj El Kiffan (18 km., 11 miles), Alger Plage (27 km., 17 miles), Tamente-foust-La Marsa (30 km., 19 miles), Aïn Taya Surcouf (35 km., 22 miles), the endless fine sand of Boumerdes (60 km., 37 miles), and Cap Djinet (80 km., 50 miles). The two main inland arteries east, N5 and N12, are the components of the motorway to Tizi Ouzou. N5 turns south at Thenia, through the wild Gorges of Beni Amran to Lakhdaria, and east again via Bouira, Bordj Bou Arreridj and Sétif on the quickest road to Constantine (423 km., 263 miles), while N12 crosses Great Kabylia due eastward.

From either Bordj Menaiel or Draâ Ben Kedha it is possible to join N24 and the sea, where Dellys, a fishing port at the mouth of the Oued Sebaou, preserves some Roman traces. Much more impressive are the Roman ruins and Byzantine basilica of Tigzirt, 26 km. (16 miles) east, one of the rare unspoilt villages left on the Mediterranean. N24 is not spectacular but pleasantly deserted for the next 39 km. (24 miles) east to Azeffoun (Roman Rusazus, not yet excavated), which is even more out of the way and constitutes journey's end, as N24 is not advisable for the remaining 93 km. (58 miles) to Bejaïa.

So inland again, best on the 35 km. (22 miles) N.R.N. (Nouvelle Route Nationale) from Tigzirt to Tizi Ouzou, the Pass of Broom, though that pass is a bare 183 m. (600 feet) above sea level. White houses climb the slopes of wooded Djebel Belloua facing south and the mountain ranges of Great Kabylia. About halfway between Algiers and Bejaïa, the sea and the snowy summit of Djebel Djurdjura, hub of eight roads along mountain crests and valleys, Tizi Ouzou has been endowed with the Institute of Hotel and Tourist Technology to train the personnel for the mountain and beach resorts developing all around, where the traditional Kabyl folk art— heavy enameled silver, jewelry, pottery with geometrical designs, wood carvings and vividly colored rugs—is an attraction.

The Kabyl Labyrinth

Narrow winding roads connect the numerous hilltop villages with characteristic pink roofs huddling round the mosque, but only two major roads, open April through November, cross the 48-km. (30-mile) east-west barrier of the Djurdjura, rising to three peaks of about 2,135 m. (7,000 feet). In the east, N15 provides a series of breathtaking mountain panoramas, with stops at the Fort of L'Arbaâ Naït Irathen, built in 1853 by order of Napoleon III to subdue the Aït Irathen tribe; at Icheridene, where a Cherry Festival is held in June; at Aïn El Hammam, another mountain resort in the making, while Aït Hichem on W17 east to Azazga on N12 is known for its fine weaving. W17 west descends to the Oued Djemaâ to rise again to the hamlet of Beni Yenni, center of the silversmiths, in a grandiose setting.

The Grotto of the Machabean and the Cemetery of the Apes, where numerous skeletons were found, are the best-known of the deep caves in this region. Tunnels pierce the chalk cliffs to the Tirouda Pass and on the descent to N26 in the Valley of the Oued Sahel.

In the center, N30 is best approached over W147 which passes through Souk El Khemis (Thursday Market), where the Maison de l'Artisanat is a veritable museum of traditional folk art, reproducing the interior of an authentic Kabyle house down to the last detail . . . with the help of Norwegian experts.

13 km. (8 miles) south, at Mechtras, where a Turkish fort guards what seems to be a town compared to the villages on the mountain crests, turn west (right) on N30 to Boghni. A forest road ascends to the skiing center of Tala Guilef above the upper limit of huge cedar and oak forests at 1,370 m. (4,500 feet). The road is being extended over Djebel Heidzer to connect with the main alpine and skiing resort of Tikjda, at the same altitude on the southern slopes. Till its completion, N33, branching east (left) from N5 at Bouira, provides the only approach to the most majestic range of the Djurdjura; a return to Tizi Ouzout is possible by N30 over Tizi N'Kouilal.

The Road to Lesser Kabylia

Impressive though these mountain trips are, most tourists are content to observe the splendid scenery from a main road, en route from one site or beach resort to another. N12 affords some views of the Djurdjura from afar, before crossing after Azazga and the mountain resort Yakouren the Forest of Akfadou on the descent to the Valley of the Oued Summam. There it joins N26 to Bejaïa, the main port of both Kabylias, but already in the Constantine Region.

PRACTICAL INFORMATION FOR
ALGIERS AND REGION

WHEN TO GO. As all Mediterranean towns Algiers is at its best in spring and fall, though only a few days in summer are unpleasantly hot. During the International Fair in May/June, hotels are booked out. Winters can be rainy—February through April are the worst months. Beach resorts open May through September, but are overcrowded July/August. Winter sports December through March, and the same mountain resorts offer pleasant freshness in summer.

GETTING THERE. From the Airport. Algiers' Houari Boumedienne International Airport (tel. 76 10 20/35) is 19 km. (12 miles) east by 4-lane highway. Half-hourly buses to the terminal on Blvd. Zighout Youcef, roughly above the Rail Station and the Gare Maritime (Car ferry embarkation); fare 10DA. Taxis to the main hotels cost around 80DA.

Bus from the Coast. E.P.T.V. buses from all major towns stop at the Nouvelle Gare Routière, Rampe Fréderic Chassériau. Buses from the west coast as far along as Ténès, Gare Routière, Rue de Béziers; from the east coast as far as Boumerdès, Boufarik and Blida, Gare Routière Tri-Postal.

GETTING AROUND. The bus network is extensive, but the buses are very overcrowded; there is little line jumping, as queues are formed only at the terminals, where they dissolve on the bus's arrival. Northern city bus terminal, Place des Martyrs; southern city bus terminal, Place du 1er Mai.

HOTELS. There are simply not enough hotels in Algiers to satisfy the demand, and those there are tend to be expensive. In the high season space is booked out in the surrounding beach resorts. It is important to book well in advance. The two top categories are airconditioned, all except the Inexpensive have baths or showers in all rooms. They all also have restaurants.

Deluxe

Aurassi, Ave. Frantz Fanon (tel. 64 82 52). 416 rooms, 39 suites. Plateau des Tagarins overlooking the town; pool, tennis, garage. Best in town.

El Djazaïr, 24 Ave. Souidani Boudjemaa (tel. 59 10 00 or 60 10 00). 155 rooms. Commands a fine view. The new block occupies most of the former garden; pool, tennis, nightclub.

Expensive

Es Safir (L'Ambassadeur), 1 Rue Asselah Hocine (tel. 73 50 40). 150 rooms. The former Aletti has kept its art deco style. Central; some rooms with sea view, others on quiet patio. Difficult parking. Good restaurant. Efficient management.

Moufflon D'Or, Parc Zoologique (tel. 56 82 25). 60 rooms. A favorite of the British consulate.

Moderate

Central Touring, 9 Rue Abane Ramdane (tel. 73 54 40).

Cinq Juillet, Complexe Olympique, (tel. 78 17 30). Newly opened three-star hotel.

Oasis, 2 Rue Smain Kerrar (tel. 73 06 20). Central; parking.

Suisse, Rue Drouillet (tel. 63 49 52). Past its prime, but still the best in this category. Central, parking.

Inexpensive

Des Etrangers, Rue Ali Boumendjel (tel. 73 32 45). Central; parking.

Ifriquia, 11 Blvd. Ben Boulaïd (tel. 63 11 12). Central; parking.

Es Salaam, 2 Rue Omar l'Agha.

Regina, 27 Blvd. Ben Boulaïd (tel. 39 14 03).

Terminus, 2 Rue Rachid Kessentini (tel. 63 61 77).

Algiers Environs

Azeffoun. *Relais de Kabylie* (M). 24 rooms. On the sea; pool.

Beni Yenni. 762 m. (2,500 ft.), 43 km. (27 miles) south of Tizi Ouzou. *Auberge le Bracelet d'Argent* (M). 24 rooms. Pleasant hotel with spectacular surroundings, friendly staff, cozy atmosphere. Clean rooms. *Hotel Djurdjura* in Ain El Hammam, Kabylia. On the N15 road between Soummah Valley and Tizi Ouzou. tel. 40 90

41 or 40 93 25. Clean and comfortable, good food, friendly staff. Hotel in beautiful surroundings.

Blida. *La Citadelle* (M), tel. 49 69 45. 17 rooms. 80 km. (50 miles) to the west of town on N1. *El Kebir* (M), 74 Blvd. Laichi Abdellah (tel. 63 49 52). *El Ancai* (I), 73 Ave. Amara Youcef (tel. 43 23 89).

Bouira. *Djurdjura* (M), tel. 52 72 70. 33 rooms. *En Nassim* (M), tel. 52 01 68. 30 rooms.

Cherchell. *Cesarée* (M), tel. 46 71 61. 31 rooms.

Chrea. 3,500 ft. up in cedar forest and 17 km. (11 miles) from Blida. *Les Cedres* (M). 29 rooms.

El Djamila. Near Aïn Benian, 18 km. (11 miles) west of the center of Algiers. *Méditerranée* (M), tel. 62 43 87. 23 rooms; beach.

Gorges de la Chiffa. South of Blida. *Ruisseau des Singes* (M), tel. 51. 25 rooms.

Hammam Melouane. *Hotel Thermale* (M), tel. 48 98 67. 30 rooms. Tennis.

Hammam Righa. In pine forests. *Les Thermes* (M), tel. 45 80 90. 50 rooms and 128 bungalows. Pool.

El Harrach. At les Pins Maritimes. 14 km. (9 miles) east of the center of Algiers. *Ziri* (M), tel. 39 72 74, at entrance to the International Fair. 108 rooms. Good restaurant. Pool and tennis.

Medea. *M'Sala* (M), tel. 50 54 24. 50 rooms.

Tala Guilef. Almost 1,520 m. (5,000 feet) up, and 49 km. (31 miles) south of Tizi Ouzou. *El Arz* (M), tel. 42 24 76. 60 rooms. Pool and tennis. There is also a refuge and a youth hostel in town.

Tigzirt. *Mizrana* (M), tel. 42 80 58 or 42 80 85. 40 rooms. Pool and tennis; on hill overlooking the sea.

Tikjda. 1,475 m. (4,500 feet) high and 70 km. (44 miles) south of Tizi Ouzou. *Djurdjura* (M), 52 72 70. 60 rooms. Pool. There is also a youth hostel and a refuge.

Tizi Ouzou. *Amraoua* (E), tel. 40 85 46. 65 rooms. Pool. *Lalla Khedidja* (M), tel. 40 29 01. On the Mechtras road. 60 rooms. *Belloua* (I), tel. 40 19 90. 60 rooms. In town.

Yakouren. In forest 53 km. (31 miles) east of Tizi Ouzou. *Tamgout* (M), tel. 10. 50 rooms.

VACATION VILLAGES. The four large, crowded beach complexes are booked out by Algerians in high season. Hotels form the central focus for apartments, bungalows, and studios; there are pools, marinas, discos, and boutiques. The distances given are by coastal road west of Algiers.

Sahel (Moretti). 24 km. (15 miles). Tel. 81 41 75. *El Minzah* (M), tel. 39 14 35. 95 rooms.

Sidi Fredj. 28 km. (17 miles). Tel. 81 44 55. *El Marsa* (E), tel. 39 10 05. 100 rooms. *El Riadh* (E), tel. 39 14 02. 125 rooms. *El Manar* (M), tel. 39 30 75. 375 rooms.

Tipasa. 70 km. (43 miles). Tipasa Plage (tel. 46 18 22). *De la Baie* (E), 111 rooms. On the sea. *Les Bungalows* (M), each consisting of 3 independent studios; also on the sea. *La Residence* (M). 352 room. 4 pools and all sports facilities; spacious grounds.

Tipasa Village (tel. 46 17 60). *Les Pavillons* (M). 600 bungalows spread over 4 quarters.

Zeralda. 31 km. (19 miles). Tel. 81 25 55. *Mazafran* (M), tel. 38 69 76. 200 rooms. This is a good alternative to central city hotels if they are booked. *Sables d'Or* (M), tel. 39 69 24. 258 rooms.

RESTAURANTS. In Algiers, beside the perfectly acceptable Algerian, French, and seafood restaurants in the city's three leading hotels, all of them Expensive, there are also—

Expensive

Alhambra, 29 Rue Ben M'Hidi Larbi. (tel. 64 60 92). Good French cooking.
Bacour, 1 Rue Patrice Lumumba. (tel. 63 50 92). Algerian specialties.
Carthage, 1 Chemin des Glycines, Place Addis Ababa (tel. 60 28 63). Up among the embassies' gardens, very convenient for government travelers.
La Casbah, 56 Rue Khelifa Boukhalfa (tel. 65 11 14). Try this place for good traditional Algerian food.
Feu De Braise, 11 Rue Khelifa Boukhalfa (tel. 58 69). Considered the best place for fine French food.
Dar El Alia, 2 Rue des Viellards (tel. 78 48 17). On the heights of Bouzaréah.
El Djenane, 2 Rue des Piliers (tel. 78 48 17). Also on the heights of Bouzaréah.
El Djenina, 10 Rue Franklin Roosevelt (tel. 59 42 92). Near the Bardo Museum.

Moderate

Le Saigon, 10 bis, Rue Valentin (tel. 64 06 23). Vietnamese cuisine.
The main downtown concentration is on Rue Didouche Mourad—**Columba,** Italian; **Cyrnos,** international; **Kheima, El Koutoubia,** and **El Maida,** all Algerian; **Victor Hugo,** French.
Up at Riadh El Feth in the Bois des Arcades—**El Boustane** is the international best, with top-of-the-range prices; then comes **El Sofra,** grillroom; **Soltane Ibrahim,** seafood; and **La Soummam,** traditional cuisine; to complete the meal, sweets and ices are served at **El Arika** and **Tikjda.**
Seafood restaurants are plentiful along the port. Among the best are **L'Auberge Phare, Le Magellan, La Sindbad,** and **Le Yacht Club.**

Inexpensive

Also in the Bois des Arcades are **Fast Burger** and the **Pizzeria La Gondole.** Downtown the best is **Le Marivaux,** 5 Rue du Coq.
Le Pourquoi Pas, 93 Rue Mohamed Belouizad, has Algerian specialties. The terrace of the **Milk Bar,** Rue Ben M'hidi Larbi is a great place to watch the world go by. For kebabs, try the kebab houses on the Rue de Tanger.

Algiers Environs

Aïn Taya. To the east. Le Gourbi (M), Ave. Principale.

Bologhine. 12 km. (8 miles) west on the coast road. *Chez Madeleine* (E), for seafood. *Villa d'Este* (E), for French cuisine. Both on Blvd. Taoufdit.

Cheraga. 14 km. (9 miles) west on the inland road. *Auberge du Moulin* (E), outstanding food; and *Dar el Diaf* (E), for Algerian food. *Golf* (M), French again.

Bordj El Kiffan. *Poker d'As* (E), excellent seafood.

Dellys. *Beau Rivage* (M), and *Sports Nautiques* (M), both for seafood.

Ech Chlef. *El Amir* (M), Route des Carrières.

El Djamila. *Riva Bella* (M) and *Le Sauveur* for seafood.

La Marsa. *L'Amiral* (M), fine fish.

Tipasa. *Le Progrès* (M), Rue des Thermes.

Tizi Ouzou. *Sebaou* (M), *Thala* (M), at the Piscine Olympique.

Zeralda. *La Sirène* (M), Ave. du ler Novembre.

MUSEUMS. Bardo Museum of Ethnography and Pre-History, 3 Ave. Franklin
Roosevelt, in a 17th-century mansion.
Children's Museum, Parc Mont Riant.
Museum of Classical and Moslem Antiquities, Parc de la Liberté.
Museum of Fine Arts, opposite the Jardin d'Essai.
Museum of Popular Arts, 9 Rue Malek Mohammed Akli, at the entrance to the
Kasbah.
Palace of the Dey. It is forbidden to take photographs.

ARCHEOLOGICAL SITES AND HISTORIC MONUMENTS. Dolmens: Azze-
foun and Beni Messous.
Berber Monument: Royal Mauretanian Tomb, Tipasa.
Islamic Monuments: Kasbah of Médéa; mosques in most towns.
Roman Monuments: Azzefoun, Cherchell, Dellys, Ténès, Tigzirt, Tipasa.

NIGHTLIFE. For conventional orientalism at unconventionally high prices there
are nightclubs at the three top hotels and in the beach resort hotels. There is also
Dar El Alia (see restaurant listing) on the heights of Bouzaréah; *El Koutoubia Club,*
next to the restaurant, 56 Rue Didouche Mourad, and at 97 in the same street, *Blue
Note.*

ENTERTAINMENT. The National Festival of Popular Arts in August. Regular
and somewhat phoney folklore evenings in the beach resorts. These performances
should be enjoyed in their natural setting, in the mountains of Kabylia or the oases.
An Arab play may be interesting *once* at the National Algerian Theater, Place
Mohammed Touri. *Cinémathèque Algérienne,* 26 Rue Larbi Ben M'hidi, and *Ciné-
ma El Mouggar,* 2 Rue Asselah Hocine, show foreign films, mostly French.

SPORTS. Golf. 18-hole golf course, Route de Chéraga, near the Olympic Stadi-
um, Dely Ibrahim, on the heights of Algiers.
Mountaineering and Skiing. Chréa, Tala Guilef, and Tikjda, November through
March. Fédération Algérienne de Ski, 30 Blvd. Zighout Youcef, Algiers.
Sailing, Waterskiing, Underwater Fishing. The Yacht Club, and the Federation
of Underwater Sports, Darse de l'Amirauté; Club Nautique de Tamemtefoust; hotels at Moretti, Sidi Fredj, Tipasa, and Zéralda.
Swimming. Pools—El Anassers, 199 Rue Mohammed Belouizdad; C.N.E.P.S.,
Ave. Mohammed Ghermoul; Olympic pool, Route Chéraga. Beaches—besides the
adequate beaches at Club des Pins, 23 km. (14 miles), Palace of Nations for Interna-
tional Conferences; Bou Ismail, 48 km. (30 miles), Aquarium; Berard, 40 km. (30
miles), near the Royal Mauretanian Tomb; there are others along the Corniche des
Dahara, especially at Gouraya, the mouth of the Oued Bou Cheral, and at Ténès.
On the east coast: Bordj El Kiffan, 18 km. (11 miles); Alger Plage, 27 km. (17 miles);
Tamentefoust–La Marsa 30 km. (19 miles); Ain Taya Surcouf 35 km. (22 miles);
Boumerdes, the best of all; Le Figuier 60 km. (37 miles); Cap Djinet 80 km. (50
miles).

Tennis. At most of the (E) and (M) hotels. Or contact—Fédération Algérienne de Tennis, 60 Rue Larbi M'hidi, Algiers; Tennis Club, Chemin Abdelkader Gadouche, Hydra; Complexe Sportif de Badjarah, Hussein Dey.

SHOPPING. The Société National de l'Artisanat Traditionnel (S.N.A.T.) offers a wide range of local handicrafts: handwoven fabrics from lambswool, goat- and camel-hair, laces, silver and gold embroideries, leather articles, copper ware, silver and gold jewelry, amethysts, ceramics; fixed prices, no bargaining at the Handicrafts Houses, 2 Blvd. Mohammed Khémisti; 1 Blvd. Front de Mer, Bab El Oued; 1 Rue Didouche Mourad.

There are also good craft boutiques at the Riadh El Feth shopping complex.

There are no souks comparable to those of Fez or Marrakesh in Algiers, but you may buy—and bargain—from the local artisans in all the villages of Kabylia.

THE ANDALUSIAN WEST

Wine and the Fifth Imperial City

Pre-historical Berber Ifri, in the center of a splendid bay, was bypassed by Phoenicians, Carthaginians and Romans, as the anchorage afforded no protection against the winds. The foundation of Ouahran is ascribed to Andalusian Arabs, who probably built the first breakwater in 903. Fairly prosperous under the Almohads and Zianids of Tlemcen—though, because of the distance, less than Honaïn and Rachgoun—the port was occupied in 1509 by the Spaniards who remained till 1791. After a devastating earthquake, which left over 2,000 dead, and under constant attacks from the Bey of Mascara, King Charles III of Spain ceded the enclave to the Dey of Algiers.

Under the French, Oran became Algeria's second town, a position it has retained together with its 19th-century aspect, despite the recent rapid growth to accommodate some 900,000 inhabitants, many crowded into the featureless expanses of housing beyond the old garden suburbs. In spite of this recent expansion, Oran has little to envy the capital itself. The famous French writer Camus was born in Mondovi, just south of Annaba, and lived for a while in Oran, which provides the setting for his masterwork *The Plague*.

Under the Romans, Columnata, now Tiaret, in the eastern High Plateaux, was the region's most important town, to become after the withdrawal of the Byzantines the capital of a Berber kingdom conquered in 683 by Sidi Okba. Neighboring Tahert was the first capital of the Ibadites, whose dominion included most of present Algeria, and remained a reli-

218

gious center till in 911 the Fatimids imposed their rival doctrines in their victorious sweep across the Maghreb.

Pre-eminence then moved west, where Idriss I, on his flight from the Abbasid caliph to the far Maghreb, had founded the first Moslem settlement in 771 on the site of the ancient Roman garrison post of Pomaria, and called it Agadir (fortress). The actual site of present day Tlemcen (the name is derived from the Berber *tilmisane,* meaning springs or water sources) was chosen by Yusuf ibn-Tashfin after the area came under Almoravid rule in 1079. He founded a new city, Tagrart, and joined it with the adjacent settlement of Agadir. His successors built the Great Mosque and a palace, the Qsar al-Qadim, which has since disappeared, on the site of the present mechouar. Almohad rule followed a two-year siege by Abd al-Mumin which ended in 1145; and in the following years, the walls and fortifications were greatly enlarged.

The power vacuum which resulted from the decline of Almohad authority in the 13th century left the Maghreb once again open to Berber invasion from the Sahara. Two tribes from the related group of Zenata Berbers were to emerge as the new rulers: the Beni Marin—or Merinids—at Fez, and the Beni Abd al-Wad—or Zianids—at Tlemcen. Throughout the 14th century and after, the history of Tlemcen is largely that of its relations with the Merinids who successively laid siege to the city—and occupied it three times—in the attempt to establish a North African empire to compensate for the loss of their Spanish territories. Tlemcen remained the capital of the Central Maghreb for 300 years and owes much of its splendor to the Zianids and Merinids who alternately rivaled each other in embellishing the city with religious foundations and palaces. The Zianids, originally from Figuig and the M'zab in the Sahara, had been settled in the area between Oran and Tlemcen by the Almohads and had acted as their governors. Almohad rule ceased when Yaghmoracen, the founder of the Zianid dynasty, established an independent kingdom in 1236. For the remainder of the 13th century, the city prospered and consolidated its control of the Saharan trade routes from Sijilmassa to the Mediterranean, establishing commercial contacts with Europe, especially with the Kingdom of Aragon.

The 14th century was Tlemcen's golden age, and despite the frequent Merinid sieges and occupations, the population grew to more than 125,000; its opulent court and its prestige as a center of Arabic culture and learning rivaled that of Fez to whom it often had to pay tribute and nominal allegiance. Both Merinid and Zianid decline started at the same time, and both fell victim to internal dissensions and corruption. The Spanish who had settled at Oran fought over Tlemcen with the Turkish governors of Algiers and eventually the city came under Ottoman rule in 1555. A long period of decay set in. With the French occupation of Algiers in 1830, the city once more divided—the Moorish elements and Berbers favoring union with Morocco, and the Turks and Kouroughlis supporting the French. However, the weak Alaouit sultans of Morocco could give little assistance, and Tlemcen became part of French Algeria in 1842.

Exploring Oran

Allah be praised! For once the fierce Arabization has not blotted out the French street signs, so that orientation in traffic as hectic as in the capital is greatly facilitated. And here a slight digression is in order. The mutability of street names in this part of the world will strike the Anglo-Saxon as strange, for he is not used to the maps of his cities being living testaments to the current political situation. In Algeria the frequent changes of street names can be attributed to any of three reasons: either they have been replaced to expunge the French past—a practice shared by Morocco and Tunisia; or they reflect changes in foreign policy, when, for example, Eisenhower and Kennedy might fall victims to an anti-American phase; or, finally, when an event or person has been commemorated prematurely, then disgraced—most leaders of the Revolution fall into this category.

Not that the Route de Ravin at the bottom of the chasm dividing the town needs much indication; west (left on the descent) the Hispano-Moorish Kasbah, gradually demolished to make way for more salubrious habitats, is entered by the Porte d'Espagne, decorated with sculptured escutcheons, and the Arab Porte du Caravanserail; opposite, the much larger 19th-century quarter is centered on the Place du 1 Novembre, where the very French town hall faces the National Theater, long closed, across the obelisk bearing medallions of Emir Abdelkader.

The Boulevard Emir Abdelkader, the main artery, rises gently past the O.N.A.T. office, the S.N.A.T. shop and restaurants, lined higher up by travel agencies and airline offices, to the plateau where the cathedral—till recently the churches outnumbered the mosques—the railway station and administrative buildings are situated. Also the Museum Demaeght, prehistory, archeology, natural sciences in the basement; 17th-century Dutch and more recent French painters at street level; prints and pictures of old Oran on the first floor.

The first crossroad, Rue M. Khémisti, leads left to the quiet Place du Maghreb, where the post office and the Grand Hotel overlook some palm trees; the next, Avenue Larbi Ben M'Hidi, is the main shopping center. In the parallel Rue des Aurès a well-stocked but expensive open-air market is held.

A Pleasing Whole

For the one mile between the Château Neuf and the beginning of the motorway to Algiers, the Boulevard du Front de Mer, above the rail line to the Gare Maritime and the Nouvelle Route du Port, greatly resembles its equivalent in the capital; less imposing official buildings, but the same frontage of unobtrusively elegant arcaded French houses, the same orderly palm trees and, best of all, the view over the magnificent bay and the busy harbor, carefully protected by breakwaters to the lighthouse far out at sea.

The Jardin du Château Neuf is a small oasis of greenery round a group of fortifications dating from various periods and still occupied by the military and therefore inaccessible. The nearby 4-star hotel, long under construction, will eventually relieve the chronic lack of accommodation. Below the Château Neuf is the 18th-century Turkish Mosque of the Pasha, whose fine porch and semicircular peristyle open on to a small garden.

Among the labyrinthine lanes of Old Oran, the triangular Place de la Perle was the Spanish Plaza Mayor, dominated by the original cathedral, now deconsecrated as well as the adjoining mosque. The whole dilapidated quarter is vowed to destruction.

Beyond, the wooded cliff of the Mudjadjo dominates the sea. Several roads serpentine the 365 m. (1,200 feet) up to the 16th-century Fort of Santa Cruz, below which the enormous agglomeration spreads its tentacles ever wider. The Sacré Coeur Basilica stands a little lower, while on the landward slope the oaks, Aleppo pines and carob trees of the Bois des Planteurs preserve the memory of the French Planteurs Militaires.

The Coast near Oran

The Corniche passes Fort Lamounne, constructed by the Spaniards in 1742, on the way to Mers El Kebir (The Great Port), 8 km. (5 miles) west. The French fleet took refuge in this splendid anchorage after the fall of France in 1940, but refused to continue the fight against Germany or even to be interned in a neutral country. A British squadron sank several of the ships with considerable loss of life, while the rest, breaking anchor, escaped to Toulon. This incident almost lead the Vichy government to declare war on Great Britain. Too good a harbor to be neglected, Mers El Kebir is the main base for the Algerian navy.

The beaches of Trouville, Paradis Plage, Les Sablettes and Claire Fontaine follow close on one another to Aïn El Turck (16 km., 10 miles), named to commemorate the landing of the Turkish janissaries among some vague Berber ruins. The Corniche negotiates Cap Falcon, with the lighthouse on the western extremity of the bay, to end at the fine beach of Les Andalouses (25 km., 16 miles), the western region's only holiday village, where the swimming competitions of the 1975 Mediterranean Games were held. There is good underwater fishing round l'Ile Plane, an islet favored by wild swans.

East of Oran, W75 hugs a more rugged coast to the Cliff of Kristel (19 km., 12 miles), where a tiny fishing port is squeezed into a geological fault splitting Djebel Kaar (457 m., 1,500 feet), which bars the way to the lighthouse of La Pointe de l'Aiguille (The Needlepoint) on the eastern headland closing the immense bay of Oran.

The Coastal Road to Algiers

As in the previous chapter the outward journey follows the coast, on a narrower but less frequented and much lovelier road than the shorter inland return. Yet the first impression is overwhelmingly horrifying. No need to return to Oran from Kristel, W75 leads inland through a gorge to Gdyel on N11 which winds through vineyards to the petrol port of Arzew (40 km., 25 miles), whose flames burning off the surplus gas of the refinery can be seen from afar—and smelt even further. Terminal of the third oil pipeline from Hassi Messaoud to the coast, and the first gas pipeline from Hassi R'Mel, the construction of a third liquefaction plant, for natural gas—Arzew claims the world's first—was temporarily suspended as part of the present austerity drive. Gas also powers an electricity plant.

That the Algerian Tourist Office still praises the charms of the surroundings and even of the port itself is, to say the least, surprising, as industry in a particulary unattractive though vastly lucrative form has obviously precluded tourism, all the 8 km. (5 miles) along the Corniche northwest to Cap Carbon; nor is the view from the Djebel Der Amara as splendid as claimed—to anyone but a petrochemical engineer.

The next 48 km. (30 miles) between the sea and the vast Plain of Habra, a drained swamp given over to rice and cotton plantations, is fairly uninteresting. Nor have the miles of fine sands at Mostaganem escaped industrialization, necessary, no doubt, but still unattractive, to recapture the prosperity of the Turkish era while Oran was occupied by the Spaniards. Founded by the Almoravid Yusuf ibn-Tashfin, Mostaganem passed from the Zianids of Tlemcen to the Merinids of Fez, who constructed the Djemaâ Abou El Hassan in the 15th century.

After bridging the mouth of the Oued Chéliff (11 km., 7 miles), N11 leaves the coast for endless vineyards to return only at Cap Magroua, narrowly squeezed between the sea and densely wooded cliffs. There are some small beaches in lonely creeks and hardly any traffic till joining the Corniche des Dahra at Ténès.

The Wine Country

N4 follows the railway, the pipeline and, at least for the first part of the return journey, the Oued Chéliff, Algeria's main river, which flows for a long time parallel to the coast, unfortunately too often out of sight. Not a very remarkable journey by Algerian standards, vineyards alternating with orchards but gradually overwhelming all other cultivation to Relizane.

If the Phoenicians did not introduce the grape, they certainly introduced the art of winemaking into North Africa, but the wine of antiquity was so heavy and concentrated that it was drunk mixed with water or raisin juice. This practice was continued under the Romans, who were great drinkers while unsuccessfully trying to enforce teetotalism in the army.

Far from uprooting the vines, Islam trained them along mosques and marabouts, as the Koran recognizes the grape as an excellent fruit though forbidding alcoholic drinks. The French increased the area under cultivation ten times within the first 50 years of the occupation, simultaneously greatly increasing the yield, as this was the time when phylloxera had wrought deadly havoc among the vines of France. Since independence a policy of reconversion has led to a considerable decrease in the vineyard acreage, but quality wines have been exempted and among these none equal the red and white Mascara.

All along N4 from Relizane to Mohammadia (53 km., 33 miles) and N7 from Relizane to Mascara (64 km., 40 miles), and well into the foothills of the Beni Chougran mountains to the west, the limitless green ranks of the orderly vines marching across the red-brown earth are only occasionally broken by olive groves, meadows or clumps of oaks, while on the crests of the gently undulating hills white, green and blue *koubbas* stand out against the deep blue sky.

In sharp contrast W12, connecting the two national roads, passes a wild forgotten vale, where four villages of flat-roofed houses cling like fortresses to the abrupt sides of gorges, the ancestral home of the Beni Rached tribe.

The higher regions of the Beni Chougran mountains are just as desolate, but the artificial lake created by damming two rivers has contributed to the development of Hammam Bou Hanifa, Roman Aquae Sirenses, whose hot springs are strongly radioactive. The village of El Guethna, 14 km. (9 miles) north, is the birthplace of Emir Abdelkader. Closer to Mohammadia, another dam retains the waters of the Oued El Hammam, allowing the irrigation of the vast plain stretching to Arzew and Mostaganem.

Situated on the Oued Toudmane in the heart of the fertile Plain of Eghris, Mascara was the seat of a Turkish bey from 1701 to 1791, before he moved to Oran. Capital of Abdelkader in 1834, it changed hands several times, and the heavy fighting accounts for the absence of historical monuments, only the Djemaâ El Kebir dates from 1750, in this capital of the wine, which is, moreover, an important crossroad.

Mineral Water

Though usually labeled in Arabic script only, the bottles of Saïda (the Happy), the flattish mineral water served throughout the country, are known to all tourists from their first meal on. Yet few know the whereabouts of the town and even fewer visit this important agricultural center between the fertile Tell of vines and wheat and the stony High Plateaux that grow only alfa, a dark green plant which serves equally well as pasture for vast flocks of sheep and raw material for paper and plastics.

On the Oued Saïda, 76 km. (47 miles) south by railway and N6, burnt by General Bugeaud in his campaign against Abdelkader, Saïda lacks touristic interest and is only touched on the way to El Bayadh or Aïn Sefra in the deep south. Likewise destroyed by Bugeaud in 1841, Tiaret has risen larger but no more attractive in standard colonial style on a last spur of the Ouarsenis range dominating the immense High Plateaux with its extensive alfa, brought by camel caravans to compressing stations along N23 south from Tiaret to Aflou. 95 km. (59 miles) northwest, N23 leads to Relizane, while N14 provides a direct connection with Mascara (103 km., 64 miles). La Jumenterie, 5 km. (3 miles) northeast, is Algeria's largest studfarm of Arab thoroughbreds.

The First Heresy

No trace remains of Roman Columnata (which became the capital of a prosperous Berber kingdom destroyed at its very gates by Oqba ibn-Nafi in 683), and little more than shapeless heaps of stones at the village of Tagdemt, 6 km. (4 miles) west on W11. Yet these are the remains of proud Tahert—from which the name of Tiaret is derived—the first capital of the Ibadites, whose history began with the murder of Othmar, the third caliph.

To avenge this murder, Mu'awiya, founder of the Ommiad dynasty of Damascus, forced Ali, son-in-law of the Prophet and fourth caliph, to accept arbitration, but some of Ali's followers rebelled against this sacrilege, as Allah's judgment could only be delivered by the vote of the entire community. After Ali's murder in 661, these first Islamic heretics, known as Ibadites or Kharijites (from *kharej,* to secede), were led to North Africa by the Iranian General Ibn Rostem, hence for a while yet another name, Rostemides. When driven from their temporary refuge at Kairouan, the Rostemides moved further west and founded Tahert, the City of Allah, in the 8th century.

The Berbers of the region embraced Rostem's strict puritanism, so that unusual order and security reigned in the flourishing kingdom which extended over most of Algeria till its destruction by the Fatimids in 911. The Ibadites sought safety at Sedrata on the northern confines of the Sahara, but religious fanaticism is unforgiving and in 1072 the Hammadit El Mansour not only razed the houses but also cut the palms and blocked the wells, so that the surviving Ibadites had to join their brethren in the M'Zab hidden deep in the desert.

The Tombs Remain

There are rupestrian shrines near Dahmouni, 19 km. (12 miles) east, where N14 and N40 part company. Protohistoric tombs or sacrificial stones, among which the Dolmen of Tiaret, can be seen near Guertoufa, 8 km. (5 miles) northwest along N23. But for addicts of sepulchres the Djeddars are unbeatable, at least in those parts. These Berber mausoleums of the Byzantine period are large tiered cones rising from a square base of dressed stone, reminiscent of the Royal Mauretanian Mausoleum at Tipasa and the Medracen near Batna.

29 km. (18 miles) south on N14, then 3 km. (2 miles) east (left) lead to the ten Djeddars scattered at some 1,100 m. (3,600 feet) along the crest of Djebel Laghdar; the largest is called Kèskès, because in its present form it resembles the pot in which the couscous is boiled; narrow passages open on twenty rooms, of which the central two were certainly burial chambers furnished with objects lifted from Columnata. Three more Djeddars crown the summit of Djebel Araoui, 5 km. (3 miles) south, amidst endless waves of barren mountains.

23 km. (13 miles) further south, Frenda lies at the border of the Saïda Mountains, which have grown even greener since the Dam of Bakhada (45 km., 28 miles north) created a vast artificial lake, and the desolation of Chott ech Chergui. 6 km. (4 miles) southwest, on a rocky spur at Taoughzout, some grim stone huts indicate the site of the Beni Salâma castle to which the famous historian ibn-Khaldun prudently retired in 1375 for nearly four years after having fallen out with his protector of the moment, the Sultan of Tlemcen. For once removed from his hectic involvement in the making of Moslem history, he found time to write about it in the *Muqaddimah* (see page 39), which is not just the mere *Introduction to History* of the title, but a brilliant analysis of nomadic and settled states. His description of the battlefield where Oqba ibn-Nafi defeated the Berber princes of Tahert is based on an on-the-spot study.

Tlemcen—The Maghreb's Fifth Imperial City

One of the joys of this vast country is the efficient road network, which offers sufficient alternative east–west and north–south connections to avoid retracing one's steps. Among several possibilities to proceed westwards, N7 provides the most direct approach coming from Mascara, via Sidi Bel Abbès (90 km., 56 miles), where it intersects N13 from Oran to El Aricha and on into south Morocco to Algeria's finest Arab town, Tlemcen (93 km., 58 miles).

From afar, minarets and green-tiled cupolas of mosques rise above white houses on a plateau interposed between the olive trees and vines of the plain, and a pine-clad hill, while a fortified russet enclosure with strong square towers is half hidden by trees. But though the map in the museum indicates 42 historical monuments, while the O.N.A.T. folder enumerates 11, the historic "museum town" has been allowed to be encircled by concrete blocks of doubtful taste.

A tour of Tlemcen usually begins at the Place du Mechouar. This site has been the center of the government of the city since the 11th century. Tradition says that it was here that Yusuf ibn-Tashfin pitched his tent before the conquest of neighboring Agadir, and it was here that the Almoravids built their palace, the Qasr al-Qadim which also was the residence of the Almohad governors. The Zianids constructed administrative buildings and barracks out of the ruins of the 12th-century palaces destroyed during their fight for control of the city and the subsequent Merinid sieges. Both Ottoman and French governors had their offices behind the high walls which date from the French occupation and in no way resemble the romantic prints beloved by Algerian hotels. It now houses the Cadet School of the Sons of the Revolution. The university comprises a center for the study of Andalusian music in North Africa.

From the Place du Mechouar, all streets lead to the main square, the Place Emir Abdelkader, typical of a French colonial town with the bandstand in the center of the gardens and the old town hall dating from 1843, the year after the French occupation of the city. The clock has stopped at 11:30, and one wonders if that was the hour the last French official left. Opposite is the rear facade of the Great Mosque which can be entered from a small arched street at the side (open to non-Moslems daily except Friday 8–11). Founded by Ali ibn-Yusuf in 1135—the same year that he ordered the rebuilding of the Qarawiyin Mosque at Fez—it is the most notable sacred building in the Maghreb which foreigners may visit.

In the first half of the 12th century the style of Cordoba inspired two completely diverse achievements—the Romanesque churches in the Pyrenees and in France, and the great mosques of Tlemcen and Fez. It was the Almoravids who were the liaison between Moslem Spain and the Maghreb. Their mosques at Tlemcen and Fez are the first and most notable products of Andalusian Islam in North Africa.

The prayer hall, consisting of 13 naves and 6 transverse arcades supporting white horseshoe arches, is monumental in its simplicity. Most decoration is in the central nave, in which there are two domes—one at the first crossing (entrance) which is ribbed, and the other before the mihrab which contains the earliest known stalactite decoration in the western Islamic world. Both are supported by high scalloped arches which recall, and were certainly modeled on, the Great Mosque of Cordoba—as was the mihrab, which was very elegant stucco work but much restored. The tall minaret, in brick with traces of polychrome tiles, was added by Yaghmoracen (1236–83). On a corner of the facade of the mosque facing the main square is a koubba (domed chamber) which served as the necropolis of all the Zianid sultans except Yaghmoracen, who, tradition says, is buried within the mosque to the right of the mihrab.

At the opposite end of the Place Abdelkader is the small mosque of Sidi Bel Hassen, which is now the Antiquities Museum (open 9–4, closed Fri.). It was built in 1297 by the second Zianid sultan, Abu Said Uthman ibn-Yaghmoracen (1283–1303) in memory of his father and is named after a prominent contemporary theologian who taught there. Its small size and extremely opulent decoration suggest that it was an oratory for use by the sultan and high court officials. The horseshoe arch of the mihrab is supported by two finely sculpted columns of onyx, and its stalactite vaulting rests on colonettes of similar design. Surrounding and framing the mihrab opening are remarkable stucco panels of floral and geometric designs alternating with bands of calligraphy, all deeply carved and often in open-work, with some of the painted decoration remaining. This is the only surviving example of Zianid art at its height, and it certainly rivals the achievements of the Merinids. In the museum, which is housed in the former prayer hall, are excellent examples of 13th- and 14th-century woodwork, including fragments of the original ceiling beams and lintels with painted floral motifs from the oratory of Sidi ben Hassan, a door from the Merinid mosque at Mansoura, and a magnificently carved grille from the Great Mosque. There are also two large Merinid ablution basins and fragments of faience mosaic tiles from the Almoravid palace in the Mechouar. In the small garden are several onyx columns from Mansoura, the capitals of which are the finest and only remaining examples of such Merinid carving in stone.

The Merinid Suburbs

In the first half of the 14th century, the Merinids occupied Tlemcen three times; their impact was felt not so much in the city itself, as in the suburbs outside the walls, where they not only constructed a new city but were responsible for two shrines which represent the apogee of Hispano-Moorish art in the Central Maghreb. The first Merinid siege was led by Abu Yakub Yusuf from 1299 to 1307. During this time, the Merinids camped west of the city, and by the fourth year of the siege, their fortified settlement had grown into a town, called Mansoura (the Victorious). The site lies about one mile outside the city limits on N7 to Maghnia. Surrounded by impressive fortifications Mansoura covers a vast area, but only ruins of the mosque and minaret remain. Of the mosque, there are some magnificent onyx columns on the site, the rest having been moved to the museum or incorporated in later buildings. One side of the minaret of reddish-orange stone still stands, and it is the best example of a Merinid minaret extant. The ramps which led to the summit can be seen on the open side, and the mosque is entered through a monumental door at its base. The whole ensemble distinctly resembles the Hassan Tower and Mosque in Rabat, while the door at the foot of the minaret is certainly modeled on the great gate of the Kasbah of the Oudaias, even having the same bluish tinge in the stone.

Both the Rabat of the Almohads and the Mansoura of the Merinids were really military encampments, and it is interesting that even after more than a century, the buildings of Yakub al-Mansur were still the models for fortified settlements in the Maghreb. After the assassination of Abu Yakub Yusuf in 1307, Mansoura was deserted, but during the ensuing two sieges, it was again the Merinid headquarters. After 1359, when the Zianids finally repelled the last invasion, Mansoura fell quickly into ruin, and its buildings became a quarry from which the monuments of Tlemcen were enriched.

Sidi Bou Mediène

The second Merinid occupation under Abu el Hassan, the Black Sultan, lasted from 1337 to 1349. Previously responsible for so many Merinid buildings in Fez, Meknès and Salé and buried at Chellah near Rabat, he built Tlemcen's most famous shrine, the mosque, tomb and medrassa of Sidi Bou Mediène. To reach it, follow the road past the Zianides hotel and the Islamic Institute in pure traditional style, and bear left at the large gate to the cemetery of Sidi Yakub to the village of El Eubbad on the hillside. On the way, you should pause at the Sacred Wood of Sidi Yakub with its ancient trees and small koubbas dating from the time of the Almoravids (open daily except Mon. and Thurs. 8–12, when it is reserved for women). Set on a hill amongst orchards of olive and almond trees, the landscape around El Eubbad recalls Andalusia—not the Andalusia of the city seen so well in Fez, but that of the sierras and the orange groves of Granada. Sidi Bou Mediène (or ibn Husain al-Andalousi) was a mystic born in Seville in 1126. He spent much of his life wandering and teaching in the Maghreb, and it was while he was on his way to Marrakesh in 1198 that he died at El Eubbad, which quickly became a place of pilgrimage and Abu el Hassan built the present shrine in 1339.

The shrine is entered by a long white open gallery to the left of which is the tomb of the saint to which a portico of painted wood gives access. In the tomb, as well as Sidi Bou Mediène, other holy men are buried, one being the Merinid sultan al-Said (1242–48), who was killed in a campaign against the Zianid Yaghmoracen. The present tomb dates from the 14th century, but successive restorations have destroyed any traces of the original decoration. To the right is the monumental entrance of the mosque decorated with faience tile mosaics and elaborately sculpted plaster work. The cupola of stalactites, with some of the gilt remaining, is one of the finest examples of stalactite decoration in plaster in North Africa. The great cedarwood doors covered with bronze plaques of geometric design came from Spain, and the whole ensemble—portico, cupola, and door—is one of the greatest achievements in the history of Islamic architecture. It is the only building of such stature between Fez and Qairawan and Cairo more than 2,000 miles away. The courtyard, which has a brilliantly tiled pavement with a tank for ablutions in the center, opens into the small prayer hall of five naves and four transverse arcades. Carved stucco arabesques decorate the horseshoe arches, and two elegant marble colonettes support the arch of the mihrab. Adjoining the mosque is a small minaret of brick in geometric patterns of the same date and a medrassa constructed in 1347. Very different from those in Fez, its layout is similar to that of the mosque, and the students' cells surround the open courtyard. The entire sanctuary is Moorish Andalusia still existing in the present day in the Maghreb.

The Mosque of Sidi al-Haloui

Abu Inan led the third and last Merinid occupation of Tlemcen, which lasted from 1353 to 1359, and it was during that period that the mosque of Sidi al-Haloui was constructed. Situated to the east of the town outside the walls in what used to be orchards, the mosque lies in a valley below the road. Unfortunately the encroachment of modern buildings detracts much from the site, but there are still fine perspectives of the court and the minaret from the hill above. Similar in size and style to Sidi Bou Mediène, the horseshoe arches of the prayer hall are supported by eight green onyx columns similar to those of the mosque at Mansoura. The building has been over-restored, and much of the elegance of the original design has been lost. Nearby on the plain, you can see the site of the old settlement of Agadir; only a 13th-century minaret remains of the mosque founded by Idriss I in 790, but among the white cupolas hidden by trees, the Koubba of the Sultana, eight arches forming an octagon, is a good example of Almoravid architecture.

Before leaving Tlemcen, it is pleasant to walk up to the Kalaa, the hill which dominates the city. This was the domain of the French settlers, and villas with names like "Les Bougainvilles," "Carpe Diem," and "Villa

Mauresque" lie in overgrown and tangled gardens. Arab families camp in some, and the whole area, with its shuttered verandas and rusting iron gates, has the melancholy air of an epoch now dead. But from here the view over the town and the rich surrounding countryside is magnificent, and you can readily see how centuries ago the landscape must have reminded immigrants from Andalusia of their lost homeland.

Tlemcen enjoys doubtless the most luxuriant setting of any of the ancient capitals. At Ain Fezza, 11 km. (7 miles) east on N7, is the Grotto of Beni Abd El Oued, well-lit to display the multicolored concretion. At El Ourit a waterfall cascades in seven tiers from an artificial lake down a verdant valley. Another artificial lake, Beni Bahdel, 32 km. (20 miles) southwest by N22 and W54 is surrounded by a dense forest. From the dam, W46 ascends the incredibly fertile valley of the Oued Tafna to its sources near Sebdou, whence N22 continues south via El Aricha to join N6 to Aïn Sefra.

The Western Confines

The same variety of orchards and vineyards extends west beyond the Tlemcen mountains to Maghnia, a market town 13 km. (8 miles) east of the Moroccan border. 10 km. (6 miles) northeast is Hammam Boughrara, visited since antiquity by sufferers from skin diseases, at the confluence of the Oued Mouilah and the Oued Tafna. N35 follows the latter downstream, joined by N22 just before the gorges, to reach the sea at Beni Saf.

N7a hugs the border northward to Mersa Ben M'Hidi on the sea, separated from its Moroccan counterpart Saïdia by the Oued Kiss. Twin bays with lovely beaches, broken by dramatic cliffs and backed by a eucalyptus forest, are scheduled to be opened up by the building of a hotel. W108 winds east through the coastal brushwood to Ghazaouet (40 km., 25 miles), where squat towers of a Berber fortress guard the busy port with an evil-smelling zinc and lead plant. Pine and cypress trees fringe the beach at Sidna Youcha.

18 km. (11 miles) southeast on W46 across the afforested Traras Mountains, Nédroma lies at almost 396 m. (1,300 feet) between the Taza Pass and Djebel Fillaousène, highest in the west. Important under the Almoravids and Almohads, the mosques of Sidi Bou Ali, Sidi Yahia, multidomed Ben Aoufine and particularly the great Almoravid mosque bear eloquent witness to a proud past, but the ramparts are ruined and the 11th-century hammam dilapidated. Yet there is an effort to revive the age-old local crafts by training 300 students in the Unité Technique Artisanale in pottery, weaving and embroidery.

To the east along W38, three green and white cupolas stand out on the crest of a hill; the Zaouïa (Religious Fraternity) of Sidi Amar, the fame of whose founder has continued to grow after his death, as his son is no less versed in curing sciatica by implanting a brass wire in the ear lobe. A narrow road recrosses the Traras Mountains northeast back to the sea at Honaïn, main port of Tlemcen in the time of its glory, terminus of caravans from the distant Tafilalet. Later a pirate hideout, but today only ruins of walls flanked by towers, of the Kasbah and broken minarets.

The same narrow road connects east with N22, which follows the Oued Tafna to the sea at Rachgoun, an ancient Phoenician trading post, as so often opposite an islet. On the fine beach are the insignificant ruins of Siga, capital of the Numidian Kingdom of Syphax. 10 km. (6 miles) east, Beni

Saf is the biggest and busiest port west of Oran (106 km., 66 miles). The houses occupy the narrow seafront between the beach and the slopes of a green hill.

PRACTICAL INFORMATION FOR
THE ANDALUSIAN WEST

WHEN TO GO. Coast, in summer, if you can find accommodation; inland, spring and fall. June/July: Cultural Fortnight at Tlemcen. September: Horse races and fantasias at Tiaret; Vintage Festival at Mascara.

GETTING THERE. By Train. The line from Oujda in Morocco is at present not operating. S.N.T.F. (tel. 34 06 21 in Oran) operates from Maghnia via Tlemcen, Sidi bel Abbès and Oran to Algiers; express diesel trains between Oran and Tlemcen. North–south from Oran and Mostaganem via Mascara and Saïda to Aïn Sefra in the deep south.

By Plane. Daily flights by Air Algérie from Algiers to Es Senia airport, 15 km. (9 miles) south of Oran, and Tlemcen. One flight per week from London to Oran, more frequently from the main French towns, Geneva and Zurich. To Tlemcen from Lyon, Marseille and Paris.

By Boat. Regular C.N.A.N. ferry boats from Marseille, Sète and Alicante (Spain) to Oran.

By Car and Bus. Adequate roads throughout the region. Frequent E.P.T.V.O. coaches between all towns. 30 km. (19 miles) motorway Oran-Oued Tlélat. The coach station in Oran is located at Blvd. Abderrahmane Mira; tel. 39 32 55.

HOTELS AND RESTAURANTS. Accommodations in Oran and particularly along the coast are insufficient for demand. It is advisable to book well in advance and double check shortly before the actual date of arrival.

Andalouses. *Les Pavillons* (M), tel. 38 52 51. 125 bungalows with 2 rooms each, and 50 family villas. Holiday Village on the beach. *La Residence* (M), tel. 38 52 53. 402 rooms.

Arzew. *Tassili* (M), tel. 37 32 13. 37 rooms. *Neharia* (M), tel. 37 33 37. 45 rooms. **Restaurant.** *Les Palmiers* (M), 30 Blvd. Emir Abdelkader.

Beni Saf. *Siga* (M), 37 rooms. On the sea-front.

Hammam Boughrara. *Hôtel Thermal* (M), tel. 22 85 24. 83 rooms. Tennis.

Hammam Bou Hadjar. *De la Poste* (M), tel. 21 63 82. 23 rooms. *Hôtel Thermal* (M), tel. 21 63 77. 70 rooms. Pool.

Hammam Bou Hanifa. *Hôtel des Thermes* (M), tel. 32 73 21. 75 rooms. Pool.

Maghnia. *Tafna* (M), tel. 03 75 22. 3 km. (2 miles) along the road to Morocco. 44 rooms.

Mostaganem. *Albert* (I), tel. 29 23 12. 40 rooms, some with showers. Elderly.

Oran. *Timgad* (E), 22 Blvd. Emir Abdelkader (tel. 39 47 93). 200 rooms. Good restaurant. *Royal* (E), 8 Blvd. de la Soummam (tel. 38 31 44). 82 rooms.

El Amir (M), 34 Blvd. Emir Abdelkader (tel. 39 16 72). 24 rooms. *El Antissar* (M), Rue Larbi Ben M'hidi (tel. 39 31 75). 42 rooms. *Balabek* (M), 6 Rue Ozanam (tel. 39 14 12). 36 rooms. *El Djoumhouria* (M), 3 Rue Ampère (tel. 39 45 68). 68 rooms. *Grand Hotel* (M), 5 Pl. Colonel Athmane (tel. 39 15 33). 119 rooms. Staffed by pupils of the hotel school; opposite the post office. *El Hamri* (M), 15 Rue Thierry (tel. 33 10 42). 50 rooms. Above average. *De L'Ouest* (M), 6 Rue Mellah Ali (tel. 36 43 98). 43 rooms. *Terminus* (M), Place de la Gare (tel. 37 13 15). 27 rooms.

Afric (I), 66 Blvd. de l'Independence. *Afrique-Asie* (I), 15 Rue Toula Houari. *Saada* (I), Rue Haoues El Aouafi. *Tipaza* (I), 37 Rue Audebert.

Restaurants. All the following are (M). On the central Rue Mohamed Khemisti—*L'Atlas* at #58, *Le Chalet* at #42, *La Lorraine* at #38, *Maurétania* at #20, *Le Sphinx* at #11.

Alhambra, 4 Rue Ampère, serves Algerian food. *Ibn Wassel,* Blvd. Emir Abdelkader, also has local specialties.

Chez Mémé, 5 Rue Pierre Tabarot, has French specialties.

Chez Papa, 73 Blvd. Des Falaises, serves traditional cuisine. *Le Panorama,* 15 Blvd. De L'Aln, features European cuisine.

On Rue Larbi Ben M'hidi are—*El Bacour* at #64, *Davilda* at #18, and *Le Hoggar* at #74. All three have mainly Algerian cuisine.

At **Mers El Kebir:** *El Mounia* (M), and *Okba* (M), serve fresh seafood.

Saïda. *Forsane* (M), tel. 25 58 38. 65 rooms. Pool.

Sidi Bel Abbès. *El Djazaïr* (M), tel. 24 61 95. 40 rooms.
Restaurants. *La Bohème* (M). French cuisine. *Le Riadh* (M). Algerian dishes.

Tiaret. *Tagdempt* (M), tel. 28 26 26. 55 rooms.
Restaurants. *Auberge du Cheval d'Argent* (E). *Le Tassili* (M).

Tlemcen. *Les Zianides* (E), Blvd. Khedim Ali (tel. 26 71 18 or 21 24 31). Only 4-star hotel in the region; fine garden round the pool; tennis.

Maghreb (M), Rue Commandant Ferradj (tel. 26 35 71). 78 rooms. *Villa Marguerite* (M). In gardens on the Upper Kalaâ. 34 rooms.

SPORTS. Swimming. There are one covered and five open-air pools at Oran. Best beaches west of Oran are between Trouville Plage and Les Andalouses, the latter also excellent for underwater fishing. To the east, Canastel and Mostaganem.

Tennis. Le Rail Club Oranais, Blvd. Colonel Ahmed Ben Abderrazak; Le L.T.C.O., Ave. de l'Indépendence.

NATIONAL TOURIST OFFICES. Algerian National Tourist Offices (O.N.A.T.)—**Maghnia:** 52 Ave. du ler Novembre. **Mostaganem:** 2 Blvd. Khemisti. **Oran:** 10 Blvd. Emir Abdelkader. **Es Senia:** Airport. **Sidi Bel Abbès:** 2 Rue Bendida. **Tlemcen:** 15 Blvd. de l'Indépendence.

CAR HIRE. Oran: 17 Blvd. Abane Ramdane, tel. 39 65 85 or 33 32 67. Garage Residence Leclerc, Place Murat, tel 39 61 86. **Arzew:** 43 Rue Aissat Idir, tel. 37 22 81.

THE ROMAN EAST

Ruined Grandeur in a Majestic Landscape

For Algeria's East we have combined two regions, Constantine and the Aurès, for the simple reason that few if any tourists would visit the latter without staying at the former. Moreover, there is as yet no accommodation whatsoever in the formidable Aurès Mountains, rising a mere 145 km. (90 miles) south of Constantine to North Algeria's highest peaks, Djebel Malmel and Djebel Chelia, over 2,280 m. (7,500 feet), in a dramatic transition from the Mediterranean vegetation of the high northern plains to the southern desert.

True, the Chaouïas of the Aurès live in characteristic *dechras,* terraced hamlets topped by fortress-like silos which could at best be described by an ambiguous "quaint," hardly deserving a special visit. The Oued El Abiodh Canyon as well as the El Kantara and Tighanimin Gorges opening into the Sahara, on the other hand, make a perfect complement to a stay on the lovely coast and a tour of the magnificent Roman ruins.

The landscape between Kabylia in the west and Tunisia in the east, the sea in the north and the desert in the south, is indeed so varied that instead of enumerating all the attractions it is easier to say that there are very few missing. The unique site of Constantine alone would warrant a visit, besides its convenient central position among the world's greatest concentration of remarkable Roman cities.

Punic Cirta became the capital of the powerful Numidian King Massinissa, who enlarged and beautified the town. His grandson Jugurtha defeated his cousin Adherbal who had sought refuge in Cirta, but Jugurtha himself was finally defeated by the Romans who renamed Colonia Cirta after the Emperor Constantine. Despite the heroic resistance of the Christian Berber King Kosaïla in the Aurès, Hodna and Nementcha Mountains, Numidia was quickly conquered by the Arabs, passing from the Governors of Kairouan to the Fatimids, Zirids, Almohads and back east the Hafsids of Tunisia. Under the Turkish Regency, Constantine became once again a capital, of the Beylik of the East.

The East's main port, Annaba, was the Roman Hippo Regius where Saint Augustine was bishop from 392 to 430.

Exploring Constantine (Qacentina)

Algeria's third city spreads over the summit of an immense chalk cliff cleft by the vertiginous Gorges of the Rhumel. The fabulous site bursts into view on arrival from the north and west, when N3 and N27 emerge from a eucalyptus forest; hewn into the precipitous rocks, N27 enters the gorge and, as Chemin de la Corniche, passes under the suspension bridge of Sidi M'Cid and through several tunnels to the stone arches of the bridge El Kantara before the railway station.

No less exciting is the approach along W44, branching right off N3, at the foot of the high cliff from which the Rhumel gushes forth. The thermal establishment of Sidi M'Cid—water temperature 27°C—is flanked by the ruins of Roman Baths and the huge Olympic Pool. The Pont des Chuttes (Bridge of the Falls) leads through the popular quarters of the Place des Martyrs connected by the Avenue Ben Boulaid to the Place du Ier Novembre, with the Post Office, Theater, Cultural Center and Coach Terminal, while the Town Hall and Wilaya Administration are close by. Parking is impossible—and so is driving—but the Old Town is sufficiently compact for a tour on foot.

The Eagle's Lair

Quite a commonplace description for a mountain village, but for a large provincial capital . . . And yet uniquely fitting, because of the chasm, despite the numerous bridges ranging from the spiderlike iron foot variety to the 27 stone arches of the Pont de Sidi Rached. The last, notwithstanding some unfortunate highrises, still dominates the town from the southwest, shortly after the Rhumel divides into two branches.

The aptly named Boulevard de l'Abîme (of the Abyss) offers the most spectacular view from within the cliff to which tall houses cling perilously, before ascending to the Kasbah. In the center is the Djemaâ of Salah Bey, who was murdered by order of the Dey in 1792 and in whose memory the women of Constantine are said to wear black *haïks* instead of the usual Algerian white. Also in Turkish style is the Djemaâ Sidi Lakhar, but the Djemaâ El Kebir (Great Mosque) is pure 13th-century Hafsid. Nearby, where the footbridge abuts on central Boulevard Larbi M'Hidi, the University Office occupies an ancient medersa decorated with colored tiles. But in a reversal of the usual process by which medieval medersas are put to mundane use, an Institute of High Islamic Studies was attached to the Djemma Emir Abdelkader which opened in the university city in 1983.

Richer tiles, varying with naïvely conceived murals of Constantine and Mediterranean ports, ornament the flowering patios and courts of the Palace of Ahmed Bey, constructed in 1826. He was a potent villain, master of 385 odalisques in addition to his four lawful wives, one of whom, an

Italian, left hair-raising accounts of his misdeeds, which were redeemed by his defense of Constantine in 1837 and his heroic death in the Aurès Mountains the following year.

In the residential Koudiat Aty district, on a flat hilltop to the southeast, the Museum Mercier houses a lot of rather dull 19th-century paintings, to be borne for the sake of the finds from Cirta—especially a fine bronze Victory—and from Tiddis; from Kalaâ des Beni Hammad; and, most intriguing, the dagger in the cedar sheath and the chain armor might have belonged to the Numidian King Massinissa, from the Mausoleum Es Souna.

Numidian and Roman Environs

The appetite having been whetted, the first excursion is, therefore, to Es Souna (The Tower) near El Khroub, 14 km. (9 miles) south on N3. From the highest point of the plateau rise the remains of a pyramid surmounted by columns where, in 1915, the body of a warrior was found. As the arms date from the 1st century B.C., it might well be the Mausoleum of the Great Numidian king. Further south along N3 are the Dolmens of Ouled Rahmoun.

Northward, N3 leads in 8 km. (5 miles) to the verdant Spa Hammam Bouziane; N27 follows for a while the Rhumel before the branch to the region's first great Roman site, Tiddis the Red (29 km., 18 miles).

The steep blood-red hill forced the builders of Castellum Tidditanorum to abandon the usual rectangular city plan in favor of a single paved main street, rising on the south side in the shape of an S, too steep for chariots, but negotiable by horses which, on the summit, were attached to iron rings before a manger hewn into the rock. Staircases connected the various street levels, on which natural caves were used as shops and one even as a temple of Mithras, while hot vapours emanate from a grotto almost hidden by asphodels.

At Tiddis, as throughout Roman Africa, Christian churches faced the temples of the gods of many nations in remarkable tolerance, like the winged phallus indicating another Mithraic shrine opposite a chapel at the town's entrance. The Baths, however, were probably the only in the Roman Empire to use rainwater exclusively, collected in an immense *impluvium* (rainwater reservoir), on the summit and canalized from a well-preserved cistern of 350 square yards throughout the town which was devoid of any wells. The Forum, in contrast, is a mere 30 by 10 yards on an artificial terrace.

A luxurious villa is partly covered by the medieval potters' quarter, dating from the time Tiddis was nearing its end under the Almohads. Pre-Roman ramparts encircle the crest of the hill whose north side falls abruptly to a valley cleft asunder by the Gorges of the Rhumel in the best Constantine manner, thus justifying the Arab name Ksantina El Kdima, Ancient Constantine.

Emperors from Africa

N5 is the main artery west, roughly paralleling the railway via Sétif to Algiers through the not particularly interesting high plateaus; W5 branches north (right) to Djemila. To avoid the fairly heavy traffic, an equidistant alternative, though on narrower roads, is offered by W2 west from Constantine to Mila, still surrounded by the walls built by the Byzantines in 540. A colossal statue represents Saturn. In the mountains of Lesser Kabylia that bar the way north to the sea, Abou Abdallah raised the Berbers of the Kutama tribe against the Aghlabids of Kairouan and led them to the conquest of the Maghreb.

W25, 154 and 117 lead quite comfortably to Djemila, spreading its columns and walls over the slopes of a gentle hill against a backdrop of blue mountains. As usual, the Roman veterans chose with an eye to the beauty of the site as well as to practical considerations of supply from a fertile countryside at the confluent of two brooks. But Cuicul differs from most Roman ruins in its exceptional state of preservation; temples missing only their roofs, whole streets clearly lined with houses, the theater ready to receive spectators, and everywhere columns rising to a respectable height.

Septimius Severus, who reigned from 193 to 221, was born at Leptis Magna in Tripolitania, and the African provinces remained the power base of his dynasty in the fierce struggle within the Roman Empire. He thus endowed Cuicul with a large temple, while his son Caracalla added a triumphal arch. Yet the most remarkable building belongs to the following century, a Christian basilica with a round baptistery, whose fine mosaics have been protected by a new dome. Mosaics are also the pride of the Museum, the delicate coloring and realistic representations of hunting scenes covering the 30 ft.-high walls from top to bottom, beautifully setting off the marble statues.

Though Cuicul escaped destruction by the Vandals and its bishop participated in a Church Council in Constantinople as late as 533, it was only to splendid ruins that the Arab conquerors gave the name Djemila, the Beautiful.

It is only 45 km. (28 miles) on W117 to Sétif, as Sifitis capital of Mauretania Sifitensis, and now, still very much marked by the French colonial style, at over 910 m. (3,000 feet) Algeria's highest wilaya capital. The center of Sétif has retained a pleasant provincial atmosphere despite the recent rapid extension of the suburbs along the east–west N5 or north–south N28. Not that Roman remains are missing, some can be seen on the Square Emir Abdelkader at the town's entrance coming from Algiers, but most have been submerged by modern development. Some large mosaics have survived in the Museum, the former Palais de Justice, where the broken ornaments from Kalaâ des Beni Hammad are a foretaste, albeit deceivingly fragmentary, of the province's Arab highpoint. The "Triumph of Bacchus" is especially worth seeing; it has been described as the finest mosaic in the Roman world.

The Hammadid Capitals

At about the same altitude, 137 km. (85 miles) southwest including 19 km. (12 miles) off N40, a huge town began to be excavated in 1964 behind the village of Bichara. Emir Hammad, son of Algiers' founder Emir Bologuin, assembled in 1007 architects and craftsmen from the whole Maghreb to build a new military, political and spiritual capital. 8 km. (5 miles) of ramparts protected the palaces on terraces along the southern slopes of Djebel Maâdid where the Hammadid dynasty—despite the destruction wrought by the Beni Hilal between 1053 and 1057—resided till 1090. In that year the Citadel of the Beni Hammad was abandoned for Bejaïa, to be burnt by the Almohads in 1152 and eventually forgotten.

The site was admirably chosen, in a valley of the Hodna Mountains, facing south above a stream flowing clear even in the height of summer. But the oriental splendor described by contemporary travelers is difficult to evoke from the scanty remains of the Palace of Salvation and many others, even though the minaret of the Great Mosque, still rising 23 m. (75 feet), resembles the Giralda of Seville.

Having come so far south, it is tempting to continue southeast on N28 via Barika to N3 and return to Constantine via Batna, with calls at Tazoult and Timgad, but such a trip is invariably connected with a visit to the Oasis of Biskra. We therefore leave that southern region last, as a stepping stone for the exploration of the Sahara, and for the sake of historic sequence turn north from Sétif to Bejaïa, 109 km. (68 miles) on N9 through the center of Lesser Kabylia, passing the artificial lake of Ighil Emda and descending the 6-km.-long (4-mile) Chabet El Akra, the Chasm of Death cut by the Oued Agrioum into the Barbor range, to the Cascade Kéfrida and the sea at Souk El Tenine.

For the last 35 km. (22 miles) N9 hugs the flat coast northwest, past Cape Aokas and the fine sands of Tichy. At the mouth of the Oued Summam, which separates the two Kabylias, Bejaïa is seen—and smelled, especially when an east wind wafts the odors from the terminal of a gas pipeline, where once sweet-smelling beeswax from the mountain was exported to all Europe.

Attractively climbing a hill which rises steeply from the sea, Bejaïa was called Vaga by the Berbers, Saldae by the Romans, and then En Nassria when the Hammadid Emir En Nasser constructed in 1607 the fortifications in which his son Mansour built 23 years later the Palaces of the Star and of the Pearl. Conquered by the Almohads in 1152, base of Barbary coast pirates as early as 1360, besieged by the Spaniards in 1509, the Turks in 1555, the French in 1833, constant rebuilding left only a vaulted cistern and a mosaic in the town hall from Roman Saldae; and from the great days of Hammadid rule the Bab El Bahr (Gate of the Sea) and the Bab El Bounoud (Western Gate), flanked by two towers, as well as the Marabout of Sidi Touati. That saint founded a Moslem university which functioned till the last century and for that reason an Islamic Institute was opened in the upper town near the ancient site in 1972. The Kasbah and Fort Moussa on the summit of Gouraya belong to the Spanish occupation in the 16th century.

Bits and pieces representative of Bejaïa's long history have been assembled in the Museum, plus a collection of African birds and insects, complemented by pictures of local landscapes. Yet the magnificent view from the Museum terrace is really the prize exhibit: over the vast Gulf from Cape Carbon to El Alouana, an irresistible invitation to excursions through the pines and olive trees of Gouraya. Cape Sigli, 40 km. (25 miles) north, is reached on inland W43 and 34, past the Roman aqueduct at Toudja, as coastal N24 is impracticable.

The Sapphire Coast

Not even the most blasé Mediterranean connoisseur would begrudge the short retracing of steps along this loveliest stretch of the Algerian coast to the mouth of the Oued Agrioum, to continue then on N43, the Corniche Kabyle, winding through the cliffs of the Babor range meeting the sea ever more precipitously.

The first beauty spot is aptly called les Falaises (the Cliffs), pierced by grottos and tunnels. The fishing ports Ziama Mansouria—protected by Mansouria Islet while the ruins of Roman Choba Municipium lie at the foot of Djebel Brek—and El Aouana—on a bay with two islets and some dolmens in the neighborhood—have all the prerequisites for beach resorts. In between is the Grotte Merveilleuse, stalactites and stalagmites aplenty.

The Corniche ends at Jijel, Punic Igilgili, which the Romans, despite the formidable mountain barrier, linked to Cirta and Sitifis by roads the French engineers largely followed. Count Theodosius landed here to suppress the rebellion of the Berber Chief Firmus, but though successful the Romans faded away and Jijel was only heard of again when the Hammadid Emir Yahia Ibn El Aziz built a palace to indulge in debauchery at a safe distance from his capital Bejaïa. This palace was destroyed by the fleet of Roger II of Sicily in 1143, but the Normans left trade first to the Pisans and then to the Genoese, who occupied Jijel on the eve of the conquest by the Barbarossa brothers in 1514. Expelled from Algiers, Kair Eddin found refuge in Jijel from 1520 to 1525, which on his restoration he gratefully exempted from all taxes.

The Spaniards burnt the town in 1611, but the French under the Duc de Beaufort were repulsed in 1644. A Turkish garrison occupied the Genoese fortress, but local marabouts exercised authority under the deys of Algiers. A fanatical Moroccan expelled the Turks in 1803, and an independent pirate republic had only just been suppressed when the French reentered the scene. The terrible earthquake of 1854 flattened the whole town, so that the port is mostly late 19th-century, with a long beach waiting for the inevitable development.

Industry Versus Tourism

East of Jijel N43 follows a gentler coast before ascending through the Gorges of the Oued El Kébir to El Milia (69 km., 43 miles) in the midst of large forests. N27 continues south 87 km. (54 miles) following the Oued Rhumel to Constantine, while N43 turns again east, separated by vast cork-oak forests from the sea. There are, however, several minor roads, especially W6 descending along the Oued Guebli to Collo, a pleasant fishing village between Cape Bougaroum and the Gulf of Stora, complete with the usual miscellany of dolmens, a necropolis of Punic Chullu, a Roman fortress, grottos used by Barbary pirates and the latest addition, a yacht marina in the fine setting of the Djerba Peninsula.

N43 returns to the sea at Skikda, Algeria's main petrol port where nine giant tankers can be filled simultaneously from the pipeline bringing gas 375 miles from Hassi R'Mel to the liquifying plant of 6 billion cubic meters capacity per annum. Six seems Skikda's destined number, because the refinery processes 6 million tons. The petrochemical complex is the largest of a dozen of ancillary industries scattered along the littoral of antique Russicada, later French Philippeville in honor of King Louis Philippe.

Add the mercury from the mines of Ismaïl near Azzaba, 29 km. (18 miles) southeast; iron from the mines of El Hallia and marble from Filfila, both about 21 km. (13 miles) east; lead from El Koll, 24 km. (15 miles) west; the gigantic cement works of Hadjar Soud, 39 km. (24 miles) southwest; and any tourist might be excused if he considered the remains of a Roman theater—mysteriously hidden within the grounds of a high school; the mosaics, tiles and marbles of the neo-Moorish town hall; and the railway station, the latest in modernity in 1936, but feeble compensations for the appalling air and sea pollution. Even if the much-touted charms of Stora, a pretty village 5 km. (3 miles) northwest which has given its name to the Gulf, are thrown in.

So unless detained by business, there is no reason to linger in Skikda. Constantine is 90 km. (56 miles) south on N3, Annaba 103 km. (64 miles) west on N44, inland as the wild Edough Mountains bar the access to the sea. But here, too, forest roads are practicable, especially the 37 km. (23 miles) on W107 to Chetaïbi, a particularly attractive fishing village also accessible from Annaba, 64 km. (40 miles) on W16. There is, unfortunately, no accommodation yet.

The City of God

It would have been surprising indeed had the Phoenicians not implanted a trading post on the last spur of the Edough Mountains on the west side of a huge bay. By the 3rd century B.C. Punic Hippo (Shelter), to which the Romans later added Regius (Royal) had shifted to the small coastal plain where it prospered for some 700 years and existed for 200 more. Not that Hippo Regius ever resembled a City of God, even during the 34 years Saint Augustine was its bishop, but it was there that he wrote *De Civitate Dei* which crystallized Christian ethics for ever. He died in 430, just before the Vandals took the town.

After the withdrawal of the Byzantine governors, the remaining inhabitants returned to the hills of the Phoenician settlement, to escape from the malarial swamp that had formed when the sea receded.

From the vicissitudes common to Algerian coastal towns, Annaba (Jujube Trees) has emerged as the country's fourth city and third port, with almost 500,000 inhabitants. The half-mile of the wide treelined Cours de la Révolution, bordered by arcaded houses beloved by the French colonists, joins the new administrative quarter to the port and railway station. To the left, Old Annaba occupies a rocky eminence round the 11th-century Zirid Djemaâ Sidi Bou Mérouan and the 16th-century Turkish Djemaâ Salah Bey. The highrise apartment blocks dotted over the barren hills are all the more incongruous for the empty spaces in between, but at least the industrial zone is some miles distant—well beyond the Roman ruins.

Of these the most complete view can be gained from the highest hill, taking a non-signposted lane right, after the circular mosque on the Skikda road. Though the lane is difficult to find, the huge Basilica of Saint Augustine is in the typical French colonial mixture of Moorish arches, Byzantine cupola, and Roman roof. Built in 1881 by a clerical architect, the Abbé Puguet, with lavish use of onyx from Skikda, the stained-glass windows direct the sunlight from dawn to dusk to the altar. The patron saint's embalmed body had been taken in the 7th century to Italy, but on the brief return of Christianity to his see, the first French bishop obtained the saint's arm as a relic, now included in his wax likeness lying in a miniature tumulus above an altar of many marbles. The greater part of his remains is the pride of the Church of San Pietro in Ciel d'Oro in Pavia.

Italian Augustinian monks are allowed to say mass, while Sisters of the Poor maintain an Old People's Home. From the terrace in front of the Saint's bronze statue, the whole layout of Hippo Regius becomes apparent.

Though the 19th-century basilica is close to the site of the 3rd-century Basilica of Peace, the largest of seven during St. Augustine's bishopric, the entrance to the archeological site is from N16 to Souk Ahras. To the right is the quarter of the elegant seaside villas, with colonnaded patios, fountains and private baths; some mosaics have been left *in situ* to convey an idea of the refined luxury prevailing in the 3rd and 4th centuries. Behind the antique Basilica and the Baptistery is a circular Market on a colonnaded square and the Public Baths. The Forum is distinguished by bigger and better columns, with the Theater at the foot of the modern Basilica's hill.

From the slight eminence of the Museum the plan of Roman Hippo is clearly revealed and artistically confirmed—in the surviving half—by one of the large mosaics which, once again, are the prize exhibits, though statues, busts and finely-worked household articles are also well represented.

To the north, a winding road hugs the coast for 10 km. (6 miles) past once-grand villas, beaches and rocky creeks to the lighthouse of the Cap de Garde. Northwest W16 rises to almost 910 m. (3,000 feet) through an oak forest to Seraidi, where an excellent hotel commands an unusually fine view over mountains and sea. W16 continues northwest to Chetaïbi.

The Eastern Confines

N44 continues 101 km. (63 miles) east to the Tunisian border, through a marshy plain of lakes and lagoons, providing good pasture for Algeria's largest herds of cattle. The huts are usually surrounded by high reed fences.

The sea is only touched again at El Kala (89 km. 55 miles), still an important fishing port, though not any more for corals—for which the Bey of Constantine granted a monopoly to traders from Marseille in the 14th century and which was exploited for some 400 years—a beach resort and last town before the frontier.

Retreating into wooded hills, N44 turns south to El Aïoun and the main border crossing, while a narrow but scenically much lovelier road affording fine views over the sea leads directly to Tabarka in Tunisia.

N16 and N21 south from Annaba divide at the huge iron and steel plant of El Hadjar, the former leading south to Souk Ahras and Tébessa, the latter to Guelma.

That important railway and road center, 66 km. (41 miles) from Annaba, 117 (23) from Constantine, 77 (48) from Souk Ahras, is approached through the vast olive and orange plantations north at Heliopolis, next to Hammam Berda whose circular pool dates from Roman times. One-story houses standing at right angles accommodate over 50,000 inhabitants, working in the sugar plant, the bicycle factory and in the manufacture of porcelain, using the china clay of Djebel Delagh.

There are vestiges of antique Baths and Cisterns, but the Theater of Roman Calama was restored in the beginning of this century and is used for cultural performances. The adjacent Museum contains finds from the numerous Roman sites of the region.

At a mere 23 km. (14 miles), Announa is the closest, 3 km. (2 miles) off N20 southwest to Constantine. The astonishingly large area of broken stones and columns strewn over the slopes and flat summit of a hill, which falls steeply to a valley in the north, rather than any recognizable building, implies the importance of Roman Thibilis. Little visited, the Roman coins offered by shepherd boys are for once the genuine article.

Nature comes dramatically into its own northwest on W122 at Aquae Thibilitanae, now Hammam Chellala, the less off-putting substitution of Hammam Meskoutine, the Bath of the Accursed. No wonder the Arabs gave this name to the sulphurous waters bubbling from fissures in the ground, at a temperature of 97° Celsius the hottest known except for the Icelandic geysers.

Some of the water has been channeled into an antique reservoir covered by a cupola pierced by aeration shafts; more cascades down a cliff, depositing part of its lime content over a wide area, so that the waterfall has over the centuries been doubled by an extraordinary petrified ocher drapery of gigantic stalactites enveloped in convincing hellfire fumes. The water, used for the treatment of rheumatic and respiratory diseases at the thermal establishment, flows at a rate of 48,000 cubic meters per day from adjoining sources.

11 km. (7 miles) further north on W122 is the vast megalithic necropolis of Roknia, some 3,000 dolmens, two- to three-foot-high rocks, scattered for thousands of years over the hillside.

The railway and N20 continue east from Guelma to Bouchegouf to join N16 on the southeast course to Souk Ahras, Roman Tagaste, where Saint Augustine was born in 354. In 388 he installed in his own villa a community which developed into a form of monasticism as important as that of St. Benedict. Byzantine walls still surround Roman ruins under the remains of a citadel.

The railway then follows the Oued Medjerda east to the Tunisian border, while N20 climbs northeast into the Medjerda range and after skirting the highest peak, Djebel Msid (over 1,280 m., 4,200 feet), turns east into the Oued Medjerda Valley just before the border; scenic W9 continues north to join N44 before El Qala. W118 leads to the La Chéffia Dam which has formed a lovely artificial lake in the densely wooded northwestern part of the range.

And Still They Come

There seems to be no end to Roman sites. At Khemissa, 39 km. (24 miles) west following the Oued Medjerda upstream almost to its source, are the impressive remains—Forum, Capitol, Baths, Triumphal Arch, Theater, Monumental Gate, Basilica, Byzantine Fortress—of Thubursicum Numidarum, raised to a Roman *municipium* by Trajan.

W7 returns east to M'Daourouch on N16. Coming from Souk Ahras on that main artery running south roughly parallel with the border, addicts of Roman/Byzantine antiquities might want to branch off to Taqura, now Taoura, 29 km. (18 miles) southeast. As there is so much bigger and better to come, leave it to the archeologists and continue the full 40 km. (31 miles) south to Drea, then branch southeast (left) 5 km. (3 miles) to Numidian Madaura which became a Roman colony in the first century. Birthplace of Apuleius, author of *The Golden Ass,* one of the first pornographic novels, and of Martianus Capella, the encyclopaedist, it also witnessed the early studies of Saint Augustine; a Mausoleum, Theaters, Baths, Basilica and Byzantine fortress.

6 km. (4 miles) west back to M'Daourouch and south on N16 to Tebessa, the outstanding eastern antique site. Dolmens and Punic tombs prove that since prehistoric times settlers have appreciated the healthy position. The 3rd-century Temple of Minerva houses the Museum, once again en-

dowed with fine mosaics. In 214 the Emperor Caracalla erected the Triumphal Arch which the Byzantine General Salomon incorporated in 535 into his mighty ramparts flanked by 13 towers. These, together with the unusually large Amphitheater and a well-preserved Christian Basilica surrounded by chapels, catacombs, a baptistery and a hostel indicate the importance of antique Theveste.

N16 continues seemingly forever south, roughly parallel to the Tunisian border, meeting N48 at El Oued before turning westward to its terminal at Touggourt.

Southeast along N10 it is, however, only 45 km. (28 miles) to the border of South Tunisia. Northwest, N10 leads back to Constantine, but at Meskiana (90 km., 56 miles) W20 branches southwest along the Oued Meskiana to Khenchela in the Aurès Mountains.

The Aurès

This region of exceptional variety is exciting for the dedicated traveler if he is prepared to put up with sparse accommodation. The adventurous might venture 108 km. (66 miles) southeast from Constantine by rail or N10 to Oum El Bouaghi, then on a comfortable new road south to Khenchela. W1 strikes south on a spectacular crossing of Nementcha Mountains to Khangat Sidi Nadji before turning west to Zeribet El Oued and a string of oases including Sidi Okba to Biskra. A lovely trip for the caravan/trailer/tent travelers.

The less adventurous had better turn west at Khenchela on W20, for the 103 km. (64 miles) to the junction with N31—though W172, rounding the highest peak, Djebel Chelia, well over 2,280 m. (7,500 feet), or W45, branching south at Touffana, both meeting at Medina to join N31 at Arris, are perfectly practicable alternatives as by evening the hotels at Batna or Biskra can be reached.

Not that arrival by railway or from N3 from Constantine to Batna (121 km., 75 miles) entails any lack of choice. The recommended roundtrip is N31 through the heart of the Aurès range via Arris to spend the night at Biskra, and return by the slightly shorter N3 (119 km., 74 miles) via El Kantara north to Batna. To which the splendid, if somewhat adventurous, middle W54 must be added, skirting the second highest peak, Djebel Mahmet, before passing the apricot orchards of the valley of the Oued Abdi, the Gates of the Desert, to the typical Auresian village Menaa, where little earth-colored cubes of houses are piled into the characteristic *dechra* on the crest of a cliff, to Amentane, a foretaste of Djemorah, an outstandingly beautiful oasis framed by mountains; W54 then improves, but not the landscape, to the junction with N3 shortly before Biskra.

Rome at Its Most Overwhelming

Such a statement certainly raises high expectations which remain unfulfilled at Khenchela, antique Mascula, now mainly given over to the weaving of wool and goat hair rugs in simple striped patterns or vividly colored lozenge designs; nor at Aïn El Hammam, with remains of the Baths of Aquae Flavianae; nor yet at Ksar Baghaï, where some ruins are surrounded by Byzantine walls in the immense cedar forests of Ouled Yakoub.

To keep the fiercely independent Berbers—who still cling to their age-old way of life in inaccessible valleys—from sweeping northward into the fertile colonized highlands, the Romans stationed a crack legion, the Tertia Augusta, at Lambesis, now Tazoult, 10 km. (6 miles) southeast of Batna on W20. Though the provincial capital before Cirta, Lambesis was first and foremost a garrison town and the only recognizable building, wrongly designated *Pretorium,* served as barracks; and looks it. The very fine mosaics and numerous broken statues in the small Museum on the village square show, however, that in the declining Empire even the soldiers had developed an appreciation of luxurious housing.

And then, at last, 19 km. (12 miles) east on W20, superlatives become justifiable. In 1765 an English traveler mentioned some ruins, but nobody expected that the excavations begun in 1880 would bring to light a whole town, as well preserved as Pompeii, as revealing of the lay-out of a late imperial foundation as Pompeii was of an earlier period. What the thick layer of cinders did for the latter, the eternal sands of the desert, aided by total oblivion, achieved for Timgad.

The soldiers of the Tertia preferred their entertainment at a safe distance from their superiors; and on finishing their military service the veterans were entitled to land. To satisfy this double need, at the end of the first century the Emperor Trajan founded the military colony Thamugadi, which during the remaining *Pax Romana* grew into an elegant and sophisticated town.

The Romans have never been surpassed in combining the esthetic with the useful. At well over 900 m. (3,000 feet) the air is wonderfully pure even in an African summer, though the snowcapped peaks to the south obviously failed to keep out the desert sands. Thamugadi only covered some 350 square yards, yet thousands of russet columns rise from the soil of the same color, with occasional grey marble standing out against the deep-blue sky. Two well-paved axes cross at right angles at the Forum in the center.

Left of the entrance, the Museum excels in 3rd- and 4th-century mosaics, besides the usual statuary and household articles. The access road is lined with votive *stelae,* probably funeral stones representing the dead.

Rolls of manuscripts filled the semi-circular niches of the Library, while the Theater provides an incomparable setting for the International Festival in May. Trajan would have deserved his Triumphal Arch for the foundation of Thamugadi alone. To the right, the Temple of the Colony's Genius is distinguished by two Corinthian columns still supporting an architrave. Opposite is the Market of Sertius, named after the provincial dignitary who paid for its construction.

Tall colonnades line the paved esplanade leading to the main temple, the Capitol. To the south is a large Basilica and the Palace of the Donatist bishop, as during the 4th century Catholics and Donatists constructed rival ecclesiastical establishments in their ferocious fight for supremacy.

After the withdrawal of the Lambesis garrison to defend Rome itself, and weakened by religious dissensions, Thamugadi fell to the Berber tribes of the Aurès Mountains, who destroyed this hated Roman settlement. But here, too, as everywhere in Roman Africa, an uncertain revival occurred under the Byzantine rule, when the great general Salomon constructed a strong fortress; but in the 7th century sand and silence covered all traces.

Anyone wanting to look at yet more stones should proceed 10 km. (6 miles) southeast to Icchoukane, a very ancient Berber village, where several circular megalithic monuments stand 7 to 9 feet high. From the sublime to the . . . well, almost!

The Abiod Valley

After so much Roman glory, straight unadulterated nature is welcome along N31 from Batna to Biskra. Leaving W20 east to Timgad, W54 southwest to the gentle Abdi Valley, and W45 to Medina behind, N31 penetrates into the heart of the mountains to Arris (61 km., 38 miles), 'capital' of the Aurès, at 1,097 m. (3,600 feet) only slightly higher than Batna, but exposed to the icy winter winds from the northeast, against which the brown bournous commonly worn seems to offer very insufficient protection.

Partly *dechra,* climbing the north slope of the Abiod Valley, partly *mechta,* spread over a mountain spur, Arris lacks a hotel but boasts the Museum of the Aurès, where the region's folk art is displayed; heavy silver jewelry, coral encrusted pectorals, enamelled clasps and enormous anklets as well as rugs and carpets with the characteristic black background ascribed by romantics to the austerity of the mountains.

The 13 km. (8 miles) of mountain road connecting with W54 in the gentler Abdi Valley make a roundtrip from Arris to Biskra and back possible. Shortly after Arris N31 enters the spectacular Gorges of Tighanimine, carved by the Oued El Abiod, through gigantic white chalk cliffs. Exiting at Tiffelfel, a different world opens up, of olive and orange trees soon giving way to the palm groves of the desert.

But the branch northeast (left), past the carefully cultivated terraces of T'Kout, skirts the wild northern slopes of Djebel Ahmar Khaddou to climb to a windswept plateau and the mighty forest round the Canyon of Djemina. From the track along the left height, the regular openings cut by troglodytes halfway up the high vertical rockface opposite provide rather uncomfortable though certainly well-protected homes.

At Rhoufi a signboard points left to the Balcon de Rhoufi, a large flattened space affording a splendid view over the precipitous gorges where dense palm groves shade the limpid water of the Oued, while fig trees climb the steep cliff to the ruined houses of the old village of Baniane, destroyed during the Revolution. From the new village of cubic houses round a green-and-white mosque, 19 km. (12 miles) southeast on N31, a track of well-worn paving stones leads into the canyon, among the orange and lemon trees hidden below the palms.

The next branch left passes through a natural rock-circus to the oasis of M'Chouneche, another graceful palm grove, whence it is possible to follow the Oued upstream—if the water level is sufficiently low—2 hours on foot to Baniane, 5 hours to Rhoufi.

After 23 km. (14 miles), the blue sheet of the artificial lake of Foum El Gherza appears on the left among forested green hills and the limitless red rocks beyond. The remaining 19 km. (12 miles) descend between these rocks to Biskra.

The Threshold

Return on N3 is through the Défilé. From the Col de Sfa the Village Rouge appears so romantically oriental that few can resist crossing the Oued Fedhala. Children—no lack of those—will act as guides through the covered lanes to the Roman Museum, where the meager remains of Calceus Herculis, Heel of Hercules, are displayed.

When naming the cleft in the ocher cliff of Djebel Metlili, gnawed by the sparse water of the oued, the Arabs produced the appropriate El Kantara, Threshold or Gate. Here is the same sudden change to the vegetation of the highlands as on the outward journey, while at Aïn Touta the roofs revert to rounded tiles.

The last branch off N3 ascends northwest (left) to Chaabat Ouled Chelih in the Belezma Mountains, where a forest road climbs to the Djebel Rafaa (1,981 m., 6,500 ft.).

Batna is another wilaya capital hardly visited for its own sake, but necessarily on the road or railway to somewhere else. Instead of taking N3 straight back to Constantine (121 km., 75 miles), a detour to the last— promise—Roman town of the eastern region can be made by taking W5 over the Col de Telmet to Zana, antique Diana, to whose forum and colonnades (dating from the 2nd century) the Byzantines added a church and fortress some 300 years later.

W135 returns east to N3 and the Medracen, a cone of dressed stones rising in vast tiers from a short cylindrical socle decorated with 60 Doric columns supporting a typically Punic cornice. Built in the late 3rd century B.C. by the Numidian King Massinissa or his son Micipsa, it must have served as model for the much larger mausoleum at Tipasa.

Except for the Dolmens of Ouled Rahmoun, the only other site along N3, Es Souna at El Khroub, is likewise ascribed to Massinissa and quite probably even his tomb.

PRACTICAL INFORMATION FOR
THE ROMAN EAST

WHEN TO GO. Coast in summer, if you book well in advance; inland spring and fall. Winters can be very rainy on the coast, cold inland. In May: Festival in the ancient theater of Timgad.

GETTING THERE. By Plane. Daily flights by Air Algérie from Algiers to Annaba, Bejaïa, Constantine, Jijel and Tébessa. Frequent flights from the major French towns to Annaba and Constantine, to the former also from Geneva, Rome and Zurich. Three flights per week from Marseille to Tébessa.

By Boat. Regular C.N.A.N. ferry boats from Marseille to Annaba, Bejaïa and Skikda; from Algiers to Annaba.

By Train. S.N.T.F. west–east from Algiers via Sétif, Constantine. The Algiers–Tunis train runs weekly. Guelma, Souk Ahras to Tunis. North–south from Annaba and Skikda via Constantine, Batna, Biskra to Touggourt. Mostly very slow, Constantine–Tunis, 20 hours. The Constantine–Tunis train goes daily.

By Road. Adequate roads to all important sites. Frequent E.P.T.V.E. coaches between all towns.

HOTELS AND RESTAURANTS

Note: both restaurants and nightclubs are almost exclusively in hotels.

Annaba. *Seybouse International* (E), tel. 82 35 77 or 822125, airconditioned rooms, 24 suites; in the panoramic restaurant on the 14th floor, the view surpasses the food. *El Alami* (M), 9 Rue des Frères Boucherit. *Ezzarah* (M), 11 Rue Lamara Abdelkader. *Hoggar* (M), 4 Place Alexis Lambert. *Paradaes* (M), Blvd. Fillali Rachid. 43 rooms; not quite Paradise—but still an excellent restaurant. *Nouzha* (I), Rue Emir Abdelkader. *Regina* (I), 6 Rue Bakhli Mokhtar.

Restaurants. *Le Bosphore* (M), Cours de la Revolution. *Caravelle* (M), Route de la Corniche, and *Le Lavandon* (M), Ave. Benghazi, *good seafood.* for seafood. *Mataâm Salim* (M), 13 Rue Lamara Abdelkader. *Le Tindouf* (M), Rue Jean Jaurès, for Algerian specialties. *La Baie El Khalid,* Place Rizzi Ammar, for kebabs.

At **Seraidi** 12 km. (8 miles) west is *El Mountazah* (E), tel. 82 26 99 or 82 98 94. 102 rooms. Located in an oak forest some 1,000 m. (3,000 feet) high and overlooking the sea; pool and tennis.

Batna. *Chelia* (E), Allée Ben Boulaïd (tel. 55 62 04 or 55 18 62. *Amin* (M), 2 Rue Mohammed Khemisti (tel. 87 16 34). Clean and comfortable.
Restaurant. *Tassili* (M).

Bejaïa. *Auberge d'Aokas* (M), Cap Aokas. *Corniche* (M), Baie de Sidi Yahia. On the sea.
Restaurants. *A* (M), Rue Abdelkader Idjraoui. *La Brise de Mer* (M), Baie de Sidi Yahia. For seafood. *Les Sables d'Or* (M), at Cap Aoakas. *Le Seville* (M), 8 Rue Cheikh Amar Salah. European food.

Bordj Bou Arreridj. *Orient* (M), 19 Rue de la République (tel. 99 18 87).

Bougaâ. *Tafet* (M), Rue Abdelhak.

Collo. *Bougaroun* (M), tel. 91 55 00. On the sea.

Constantine. *Cirta* (E), Ave. Rahmani Achour (tel. 94 30 33). 126 rooms; reasonable restaurant. *Panoramic* (E), 59 Ave. Aouati Mustapha (tel. 94 24 77). 35 rooms. As named, with fine view. *El Oumara* (M), 29 Rue Abane Ramdan. 46 rooms.
Restaurant. *As Sahri,* south of Constantine on Batna Road, at Khadr, Oued Hamimime; outstanding food.

El Kala. *El Mordjane* (M), tel. 86 02 40. 103 rooms. Pool and private beach.

Guelma. *Mermoura* (E), tel. 86 36 49/58. 60 rooms. Comfortable.

Hammam Chellala. *Hôtel Thermal* (M), tel. 86 80 18. 150 rooms.

Hammam Gouergour. *Hôtel Thermal* (M), tel. 80 04 42. 130 rooms. Very scenic, with modern spa. Tennis.

Jijel. *Glagier* (M). *Littoral* (M). *Tindouf* (M). All modern.
Restaurants. *Beau Rivage* (M), Blvd. Zighout Youcef. *Dolce Vita* (M), Blvd. Zighout Youcef.

Khenchela. *El Mourad* (M). 36 rooms.

Sétif. *El Hidab* (E), Blvd. Cheikh Laif (tel. 90 40 43). 131 rooms, 3 apartments. Pool. Centrally sited close to the museum. Modern, clean, and friendly; good food. *Guergour* (M), tel. 86 910. 43 rooms. Less central. *El Mountazah* (M), 12 Ave. Ben Boulaid (tel. 90 50 48). 72 rooms. *El Riadh* (M), 2 Rue des Frères Meslem (tel. 90 78 47). 60 rooms. *Setifis* (M). 45 rooms. Good restaurant.

Skikda. *Es Salem* (E), Pl. du 24 Février (tel. 74 67 93 or 74 65 53). 152 rooms, 5 apartments. Pool, tennis, bowling alley, large garden. *El Mountazah* (M), 2 Rue Didouche Mourad (tel. 39 70 57). 47 rooms. Good restaurant.

Outside town on the corniche: *Château Vert* (M), tel. 95 90 01. *Paradis Plage* (I). 59 rooms.

Tebessa. *Aigle* (M), tel. 97 03 54 or 97 00 79. 70 rooms in a 4-story building; clean, water supply erratic, dining room cozy but only set meals are served.

Tichy. *Les Hammadites* (E), tel. 92 66 80. 150 rooms. Beach, pool, and tennis. *Grande Terrasse* (I). 30 rooms. In the village.

Timgad. *Timgad* (M). 70 rooms. Closed during the Ramadan.

ARCHEOLOGICAL SITES AND HISTORIC MONUMENTS. Dolmens: Ouled Rahmoun and the vast megalithic necropolis at Roknia.
Berber Monuments: Le Medracen, Icchoukan, Kenchella.
Islamic Monuments: Kalaâ des Beni Hammad, Kasbah of Bejaïa, Arris in the Aurès.
Roman Monuments: Djemila, Tebessa, and Timgad are all outstanding. Announa, Bejaïa, Guelma, Khemissa, Lambese, Mila, M'Daourouch, Sétif, Skikda, Souk Ahras, and Zana.

SPORTS. Swimming. There are pools at Annaba, Constantine, Jijel, and Skikda, besides the hotel pools mentioned in the above listing. Best beaches between Bejaïa and Jijel, at Collo, Skikda, and El Kala.
Tennis. Club de Tennis Universitaire, Ave. des Arcades Romaines, Constantine.

SHOPPING. S.N.A.T. shops—Annaba: 2 Cours de la Révolution. Constantine: 22 Rue Aban Ramdan.

NATIONAL TOURIST OFFICES. Algerian National Tourist Offices (O.N.A.T.) at—**Annaba:** 1 Rue Tarik Ibn Ziad. **Batna:** Allée Ben Boulaid. **Bejaïa:** 31 Rue Ahmed Ougana. **Constantine:** 6 Rue Zaâbana, and Airport. **Skikda:** 1 Rue Rezki Kahal.
Touring Club offices at—**Annaba:** 1 Blvd. Zirout Youcef. **Sétif:** 4 Rue des Frères Meslem.

THE SAHARA

Solitude in a Limitless Land

Twenty-one countries encircle the Mediterranean, vying with one another in beaches, mountains, classical ruins and medieval towns, but only three share an equally fabulous sea, the immense, the stunning sea of sand, the Sahara, of which Algeria possesses the lion's share.

The desert is a shock that gradually becomes a drug. Limitless silence over endless miles of naked earth, a deadening sun reducing all desires to thirst, a punishing wind whipping up the sand, all combine to chastise the body and chasten the spirit. Poets and painters alone are qualified to describe the absence of lines, the substitution of shadows, the density of reflections, the vibrations and densities of colors from sunrise to sunset; while the singular clarity of the nights would suffice to account for the nostalgia felt forever by anyone who has experienced their awe-inspiring solitude.

Camus, out of his deep love and understanding of his native country, wrote: "The desert is a land of useless and irreplaceable beauty." Charles de Foucauld stressed the spiritual level on which the desert exerts its deepest influence: "It is necessary to pass through the desert and to live there in order to receive the grace of God." Shattered by so inhuman and immeasurable a setting, man leaves behind all that is superfluous and inessential to turn to the transcendental and thus, perhaps, to find himself.

It is not for nothing that the temptation of Christ took place in the desert, which has always attracted mystics and witnessed the birth of religions. Though no longer inaccessible, no longer even an adventure, the Sahara has preserved its magic and mystery.

Airports, a network of excellent roads, comfortable hotels, by far the best in the country, only serve to reveal the poignant beauty of an unconquerable nature. Flying over what is so wrongly believed to be a flat, monotonous and empty plain is a true voyage of discovery of constantly changing facets, enhanced by cities straight from the *Arabian Nights*. The Saharan circuits, either in airconditioned coaches or by ordinary car, at least in the North Sahara, naturally allow a much better acquaintance and a true appreciation of the bliss when the palm groves at last emerge from the burning sands.

The Oases

At the gateway of the Grand Erg, a string of oases, hidden in the folds of sand dunes, among arid cliffs ever spreading their luxuriant green amidst endless plains, offer delightful cool and freshness in an amazingly varied combination of the simple basic ingredients: an oued, palm trees, a village. Even the architecture emphasizes this diversity, though mosque and minaret dominate one and every village regardless of the local style. The delicately shaded hues of sands and rocks ranging from the palest ocher to deep red, violet, brown and grey are more often than not accentuated by the dazzling whiteness of the houses visible from far away, while occasionally they are hardly distinguishable below the tall trees, their unbaked mudbricks the very color of the soil.

Which to choose amongst this embarrassment of riches? If hard pressed for time, a flight to either Biskra, Ghardaïa or Touggourt will yield the maximum return of local color, though a drive from Algiers to the closest oasis, Bou Saada, may likewise be considered.

An excellent circuit of initiation into the wonders of the Grand Eastern Erg lasting about a week would start at Ghardaïa and the five villages of the M'Zab, proceed to Ouargla on the Oued Mya and Touggourt on the Oued Rhir, two of the largest oases with together more than two and a half million palm trees; to El Oued, capital of the Souf, a conglomeration of palm groves which owe their existence to funnel-shaped holes dug into the sand so that the roots of the trees can reach the actual sheet of subsoil water; to end at Biskra, a town in the center of a veritable archipelago of oases, offering some remarkable excursions.

A longer circuit of the Grand Western Erg, requiring a minimum of ten days, would include lesser-known but therefore all the more characteristic oases; likewise starting at Ghardaïa and the M'Zab, the Grand Erg itself would be penetrated to El Goléa, a sprawling village flanked by a picturesque ksar. Next stop at Timimoun, the red oasis, capital of the Gourara, a group of ksour carved into the almost violet clay of a cliff facing the golden sands; Beni Abbès, where the white crest of the ksar stands out against the reddish background of the Erg, while the hotel stands at the foot of an immense orange dune; Taghit, one of the Saoura's outstanding sites, hidden behind the wall of desolate sand; to end at Aïn Sefra, which controls a splendid gorge on the Ksour Mountains and presents a startling mixture of typical Sahara features and Mediterranean vegetation.

With a few more days available, this tour can be extended southward to include the Plateau of Tademaït, 402 km. (250 miles) without a blade of grass, in Salah, the Plain of Tidikelt, Touat and Adrar.

To see the lot—and no one sensitive to so unique an experience has ever regretted it—several main arteries traverse the Sahara from north to south and west to east, crossing one another in the middle of nowhere. The three main vertical axes are: in the middle, N1 starting at Algiers, leads south via Blida, Médéa to Djelfa—where it is joined by N8 from Algiers via Bou Saada—Laghouat, Ghardaïa, El Goléa to In Salah, where a dirt road, perfectly practical for Land Rovers, takes over to Tamanrasset and Agadès in Niger, the future Trans-Sahara Route; in the west, N6 starts at Mascara, to be met by N22 from Tlemcen north of Aïn Sefra, to continue southwest to Béchar and Abadla, then southeast to Beni Abbès and Adrar, whence a dirt road ventures to Reggane and Gao in Mali; the middle axes can be joined by paved N51 via Timimoun to south of El Goléa or over a dirt road from Reggane to In Salah.

N50 branches west shortly after Béchar, paved all the 805 km. (500 miles) to Tindouf, but at present far from advisable, as this is a dead end while the border with Morocco remains closed, and Tindouf is definitely not worth retracing one's steps over such a distance. Moreover, the Polisario guerrillas operating from this region might just think you are their favorite hostage, if the Algerian authorities should allow you—which is unlikely—into the Far West.

A settlement of the Western Sahara dispute would, of course, reopen this first section of the principal west to east axis, which begins at Agadir in Morocco, crosses N6, as stated above, to Ghardaïa on N1, whence N49 leads via Ouargla to N3, north of the oilfields of Hassi Messaoud.

N3 is the eastern north-south axis, starting from Skikda via Constantine, Batna, Biskra to Touggourt—N16 branches east via El Oued to Tozeur in southern Tunisia—Hassi Messaoud and straight through the center of the Grand Eastern Erg to Hassi Bel Bouebbour, where it divides into a paved branch east to Mazoula and Tin Fouyé, then south to In Aménas and El Abed Larache, whence dirt roads lead to Djanet and the other sites in the Tassili; the second, unpaved, branch strikes south via Amguid into the Hoggar.

With all those routes nationales and pistes, not to mention airports and hotels, what has happened to the solitude, the desert's most marvelous feature, beloved by mystics, poets and this guide? All this modernity is but a grain in the sand. The Sahara has been inhabited since time immemorial, criss-crossed by countless caravans, and if only along the few roads the camels have partly been replaced by trucks and coaches, the Sahara can dwarf even the functional ugliness of the derricks in the oilfields.

Black Gold

Yet to some the Sahara is mainly known because of the oil and gas. From the vast oilfield of Hassi Messaoud pipelines have for years brought oil over sand and mountains to the refineries of Annaba, Arzew, Bejaïa and Skikda. With the discovery of the even vaster natural gasfield at Hassi R'Mel, between Laghouat and Ghardaïa, gas pipelines were added, first to Arzew, later to Skikda, while a third and largest annually brings 17.5 billion cubic meters of gas via Tunisia, Sicily and the Straits of Messina to Italy and France.

The State Oil Company, now split into 24 autonomous units, has developed several vast oil and gas fields south of Hassi Messaoud as well as round In Aménas near the Libyan border. Wells have been sunk in so many promising places in the southeastern Sahara that the production of hydrocarbons has kept fairly steady, the decrease in petrol production being compensated by an increase in gas deliveries. The 1985–89 Five Year Plan reduced the colossal investments needed to maximize production in order to avoid exhausting the proven reserves—one billion tons of petrol and a gigantic 3,500 billion cubic meters of gas—too rapidly.

Yet flying over the desert or even driving through, it is most unlikely that a unique experience should be disturbed by mundane appurtenances. Immensity has defeated the temporary.

The Oldest Industry

Beautifully fitting into the landscape, and, what is more, forming an essential part, are some 70 kinds of date palms which produce an equal number of different fruits. Outstandingly popular are the *deglet nour* (finger of light), large, light in color, and succulent, accounting for almost one half of the production, and mainly reserved for export; the *deglet beida* (white finger), smaller and less juicy, mostly for interior consumption; and the *ghars,* soft, syrupy, very sweet, pressed for preservation into "the bread of caravans."

Almost seven million date palms yield some 85,000 tons of dates, only a rough figure, as the very important direct consumption which does not reach the market is difficult to evaluate. The palm requires abundant water, brackish will do, during its 70-year lifespan, which accounts for the intensive irrigation as well as careful replanting in all the oases. After the picking of the fruit in fall, the lowest circle of fronds is cut off; the scars of the annual pruning indicate the age of the tree. The wood fuels the potter's kiln, is carved into household articles and supports the arcades of mosques and markets. The trunk, cut lengthwise and hollowed out, serves for the canalization of the water. The leaves are woven into mats, fans or roof coverings. Nothing is wasted, though the delicious *coeurs de palmier,* the young shoots of palms served as vegetable or salad, come from another, less valuable variety of the tree and are, even in North Africa, mostly imported from Brazil.

The Gateway

Bou Saada is an obvious first example of an oasis, offering, at a mere 251 km. (156 miles) south of Algiers along N8, the closest Saharan specimen, complete with palm groves, sand dunes, white *koubbas* and camels; it is, moreover, at the apex of the triangle formed by N46, west to Djelfa, east to Biskra, for those wishing to sample more oases by car.

The S.N.A.T. shop displays beside the usual ceramics, thick camel-hair rugs, silks and jewelry, long thin knives in red leather sheaths, called *bousaadi,* all well as embroidered palmleaf fans. Accommodation is attractive and in the evenings the famous dancers of the Ouled Naïl tribe present in their multicolored veils an almost authentic folkloric spectacle. More than enough to justify the Arab name of Father (or City) of Happiness. A favorite location for filming, with a bit of luck a genuine *fata morgana* over the torrid Chott El Hodna might be thrown in.

This plethora of advantages has, inevitably, caused a very serious drawback: the Oued Bou Saada, flowing at the foot of a huge cliff before losing itself in the Chott El Hodna and sustaining a mere 25,000 palm trees along a 2-mile ribbon, is no longer able to supply all the multifarious activities. Water is often rationed in the hotel, while the new quarter that has sprung up round the textile factory has further aggravated the problem. A mile upstream, the oued passes through the Gorges of the Gobr El Oucif, dammed up to provide water for the ruined—and thus all the more romantic—Moulin (Mill) Ferrero.

The original village lies in the valley's lowest part; narrow lanes—one occupied exclusively by the smiths sharpening the *bousaadis* —ascend to the Djemaâ Sidi Brahim, one of 25 mosques, from which the view extends over the whole oasis. Three simple tombs lie under the whitewashed *koubba* in the middle of an abandoned cemetery; the French painter Etienne Dinet, whose work is represented in the Museum of Algiers, was sufficiently seduced by the charms of Bou Saada to reside there for some 40 years after becoming a Moslem. He rests next to his friend and the latter's wife.

In the middle of the last century, Sidi Mohamed Ben Belkacem founded a zaouïa at El Hamel, 13 km. (8 miles) southwest off N46. This religious fraternity soon acquired a great reputation as center of Islamic studies, all the more as the local inhabitants claimed descent from the Prophet and insisting on racial purity resisted any intermixture with the Ouled Naïl. The simple but graceful dazzling white koubba is surmounted by six irregular cupolas. Glazed tiles are advantageously used round the door and in the interior, which serves as mosque, study center and tomb simultaneously. In the large hostel on the square, coffee is dispensed to pilgrims and even non-Moslems.

An Oasis for All Tastes

74 km. (46 miles) east on N46, Tolga is, thanks to artesian wells, the most luxuriant of the Ziban oases, famous for their deglet nour, packed on the spot for export. The almost cyclopean walls are ascribed to the Byzantines. The curious pyramidal minaret is surmounted by a lantern of palmwood.

42 km. (26 miles) further, Biskra is everything an oasis should be. 245 km. (152 miles) south of Constantine by N3 through the Aurès Mountains, the airport is surrounded by some two million palm trees, stretching almost to the mountains barring the northern horizon. The red and ocher soil is scarred by the dry beds of oueds only running after rare cloudbursts, because in the Sahara it never rains but it pours, as during the terrible inundations of 1969.

The Romans built Vescera between mountain and desert on the bank of the largest all-year oued, where new quarters spread in a checkerboard pattern to form the biggest Saharan town. Because of its exceptionally mild climate recommended for tubercular patients, even before it was made famous by André Gide in the last century, Biskra became easily accessible by the construction of the railway to which it is connected by a fine tree-shaded avenue.

The Hotel Les Zibans, southeast of the town, is a modern copy of the 14th-century Koubba of Sidi Zerzoug, on an islet in the midst of the oued, which is over a quarter of a mile wide. From the Turkish fort the panorama includes grove after palm grove, irrigated by open *séguias* (irrigation ditches) which assure an equitable distribution of water in a three-story cultivation: vegetables, fruit trees, date palms. Horse carriages are best suited, beside being part of the local color, to penetrate the luxuriant vegetation for a drive on the twisting lanes round Old Biskra to the hamlets scattered among the trees, whose shade makes walking in this truly idyllic surrounding an equal pleasure.

Biskra possesses sufficient attractions to confine even a longish stay to the main oasis, with nothing more strenuous than a swim in the pool, a leisurely walk or drive. Yet even sightseeing requires little effort, beginning painlessly with a mere mile east across the Oued to Chetma, a small off-beat oasis of lovely gardens under magnificent palms. 5 km. (3 miles) northwest, the Romans treated their rheumatisms and skin diseases in the 50°C water of Ad Piscinam, which as Hammam Salahine (Bath of the Marabouts) has become one of Algeria's leading spas.

The Herald of Islam

On his return from Massa where he had ridden his horse into the Atlantic claiming that he had extended Islam to the end of the world, Oqba Ibn Nafaa (Oqba ibn-Nafi) was confronted by the indomitable Berber tribes of the Aurès Mountains under the Christian King Kosaïla and the Prophetess Kahina. Oqba was killed outside Biskra in 682, the year 62 of the Hegira, and his tomb, Algeria's oldest Moslem shrine, has attracted pilgrims ever since.

Built from the pebbles of the small oued, held together by beaten earth over a framework of palm trunks, the 10th-century mosque, greatly enlarged in 1913, was threatened with collapse after the disastrous inundations of 1969. Restoration has, on the whole, been successful, and despite the inevitable cement reinforcement much of the latter adjuncts have been removed in a return to the original purity. The carved cedar gate is pre-Islamic, some columns are Roman as probably also the stones found during the enlargement of 1964.

The entire village, 14 km. (9 miles) along W1 to Khenchela, is built of mud-bricks, the best of all thermic insulators. Since the construction of the Foum El Gherza Dam, the waters from the Aurès Mountains have irrigated the ancient battlefield into a vast vegetable garden.

A Chain of Oases

For the next 222 km. (138 miles) south it is for once preferable to take the railway, right to the terminus at Touggourt, because it touches on most of the pretty oases—El Ourir and M'Raïer on the confines of the Chott Meranane, El Arfiane, Djamaâ and Tamena, with an impressive ksar—while N3 bypasses them. From the tower of the Hotel Oasis as well as from the minaret of the main mosque, it becomes apparent that Touggourt is only a link—though by far the most important—in a chain of palm groves extending for 145 km. (90 miles) along the course of the Oued Rhir, whose subterranean waters have been tapped with a resulting increase in the number of trees to about 1,300,000. The pyramids of fresh dates in the market in the fall are a sight not to be missed.

Four simple domed koubbas, one white, three earth-colored, hide behind a screen of tamarisks on the large cemetery to the west. Below irregular low vaults are the tombs of the Ouled Djellab dynasty, two vertical slabs for the men, three for the ladies, or at least in theory. These blood-thirsty princelings, who kept their independence from the 15th century to the death of the last in 1854, were so hated by their luckless subjects that, fearing revenge beyond the grave, they resorted to a certain amount of camouflage.

It is only a few steps from the legerdemain of medieval tyrants to the beginning of motorized Trans-African transport; a simple pillar on the

main square commemorates the departure of the Citroën caterpillars
which accomplished the first crossing of the Sahara in 1922. An arcaded
avenue leads to the old town, where partly covered, winding lanes surround the mosque, the interior of whose dome is decorated with mosaics
and stucco work.

The chain of oases continues south along N3, which follows the Oued
Rhir, though it is more picturesque to take the piste—no problem for the
car—starting at the Hotel Oasis to pass through some particularly fine
groves round a marabout with five small green pear-shaped cupolas culminating in pink nipples, a busy potters' village, to the Sea of Temacine,
which is not all that grand but a very small lake of clear though brackish
water. The derrick towards the Sidi Mahdi Airport is employed in the
search for subterranean water reserves and not for oil.

Temacine (11 km., 7 miles) is a fortress town, whose houses are built
into the ramparts, crumbling despite their palm-trunk reinforcement.
Here, too, there is a fine view from the square minaret, decorated with
a geometric design of unbaked bricks over the labyrinthine ksar, tightly
encircled by the grove which in turn is hemmed in and threatened by the
eternal enemy, sand. A mile further south, Tamelhat, Zaouïa of the Tidjani, is a ksar on a lesser scale, but the domes of the 18th-century Mosque
and Mausoleum of Sidi El Hadj Ali are elaborately decorated with colored
tiles and stucco.

The journey south along N3 is interrupted for a touristic *must,* a visit
to El Oued, capital of the Souf, 97 km. (60 miles) northeast on N16.

Town of a Thousand Domes

Here, a very different view presents itself from the pointed minaret of
the Djemaâ Sidi Salem or the hotel terrace. The ubiquitous flat roofs have
been superseded by cupolas and vaults over the white, one-storied, arcaded
houses which, by extending the surface of refraction, lessen the deadening
heat of the summer. The unusual architecture inspired Isabelle Eberhardt,
a young explorer and novelist converted to Islam, to coin the name in 1900
during her adventurous stay. Not only more romantic an appellation, but
also infinitely more fitting than the official El Oued, as there is no trace
of a river, which explains the second, equally startling difference: the absence of the customary ring of extensive groves, expected for a town of
20,000 inhabitants, so that the menacing golden sand dunes seem to engulf
the town itself.

Fear not! The dunes are artificial. Joke of the century, artificial dunes
in the Sahara, as if the billions upon billions of the indigenous variety were
not sufficient. But there is surprising method in this apparent madness,
which is a heroic manifestation of the eternal struggle of man against unpropitious nature. Backbreaking labor has excavated huge craters of diam-
eters up to half a mile and a depth of 60 to 90 feet to allow palm trees
planted at the bottom to reach the subterranean water without any canalization and the ensuing waste by evaporation. These gigantic funnels have
proved so eminently successful, that the half million palms cultivated bear,
according to connoisseurs, the world's finest dates.

Yet the fight against the sand is never ending; the natural slow slide
of the fine grains from the crest of the dunes might be stopped by a system
of dried palm-leaf fences, which have to be constantly repaired, but they
offer no protection against the fierce desert storms. So day after day, year

in year out, men aged before their time by the merciless sun toil with their donkeys up to the crests, to remove on each journey 120 lbs of the all-pervading enemy. The proverbial silver lining? Not much of it, children joyfully gliding down the dunes as if they were snowhills. And in some hollows, a few wells supply water—raised with a balance-pole and a lever—for vegetables and the Sahara's only tobacco, of exceptionally high nicotine content.

Better than Taxes

It would appear that there must be less strenuous ways to earn a living. Not for the ancestors of the hardy Soufis, who left their native Yemen in Arabia some 500 years ago and after driving their meager flock across Egypt and Libya settled in Tunisia. Harsh taxation sent them once again westward, but the arid Souf seemed no place to tarry. The price of the Oued Rhir's abundant water was, however, malaria.

Between diseases and the tax gatherer they preferred the latter, but on the return journey through the Souf, as they dug for the desperately needed water, they revealed a vast sheet of that precious liquid, exceptionally soft to boot, which has determined the Soufis' way of life ever since. Near this first excavation grew the main town, which is intersected at right angles by two wide streets lined by the principal buildings.

The Museum of the Souf gives an exceptionally clear picture of the region, geology, fauna—including the bluish bird-of-passage whose predilection for scorpions and snakes has earned the name of Gendarme of the Oasis—flora, folklore and household utensils. The most useful article in the market (Friday is the big day) are the slippers, whose exceptionally thick soles of wool and camel hair make for easy walking on the burning sand, when the temperature rises to 60°C.

This is fairly high even by Sahara standards, but then some of the region lies below sea level and the average altitude is zero; yet at its closest, at the Gulf of Gabès, the sea is 322 km. (200 miles) away. To these cooler climes N16 continues through the eastern Souf villages, turning north to Negrine and Tébessa parallel to the Tunisian border, which another branch passes in the direction of Tozeur and Gafsa.

Though camels and donkeys greatly outnumber the cars, the Souf's secondary roads present no difficulties till the unsurmountable walls of loose golden sand or cliffs of white limestone encrusted with pebbles that mark the beds of ancient rivers. W405 advances 13 km. (8 miles) southeast to the largest craters with the finest groves at Nakhlat; from then on the renowned Soufi trackers take over, for whom the sands apparently hold no secrets.

N48 passes north through the other main settlements, the picturesque Ksar of Kouinine, and Guemar, where once again ruined fortifications, an elaborately decorated mosque and medersa witness the former importance of a Tidjani Zaouïa. Here, too, the rare *Narh* (Dance of the Hair) is still practised at marriages.

After the airport, N48 is hemmed in for over 97 km. (60 miles) by the two huge salt depressions, the Chott Méranane, whose center lies 100 feet below sea level, and the even larger though shallower Chott Melrhir. They are a prolongation of the Tunisian Chotts, one of the most desolate landscapes in the world. Yet even here sparse saltbushes provide pasture for sheep, goats and camels.

Where Oil Is King . . .

. . . and tourists fear to tread. 64 km. (40 miles) off Touggourt along N3, W33 branches west (right) to the fertile group of oases round El Hadjira, but is then somewhat lost in the virginal infinity of golden waves till Guerara, founded in 1651 to accommodate the surplus population of the M'Zab. W33 emerges for the remaining 74 km. (46 miles) as the shortest—albeit most precarious—link to N1 at Berriane, founded in 1690 by a religious faction expelled from Ghardaïa and specializing in the finest Ibadite funerary monuments, 40 km. (25 miles) north of their home town.

16 km. (10 miles) further south on the main axis, N56 branches southwest to Ouargla (80 km., 50 miles), while N3 continues almost due south, with another connection, N49, to Ouargla after 72 km. (45 miles). From this crossroad, Algeria's first oilfield makes its presence increasingly felt: a network of pipelines, abandoned and active derricks. The thick clouds of black smoke that signalled Hassi Missaoud from far away have now disappeared, as the gas is no longer burnt off but utilized, though minor flames still light the night sky. Wells, pipes, giant tanks, complicated installations pertinent to extraction and the pumping of oil over vast distances are scattered along the road for 32 km. (20 miles), impossible to escape or ignore on the way south to Tassili.

Group visits to Base 24 Février—the Algerian petrol industry was nationalized on 24 February 1971—can be arranged. The Petroleum Museum illustrates the remarkable development that has taken place since the first strike in 1956 at a depth of 2,134 m. (7,000 feet) below the sands of the Sahara to the recently reduced production of *only* some 70,000 tons of crude oil and 1.8 billion cubic feet of gas per day. About 1,000 technicians, almost exclusively Algerians, live with their families in comparative comfort in bungalows surrounded by gardens, with sports facilities, the most welcome of which are the pools. But the prevailing functional ugliness is overwhelming and the climate, unrelieved by any oued and the resulting freshness of palm groves, ranges between extremes of +65°C and −10°C.

So one might be forgiven continuing somewhat hurriedly to Hassi Bel Guebbour and In Aménas; if sufficiently adventurous attempting the Tassili by car, which means most decidedly a Land Rover. When flying, which is safer, one will see isolated derricks seemingly lost in the sand that tell of determined efforts to conquer the unconquerable.

Return to Saharan Normality

Ouargla provides the picture of an open oasis, pleasantly familiar by now, half a million trees round the town, twice as many again along the wide north-south depression of the underground Oued Mya. The romantic ksar of bluish-white houses, dominated by a tall minaret, is encircled by ramparts pierced by fortified gates. But activity, even of the arcaded market, is gradually moving south to the new town, which includes an industrial zone of doubtful esthetic merit.

The Museum of the Sahara, built in the typical pink local style beloved of film producers, contains the well-tried mixture from prehistoric arrowheads to local arts and crafts, culminating in a fine collection of rugs from many regions. The usual heavy jewelry and silica arrowheads are on sale.

The hotel adopted the same fortress architecture. The Wilaya Administration building is simple but effective, but the pink elliptic town hall failed to combine the old with the new. The Spring Festival here is particularly lively, with dancing and fantasias. Yet Ouargla would not make the first in the Sahara League, were it not for the ruins of Sedrata, not all that wonderful, to be sure, but not bad for a change.

After the destruction of Tahert by the Fatimids, the Ibadites sought refuge in the inaccessible South and in 911 established themselves at Sedrata (Isdraten), where the fanatical energy of the Possessed by God created the desert's most illustrious town. Puritanism, as elsewhere, engendered prosperity which, equally predictable, aroused jealousy in the guise of religious orthodoxy. In 1072, the Hammadid ruler of Bejaïa razed Sedrata to the ground and the survivors joined their co-religionists in the less propitious climate of the M'Zab. The faithful possess long memories, and their descendants still return for a mass picnic every April.

14 km. (9 miles) southwest, across the pipelines, the piste ends in the sand which has swallowed up the remains of Sedrata. From the crest of the highest dune, a labyrinth of low walls vaguely indicates the layout of a city, but of the horseshoe and lobed arches there are no traces, though some decorative slabs have been taken to the Bardo Museum in Algiers. The main interest lies in the constantly changing aspect, as the wind shifts the clean golden sand, covering some broken stones and uncovering others.

To the south rises the pink, red and violet cliff of the Gara Krima, whose irregular crest dominates the stony, yellow, salt-encrusted infinity of the limestone plateau, eroded and furrowed by entwined blackish ravines, the beds of long-dead rivers, which fully justifies the only name it ever possessed, the Chebka (Net or Trickle). Glittering blindingly in the sun, the salt desert assumes the softest pastel hues whenever some humidity is present.

To the north, W202 descends the valley of the oued for 27 km. (17 miles), through a string of pretty oases before petering out in the Chebka into which the subterranean Oued Mya and the even more deeply submerged and longer Oued M'Zab finally give up.

The Envy of Architects

The 190 km. (118 miles) northwest on N49 through the most arid Chebka explains the seclusion ordained by hostile nature on the M'Zab. How this isolation was consummately exploited can best be judged on arrival by plane. A winding green ravine, only 10 km. (6 miles) long, clefts the Chebka, with five pyramids of regular cubes, topped by a minaret-watchtower and encircled by ramparts, clinging to the larger bends.

Only in the 20th century have pioneers like Frank Lloyd Wright and Le Corbusier rediscovered what had been accomplished in the M'Zab almost a thousand years earlier, a spontaneous architecture embedded in and belonging to the soil, wedded to the landscape, but also adapted to the life of the people. Nowhere has this been more strictly adhered to than in the Pentapolis of the M'Zab, where houses and enclosures are built with the stones of the Chebka, held together with a mortar of the same origin, which gives the surface a uniform rough texture and a predominant ocher coloring, though white and soft blue are not uncommon.

The plan of a city as a reflection of its society—in this case withdrawn religious austerity—was unmistakably expressed by the impenetrable walls that completely insulated the houses from the promiscuity of the street. No building could rise higher than 21 feet, lower towards the top in respect for the mosque crowning the pyramids. Building regulations at that time and place may seem strange indeed, but living space is more restricted in the desert than elsewhere. Religion forbade class distinction, the notables lived no differently from the ordinary people, hence the absence of palaces. More surprising in so theocratic a community, there was no structural or ornamental enhancement of the mosques. Economy forbade waste and dictated the piling up of regular cubes. Yet this emphatic functionalism resulted in a harmonious whole, aided by the purity of lines and the simplicity of proportions.

But was the Chebka able to sustain all this intelligent town planning?

None but saints or the persecuted would choose so inhospitable a land to comply with their moral code. As for saints, the earliest manuscript mentioning the M'Zab Valley dates from 824, heyday of the Ibadite Kingdom of Tahert, so the earliest settlers must indeed have come of their own chosing. The persecuted appear only a hundred years after the fall of Tahert, with the foundation of the cities, El Ateuf (The Turning of the Valley) in 1011, followed by Bou Noura (The Luminous), Melika (The Queen), Beni Isguen (The Pious) and, in 1053, Chardaïa (Cave of Daïa, a pregnant girl, repudiated by her parents and befriended by a saintly man), completing the Pentapolis.

Life depended on water, supplied by the subterranean oued which flows, however, exceptionally deep. Wells had to be dug to between 7.6 and 52 m. (25 and 170 feet) down, though even 61 m. (200 feet) was not uncommon. At such depths, the usual balance pole proved insufficient and had to be substituted by a long sliding cord on a pulley, worked by a camel or donkey, which lowers and raises a waterskin to be emptied into the irrigation ditches, which only in the M'Zab were coated with lime to prevent any soil infiltration. Not so long ago, some 3,000 wells assured the necessary irrigation, supplemented by a dam across the usually dry riverbed, so that the rare torrential rains would not be lost.

But despite the meticulous care with which the oasis had been created and maintained, the underground river eventually was unable to supply the needs of a growing population. The wells began to dry up and the Mzabites took to commerce or emigrated, to earn enough money to enable their families to live in the M'Zab to which they themselves would return one day. Now, an ingenious network of pipes connected to watertowers supports the lives of over 50,000 Mzabites in their luxuriant if diminutive gardens, round the summerhouses in which every family spends the better part of the year. Meters have been installed, but it is unthinkable that anyone should exceed the allocation fixed by the Halqah (Council of Twelve Clerics).

Salient common features of the Five Towns are the underground mosques round arcaded sunken courtyards, flanked by high tapering minarets, daubed with ocher mortar and crowned by strange fingers pointing skyward. On houses these whitewashed fingers alternate with decorative earthballs, but the most vigorous ornamentation is reserved for the tens of thousands of funerary monuments, vacillating between pyramids and cones, in their lack of symmetry not unlike modern sculptures. The most interesting of these vast cemeteries are at Ghardaïa and Melika, on the slopes of the valley.

The market of Ghardaïa is surrounded by arcades; the Museum of the M'Zab reproduces the interior of a Mzabite house; from the hole in the rock Daïa was rescued by her saintly man; beyond the dam is the underground 12th-century Djemaâ Chaaba, where evening prayers are held on the roof.

Beni Isguen, the M'Zab's holy town, is at prayers from midday to 3:30 P.M., when it closes its gates to strangers, who are permanently excluded from some quarters and forbidden to spend the night anywhere. The ten thousand inhabitants are not allowed to marry outside, but the betrothed have recently been allowed to see one another before the wedding. Other concessions to modernity are that the few wells still operative in the valley's finest palm grove have been equipped with motor pumps; natural gas from the Hassi R'Mel field has been installed in many houses; a mini industrial zone has been established. But one tenth of the crop is still distributed to the poor.

Melika, where red predominates, offers the best view over Ghardaïa and its cemetery. Near El Ateuf, the Oued M'Zab rises sufficiently to form a stagnant pool with small fish. The irregular plan and asymmetrical arcades of the Djemaâ Sidi Brahim are supposed to have inspired Le Corbusier's Chapel at Ronchamp.

Of the three Chaamba oases, often opposed to the Ibadites, Daya Ben Daoua, 13 km. (8 miles) northwest, is the closest, but Metliki (The Cradle of the Chaambas) off the El Goléa road, the most interesting. From the white mausoleum on a rocky eminence there is a fine view over the picture postcard ksar on a promontory, the village below and the extensive palm grove along the oued, where water occasionally flows above ground.

And then there is nothing but the stony, monotonous Hammada, where the few hardy bushes and tufts of wiry grass provide insufficient pasture even for dromedaries, though there are cafes at Hassi Touiel and Hassi Fahel as well as a gas pump at the latter on the well-maintained 274 km. (170 miles) south to El Goléa.

Lakes in the Desert

El Goléa is as different from the M'Zab as two oases could possibly be. Where the narrow vaulted lanes of blank walls in the latter are decidedly claustrophobic, the wide shady boulevards and squares confer a feeling of peaceful tranquility in the former. Hard to believe, not only in the Saharan but the entire North African context, there is no labyrinth of tortuous passages at all, at least not one in use, as those in the ocher-colored ruined ksar on the hill dominating the groves have long been abandoned for the spaciousness of the white town below. Only the name, signifying Citadel, persisted, though the 14,000 inhabitants enjoy an unwonted comfort surrounded by 200,000 palms interspersed with eucalyptuses, pines and tamarisks, at the boundary of the inhospitable Hammada and the impenetrable Grand Western Erg.

Swans favor a small brackish lake, while wild ducks prefer the two-mile-long sheet of water off the In Salah road, so salty, however, that bathing is problematic. Another Saharan curiosity: at Bel Bachir, 3 miles north, a white church is topped by two clocktowers, but decidedly African vaults in the interior.

Charles de Foucauld, the Hermit of the Hoggar, was buried in the small cemetery in 1929, in a cement grave of which, no doubt, he would have strongly disapproved. Church and cemetery, deprived of the Christian community flourishing under French rule, are slowly but inexorably submerged by sand.

The Lost Source

This common Sahara menace is the only feature shared with the next facet of desert variations, In (Aïn) Salah, or the Brackish Source, seems as misnamed as El Oued, the River. Unsuspected desert humor?

412 km. (256 miles) across the Plateau of the Tademaït is, however, no laughing matter, even on asphalted and swept N1. Absolute desert, flat as a pancake, devoid of even that trace of vegetation that sustained the frugal dromedary and goat in the northern Hammada. An eternal wind whirls the thin layer of yellow sand above the steel-grey flint encrusted with pebbles, while occasional gusts raise terrifying eddies. The encircling dunes tower above the minaret of the Djemaâ Ouled Bahamou, built like the entire village, because it is no more than a village of red clay. The sand encroaches on house after house, and even the tamarisks of the alley leading to the hidden palm grove are half submerged. If any practical demonstration of the need for a *litham,* the double veil which protects the face, was required, this is it.

So why come to In Salah? The answer is don't, though quite a number of Trans-Saharan trucks and station wagons make the crossing to Tamanrasset in the Hoggar, which means 705 km. (438 miles) more on still asphalted and swept N1 over the Plain of Tidikelt. But it is no improvement; the same utter desolation, with the added agony of powdery sand dunes affording the wind larger opportunities to play with; even the limitless horizon, which is grandiose indeed, loses a lot of its magic after endless hot hours, if it is not blotted out anyway by a sandstorm.

Bad enough as these storms are along N1, they are even more terrifying on the 290 km. (180 miles) of N52, a well-maintained piste to Reggane, southernmost of the Touat oases. Yet the awful emptiness of the Tidikelt on this westward crossing is pleasantly interrupted by a scattering of tiny oases round Aoulef which, since the revival of the ancient *foggara* system by motor pumps, produce early spring tomatoes and cantaloupe melons, much appreciated in Europe. Besides, Aoulef has remained what it has been for thousands of years, a major Touareg market.

The Desert of Thirst

Having ventured so far south, we shall dutifully go the whole hog, as if we had taken N52 which, however, we most emphatically do not recommend, except to the explorer/adventurer type for whom it will be all they could ask for. The more conventional tourist should stick to the much easier and also much more rewarding link between N1 and N6 offered by N51 further north, without detracting from the glowing satisfaction of doing a thorough circuit of the Sahara. Enough is enough is enough.

Reggane—if possible even redder than In Salah, because as in all the towns of the Touat dark-red pisé is the exclusive building material—is a border town, though the frontier with the Mali is 705 km. (438 miles) south. But what miles!! N6, degenerated into a piste, traverses the Tanezrouft, the notorious Desert of Thirst, so completely devoid of life that it served as experimental ground for the first French atom bomb explosions, to nobody's discomfort. No wonder that the crossing requires a permit, issued by the authorities at Adrar after careful inspection of car and equipment.

The grim mercilessness of the south is beyond doubt; to the west, the Erg Chech, the largest of all Saharan sand deserts, extends for ever and ever; Tademaït and Tidikelt are no improvement in the east; only northward, amidst the rather unattractive off-white sterility covering the violet-red clay of the Touat, is a string of oases able to sustain life, though not as well as once they did. Malfante, an Italian trader, reported in 1447: "this region is a commercial halting place in Moorish country, composed of between 150 and 200 villages, 18 enclosed within walls." For centuries caravans passed from Gao and Timbuctoo to Sijilmana and Tlemcen through the Touat.

But the valley was then watered by a succession of great rivers, of which the northernmost, the Oued Guir, still carries the waters of the Ksour Mountains south to the Oued Saoura, but the Oued Messaoud has gone underground when not completely dried up. The ingenious *foggaras,* a system of underground canals extending in its heyday no less than 2,750 km. (1,700 miles) (the only comparable irrigation on that scale is by *quanats* in far away Iran), pinpointed by wells between six and thirty feet deep, maintained cultivation until replaced by more efficient motor pumps. But the foggara wells are still a prominent feature throughout the region, even in the very center of the towns.

The Palm Grove Trail

The return north along N6 pleasantly differs from the outward drive on N1, as the distances between the oases are much shorter and there is no comparable immensity of desolation near the road, though plenty further away.

Each oasis sustains at least one kasbah, a rectangular fortress surmounted by crenelated square towers, the single gate approached by a bridge over the surrounding moat. The yard-wide winding lanes are often covered with palm fronds. The clay, hardened in the sun but still unable to support more than one floor, determined not only the basic red color, faded by the rare yet violent rains into many lighter hues, but also the thickness of the walls. This style is similar to the kasbahs of southern Morocco, but usually called Sudanese architecture, as it spread south beyond the Sahara. Verses from the Koran are carved round the doors, accompanied by a hand, an eye, symbolic triangles and lozenges painted in whitewash.

Only broken walls rising from a rocky base remain of the 9th- and 10th-century fortified granaries, different from the usual ksour, because they served first and foremost as stores for the food reserve, gold and ivory, built on high ground, while the kasbah, to which the entire oasis population withdrew in time of danger, extended below. In better shape are the zaouïas, where religious brotherhoods still pray and preach.

The trail is sufficiently short, a mere 135 km. (84 miles), for the charm of the kasbahs to last; Bou Ali, Tazoult, Tiorinine, El Ahmar, Djedid, El Mansour hide their crumbling walls amidst luxuriant vegetation, palms, of course, but also barley and vegetables. Tamentit is grander, the wide moat dug to the rock bed surrounds 45ft.-high walls, the market is larger, there are some ruined religious buildings, because this was the Touat's most powerful city, with a considerable Jewish colony, till a destructive civil war in 1492. The shrinking of the Oued Messaoud's flow, coupled with a similar decline in the caravan trade, prevented a recovery, though Tamentit remained an independent republic, administered by a sheikh and the djemaa (local assembly), till the beginning of this century. Craftsmen continue to melt silver for the heavy jewelry, though the gold of better days is out, while the potters are turning out lovely black earthenware according to age-old methods.

Pre-eminence passed to Adrar, then called Timmi, which is entered by a monumental gateway reminiscent of the Sudan. Rectangular avenues end in the two main squares, one so large that it accommodates the fantasias of the Spring Festival at the end of March, while trade and craft fairs are held in the surrounding arcades, interrupted by triumphal arches with ogives and pylons; the other features two rather incongruous monuments, a gigantic concrete fountain facing yet another red triumphal arch topped by a white pear-shaped dome; nobody has the vaguest notion which triumphs are so emphatically commemorated; the finishing touch is a pink minaret rising above a green cupola. Not a place for the color-blind.

The excursion westwards to Bouda is for the truly insatiable, as it presents, however attractively, more of the same. The red hamlets are so deep in sand that it is hard to distinguish between the occupied and abandoned, yet the groves produce henna, wheat and tobacco besides dates.

The Red Gourara

The red climax, and one that should not be missed, is, however, yet to come. The 217 km. (135 miles) to Timimoun, first northwest on N6, then east on N51, are dreary, but the Sebkha of these parts is far less deadening than the Chebka round the M'Zab (semantics at their etymological best). Charouine is the first of the Gourara oases, all that is to come in a minor key, so description had better wait for a major.

Which is not far away. Timimoun would rank as a "maximum key," if there were such a thing. Its attractions are almost impossible to describe: a wine-red *gara* (table-topped cliff) rising from deep-green palm groves, encircled by the pale pinkish-white Sebkha, the salt-encrusted bottom of a vast dried-up lake; with the orange sand dunes of the Grand Western Erg in the distance. A combination which must be experienced to be appreciated.

In this magic setting architectural details—again the so-called Sudanese style—matter little. A main street as wide as Algiers' Boulevard Mohammed Khemisti, though shorter; a fountain of water flowing freely out of the twin humps of a stone camel; the hotel, happily imitating the Ksar model, also followed by the administrative buildings; the Ksar itself, golden crenellated ramparts in ruins as are all the medieval fortifications throughout the Gourara, now that the *rezzous* (raids) by savage Chaamba or Touareg tribes are a thing of the past.

Yet these ruins constitute an essentially romantic element on the Piste Touristique recommended, and rightly, by the local tourist office, 90 km. (56 miles) through scanty groves (hardly holding their own against salt and sand) as well as luxuriant oases, where barley, wheat and vegetables grow, thanks to a combination of foggaras and open irrigation ditches. Allamellal, Akekour, Irher (Ighzer), on top of a cliff above a deep cave offering welcome freshness; Oumrad and Feraoun, whose fine gardens are watered from big tanks; Tindjillet, the highest and mightiest ksar, on a cliff which only a few millennia ago was lapped by the waves of the lake; Semouta, Taghouzi and Tinerkouk, at the boundary of the Grand Erg. Lovely sand-roses are on sale where they are found, also petrified pieces of wood from a primeval forest that once covered the plateau to the south. The outstanding local handicraft, the *fatis,* a handwoven material with Berber and Malian geometric designs in fast colors, can be purchased in the S.N.A.T. shop next to the tourist office.

140 km. (87 miles) northeast on N51 M'Guiden is an oasis in the making, and it is interesting to watch that arduous process while returning to El Goléa on N1. But the Saoura is waiting to be explored, so back to the road fork and northwest by N6 which, unfortunately, mostly keeps its distance from the Oued Saoura and thus from the groves. At Kerzaz the balance-poles dip into the wells only a few feet from the first dunes of the Grand Western Erg. El Ouata is the next oasis and then, at last, the branch to Beni Abbès, 351 km. (218 miles) northwest of Timimoun, 386 (240) from Adrar.

White, Green and Orange

Not the flag of the Saoura, but the colors of Beni Abbès, and a welcome rest after all that intense red. The table-topped cliff, the Ghar Arba, is off-white chalk instead of clay, with the whitewashed crenellated ksar on the crest, dazzling white houses, climbing the eastern slope, and blinding-white administrative buildings half-hidden in gardens in the center. The bulge of the Oued Saoura, lined with laurel bushes, frames the grove stretching to the foot of the cliff, and to the north rises the menacing orange dune of the Grand Western Erg's advance guard. The reverse view from the top of the gara is no less stunning.

In the gardens of the Center of Saharan Research and Studies below the cliff is a small zoo, whose most remarkable inmates are huge lizards with black-and-red or black-and-yellow scales. Another Saharan Museum is strong on useful information concerning the formation of dunes and similar geological titbits, but ominous about vipers which though usually measuring half-a-foot come also in a 6-foot size. To quote, greatly abridged: "the horned viper is the plague of the ksour, to be met everywhere; its bite may be deadly, if not immediately attended to." As for scorpions . . .

On the plateau, at a distance from the settlement, a clay wall surrounds a few cells, where some brothers have been living since 1935 in the fraternity dedicated to meditation and prayer that Charles de Foucauld had tried to establish in 1901.

The 129 km. (80 miles) branching northeast via Igli to Taghit (Tarrhit) are somewhat hard on ordinary cars, but almost two thirds shorter than the admittedly more comfortable roundabout on N6. Back into the red country, though with a browner tinge, between the thornbush and wire-grass of the Hammada and the old-gold dunes of the Grand Western Erg into which few trees straggle forlornly. From a promontory, facing the comfortable hotel, the ksar dominates the winding ribbon of palms confined to the banks of the oued, whose clear water flows the whole year round. Hardly a new scene, but in accordance with the glossiest pamphlets. This is far from being the case of Béchar, 97 km. (60 miles) north on an excellent road.

The Capital in Shocking Pink

Béchar is singularly devoid of any redeeming feature, with a grove of a negligible 80,000 trees. The color is pleasant enough, but ugly five-story blocks of flats break the simple harmony which graces most Saharan towns. There are some white islands in the pink sea: the tall hexagonal minaret features both colors; the clocktower of the former church is pure white; the arcades of the administrative buildings are whitewashed and there is even a sprinkling of green glazed tiles.

Béchar, capital of the Saoura, is the West Sahara's largest town, the last chance to provision and check the car before the desert crossing. It retains its position as the hub of a road network—yesterday's caravan trails—at the intersection of the west/east axis from the Draa Valley and the Tafilalet in Morocco to the Gourara and the Touat, and the north/south artery, ranging even further, from the Mediterranean coast of Algeria and Morocco, doubled by railway lines, to the Mali.

66 km. (41 miles) due west, the Dam of Djorf Torba retains the Oued Guir in one of Algeria's largest, though shallow, artificial lakes, sufficient to irrigate an enormous extent of barley and wheat stretching mile after mile south to Abadla, near the road fork of N50 southeast to Tindouf and N6 southeast to Beni Abbès.

Abadla and Amaguir, from which the first French satellite was launched, are the only relief on the 808 km. (502 miles) of pebble-strewn Hammada to Tindouf, and they are still fairly close to Béchar. It is unlikely that you have heard of the Mouggar, and long may you remain in ignorance. It used to be a colorful gathering of nomads from all countries adjoining the Sahara; the crowd is still growing, every May, but camel caravans are out and dusty convoys of lorries are in, bringing besides the occasional genuine craft work vast amounts of plastic rubbish. The fantasias are what they always are all over North Africa, no more no less. But then, according to an official publication: "a fascinating population with bewitching dances in which mysterious gestures combine in harmony with an insistent beat." So if you cannot resist "to be received naturally, to the sound of rifle fire in rhythm with the tom-tom," go there by plane, the airport is opened for the brief season.

Even if the road to Morocco is re-opened, there are less strenuous crossings. And yet Tindouf may make it, in the not too distant future. 145 km. (90 miles) southeast, at Gara Djebilet, three billion tons of iron ore with a concentration of 58 percent are waiting to be exploited.

Rock Carvings Galore

Northeast of Béchar, N6 crosses the Ksour Mountains, for 274 km. (170 miles) parallel to the railway to Aïn Sefra (The Yellow Source), where the Sahara's sea of sand meets the High Plateaux's sea of alfa in a setting differing from either. At 1,006 m. (3,300 feet), in the shadow of the 914 m. (3,000 feet) higher Djebel Mekter, among silver-grey poplars and dark cypresses topping the palms in luxuriant orchards, multi-storied houses are no longer incongruous, nor the huge Moorish barracks from which the French once controlled the Gorge of the Oued El Breidj, one of the gates in the Saharan Atlas.

And along that Atlas, not as high but a longer chain than any of its three Moroccan counterparts, we are going to rejoin Bou Saada, point of departure, exercising on this last leg a wise restraint on the visits to the vast number of rock carvings on show. The first are a mere 10 km. (6 miles) east along N47, in the cliff face near the orchards of Tiout; buffaloes, elephants, ostriches and groups of hunters were carved some 5,000 years ago into well-delineated panels. More, many more, at Hadjra Mahisserat and the entire Tazina Region.

The only chance to stock up, for man and car alike, is after 232 km. (144 miles) of unremarkable but not unpleasant mountain driving at El Bayadh; N47 continues through the same setting for the remaining 126 km. (78 miles) northeast to Aflou. But before reaching that capital of a 13th-century Beni Hilal confederation which subjected the local Berbers, the biggest and best in the rock carving line that Algeria has to offer beckons 35 km. (22 miles) south at El Ghicha (Rhicha), at the head of an idyllic valley of evergreen oaks, junipers and fruit trees hidden in the Djebel Amour. A cross-section of the animals that once populated these mountains and nourished the neolithic hunters is engraved on the rocks behind a disused mill, only a naked praying man is chiselled in bas relief. At Aïn Sfisifs, 6 km. (4 miles) west, are extraordinarily vivid scenes involving aurochs, elephants, lions and vipers.

But there is a limit to the enjoyment of rock carvings and a break, a particularly pleasant one at that, is dictated by the termination of the west/east N47 at Aflou, and N23 taking over, 174 km. (108 miles) north through the alfa of the High Plateaux to Tiaret, and 122 km. (76 miles) southeast to the one remaining oasis, Laghouat.

Garments of God Interchanged

And one not to be missed, familiar though that may sound. Already near the approach, west along W231, are above average appetizers, a picturesque ksar at Tadjemout, followed by another at Aïn Mahdi, out of bounds for non-Moslems, because it is the seat of the zaouïa founded by Sidi Ahmed Tidjani. After his death in 1897, his French wife, a fervent convert to Islam, directed her husband's renowned center of Koranic studies till 1933 from her nearby property at Kourdane, a lovely period piece.

Laghouat (pronounced Larrhouat, The Gardens) is sharply divided by a long rocky eminence, to the west and wide avenues of the modern city, lined by shops which would not disgrace Algiers, converging on a central square; to the east, the typical Saharan quarter of low white-washed houses in narrow alleys, little changed since its foundation by the Beni Hilal in the 11th century.

Near the crest, an imposing construction with ogival stained-glass windows and square lantern towers . . . the Djemaâ El Attik. Equally impressive, with a large central dome supported by half-domes and smaller cupolas, flanked by two minarets . . . the Cathedral of the Bishop of the Sahara. The interior of both is similarly austere, in keeping with the Islamic prohibition of representative art as well as with modern sacred architecture. The ksar facing the mosque is framed by two square marabouts with arcaded porticos; the larger is the tomb of Sidi El Hadj Aissa, 17th-century patron of Laghouat. From the terrace in front, the view extends over the town, grove and dunes to the precipitous wall of distant Djebel Dakhla.

A palm-lined avenue descends from the cathedral past the square white tower of the wilaya, the courts and the Parc de Jerusalem to the post office.

Just behind is the Artisanat de Laghouat, the official arts and crafts shop as distinct from numerous souvenir shops. The main local products, carpets and rugs, are in the Ouled Naïl colors, black and red.

The branch to the gasfield of Hassi R'Mel is within the last third of the 203 km. (126 miles) south on N1 to Ghardaïa. 109 km. (68 miles) north of Laghouat is Djelfa, a little less than halfway to Bou Saada.

A Pinch of Salt

First a reunion with rock carvings, three large panels of elephants and bubal antelopes on an orange cliff, on the Oued Hesbaia, 10 km. (6 miles) east (right) of Sidi Makhouf on N1. But the big stuff is to be found along W162, which branches southeast 39 km. (24 miles) to Messaad, where palms and apricot-trees surround the Saharan-type town of flat-roofed houses. The 10,000 inhabitants make, wear and sell attractive burnouses. Plenty of carvings at Hairat Boubaker, Theniet El M'Zab off W162, and the finest in the prettiest but least accessible site, off the piste to Djelfa, a spring amongst gardens at Aïn Naga. Much easier is the short detour west, (left) off W76 to Bou Saada, to Amoura, an eagle's nest on a spur of Djebel Boukahil, from which the view embraces the first dunes of the Sahara.

More original, but harder on the car, is a visit to the *daïas,* large indentations once filled with water but now sheltering groves of jujubes, pistachios and terebinths. After the endless barren grey limestone hills, this meager vegetation takes on a park-like look. A few miles south of Messaad the piste crosses the Ifri Pass in the last range of the Atlas to the edge of the Sahara. This is the daïa country, at whose rare wells nomads congregate to water their flocks.

Back along N1, the next branch right is a short 8 km. (5 miles) to Zaccar, as characteristic as any of the mountain villages, whose pisé houses miraculously support the heavy beams of the roof covered with pebble-encrusted flint slabs. The carvings on two large rocks depict a bubal antelope brought down by a lion, and a mouflon with enormous horns; others are scattered over the mountainside, towards the ruins of medieval Zaccar perched on the highest escarpment. Carbon 14 tests date the flint tools found throughout the area at 6000 B.C.

N1 negotiates the Caravan Pass at 1,189 m. (3,900 feet) and descends just a little to Djelfa, at 1,067 m. (3,500 feet) Algeria's highest wilaya capital. Hence the long cold winters in this important communication center and market town of low grey houses set out in a checker-board pattern in a depression of the Ouled Naïl Mountains. Djelfa has been a provincial capital only since the administrative reforms of 1974, but for centuries it was the main meeting place of the Ouled Naïl. That Arab tribe claims descent from the Prophet through Moulay Idriss and Sidi Naïl, the latter coming to the mountains that bear his name 350 years ago.

On a small square stand some twenty 6-ft.-high stone slabs with—you would never have guessed—copies of rock engravings. Only a few of the White Fathers remain, the order of monks that carried out highly beneficial cultural activities throughout French North Africa. They have a large comprehensive picture of the major sites in their Museum of History and Folklore. Reproductions on panels of red-brown stone are on sale as a slightly bulky souvenir.

To the west W164 traverses the afforested Djebel Senalba to Charef, a spa in Roman times. Other Roman vestiges are found 5 km. (3 miles) north along N1 at an antique Berber village with citadel, beyond hundreds of dolmens scattered over the hillside. 19 km. (12 miles) further along N1, which parallels the railway line the 291 km. (181 miles) to Algiers, to the west (left), is the shattered mass of the Saltrock, sculpted by erosion into extraordinary shapes. A piste continues into the vast depression, where rain or water rising from subterranean oueds occasionally forms shallow lakes which quickly evaporate, to leave millions of crystals sparkling in the sun, while astonishing white salt flowers have formed in the innumerable gullies of that tortured landscape. The salt desert is more easily accessible by W163, branching left 5 km. (3 miles) further north, to the yellow sand dunes of Zahres.

The 130 km. (81 miles) northeast of Djelfa on N46 lead back to Bou Saada, starting point of this all-comprehensive tour of the Saharan oases.

PRACTICAL INFORMATION FOR THE SAHARA

WHEN TO GO. Not in summer, but remember the Sahara is a very cold region where the sun is very hot. The differences in temperature are considerable; an average of $+36°C$ by day and $-5°C$ by night, but $-10°C$ is not unusual. These climatic conditions require special precautions, like warm woolen clothes, blankets and, when camping, a sleeping bag against the cold. But simultaneously strong sunglasses, sunhats, a *chèche* (head veil against the sandstorms), a chap stick for lips, sun screen and moisture creams for the face, mint or lemon lozenges against sore throat due to the excessive dryness; for the same reason avoid chewing gum.

No real rain might fall for twenty years, but a sudden cloudburst transforms dry oueds into raging torrents, drowning men and beasts.

March and April: Spring Festivals in most oases, folkloric performances, dancing, fantasias.

May: Mouggar at Tindouf, folklore plus a general fair.

December: Date Festivals.

HOW TO GO. By Plane. Frequent flights by C.N.A.A. from Algiers to Béchar, Biskra, El Oued, Ghardaïa, Hassi Messaoud, Ouargla, Timimoun, Touggourt; to Tindouf only during the Mouggar in May. Also flights between Oran and Béchar, Annaba and Ourgla.

By Train. Constantine via Batna–Biskra–El Meghaier to Touggourt. From Oran via Mohammadia–Saida–Mecheria–Aïn Sefra–Beni Ounif to Béchar.

By Coach. There are frequent E.P.T.V.S.E. and E.P.T.V.S.O. coach services to all oases.

By Car. The roads are divided into three categories:

1. Without any risk and open to all cars: N1 as far as In Salah. N3 as far as In Aménas. N16 Touggourt–El Oued–Tébessa and N48 to Tozeur (Tunisia). N6 as far as Adrar. Also N49, N50 and N51.

2. A permit must be obtained from the wilaya or daïra at the point of departure; this may be refused if the car or equipment is found unsatisfactory. The permit will be checked by the traffic police along the roads. The permits imply no responsibility by the state, and travelers drive at their own risk and peril. Assistance in breakdowns or search is charged to the travelers. Cars are allowed to proceed on their own in category A below, in convoys of at least two in category B below, where it is also forbidden to drive by night. It is strictly forbidden to deviate from the pistes or to leave the car in case of breakdown or on losing the way.

A: N52 In Salah–Reggane. N6 Adrar–Reggane. N54 Hassi Bel Gebbour–Bordj Omar Driss.

B: N6 Reggane–Bordj Mokhtar–Gao (Mali).

3. On all other pistes a special authorization stipulating special security measures is required.

HOTELS AND RESTAURANTS

Adrar. *Touat* (M), tel. 25 99 33 or 25 91 92. 120 rooms. Pool. *Djemila* (I). 21 rooms.

Aïn Sefra. *El Mekhter* (M), tel. 31 71. 60 pleasant and simple rooms. Pool and tennis; to the south of the town.

Béchar. *Antar* (M), Ave. du ler Novembre (tel. 23 71 61). 114 rooms. Pool; the best. *Saoura* (M), 24 Rue K. Belahrèche. 29 rooms.
Restaurant. *Rose des Sables* (E), 3 Rue Mohamed Ben Mohamed.

Beni Abbès. *Rym* (E), tel. 23 52 14 or 23 32 14. 60 rooms. At foot of dune with pool and tennis. *Grand Erg* (M). 19 rooms.

Beni Ounif. *Afric* (M). 50 rooms. Pool.

Berriane. *Ballouh* (I). 20 rooms.

Biskra. *Les Zibans* (E), Route M'Cid (tel. 71 30 67). 104 rooms. Pool, tennis. On the banks of the oued. *Gouendouz* (M), Blvd. Abdelkader (tel. 71 57 69). 60 rooms. *Oasis* (M), tel. 71 76 08. 40 rooms.
Restaurants. *Cuifa Gorge* (M) On road going south from Biskra toward mountains; outside M'Chouneche village. The food here is outstanding as the owner flies in products from France. On the same road, you'll find *Kchina,* a gourmet restaurant which serves such specialties as pigeon and squid.

Bur Saada. *Le Caïd* (E), tel. 54 43 96/97. 78 rooms. Pool, in the palm grove. *Transat* (M). 50 rooms. Pool and garden.

Djelfa. *Senalba* (M), tel. 53 46 02. 38 rooms.

El Goléa. *El Boustan* (E), tel. 73 60 50. Pool and tennis; in the palm grove. Fair service, clean, and comfortable. *Vieux Ksar* (M). 30 rooms.

El Oued. *Le Souf* (E), tel. 71 85 23. South of the town with pool and garden. *Or Noir* (M), tel. 72 82 99. 40 rooms. Pool.
Restaurant. *Sept Coupoles* (M). Food and setting well above standard.

Ghardaïa. *El Djenoub* (M), tel. 89 06 30 or 89 39 91. 252 rooms, 26 cabanas. This new, state-run hotel, situated on pleasant gardens, has a restaurant (food indifferent), snack bar, lounge, and pool. *Transat* (M). 37 rooms. Pool.

Hammam Salahine. *Izorane* (M), tel. 89 15 60. 40 rooms. Well-kept hotel with clean rooms and good food. *Hôtel Thermal* (M), tel. 71 47 88. 150 rooms in hotel and bungalows. Pool.

Hassi Messaoud. *Sonatrach* (M). 120 rooms.

In (Aïn) Salah. *Tidikelt* (M), tel. 73 03 93. 120 rooms. *Badjoudas* (I). 15 rooms opposite the market.

Laghouat. *Marhaba* (M), tel. 72 46 67. 49 rooms. Pool and garden.

Ouargla. *Transat* (E), 47 rooms. *El Mehri* (M), tel. 70 20 66. 60 rooms. Near wilaya. Pool. *Marhaba* (I). 16 rooms.

Taghit. *Taghit* (E), tel. 25 64 93, 40 airconditioned rooms, simply furnished and clean; fine restaurant, good service. Pool and tennis.

Timimoun. *Gourara* (M), tel. 23 44 51. 60 rooms. Pool and tennis; on a lovely site to the north of town. Reasonable food and agreeable service.

Tindouf. *El Mouggar* (M). 40 rooms. Pool and tennis.

Touggourt. *Oasis* (E), tel. 72 69 16. 60 rooms. Pool and tennis. South of the palm grove.

TRAVELING IN THE DEEP SOUTH. You will need rather a lot of supplies—a comprehensive repair kit, special Sahara tires, special filters against the sand, a spade, perforated metal sheets, an emergency medical kit including scorpion and snake bite serum, water, gas and oil reserves, food for two days, a compass, a mirror or white sheet for signaling, and two smoke bombs, one black, one red.

Drinking water and gas are obtainable only in the main oases; south of Adrar only at Reggane and Bordj Mokhtar before the border with Mali.

Needless to say, all these regulations are for the protection of the travelers and must be strictly adhered to.

Still want to go? Our advice for the Deep South, unless you are the adventurous type, is to choose one of the tours offered by O.N.A.T., usually a combination of air and coach traveling. There is only one point against it: you might be missing the desert's greatest gift, absolute solitude in a limitless land.

SHOPPING. S.N.A.T. or local handicraft shops in all major oases.

SPORTS. Swimming pools and tennis courts in the better hotels. Riding on horses and camels is available in all oases.

NATIONAL TOURIST OFFICES. Algerian National Tourist Offices (O.N.A.T.)—**Biskra:** Rue Gamri. **Bou Saada:** Rue Emir Abdelkader. **Ghardaïa:** 2 Blvd. Emir Abdelkader. **Timimoun:** Hotel Gourara.

HOGGAR AND TASSILI N'AJJER

To a World Beyond

Hoggar and Tassili N'Ajjer, mountain range and plateau, constitute the southern and southeastern part of the Sahara, but differ so completely from Chebka, Erg, Hammada, Reg or Sebkha, indeed from any landscape on earth, that they deserve a chapter on their own. They are, moreover, so isolated and remote that most visitors will avoid the endless, tiring and, in parts at least, frankly monotonous drive and take the plane from Algiers. The world of the oases should best be sampled separately from so overwhelming a sightseeing experience, which requires freshness of mind and body to an unusual degree, and involves a fair amount of walking.

Making a virtue of necessity, an enterprising French travel agency organizes walking tours in the remotest part of the remote Sahara, the Tassili of the Hoggar, near the border of the Niger, under the slogan *Experience of Solitude*. And this crushing solitude is the connecting link with the other forms the desert assumes, a common subordination of the works of man to the grandeur of nature. Fascinating as the rock carvings of the Hoggar and the rock paintings of the Tassili may be, from almost every point of view, artistic, anthropological, zoological, climatic, the lasting impression that will remain for ever unforgettable is of the extra-terrestrial setting.

Volcanic contortions twisted the basalt ranges of the Hoggar into an unearthly maze of metallic-colored mountains, rising to 2,780 m. (9,120 feet) on the Plateau of Assekrem. This is chaos on the grandest scale, the world's bare bones stripped of all softening embellishment for final despair or redemption. It was inevitable that Charles de Foucauld, one of the rare Europeans capable of understanding the interplay of nature and religion, even if his was not the one now practiced in the desert, should end his life as the Hermit of the Hoggar.

Northeast towards Libya, the sandstone Plateau of Tassili N'Ajjer, topped by craggy peaks and cleft by bottomless canyons, presents even more bizarre forms, but the colors seem less borrowed from the Great Beyond.

Exploring the Hoggar

The package tours organized by O.N.A.T., the Algerian State Travel Agency, promise *The Unusual Hoggar.* Never a truer word, from the landing at Tamanrasset—Tam to the smart set (which is discovering but has so far failed to make its mark on the Hoggar, defeated by sheer size and lack of accommodation). True, most of the 3,000 Touareg inhabitants have abandoned the traditional indigo veil, whose dye impregnated the skin of the mysterious Blue Men, but because of import restrictions and not by choice. Some have even completely renounced the *litham,* at their own risk and peril when facing a sandstorm. Many have exchanged the dromedary for a Land Rover or coaches able to mount dunes and rocks like camels. By the way, the individual traveler should book for one of the conducted tours immediately on arrival, as in season there might be a waiting list, while in winter it may take some days to get a party together. Those insisting—unwisely—on using their own car should at least hire a guide.

The exceptionally large proportion of cars to inhabitants is not entirely due to the tourist industry. The N1 is the great Trans-African highway to West, Central and even South Africa beyond. This brings in geopolitics. About halfway between the Mediterranean and the Gulf of Benin, 1,967 km. (1,222 miles) from Algiers and 2,473 km. (1,536 miles) from Lagos, Algeria's smallest wilaya capital holds a key position in the economic exchanges between the Maghreb and Black Africa. But the subterranean watersheet is insufficient for the ever-increasing permanent population, not to mention the migratory one, competing for insufficient hotel accommodation. Tamanrasset, locally called Tamenghest, has retained its much older capital role as seat of the *Amenokal,* supreme chief of the Kel Rela Touaregs, who still exerts a decisive influence, even if his political power has been limited.

At 1,585 m. (5,200 feet) it's rarely excessively hot even in the height of summer. The red-brown pisé walls of the low houses enlivened by blue and green doors, extend their very Saharan architecture on both banks of a dry oued, which after the rare cloud bursts becomes a raging torrent. The main street, shaded by large tamarisks, is always crowded with shoppers coming from anywhere up to a thousand miles.

The Museum of the Hoggar is dedicated to the proud "Masters of the Desert," as the Touaregs like to be called. As so often in a society of warriors, arms and jewels take pride of place. Nearby is the residence of the Amenokal—though he usually lives in an encampment of camel-skin tents enclosed by a rush fence 27 km. (17 miles) away—the Wilaya and the Municipality, in whose social services the Sisters following Charles de Foucauld are working. They live in his modest house, built in the local style south of the village across the oued, while his Bordj, a solid fortified square of crenellated walls he intended as a refuge for the local population, is near the administrative buildings.

The Hermit of the Hoggar

Count Charles de Foucauld has been mentioned several times, but nowhere is he so intrinsic a part of the local scene as in the Hoggar, which he brought for the first time to the notice of a world completely ignorant of its existence. He is, moreover, the most spiritual member of that group of enlightened Frenchmen who considered the Maghreb not simply as an extension of France and in need of French culture, but possessing great culture and wisdom of its own, able to give as much as to receive. There is no doubt that Foucauld's appreciation of the Arabs and their way of life inspired the greatest of all French colonizers, Marshal Lyautey, in his highly successful attempt to reconcile Moroccan tradition with 20th-century France.

Born in Strasbourg in 1858, Foucauld was educated at the prestigious Cadet School of Saint Cyr and the Calvalry School of Saumur, where he acquired a certain notoriety. Despite his outstanding military capacities displayed in the campaign in the Oran Region in 1881, he was so fascinated by native life that, disguised as a Jew, he explored the forbidden towns of Morocco in 1883 and revealed an unknown country to the world in his *Reconnaissance of Morocco.* Deeply impressed by Moslem devotion, he opted for Christian precepts and after stays in Trappist monasteries and at Nazareth was ordained a priest in 1901.

On his return to North Africa, he tried to establish a Benedictine community at Beni Abbès near the border of Morocco, which, however, he never re-entered. But after the Touaregs of the Hoggar made their submission to France, he explored that other forbidden country. In 1905 he built his first tiny hermitage, replaced five years later by the house still used, at Tamanrasset, then consisting of a dozen huts in the bed of the oued. In the same year, 1910, he constructed another hermitage high up on the Plateau of Assekrem, in a poignantly austere site, conducive to a life of meditation and study as still practiced by some Fathers.

Foucauld himself divided his days in accordance with the Benedictine rule of *ora et labora,* pray and work; he compiled a French-Tamalaq (the Touareg's language) dictionary and a comprehensive collection of Touareg poetry, while trying to improve the lot of the local population, even after the outbreak of the First World War. In 1916 the Meharists—Touareg auxiliaries mounted on dromedaries—were fighting in southern Morocco, when Senussis from Libya occupied Tamanrasset. At the call of an inhabitant known to him, Foucauld went outside the Bordj, where he had gathered the villagers and had readied some arms. Forced to his knees, bound hand and foot, he was shot in the head on the night of December 1st, 1916.

Mother of the Touaregs

Except for the village of Hadriane, below a huge cliff 5 km. (3 miles) east, where smiths are equally adept in making knives, tools and silver jewelry—triangular pectorals, bracelets and rings—the only excursion not involving walking on a largish scale and thus possible without a guide, is to Abalessa, 101 km. (63 miles) west, by N1 to Tit and then piste.

Several miles of foggaras irrigate at a depth of 12 to 15 m. (40 to 50 feet) the oasis, which dominates a ruined fortress. Henri Lhote, the great authority on the region, maintains that this was the furthest Roman outpost in Africa. In 19 B.C., Cornelius Balbus led an expedition from Lybia via Vescera (Biskra) and Alasi (Illizi) to Balba, which became Abalessa or also Kasbah of Tin Hinan. Not only were Roman coins, lamps and vases dating from the 2nd to the 4th century found in the fort, but excavations undertaken in 1925 brought to light a female skeleton—now in the Bardo Museum of Algiers—ascribed to Tin Hinan, Queen of the Kel Rela Touaregs, whose legend inspired Pierre Benoît's *Antinéa*.

According to this legend, a Berber princess arrived from the distant Tafilalet in Morocco with a faithful slavegirl as sole companion—only trouble of exceptional severity could justify so desperate a journey through the desert—and thanks to her incomparable courage she was chosen as leader by the local tribes. As good an explanation as any for the long line of Touareg queens.

A Dead World

The visit to the Assekrem Plateau is feasible in a sturdy car without a guide, but only just and not advised. It can easily be made in one day, as the distance is a mere 34 km. (21 miles), but about 3½ hours are needed for the ascent—on foot of course—2 hours on the site and the same time for return to the base.

It is advisable to start at sunrise, along the western piste, so that the morning sun illuminates the sugarloaf peak of Illamane, only topped by the 2,918 m. (9,573 feet) of Algeria's highest mountain, Tahat, in that grandiose volcanic chain of sinister metallic hues. The first carvings can be seen on the black rocks hurled by a gigantic fall into the dry bed of the Oued Otoul, their evil, fantastic shapes vying for attention with the prehistoric designs. The two pistes meet at the refuge, 180 m. (600 feet) below the plateau, whose stark nakedness of extraordinary colors contrasts dramatically with the basalt pyramids and porphyry fingers rising in a diabolic circle below the cataclysmic mountains.

Yet man persists in imparting life to the white sand and the black stones. Some corners of the most ungrateful soil on this planet, to which this dead chaos hardly seems to belong, are cultivated to support a few Touareg families and their goats. They worship in the mosques of the mountains, simple stone enclosures from which all impurities have been removed, with a heap of stone indicating the east and Mecca. And then the Christian contribution to the search for God, the Hermitage of Charles de Foucauld, maintained by dedicated Fathers. In the chapel, light falls—through one narrow slit in the thick walls built to resist the gales—on the stone slab that serves as altar below a severe crucifix; the only room still containing his books.

The return is made along the eastern piste, below the tower of Djebel Akar-Akar. But guided groups spend the night in the dormitory of the refuge, after a visit to the Touareg village of Terhehanet and the engravings of Daouknet, a walk of about two hours. Next day, they follow the Route of the Gueltas, numerous pools of fresh water scooped into the slopes of the mountains. After the verdant gardens of Hirafok it is 27 km. (17 miles) past the rock carvings of Oued Zarzoua, Immaara and Oued Isharrar, where the first paintings can be seen in the rock panels, to the attractive village of Idelès, where the night is spent in tents. It is 64 km. (40 miles) across arid Djebel Taderaz to Tazrouk, the Hoggar's highest village, set amidst poplars, giant fig, apricot and peach trees. The camp faces the splendid rock needle of the Aokasit. After climbing the 1,706 m. (5,600 feet) of the Azrou Pass, the piste follows the oued down to the extensive orchards of Tahifet and the night is spent at the waterfall of Tamengrets, the Impassable, near Tarhaouaout. On the last day on that circuit a dromedary ride, a very long three miles for some, is thrown in for good measure.

That still leaves the richest but most inaccessible carvings and paintings of exceptional quality in the south of the Tefedest, in the valleys round Djebel Akoulmoun, over 2,130 m. (7,000 feet). After 121 km. (75 miles) north on N1 to In Amguel, a piste branches east into the Plain of Arechoun, where the last waves of lava from the volcanic Hoggar give place to the granite rocks of the Tefedest, an alpinist's dream, extending in a narrow sweep 129 km. (80 miles) northeast. The track follows the Oueds Ifraq and Timesdelessine past Hirafok to Idelès, whence an even lesser track turns north into the granite wilderness to the village of Mertoutek, center for the exploration of the prehistoric sites.

Mountaineers will prefer the northern region round Garet El Djenoun, the Mountain of the Genii, which rises steeply 1,280 m. (4,200 feet) above the surrounding plain, reached by round-about pistes, the best being the Amguid.

The last (or first) site for motorists coming from In Salah on N1 is the Gorges of Arak, impressive canyons cut several hundred feet deep by oueds that have now dwindled to a trickle among pink oleanders.

Exploring the Tassili N'Ajjer

Neither the 721 km. (438 miles) of piste from Tamanrasset northeast via Idelès to Djanet, nor the 504 km. (313 miles) from the end of tarred N3 at El Adeb Larache south via Illizi and Zaouatanlaz are suitable for anything but the sturdiest vehicles. Camel caravans proceed leisurely from waterhole to waterhole in about 12 days. But the ordinary traveler will do well to choose the plane, either from Algiers with stops at Ghardaïa and In Aménas, or better still from Tamanrasset. From the air it is easy to see the changes within these geologically different regions, from the basalt of the Hoggar to the sandstone of the Tassili, from a world that has died in chaos to one seemingly giving birth to peaks from a chaotic earth crust.

The Tassili N'Ajjer, the Plateau of Rivers reduced by the change of climate to a Plateau of Chasms, stretching to the Fezzan in Libya, first appears from the air as a bluish wall, torn by fissures and crevasses, dissolving into a forest of rock needles, petrified sand eroded into gigantic canyons, isolated castles, cathedrals or whole towns. For hundreds of square miles of this incredible setting, the world's finest rock paintings teach the most comprehensive lesson of pre- and proto-history.

The Last Turkish Fortress

Djanet, in a narrow valley between the escarpment of the Tassili and the lava hills framing the sand depression of Admer, raises its 40,000 date palms from the finest white sand. At 910 m. (3,000 feet) the Kel Djanet Touaregs, dark-skinned but with sharper Berber features, enjoy a mild climate, the thermometer hardly ever descending below freezing point and rarely registering a maximum of 40°C. Even in the driest years, rivulets of abundant water irrigate the luxuriant orchards linking the oasis's four distinct settlements.

The piste approaches from the south, leaving to the left the geometric cubes of Adjahil and a Turkish fortress on a mountain spur. In one of those ironic twists of history, the Turks subjected the Tassili only at the end of the 19th century, long after their ejection from Algeria, to be driven out by the French when Tripoli was occupied by the Italians in 1911. Leaving Ksar El Mihan to the right, the piste enters Djanet itself, whose flat-roofed houses surround a hill crowned by a former Senoussi zaouïa. North, at the edge of the sand, is the more warlike 16th-century Ksar of Sultan Goman, ruler of Djanet and Chat, on the Tassili's Libyan slope.

In the absence of imported entertainment, the Djaneti are keen on local festivities, religious and private. Music and dancing are common, the most original being the Sebiba, where masked warriors sing, dance and beat the drums while the Djaneti, their long black haïk leaving the face uncovered, wave garishly colored bits of muslin.

But all these attractions are a bonus over and above the unique object of any visit to so remote a place, the sensational rock paintings discovered by the French Lieutenant Brenans in 1933 and systematically explored by Henri Lhote since 1956.

The World's Finest Open-Air Museum

The Tassili N'Ajjer, extending some 12,950 sq. km. (50,000 sq. miles) southeast from Djanet to the Libyan frontier, contains tens of thousands of paintings in ocher schist as well as carvings from the seventh to the first millennium B.C., equally remarkable for their number as for their artistic qualities. So far, a mere 15,000 have been classified, testifying to the existence of a large and ingenious population amidst a rich and diversified flora and fauna where is now abandoned desolation.

Four clearly defined periods have been established:

1. The Period of Roundheaded Men, prior to 4000 B.C., with some carvings, e.g. the elephant at Timenzouzin, dating back to 6000 B.C. Faces are featureless disks on bodies increasing in size with the passing of time from very small to gigantic, e.g. the so-called Martians at Jabbaren, 18 feet tall. The negroid population are shown hunting bubal antelopes, elephants and mouflons with enormous horns, but there are also scenes of magic and worship.

2. The Period of the Cattle herders, lasting till 1500 B.C., when during a time of unusual humidity domesticated cattle first appeared, naturalistically displayed together with their negroid masters, now possessed of eyes, mouth and nose, in pastoral and hunting pictures, first carved and then painted in. It seems that the peaceful existence of these herdsmen came to an end with the arrival of white warriors dressed in the Cretan fashion and mounted on horse-drawn chariots.

3. The Period of Chariots and Horses, both introduced by the Hyksos, the Sea People, who slowly made their way westwards from Egypt, as witnessed by countless carvings and pictures from Libya to Morocco showing two- or four-wheeled chariots in the tradition from pre- to proto-history, when yet another animal was introduced which has remained above all connected with the Sahara.

4. The Period of Camels. Though marked by an artistic decline, frequent inscriptions in an early version of the present Tamalaq letters add an historic interest.

No Gain without Pain

The basic guided circuit requires five days and with all that walking it may be wise to avoid the three summer months, but at 1,585 m. (5,200 feet) the nights are fresh, if not outright cold, on the Plateau. The cars leave at sunrise to stop after miles at the foot of the first akba, the mountain paths climbing the sandstone cliffs separating the three ledges of the giant stairway to the Plateau. It takes the donkeys about one hour to the first ledge, which dominates some impressive gorges, half-an-hour of level ground to the second akba in the Aabaraka Tafelalet, altogether five hours to reach the tent village of Tamrit below a dozen 1,000-year-old cypresses in the bed of the Oued Tamrit. To avoid exhaustion, the Elephant of Timenzouzin can be viewed in the afternoon.

Departure on the second day is again at 5:30 A.M., on foot past the first paintings at Itinen to the prehistoric settlement of Sefar, with the most impressive frescos of the First Period, *God before Worshippers,* covering 90 square feet; horned devils and giant mouflons, but also war scenes with archers from the Third Period, fish with legs, and animals with disproportionately long tails from the Last Period. The encampment is near the streets, squares and monuments eroded from the sandstone rocks. The third day's short walk leads through one of these natural streets to Tin Tazarift, where nature has created cathedrals, mosques and minarets, to which man has added hunting scenes and animals from all four periods.

The fourth day allows a late departure at 8 A.M. for Tin Aboteka, which dominates the Plain of Fezzan in Libya, the antique Kingdom of Garamantes, whose war chariots the Greek historian Herodotus described in the 5th century B.C. More paintings, followed by a 2-hour walk to the huge Cave of Tan Zoumaïtok, painted in the 6th millennium B.C. from top to bottom, men with disk heads and little horned devils. The last night is spent in the tent village below the magnificent cypresses, last of their kind since the deterioration of the soil and the lack of humidity has put an end to their reproduction; the diameter of the survivors is more than 5.8 m. (18 feet). The locals maintain that they can twice recite their prayer before a stone thrown into the abyss of the Tamrit Gorges resounds from the bottom.

Of equal interest is the three-day excursion beginning with a 19-km. (12-mile) drive to the foot of the Akba Aroun to ascend to the Plateau of Jabbaren (The Giants) and, indeed, some of the 5,000 paintings belonging to all the four periods are gigantic, e.g. the *Great Martian God.* 900 feet higher at Aouanrhet is the sanctuary of the *Horned Goddess* or *White Lady,* flanked by an odd nude with her bosom on the back, and a *Negro Mask.*

This is by no means an exhaustive list of the sites, but the remainder, as for instance at the Oued Djorat or at Tadjelamine, are too difficult of access for anyone but mountaineers.

The Depredations of Homo Touristicus

Miraculously preserved due to the exceptional dryness which has prevailed for some 3,000 years, the paintings are at present under attack by a more dangerous enemy than the elements: modern man. In order to invigorate the delicate colors, photographers—and that means practically every visitor to the Tassili—do not hesitate to use all kinds of harmful liquids, or even to trace the outline in colored pencils, before proudly engraving their initials.

This vandalism has assumed such alarming proportions—this is, after all the homeland of the Vandals, even if they never penetrated so far south—that in 1978 the Algerian Ministry for Information and Culture organized with the assistance of U.N.E.S.C.O. a conference of archeologists, climatologists, biologists and geologists from 13 nations to study on the spot the problems of preservation.

The effects of varnishes applied experimentally since 1968 were examined, but the greatest emphasis was laid on the needs of strengthening supervision in the National Park of Tassili, entrusted to a totally insufficient number of guards and guides. In the absence of any roads to the plateau, which is accessible only on foot or by donkey, the number of visitors rarely passes 5,000 per year, despite the airport at Djanet. Though tourism here requires physical stamina for a spiritual adventure, the paintings have to be protected more efficiently from the public. This is potentially one of the major threats of "tourist pollution," as experienced by the cave paintings at Lascaux in France. Besides the foundation of study centers for the appreciation of the natural and artistic wealth that is here, and for its preservation, the experts propose to include the Tassili National Park among the sites listed as a world heritage. And there is no doubt that it is on this highest of international levels that the scientific opening up and protection of the Tassili must be carried out.

PRACTICAL INFORMATION FOR
HOGGAR AND TASSILI N'AJJER

WHEN TO GO. Because of the high altitude, summers are cooler than in the oases of the Sahara, but because of the distances to be walked package tours concentrate on the winter months. Remember that nights on the Tassili Plateau are then very cold. Annual Festival of the Hoggar and Tassili, folkloric performances at Djanet and Tamanrasset in spring. Much the same at the Assihar, December 25 to January 10, at Tamanrasset.

GETTING THERE. By Plane. Twice weekly from Algiers via Ghardaïa to Djanet as well as to Tamanrasset, once weekly between Djanet and Tamanrasset.

GETTING AROUND. By Car. Only N3 El Adeb Larache–Illizi–Djanet is in the B1 category. All the other pistes open to traffic are B2. The advice we give elsewhere (in *Planning Your Trip* and *Practical Information for the Sahara*) naturally holds good. O.N.A.T. offers a choice of several tours, either each region separately or both combined, 8 to 10 days, by air from Algiers, then Land Rover, cost from 2,000 to 2,700DA. The most original tours are organized by Terres d'Aventure, 16 Rue Saint Victor, 75005 Paris, walking in small groups with fairly comfortable camps, under the very appropriate name *Experience of Solitude* in the Tassili of the Hoggar, south of Tamanrasset.

HOTELS

Tamanrasset. *Le Tahat* (M), tel. 73 44 72. 120 airconditioned rooms In season reserved entirely for O.N.A.T. On the outskirts of town. *Ilhamene* (M). 30 rooms. *Tinhinan* (M) in the airconditioned new section, but (I) in the very simple older half.

NATIONAL TOURIST OFFICES. Algerian National Tourist Offices O.N.A.T.—**Djanet:** Place du Marché. **Tamanrasset:** Blvd. Emir Abdelkader.

Tours. The Mero-N'Man Agency, B.P. 150, Tamenrasset (tel. 73 40 32 or telex 63055) does organised tours of the Tassili N'Haggar and the Hoggar Massif. Each tour lasts two or three days.

TUNISIA

278

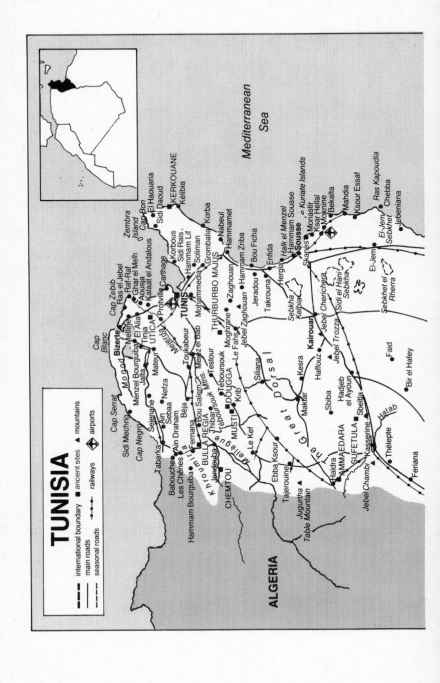

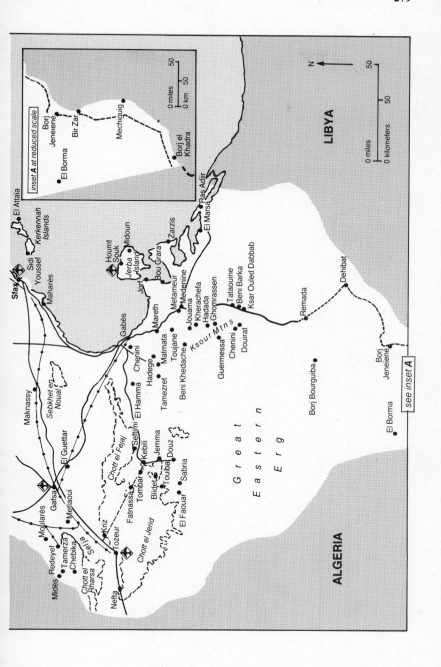

PRELUDE TO TUNISIA

Covering 164,150 square km. (63,362 square miles—slightly larger than Georgia, or England and Wales together) Tunisia's attraction does not lie in any grandiose natural features, but in its superb sandy beaches, fringing almost the entire 1,440 km. (810 miles) of Mediterranean coastline, which have catapulted Tunisia into the forefront of international tourism.

The country's relief is varied, revealing mountains which are densely wooded to the north, barren in the center, often arid and wild to the south. The steppe, which forms the dusty heart of the country, becomes verdant along the shore and, as it descends towards the south, levels off into the Sahara.

The shorter north coast, from the Algerian frontier to Cap Bon, offers two different aspects. From the west to Cap Blanc, to the north of Bizerta, it consists of a few narrow plains wedged between the mountains and the sea. From Bizerta to Cap Bon, the coastline is picturesque interrupted by Lake Bizerta, Ghar-el-Melh bay, the gulf and lake of Tunis, and Cap Bon, a mere 140 km. (87 miles) from Sicily.

The long low curve of the eastern coastline is scalloped by the gulf of Hammamet and then further to the south by several capes sheltering the harbors of Sousse, Monastir and Mahdia. Then follows a vast coastal plain covered with olive trees growing in sandy, dry soil. To the south of Sfax lies the Gulf of Gabès with its strong tides, making a vast indentation in the shore which is low and flat, rimmed with shallow lagoons and sand banks. The Kerlenna islands facing Sfax, and Jerba in the far south have unbroken coastlines and are covered with palm trees. The African sun shining down on this rather shallow sea evaporates it very quickly and the sea breeze carries the water vapor far into the interior. It is this atmo-

spheric humidity which provides enough water for cultivation from Sousse
up to the southern hills.

A Dorsal of Jebels

More than half of Tunisia is less than 500 ft. above sea level, but the
last, occasionally impressively rugged, more often somewhat puny spurs
of the Atlas and Anti-Atlas intersect the country from southwest to northeast near the coast and in the center, the latter higher chain of dome-
shaped peaks named slightly pretentiously the Great Dorsal.

The Great Dorsal stretches diagonally from the highest point, Jebel
Chambi (1,544 m., 5,065 ft.) at the Algerian frontier, to Jebel Bou Zaghouan, the backdrop of Tunis. Seen from the plain, the Chambi looms
nobly, and despite less than 16 inches annual rainfall, its fragrant shrubs
provide pasture not only for the frugal goats, but also for cattle and sheep,
beside a multitude of game.

The Dorsal's gentle hills and rocky slopes which encircle its valleys start
deep inland at Jebel Chambi and reach down to the sea. Some summits
are worthy of interest, such as Zaghouan, a reservoir dating from ancient
Carthage and the starting point of a Roman aqueduct and Jebel Bou Kornine, the two-horned mountain overlooking Tunis, venerated by the Carthaginians because of its resemblance to the crescent moon.

Although the jebels are charming—rose-colored in the morning, ocher
at noon and mauve in the evening—Tunisia is not a mountaineering country. The Great Dorsal is an unfortunate geographical feature of Tunisia
because it prevents the rain clouds coming down from the north from
reaching the southern part of the country, thus depriving it of the water
needed for cultivation. The only waterways worthy of mention are to be
found to the north of the Dorsal—the Mejerda, and its tributary the Oued
Mellegue.

The Mejerda, the longest river in Tunisia, runs for 418 km. (260 miles).
Like the Oued Mellegue, it originates in Algeria but soon crosses the frontier and flows through the most fertile regions of Tunisia. Although never
drying up completely, it changes like many irregular oueds with incredible
rapidity from a trickle of water to a roaring torrent. The Mejerda empties
into the sea near the neck of Ghar el Melh. Towards the end of its course,
it digs its bed through the alluvial deposits that it has accumulated since
antiquity, filling with rich silt the gulfs through which the Carthaginian
ships once passed.

The Oases

The oases closely resemble those of Morocco and Algeria in a minor
key. Rustling palm branches, bubbling water, cool shade, exquisite dates
in the middle of a desolate and sandy desert or on the edge of a salt basin
burning to the eye. You can reach them without playing the role of explorer since the main roads are excellent. The most remarkable oases are situated to the northwest of Chott el Jerid, Tozeur and Nefta, and in the southeast Blidet, Sabria and Douz, hemmed in by sand dunes.

In the Deep South, in the region of Foum Tataouine, the Berbers, fleeing
the invasions, took refuge in villages perched on harsh mountain peaks
and hollowed out their dwellings in the rocks of the rugged Ksour Mountains. They still to this day keep to their ancestral traditions. Beyond these

last outposts of humanity is the Great Eastern Erg, the endless sands of the Sahara.

The sea, the Dorsal and the Sahara divide the country into different climatic regions, and what nature divides should be taken into account when planning a holiday.

Sahel, Steppes and Tell

Touristically most important is the Sahel, the coastal plain that extends from the Gulf of Hammamet to that of Gabès. The two main towns, Sousse and Sfax, are busy ports, surrounded by vast olive groves, orchards and cornfields moistened by the sea breeze. Gabès is a coastal oasis, whose extensive gardens are cultivated in the shade of palm trees. The larger palm groves of the island of Jerba provided an idyllic setting for intensive touristic overdevelopment.

The steppes south of the Dorsal are least visited. Because of the low rainfall there is little cultivation, except in the Kairouan region. Elsewhere it is grazing on sparse pastures, mainly along the oueds that hollowed their beds in the arid soil. The main towns are Sbeïtla in the upper steppe (above 305 m., 1,000 feet) in the north, Kairouan in the central lower steppe, and Gafsa, the northernmost oasis.

The Tell, north of the Dorsal, is good farming and cattle grazing country, gently sloping from the High Tell's average altitude of 700 m. (2,300 feet) to the rich black soil of the Mejerda basin, which produces Tunisia's finest wheat crops. The refreshingly green Northern Tell consists of the Khroumiria and the Mogod mountains, covered with dense forests of cork oaks, which gradually give way to olive groves on the north coast between Tabarka on the Algerian border and Bizerte. The Lower Tell centers on Tunis, the country's most populous and prosperous region, in which olive groves, orchards and vineyards stretch from Bizerte to Cap Bon.

Climate, Flora and Fauna

Tunisia is sufficiently small and the main roads sufficiently good to pass easily from the coast to the oases, from the desert to forest, from the shade of date trees to that of pines and cork oaks.

The temperature is mild, though it can be quite cold in the winter. Rainfalls, though not rare, are brief, sunshine almost guaranteed. Only the occasional high winds throw a shadow on this idyllic scene, but many of the holiday sites are sheltered by trees or mountains. The scorching wind from the south, which is sometimes almost unendurable in Tunis during the summer, is cooled by the time it reaches Hammamet or Monastir, while conch-shaped Sidi Bou Saïd turns its back to the prevailing winds. Moreover, the sea makes a summer visit enjoyable, particularly on the island of Jerba, even though it is located in the far south.

Tunisia is certain of enjoying sun at all seasons, but the rainfall is irregular and badly distributed: an average of 60 inches on the Khroumiria forests, 22 inches on the Kef Plateaux, 12 inches on the olive trees of Sfax, 8 inches on the date trees of Gafsa and less than 4 inches on the oases in the south. These figures are only averages; they vary considerably from one year to the next. Seventeen reservoirs greatly contribute to stabilizing irrigation, but in the south scarce rains swell the oueds which disappear into the salt basins.

Four characteristic types of vegetation can be distinguished—cork oaks in the north, Aleppo pines near the coast, esparto grass and jujube trees on the steppe, date palms in the oases. But the land is increasingly cultivated. The vineyards and orchards of Cape Bon, the cereal fields of the Mejerda plain, the olive groves of Sousse and Sfax were considerably expanded by the French landowners and their efforts have been continued by the Tunisians. Some 55 million olive trees may produce up to 180,000 tons of oil in a particularly good year.

Wherever man has found water, the land has become lush and productive. The aloes in the shade of the giant eucalyptus trees, spreading out their silhouettes like modern sculptures crowned by the thrust of a slender taper, are sometimes several meters high. The prickly pear plants protect their fruit with the spikes of their cruel thorns, the bougainvilleas cover the walls with blobs of purple, the hibiscus display their red petals in the shade of the thick foliage, the orange and pomegranate trees bow under the weight of their fruit. In the south, the orchards lie under the palm trees of the oases. Harvesting occurs several months before it does in Europe. The dates begin to ripen in September but the deglet dates, reserved for export, are not picked until November and December.

Considerable attention has been given to increasing the area of the existing oases as well as to creating a belt of new ones from the Algerian to the Libyan border. Reserves of underground water have been trapped and this slightly salty water is adequate for palm trees. Young trees are encircled by tubular braids of palm branches which protect them from the sun and the animals, although another menace faces them: sand. Long palisades are used in an attempt to protect them from the sand dunes. The expansion of cultivated land necessitates a continuous battle against drought, sand, sun and wind.

Though goats have been restricted because they destroy vegetation and thus create deserts, they are as ubiquitous as of yore, ruminating in reafforested areas. There are some bovines in northern Tunisia. Bushy-tailed sheep graze on the wild hilltops and descend after the harvest to feed on the stubble left in the fertile hollows. In central Tunisia, sheep and dromedaries graze on the sparse grass which appears in patches and they then move on depending upon the caprices of the rain. Half of the cattle sometimes die because of drought. The dromedaries hold out rather well against the competition of trucks. They eat what the sheep do not want and also have an additional advantage—their manure fertilizes the cultivated land and so they are in demand after the harvesting.

Game is abundant. Wild boar thrive in the jebels. Although they are Moslems, the Tunisians do not believe they will be damned if they participate in hunting them. Partridges and hares are also available. Gazelles abound in the south. Hunting is strictly regulated, but everywhere the traveler is offered skins and even sad stuffed victims.

Because of the climate, bird life is not rich in the south. The most conspicuous are the buzzards which revolve tirelessly in the still sky, their metallic eyes taking in the mountain crevices and the bleak expanses of the steppe, searching for prey or carrion overcome by heat and thirst. Others, perched on the crags or telegraph poles, stand guard silently and stare at the passerby. In the north, the pink flamingos of Tunis lake flee with a noisy batting of their wings when cars or the suburban train pass over the causeway. Others lead a more tranquil existence along the half-deserted river banks of the Gulf of Gabès.

The storks build their nests at the top of the minarets and on the pieces of remaining walls of the Roman ruins. Nobody disturbs them—it is regarded as a sign of good luck to have one's roof chosen by a family of storks.

The somewhat shallow sea skirting the Tunisian shore is full of fish. The lobster and fish have not yet understood the danger they risk from the deep-sea fishermen. In the south, nature gives a helping hand to the fisherman: the shore of the Gulf of Gabès is not very deep. There are long palisades of palms in the sea. The fish rise to the surface with the flow of the tide and when the sea ebbs the giltheads, the red mullets and their like are stranded at the foot of the palisade. The octopuses, dried and blackened by the sun, their heads encircled with tentacles, are sold in the markets and are used by the poor as the main trimming of their couscous. Sponge-fishing is practised by some divers from Jerba and the Kerkenna Islands.

Off Cap Bon, fishing is a more violent sport. In spring, the schools of tuna are routed towards a death chamber by means of a masterly disposition of nets. Then the nets are drawn on board small boats, the long silver tapers, heaped in the puckered meshes of the net, flounder and try to slip out and back into the sea, the men jump into the net and bludgeon them to the accompaniment of cries. The sea becomes red and frenzy takes possession of fishermen and spectators alike.

Fading Variety

The eight million inhabitants are, as in the other two countries, very unevenly distributed between the thickly populated north and east coasts, and the empty south. In the southern oases there are blacks who are the descendants of the Sudanese slaves, but only the Berbers of Jerba and the deep south still speak their own language.

In the upper class, clan consciousness is based upon regional origin, and among the common people on tribal origin. For example, an ambitious young man from Sousse who has "gone up" to Tunis and become successful will send for his family and will find work for them. Berbers are "in control" of certain types of commerce—they are newspaper dealers, candy merchants, etc., in a closely knit world where nepotism is the order of the day. Family, village and regional connections also played a role among Tunisian workers in France and in the Tunisian villages they counted a great deal on "the uncle who works for Renault" to find a job there for the boys, when emigration was possible.

The current Five Year Plan concentrates like all its predecessors on job creation, but though the annual population increase has been reduced to a *mere* 2.4% it is economically impossible to provide employment for ever more youths entering the labor market, while a constantly increasing number of women are clamoring for work, due to emancipation. Women are even employed as traffic police, no mean achievement in downtown Tunis. A family planning campaign has been part of the National Development since 1964. Abortions are legal for mothers of more than five, contraceptives are distributed freely and prominently advocated in newspapers. Mobile clinics bring modern medicine with encouraging results to the outback. Infant mortality has been reduced to below 1%, North Africa's lowest.

Pragmatism over Dogma

Tunisia of today is a phenomenon of Bourguiba. "Father of the Nation," "Supreme Combatant," the President skillfully adapted Moslem traditions to modern life. Women's Day, August 13, commemorates the promulgation of a family code in 1956, barely six months after independence, granting women almost equal rights with men, at least in law. Unique in Arab countries, polygamy was forbidden, but this is still a hotly disputed point, especially among the increasingly strong fundamentalist student movement. With the succession of a younger president in 1987, Zine el-Abidine Ben Ali, the presidential regime has remained centralized though apparently more flexible. The PSD (Destourian Socialist Party), now renamed Constitutional and Democratic Rally (RCD), has kept its complete control of the administration and professional organizations.

The President appoints the government, which is responsible to him as well as the National Assembly, elected by universal suffrage for five years. The twenty administrative regions, called governorats, are each subdivided into several delegations.

Among developing countries Tunisia was the first to turn successfully away from full-blooded socialism towards economic liberalism and encouragement of the private sector. Private enterprise enjoys greater freedom than at any time since independence; state marketing monopolies have been disbanded; farms and shops returned to their owners; private investors, both Tunisian and foreign, are encouraged to take a stake in light industry and the tourist business. Though the government continues to control the major industries, Western and Arab consortium investment banks now compete with the state-dominated local commercial banks. The liberal approach is paying off, the retreat from state socialism and the country's stability are attracting much needed foreign capital and the growth rate is second to none in Africa.

About half the population still work in agriculture and fishing which, however, contribute less than 18% of the gross domestic product. Among the main crops are cereals, particularly the soft grain wheat for making bread and another wheat used to make semolina which is the basic staple of the Tunisian diet. The vineyards provide wines which are rich in alcohol (12 to 13.5%). The Tunisians drink very little of it, but the tourists prove helpful in diminishing the difficulties of exporting the surplus. Tunisia is the largest exporter of olive oil outside the E.E.C.; receipts amount to almost 8% of foreign exchange earnings. Market gardening flourishes, while orchards provide all kinds of fruit, with citrus fruits playing a dominant part. In the south, dates constitute an additional food, but the choice deglet are for export only.

Industrial farming consists of cork oaks, sugar beets and esparto grass that is gathered on the steppe and from which cellulose is extracted.

Complemented by the 5.25% transit fee from the Algeria–Italy gas pipeline, the largest export earner remains, despite falling prices, the other oil mainly produced on the off-shore field in the Gulf of Gabès. The refineries at Bizerta and Gabès fully meet domestic demand, leaving more than half of the crude oil for export. A chemical plant at Sfax, a paper factory, three cement factories, a textile mill in the Sahel, a sugar refinery at Beja and a steel works near Bizerta, all produce for the home market, but the canning factories around Tunis concentrate on export. Light industry provides the best chance of lessening unemployment, as for example, the car assembly plant at Monastir which has brought about the creation of numerous subcontracting workshops. The I.C.M. (Industries Chimiques Maghrèbines) complex at Gabès annually transforms about two million tons of phosphates into fertilizers, badly polluting the once lovely bay in the process.

The Tunisian subsoil contains important deposits of phosphate rock, but with an average of only 66% of tri-phosphate of lime against Morocco's 72%. The principal mining areas are in the region of Gafsa with a production of about five million tons a year. Other minerals include: 800,000 tons of iron deposits; 6,000 tons of zinc; 30,000 tons of lead; 6,000 tons of mercury; rock salt and fluoride deposits.

Education

Of the 1,200,000 students, girls number 40% in primary schools, 35% in secondary and over 25% at universities, the highest percentage in any Islamic country. Little schoolchildren in blue smocks sometimes travel ten miles to attend classes and are happy to hitch a ride; they are lively, intelligent children, speaking in a colorful French which they are proud of using. France and Belgium provide a great deal of cultural assistance, with young technicians working during a period corresponding to their military service obligations.

Islamic fundamentalists and communists have caused sporadic disturbances at the universities, largely because there are insufficient openings for graduates and unemployment presents an ever-increasing problem. And though civil servants are often very young, promotion possibilities are blocked. Under these conditions, there is a temptation to call into question the society's structure.

Looking Forwards

Tunisia represents a subtle synthesis of Islamic and occidental cultures. Far from repudiating the French contribution, it has integrated it, and thus gives a strong impression of rare malleability. It acquired independence without unnecessary drama and has avoided monolithic doctrines and ideological structures. Though Islam is the state religion, the constitution provides that the laws are made by parliament, and not by theologians.

Served unkindly by its climate for agriculture though not tourism, threatened with a tidal wave of population increase, Tunisia has largely succeeded in remaining itself. It is not fortuitous that the future seems less dark here than in most of the developing countries, despite foreign debts amounting to more than 40% of the G.N.P., inflation of about 15%, while the safety valve of emigration has been shut off with a resulting decline in remittances from Tunisians working abroad, strikes and some labor unrest. These problems have been greatly aggravated by the steep drop in earnings from hydrocarbon exports, while tourist receipts are only just recovering after a period of stagnation. The number of British tourists has been steadily increasing, so that they now hold third place among European visitors. North American tourists still account for less than one percent.

Arab, Moslem, African and Mediterranean, Tunisia has been the seat of the Maghreb Consultative Council since its creation in 1966, of the

Arab League since 1979, though a decision has been taken in principle to move it back to Cairo, and since 1983 of the P.L.O. (Palestine Liberation Organization), on a much diminished scale since the amazingly accurate Israeli air raid on its headquarters in 1985.

FACTS AT YOUR FINGERTIPS

WHAT IT WILL COST. Tunisia offers a wide choice of modern and well-situated hotels, and tourists can expect to pay about the same as in Morocco for equal quality (see *Planning Your Trip* at the beginning of the book; also for tour operators). In Tunis there are still some cheaper hotels that were built before World War II and are showing it.

The average daily cost per person for each of our standard categories, including transportation within the country, entertainment and extras, is for Luxury about 150DT; Expensive 90DT; Moderate 60DT; Inexpensive 25DT.

For hotel and restaurant costs, see below under *Staying in Tunisia*.

The price of drinks varies according to the place: a Coca Cola between 400 and 800 millimes, likewise a cup of Turkish coffee; and orange juice at the counter in the street 1.2DT, while at a hotel bar it costs 3.5DT; a mint tea between 400 millimes and 1.2DT. The government levies a heavy tax on alcoholic beverages and imports are disproportionately expensive, from 4 to 7DT for a Scotch, gin, vodka, etc., aperitifs 1.5 to 3DT. Local brands are much cheaper, beer from 1DT up, wine from 4.5 to 13DT a half bottle and most brandies around 1.8DT.

A pack of foreign cigarettes costs from 1 to 1.5DT, depending on the brand; a pack of Tunisian cigarettes between 300 and 600 millimes. The most widely sold are *Kim*, which resemble French Gitanes.

A cut and set for ladies at a good hairdresser in Tunis costs 5 to 15DT. A haircut for men 2.5 to 7DT. Festival tickets cost 4 to 8DT. A movie seat in Tunis costs from 1 to 2DT.

WHEN TO GO. A visit to Tunisia is agreeable most of the year round. In winter, the bay of Tunis offers the seductions of the Riviera (including occasional freezing fog and rain), but the Sousse coast is warmer. Even further south it can be chilly. The small amount of rain it receives generally falls in December, January and February.

Spring is particularly beautiful. The gardens of the gulf of Carthage are resplendent, it is still only moderately hot on the steppe, which is dotted with wild flowers, and this is a time for a trip to the deep south.

In summer, the proximity to the sea and its occasional high wind provide a pleasant coolness at the seashore. The steppe is often very hot, but the air is dry. In the south brief and violent storms may make the roads impassable and the hot Saharan wind can bring the temperature up to over 40°C (104°F) in Tunis. However, Khroumiria and particularly the region of Ain Draham with its forests and streams remain pleasantly cool. Autumn is beautiful and quiet, but the vegetation, dried out by the summer heat, has lost its vernal splendor. Towards the end of autumn there are several showers.

The climate varies widely due to the existence of mountain chains and proximity to the Sahara. The annual sunshine averaged over the entire territory comes to 3,000–3,250 hours per year.

Average afternoon temperatures

	Jan.	Feb.	Mar.	Apr.	May	June	July	Aug.	Sept.	Oct.	Nov.	Dec.
Casablanca												
F°	63	64	67	69	72	76	79	81	79	76	69	65
C°	17	18	19	21	22	24	26	27	26	24	21	18

Tunis											
F°	58	61	65	70	76	84	90	91	87	77	68	60
C°	14	16	18	21	24	29	32	33	31	25	20	16

SPECIAL EVENTS. Of some 240 so-called festivals presenting 450 programs, only the few of general touristic interest are listed here. Though touted as "colorful spectacles, culturally rich and entertaining," most are variable mixtures of cultural, folkloric, regional, and religious elements. Dates and durations vary just as much. The inevitable weekly *Folkloric Evenings* in the bigger resort hotels are as phoney as in Morocco, largely non-events.

March	Festival of Tarouine; Berber tribes gather for traditional festivities, including displays of horse riding.
April	*Sound and Light* at the Ribat April through September.
May	Monastir Festival; theatrical performances spaced till August. Festival of Meknassy; an exhibition of Arab thoroughbred horses.
June	First fortnight, Dougga Festival. Classical plays performed in French in the Roman theater. Three days, Hawking Festival at El Haouaria. International Festival of Classical Music; this takes place around June 23 for three weeks. Orchestras from France, Italy, Germany, Russia, and other parts of Europe perform well-known pieces at the El Djem Roman amphitheater outside Sousse.
July/August	Festival of Carthage, Tunisia's most glamorous and the only one deserving to be called International. Theater, ballet and folklore. An original and very noisy contribution is the nine-piece jazz-rock-traditional fusion band where the modal and linear Tunisian music is intermingled with western harmonies. El Jem Festival: the setting, at least, is always spectacular. Siren Festival, Kerkennah Islands. Traditional wedding customs, boating. Hammamet Festival: the Euro-Arab Summer University coordinates musical and theatrical performances in the open-air theater of the Cultural Center. Tabarka Festival: avant-garde music and theater, coral exhibition and sale.
	Layali of Sidi Bou Saïd. Traditional performances culminating in the religious Kharja celebrations in August. Ulysses Festival at Houmt Souk, Jerba. The usual folklore is livened up by tourists participating in inter-hotel competitions. Election of Miss Ulysses, of all loony titles.
August	Aoussou Festival at Sousse. Musical entertainment, parades.
October	Biennial Film Festival of Carthage: films from Third World.
December	Festival of Tozeur. Ending the year on the same Saharan note—and probably with the same camels—as the beginning across Chott el Jerid. Sahara Festival at Douz. Folklore, camel fights and races. The camels are employed on a lesser scale in the grandiloquent *Ballet of the Sahara* twice weekly.

EXCURSIONS. As the lure of the sea is usually the determining factor for visiting Tunisia, emphasis has been laid on the coastal regions, though the Sahara and the remote south are certainly worth a trip. A two-week trip with a maximum of sea and desert should include part of the interior with its monuments. But even the briefest visit to Tunis should allow a visit to the Punic and Roman ruins of Carthage as well as the charming hillside village of Sidi Bou Saïd.

Two recommended 2-day excursions. Northwest in the direction of Bizerta, through La Marsa and Gammarth, the Punic and Roman remains at Utica, the lagoon of Ghar-el-Mehl where the ancient forts are reflected in the still water, the picturesque village of Raf-Raf, the village of Metline hanging on a steep slope and the large Andalusian village of El Alia. Bizerta's *medina* surrounds the old port below the Spanish fortress. The coastal route from Bizerta to Cap Blanc, Africa's northernmost point (8 km., 5 miles), is worth being included in this excursion.

The second excursion leads southeast to Cap Bon, on the motorway till Borj Cedria, then along the beautiful coastal road of Korbous, past the fisheries of Sidi-Daoud, the excavations of the Punic city at Kerkouane, the fishing port of Kélibia, the potters and ceramists of Nabeul. The incomparable gulf of Hammamet offers a wide choice of hotels (200 km., 125 miles from Tunis).

Return to Tunis inland via Zaghouan (a steep jebel and Roman nymphaeum) and visit the Roman ruins of Thuburbo Majus, passing the Roman aqueduct between Zaghouan and Carthage. At La Mohammedia are the ruins of a Bey-like version of Versailles (140 km., 90 miles).

Two-week itinerary. Continue from Hammamet south to Sousse. At 6 km. (4 miles) from Enfida, take a detour to Takrouna village perched on a rock. At Kairouan, visit the Great Mosque, the Barber's Mosque, the ramparts and the pools of the Aghlabids. The museum at Sousse possesses dazzling Roman mosaics; the *ribat* (fortified monastery) is also interesting but less impressive than the one at Monastir. Stop at the rocky point of Mahdia to enjoy the view of the town and the sea. But the region's highlight is the amphitheater of El Jem which is comparable to the Colosseum in Rome.

Sfax, with its forests of olive trees, is the second largest city in Tunisia, and its medina is encircled with handsome ramparts. Gabès is a seaside oasis. If you are not familiar with the Sahara, a visit to the palm-grove is ample justification for the rather monotonous route after Sfax.

There is a choice between an excursion to Kebili, Douz and the surrounding oases of the Nefzaoua—where the white sand dunes undulate around the palm trees—or the rugged hills of the Matmata, where the Berbers dug their houses around central wells. On the beaches of the island of Jerba it is said Ulysses met the somnolent lotus eaters. On the way from Gabès, to Jerba at Medenine and on a detour towards Metameur are the *ghorfas,* superimposed vaulted granaries in which the semi-nomads stored their harvests.

If you have time continue south from Medenine to Tataouine, not so much to see this village as for the sake of the *ksar* (fortified village) and the cave villages where the Berbers took refuge on the rocky peaks in the 11th century.

The ghorfas at Ksar Ouled Debab 10 km. (6 miles) to the south of Tataouine; the cave villages of Chenini, Douirat and Guermessa; as well as Ksar Haddada, 6 km. (4 miles) beyond Ghoumrassen are accessible by car.

TUNISIAN NATIONAL TOURIST OFFICE. In the U.S.: Tourism Division, Embassy of Tunisia, 1515 Massachusetts Ave. NW, Washington, DC 20005. **In the U.K.:** 7a Stafford St., London W1X 4EQ (tel. 01–629 0858).

There are National Tourist Offices (O.N.T.T.) and Syndicats d'Initiative (local information offices) in all major towns and touristic centers with Tunisia. See *Practical Information* sections for regional chapters.

Getting to Tunisia

FROM NORTH AMERICA

By Plane. There are currently no direct flights from North America. Most convenient way is to fly to London, Paris, Milan or Rome and go on from there.

By Boat. There are no passenger sailings. See section *From the Continent* below.

FROM BRITAIN

By Plane. Tunis Air runs four flights a week from London to Tunis, and one flight weekly to Monastir. There are also occasional scheduled flights to Monastir. But the bulk of vacationers from the U.K. fly by charter from as many as eight provincial airports as part of an inclusive tour. These flights go mainly to either Tunis or Monastir, with one or two direct to Jerba. A new British Airways and Gibair (Gibraltar) joint airline—GB Airways—now runs two flights a week from London to Tunis. It provides extremely good service. The planes are new, comfortable, and the flights generally leave on time. Flights run from Gatwick and tickets can be booked from the London GB office (tel. O1 897 4000), or from offices in Bristol (tel. 0272 298181), Manchester (tel. 061 2286311), Birmingham (O21 2367000), Newcastle (O91 2611552), and Tunis (O1 244261). Internal flights are available from Tunis to Monastir, Sfax, Jerba, Tozeur, and Tabarka.

APEX fare from London to Tunis is likely to remain around the £175 mark for 1991. The first class roundtrip fare costs about £700.

By Boat. There are no direct sailings from the U.K. to Tunisia, but Tunis is a port of call for some cruises. There are ferry services from the Continent (see below).

FROM THE CONTINENT

By Plane. Tunis Air runs flights to Tunis from Amsterdam and Barcelona, to Tunis and Monastir from Brussels, and to Tunis, Monastir, and Jerba from Frankfurt, Geneva, Marseilles, and Zurich.

By Boat. S.N.C.M. in conjunction with Cie. Tunisienne de Navigation operate modern car ferries from Marseille to Tunis (La Goulette). There are up to three sailings a week in summer, and the crossing takes around 22 hours. Note that the sailings are not to a regular pattern so it is essential to check with your travel agent at the planning stage. C.T.N. offer a service, with a similar frequency, from Genoa to Tunis which takes 24 hours. Tirrenia Line operate weekly sailings from Naples via Palermo, and from Trapani (in Sicily) to Tunis. In addition Costa Line operate regular services throughout the Mediterranean. Their sailings connect Genoa, Barcelona, Villefranche, Palma, Palermo and Naples with Tunis. There is also a service from Malta.

Hydrofoil for 180 passengers from Trapani (Sicily) to Kelibia, four hours including a one-hour stop at the island of Pantellaria; June 15 to September 15.

FROM ALGERIA

By Train. There is a daily through train, the *Transmaghreb,* from Algiers to Tunis via Annaba. This takes just over 25 hours for the 1,000 km. (621 mile) run. There are through day carriages from Algiers to Tunis, but no couchettes or sleepers.

By Car. From Algeria there are several access roads, starting in the north from El Kala to Tabarka, from El Aïoun to Ain Draham, from Souk Anras to Jendouba, from Tebessa to Kasserine, from El Oued to Gafsa. Roads from Libya are open or closed according to the political climate.

Staying in Tunisia

MONEY. The monetary unit is the Tunisian dinar (DT for short) divided into 1,000 millimes (M for short). Exchange rates (subject to constant fluctuation) are:

$1 equals one dinar, £1 equals 1.500DT. Small sums are usually given in millimes. The figure 5,500, therefore, means 5½DT.

There are 2, 5, 10, 20, 50, 100, 500 millimes and 1DT coins, and bills of 1, 5, 10, and 20 dinars. Small change is rather hard to come by, so it is best not to run short.

Traveler's checks are sometimes difficult to cash in hotels which, moreover, give a less favorable exchange rate. Banks, especially in the provinces, do not change money on a Monday morning until the rates valid for the week are fixed.

HOTELS. The prices we quote are high season rates for double rooms with bath or shower and include breakfast and service charges. Luxury 90DT and up; Expensive 40–80DT; Moderate 20–40DT; Inexpensive 10–20DT. During the low season, November 1 to March 28, rates are 10% less in towns and up to 30% less in the few resort hotels that remain open.

There is a wide choice of adequate expensive and moderate beach hotels, but only a few of the international luxury chains, the Hilton and Meridien in Tunis, the Sheraton at Hammamet. Total capacity amounts to some 60,000 rooms. The State Tourist Organization (O.N.T.T.) is much stricter than in the other two countries, and occasionally closes even three-star hotels and restaurants for not being up to standard. The integrated vacation complexes of Port El Kantaoui and Dar Jerba, the former arguably the best, the latter plain touristic mass production, are among the largest in the Mediterranean. The tourist sites and smaller towns in the interior are provided with at least one modern hotel (advance booking essential in season).

A state-run chain of hotels, the S.H.T.T. (Société Hotelière et Touristique de Tunisie), competes with several private chains, among which the Abou Nawas is outstanding. (L) and most (E) hotels are airconditioned; beach hotels down to (M) have pools and feature weekly folklore evenings of somewhat spurious quality. The Touring Club of Tunisia, 15 Rue d'Allemagne, Tunis (tel. 24 31 82), has adapted some former caravanseries, ghorfas, and constructed simple but clean inns, called marhalas, in the south and at Kairouan.

Youth hostels at Radès, five miles from Tunis and all major towns. Tunisian Travel Bureau, 1 Coleherne Rd., London SW10, tel. 01–373 4411, holds block bookings in some 40 leading hotels and collaborates with the Tunisian National Tourist Office.

The five holiday villages of the Club Méditerranée, three of bungalows (E), and two of thatched huts, are in a class of their own, but there are occasional vacancies for independent travelers. A knowledge of French is a great help. For booking see page 7; also locally Rue Salem Hamida, El Menzah, Tunis (tel. 233 462).

In the U.K., Tunisian hotels are bookable through Tunisian Hotel Associates, 304 Old Brompton Rd., London SW3 (tel. 01–373 4411).

RESTAURANTS. The possibilities on the restaurant front are varied, especially in Tunis which offers perhaps the widest choice in the three countries. Though the hotel menus are of the same unimaginative international variety, there is often one local dish, adequate but not particularly choice. Hotels at beach resorts sadly neglect the more expensive seafood for the sake of cheaper "traditional" dishes. Fortunately, seafood establishments abound all along the coast, though they tend to be expensive.

Meals will be from 15–20DT per head in an Expensive restaurant; 9–15DT in a Moderate one; and 4–9DT at the Inexpensive restaurants frequented by locals, which are more likely to serve alcoholic beverages than in the other two countries.

TIPPING is expected, even though the hotel bill almost always says "all-included." Tip the maid or room-boy 4–8DT per week, according to the class of hotel; 10DT to the head waiter. 500M per suitcase for the porter. If you deal with a voluntary guide, decide with him on the payment before accepting his services. Do not let yourself be victimized by impromptu car-guardians, and beware when they try to polish your windscreen with a sand-laden cloth!

MAIL. Postal rates for abroad: Letter up to 20 grams to France 300M, rest of Europe 400M; to the U.S. 500M. Postcard to France 200M, rest of Europe 250M; to the U.S. 300M. Liable to change.

TELEPHONES, TELEGRAMS. The telephone functions normally in the cities and in the north. In the south, it is not really deficient but sometimes a rather long wait is necessary. It costs 5DT per 3 minutes to telephone the U.K., more (and slower) to the U.S. During rush hours, it may be necessary to wait for an hour. The Telecommunications Center, 15 Rue Jamel Abdel Nasser, provides a public telex service.

SHOPPING. The best buys in each city are: In Tunis: rugs, leather articles (traveling bags, handbags, writing-pads), boxes decorated with metal or jewelry, carved or enameled jewelry, lace. At Sfax: carved wood, copper articles (trays, vases, pitchers). At Bizerte, Gafsa and Gabès: rugs. In Kairouan: knotted rugs and nomadic carpets (Klim, Ksaya, Mergoum). At Nabeul: ceramics and wrought iron. At El Jem and Oudref: carpets. At Sousse: lace. On the Kerkenna and Jerba islands: reed or grass mats, cotton or silks in pastel colors. At Sidi Bou Saïd: graceful metal bird cages.

There are stores of the National Office of Tunisian Handicrafts (Office National de l'Artisanat Tunisien, O.N.A.T.) in Tunis and the port of La Goulette, Beja, Bizerte, Gabès, Gafsa, Hammamet, Jerba (Houmt Souk), Kairouan, Monastir, Nabeul, Sfax, and Zarzis. 6% discount for payment in foreign currencies.

Antique Shops. Oil lamps and small terracotta vases, offered to you at Carthage and at several archeological sites, will often have been buried in the back garden for several months and are always fakes. On the other hand, coins and intaglios are sometimes authentic, but the price asked is much higher than that proposed by serious antique dealers with their own established shops. The latter will not sell you exceptionally fine objects because these are reserved for the museums and moreover their export is forbidden. If you are an amateur collector of old jewelry (Berber or other), fire-arms or side-arms, glass paintings, hope chests or small pieces of furniture, you can rummage about in the antique shops which exist in the main towns.

PUBLIC HOLIDAYS. Sunday is the legal holiday, though Friday is also vaguely kept in the country. The Tunisian Republic faithfully but without too much exuberance commemorates the memorable dates in its short history. Unless he is passionately interested in Tunisian political life, the foreign visitor will find little of interest in these official ceremonies. The following dates are public holidays: January 1, New Year; January 18, Anniversary of the Revolution; March 20, Independence Day; March 21, Youth Day; April 9, Martyrs' Day; May 1, Labor Day; June 1, Victory Day; July 25, Anniversary of the Proclamation of the Republic; August 13, Women's Day; October 15, Anniversary of the Evacuation of Bizerte. For the moveable religious holidays see page 2.

The small Tunisian Jewish community celebrates its religious holidays according to its own calendar. There are annual pilgrimages to the various synagogues, especially to Ghriba on the island of Jerba, about the 33rd day after Passover.

OPENING HOURS. Stores are generally open in winter 8:30–12 and 3–6 (4–7 in summer), except for food stores which open 7–1 and 3:30–9 all year round. In the towns shops close on Sundays, but in the beach resorts on Mondays, if at all. The souks are open all year round 8:30–7, and are closed on Sundays. Banking hours are Monday to Friday, 8–11 and 2–4:15 in winter, closed all afternoon in summer. All better hotels change money and travelers' checks, for a small commission.

NEWSPAPERS. English papers, the *International Herald Tribune* and French morning newspapers are on sale in Tunis in the afternoon. Tunisian dailies in the French language are *La Presse, Le Renouveau,* and *Le Temps.*

GOLF, TENNIS AND HORSES. At Tunis, golf and riding are available at La Soukra, not far from Carthage, and tennis at the Tennis Club, Rue Alain Savary, and Parc des Sports, Ave. Mohammed V. Another 18-hole golf course is at El Kantaoui. Many hotels have their own tennis courts, minigolf and organize horseback riding trips. Horse races take place each Sunday from October to May at the Kassar Saïd race track, 10 km. (6 miles) from Tunis, where you can also join the Club Hippique.

SWIMMING, SAILING, AND YACHTING. The beaches are one of the main attractions of the country. The most beautiful are, from north to south: Tabarka, Bizerte, La Marsa, Carthage, Radès, Hammam Lif, Nabeul, Hammamet, Port El Kantaoui, Sousse, Monastir, Mahdia, Maharès, Gabès, Jerba (east coast), Zarzis. Horseback and camel rides, beside tennis and windsurfing are available in most beach hotels. More sophisticated nautical sports are on the whole restricted to luxury hotels, the Club Méditerranée, Club Nautique, Sidi Bou Saïd and the Nautical Center on Zembra Island. The sea from Dec.–Mar. is always *below* 60°F. (15°C.). There are 12 marinas between Tabarka and Zarzis.

UNDERWATER FISHING. It is practised along the entire coast but above all on the north and northeast coasts. For good catches we recommend Tabarka, the coast road of Bizerte, the island of Zembra, the entire coast of Cap Bon and the Kerkenna Islands. Centre Nautique International de Tunisie, 22 Rue de Medine, Tunis.

Traveling in Tunisia

BY PLANE. Tunis Air operates daily domestic flights between Tunis and Jerba, some via Skanès–Monastir. Monastir to Jerba—flying time about 45 minutes. There are now also frequent flights between the capital and the desert oasis of Tozeur. Another domestic company, Tunisavia, 38 Rue Ghandi, Tunis, has flights between Tunis and Jerba and between Tunis and Sfax. Tunisavia also runs an air taxi service to any point in North Africa and Europe, including some of the remote oases within Tunisia.

BY TRAIN. Although few tourists use the railways for getting about, they have improved substantially in recent years even though they are still slow by European standards. New rolling stock has been introduced on all main routes making journeys fairly comfortable, especially in the "luxe" class. Trains are cheap: A first-class ticket to Gafsa or Gabès will cost around 12 DT.

The early morning train from Tunis arrives at Sfax 3½ hours later, continuing south to Gabès; from Sfax it takes 6 hours via Gafsa to Metlaoui in the west, stopping at all the little stations on the way. Train lines to Tozeur were destroyed during heavy floods in 1989 and in mid-1990 this southern town could only be reached by bus or plane. Return fares, valid for 8 days, when the distance between traveling points is at least 300 km. (188 miles). To break a journey, ask for a *bulletin d'arrêt* at each stop and have it stamped on arrival and departure at the station. Main Tunis Railway Station is in Place Mongi Bali.

It is recommended to travel 1st class; but on the express trains from Tunis to Sfax it is possible to pay a supplement and travel 2nd class in fair airconditioned comfort. Even some not airconditioned trains (e.g. Sfax–Tozeur) are quite bearable.

BY BUS OR SHARED TAXI. Ordinary motor coaches serve the principal cities on fixed timetables. Overcrowding and price are similar to the railroad.

There are also long-range shared taxis (*louages*), authorized to take five passengers, though they often try to squeeze in more. They are privately owned and operate from a *gare routière* in Tunis at 72 Ave. Farhat Hached. They circulate between the principal towns with no fixed timetable, but start when five passengers have congregated. They are faster and only slightly more expensive than the buses, but are not always reliable.

BY TAXI. There are two kinds of taxi: the *petit taxi* for up to four passengers within the respective townlimits; meters are used, rates are reasonable. The *grand taxi* for any distance; if not metered, it is essential to agree on the price beforehand.

BY CAR. There are 10,400 km. (6,500 miles) of paved road, mainly narrow except for the Tunis–Hammamet motorway. They are well maintained, classified, and numbered, GP for the principal, MC for the secondary roads. The 5,300 km. (3,300 miles) of unpaved tracks (*pistes*) are negotiable, except after rare cloudbursts, or when the oueds flood.

The maps issued by the Office of Tourism are fairly up to date, but sometimes out of print. Street signs and signposts are everywhere in Arabic and French.

Parking in the cities is often charged for, but there are no "no-parking" zones or "limited hours" parking. In some streets in Tunis, parking is on alternate sides on alternate days. The traffic police do not give parking tickets; they telephone the car-impounding section of the police and the car is towed away. If your car has disappeared, hail a mini-taxi and ask the driver to take you to the car-pound. It will cost you 10DT to get back your car. It is useless to try and bargain as the personnel of the pound are rather cantankerous—which is rare enough in Tunisia to merit being pointed out.

Motor Fuel. There are filling stations on all the main roads. On the pistes, an auxiliary tank of 10 or 20 liters, say 4 gallons, is essential. At presstime, super gasoline (high octane petrol) costs 500M the liter and ordinary 86 octane petrol 470M the liter.

Car Hire. The big rental agencies (Avis, Hertz) have offices in Tunisia; advanced booking always advisable during the tourist season. Rental rates start at 20DT per day, plus 200M per km. For longer periods unlimited mileage rates are more advantageous: about 160DT for three days, 240DT for five days, 320DT for a week, and 1,500DT for a month. Guide-chauffeurs are available from the car hire firms.

For further information see *Traveling by Car in North Africa* in *Planning Your Trip*.

BICYCLES AND MOTORCYCLES. These can be hired in all the larger towns and resorts. The greatest choice can be found in Tunis, Rue de Palestine.

TUNIS AND CARTHAGE

Land of Myth and Legend

The hunters of prehistory preferred the harsh environment of the interior to the gentle attractions of this beautiful bay, but with the domestication of animals the primitive herdsmen became aware of the coast's grazing potentials. The second millennium B.C. brought Cretan merchants and pirates, though the semi-nomadic indigenous settlers might have been hard-pressed to tell the difference.

By 1000 B.C. larger vessels manned by bold seamen stopped in the gulf. A powerful city was born, Carthage, founded by Dido the Phoenician, who was banished from her homeland and abandoned by the fickle Aeneas; Carthage, doomed for defying Rome; Carthage, with its children sacrificed to Tanit; Carthage, with its carnage, turmoil, battles and flames; the clamor of the Vandals; the death of Saint Louis, King of France.

The history of Tunis is less grandiose. The Carthaginian stronghold of Thynes, destroyed together with Carthage, rose again as Tunes, a small but prosperous Roman and later Byzantine town, till the fourth Aghlabid ruler, Ibrahim Ahmed I, made it his residence in the 9th century. After the conquest of Sicily in 827 the capital also had to be a port, and a canal was dug across the shallow lake, while the ruins of nearby Carthage were an inexhaustible quarry. Temporarily eclipsed by Mahdia, Tunis flourished again under the Zirids, when it rivaled Kairouan, the capital of the steppes.

In 1054 the Beni Hilal ravaged Tunisia but spared Tunis. These nomads had no use for a port; the great desert of water did not attract them. The destruction of Kairouan left Tunis the undisputed capital. The Almohad governors resided in a formidable new Kasbah, but the town's golden age belongs to the following century. Under the benevolent rule of the Hafsids over 100,000 inhabitants prayed in innumerable mosques and studied in one of the most famous universities of Islam, protected by mighty ramparts. In 1236 Tunis gave its name to the country as a whole. Ingenious refugees from Andalusia made it into a garden city, with Moorish villas. The first Bardo Palace was built in 1420. Judeo-Spanish banks opened branches, making possible European economic penetration. Special quarters, *fondouks,* were assigned to the trading community consisting of all Mediterranean races, while each guild displayed its products in its own souk.

But prosperity and tolerance succumbed to the bloody struggle between Spaniards and Turks in the 16th century; trade was restricted to slaves, albeit on a gigantic scale, which made Tunis second only to Algiers as a market of human misery.

At the end of the 19th century, a French town of broad boulevards grew up alongside the souks and holy mosques of the Arab city. Since Tunisian independence, the city has spread in all directions to contain two million inhabitants. The elegant quarters are around the Belvedere Park to the north, especially on the heights beyond. The populous and popular suburbs stretch south and west, divided by the Sebkhet Es Sejoumi, a vast dreary salt marsh.

To the southeast, the wide-open Bay of Tunis is dominated by the Jebel Bou Kornine, the two-horned mountain, where the Carthaginians practised a moon cult. East, in front of the town, extends a smelly, stagnant lagoon stopped up by thousands of years of mud. On the causeway across the lagoon a road and electric railway lead to La Goulette, the port, and from there to Carthage, Sidi Bou Saïd, blue and white on its flowered hillside, and the sandy beaches of La Marsa and Gammarth.

Exploring Tunis

Eucalyptus-lined GP9 from the northern coastal suburbs passes the Tunis-Carthage airport to link with Liaison Nord—Sud (North—South Connection), which runs along the lagoon, euphemistically called Lac (Lake) de Tunis, in an easy approach to the lower end of Avenue Habib Bourguiba. This wide, tree-shaded central artery slopes gently down from the Place de l'Indépendance toward the lake. At the top, the French Embassy faces the heavy no-style Catholic cathedral which now only rarely opens for worship. Opposite is the white Municipal Theater, and at the corner of Avenue de Carthage is the Office National de l'Artisanat, whose windows display caftans in pastel colors that no Tunisian woman would dare wear in public.

From the T.G.M. station at the lower end of Avenue Bourguiba, the electric train and a road follow the causeway across the lake to La Goulette and then on to Carthage.

Retracing Avenue Bourguiba, an equestrian statue of the former President marks Place de l'Afrique, from which palm-lined Avenue Mohammed V branches right past the Tourist Office (O.N.T.T.), the Congress Hall, the Kennedy Garden, the Palais de la Foire (Fairground), and the Parc des Sports to Avenue Khereddine Pacha, widening soon into GP9 leading to the airport, Carthage, La Marsa, and the beaches.

Along the city's backbone, airline and tourist offices, cafes, restaurants and nightclubs, antique and candy shops mailing Tunisian specialties abroad, all jostle for place and overspill into the avenues crossing at right angles, but bearing different names on each side. The next is to the left, most confusingly called Avenue de Carthage though it heads in exactly the opposite direction, dividing before a huge cemetery into GP1 to Hammam Lif and Sortie Sud (Exit South) to the Hammamet motorway. To the right, Avenue de Paris turns into Avenue de la Liberté leading to Place Pasteur, a main crossroads in front of the Belvedere Park.

To the left of the main artery, Rue de Grèce and Rue de Hollande provide access to the rail station in Place Mongi Bali. After the Place de l'Indépendance, Avenue de France continues Avenue Bourguiba and leads to Place de la Victoire, beyond which lies the medina.

Belvedere Park

The several Avenues Habib Bourguiba beside the main thoroughfare are likely to be renamed soon. The two Avenues de la Liberté commemorate the event more than 30 years later. But two Avenues Taieb Mehiri, both major arteries within walking distance, really seems overdoing planned confusion. However, you will have to take one of the Liberté or Mehiri to get to the Belvedere Park, Tunis' only sizeable green space, equally popular in the heat of the day and the cool of the evening. More than a 100 acres in area, on the side of a hill shaded by sycamores, pine, orange trees, palms, and eucalyptus, the park is for the greater part sadly neglected, and the few benches are broken. Below the mini zoo is a tiny lake. Except for an occasional interesting exhibition, the Museum of Living Art in the former casino can be given a miss without much loss. More interesting is the rebuilt 18th-century *midha* (bath-house) from the souks, its three rooms decorated with arches and slim columns. The central room is the patio. Another graceful building from the same period re-erected here is the koubba: its marble-columned portico opens out on to the surrounding foliage, while the sun plays over the brightly colored glass set into its ornate white stucco.

The Park extends to the Chedly Zouiten Stadium. Beyond the higher ground, amid ocher-colored hills, rises the Hilton, while further west, across Voie X the northern ringroad, cluster the main faculties of the scattered university campus.

The Medina

In the lanes and covered passageways of the old city the atmosphere matters more than the monuments. Besides the souks, the quietest and cleanest of any major city in the Maghreb, the patrician houses built around the Great Mosque turn their backs to the street and open on to interior courtyards; their high nail-studded gates, adorned with wrought-iron knockers, the *moucharabieh* (wooden window-lattices) set high in their warm colored walls, their columned porches and marble floors reveal the luxurious refinement of the rich Tunisians of long ago.

The British Embassy stands on the right on Place de la Victoire before Bab Behar, the Sea Gate better known as Porte de France, one of the 17 gates in the medieval rampart which, for the greater part, was pulled down at the end of the last century. Beyond Bab Behar, Rue de la Kasbah and Rue Jamaâ ez Zitouna ascend through the medina's labyrinth of lanes.

Never particularly vivacious and almost deserted on Sundays, when the shops are closed, the souks along the Rue Jamaâ ez Zitouna display the

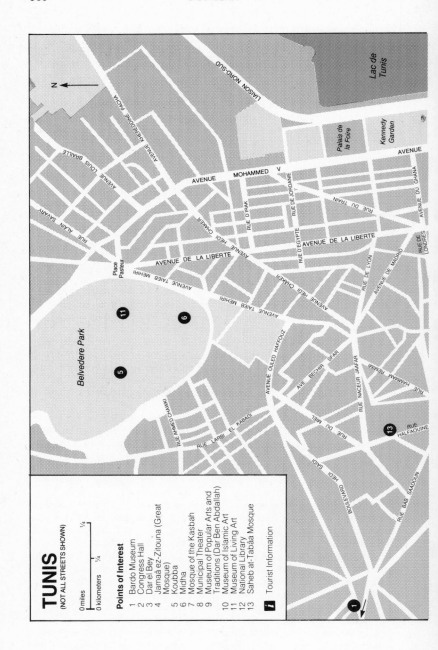

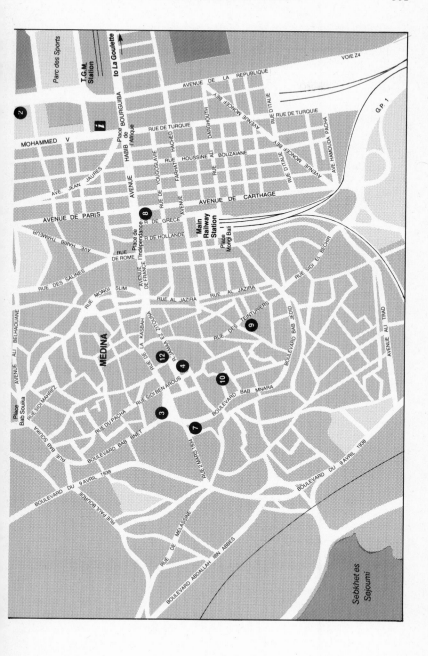

expected handicraft miscellany, emphasizing birdcages, and fish made out of brightly colored fabrics to serve as lucky charms.

To the left, in the same street, opens the portal of the 17th-century chapel of the Holy Cross, founded by the disciples of St. Vincent de Paul dedicated to buying back captive Christians from the Barbary pirates. On the right, farther on, is an annex of the Faculty of Arts and Letters.

At the top of the street, to the left, just before the Great Mosque, lies the domain of the *tarbouka*—the ritual marriage drum, covered with sheep or fish skin.

The Great Mosque

The National Library is on the other side of the street; in front is the Great Mosque, Jamaâ ez-Zitouna (Mosque of the Olive Tree), founded in 732 and continually altered since then. There were times when the fame of its school shed its luster over the whole of Islam, and made Tunis the intellectual rival of Cairo, Baghdad and Fez.

Tourists may enter only the courtyard of this mosque which follows the Malikite rite. The forbidden prayer hall is dark and cool, with ceilings whose exposed beams are supported on six rows of columns. The ground is covered with mats. In line with the mihrab, abundantly decorated with carved stucco and surmounted by a faceted cupola, the capitals of the columns shine with bright pink and green color. Cupboards against the wall hold precious manuscripts, and the minbar is a striking construction of carved wood. A row of large wooden doors studded with nails separates this place of prayer from the courtyard, which is surrounded by a colonnade and arches.

The busy life of the souks flows round the mosque. Merchants and craftsmen are grouped into guilds. Almost all the alleys have name plates and sights are adequately signposted in French. To the right, in the shoe and slipper souk, stands the tomb of Princess Aziza who died in 1646 and was famous for her kindness. The el-Attarine souk, the souk of perfumes, huddles against one of the walls of the Great Mosque. Here they sell everything necessary for weddings, in particular the lined baskets that men send their fiancées a week before the wedding. In it they put candles in the shape of a hand, soap, perfumes, and grayish green powdered henna, with which the bride will dye her feet and hands red three days before the wedding. The gift in addition includes lumps of ambergris; these will be mixed with other plants and used to make the girl's hair an ideal black. The gold- and silver-embroidered vests worn by brides are also here.

The el-Attarine souk runs into the Rue Sidi Ben Arous, where the 18th-century Hamouda Pacha Mosque, of the Manafite rite, is roofed with green glazed tiles. The interior is decorated with a beautiful balcony of carved wood painted sky blue, which the women reach by means of a ladder.

The chechias souk runs at right angles into Rue Sidi Ben Arous, on the opposite side from the mosque. All the tailors are in Souk et-Trouk, which follows on from the el-Attarine souk. Here, on the right, the cafe-restaurant M'Rabet ("of the holy men"), offers welcome refreshments. The upper story has a good restaurant with an interesting view over the souks and mosques through moucharabieh.

The cloth souk skirts one of the walls of the Great Mosque, at right angles to the el-Attarine souk. At the end of it is the souk of the women, not of luscious slave girls as of yore, but simply of beauty products. #58 in the el-Leffa souk proclaims itself the "Palace of the Orient." From the terrace you can see ruined arches covered with tiles (some of them dating from the 14th century), the souks and the city. A golden canopied throne is called the "bed of the bey."

The slave market used to be located in the el-Berka souk, which opens off the el-Leffa souk to the left as you face away from the Great Mosque. Also to the left of the el-Leffa souk, a series of blind alleys makes up the gold- and silversmiths' souk.

The 18th-century palace of Dar Hussein closeby houses the Museum of Islamic Art, and merits as much attention as the collections it contains. The palace is built around a large courtyard with a surrounding arcade and tile-covered walls, and is richly decorated with stucco. Of the four rooms that make up the museum, the first, devoted to paleography, contains illuminated manuscripts, miniatures in Persian style, copies of the Koran, standards of weight, and coins. The second is the ceramic room: here are pieces of iridescent glass, glazed Mameluk and blue Persian plates, little glass figurines, embossed silver plaques from harnesses and ancient weapons. The third room contains silk embroidered clothes from Persia, women's tunics, and panels of wood inlaid with ivory and mother-of-pearl. The stucco in the fourth room, its ceiling festooned with a huge chandelier, is encrusted with colored glass; Fatimid ceramics, and earthenware jars contain silver coins minted by the Spaniards under the last Hafsid sultan at the beginning of the 16th century.

Near the museum is the El Ksar Mosque, dating from the 12th century, with a minaret rebuilt in the 17th century. Not far is the Sidi Bou Krissan Museum of Epigraphy (open 9–12 and 2–5), more easily reached by taking Boulevard Bab Menara on the edge of the old town. By the mosque a quiet garden contains tombstones whose inscriptions date from the 11th to the 19th century, and an interesting mausoleum.

The Governmental Palace, Dar el Bey, the 19th-century residence of the beys, stands at the upper end of Rue de la Kasbah, but can also be reached by car along one of the boulevards, Bab Bnet to the right, Bab Mnara to the left, which encircle the medina. The Palace, seat of the prime minister and cabinet (not open to visitors), faces the Place du Gouvernement, a square shaded by trees. To the left rises the Sidi Youssef Mosque, built by the Turks in 1574 and restored by Youssef Dey in 1616. To the right, the Ministry of Foreign Affairs features a large clock with a single hand and a weight in the shape of a crescent moon. On one wing of the building a sundial bears two plaques ornamented with astrological symbols.

Tours of the Medina

Seeing that most guides turn a visit to the old town into a shopping tour, the O.N.T.T. has elaborated the Circuit of Ibn Khaldoun, concentrating on sites. We opt for a tour easily followed by car. As the medina is encircled by a wide boulevard, changing name at each gate, several interesting places on the edge of the old city can be reached without too much effort.

In front of Place de la Victoire, take Rue Mongi Slim to the right, then Rue Bab Souika to the square of the same name. To the left, Rue Sidi Mahrez leads to the 18th-century Sidi Mahrez Mosque which is Turkish in style and contains some beautiful tiles. The cupola of the Sidi Ibrahim Mausoleum is decorated with stucco work.

To the right of Place Bab Souika, the Gate of the Small Market, destroyed in 1885 at the construction of the wide square, Rue Halfaouine leads to Place Halfaouine, where there are picturesque cafes. On one side of the square, the 19th-century Halfaouine Mosque, also called the Saheb at-Tabâa, has a prayer hall with arcades decorated with carved stucco, a marble mihrab and, in the courtyard, the mausoleum of the founder and his family. The Medersa, a religious school, now disused, has an arcaded courtyard surrounded by cells for students, with attractively tiled walls. From Place Bab Souika and the street of the same name, Boulevard Bab Bnet (Benat)—the Gate of the Girls, named after the daughters of his defeated rival, whom Emir Abu Zakariya (1229–49) brought up like his own children in a palace near this long-vanished gate—continues past several ministries to the large Place du Gouvernement, with the Dar el Bey on the lower left. To the right, only a few crumbling walls remain of the Kasbah below the modernistic headquarters of the Destourian Socialist Party. At the corner of Bab Mnara (Menara), the Gate of the Lamp, from here on the name of the encircling boulevard, stands the 13th-century Mosque of the Kasbah with a lovely minaret, brashly restored.

Some distance to the right, on the heights of El Houa, is a bastion-defended Bab Sidi Kacem el-Jalizzi, named after a pious Andalusian who founded a *zaouïa* here in which he was buried in 1497. The mausoleum's graceful marble arcades, within the enclosure of carved wood, stuccos and ceramics, are topped with green tiles. To the southwest extends Sebkhet Sejoumi, an immense saltwater marsh that dries up in summer.

Inside the medina, Sekkajine souk leads to the Sidi Bou Krissan Museum of Epigraphy, already mentioned. The boulevard then takes the name of Bab Jedid, after the 13th-century fortified Hafsid New Gate which it passes, and continues to skirt the medina. On the left, Tourbet el Bey, since Ali Bey (1758–82) the mausoleum of the Husainid family, with an Italianate facade and green tiled domes. The 18th-century Mosque of the Dyers is attached to a mausoleum and religious school. Nearby are Dar Othman, a 16th-century palace faced with stones of alternate colors, and also Dar Ben Abdallah, a 19th-century palace which houses the Museum of Folklore.

Bab Jedid opens on the souk of weapons—still so called, though the gunsmiths have gone—where the 14th-century El H'Laq Mosque is remarkable for its austere style. The encircling boulevard becomes Rue Al Jazira at the Gate of the Peninsula, thus named because it faces towards Cap Bon, returning to the starting point at the Place de la Victoire.

The Bardo Museum

The Bardo Museum, by far Tunisia's most important, stands 5 km. (3 miles) from the center in the not particularly western suburb to which the palace has given its name. It excels in Carthaginian, Roman, Byzantine, and Arab collections.

Until 1957 the Bardo Palace was the official residence of the Beys. Established in the harem quarters in 1882, the national collections have continued to grow, and now spread over 3 overcrowded stories. Included are the former state apartments, but gone are the troupes of dwarfs, male and female, about 15 to 20 in number, which amused the Beylical court until as late as 1939, and the eunuchs who waited upon them.

The National Assembly building next to the museum is barred to tourists by the Presidential Guards in resplendent red and gold uniforms, who are not averse to posing for photos.

On the Museum's ground floor, Room I contains the publications desk, where an excellent catalog is available (French only). Several instructive models of Roman sites precede the Punic exhibits, which have been rearranged recently and partially transferred to the Carthage Museum. At present, Room II displays Punic funerary stelae from the Tophet at Carthage—markerks designating the graves of the first-born of the greatest families, sanctified to Tanit and Baal-Hammon in periods of great national disaster. Showcases contain grimacing Carthaginian masks of religious significance, of glass as well as of terracotta, beside archaic and classical Greek statuettes in terracotta from Punic tombs.

A small room to the right holds a unique collection of Punic jewelry and amulets found in the tombs at Carthage, Utica, Dougga and Cap Bon.

The funerary stelae from Ghorfa (in a passage between Room IV and the corridor of the sarcophagus) date from the 2nd century A.D.; they were produced by Berbers near Dougga but they reflect Punic and Roman influence; although fairly crude in workmanship, they offer interesting evidence of the penetration of Semitic and Indo-European civilization into the Berber milieu.

In Room VII are exhibited another group of neo-Punic statuary, the 1st century A.D. terracotta sculptures from Thinissut, a rural settlement on Cap Bon. Statues of Tanit with a lion's head and winged and feathered bodies. Also three sphinxes—it was believed that the dead took the form of the sphinx to return and haunt the living, a fascinating evidence of the persistence of the Punic religion into Roman times.

Finds from Bulla Begia (Room VI) and Thuburbo Majus (Room VIII). The early Christian antiquities give ample evidence of the importance of the North African provinces in the development of Christian iconography. The 5th- and 6th-century polychrome terracotta plaques from the walls and ceilings of the basilicas at Carthage, Kassarine, El-Jem and other sites displayed in the passage to Room VI—the whole panorama of the Old and New Testaments, Adam and Eve, Daniel and the lions, Jonah and the whale, the Virgin, scenes from Christ's life, St. Theodore, along with a gallery of animals known in the region at the time—lions, stags, peacocks, even elephants—are all depicted with a touching naïveté.

Mosaics of the 4th to 6th century from various basilicas and tombs are displayed in Room V and on the walls of the staircase that ascends from it. On the right of the stairs, the schematic reconstruction of the plan of a Byzantine church with 3 naves, the mosaics from the baptistery at Kelibia, and the beautiful sarcophagus cover in mosaic from Tabarka, depicting on the upper register a scribe (perhaps an ecclesiastical notary), and on the lower register an aging woman (the inscription names her Victoria) portrayed in the *orans* posture—arms held almost vertically with the hands pointing outward. The occupier of the tomb strove to have herself identified closely with the Virgin by assuming the stance in which Mary so often appears in early Christian iconography as the personification of the Holy Church.

The best mosaics from the Roman period, along with finds from the Roman sites at Carthage, Sousse, Dougga and El-Jem, are displayed on the second floor. The mosaics illustrate the life of wealthy Roman colonists in the 2nd and 3rd centuries A.D.

Room IX, the old courtyard of the harem, contains many sculptures from Roman Carthage; in Room X, originally the banqueting hall extending over two floors in white and gold under a sculpted wooden stalactite ceiling, a magnificent mosaic from Sousse, set in the floor, depicts the triumphs of Neptune. Numerous sculptures from Dougga in Room XI are dominated by an immense mosaic portraying a scene from Virgil (*Aeneid,* Book VIII, verse 146) of the cave of the Cyclops with the three giants, Brontes, Steropes and Pyracmon, forging the thunderbolts of Jupiter. In Room XII, the vivid hunting mosaic of El-Jem recalls the Assyrian bas-reliefs from Nineveh in the British Museum.

Rooms XVII to XXII, called the Mahdia Rooms, contain the rich cargo of a Roman ship which sank off the coast at Mahdia in 81 B.C. and was discovered at a depth of 39 meters (128 feet) in 1907. The most remarkable objects are two Greek bronzes of the 3rd century B.C., originally forming a single ensemble—the winged youth Agon, with the Hermes of Dionysus. There is also a bronze Eros, the replica of a work by Praxiteles, along with numerous and delightful satyrs and cupids. Marbles found half-buried in the sand are deeply scarred on the side that was exposed to water. Moving relics include blackened pieces of wood from the hull of the boat, its anchors, the remains of its rigging, the everyday objects used by the crew such as oil lamps, fish hooks and weights for fishing nets.

In Room XXIII large mosaics show Amphitrite playing with dolphins; a panorama of the coast with villas, gardens and beaches; a scene of fishing with nets and a seascape of fish and crustaceans. Room XXIV, a Roman mausoleum, has mosaics of hunting scenes where the quarry is wild animals, antelopes and gazelles; also, Venus in a chariot drawn by cupids; and a scene of fishing with nets and hooks.

Among the mosaics in Room XXIV are Ulysses and the Sirens; Dionysus fighting the pirates; Apollo and Marsyas surrounded by the four seasons; there is an amusing Roman Hercules in bronze of the 3rd century A.D. In Room XXVII (the "Peacock Room"), little horses graze among flowers; female centaurs, their large eyes ringed with kohl, crown a sensual Venus; and a strutting peacock spreads his tail.

The top story contains more mosaics. The light in these eight rooms (XXIX–XXXVI) is much better, owing to the many skylights; and from the balconies you can get a perspective on the mosaics on the second floor.

The small palace which houses the Arabic Museum is connected to the Bardo. Notice the ceilings of worked stucco, and the bright tile facing. T-shaped rooms with alcoves in traditional Tunisian fashion, surround a patio with a marble pool and fountain. Among the embroideries, jewels, objects decorated with silver filigree, and ceremonial tunics embroidered with gold and silver and furniture inlaid with mother-of-pearl, a seven-branch candlestick oddly labeled "Instrument for Circumcision."

The Gulf of Tunis

To the southeast, the motorway to Hammamet bypasses Hammam-Lif, once the bey's winter residence, now grown into a town extending from the sea to the slopes of Jebel Bou Kornine, the Two-horned Mountain. A road climbs through the Aleppo-pine groves, carpeted with wild cyclamen in the spring, to the twin peaks, the Gulf's landmark. The view is outstanding from every bend up to the T.V. and radio relay stations broadcasting in Arabic and French. Nearby are the remaining vestiges of a Punic sanctuary.

An attractive return can be made along the coast via Borj Cedria, Ez Zahra and Radès, the last perched picturesquely on a hill between the sea and the Lake of Tunis.

To the northeast stood Carthage, founded by Queen Dido from Phoenician Tyre. The maritime republic's almost millenary pre-eminence in the western Mediterranean was challenged by Rome in the three Punic wars, to end in 146 B.C. with the accomplishment of Cato the Censor's notorious *"Carthago est delenda"* (Carthage must be obliterated). This dictum rang true down the ages, heralding what was believed to have been history's most thorough destruction after a siege of three years ending in a conflagration that raged for 17 days, followed by a systematic leveling and plowing-up of the ground that was sprinkled with salt to assure both symbolic and lasting sterility. Yet excavations carried out by 12 national teams under U.N.E.S.C.O. auspices, and documented by some 60 volumes, found the walls and foundations had somehow resisted this seemingly implacable combination of onslaughts on the town of some 30,000 inhabitants, described by the near-contemporary writer Appian.

The final blow came, ironically, only with the Roman recolonization just over 100 years later, by the use of the building materials so conveniently to hand in the Punic ruins. Within another century, Carthage was again one of the Mediterranean's dominant cities, a status preserved as capital of the Vandal kingdom from 430 to 534, and even after the Byzantine reconquest up to the sack by the Arabs in 695. Then, for over 1,000 years, the ruins served again as a splendid quarry, so that the Arab writer of the 15th century noted that "every ship that pulls out of Carthage must have its load of stone." Yet a site so blessed by nature could not remain for ever wasted by man. The villas of Tunis' garden suburb spread northward along the coast, while modern Tunisia, roughly covering the same area as the Punic republic and the Roman province of Africa, is ruled from the presidential Palace of Carthage, a mere catapult's throw from Dido's palace on the hill of Byrsa.

The 2,800th anniversary of the foundation of Carthage was duly celebrated, and 2,131 years after the first and greatest destruction, the mayors of Carthage and Rome signed a peace treaty in 1985. The former has adapted the slogan to read "Carthage must *not* be obliterated," to prevent the historic site from being engulfed by unzoned development. To this end in 1985 a presidential decree established a National Archeological Park of 500 hectares including the most important ruins.

Excavations still reveal Punic remains beside and below the important Roman ruins, easily reached by T.M.G. train from Tunis Port over the 10-km. (6-mile) causeway across the shallow and smelly Lake of Tunis. The causeway which also carries the road, serves as a dike for the deep canal dug by the French at the end of the last century to develop the port of Tunis. The first stop is at the much larger outer port, La Goulette, whose bleak fortress, conquered and rebuilt by the Emperor Charles V and Don John of Austria, once held 10,000 Christian slaves, including St. Vincent de Paul. Except for arrival and departure by sea, the unattractive port is visited for some good and relatively inexpensive seafood restaurants and for its colorful fish hall with its array of bream, red mullet, groupers, gar-fish, mantis shrimps, tunny, shark, and octopus, which provides a tempting scene for photographers not put off by the overwhelming smell.

Villas in pretty gardens, but not yet beaches, begin at Khereddine, named in fond memory of that particularly objectionable 16th-century pirate, Khair al-Din Barbarossa.

Carthage-Salammbô, a compliment to Flaubert for his famous novel, is the first of six stations within the vast expanse of Roman and modern Carthage through which the T.G.M. passes.

Infanticide and Engineering

Avenue Jugurtha turns seaward to the first fragment of the widely scattered Parc Archéologique, the Tophet, discovered in the best detective-story tradition in 1921. Two minor French officials purchased from a Tunisian a fine black stele, over a meter high, representing a man with a child in his arms. The vendor refused to give any indication as to its provenance, but was trailed by the amateur archeologists to a site of unique horror and major importance. Below six meters (20 feet) of earth, thousands of urns surmounted by stelae were brought to light. The sanctuary is now once again abandoned, the embankments have crumbled back into the ditches and wild herbs cover the ground where the Carthaginians buried the ashes of their firstborn, burned on a sacred pyre as a sacrifice to Baal-Hammon and Tanit.

The successive archeological levels illustrate the stylistic evolution of the infant burials: very simple pottery in the 8th century, rough coffins in the 6th century. The position of the burials is indicated by stelae of Egyptian design, which in the fifth century acquired classical pediments. Around the fourth century small obelisks and stone parallelepipeds ending in pyramids appear, as well as flat stelae with triangular tops engraved with the symbol of Tanit, a solar disc on a crescent moon pointing upward. The stylistic progression is well represented in Room II of the Bardo Museum.

The sacrifice took place at night at critical moments in the city's history. According to legend, the children—supposed to be the first-born of the most distinguished families of Carthage—were strangled in public before they were burned. Often, however, the children of slaves or foreigners were exchanged at the last moment and became the unhappy victims; and at times not unduly calamitous, even sheep were offered up. Examinations of teeth found in the ashes shows that the victims were babies or children two or three years of age. Their bones were buried in urns alone or mixed with those of young animals. In conclusive proof, the tablets recording the gruesome sacrifice use the dedicatory formulae associated with consecration, are totally different from normal epitaphs.

The Tophet is close to the Punic commercial port, but the easiest approach is from the next T.G.M. stop, Carthage-Byrsa; follow the sign to the Ports Puniques, through roads winding past villas smothered by bougainvillea, to the perfectly crescent-shaped military port of Carthage and the originally rectangular now oval commercial port to which it is connected by a narrow channel. The slipways into the tiny twin pools were discovered by the British who excavated the dockyards and built models of the Punic as well as of the Roman naval base. The Carthaginians were brilliant engineers, moving some 250,000 cubic meters of earth—a feat comparable with the building of the Pyramids. A complex of ship-building and repair yards were built on stone at a time when Rome was still a city of mud and wood. The Romans learnt not only naval warfare, but also engineering from Carthage.

The admiralty buildings stood on a circular islet in the middle of the harbor; recesses in the shore sheltered 220 war galleys. Hard to imagine,

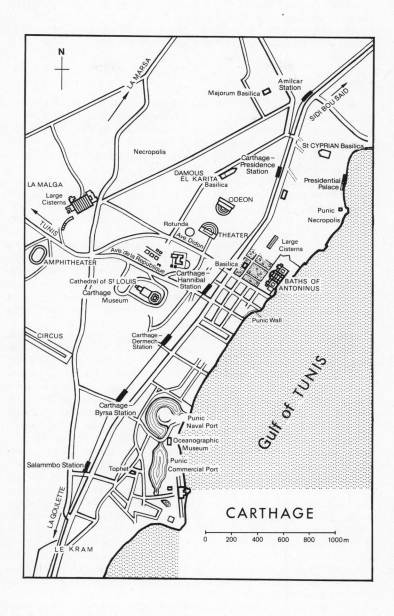

N

TUNIS AND CARTHAGE

LA MARSA

Amilcar Station

Majorum Basilica

SIDI BOU SAID

Necropolis

St CYPRIAN Basilica

Carthage–Presidence Station

DAMOUS EL KARITA Basilica

LA MALGA

Large Cisterns

Presidential Palace

ODEON

Punic Necropolis

TUNIS

Rotunda

Ave Didon

THEATER

Ave de la Republique

Large Cisterns

AMPHITHEATER

Basilica

BATHS OF ANTONINUS

Cathedral of St LOUIS

Carthage Museum

Carthage–Hannibal Station

Punic Wall

CIRCUS

Carthage–Dermech Station

Gulf of TUNIS

Carthage–Byrsa Station

Punic Naval Port

Oceanographic Museum

Salammbo Station

Tophet

Punic Commercial Port

LA GOULETTE

CARTHAGE

LE KRAM

0   200   400   600   800   1000m

seeing the minute dimensions of the installations; yet here, according to Virgil, the Trojan fleet anchored, and here the ghosts of Priamus and Hector and Cassandra appeared before the faltering Aeneas, and here the founder of Rome bade farewell to the distraught Queen Dido and set forth to Italian shores. Nearby is a rather uninspiring oceanographic museum (open daily except Monday, 4–7 in summer and 2–5 in winter).

The Upper Town

Carthage-Byrsa is, paradoxically, far from the hill of Byrsa, and though the following stop, Carthage-Dermech, is just underneath, the most convenient ascent is from the Carthage-Hannibal station by the wide Avenue de la République, lined with the villas of diplomats surrounded by lovely gardens. At the beginning of the French colonial era, Cardinal Lavigerie built a religious complex on the hill's summit. For half a century this was the focus for the see of the ancient Diocese of Africa, revived after 1250 years and now once again defunct. The imposing ocher Cathedral of St. Louis, basically neo-Byzantine—with practically every conceivable neo-added—is now deconsecrated and scheduled to house a Paleo-Christian museum.

The entrance to the Carthage Museum, the former Monastery of the White Fathers, is within the excavation precinct. Divided into Prehistoric, Punic, Roman, and Paleo-Christian sections, sarcophagi, stelae, amphorae, and heavy Roman statuary overflow into the garden, where a recumbent statue of St. Louis serves as a reminder that France's greatest medieval king died hereabouts of the plague just two hours before his brother, King Charles of Naples, landed with a relief army.

In Room I is a mosaic representing Tellus, a personification of the earth. In Room II there are Hellenistic, Etruscan and Punic objects found in tombs, among them an unusual collection of babies' feeding bottles in terracotta, some with eyes painted on them to frighten away evil spirits; the bottles were designed to be held in two or three fingers, the thumb staying free to stop up the air hole and thus control the flow of milk. Room III contains oil lamps and several terracotta plaques modeled with allegorical animals, used in the decoration of Christian chapels; also in this room is a striligated sarcophagus bearing the figure of the Good Shepherd.

The museum's two unique treasures are the only significant Punic sculpture ever found—the lids of two sarcophagi. One lid represents a man in seemingly Greek dress, right hand raised, left hand holding an unidentified object. The other lid, a woman, is far more interesting. As if enfolded in the wings of a bird, holding a dove in her right hand and the same object as the man in her left, she is reminiscent of the tomb sculptures from Palmyra in Syria. Both probably date from the 4th century B.C.; there is nothing to compare them with, so they cannot be identified, be they priests or heroic dead. But the most puzzling feature of Carthaginian culture is the lack of style, of any esthetic distinction. Even the most advanced pottery is crude and functional, verging on the ugly, without the grace of contemporary Greek products.

Yet Carthage was a splendid city in stone, of vaguely Greek aspect, not at all the expected oriental medina with narrow twisted lanes, but—as the recent excavations established—of parallel unpaved streets, six to seven meters wide (just over 20 feet), that crossed at right angles. The north slope of the Byrsa is taken up by Roman buildings, but on the south slope the foundations along five streets permit the tracing of the elegant upper town, despite the destruction of 146 B.C. The view from the citadel embraces the entire Gulf of Tunis, and it is quite likely that on the crest of the hill stood the palace of Dido, and that near this spot, wearing the toga of Aeneas, she mounted her funeral pyre, proclaiming the name of her descendant who should one day avenge her honor and redeem the city—Hannibal.

Roman Carthage

To the west, in the inland plain, portic myths give way to still fairly solid history. There is a large circus and amphitheater where, in 1943, Churchill addressed the victorious Allied troops in an appropriate setting of fallen columns and broken marbles. Almost as large as the Colosseum in Rome, and standing nearly intact until the 16th century, when it began to be used as a convenient quarry, only the arena and an underground passage remain of the original structure. It was the scene of gladiatorial combats, animal fights, and the martyrdom of Christians. Impressive even in their decay, these remains of imperial Rome are difficult to visit without a car.

But there are plenty more, better preserved and partly restored, within easy walking distance. Descending from the Byrsa by Avenue Didon, an entire quarter lies to the left. After passing a large Mausoleum, a modern road as well as Roman cobblestones—bearing the marks of hopscotch games engraved most likely by Roman children—branch past the badly ruined Odeum and remains of the Emperor Theodosius' wall to the Quartier des Villas. One villa has been sufficiently restored on a spacious terrace with mosaic floors around fountains to illustrate how very pleasant life must have been here for several centuries.

Further on, a rare circular monument once rose two stories of 12 columns, within a rectangular arcade, probably an early-Christian *martyrium,* where relics of the martyrs were displayed for public devotion. This Rotunda was probably part of a religious complex that comprised the Damous El Karita, the *domus caritatis* (House of Mercy), a large 17th-century basilica, flanked by a trefoil-shaped chapel and the polygonal baptistery. The surrounding Christian cemetery of antiquity was used again by the White Fathers under the French Protectorate.

The next branch left leads to the Theater, heavily restored in utilitarian concrete to accommodate the annual Festival of Carthage, the country's most important cultural event. The guards look the other way when touts offer coins that may conceivably be Roman, and clay idols that by no stretch of the imagination could be Punic.

Below the T.G.M. lines, at the bottom of the Avenue des Thermes d'Antonin, and divided by palms, is the grandest of the Roman monuments, the Baths of Antoninus. Begun by the Emperor Hadrian in A.D. 112 and completed by Antoninus Pius about A.D. 146, near the sea, the baths were among the largest in the Roman Empire. Two tall columns have been reerected, but the floor above, twice as high, the vaulted baths proper, has almost completely disappeared; the ground floor is occupied mainly by the elaborate heating arrangements—ash and cinder still cover the central octagon—and large rest rooms, shady and cool, for use during the hot siesta hours.

By the sea, granite and porphyry fragments are scattered over an area of 200 square m. (some 240 square yards). A Corinthian capital 1.80 meters (6 feet) high, weighing four tons gives some idea of the former grandeur. From huge octagonal halls the remains of a staircase mount to the upper floor.

Behind the baths, a pleasant garden has been laid out on the site of a Roman residential quarter, where some of the villas and a nympheum have been restored. A row of palm trees on the left leads to a semicircular esplanade paved with mosaics: this remarkably large area is the site of the latrines of the baths.

Among the paths lined with Punic and Roman stelae and caskets there are signs marking the roads that crossed at right angles (*Cardo*).

At the corner of Cardo XV, you can go down into a restored Christian tomb—of interest only for its pavement. At the corner of Cardo XIV are the ruins of two Christian basilicas. One of them still retains part of its pavement, its baptistery and a few column shafts.

At the far end of the garden, where excavations have left deep pits, the Punic necropolis with its little stelae lies on a hill planted with pines. Votive offerings and epitaphs mention Saturn (Baal) and Caelestis (Tanit): the Carthaginian gods had Romanized their names.

Rue Septime Severe, named after the first Roman emperor born in Africa, leads to another luxurious group of villas, the Quartier de Magon, somewhat arbitrarily called by archeologists after the Punic agriculturist Mago who wrote a treatise on the cultivation of grapes and olives in the 6th century B.C. It is noteworthy that the only Carthaginian books translated by the Romans concerned farming. The meager Punic foundations abut on a seawall restored by German excavators.

The Carthage-Presidence stop is near the entrance of the Palais de Carthage, the former beylical summer palace and now the official residence of the country's president. From Carthage-Amilcar a track to the right (past the steep descent to the Hotel Amilcar) descends to the Basilica of St. Cyprian, whose impressive seven aisles were unearthed in 1915; closer to the sea is the Spring of the 1,000 Amphorae, the only source of water for Carthage—which explains the prevalence of huge rainwater cisterns scattered over the Punic town.

Inland from the Amilcar station is the entrance of the American Military Cemetery and Memorial. Covering an area of 27 acres, the site was selected in 1948 and construction was completed in 1960. Here rest 2,840 Americans who fell in World War II. Within the Visitors' Building near the entrance is a Roman mosaic given by former President Bourguiba. From there stretches the Mall, on the south side of which is the Wall of the Missing, with names and particulars of 3,724 Americans missing in North African campaigns. The cemetery is beautifully maintained by the American Battle Monuments Commission and is a spot of peace and tranquility.

An Oriental Stage Set

From the Sidi Bou Saïd station it is a short ascent to the town. Cars are not permitted in the narrow lanes of dazzling white cubes, smothered in bougainvillea and convolvulus beneath the all-pervading smell of jasmine, which not only grows in profusion but is tucked behind the ears of most men or worn in chains round their necks. The little village, miraculously preserved despite its fame, looks out over the bay from the slopes of a steep headland. The streets lined with white houses, their windows, doors and ironwork painted blue, could not have been more attractive when the town's patron, Abou Saïd al-Baji, taught here in the *zaouïa,* still a place of pilgrimage from all over the country. Though he died in 1231, local tradition maintains that he was none other than St. Louis, who abandoned his army for the charms and religion of a Moslem beauty. In so delightful a setting a few feel sufficiently pedantic to bring up the date of the saintly king's arrival, which happened to be 1270. Be that as it may, Bou Saïd became the patron of the Barbary pirates, who fortified the village only to lose it promptly to the Spaniards. Cervantes was a member of the garrison placed on the strategic rock by Don John of Austria. The future author of Don Quixote became thus the first—though hardly by his own choice—of several distinguished writers inspired by the superb position. *Their* patron, though saint only to a very few, is André Gide, who wrote here his *Thésée* and translated *Hamlet* in 1942. As usual, the upper crust followed the lead of the artists; after World War II, first the French élite then the higher Tunisian dignitaries built villas at the approaches, in perfect keeping with the local architecture.

Dar Khosroff, a lovely old mansion, houses a Museum of Traditional Arts. Next to the saint's marabout, near the square, stairs lead up to the Café des Nattes (of the Straw Mats), a must with the tourists who, however, by sheer weight of numbers, have destroyed the dignified atmosphere of repose on the mat-covered benches. Mint tea, rather sickeningly sweet, is the thing. The Café Le Chergoui with its caves and its view of the bay is, if possible, more tourist-oriented. Yet the view is as lovely as ever, the magnificent crescent of the sea extending to the perfect backdrop of Mount Bou Kornine; its breathtaking beauty tames even the most persistent of all invaders, the tourists.

La Marsa is the last of the suburbs of Tunis, and also the terminus of the T.G.M.—after the stops at La Corniche and finally the station at Marsa-Plage. Much frequented by Tunisians in summer, the most imposing among the many fine residences is a beautiful, domed white mansion near the post office. The great local attraction is the Cafe Saf Saf whose customers sit under awnings in the courtyard where a blindfold camel circles drawing well water into earthenware jars attached to a wheel.

Gammarth, 4 km. (2½ miles) farther on, a country retreat much sought after by rich Tunisians in the 19th century, has now been taken over by hotels. High above, reached by a steeply winding road, the crags and swiftly-flowing streams of the Jebel Khaoui and forests are still untouched. This is the Megara on the edge of Carthage where Dido and Aeneas hunted stag; the same forest where Berlioz set the *Royal Hunt and Storm* music.

PRACTICAL INFORMATION FOR
TUNIS AND CARTHAGE

WHEN TO GO. The climate is typically Mediterranean. The average temperature in winter is 11°C (52°F), and in spring 16°C (61°F). The autumn is generally dry, with the rainfall concentrated in a few heavy storms. In the summer the wind from the south raises the temperature unpleasantly, when it is time to take refuge on one of the numerous beaches.

Businessmen will be interested in the biannual Tunis Fair in June; buffs of Third World films and discussions on Arab-African cinema in the biannual Carthage Film Festival.

GETTING INTO TOWN. From the Airport. A small taxi to the Hilton or the hotels in the town center costs about 3.5DT, a large taxi roughly double that. The half-hourly 35 bus costs only 400M, but becomes very crowded at the numerous stops before arriving at the Ave. Habib Bourguiba terminal. Transtour buses to the town center as well as buses from some Hammamet hotels meet planes from main starting points.

From the Port. Taxis from La Goulette are cheaper to the center, dearer to the Hilton. Trains every ten minutes to the T.G.M. terminal.

GETTING AROUND. By Electric Train. The hub of public transport is the T.G.M. station at the Tunis Port end of Avenue Bourguiba. Frequent trains cross the causeway at La Goulette and then follow the coast north via Carthage and Sidi Bou Saïd to La Marsa in 20 minutes; return ticket first class 800M, overcrowded second class 500M. On the Port to the right is the metro terminal to the touristically uninteresting southern Ben Arous suburb. A new tram system, covering the entire city and extending to Ariana and the Bardo, operates from Place Barcelona.

By Bus. The main terminal is close to the two train terminals. #1 and #2 go to the Medina; #3 to the Bardo; #5 to #5D and #7 to the Belvedere; #35 to the airport. Another bus terminal is in front of the S.N.C.F.T. Gare Centrale (Main Rail Station), Place Mongi Bali, from which trains depart half hourly for the southern coastal suburbs. Even in the rush hours few are hardy enough to try for a free ride as the number of inspectors seems equal to the number of buses.

By Taxi. *Petits taxis.* Call 241 312/3 for the small red and white cars that carry up to 4 persons within the city and inner suburbs. They are reasonable and the meter is always used. *Grand taxis* —station in Avenue Bourguiba (tel. 259 373). The price should be negotiated in advance.

TUNIS

Hotels

Deluxe

Abou Nasas, Ave. Mohammed V (tel. 350 355). 300 rooms. This new hotel opened in the summer of 1990 with well-appointed rooms, 2 restaurants, bars, heated pool, gym, and conference facilities.

Africa Meridien, 50 Ave. Bourguiba (tel. 347 477). 168 rooms. Highrise with two luxury floors, *Club President,* set apart; conveniently central. *La Rose des Sables* restaurant, *Les Caravaniers* coffeeshop, and for dinner dances *L'Etoile du Sud* on the 20th floor; pool and conference facilities.

International Tunisia, (El Hana), 49 Ave. Bourguiba (tel. 254 855). 228 rooms. *La Sofra* restaurant, and the popular *Brasserie des Deux Avenues.* The hotel has begun to take on a dingy appearance.

Oriental Palace, 29 Ave. Jean Jaurès (tel. 342 500). 388 rooms. Facilities include 2 restaurants—one specializing in North African dishes, the other in International cuisine—heated pool, gym, sauna, and conference room.

Tunis Hilton, Notre Dame Le Belvedere (tel. 282 000 or 800–HILTONS in U.S.). 236 rooms. Rather a remote location, but with a fine view. Grillroom, *Le Patio* restaurant, coffeeshop, bars, nightclub; conference facilities; large pool and terrace. Free bus service to downtown Tunis—less than 10 minutes' ride—every hour, and in summer to the hotel's private beach at Gammarth.

Expensive

Du Lac, 2 Rue Mont Calmé, at the beginning of Ave. Bourguiba (tel. 258 322). 202 rooms, 1 suite, forming an inverted pyramid. Quiet, fine view from the upper rooms. Many package tours; cheapest in this class, but efficiently managed.

El Mechtel, Ave. Taieb Mehiri, at the city end of the Belvedere Park (tel. 783 200). 450 rooms. Pool.

Khredding Pacha, 2 Ave. Khereddine Pacha (tel. 788 211). This new hotel has 96 modern and comfortable rooms with TV; coffee shop and restaurant.

Sofitel Diplomat, 44 Ave. Hédi Chaker (tel. 785 233). 136 rooms, 14 suites. 2 restaurants. Almost in the luxury class.

Moderate

Ambassadeurs, Ave. Taieb Mehiri (tel. 288 011). 90 rooms. Best choice in this class.

Carlton, 31 Ave. Bourguiba (tel. 258 167). 40 rooms. Central location, with adequate if sometimes noisy rooms.

Golf Royal, 51 Rue de Yougoslavie (tel. 344 311). 60 rooms. No golf course in sight, but it is central; also no restaurant, but there are lots close by.

Maison Dorée, 6 bis Rue de Hollande (tel. 246 254). 54 rooms, 30 with bath. Pleasant atmosphere and excellent service. Good restaurant.

Saint Georges, 16 Rue de Cologne (tel. 282 937). 36 rooms, 26 with shower.

Majestic, 36 Ave. de Paris (tel. 242 848 or 242 266). 90 rooms. Central, with pleasant coffee terrace; most expensive—but also best—in this grade.

Tunis Parc, 7 Rue Damas (tel. 286 696). 28 rooms. Near the Belvedere.

Inexpensive

Capitole, 60 Ave. Bourguiba (tel. 244 997). 43 rooms.

Commodore, 17 Rue d'Allemagne (tel. 244 941). 48 rooms.

De France, 8 Rue Mustapha M'Barek (tel 245 876). 50 rooms with bath or shower at this budget-rate place.

Dar Masmoudi, 18 Rue du Maroc (tel. 344 713). 33 rooms. Partly airconditioned.

Metropole, 3 Rue de Grece (tel. 241 377). 55 rooms.

Salammbô, 6 Rue de Grece (tel. 244 252). 52 rooms.

Suisse, 5 Rue de Suisse (tel. 243 821).

Transatlantique, 106 Rue de Yougoslavie (tel. 240 680).

Restaurants

Expensive

Reservation is recommended

L'Astragale, 7 Rue du Dauphiné, Le Belvédère (tel. 890 455). Fine French cuisine.

Belle Epoque, 16 Rue de l'Arabie Séoudite (tel. 281 704). Appropriate turn-of-the-century decor.

Dar Jeld, Souk, in the medina (tel 260 916). You may hear about this chic African restaurant from touts in the souk, but there have been complaints that the meals are too pricey. Show included.

El Khalil, 32 Ave. Louis Braille (tel. 893 609). Oriental atmosphere.

M'Rabet, Souk et–Trouk in the medina (tel. 263 681). Tunisian specialties in restored traditional setting; oriental dances.

Le Regent. Off Ave. Habib Bourguiba, behind Hotel Africa (tel. 340 417). Excellent French cuisine served here, considered the best in Tunis.

Saadi, Cité Olympique (tel. 247 599). Handy after sporting events.

Moderate

Le Babylon 32 Rue Amohides, El Menza 1 (tel 243 002) Simple but excellent seafood dishes prepared here.

Le Baghdad, 29 Ave. Bourguiba. Oriental.
Capri, 34 Rue Nahas Pacha. Pizzeria.
Chez Nous, 5 Rue de Marseille. French.
Chez Slah, 14bis Rue Pierre de Coubertin. Best Tunisian in this category.
Hong Kong, 85 Ave. Taieb Mehiri. Chinese.
Malouf, 10 Rue de Yougoslavie. Touristy Tunisian with good specialties.
Le Palais, 6 Rue de Carthage. A bit of everything.
Steak House, 31 Rue Garibaldi. As promised.

Inexpensive

Brasserie and **Pizzeria Schilling,** 93 Ave. Mohammed V.
Cosmos, Rue Ibn Khaldoun.
Le Grill, 17 Ave. Bourguiba.
Strassbourg, 100 Rue de Yougoslavie.

Cafes. Among the pleasant outdoor cafes on Avenue Bourguiba *the* meeting places of Tunis society are the **Café de Paris** (E) and the terraces in front of the Africa Meridian and the International Tunisia.

Le Cartage (M) under the arcades of the Ave. de France is a good place to watch the world go by. Most original is the terrace of the Majestic with its sun umbrellas and swings.

HOTELS AND RESTAURANTS

Northeastern Coast

Carthage (Amilcar). *Amilcar* (M), tel. 740 789). 250 rooms. On the beach near Sidi Bou Saïd; filled by package tours.
Restaurant. *Amphitrite* (E), near the hotel and station. *Neptume* (E) and *Tschevap* (M), on the beach near Sidi Bou Said, both good seafood.

Carthage (Hannibal). *Reine Didon* (E), tel. 275 447. 40 rooms. New edition of a famous old establishment. Splendid view. On the hill of Byrsa next to the museum and the cathedral.

Carthage (Salammbô). *Residence Carthage* (M), tel. 731 072. 18 rooms when open. Restaurant.
Restaurant. *Ball* (M), tel. 270 792. This newly opened place serves African and international cuisine.

Gammarth. *Abou Nawas* (L), tel. 741 444. 160 rooms. 2 fine restaurants, 2 pools, good beach, tennis. Set in a garden. *Residence Abou Nawas* (E). 60 apartments and studios.
Karim (M), tel. 741 533. 179 rooms, restaurant and snack bar; 2 pools, tennis courts, dialysis center for patients with blood and kidney disorders.
Megara (M), tel. 740 366. 77 rooms. Attractive Moorish decor; large pool and extensive garden. *Tour Blanche* (I), tel. 271 788. No showers in any of the 100 rooms, but a pool. Good *Le Soleil* restaurant.
Restaurants. *Les Dunes* (E). Restaurant-grill-pizzeria-nightclub by the sea. *L'orient* (E). This restaurant on the coast has a mixed menu and loyal clientele. *Les Ombrelles* (M). *Sinbad* (M), for seafood.

Gammarth-Raouad. *Cap Carthage* (E), tel. 740 064. 162 rooms. *Club Dar Nour* (E), tel. 241 000. 500 rooms in Moorish bungalows. Open-air theater, large pool on endless beach backed by eucalyptus forest.
Touring Club Village de Vacances (I), tel. 270 904. 250 thatched huts. Disco.
Restaurants. The coast's best and most expensive seafood. *Les Coquillages. Le Pêcheur, Select Club,* weekend dinner shows.

La Goulette. Restaurants. Not much of a setting, but tasty fish at moderate prices. *L'An 2000,* the newest in the port. *Canal 11. Monte Carlo. Petite Etoile.*

La Marsa. *Corniche Plaza* (I), tel. 270 098. 13 rooms. Restaurant; disco; noisy. Despite its name, it's in town.
Restaurants. *Au Bon Vieux Temps* (E), with a nostalgic touch. *Forum* (E). *Le Golfe* (E), at Sidi Addelaziz. *El Hafsi* (M), opposite the T.G.M. station.

Sidi Bou Saïd. *Sidi Bou Saïd* (E), tel. 740 411. 28 rooms, 4 suites. Heated pool and dining terrace.
In the port below, *Residence Africa* (M), tel. 740 600. 100 furnished flats.
Restaurants. *Dar Zarrouk* (E), tel. 270 703. Reservation necessary in this small ex-beylical palace high on the hill; justifies the very steep prices. *Le Pirate* (E), with the expected piratical trappings. *Le Chergoui* (M), also a cafe, on a terrace overlooking the port. *Le Café des Nattes* (M), is equally touristy, but serves little else beside mint tea.

Southeastern Coast

Borj Cedria. *Dar* (M), tel. 290 188. 144 bungalows on beach; geared for package tours. *Salwa Club* (M), tel. 290 764. 172 rooms. Pool. *Les Pinedes* (I), tel. 206 036. 200 huts in holiday village. Open summer only.
Restaurant. *Les Coupoles* (M), with nightclub.

Ez Zahra. *International Ez-Zahra* (E), tel. 482 550. 123 airconditioned rooms. Beach and large pool. *La Siesta* (M), tel. 480 959. 44 rooms, 14 baths. Good restaurant.

Hammam-Lif. *Bon Repos* (M), tel. 291 458. 12 rooms; restaurant. *Casino* (I), tel. 290 010. 16 rooms.
Restaurants. *Le Chalet Vert* (E), on the slopes of the Jebel Bou Kornine, commanding a fine view. *Les Sirènes* (M), near the beach.

NIGHTLIFE. Except for the nightclubs in the leading hotels, there is very little night life of high quality. In the Hotel Mechtel, *2001* is a popular disco. In the heart of the city, *Monseigneur* (E), at 2 Rue de Marseille, offers a variety show (airconditioned), as also the *Crazy Horse Club* (E), in the Colisée, the gallery off 45 Ave. Bourguiba.
The *Tunis Club* (M) tea room, Ave. Bourguiba, becomes a nightclub around 11 P.M. (airconditioned) and the *Pub-Sandwich* (M), Avenue de Carthage, is *the* rendezvous in winter. If you are looking for somewhere more intimate, try *La Potinière* (M), 11 Rue de Hollande. *La Source* (M), 11 bis Rue de Marseille is a discothèque, as is the *Black and White* (M), 93 Ave. Mohammed V. Men on their own may want to try their luck at *Champs Elysées* (M), 2 Rue du Caire, or at *La Grotte* (M), 25 Ave. de Paris. Most of these places have now grown seedy and run-down. A far better bet is a trip to *La Baraka* at Sidi Bou Saïd or *La Palaza Corniche* at La Marsa.
The northern suburbs offer more opportunities for entertainment, since one can dance in several hotels and restaurants, for instance at *La Cave du Roy* (E) in the *Reine Didon* (E) at Carthage. *La Baraka* (E) and the *Olivier Rouge* (E) at Sidi Bou Saïd are very fashionable.
In Gammarth, there is dancing at *La Caravelle* (E) in the Abou Nawas.
On the south coast the only real nightclub is *La Gaieté* (E) in Ez Zahra.
The oriental dancing at the *Malouf, M'Rabet* and *Le Palais* in town pleases some but is considered overpriced and unduly shifting the emphasis away from food by others.
The Gulf of Tunis by Night (M) is a boat ride lasting about two hours, organized by the Compagnie Navitour, 39 Ave. Bourguiba, with refreshments and music on board. Departures are from La Goulette.

ENTERTAINMENT. Performances of plays featuring actors from Paris are given during the winter at the Théâtre Municipal. The Tunis Symphony Orchestra gives a concert at least once a week. Your hotel porter should be able to advise you about current folklore events.

MUSEUMS. The Bardo Museum. Bus #3 from the port bus terminal; by car take Rue Bab Saadoun and Blvd. du 20 Mars beyond the medina. Open daily except Monday—9:30–4:30. Admission 1DT; 2DT surcharge for photographing. The exhibits from all parts of Tunisia are divided into four historical periods: Punic, Greek and Roman, Paleo-Christian and Arab-Moslem. The underwater finds from Mahdia contain some particularly fine Hellenistic bronzes. The pride of the collection of Roman mosaics is the unique picture of the poet Virgil seated between two Muses.

Carthage Museum. Open daily 8:30–6:30.

Coin Museum, 27 Rue de Rome. Coins from Carthage to the present day.

Museum of Folklore, in the Dar Ben Abdallah, Medina.

Museum of Islamic Art, Dar Hussein Palace, Place du Château, reached by Blvd. Bab Menara. Open daily 9–12, 3–6.

Museum of Living Art, Belvedere Park. Occasional interesting exhibitions.

Museum of Traditional Arts, Dar Khosroff, Sidi Bou Saïd.

Postal Museum, 29 Rue Gamel Abdel Nasser. History of the postal service; stamp collections; current issues on sale.

EXCURSIONS. A great variety of organized tours are available. Bookings can be made through hotel porters. The Roman site of Thuburbo-Majus and Zaghouan (½ day); Sousse and Monastir (1 day), Kairouan (1 day), Nabeul and Hammamet (½ day), Dougga (1 day), Carthage, Sidi Bou Saïd and the Bardo (½ day), and the oases of Tozeur and Nefta (2 days). For those traveling further south, many of these excursions are offered from other centers, but Dougga, one of the finest Roman cities in North Africa, is most easily accessible from Tunis.

SWIMMING. The pools of the luxury hotels are heated, but not usually open until the beginning of April and are closed in winter. A heated indoor pool at the Cité Olympique in El Menzah is heated and open year-round but has few opening times for the public until the summer. The municipal pool in Belvedere is heated and open only during the summer. At La Marsa Corniche a heated pool by the beach stays open all year-round.

SHOPPING. The Office National de l'Artisanat Tunisien (O.N.A.T.), at the corner of Ave. Bourguiba and Ave. de Carthage, in Ave. Bourguiba displays and sells the most beautiful products of Tunisian handicraft—souvenirs, fabrics and carpets. The luxury shops are all in and around the Ave. Bourguiba. All articles are sold under State control at fixed prices. The souks are rather disappointing, and hardly worth the endless bargaining.

For antiques, Ayoub, 27 Ave. Bourguiba and Evangelisti, Rue Jamâa ez-Zitouna in the medina, are expensive. More reasonable are the numerous shops in the Rue Zarkoun (right from Place de la Victoire, past the British Embassy along the Rue Mongi Slim and first left). This is the "flea market" of Tunis and you can find numerous reminders of the beylical and French colonial past—Berber jewelry, *marfas* (the ornate painted wall racks which once held Ottoman rifles), antique firearms, *objets d'art* of every description, fine examples of art nouveau and art deco, and above all, the enchanting primitive paintings on glass, an art that is fast dying. Bargaining is the rule here too, but it is less hard than in the souks.

USEFUL ADDRESSES. Tourist Information. Office National du Tourisme Tunisien (O.N.T.T.), 1 Ave. Mohammed V (tel. 341 077); 1 Ave. Moncef Bey (tel. 256 957); Port La Goulette (tel. 275 300); and at the Tunis-Carthage airport (tel. 236 000).

Travel Agencies. The largest are in Ave. Bourguiba: American Express, #59 (tel. 254 304); Cook, #65 (tel. 242 673); Afrique Voyages, #27 (243 310); Agence de Tourisme, #45 (tel. 258 240); Atlas Voyage, #29 (tel. 255 333); Carthage Tour, #59 (tel. 254 695); Oasis, #45 (tel. 244 325); Tourafric, #52 (tel. 245 066); Tunis Tour, #21 (tel. 244 243).

Car Hire. Avis, 90 Ave. de la Liberté, Hotel Africa, and at the airport; Hertz, 8 Rte. de la Charguia, the Hilton, and at the airport; Africar, 52 Ave. Bourguiba, and at the airport. Budget and Europcar also have offices at the airport along with a variety or rental agencies; it is worth shopping around as prices can vary substantially.

Airlines. GB Airways, 17 Ave. Bourguiba; Air France, 1 Rue d'Athènes; Tunis Air, representatives for TWA, 48 Ave. Bourguiba.

Shipping Agencies. Compagnie Tunisienne de Navigation, 5 Rue Dag Hammarskjold; D.F.D.S. Seaways, Atlas Voyage, 29 Ave. Bourguiba; Navitour, 8 Rue d'Alger; Tirrenia, 127 Rue de Yougoslavie.

Consulates. American, 144 Ave. de la Liberté (tel. 282 566); British, 5 Pl. de la Victoire (tel. 245 100). The Commonwealth War Graves Commission, 8 bis, Ave. des Etats-Unis.

Medical. Habib Thameur Hospital, Rue de Valence, Montfleury (tel. 490 600); Charles Nicolle Hospital, Ave. 9 Avril, Bab al Alauj (tel. 663 101); Aziza Othmana Hospital, Pl. du Gouvernement (tel. 663 655); SOS Doctors (tel. 341 250); SOS Ambulance (tel. 245 339).

Miscellaneous. Automobile Club, 29 Ave. Bourguiba; Touring Club, 15 Rue d'Allemagne.

Police (road safety and information), 1 Ave. de Carthage (tel. 254 427); Police for Foreigners, Ave. Bourguiba (tel. 262 088).

Central Post Office (P.T.T.), Rue Charles de Gaulle.

HAMMAMET AND REGION

The Tunisian Riviera

Hammamet is a walled village flanked by two vast beaches of fine sand, backed by luxuriant gardens, mild in winter, never too hot in summer. The Tunisian riviera curves along fertile land where vines, orange and lemon groves are shaded by tall cypress trees. Cap Bon enjoys the same delightful climate, but its beaches are still comparatively undeveloped. Inland, Jebel Zaghouan, the water tower of Roman Carthage and of modern Tunis, makes a pleasant excursion. At Thuburbo Majus the ruins of temples, houses and baths spread over a sun-baked plain.

Exploring Hammamet

Modern Hammamet is one of Tunisia's largest beach resorts. The huge hotel complexes usually consist of bungalows or pavilions around a main building, enclosed by trees in spacious gardens. Though the original plan that the buildings should not tower above the landscape has not been strictly followed there is little overcrowding—covering so large an area, and with hotels placed far apart, even in high season the resort seems to absorb tourists. The seemingly endless sandy beach is really the best route from hotel to hotel and in and out of town; the road at the back, lined with souvenir shops and bars, winds about between the hotels, making distances far too long for a comfortable walk.

Antiquity's not particularly distinguished Siagu-Puput, whatever that may mean, was sensibly renamed Hammamet by Arab conquerors, meaning either Bathing Places or, more romantically, Doves. Only in the 13th century was a kasbah built on the present site, but the existing fortifications and medina were constructed in the 15th century and extended during the Spanish occupation of Tunis (1535–69) by Charles V. Foreign legionnaires occupied it during the war, and for a time Rommel made his headquarters in the hotels. The narrow twisting streets are worth a visit, and the view from the kasbah walls, with the Moslem cemetery by the sea and the small boats on the beach below, is full of charm. The small museum houses a collection of regional costumes.

But to appreciate the uniqueness of Hammamet it is necessary to go back several decades, to an era when a few foreign artists and intellectuals built villas on this most beautiful of hitherto "undiscovered" beaches, and when Paul Klee and André Gide came here to draw inspiration among the groves of palm and eucalyptus, from the gleaming white houses of the fishing villages, the purple sea at sunset and the wonderfully changing sky.

The villa of Georges Sebastian, the great French conductor, acquired by the Tunisian Government in 1959, which Frank Lloyd Wright termed "the most beautiful house I know," sums up the spirit of the place. Seeming to fuse the Sudan with Capri and Santorini, and drawing inspiration from the Arab style of Kairouan, it is among the great achievements of modern architecture. From the outside it is a low square block in complete harmony against the sky. The interior is mainly one immense room with little furnishings—only low divans strewn with snow leopard skins brought from China. The ceiling is low, distorting and enhancing the apparent size and length, and the whole effect is cool and conducive to calm and comfort. The dining room, with a refectory table of monolithic marble, is contrived in such a fashion that it forms an open room beside the green tiled pool, with arcades all around. There are no guest rooms, but three or four bungalows, like koubbas, set in a garden of white oleanders and cypresses: and featuring high-vaulted bedrooms with antique mirrors and sunken Roman baths.

This delightful model has been debased in the relentless spread of vast vacation factories; only the luxury hotels attempt valiantly to recall the charm of those heady days. The Sebastian Villa has become the nucleus of the International Cultural Center (C.C.I.H.), where the annual Summer University is closely linked with the July/August festival. The standard of concerts and plays needs to be raised, but beyond the circular stage is the beach, the sea, the scent of lemon and orange, and the African night!

The Cap Bon Region

The Cap Bon roundtrip of 201 km. (125 miles) is most enjoyable, as from Soliman it is easy to get to Hammamet via Grombalia.

Nabeul starts appropriately some 15 km. (9 miles) from Hammamet with abandoned pits of red clay, as the finer white kaolin now predominantly used is brought from the Kroumirie. To the right are several truncated columns, sole remains of Punic and Roman Neapolis. Pottery and ceramics shops line the streets, olive stones, and even esparto grass, send black smoke spiraling into the blue sky. Most of the wares are of a showy vulgarity climaxing in paranoic inspiration, like a bust of Beethoven tattoed with traditional Islamic arabesques and flowers, his open skull sprouting a pot of poinsettia. Chemical colors have replaced the oxidized-metal powders, and only a few craftsmen follow tradition and make vases and water-coolers in the old shapes.

Nabeul is also an important center for wrought-iron work and elegant gates and grilles for the façades of grand houses. While the men work around the oven and the forge, the women sew. Friday is market day, a colorful sight. In Dar Chaabane, at the northern exit of town, the ceramists and stone-carvers work side by side. Here sculpted lintels and carved door-posts are made for the well-off homes of Tunisia. Nabeul beach is a continuation of Hammamet beach, with the same fine sand but without shady gardens. Blanket and rug weavers live in Beni Khiar. At Mâamoura the road is bordered by majestic eucalyptus trees shading the rich dark red earth.

After Korba, Roman Curubis, a narrow strip of sand separates the open sea from a salty lagoon, with darting birds. Shady avenues lead to attractive estates which were built by French settlers and today have become cooperative farms. Vines, olive trees, cereals, and orchards have made Cap Bon rich ever since the Punic era.

Two *marabouts* perched on hillocks at either end of the beach keep watch beyond Menzel Temime as you leave the village. Rocky shoals, rich in fish, tempt you towards the sea, but it is better to wait until Kélibia, where the steep headland overlooks the shore.

In the port below, the Fishing Office runs a training school for Tunisian fishermen, but many of them go back to the methods of their ancestors. In front of the peninsula, fish are plentiful in the rocky depths, which are also ideal for underwater fishing. The best beach is 2 km. (1 mile) to the north at Mansoura where cheap villas have been built by Belgian developers along the road which goes around the headland. Borj Kélibia, the Roman fortress Clupea, on top of its 81-meter (266-foot) rock, has been restored. One of the eight square bastions houses a museum amid the vaulted walks with thick-set columns, plus a Byzantine chapel and a modern lighthouse.

The Ruins at Kerkouane

After Kélibia, the road passes through fields or pine and eucalyptus groves. 9 km. (5 miles) further on, a road branches right to the sea; the excavations at Kerkouane have brought to light the best preserved Punic town, founded in the 6th century B.C. and destroyed 400 years later. The layers of sand protected the ramparts, the baths with mosaic-decorated pools and the drainage system; in many cases the house walls still have their facing of colored clay. Columns tower up from the site of a sanctuary. In a small atrium with a well there are fragments of figurative mosaics. Here and there at bends in the streets there are curbstones, doorsteps, well-worn thresholds, red mosaic flooring picked out with white stones.

The sea is slowly eroding Kerkouane. Floors stop at the edge of fish-filled shoals. An oven clings to the cliff face. But the archeologists continue to reveal traces of a community which Rome thought she had consigned to oblivion. The necropolis lies 1 km. (½ mile) inland.

El Haouaria and Sidi Daoud

After Kerkouane the road moves away from the sea and passes to the south of Jebel Abiod. At its foot the inhabitants of El Haouaria still practise falconry and birds captured in the jebel are used for hunting at sunrise or sunset. In a wild region 3 km. (2 miles) from the village, the "cave of the bats" is worth a visit. And 2 km. (1 mile) from there, at Ghar el Kebir, you can see the enormous caves where shelly limestone of first-rate quality has been quarried since ancient times. You can also make a trip to the tip of Cap Bon (Ras Addar) with its lighthouse. And behind it, from the top of Jebel Abiod (393 m., 1,289 ft.), you can see Sicily and part of the Tunisian seaboard.

A piste branches for 4 more km. (2½ miles) to the remote Ras el Drak beach, a paradise for campers, underwater divers and fishermen. Between El Haouaria and Sidi Daoud, Roman Missua, the road passes through a landscape of trees stunted by the wind. The Fishing Office runs a tuna-canning factory here, which is in operation during the months of May and June. Fishing methods are the same as in Sicily and Portugal: the shoals of tuna try to swim around the enormous tunny net which stretches several kilometers from the shore, a hundred feet from the surface to the sea bottom. But other nets gradually force the fish, twisting and turning, into the trap, a "corpo" net which is surrounded by large fishing boats. The men sing the *chaloma* while hauling in the net. The singing gives way to shouts as the men jump into the nets, stabbing the fish till the sea turns red.

Pliny gives a vivid description of the annual tuna migration and Romans used this knowledge, setting out from the port of Missua, whose remains lie to the south.

The Island of Zembra and Korbous

15 km. (9 miles) offshore from Sidi Daoud, a rock island covered with undergrowth emerges from the sea: Zembra, separated from Cap Bon by its small sister Zembretta, which is just a reef. In the bay with cliffs as high as 430 meters (1,410 ft.), the International Nautical Center runs a sailing and water-sports school.

7 km. (4 miles) from Sidi Daoud, MC26 loses sight of Zembra and Zembretta and plunges into pinewoods. Here and there tracks lead to deserted beaches, while inland rises scrub-covered Jebel Sidi Abd-er-Rahmane (637 meters, 2,089 feet). In a series of hairpin bends MC26 crosses the Douela pass, then descends through vineyards and olive groves. Eucalyptus-lined avenues lead to Provençal-style farms established by French settlers.

Before Soliman, MC128 is cut into the cliff face, leading to the right (north) towards Aïn Oktor and Korbous. After the hamlet of Sidi Raïs—lost in vineyards which produce a fruity white wine—the view alone makes the detour worthwhile, even for those not afflicted with any of the increasing number of ailments for which cures are promised at the local spa. The panorama of the entire Gulf of Tunis to La Marsa on the western headland is particularly impressive at sunset.

MC128 overlooks the valley at whose bottom is the little white town of Korbous, once Aquae Caldiae Carpitanae, where the Romans used the hot springs (50–60°C) for rheumatism. Snuggling between the ocher-colored slopes of the valley, Korbous opens towards the sea. The thermal establishment on the shore is based on the principal spring, Aïn el-Kebira, now also recommended for the treatment of arthritis, cellulitis, and hypertension. It is connected with a pavilion built by Ahmed Bey, and is flanked by a small minaret. Much grander is the President's villa which commands the valley; below, the rock of Zerziha has been worn smooth by the many women who have slid down it in the belief that it would bring fertility.

MC128 continues north along the coast for 2 km. (1 mile) to the warm spring of Aïn Atrous, site of a Greek oracle, the cliff face bright with sulphur yellow, green and red from the high mineral content of the water. A track leads to the charming cove of Kallat Sgira. Beyond Soliman the motorway leads south to Hammamet via Grombalia 35 km. (22 miles) and west to Tunis 30 km. (19 miles) via Hammam-Lif.

Zaghouan and the Aqueduct

The day excursion from Hammamet to Thuburbo Majus, 80 km. (50 miles), includes the Roman ruins of Zaghouan. 10 km. (6 miles) south of Hammamet, to the right of GP1 at Bou Ficha, stands a massive Roman mausoleum, Ksar Menara—the lighthouse castle. The squat round tower, damaged at the top, on a square pedestal, resembles in miniature the tomb of Caecilia Metella in Rome. Close by, the ancient road runs alongside GP1, and passes over a strong Roman bridge with its thick arches still in good condition. A little further along GP1 moves away from the brilliant blue gulf.

MC35 branches right (northwest) to Zaghouan, across a rich and well-cultivated plain. After 8 km. (5 miles), a track leads to Jeradou, an old Berber village, perched on a mountain peak. Nearby, at Bir el Fouara, are Roman temple ruins within a Byzantine castle. Scenic MC35 turns right (north) to Tunis, while MC28 takes over straight (west) to the junction with MC133 just outside Zaghouan. The latter road comes from Enfida on the coast, via the very simple thermal installations of Hamman Zriba, and the Défile de la Hache (the Defile of the Axe) where Hamilcar hemmed in the rebel mercenaries. MC133 continues right (northwest) through Zaghouan, a pleasant little white town on the slope of Jebel Zaghouan, whose springs water luxuriant orchards. A small Roman triumphal arch is almost the only remaining trace of ancient Ziqua. A sideroad branches to the marabout of Sidi Ali Azouz, covered with polished green tiles and decorated with intricate stucco-work and ceramics. There is an extensive view, taking in a modern Provençal-style church, converted into a mosque since the departure of the French whose farms were scattered over the plain.

2 km. (1 mile) beyond another of the President's villas, MC133 passes the Nymphaeum, the Temple of the Nymphs, built in the 2nd century in the reign of the Emperor Hadrian at the foot of the Jebel's steep slope. The sanctuary forms a semi-circle 30 meters (100 feet) wide by 35 meters (115 feet) long, built against the rocky cliffs. The only remains are the outside walls, with 12 niches which once contained the statues of the nymphs.

The water still gushes forth into a reservoir with two chambers before entering Hadrian's tremendous aqueduct, 55 km. (34 miles) to Carthage. MC36 follows the impressive remains on the shortest but largely unpaved route north to Tunis. Since there were no pumps, an even slope was indispensable and the water crossed the valleys on high arches which can still be seen, while it passed through the hills by means of an underground canal. The modern canal network which today brings water from Zaghouan to Tunis incorporates the underground Roman canals in some places.

From the Temple of the Nymphs a piste climbs the Jebel past the Zaouia de Sidi Bou Gabrine to the television relay station at an altitude of 950 meters (3,117 feet). The view on a clear day embraces a large part of northeastern Tunisia; it is even better from Raz el Guessa 1,295 meters (4,249 feet), the summit. Though an easy climb, it is advisable to leave at dawn to get back during the afternoon.

For a less dusty return to Tunis keep on MC133 via Moghrane and Sminja to Jebel el Oust, a minor thermal station for the treatment of rheumatism, more frequented by the Romans than it is now, as witnessed by the considerable ruins. From here it is 31 km. (19 miles) north on GP3 to Tunis.

Thuburbo Majus

Coming from Zaghouan, MC28 crosses GP3 just north of Le Fahs to the well-signposted ruins of Thuburbo Majus, 56 km. (35 miles) southwest of Tunis. The fertile plain was inhabited by Numidian farmers before the arrival of the Romans. A colony of veterans was established under Augustus in the year 27 B.C. and prospered in Hadrian's time under the name of Colonia Julia Aurelia Commoda. Like all the towns of the African province, it had beautiful monuments and splendid houses, but always remained a place of secondary importance. The name Thuburbo Majus was not given to it until the 4th century, when it was rebuilt after a period of eclipse lasting 150 years. The excavations are fairly limited and can be visited easily.

The Capitol was built on a platform as the Roman planners wanted to dominate the forum. There are vaulted rooms on the platform where the municipal treasure and archives were kept beneath the feet of Capitoline Jupiter. The temple still has part of its colonnade. Four columns with Corinthian capitols have been restored. Climb the steps from the Forum to the Capitol, and you are at the religious and political center of the small town. As in Rome, it was here that all the official religious ceremonies took place. Fragments of a monumental statue of Jupiter lie on the floor of the *cella*.

At the foot of the Capitol steps lies the 40 meters (130 foot) square Forum. The paving has almost completely disappeared, although several columns of the porticos still remain. In the left-hand corner of the Forum—facing away from the Capitol—is the Curia (the municipal senate), which is reached by steps. Notice the two bases of columns from the portico and a stele decorated with a rather worn Pegasus. At the far end of the Curia is the council chamber, where there are the bases of a few statues and fragments of well-sculpted soffits.

At the far end of the Forum, in the right-hand corner, is the market. It is a smaller square with a well in the center. Some of the shops are still decorated with parts of mosaics. They were not unlike the booths or stalls in Tunisian souks today. On two sides the market had porticoed rooms, one of which still has its mosaic floor.

In the middle of the right-hand side of the Forum is the little round Temple of Mercury, which must have been a most elegant building. Behind this rotunda was a square cella overlooking the Street of the Waggoner. The streets of Thuburbo Majus do not follow the geometric layout of the great Roman cities, but are of varying width and there are no clearcut intersections. The Forum could only be reached by alleyways that emerged into the corners, whereas traditionally there would have been broad avenues leading to the center of the four sides.

Following the Street of the Waggoner we pass in front of the ruins of some houses. One of these, the House of the Labyrinth, on the left, completely filled the space between the Street of the Waggoner and the Street of the Labyrinth. The intersection of these two streets is marked by a large stone with an inscription. After the intersection, again on the left, lie the ruins of the House of the Waggoner. The road continues to the end of the excavations.

Here, to the left, the Street of the Winter Baths leads the few meters to the portico of the baths. Although a town of secondary importance, Thuburbo Majus still had two public baths, one for winter, the other for summer. The layout of the Winter Baths is irregular. This lack of order, unusual in a Roman town, is also apparent in the houses of Thuburbo Majus, which are "made up of haphazardly placed rooms, lit by tiny court-yards which are not necessarily in the center of the building."

You enter the Winter Baths through a doorway with columns, three of them still with their capitals. After passing through the tiled vestibule, you cross several rooms to get to the *frigidarium* (cold room), where the walls were once covered with marble and where the green mosaics, deco-rated with black lines fringed with white, suggest cool water. The other rooms make up the *caldarium* (the hot rooms). To the right is a hall with geometrical mosaics, and three out of four original columns still standing.

Beyond the Street of the Waggoner the small temple of Baal is an inter-esting reminder of the local religion's persistence. The raised cella is sur-rounded on three sides by a polygonal portico. To the right—facing the steps leading to the cella—an arch leads to a small forum formerly sur-rounded by porticos.

The Street of the Petronii leads to a Palaestra with a very fine Corin-thinian portico with black marble columns. A long dedication engraved on a frieze shows that it was offered by Petronius Felix and his sons. Vari-ous rooms open onto the Palaestra. One to the southeast, paved with mar-ble and preceded by two columns, is a sanctuary of Aesculapius. Nearby are the ruins of a Byzantine church.

The Summer Baths are to the southwest of the Palaestra. They are larg-er than the Winter Baths (about 2,800 square meters instead of 1,600). The floor of the vestibule and the pools were covered with mosaics, the walls of the cold rooms with marble. The hot rooms were heated by several fires. A very deep well ensured a good supply of water.

Backing onto these baths, a semicircular building, with columns and a sculptured ceiling, housed the latrines which were probably the most luxurious urinals in the world.

To the southeast, near the excavation site, a church was built during the sixth century over an ancient temple of Baal and Tanit. The ocher-colored stone subfoundation still survives. The black limestone columns were re-used, a part of the courtyard was transformed into a cemetery and a baptismal font installed in the pagan cella. On a hill to the east, a Byzan-tine fortress was built on the site of a temple of Saturn.

Returning to Tunis on GP3, visit Mohammedia, named after Moham-med Bey who built here a first palace in 1758. Not quite a hundred years later Ahmed Bey started no less than three, but for lack of money the vast palace complex on the hill side was never finished, the lovely wall- and floor-tiles were used for the decoration of the Bardo and the Carthage resi-dence, so that only romantic arcades and towers, dotted over extensive gardens grown wild, remain of what is grandiloquently but misleading called Tunisia's Versailles.

The road back to Tunis leads through flat and barren country.

PRACTICAL INFORMATION FOR
HAMMAMET AND REGION

WHEN TO GO. Hammamet and the southeast coast of Cap Bon are pleasant at any time of the year. The coast is sheltered from the north winds and the scorching sirocco from the south has been cooled by its journey over the sea by the time it reaches Hammamet. But it may rain quite heavily from December through February. Bathing is enjoyable from May through October.

The International Cultural Center in Hammamet organizes an International Festival of ballet, theater and music in July and August. It was set up to provide accommodation for artists and writers and it promotes lectures and conferences.

The Nabeul Fair (April) has other attractions, as well as its commercial side— evenings of folk dancing from different regions, processions of newly married couples and other entertainments.

GETTING THERE. By Car. Distances from Tunis: to Soliman 30 km. (19 miles); to Korbous 49 km. (30 miles); to Hammamet on Tunisia's only motorway 63 km. (39 miles); to Nabeul 65 km. (40 miles); to Kélibia 95 km. (59 miles); to Sidi Daoud 89 km. (55 miles); to Thuburbo Majus 62 km. (38 miles); to Zaghouan 57 km. (35 miles).

By Train. Regular trains from Place Mongi Bali, Tunis, to Hammamet and Nabeul.

Group Taxis. This is a better way of getting around. Many departures daily for Hammamet and Nabeul from Garage Soudan 2, 4 bis Rue Soudan, in Tunis. Fare about 30DT–5DT, depending how successful you are at bargaining with the taxi driver. Taxis back to Tunis leave from Hammamet station.

By Bus. There are frequent bus services every day between Tunis, Nabeul and Hammamet and the main towns of Cap Bon. Bus station on both sides of the junction of the Rue Djazira and the motorway. Ask your hall porter in Tunis or the hotel at your destination to arrange your transfer.

HOTELS. Almost sixty hotels, with not a single highrise among them, are strung out along the beautiful sandy beach that stretches on both sides of Hammamet. The deluxe hotels are on the south beach, which is the smarter side. Most hotels lie in gardens and even Moderate establishments have swimming pools, tennis, riding and nightclubs, with airconditioning in the public rooms. The hotels are farther from the town and more spaced out than at most resorts, but all are filled with package tours. Many hotels remain open all year round.

Area code 02.

Deluxe

By price and most other standards these are deluxe though not officially listed as such, except for one.

Abou Nawas (tel. 81 344). 225 rooms. Large pool. Available here are restaurants, a nightclub, sports facilities, and baby-sitting services.

El Minar (tel. 81 333). 203 rooms. This is considered the finest resort hotel in Tunisia. There are 3 restaurants plus a beach restaurant in summer, satellite TV, 3 pools, 2 nightclubs, and baby-sitting services. Sports facilities include waterskiing, fitness rooms, and sauna.

Phoenicia (tel. 80 336). 372 rooms. 2 pools, one half covered for bad weather. *La Panache* is the best of several restaurants. Many rooms do not face the sea but have terraces.

Sheraton (tel. 80 555 or 800–325–3535 in U.S). 205 rooms in six Moorish buildings. Attractively furnished with a good bar and a band for dancing. White arches and vaults abound in the restaurant and the food is excellent. Large heated pool with a bar in a sunken domed pavilion, as well as extensive patios and gardens.

Sinbad (tel. 80 122). 149 rooms, 7 apartments. Pleasing architecture in particularly lovely gardens extending to the beach. Close to the town; small pool.

Expensive

Bel Azur (tel. 80 544). 289 airconditioned rooms. North of town. Beach is not entirely up to standard, but lovely pool and terraces. Two restaurants.

Dar Hammamet (tel. 81 440 or 81 610). This 500-room resort is owned by Club Med and offers all the amenities and facilities associated with the organization.

Dar Khayam (tel. 80 454). 232 rooms. North of town. Unfortunately shares some of its facilities with the Moderate *Omar Khayam* (see below).

Fourati (tel. 80 388). 340 rooms, 20 suites. South of town. Much enlarged round the original villa, with some rather cramped additions amid exotic plants.

Grand Hotel (tel. 80 177). 125 rooms. North of town. Good service; poolside barbecue and large pool.

Le Hammamet (tel. 80 160). 225 bungalows. South of town; not on beach, but with large pool and good food.

Hammamet Beach (tel. 80 400). 250 rooms. North of town. Rather sterile complex in several buildings, but above average terraces and pool.

Hammamet Club (tel. 81 882). 200 rooms. This newest resort, owned by the French chain, Nouvelle Frontières, is operated similar to a Club Med.

Miramar (tel. 80 344). 140 mostly airconditioned rooms in 2 blocks and 18 bungalows. Set in spacious gardens. In the S.H.T.T. chain. South of town.

Les Orangers (tel. 80 144). 228 rooms, 20 bungalows. South of town. Pleasant indoor and beach restaurants, where service is friendly but slow; large indoor pool open to non-guests.

Le Paradis (tel. 80 300). 221 bungalows. Some distance south of town, on quiet beach.

Parc Plage (tel. 80 111) and **Continental** (tel. 80 049). 198 and 178 airconditioned rooms respectively. South of town. Under the same management, with services shared. In large park; pool.

Le Président (tel. 81 100). 205 rooms. Better than most.

Sultan (tel. 80 705). 250 rooms. South of town. In the Iberotel chain.

Yasmina (tel. 80 222). 96 rooms. South of town. Closest to the medina, with large pool.

Moderate

El Bousten (tel. 80 126). 380 rooms for mass tourism. South beach.

Les Charmes (tel. 80 010). 170 rooms. Restaurant, nightclub, pool.

Du Golfe (tel. 80 010). 170 rooms. South of town. Reception, bar, and dining-rooms are all in one room.

Méditerranée (tel. 80 433). 224 rooms. North of town.

Omar Khayam (tel. 80 355). 97 rooms, 145 bungalows. North of town. Popular with large groups.

Pacha Club (tel. 80 077). 100 rooms in central block, and 50 bungalows. South of town.

Residence Hammamet (tel. 80 408). 184 airconditioned apartments in the town center. Small roof pool.

Sahbi (tel. 80 807). 105 rooms. In town center; no pool; family-run with pleasant atmosphere.

Tanfous (tel. 80 213). 250 bungalows on the beach, with restaurant, nightclub, pool, and sports facilities.

Inexpensive

Baie du Soleil (tel. 80 298). 225 bungalows in a resort setting; restaurant but no pool.

Bennila (tel. 80 356). 27 rooms in a friendly boarding house. 300 yds. from the beach.

Samira Club (tel. 80 016). 544 beach huts. South of town. Holiday village.

RESTAURANTS. As package tourists mainly eat in their hotels, these greatly outnumber the eating establishments. Among the *Expensive,* the best bet is shared by **Le Berbère** and **Chez Achour** serving seafood in the port, and **La Perle Du Golfe,** a new restaurant that is gaining an excellent reputation.

Also (E)—**La Pergola** and **Les Trois Moutons** are in the town center. **Sidi El Bahri** emphasizes Tunisian specialties in the Ave. Bourguiba. **Jugurtha** and **Orangerie** are in the Ave. des Nations Unies. **La Mama** is valiantly Italian, further south.

Moderate are **Bella Italia, Barberouss, Sand Pub, Quick L'Orient, Belle Vue,** and **Latos** in town.

NIGHTCLUBS. Beside those in luxury hotels, the *Sidi Bou* (E), *Le Pacha* (E) to the south, and *Sahara City* (E) at km. 64 on GP1 offer folkloric shows.

Nearly all other hotels feature discos, supplemented by a few outside disco-restaurants. *Mexico, Ranch Club, La Tortue* and *Tropicana,* south, *Top Kapi* north. All are (M).

HOTELS AND RESTAURANTS FOR THE HAMMAMET REGION

El Haouaria. *Epervier* (M), tel. 97 017. 11 rooms.

Jebel el Oust. *Cheylus* (M), tel. 79 977. 45 rooms.

Kélibia. *Ennacim* (I), tel. 96 245. 30 rooms. *Florida* (I), 96 248. 13 rooms. Both in port and facing each other. *Mamounia* (I), tel. 96 088. 81 bungalows in a holiday village. *El Mansourah* (I), tel. 96 156. 116 rooms in a holiday village. Best of the four.

Korba. *Club Méditerranée* (M), tel. 88 411. 600 thatched huts.

Korbous. *Aïn Oktor* (E), tel. 94 552. 27 large rooms overlooking the Gulf of Tunis from a cliff; no beach. *Les Sources* (E), tel. 94 533. 140 airconditioned rooms. Apartment hotel. Thermal pool; thermal cures for kidney and liver complaints.

Restaurant. *La Touristique* (E).

Nabeul. *Kheops,* (L), tel. 86 555. Newly opened deluxe hotel, the first in Nabeul. *Al Diana Club* (E), tel. 85 400. 230 rooms. Halfway between Hammamet and Nabeul. Sports facilities; but a little remote. *Iniem* (E), tel. 22 310. 80 rooms, restaurant, pool, and sports facilities. *Lido* (E), tel. 85 104. Vast holiday complex of 194 airconditioned rooms in a central block, and 300 bungalows.

Aquarius Club (M), tel. 85 777. 86 rooms in central block, 252 bungalows. *Les Mimosas* (M), tel. 87 964. 132 rooms. *Nabeul Plage* (M), tel. 86 111. 285 rooms. Not directly on beach. *Le Prince* (M), tel. 85 470. 216 rooms in bungalows. *Les Pyramides* (M), tel. 85 444. 350 bungalows. Large pool and playground for children. *Ramses* (M), tel. 86 363. 150 rooms, 64 simple bungalows. *Riadh* (M), tel. 85 744. 57 rooms, 38 bungalows.

Club Maamoura (I), tel. 85 717. 254 simple huts. Far to the north. *Les Jasmins* (I), tel. 85 343. 32 rooms, 15 bungalows. Behind the rail tracks.

Restaurants. *Karim* (M), *Monia* (M), and La Rotunde (M), all with a variety of dishes. *L'Olivier* (M), pizzeria.

Soliman Plage. *Solymar* (M), tel. 90 105. 30 rooms, 155 bungalows. On own beach close to Tunis (30 km., 19 miles). *Les Andalous* (I), tel. 90 280. 135 bungalows. Also on own beach.

Zaghouan. *Jebel El Oust* (E), tel. 79 740. 45 rooms. *Les Nymphes* (M), tel. 75 094. 40 rooms.

Zembra. *Club Nautique* (I). 24 bungalows in a holiday village.

EXCURSIONS. The hotels and travel agencies offer a variety of excursions from both Hammamet and Nabeul. Included are day trips to Tunis and Carthage, Kairouan, Sousse and Monastir, also a two-day trip to the southern oases of Tozeur and Nefta on weekends. Visitors can rent a car through their hotel porter (often the hotel has its own vehicles) to visit nearby Zaghouan and the Roman ruins at Thuburbo Majus.

MARKETS. If you like picturesque sights you can visit the country markets: Monday at Kélibia, Tuesday at Menzel Temime, Thursday at Menzel Bou Zelfa, Friday at Nabeul (colorful and good for snaps), Sunday at Korba. Pottery at O.N.A.T. shop, Ave. Habib Bourguiba, Nabeul.

FISHING. For tuna-fishing at Sidi Daoud from May to June ask at the National Fishing Office, 26 Ave. de Paris in Tunis. At the Ras el Drak beach, 4 km. (2½ miles) from El Haouaria, sheltered by the Jebel Sidi Aboid, the coves are full of fish, including the famous gilthead. The port of Kélibia is a fishing center. Underwater fishing is also possible.

WATER SPORTS. The Island of Zembra, a huge mass of rock facing Sidi Daoud, is famous for its **sailing, cruising,** and **diving** schools. People aged 18 to 35 (in June and September 18 to 40) who wish to take a course at the Island of Zembra should contact the Centre Nautique International de Tunisie (C.N.I.T.), 22, Rue de Medine, Tunis. Three different courses are offered: 1) for everyone: sailing—beginners and refresher courses—introduction to underwater diving; 2) for keen yachtsmen—cruising; 3) for underwater diving enthusiasts—a 15-day course. Accommodation at Club Nautique de Zembra. Travel connections are arranged by the C.N.I.T. from Sidi Daoud. There is also waterskiing and paraskiing over the sea on Hammamet beach.

TOURIST OFFICES. Hammamet: Office National du Tourisme (O.N.T.T.), Ave. Habib Bourguiba (tel. 80 423). **Nabeul:** O.N.T.T., Ave. Taïeb M'hiri (tel. 86 737).

BIZERTE

Ports, Ancient and Modern

Alluvial deposits buried the Punic city of Utica, founded in 1101 B.C., according to Velleius Paterculus; they also buried Ghar el Melh (Salt Hole), formerly Porto Farina, naval arsenal of the beys, which was succeeded by the French Navy's African version of Toulon. The fleet is gone and tourism has taken over the fine beaches round Bizerte, providing a ready market for the rich and well-farmed plain of the lower Mejerda. The large clean and busy villages with deep pools of shade beneath their arcades and arched passageways cling to the fertile hillsides where fruits and vegetables grow copiously.

Exploring the Bizerte Region

First stop on the road to Bizerte from Tunis is Ariana, a town made prosperous by its Coptic community from the eighth century, although it also has a number of 16th-century Andalusian ancestors. Sidi Abar is buried there, mortally wounded during the Crusades of St. Louis, in the battles along the coast of Carthage. Age-old vineyards and olive groves line the road to Cebala ben Ammar, 17 km. (11 miles), which has an ancient fountain reached by an arcaded gallery supported by four columns. Then the alluvial basin of the Mejerda begins and the road, here and there shaded by eucalyptus trees, runs between two tracks of loosely-packed earth, along which pack- and draught-animals trudge. From Protville a branch leads right (northeast) to Kalaat et Andalous, 11 km. (7 miles) away, built by Andalusians who hoped to dominate the vast plain from this promontory. The main road crosses the Mejerda and numerous drainage canals which sometimes contain more water during the summer than the river. A recently completed conduit brings water to the orchards and fields of Cap Bon far to the east. To the right of Zana, 30 km. (19 miles) from Tunis, is the road to Utica. Two km. (1 mile) after the crossroad the first ruins appear.

Utique (Utica)

From the end of the second millennium B.C., Utica was the first port of call along the African coast of the western Mediterranean. It traded in tin and was the oldest of the stopping-places on the way to Gades (Càdiz) on the Atlantic. Despite the shallows, which probably existed even at that time, the Mejerda estuary provided good anchorage for shallow-draught boats, while the fertile hinterland was a source of trade for the Phoenicians. However, when Dido fled Tyre taking with her eighty virgins from Cyprus for childbearing and for the benefit of the sailors, she scorned Utica and founded Carthage. This was because the sea was already retreating before the gradual advance of alluvial deposits left by the river and the light flat-bottomed boats had given way to larger, heavier vessels.

The Romans landed at Utica in 149 B.C., and three years later, after the fall of Carthage, it became the temporary capital of the Roman province of Africa, Vetus (Old Africa), but the Roman pro-consuls soon returned to the site of the former Phoenician capital. In one of those strange twists in history another Cato, a descendant of the man most responsible for Carthage's destruction, committed suicide here exactly 100 years later, after the defeat of Sextus Pompeius and the republican forces at the battle of Thapsus (Ras Dimas) in 46 B.C. In the midst of Roman prosperity Utica declined, due to the silting up of the port. From a fishing village on a marshy delta, it changed into an agricultural settlement 10 km. (6 miles) from the sea, with wheatfields growing on the quays where Phoenician and Roman galleys once anchored. An ephemeral revival by Moors and Jews, driven out of Spain in the 15th century, left no marks.

Today, although the ruins spreading over a small plateau may be moving, they are hardly impressive. What is left of the baths lies behind a reconstructed portal, with remains of basins and pools with mosaic bottoms, and fragments of marble paving stones. Further on is the Punic necropolis where rather worn sandstone sarcophagi from the 6th century B.C. have been found. A Roman columbarium has been partially restored and other traces of ancient Rome are scattered over a second fairly unspectacular excavation site.

The most evocative remains of Utica are collected in the Antiquarium and the Lapidary Museum. Several Roman mosaics are exhibited in situ. In the interior of the Antiquarium, the items are arranged according to their historical period: statuettes, pottery, Phoenician household objects found in a cemetery, Carthaginian stelae, Roman statues from villas and tombs, coins. *Sic transit gloria mundi.*

Ghar el Melh

After Utica, the road leaves the alluvial plain. To the right MC69 leads, via Aousdja, to Ghar el Melh, on a lagoon linked by a narrow channel, constantly threatened by alluvial deposits, to the open sea. Now only fishing boats can enter it, although in the 16th century the navy of Emperor Charles V anchored there before attacking Tunis. A hundred years later, the pirate Ousta Mourad built a fortress there. Later some Andalusians settled around his stronghold. Orchards grew up all over the area. The fort, however, could not in 1654 stop Admiral Blake breaking through the defenses, sailing into the lake, and pillaging the bey's navy. In the 18th century, the beys tried in vain to make Ghar el Melh their naval base. Forts and an arsenal were built but the Mejerda, more persistent than the architects, continued to silt up the harbor and made dredging impossible. Ghar el Melh is still a fortress flanked by casemates of ocher stone, with a polygonal tower, topped with cupolas. A luxury resort has long been planned, but is delayed by the crisis in tourism.

The road passes under a shady archway where peasants squatting on their heels sell their products. Back in the sunlight, another crenellated fortress appears; there are cooling fountains and further on you come to a port with crumbling quays and bobbing fishing boats. There are nets drying and flags flapping in the wind. On land, the arcades of a damaged portico mellow in the sun. Higher up, the slopes of the Jebel Nador give off the scent of brushwood.

A road leads to Sidi Ali el Mekki through groves of palm trees whose roots sometimes draw water from the lagoon, right up to a white sandy beach which disappears into the open sea. On the side of the cliff is the marabout of Sidi Ali el Mekki which looks like a small fort.

The alternatives to Bizerte are via El Alia, a lovely village of square white buildings decorated with arches, turning right after Aousdja. Or else, 2 km. (1 mile) to the right, before this place, by Raf-Raf and Ras el Jebel. Raf-Raf is a picturesque village, famous for its grapes and its sand. Coming downhill—and noticing on your way the sea and tiny rock island eroded into a curious shape—you soon reach the seashore where there are cabins to rent and good underwater fishing. Metline dominates the slopes and the summit of a hill scarred by a ravine.

Cap Zebib is redolent with tuna fish and sardines in season, out of it with the less inviting putrefying remains. You have to turn inland to rejoin the main road. Three km. (2 miles) before Bizerte you branch right to the beach of Rimel through a forest.

Bizerte

The town—or the ground it stands on—keeps its secrets well. No important remains have yet been uncovered, but the modern city stands on the site of the ancient Hippo Diarrhytus. At the junction of the two Mediterranean basins, it is backed by a huge lake, protected from silting up by the Garaet (Lake) Ichkeul, which acts as catchment area. It is not surprising that the French thought it an ideal place for an arsenal and naval base which were only evacuated in 1963. Today, Tunisia is trying to make full use of this fine natural port. Menzel Bourguiba houses a metallurgical complex. A refinery treats the oil from Borna in the south.

The modern city has not recaptured the liveliness it had when French sailors with their red pompons strolled there. Nevertheless, the old city is worth a visit. After crossing the canal—finished in 1895—turn right along Quai Trak Ibn Ziad to the Sport Nautique restaurant. Then follow Bougatfa Avenue, which runs beside the sea, past the Casino; before the bridge which runs over the channel of the Vieux Port, it comes to an old

Spanish fort with crenellated walls and the El Ksiba Mosque. Another approach to the old town is to take Bourguiba Ave. from the roundabout in Bougatfa Ave., leading away from the sea, for about 200 meters, before turning right to reach the Fruit Market (Marché aux Fruits) and the Robaa Mosque. Seventy-five years ago the canal, which is now filled in, passed through this quarter. It linked the lake to the Vieux Port, which is surrounded by arched alley-ways sometimes lined with arcades.

You can follow the quay to the Place 13 Janvier 1952. This brings you to a fountain and then to the Great Mosque, with its octagonal minaret. From there, the Rue des Armuriers and the Rue des Forgerons lead to the Place du Marché, the market-place, facing the entrance to the kasbah. This labyrinth of little streets, protected by a 17th-century mosque, dozes in the shelter of the ramparts.

You reach the Andalusian quarter by the Rue El Medda. The neighboring hill is crowned by the Fort d'Espagne, a 16th-century Turkish construction; from it there is a beautiful view of the town. Finally above the Military School there is the international cemetery where Serbian soldiers were buried during World War 1.

The environs of Bizerte—Cap Blanc, northernmost promontory of Africa, the village of Béchateur, a number of beaches—make a pleasant roundtrip as you can return via the Sfaïat pass of Jebel Nador.

PRACTICAL INFORMATION FOR
BIZERTE AND REGION

WHEN TO GO. Preferably from May to September. Although it is very hot in summer near Lake Bizerte, it will be pleasantly cool on the beaches. In the fall there may be thunderstorms.

GETTING AROUND. By Car. From Tunis by GP8: 65 km. (40 miles); from Tabarka: 148 km. (92 miles).

By Train from Tunis, 1 hour 50 minutes—several departures a day.

Louage (shared taxi) from Tunis: gare routière, 72 Ave. Farhat Hached and Kiosque Esso, 14 Ave. Ali Belhaouane. Fare, 1.5 DT. At Bizerte, louages leave from the gare routière for Tunis, Béja, Tabarka and other northern destinations.

Bus Station. Place Trak Ibn Ziad. Departures for Tunis, Menzel Bourguiba, Ghar el Melh, Mateur and Tabarka.

HOTELS. It is hard to recommend any of the town hotels with a clean conscience. Only the *Sidi Salem* (M), 30 bungalows on town beach, but of doubtful hygiene and poor food, comes even remotely close to measuring up.
Area code 02.

Along The Corniche. The only hotels that can really be recommended are on the Corniche road. All provide water sports, riding and boat trips to Cani Island (about one hour) from the coast as well as fishing. *Corniche Palace* (E), tel. 31 844. 87 rooms. *El Kebir* (M), tel. 31 892. 200 rooms in holiday village on the excellent beach; good value despite the lack of heating (though this is not of burning importance, as the place is closed Oct. through April). *Jalta* (M), 32 250. 138 rather small rooms; no pool. *Nador* (M), tel. 31 846. 100 rooms. Adjoins the Moorish cafe and is under the same management; round a lovely patio, with pool but no disco. *Petit Mousse* (M), tel. 32 185. 12 rooms. Excellent restaurant. Farther out on Cap Blanc.

Menzel Bourguiba. On the Bay of Bizerte. *Younès* (I), tel. 60 057. 16 rooms.

RESTAURANTS. *Le Bosphore* (M), Rue d'Alger. Bonheur (M) and *L'Eden* (M) are both new and serve simple, but good food, in town in the old port. *Possada* (M), Ave. Bourguiba. *Sport Nautique* (M), at the beginning of the beach. On the Corniche—*Belle Plage* (M).

EXCURSIONS. In Zarzouna (near the bridge on the Tunis side), take the road south for Menzel Abd el Rahman 4 km. (2½ miles) to enjoy lovely glimpses of the lake through the olive trees. Continue to Menzel Jemil, 8 km. (5 miles) inland. There a road to the left climbs the Ben Negro hill: beautiful view of the lake. From Menzel Jemil join the Tunis road to Bizerte. To reach Cap Blanc, leave Bizerte by the Corniche road which leads to several hotels, and runs beside the beach. Crossing Cap Bizerte the road slowly climbs to Cap Blanc 8 km. (5 miles). At the foot of the cliffs, the sea breaks over rocks. Continue to the top of Jebel Nador 260 meters (853 feet) and return to Bizerte by Nador and the Sfaïat pass: there is a panoramic view over the town and the lake.

To visit Béchateur and Sidi Abd el Ouahed beach, leave Bizerte by Ferhat Hached Boulevard. Béchateur 4 km. (2½ miles) away is a pretty village built on the top of a Roman *oppidum* amid Barbary fig-trees. From there you can reach Sidi Abd el Ouahed 20 km. (12 miles)—a series of beautiful sandy beaches, in little coves, near reefs and islets. The waters are full of fish here.

SHOPPING. O.N.A.T. shop, Quai du Vieux Port: lace, patterned long-pile carpets, wrought iron.

USEFUL ADDRESSES. Tourist Information. Office National du Tourisme, 1 Rue de Constantinople (tel. 32 897). **Post Office,** Rue d'Alger. **Police,** 20 Ave. du 20 Mars. **Hospital,** Rue Saussier.

THE TELL

The Heart of Tunisia

The Tell offers an escape from the madding crowd, in the wooded areas of the Mogod and Khroumiria and even along the little frequented coast. Visit Tabarka, a picturesque port which, though it has escaped the onslaught of tourism, nonetheless has a number of hotels. Ain Draham, in the woods, is an agreeable summer vacation center frequented by Tunisians. Nearby is the Jebel Bir (1,014 m., 3,327 ft), one of the highest points in the Khroumiria, a well-watered mountain region, pleasantly cool in summer.

Prosperous Béja, set in a fertile plain, is the successor to the Roman cities which were made rich by the granaries of the Mejerda basin. The rolling fields stretch to the horizon. After the harvest, the countryside seems all one color, with the tawny camels feeding on the yellow stubble and the houses made of brown mud.

The elaborate underground villas of Bulla Regia and the ruins of Dougga ranged against a hillside deserve a visit, as does Le Kef, a pretty village perched on a spur and protected by crumbling ramparts. If you are hardy you can go on as far as the mountain platform—called the Table of Jugurtha—which overlooks the Algerian-Tunisian border.

Exploring the Tell

GP5 from Tunis into the heart of the Tell passes the Bardo to Massicault, 31 km. (19 miles); in a grove of eucalyptus is the War Cemetery where 1,576 British and Commonwealth soldiers rest. This town, situated near the Mejerda, is heir to the ancient city of Membressa whose wheat fed Rome. On either side of the road, cultivated fields cover as yet unexplored sites; the land is so fertile that it would be too costly to expropriate it.

Mejez el Bab, 60 km. (37 miles), was the key position of the Allied front during the campaign in Tunisia. The British First and Eighth Armies fought fiercely before their final victorious advance on Tunis in April 1943. West of the town and north of the road to Le Kef is one of the largest war cemeteries in Tunisia, where 2,904 British and Commonwealth troops are buried. Near the Cross of Sacrifice runs a long wall on which is the inscription:

"On this famous battleground of the ancient world two armies converged from the west and the east in the year 1943 to set free North Africa and make open the way for the assault upon Southern Europe."

At Toukabeur—Roman Thuccabor—14 km. (9 miles) from Mejez el Bab (the road to the left as you leave the town, going towards Tebourda), children will take you through orchards and gardens to see sections of walls, bases of columns and the remains of a triumphal arch. The cisterns of long ago now house cattle pens. Two km. (1 mile) farther on are the remains of Punic tombs cut into the rock wall.

Béja

GP6 leads west to Béja, an important market town at the junction of three main highways. Béja was built on the site of Vaga, one of the principal cities of Numidia, which came under the overlordship of Rome in 105 B.C. to develop into the largest African wheat market. Béja is set in a majestic landscape of broken hills, bright green in spring and autumn, but bleached in summer. The country is fertile, growing mainly grain, but there are a few vineyards. From the keep of the kasbah there is a fine view and in the Mzara quarter some curious cave dwellings still exist.

13 km. (8 miles) south of Béja (the road becomes a mediocre track towards the end), there is a Roman bridge in excellent condition, wrongly called the Pont de Trajan as it was built in the reign of Tiberius; its 70 meters (76 yards) span the Oued Béja. To reach the ruins of Dougga take the MC75 for Thibar and Teboursouk (47 km., 29 miles from Béja).

GP6 turns southwest to the valley of the Mejerda at Bou Salem, a large prosperous market-town on the plain. Some well-kept small forts nestle in the palm and eucalyptus woods and the streams have cut their way through the rich soil. We cross the Oued Tessa and then the Oued Mellegue. Their water flows into a river whose character can change drastically, sometimes raging, sometimes sluggish. It brings in turn devastation and abundance to the plain it irrigates.

50 km. (31 miles) from Béja is Jendouba near the ruins of Bulla Regia. From Jendouba you can get to Tabarka, 70 km. (44 miles) north, via Ain Draham, by crossing the wooded mountains of the Khroumiria or else to Le Kef which is 45 km. (28 miles) south.

Lakes and Mountains

The first alternative allows for a worthwhile roundtrip, including Bizerte or, if in a hurry, a return on the GP7 to Tunis via Mateur. As many tourists undertaking this excursion may be staying at the beaches of Bizerte, we shall start from there. The GP11 leads to Mateur, which you can miss at no great loss, by taking at Tindja the scenically much lovelier MC57 facing the 511 m. (1,677-foot) Jebel Ichkeul and skirting the Garaet Ichkeul, a large lake into which the oued waters flow before they reach Lake Bizerte. In the springtime, when its banks are covered with wild flowers, it attracts water birds and hunters.

MC57 turns south through a well watered plain to join GP7 shortly before the railway stop of Jalta; MC51 continues west along the Oued Sedjenane to MC66 and Cap Serrat. On GP7, Jefna lies at the foot of the Mogod mountain range. A small stone pyramid with the inscription "Greenhill, the Argylls, November 1942," marks the place where the Allied Front held firm during the winter of 1942–3.

Once past Jefna, the landscape changes; the road winds through woods of oak and the little stone houses with their beaten earth roofs. The railway station of Aouana serves the Bazina mines further south. The entire region contains deposits of zinc and lead which are exploited in a modest way. The iron mines have been abandoned as unprofitable.

At Sejenane, a small, cool village which lives off the forest, pasture lands and mining, the MC66 branches north to Cap Serrat, through brush covered hills where wild boar abound. A track leads to the lighthouse from which you can see all the way to La Galite, a group of rocky islets.

After Sejenane, the mountains become higher and various tracks lead through oak forests to the sea. There are some Roman ruins near the Sidi Mechrig beach, 20 km. (12 miles), protected by cliffs below which the sea teems with fish. The beach of Cap Negro is even less accessible.

Along the main road, Tamera's red-tiled roofs are hidden in the trees. In the neighboring undergrowth, ferns and gentians grow and streams cut their way through the red earth. The improvement in the standard of living is indicated by the way dwellings have evolved; branch huts have given way to little houses with white walls and tiled roofs.

About a mile after Tamera the road passes under a viaduct. Immediately to the left are the openings of the Punic tombs cut into the rock; they have all been looted and are sometimes used as sheep pens. A little further on the road enters the Nefza plain, parts company with the railway line for the time being, passes through the village of Nefza and then winds along the Khroumiria mountain pass.

In spring and summer, in the shade of the cork oaks, children hold baskets of raspberries and wild strawberries. After the village of Ouchtata and the Oued Titria with its banks of sand and rock (the favorite swimming place of the strawberry sellers), a region of dunes has been driven far inland by the north wind. After Ain Sebaa, the contours of the landscape become more restrained and the road comes to a region exposed to the sea wind; matting protects the trees; and the sea is again visible.

Near the school of Ain Sebaa, a road to the right crosses the railroad tracks, runs through eucalyptus and pine woods, crosses a very pretty stretch of dunes and reaches the deserted beach of Jabbara about 8 km. (5 miles) away.

Tabarka

The port of Tabarka is hemmed in by the mountain and the sea, crowned by an old fort; a fine beach stretches to the east; the west coast is rocky. Coral fishing is a traditional pastime. Tabarka is a name of Phoenician origin, meaning "dense" or "thickly wooded." The Romans built a causeway across the narrow channel separating the island from the mainland, which is the site of the modern port. The few late Roman remains found here are mainly funerary items and have been put, along with the mosaics of the region, in the Bardo Museum. One of the mosaics illustrates what rural life was like on the edge of a forest full of wild animals. This remote region attracted Christian monks and St. Maxime is said to have been the Abbess of a convent but no traces of it have ever been found. The Vandals seized several monks here and took them to Carthage to suffer martyrdom.

Tabarka was a haunt of pirates, then a coral fishing center. It aroused the greed of the Genoese who settled on the island and built a fortress. In 1741, the Bey of Tunis destroyed their settlement and annexed Tabarka and the island to his states. France developed the town but its port, in competition with neighboring Algerian ports, never reached great importance. A jetty has been constructed partly on the foundations of the Roman embankment. Cork oak is the main export and a factory for processing cork helps to maintain the town's activity, while local craftsmen make their contribution by preparing the briar roots which are sent to the French Jura where the pipes are finished off.

In the town, in the Rue des Kroumirs there is a secularized church, which was built inside an enormous ancient cistern. Going along the sea round the port towards the west, you reach the Aiguilles, a curious group of ocher colored rocks jaggedly eroded. From the end of a pier extending into the sea, you can see the whole port and the contorted rocks of the coast.

The island, shaded by some 600 trees, is still protected by the ruins of the Genoese fort. To the east of the port lies an immense beach, where the wind has formed dunes which, in some places, reach inland. On the heights above the town there are remains of Ottoman forts. There are two of them on the way out of town on the road to Algeria. One is abandoned, the other is occupied by the Tunisian army. From the road there is a beautiful view of the port, the rocks and the island. Seven km. (4½ miles) from Tabarka, a poor track leads to the isolated Melloula beach.

There is no regular transport to the Archipel de la Galite, 65 km. (40 miles) out at sea from Tabarka, but the boats that do go there usually leave from Tabarka. Only the main island, a steep rock 5 km. by 2 km. (3 miles by 1 mile), is inhabited by a few fishermen. Crayfish are plentiful around the island and the nearby reefs. The small island of Galiton shelters a colony of seals and hunting them is strictly forbidden. Punic tombs, Roman ruins and pirate caves are in the best Tunisian tradition, brought up to date by former President Bourguiba's exile here in 1952. There is no accommodation at Galite, but the inhabitants are friendly to campers. There is a danger that in bad weather your stay there may be prolonged.

From Tabarka to Aïn Draham

GP17 from Tabarka to Jendouba runs through flat countryside and then climbs the mountain mass covered with huge cork oaks and other trees.

Babouche is a village in the forest near a pass on the road to Algeria. Near the frontier, in Tunisian territory, is the Borj el Hammam spa.

At Aïn Draham, the Source d'Argent up 800 meters (2,600 feet), the climate is appreciably different among greenery and cool springs. The town is less interesting than the surrounding countryside with its lovely walks through the forest. The Tourist Information Bureau suggests some routes so complicated that you are almost bound to lose your way. No matter, the whole forest is beautiful.

The Col des Vents, 2½ km. (1½ miles) from Aïn Draham is the departure point for a walk and a drive. In about 30 minutes you can climb Jebel Bir on foot (1,014 m., 3,300 feet). By car, there are 20 km. (12½ miles) of sometimes poor track: the Oued-el-Lil dam surroundings are worth seeing as far as the forest house of the oued. If the track is too bad further on, you can go down to the oued on foot. The splashing of a pretty waterfall will reward your trouble.

From the Col des Ruines a footpath climbs to the summit of Jebel Fersig (30 minutes).

Along GP17 to Jenouba, 44 km. (28 miles) from Ain Draham, the oak trees form beautiful glades around two simple hotels. In the village, facing the Hôtel Beauséjour Fougères, two large tree stumps cut into the shape of animal heads draw attention to the Maison de l'Artisanat, where you can find Khroumir carpets, objects of carved wood and original pottery.

Bulla Regia

Shortly after Les Chênes, a detour of about 10 km. (6 miles) brings you to the Ben Métir dam (1955). Its full capacity is 73 million cubic meters of water, which forms a large lake covering 850 acres. The purified water is conveyed to Tunis. The road crosses the dam and then runs along the Oed El Lil valley, with several fine views over the valley, and finally reaches the main road near Fernana.

The countryside changes; the cultivated steppe and the Barbary fig trees reappear. Once again, the oueds cut their deep beds through the loose-packed earth; near a metal bridge over the Oued Rhezalah, a high water marker several yards tall speaks of the unpredictability of the waters. Here is the fertile soil of the Mejerda basin with the first palm trees and olive groves among the wheat fields.

Five km. (3 miles) before Jendouba a signpost points to Bulla Regia to the left. MC59 to the ruins is bordered with eucalyptus and fruit trees and continues towards Bou Salem. A thorough visit of the ruins, north of the road, requires half a day. The baths, a large two-storied building, immediately catch the eye, but you need the custodian to visit the underground villas. There is no set charge for his services, but he won't refuse if you offer him 500 millimes.

The site of Bulla Regia was populated well before the Roman domination. Archeologists have uncovered Phoenician-type burial places with shafts and chambers. Less than half a mile south of the baths there are dolmens. The name Regia given to the town by the Romans indicates that it was a royal Numidian residence. Hiarbas, a successor of Massinissa, sought refuge there in 81 B.C. During the Roman Empire, the town grew as the grain of the Mejerda brought wealth to the settlers from Italy. On this low plateau, cut off from the sea by the Khroumir mountains, the wealthy landowners built beautiful underground villas which have survived in good shape; and are the main attraction of the site.

At the entrance, the thermal baths were so well built that some mosaics have survived. Two pools face each other from either side of a central room, where niches once contained statues. A partly excavated paved road

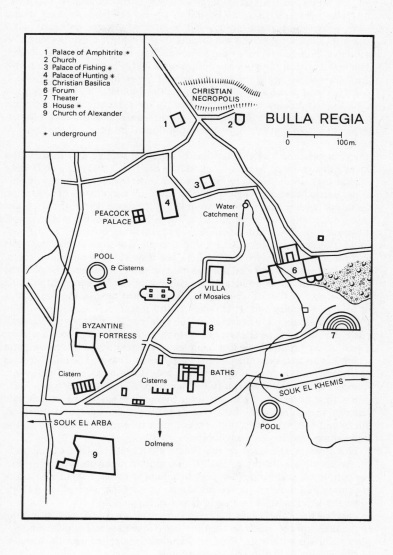

1 Palace of Amphitrite ✳
2 Church
3 Palace of Fishing ✳
4 Palace of Hunting ✳
5 Christian Basilica
6 Forum
7 Theater
8 House ✳
9 Church of Alexander

✳ underground

CHRISTIAN
NECROPOLIS

BULLA REGIA

0   100 m.

PEACOCK
PALACE

Water
Catchment

POOL
& Cisterns

5

VILLA
of Mosaics

6

BYZANTINE
FORTRESS

8

7

Cistern

Cisterns

BATHS

SOUK EL KHEMIS

SOUK EL ARBA

Dolmens

POOL

9

leads to the antique theater; another branches north alongside the baths for 150 meters to the first underground house: the Villa des Mosaïques. A staircase leads down to this beautiful summer residence situated several yards below the present-day ground level. Two cisterns collected water and also allowed light and air to pass to the central room by means of windows. This central room was surrounded by rooms with mosaic floors. The upper part of the villa has disappeared, but it is easy to imagine how the light was arranged in this cool retreat beneath the burning ground.

To the west of the Villa des Mosaïques, the foundations of a 6th-century Christian basilica have been uncovered; it has a double apse and marble columns. There is a paving ornamented with birds and fish, and a baptistery with a deep font for baptismal immersions. The altar is at the opposite end.

150 meters north of the basilica, beyond the stubble and thistles that cover ruins revealed by soundings, stands the Palais de la Chasse (Palace of Hunting), a sumptuous residence which owes its name to a mosaic now in the Bardo Museum. At ground level, there are the remains of an atrium, decorated with mosaics and surrounded by columns. From there a staircase leads to the underground part of the villa, more than 6 meters down, a fine room with Corinthian columns and the living quarters. In the bedrooms, lighted and ventilated by shafts, cupboards are cut into the walls and the little stone steps show where the beds stood. The dining room, with a beautifully decorated floor, is built on top of a cistern. The pleasant flow of cool air gives an idea of the efficient airconditioning of the Bulla Regia houses of the 3rd century A.D. The kitchen next to the staircase is lit by two air-holes and its chimney is still intact.

Cross the street on the east side of the Palais de la Chasse to the mysterious Palais de la Pêche (Palace of Fishing), unlikely to have been a private dwelling. At ground level is a complex of rooms grouped round a patio which has an apse decorated with a lovely mosaic basin. The underground part is reached by a wide ramp which goes down to a central patio surrounded by roomy archways. In the middle of the patio there was a fountain with a gutter leading to a cistern. In one apse-shaped room a mosaic representing Cupid as a Fisherman (Amour Pêcheur), surrounded by ducks and fish, has given this vast complex its name and has led to the supposition that it was a sanctuary.

The street north leads to the Palais d'Amphitrite. One of the well-preserved mosaics in the basement represents Amphitrite with Neptune; the couple are surrounded by Cupids holding crowns. Two other Cupids are riding dolphins; one is holding a mirror, the other a jewel-case. (Photography is allowed; a flash-light is not indispensable.)

Leaving the Palais de la Pêche to our right, we follow a path leading to the large spring which served the town in the past and which now supplies Jendouba with water. The modern tank is installed near the remains of the ancient shrine to the water nymph.

In front lie the remains of the Temple of Apollo and the Forum; farther back, the Capitol and a basilica. To the south, a paved way leads to the theater, reached also by a street from the baths. Chariot wheels wore away the stone and wheel hubs left their mark on the wall of the theater. The semicircular auditorium is in good condition but the back wall has almost disappeared; the stage still has a mosaic of a bear. Despite all the damage, the theater has preserved its excellent acoustics, as witnessed during occasional performances in spring and summer.

South of the theater lie the remains of a residential quarter. By taking the old street to the baths, we soon come upon a Temple of Isis: the podium still has some column shafts and its steps. Almost opposite are the ruins of a large villa opening onto a rectangular garden where the tanks for watering the garden have survived.

Chemtou

A visit to the marble quarries and the ruins of Chemtou, and even more of remote Thuburnica, which have not been excavated, can complete the visit to Bulla Regia. (Cross the road from Tabarka to Jendouba and take MC59 which is an extension of the Bou Salem road.) Chemtou, with its marble quarries, is 18 km. (11 miles) from the cross-roads over scrub-covered hills. The remains of ancient *Simittu* are scattered among the vegetation: the Forum, the semicircular theater and the remains of the baths. The foundations of a temple in the Hellenistic style from the Punic period, built north of the quarries in the second or first century B.C., on a site deserted today, have provided interesting information about Greek influence on the Punic and Numidian civilizations.

Dougga

At the entrance of Bou Salem, MC75 branches right (southeast) to Thibar, where a seminary was established in 1895 as an agricultural college by the White Fathers. This missionary society was founded in the 1870s by Cardinal Lavigerie in Algeria and spread into different parts of Africa. Although the order is credited with only one conversion in Tunisia, it was outstandingly successful in the cultural and educational spheres, establishing museums, schools, experimental farms and plantations throughout the country.

Among the extensive vineyards and farmlands surrounding the seminary, some ruins indicate the site of the Roman town of Thibari. From Thibar a track leads to the village of Jebba and from there you can make an energetic but interesting excursion into the Jebel Goraa. On the way, make someone point out to you the location of the grotto of the Sept Dormants (Seven Sleepers), with its entrance closed by an ancient great wall. According to popular folklore, seven holy young men retired there to sleep 309 years away from the world. This legend of the Eastern Christians is sacred teaching for Moslems as it appears in the Koran (Chap. XVIII).

The road then reaches Jebba, situated in a rocky landscape with caves. One cave was formerly dedicated to Our Lady of the Goraa. Others are used as dwellings or animal pens. From the top of Jebel Goraa, 963 meters (about 3,000 feet) high, you can see as far as the Jebel Zaghouan.

16 km. (10 miles) before Teboursouk, a branch left leads to Ain Melliti and its mineral springs. Next comes a track, again left for approximately 6 km. (4 miles), to Matria, ancient Numuli, built on a rise. The ruins are very dilapidated but include a temple, two basilicas, thermal baths and cisterns.

Teboursouk is built on the side of a hill overlooking the valley of the Oued Khalled planted with olive trees. The sloping streets lead to a Byzantine town, taken over by the Arabs; from it there is a good view. The modern town lies at the foot of the hill along the roads to Le Kef and Tunis.

The road to Dougga (6 km., 3½ miles away) leaves from the market place in Teboursouk and runs above the valley of the Oued Khalled beside

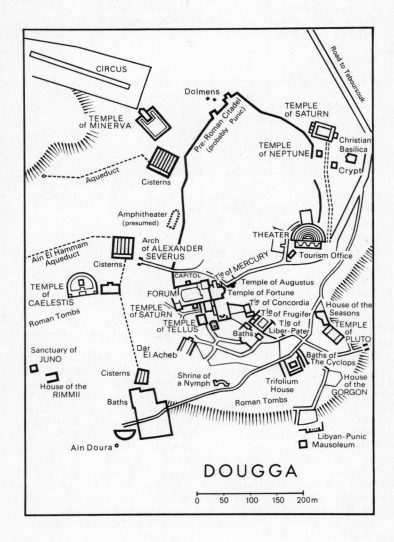

CIRCUS

Dolmens

TEMPLE
of MINERVA

TEMPLE
of SATURN

Pre-Roman Citadel
(probably Punic)

TEMPLE
of NEPTUNE

Christian
Basilica

Crypt

Aqueduct

Cisterns

Amphitheater
(presumed)

THEATER

Ain El Hammam
Aqueduct

Arch
of ALEXANDER
SEVERUS

T<u>le</u> of MERCURY

Tourism Office

Cisterns

CAPITOL

Temple of Augustus

TEMPLE
of
CAELESTIS

FORUM

Temple of Fortune

Roman Tombs

TEMPLE
of SATURN

T<u>le</u> of Concordia

House of the
Seasons

TEMPLE
of TELLUS

T<u>le</u> of Frugifer

T<u>le</u> of
Liber-Pater

TEMPLE
of
PLUTO

Sanctuary of
JUNO

Dar
El Acheb

Baths

Baths of
The Cyclops

House of the
RIMMII

Cisterns

Shrine of
a Nymph

Trifolium
House

House
of the
GORGON

Baths

Roman Tombs

Ain Doura

Libyan-Punic
Mausoleum

Road to Téboursouk

DOUGGA

0   50   100   150   200m

marble quarries which have been worked since time immemorial. The ancient town of Thugga, situated on the side of a hill up to 1,800 feet, deserves a thorough visit, but the principal remains, the theater, the Forum, the Temple of Caelestis, on almost level ground with well-marked paths, can be seen in about an hour.

Thugga, already an important town during the Punic era, became one of the residences of Massinissa, a Numidian king who was a Roman ally. A temple, which has disappeared, was dedicated to him. During the 2nd and 3rd centuries, Thugga developed like all towns of Roman Africa and the region was densely populated. There were ten cities within a radius of 50 km. (30 miles). From the second half of the 3rd century, little more was added to the town. The remains date from the same period and have great unity of style, except for the Punic mausoleum built five centuries earlier than the rest.

Immediately to the right of the entrance is the theater. Built in 168 A.D. it had 3,500 places—relatively few for a town of the size and importance of Thugga. Behind the stage was a wall which has disappeared; a colonnade behind this wall permitted people to stroll and enjoy the view during intermissions. The theater was restored in about 1910 and now is again used for performances. Tunnels below the wings connect directly with the car park.

To the right a path leads up to the Temple of Saturn, which was built shortly after the theater. The lovely columns of its vestibule can be seen from some distance and in front an esplanade affords a good view of the town and surrounding countryside. An underground tomb has been uncovered below the temple, as well as a small Byzantine church.

The antique street from the theater and the tourist office leaves to the left a small semicircular sanctuary dedicated to Augustus, next to the foundations of the Temple of Fortune partly covered by a mosque.

Three steps lead to the square of the "Rose des Vents" (the rose of the winds) where the names of the twelve winds are still visible. At the bottom is the Capitol of amber-colored stone, opening onto a remarkably well-preserved peristyle. To the right are the remains of a portico in front of the Temple of Mercury. The interior is made up of three rooms: the middle one is rectangular, the others are semicircular. An unusual plan, which is duplicated with some modifications in the Temple of Tellus.

Opposite the Temple of Mercury stood the market, which was under the protection of the god of commerce. The haste with which the Byzantines erected fortifications in about 540 from the ruins left behind by the Vandals in 438 A.D. is apparent in the poor quality of the wall which they built against the back of the Capitol. Eleven steps lead to the portico of the Capitol, one of the most beautiful monuments in North Africa. The four monolithic columns of the facade support a pediment which has suffered little from the passage of time. On the tympanum are the remains of a relief symbolizing the apotheosis of Antoninus Pius; you can make out an eagle carrying a man in his claws. The inscription carved on the frieze mentions the names of the gods to whom the sanctuary was dedicated: Jupiter, Juno and Minerva, the usual Capitoline triad, and the name of the donors, the Macii. Thugga owes its theater and Capitol, built at approximately the same time, to their generosity.

The statues of the gods have disappeared from the pleasantly cool *cella,* but the columned portico looks upon a vast landscape. Contrary to custom, the Capitol faces the plain, whereas traditionally it would have faced the Forum. Perhaps it was to thank the gods for the fertile land from which Thugga drew its wealth; or to impress travelers passing the foot of the hill on their way from Carthage to Tebessa.

In front of the Capitol is a small esplanade—a lovely rectangular square down seven steps. The bases of the portico columns are still in place.

Among the olive trees, to the right, an ancient street passes under the triumphal arch of Alexander Severus which was built about 60 years later. Nearby are some cisterns.

Another wonder of Thugga, the Temple of Caelestis, built at the same time as the triumphal arch (about 230 A.D.), is 100 meters from the Forum. The sanctuary's limestone columns have been re-erected on the platform reached by twelve steps. A semicircular courtyard, enclosed by a high wall bordered by a portico, isolates the sanctuary and allowed the processions and sacred mysteries of the followers of Juno Caelestis (the Romanized version of Tanit) to take place in private.

Near the temple is an overflow tank. Beyond the olive trees are the ruins of a little sanctuary dedicated to Juno and the remains of a burial-place. Lower down are the rather uninteresting remains of the baths. From the esplanade in front of the Capitol, a gently-sloping ramp leads to an ancient well-paved street. To the left, down from the Forum, stand the remains of the Temple of Tellus, which opens off a small courtyard with a portico. The main room is flanked by two adjoining rooms with apses, similar to the Temple of Mercury.

Residences, Baths and Brothels

The hillside road winds to the wealthy residential area. The houses are in ruins and have been stripped of their best mosaics, which have been placed in the Bardo Museum. However, we can imagine the way of life of the Roman settlers who lived in these rooms, built round little court-yards with porticos. Some of the houses, such as the house called after Dionysus and Ulysses, were built on two levels. A stairway along the side of the hill led from the upper floor at street level down to the lower floor with the traditional central courtyard.

The area is overlooked by the high walls of the Licinian baths (3rd century), entered by a long tunnel, the service entrance leading to the vestibule. A lovely room paved with mosaics was surrounded by a portico with twelve columns, seven of which have been raised again. All around were the hot, warm and cold rooms. There was also a small palaestra. From the room with the twelve columns, a large staircase leads up to the temples of Frugifer, Concord and Liber Pater, of which only the foundations remain. Lower down, the tiers of a small theater face the plain. They are all that remain of what was undoubtedly a monument in which sacred mysteries were celebrated.

The temples to which this monument belonged were dedicated to Romanized Punic deities and were built on the site of Numidian sanctuaries when the Roman town began to develop (around 125–135 A.D.).

Below the small theater was the House of Trifolium, Thugga's largest building, a brothel, whose obvious trademark—a phallus—has been modestly removed, so as not to contradict the guide's vague references to the "mansion." The usual courtyard is replaced here by a garden surrounded by a portico with the working quarters opening off it. One of these rooms which is shaped like a clover leaf has given this opulent dwelling its name. Its mosaic floor is now at the Bardo Museum.

The ancient street runs near the Baths of the Cyclops, whose entrance is on the right. These are in ruins, except for the latrines, which are remarkably well-preserved. In a stone bench shaped like a horseshoe, there are twelve holes side by side; the waste channel joins the street gutter and at the entrance there is a wash-basin. Not much privacy there, to put it mildly. Straight ahead is the badly damaged arch of Septimius Severus; to the right is the Punic mausoleum whose pointed silhouette can be seen from afar. The only important Punic monument to have survived dates from the 3rd century B.C., when Carthage and the Numidian princes dominated North Africa. The removal of an inscription (now in the British Museum) by the English consul to Tunis in 1842, led to the collapse of the funerary tower. It has been restored to the original height of 21 meters (60 feet), on a square base decorated at the corners with Ionic pilasters. Three tiers support the third story, which still has fragments of statues of horsemen in each corner. With binoculars, you can make out some bas-reliefs on this story, representing four-horse chariots with two drivers. In the corners there are pilasters with capitals with Egyptian details. The monument is topped by a pyramid with statues of winged spirits at the four corners. At the very top a crouching lion is perched.

The funerary chamber was most probably on the first or second story of the edifice. The dedication, in the British Museum, indicates that the monument was erected in honor of Ateban, son of Iepmatah, son of Palou. Then follow the names of the architects.

Other funerary towers were built in Thugga before the Roman era and archeologists have found some remains, but it has not been possible to reconstruct any of them.

For a complete view of Thugga, return to the Forum and follow the line of the Numidian wall which extends to the north, curving round from the Forum to the Temple of Saturn whose huge foundations are clearly visible for 100 meters. To the northwest, outside the wall, you can still see some dolmens, the damaged ruins of a Temple of Minerva, well-preserved cisterns and the site of a circus.

Testour, half-way between Teboursouk and Mejez el Bab on the GP5, is full of the nostalgia of the Moors driven from Spain at the end of the 15th century. Built on the site of Roman Tichilla, the village has an Andalusian atmosphere in a Tunisian setting. A wide street, tiled roofs, an unusual minaret—the base like a Christian church tower, the top clearly Arabic—all suggest Spain.

In the courtyard of the Great Mosque is a sun dial. Finally, a kind of weavers' guild has taken the place of the old religious brotherhood in the courtyard of Sidi el Karouahi mausoleum.

From Teboursouk to Kallaat-Senan

GP5 southwest passes through a prosperous region with open hollows and wooded rises. Six km. (3½ miles) after Nouvelle Dougga, with its little blue and white houses surrounded by gardens, the ruins of a Byzantine fort stand on the site of ancient Agbia to the right on a hill. At the Krib junction branch right, to see, a few yards away on your left, a Roman triumphal arch; then on the right are the columns of a portico, a temple, an oil-crusher, a paved square, a street lined with the remains of shops, including, it is believed, the sign of one very old profession. These are the ruins of Musti, one of the many Roman towns near Dougga.

The small town of Krib, soon after Musti, draws its wealth from the fertile soil; the Byzantine ruins of Aunobari are some distance off the road. 8 km. (5 miles) from Krib, there is a marabout at Borj Messaoudi, site of ancient Thacia (ruins of a mausoleum). The plain is now dotted with trees and farms. The fountains keep their age-old role as meeting-places; women gather round them, while on the roadside children offer fruit, vegetables and poultry to travelers.

The Oued Tessa flows between oleanders. Barbary fig trees, grain fields and eucalyptus trees alternate with pasture land cropped by grazing sheep. In small villages with red-tiled houses live those who work on the cooperative farms which have been set up on the land which once belonged to the French settlers.

Seventy km. (44 miles) from Teboursouk, on a steep slope, a white town enclosed by an ocher-colored wall stands on the site of Sicca Veneria, famous for the temple where sacred courtesans plied their trade. The flourishing Roman town was destroyed by the Vandals, which provided ample building material for the medieval ramparts and Le Kef's kasbah, built in 1679 by Bey Mohammed on antique foundations.

A little beyond is the Belvedere pine wood, a public park. An uphill road leads to the blue gates of one of the country houses of former President Bourguiba. Beyond to the left is the graceful Sidi Mizouni mosque with its white domes, picked out with bands of green tiles; it is now the public library. Following the boulevard which overlooks the plain and from which you can see as far as Algeria, you reach a little square with ancient columns. In one corner stands the zaouïa of Sidi Ali Ben Aïssa. Further on is the gateway to the kasbah, which is occupied by the army and cannot be visited.

Lower down the Sidi Bou Makhlouf mosque's polygonal minaret, decorated with faiences, tops the two ribbed domes. Inside, the domes are decorated with carved, painted stucco-work. The mosque contains the tomb of Sidi Makhlouf. Below a Moorish cafe stands the ancient Christian basilica of St. Peter, complete with roof over large, square pillars and columns.

To the north of Le Kef, the Nabeur Dam on the Oued Mellègue forms a lake of 1,500 hectares (3,750 acres) 18 km. (11 miles) long. The very secondary MC72 just manages the near end; a less arduous 7 km. (4½ miles) branch west (left), after 30 km. (18 miles) along GP17 to Jendouba, to the dam at the farther end of the lake.

Kallaat-Senan, the Table Mountain of Jugurtha, is 70 km. (45 miles) from Le Kef, plus several hours walking. Four km. (2½ miles) from Tajerouine, on the road to Kasserine, turn right towards Sidi Amor Ben Salem. Four km. (2½ miles) southeast of this little border town a very poor track will bring you to a curiously shaped flat-topped mountain, a natural fortress, surrounded on all sides by cliffs. It was once protected by a fortified gateway but it can now be reached by a staircase cut into the rock. On the top, outlaws who took refuge from the troops of the Bey of Tunis built water-tanks. But there is nothing to prove that this impregnable table mountain was one of the unlovable Jugurtha's operational bases in his struggle against Rome.

On his deathbed in 118 B.C., Micipsa, King of Numidia, made the mistake of leaving his kingdom jointly to his two sons, Hiempsal and Adherbal, and to his ne'er-do-well nephew Jugurtha. Jugurtha quickly had Hiempsal put out of the way and the surviving cousin, Adherbal, fled to Rome. The Senate divided Numidia between the two cousins, but Jugurtha

was not satisfied with this. He invaded Adherbal's territory and had him
put to death. Then, wise in the ways of the world, he had no difficulty
in bribing the Roman generals who were sent to depose him. He even went
to Rome to plead his cause and had young Massiva, chief witness against
him, assassinated.

Near the village of Haïdra, the fairly extensive ruins of Ammaedara include several interesting buildings which have not yet been completely excavated.

Ammaedara, near the Algerian frontier on the road from Kalaa Khasba
to Tebessa, lies at an altitude of 900 meters (2,950 feet). Until the 1st century A.D. it served as the headquarters and winter base of the Tertia Legiona
Augusta, which was responsible for guarding Roman Africa. When the
legion left this garrison at the end of the 1st century to go to Teveste (Tebessa), the town was handed over to a colony of retired Roman soldiers
who cultivated the surrounding countryside and made it prosper.

The arch of Septimius Severus is massive and severe, but graceful columns relieve the austerity, a compromise between a desire for elegance
and that military rigor that survived among the descendants of veterans.
A Byzantine bastion built up against the arch unfortunately spoils its harmonious lines. Nearby are the ruins of a three-naved basilica and a larger
Byzantine church with marble columns and two towers. The theater still
has the paving of its stage and a few tiers of seats. A mausoleum with Corinthian pilasters and two others in the form of towers stand in silent vigil.
The Byzantine citadel which controlled this important strategic point on
the road from Tebessa to Carthage has kept its proud bearing. With its
thick walls strengthened by towers it gives an idea of the energy expended
during the 6th century by the soldiers of Justinian to ensure what they
thought would be the rebirth of imperial power.

PRACTICAL INFORMATION FOR THE TELL

WHEN TO GO. This mountain region is appreciated by the Tunisians for the
greenness and coolness in summer, the snowy landscape and the hunting in winter.
Spring and fall are also pleasant. Festival of Tabarka, avant garde music and theater, summer university, July through August 31. Theatrical performances in the
antique theaters of Dougga and Bulla Regia.

GETTING AROUND. By Car. Tunis-Béja—100 km. (62 miles); Tunis-
Tabarka—175 km. (108 miles); Tabarka-Jendouba—70 km. (44 miles); Jendouba-
Dougga—70 km. (44 miles); Tabarka-Le Kef—122 km. (76 miles); Le Kef-Kalaat-
es-Senam—63 km. (39 miles).

By Train. A line connects Tunis with Tabarka and another goes to Jendouba
from the Place Mongi-Bali.

By Bus. Frequent buses from Tunis to the main towns.

Group Taxis. Several departures daily from gare routière, 72 Ave. Farhat Hached, Tunis, to the towns of the northwest.

HOTELS AND RESTAURANTS
(Area Code 08)

Aïn Draham. *Beau Sejour* (M), tel. 47 005. 30 rooms. Rather expensive considering it's officially unclassified, but good food. *Les Chênes* (M), tel. 47 211; 32 rooms. 7 km. (4 miles) to the south in the forest; comfortable. *Hotel Rihana* (M) tel. 47 391/394. 75 rooms. The best of the three.

Béja. *Vaga* (M), tel. 50 818. 18 rooms. *Phénix* (I), tel. 50 188. For emergencies only.
Restaurant. *Hachmi* (I), Rue Khreddine.

Bou Salem. *Des Agriculteurs* (I), tel. 49 239. 8 rooms. Another emergencies-only halt.

Hammam Bourguiba. *Des Thermes* (M), tel. 47 217. 40 airconditioned rooms and 20 bungalows; spa 17 km. (11 miles) west of Aïn Draham in the forest.

Jendouba. *Atlas* (M), tel. 30 566. 16 rooms. *Simitthu* (M), tel. 31 695/743. 26 rooms and restaurant. Newly opened.

Le Kef. *Sicca Veneria* (M), 32 rooms, tel. 21 561. Newly opened; comfortable and certainly the best in the area. Has a restaurant and bar and in summer guests can use an open-air private pool nearby. *La Source* (I), tel. 21 397. 9 rooms. Very simple, with few private showers.

Mejez el Bab. *Membressa* (I), tel. 60 121. 14 rooms, no private showers.
Restaurants. *Nassim El Kef* (M), simple relais-style meals. *Dyr Esso Stop* (M), for hungry passersby.

Tabarka. *Club El Morjana* (E), tel. 44 453; 165 airconditioned rooms. Disco; pool. 4 km. (2½ miles) from town on sandy beach with nearby pine forest. *Les Mimosas* (M), tel. 44 376. 65 rooms, 16 bungalows. Older Moorish-style building with modern wings on a hill above town. Private beach reached by hotel bus.; closed in winter. *De France* (I), tel. 44 577. 16 rooms. In town. The first units of the *Montazah Tourist Complex* should open shortly.
Restaurants. *Le Corail* (M), and *Le Pescadou* (M), are both small and near the port; good for fish. *Novelty* (I), in town, unpretentious.

Teboursouk. *Thugga* (M), tel. 65 713. 33 rooms. Motel on the Tnis–Le Kef road, in an olive grove below the town.
Restaurants. *Tanit* (I), cafe-restaurant at the entrance to the Dougga ruins; modest but clean. *Antic-Club* in the town is another modest cafe-restaurant.

Testour. *Ibn Zeidoun* (I), tel. 68 033. 30 rooms.

Sports. **Yachting,** snorkeling, and scuba diving at Yachting Club of Tabarka, Port de Peche, tel. 44 478.

SHOPPING. Handicraft Shop at Aïn Draham: Khroumir rugs, blankets, weaving, wood carving.

TOURIST OFFICES. Aïn Draham: Syndicat d'Initiative, Centre Ville (tel. 47 115). **Tabarka:** Office National du Tourisme, 32 Ave. Habib Bourguiba (tel. 44 491).

CENTRAL TUNISIA

Kairouan and Kasserine

The vast bare landscape of Central Tunisia supplies the setting of the holy city of Kairouan, the rocky peak of La Kesra with Berber dwellings clinging to it, the white marble ruins of Maktar, frozen there since the fall of the Roman Empire, Sbeïtla where the setting sun gilds the three temples of a well-preserved capitol, Kasserine where a modern cellulose factory is trying to cure the town of its lethargy and where little-known Roman ruins are scattered over the plateau, and Thélepte, which bears the mark of Rome and of the dawn of Christianity.

Halfway between the Khroumir forests and the desert the earth is ocher, yellow, or gray. Under a boundless sky, men cling to the unprofitable, barren soil. They cultivate whatever will grow—a few olives, a great deal of alfalfa. Sheep and a few camels wander over seasonal pasture lands dependent on a whim of the sky: if the summer drought lasts too long, plants and animals die; if the longed-for autumn rain becomes torrential, the water runs off the parched sides of the hills, silt fills the wells and the swollen oueds sweep away men and their meager belongings, transforming the cultivated hollows into lakes of mud and death.

Kairouan

Founded in 670 by Oqba ibn-Nafi (Okba Ibn Nafaa), the first Islamic city in the Maghreb changed from an armed camp into a center of civilization in 800, when Ibrahim ibn Aghlab assumed the title of Emir and founded the Aghlabid dynasty, which ruled till 909. The Aghlabids provided Kairouan with a magnificent mosque and other religious buildings. Palaces and mosques with mosaic decoration were built at Raqqada, 7 km. (4½ miles) to the south, in the midst of gardens and pools which have since almost completely disappeared. After the Fatimid conquest of Kairouan in 909, the capital was moved to Mahdia on the coast; the city thus lost its political pre-eminence, but became the bastion of orthodoxy against the heretical invaders.

When the Zirid governor declared his independence in 1048, the Fatimid, al-Mustansir, took his revenge by releasing the Beni Hilal tribe of Bedouin against the city which they destroyed in 1057. The surrounding lands, made fertile by 500 years of effort, reverted to near-desert steppe, and as late as 1217 Kairouan was still in ruins.

The city gradually revived under a newly independent dynasty, the Hafsids, in the 13th century. The Great Mosque was restored in 1294 by Abu Hafs, but Kairouan never regained its former splendor. Stripped of temporal power, it retained its religious distinction and seven pilgrimages to the Great Mosque equal one to Mecca. Because of the surrounding steppe, the Holy City of the Maghreb has so far escaped the excessive growth of other Tunisian towns. Some 100,000 inhabitants earn their livelihood mainly from pilgrims, small trade and crafts, and the ever-growing tourist industry. But the largest of the recent Tunisian dams is rapidly transforming the region.

The old town lies within brick ramparts dating from 1052, strengthened in the 18th century by towers and crowned with rounded merlons. A boulevard winds around all but a part of the northern section.

To the south are two gates, Bab Chouhada and Bab el Khoukha. The double arch of Bab Chouhada, or Porte des Martyrs, opens onto Place Mohammed Bejaoui and gives access to the Rue Ali Bel Houane, the main street of the old town. Rue de Sousse and its continuation Rue El Farabi skirt the wall and lead to the second gate, Bab el Khoukha or Porte de la Poterne. Behind this, Boulevard Brahim Ben Aghleb leads to the Great Mosque and the museum.

The eastern gate, Bab Jedid, is reached from Bab Chouhada by following Boulevard Hedi Chaker (to the left) and then turning right into Boulevard Idriss I.

To the north, next to the Porte de Tunis at the junction of Boulevard Sadikia and Rue Ali Bel Houane, the angle between two sections of wall has been pierced to help the traffic flow. If you follow the outside of the wall, you reach the kasbah, which has been expertly restored. An opening leads into the Rue de la Kasbah, which runs along the inside of the wall to the Great Mosque.

Don't try to use your car in the old town.

The Great Mosque

To reach the Great Mosque from the Bab el Khoukha gate, take Boulevard Brahim Ben Aghleb—a somewhat grandiose name for a street which is lined with houses of sun-dried brick or rough white-wash, whose wrought iron and woodwork is painted a soft green or blue.

The museum across the boulevard contains some stucco and woodwork from the mosque, together with coins, a variety of small objects found in the excavations of the Aghlabid palaces at Reqqada (Rekada), and a series of carved tombstones, mostly from the golden age of Kairouan, from the

AGHLABID
POOL

AV. DE LA RÉPUBLIQUE

RUE DES AGLABITES

TUNIS

KAIROUAN

0   150   300   450
m.

SIDI SAHAB
ZAOUIA

BOULEVARD EST

GREAT
MOSQUE

RUE ALI BEY

RUE IBN AGHLEB

Site of
CASBAH

ROUTE DU BATHEN

OUSSELTIA

RUE DE LA KASBAH

PLACE
ABDELKADER

RUE EL FARABI

PL.DE
TUNIS

PtedeTUNIS

Djama
Tleta Bibane

BOUL.SADIKIA

RUE BELHOUANE

SOUKS

SIDI AMOR ABBADA
ZAOUIA

BOULEVARD IDRISS PREMIER

Bir Barouta

Sidi Abid
Zaouia

BOULEVARD ESSAID ESSAHBI

BVD. H. CHAKER

PtedesMartyrs
PL.DE L'INDÉPENDANCE

SOUSSE

AVENUE FARHAT HACHED

RUE

POST
Office

ALI IBN FOURNAT

9th to the 12th centuries. Especially notable are the cypress beams from the original roof of the mosque, brilliantly painted in floral and arabesque motifs of seemingly Persian inspiration.

Although the prayer hall and minaret are closed to non-believers, parts of the Great Mosque can be visited by arrangement with the Tourist Office (at Porte des Martyrs), and it is worth taking the trouble. The Jamaâ Sidi Oqba stands on the site where, according to tradition, Oqba ibn-Nafi founded the first mosque in the Maghreb in A.D. 670. Rebuilt in the present form by the third Aghlabid Amir, Ziyadat Allah, in 836, this purest example of Islamic architecture in the Maghreb has been restored four times, the latest restoration coinciding with the town's 1300th anniversary. Owing to the early date of construction, without the Andalusian filigree of Tlemcen and Fez nor any of the later rococo exuberance of the tombs of the Egyptian Mamelukes, the Great Mosque stands alone, without obvious antecedents or progeny.

The severe exterior presents an irregular appearance, the outline being broken by buttresses of varying size and shape irregularly placed—the whole dominated by the minaret and five domes. Obviously the buttresses represent attempts made at different epochs to shore up the walls from collapse. The 1970 restoration removed centuries of whitewash, exposing the intricate designs and the honey color of the bricks.

There are eight doors currently in use, four to the east and four to the west. Three of the doors in the east wall are unadorned, while the fourth, the Bab Lalla Rejana, which leads into the sanctuary, is sheltered by a domed porch ornamented with antique columns. On the west front all four doors have little porches, the far gate to the courtyard being surmounted by ribbed cupolas and the horseshoe-shaped Bab al-Sultan giving direct passage into the prayer hall. The two walled-up entrances used to be the only means of access to the 9th-century building of Zigadat Allah. Until the 10th century all mosque entrances were flush with the wall. The first monumental gateway, that of the Great Mosque at Mahdia, was finished about 921. The eight gateways now in use in Kairouan date from the Hafsid restoration of 1294.

The great courtyard—or *sahn*—entered by the third door in the west wall is trapezoidal in shape, the west wall being 219¾ feet and the east 220½ feet, and paved in white marble. It is surrounded by arcades supported on single or paired antique columns which are part of the restoration of Abu Hafs at the end of the 13th century. Under the marble pavement are 9th-century cisterns from which water can be drawn through openings in the floor. In the center the paving slopes gently down to a square marble collecting basin with an intricately carved border.

Towering above is the massively square minaret (115 feet) ending in a domed pavilion, part of the Aghlabid structure of 836, which makes it the oldest existing minaret in the world and clearly reflects the early Syrian church towers which were its predecessors. On both sides of the small doorway Latin inscriptions and Roman sculptures identify stones that were re-used by Arab builders; even the floor of the entrance is paved with carvings from Roman monuments. The staircase, with its 128 steps, is not quite in the center of the tower, whose walls are of immense thickness. It is lit by three windows on the south-east side, while the other three walls are pierced by several arrow-slit apertures. The ceiling vaults rise in steps corresponding to the flights of the staircase which finally emerges under the vaulted cupola. From the upper platform, 98 feet above the ground, there is a wonderful view over the domes and cubic white houses of the city to the ramparts and the blue jebels on the horizon.

Across the courtyard the entrance to the enormous sanctuary is under the domed portico with its four elegant pillars erected by Ibrahim Aghlab at the end of the 9th century when the depth of the prayer hall was extended. The great wooden doors are largely of 19th-century manufacture. The sanctuary is truly a "hall of columns," its 17 aisles with 16 arcades of 7 arches each running perpendicularly to the back wall. The 414 columns are a living textbook of antique architectural decoration, brought from Carthage, from Roman sites all over Tunisia as well as from Sousse (Hadrumeta), the chief Byzantine city of North Africa. The taller pillars of the central aisle carry a frieze of seemingly Sassanid inspiration, and the finest and tallest—of beautifully colored marbles, granite and porphyry— support the dome before the mihrab. While round horseshoe arches surmount the colonnades, the central aisle and the octagonal dome at its end are of the pointed type.

The central aisle leads to the horseshoe-shaped mihrab, flanked by a pair of orange-red marble pillars. The recess is lined by a series of marble panels decorated with inscriptions and arabesques, some of open-work, while the face and the rectangular surface surrounding it are decorated with brilliant luster tiles, both polychrome and monochrome, placed in an irregular pattern.

Beside the mihrab is a minbar of teak, carved and inlaid with stylized plant motifs—one of the most precious Islamic works of art in wood. An inscription states that the marble panels, as well as the tiles and teak for the minbar, were imported from Baghdad by the Aghlabid Emir Ibrahim Ahmad and that he completed their installation in the mosque in 862. The tiles take their place among the world's art treasures as the earliest known examples of luster pottery of certain date.

The Town

Starting from the Bab Chouhada, the Rue Bel Houane leads to the Café Halfaouine at an intersection near the rug souk. Allah knows how rugs have made Kairouan famous. During the rug fair, held once a year, usually in May, horsemen give exciting displays of skill.

In Andalusian fashion, the walls are decorated at different levels with clay dishes in which climbing plants grow. On the upper floors trellises made of wood or iron protect carved wooden loggias.

At the top of the staircase of the Café Barouta a blindfolded camel, its chin supported by a wooden stick, is harnessed to a beam and, walking round in a circle, turns a wheel to draw water.

Around these cafes on summer evenings you can watch dancing that is not just laid on for tourists. Nobody will mind if you try out your own skill, rotating your hips without moving your shoulders.

But Kairouan is above all a holy city. Several sanctuaries are worth a visit, such as the zaouïa of Sidi Abid el Ghariani, which houses the Museum of Islamic Art, reached by a street of the same name, the second on the right from Rue Ali Bel Houane. The saint's tomb stands near a courtyard surrounded by galleries. With its decoration of tiles and ornately worked wood and stucco, it dates from the 14th century, though it has been altered several times since.

To reach the Jamaâ Tleta Biban (Mosque of the Three Doors), which dates from 866, follow the leather souk near the Café Barouta until you come to the Rue de la Mosqueé des Trois Portes. The carved façade, unfortunately disfigured in the 15th century, is a fine example of art of Arab sculptors in the very first centuries of Islam. The bands of script, set between decorations of floral and geometric design, crowned by a cornice resting on 25 corbels, was to become one of the chief characteristics of Hispano-Moorish buildings. The modern interior is of little interest.

The five ribbed domes of the zaouïa of Sidi Amor Abbada, known also as the Mosque of the Swords because of the votive weapons offered by its founder, an armorer, date from the last century. Further on, in the modern town, the zaouïa of Sidi Sahab is is also called the Mosque of the Barber, for according to tradition Abou Jamal el Balaoui, the saint in whose honor it was built, always carried with him three hairs from the beard of the Prophet. The building has been altered at different periods and was the seat of an important religious brotherhood (zaouïa).

In the courtyard to the left were the quarters of the *mokka-dem,* servants of the brotherhood, and at the far end are rooms which were used by pilgrims. Access to the minaret, from which there is a pleasant view of the town, is, in theory, possible.

A door in the middle of the wall to the left leads to the patio of the brotherhood's school, surrounded by columns taken from Byzantine buildings. Behind this arcade are the students' cells, prayer room, and study hall.

Through a door at the foot of the minaret you enter a luxurious entrance hall with a painted wood ceiling and walls covered with tiles below an area of carved stucco; this leads to the holiest part of the sanctuary. A few steps take you to a courtyard with columns decorated with tiles and stucco. The saint lies close by, in a domed room, and a marble door opens into semi-darkness. Pious pilgrims brought back from Mecca bizarre votive offerings such as enormous ostrich eggs sheathed in fine leather.

Still on the Tunis road, 1 km. (less than a mile) from the north gate, you will find remarkable proof of the skill of ninth-century Arab engineers, for here two monumental cisterns constructed by the Aghlabid Abu Ibrahim Ahmad, between 860 and 863 and originally fed by an aqueduct that has since disappeared, again serve as reservoirs since their ungainly restoration in concrete in 1969. The largest is 130 m. (426 feet) in diameter and has 48 sides and is connected to the smaller, which served as an overflow basin, by an underground channel. Both pools are 8 m. (about 26 feet) deep, with sides that are curiously reinforced inside and out by rounded buttresses. At the center of the large basin there is a group of pillars which formerly supported a pavilion, to which it is said the princes and their consorts came to enjoy the coolness on summer evenings.

La Kesra

The picturesque mountain village of La Kesra lies 85 km. (53 miles) to the west of Kairouan and 20 km. (13 miles) before ancient Maktar. The steppe turns into sparsely covered scrubland and GP12 climbs the Dorsal, skirting the north side of the Jebel Cherichera (485 m., 1,600 feet) before reaching Haffouz, an important alfalfa market; to the south the Jebel Trozza rises nearly 1,000 m. (3,300 feet).

The road continues to climb and crosses the jagged rocky barrier of Kef el Garia in a tunnel. Aleppo pines and evergreen oaks become more frequent, and figs and olive trees nestle in the small sheltered valleys. Afforestation is gaining ground on the whitish rock-strewn soil.

A road to La Kesra branches off to the right a little after the Oued Zitoun. Clinging to the mountainside, above the forest dotted with pine and olive trees, the village seems one with the rock. The men, who wear monkish hooded robes of rough homespun cloth, are descendants of the Berbers who perched their villages on the clifftops to escape from the raids of the nomads from the east.

La Kesra lies at an altitude of more than 1,000 m. (3,300 feet). A ridge of bare rock overhangs the houses, which are built of stone without mortar. The fierce Berbers who have lived here for 12 centuries come down from their eagle's nest every day to cultivate the plain, then every evening climb back up again. The stairs cut into the rock gleam from centuries of daily use. Valerian and fig trees cling to the crannies. Cool water springs up in profusion from deep gashes in the hillside and flows into stone basins where women wash clothes, and horses and sheep come to drink. Straw mats dry in the sun. At the very top of the mountain an old watch tower stands like a sentinel, and birds of prey circle overhead.

Maktar

After La Kesra, the road winds around ravines and rocky hills planted with eucalyptus and pines. At Maktar some megalithic monuments bear witness to the extremely ancient occupation of this site, the key to one of the main thoroughfares of the Dorsal. To protect their domain from the Massyls in the west and the raids of the nomadic tribes from the south, the Numidian kings built a stronghold where, in 146 B.C., Carthaginians fleeing for their lives found a refuge and a warm welcome. The affinity between their religion and that of their hosts favored good relations, and the refugees brought with them a culture from which the Numidian principalities were quick to profit.

The fall of the Numidian kingdom brought few changes as the Romans granted a certain degree of autonomy to the settlement of Mactaris. For two centuries a civilization that was Punic in origin was to survive— though in an increasingly degenerate form—in the heart of Roman Africa.

In A.D. 180, the Romans established themselves in full strength. Maktar then became one of the most beautiful towns in the African province, but like the others it started to decline during the 3rd century. By the time of the Arab invasions it was no more than a small hamlet huddled around great ruins.

These lie a few yards beyond the arch of Bab el Ain, the gateway to Mactaris, indicated by a signpost. The town, which covered an area of 600 MX 500 m. (some 650 MX 550 yards), is only partially excavated.

To the left of the entrance, a small museum houses funerary stelae. They are mediocre in quality, but they show how Punic religious traditions survived at the height of the Roman domination. Some Christian symbols of the 3rd century, as crude as the last Punic stelae, testify to the existence of a Christian colony. Above the Tunis road, the mausoleum of the Julii, hidden among modest houses, is decorated with a relief representing a ritual offering.

At the entrance to the excavated area, on the left, is a little amphitheater still in fairly good condition. A gently sloping path leads across an area that has not yet been excavated, to a noble forum, well paved and surrounded by a portico, with an arch at the far end celebrating the triumph of Trajan.

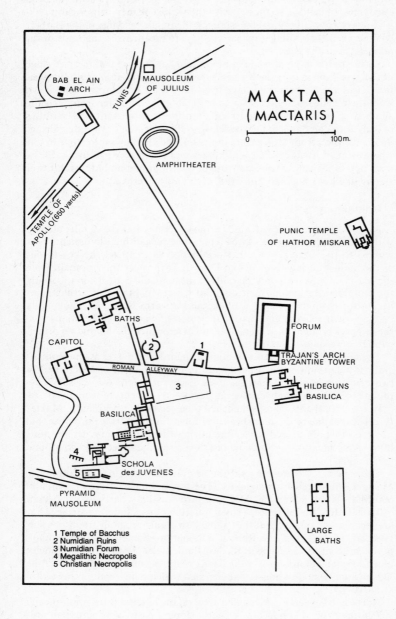

MAKTAR
(MACTARIS)

0   100m.

BAB EL AIN
ARCH

MAUSOLEUM
OF JULIUS

TUNIS

AMPHITHEATER

TEMPLE OF
APOLLO (650 yards)

PUNIC TEMPLE
OF HATHOR MISKAR

BATHS

CAPITOL

2

ROMAN   ALLEYWAY

1

3

FORUM

TRAJAN'S ARCH
BYZANTINE TOWER

HILDEGUNS
BASILICA

BASILICA

4

SCHOLA
des JUVENES

5

PYRAMID
MAUSOLEUM

LARGE
BATHS

1 Temple of Bacchus
2 Numidian Ruins
3 Numidian Forum
4 Megalithic Necropolis
5 Christian Necropolis

Beyond the arch and the fragments of a later tower, the remains of a Byzantine basilica (called the Basilica of Hildeguns) lie near a paved Roman street. Some 200 m. (220 yards) ahead are sections of the massive walls of the partly excavated thermal baths, dating from the 2nd century A.D. Below the present ground level are mosaics and elegant pavements, colonnades and friezes executed with the care for quality that characterizes the great age of the Roman Empire.

Follow the ancient street left for 100 m. (110 yards) until a paved square where the ruins of a temple stand on a platform preceded by tiers of steps. This temple, dedicated to Bacchus, was built during the Roman period above a crypt carved out of the rock, whose layout indicates that it served as a sanctuary in Numidian times.

All around fragments of marble and other debris lie scattered in the grass, and several archeological levels can be distinguished fairly easily. This was the Numidian forum, which, unlike a Roman forum, had no surrounding colonnade. The plan of the Roman town—due to financial considerations, or, more probably, to a desire to comply with local custom—was adapted to that of the Numidian town.

A street to the left leads to the Schola des Juvenes, the meeting place for an association of young people rather than a school. Around the colonnaded courtyard (used as palaestra) were various rooms, of which the largest, with an apse, served as a hall and place of worship. The local youths gathered here to train for sports and military activities, and to serve as a militia. To the south, a curious apsed building has openings connected with troughs, into which the citizens would pour the quantity of grain assessed as their tax by the authorities. The young people from the schola checked the deposits and guarded them before they were sent on to Rome. (It is estimated that 1,260,000 quintals, or nearly 9,000 tons, of wheat were sent yearly from Africa to provide for the free distribution of food to the common people in Rome.)

Still further south is a necropolis, where Roman tombs are interspersed with megalithic tombs used by the native population until the beginning of the Christian era. The mausoleum of Julius Piso and his daughter dates from the end of the 2nd century. The capitol of Mactaris, almost completely destroyed, lay northwest of the schola. The Roman funeral tower, similar in style to the Libyan-Punic mausoleum at Dougga, was inspired by old Numidian traditions, but differed in intention. While the tower of Dougga celebrated the deification of the soul of the dead, the mausoleum of Maktar (as an inscription proves) was intended only to remind the living of the deceased. Beyond the large baths are the romantic ruins of the aqueduct.

The modern town dates from the time of the French Protectorate. Lying on a high plateau (950 m., just over 3,000 feet high) it is blessed with a healthy climate, comfortable summers, and refreshing winters.

At the junction of the roads to Kairouan and Tunis, near the Roman arch called Bab el Ain, or Gate of the Spring, which was one of the gates of Mactaris, is a small public garden which contains fragments of statues and monuments. In the same area is the mausoleum of the *gens Julia,* the Roman family of Julius.

Little remains of the Temple of Hathor Miskar, which was originally a Punic sanctuary and was then altered during the Roman occupation before serving finally as a Christian church.

Archeological Excursions from Maktar

The region is strewn with innumerable Roman ruins, the most interesting of which are those of Thigibba, 15 km. (9 miles) west. At Hammam Zouarka are extensive ruins from a Roman bath establishment and, nearby, the starting point of the aqueduct which brought water to Maktar. In the middle of the ruins an arch bears the following inscription, lacking in grandeur but revealing the habits of an easy-going population: *"Si quis hic urinam fecerit, habebit Martem iratum"* ("he who urinates here will incur the wrath of Mars"). The ruins of Uzappa, 25 km. (15½ miles) by a fairly difficult track, are near the village of Ksour Abd el Melek; two triumphal arches, one of them delicately carved.

From Maktar, follow GP4 west through a cultivated steppe surrounded by flat-topped hills. The slopes are cut by parallel contour trenches designed to retain the torrential waters of the autumn rains. The deforestation of central Tunisia became widespread after the invasions of the Hilal Bedouins in the 11th century. Remains of oil presses, found here and there in the vast, bare countryside, show that there were olive groves in antiquity and in early medieval times. Such fertility explains the size and number of ancient towns in a region where agriculture is precarious, at the mercy of a capricious climate. 21 km. (13 miles) from Maktar GP4 intersects MC71, which leads right (north) to Ebba Ksour 34 km. (21 miles) and to Le Kef, left (south) to Sbeïtla, 67 km. (42 miles).

Ebba Ksour is not much to write home about, but a track to the left leads to Medeïna, the site of ancient Althiburos, which lies in hilly country on either side of a deep oued. Here are the poorly preserved remains of a forum, capitol, and theater, the podium of a temple, the foundations of villas, and a triumphal arch.

Sbeïtla

Turning left at the crossroads coming from Maktar, you cross the steppe where a system of irrigation ditches has begun to restore the plateau to its former prosperity. The huts are made of dry stones laid without mortar and often have clay roofs. As you go farther south, horses become fewer and the number of camels and donkeys increases, while tufts of alfalfa appear.

Sbiba is a well-irrigated village, with cube-shaped houses scattered in the midst of small orchards. There are gardens everywhere and prickly pear cactuses cover the hills. The crops and olive groves are protected from the grazing camels by hedges or little walls made of mud. At the entrance to the village lie the columns of a basilica, converted into a mosque by the first Arab conquerors, but nevertheless destroyed by the Beni Hilal.

To the north of Sbeïtla, the upper steppe's principal though undistinguished capital, rise the extensive ruins of Roman Sufetula. Insufficiently excavated, little is known of its history during the prosperous 2nd and 3rd centuries A.D., but in the Byzantine period it was the residence of the patrician Gregory, who probably built the three fortresses. But these are completely overshadowed by the Roman remains.

The three temples of the capitol rise on platforms above the forum, surrounded by a high wall pierced with a triple arch. The beauty of the golden stones, the proud layout of the temples, and their silhouette against the blue sky, lend an aura of nobility to the whole site. Approach the capitol by crossing the forum. The sculptures are perfect, their details carefully executed. An urge to create a spectacular overall effect obviously governed the composition of the group, but the execution of the details was on an equally high level.

Outside the walls of the forum, fragments of Roman masonry half-buried in the ground serve as gravestones in a Moslem cemetery. Turn left toward the oued, and about 160 yards farther on you come to the ruins of two churches, where three columns, the remains of a portico, indicate the position of a baptistery decorated with mosaics. The other ruins of Sufetula are in very poor condition, except the handsome triumphal arch of Diocletian near the road. The columns decorating its jambs have been put back in position, and the whole of the arch has been beautifully restored.

Kasserine and Thélepte

In the austere alfalfa steppe of the south only a few scattered olive trees make a splash of green on the wild plateau. 10 km. (six miles) before Kasserine, GP13 crosses the deep Oued El Hatab, which is lined with trees. On the rim of the areas eroded by the oued, cactus hedges have been planted on banks of dirt in an attempt to stop further erosion and to absorb the surging waters.

Kasserine is a town of 10,000 inhabitants, lying at an altitude of 670 m. (2,200 feet). The crest of Jebel Chambi—at 1,550 m. (5,100 feet), the highest mountain in Tunisia—forms the horizon to the west, turning pink at dawn and varied shades of violet at dusk. Game is plentiful, mainly wild boar, partridge and hare. A track enables cars to get as far as the lower slopes.

Kasserine's economy is bound up with an alfalfa processing plant that extracts cellulose from the grass: prosperity rises and falls with international cellulose prices, the precarious basis on which the economy of the Tunisian interior rests. Part of the modern town covers the site of ancient Cillium, whose interesting ruins have not yet been systematically excavated. Opposite the gardens of the provincial administration, the three-storied funeral tower of a Roman tomb was inspired by Numidian monuments such as those at Maktar. A poem of some hundred lines in memory of Flavius Secundus is engraved on either side of the door on the ground floor, and on the middle story there is an epitaph to Flavius and his family, while the top story has a rounded niche.

A vast number of ruins covers the plateau to the left toward Gafsa. A solitary triumphal arch dominates this monotonous stretch of land strewn with scattered stones, except for a few arches of an aqueduct. Torrential rains have cut deep ravines in the plateau and a turbulent oued has replaced the nymphaeum in which the waters were once disciplined by ancient engineers.

To the south of Kasserine the landscape becomes even bleaker, the steppe increasingly bare and scored by oueds. Green tufts of alfalfa dot the yellow earth, and some grain grows in small hollows in the ground. Here and there Bedouins, their black tents huddled together on the dusty earth, put their sheep and camels out to graze while the women spin wool beside the camp. Sometimes there are a few mud huts for the farmers round a new school.

On this almost uninhabited steppe, the village of Thélepte appears neat and clean, with earth walls protecting the orchards. Bales of alfalfa, heaped together like hay stacks, are lined up on the platform of the railroad station, where cactuses thrust upward between the tracks. On the way out in the direction of Gafsa, GP15 passes through a vast field of scattered ruins that include two Christian basilicas, the substructure of a Byzantine fortress and a theater.

Off the highway is the little village of Feriana, where the desert really begins. Just off the main street, reached from the highway through a school courtyard to the left, you'll find a fascinating village market (Monday and Thursday), with a wide assortment of pure junk, vegetables and fruits, and an occasional piece of jewelry or two. Behind the market, in a gully, the "ships of the desert," camels on which the produce was brought to market, are anchored in the sand.

Gafsa lies 80 km. (50 miles) beyond Thélepte; but it is already in the Tunisian South.

PRACTICAL INFORMATION FOR
CENTRAL TUNISIA

WHEN TO GO. It is best to visit Central Tunisia in the spring, when the steppe is in bloom. In the autumn heavy rains can cause sudden, violent floods. Kairouan holds a Regional Festival of Music and Popular Arts in April, a Summer Festival in July and August and, on Mohammed's Birthday, impressive ceremonies.

GETTING AROUND. By Train. Daily from Sfax, linking with the morning train from Tunis, to Gafsa, returning in the evening; refreshment service. Journey time is 4 hrs.

By Car. Tunis-Kairouan, 156 km. (97 miles); Kairouan-Maktar, 105 km. (65 miles); Kairouan-Sbeïtla, 107 km. (66 miles); Sousse-Kairouan, 57 km. (35 miles).

By Bus. from the bus station on the south side of Kairouan several buses daily for Tunis, passing through Le Fahs, Zaghouan, or Enfida to Sousse, Maktar, and Le Kef, Sbeïtla, Kasserine, Thélepte, Feriana and Gafsa.

Louages (shared taxis): from Tunis, Gare routière, 72 Ave. Farhat Hached, and Garage Ayachi, Bab Souika. From Sousse many louages depart daily from the Bab Jedid. Journey of one hour.

HOTELS AND RESTAURANTS
(Area code 07)

Hajeb, El Ayoun. *Relais Agip* (M), tel. 57 005. 13 airconditioned rooms. 42 km. (26 miles) from Sbeïtla on the Kairouan road; with pool.

Kairouan. *Les Aghlabites* (E), tel. 20 855. 62 rooms with uncertain airconditioning. Patio and pool, in garden; cheaper in every respect than the *Continental* (E), tel. 21 135. 175 airconditioned rooms. Large pool; Moorish cafe and garden; comfortable. *Splendid* (M), tel. 20 522. 28 rooms. Only just makes the grade. *Tunisia* (M), tel. 21 855. 11 renovated rooms. No restaurant, but central. *Marhala* (I), tel.

20 736. 30 rooms. A rest house run by the Tunisian Touring Club in the heart of the rug souk in the medina.

Restaurants. *Dar Es Salam* (E), opposite hotel Les Aghlabites; a tourist rip-off. *Cafe Restaurant El Abassia* (I), Ave. Farhat Hached. One of the best of the inexpensive eating places in the souks. *Neptune* (I), and *Roi du Couscous* (I) are both similar atmospheric haunts.

Kasserine. *Cillium* (M), tel. 70 106. 36 airconditioned rooms. 2 km. from town near the ruins. Pool and effective circular architecture. *Pinus* (I), tel. 70 164. 13 rooms with baths and restaurant. *De la Paix* (I), 71 465. 16 rooms. Good restaurant. *Maison des Jeunes* (I). 92-bed youth hostel.

Maktar. *Mactaris* (I), tel. 76 014. 20 rooms. *Maison des Jeunes* (I). 20-bed youth hostel.

Sbeïtla. *Bakini* (M), tel. 65 244. 30 rooms. *Sufetula* (M), tel. 65 074. 36 airconditioned rooms.

ENTERTAINMENT. Very near Kairouan, on the road to Tunis, the *Fantasia Club* (M) has a standard program: dinner under a tent every night, fantasias, Bedouin music, and dancing. The Tourist Office organizes free fantasias during the tourist season near the Hôtel Les Aghlabites.

SHOPPING. O.N.A.T. shop is on Rue Ali Zouaoui, Kairouan.

TOURIST OFFICES. Kairouan: Office National du Tourisme, Ave. Habib Bourguiba (tel. 21 797); Syndicat d'Initiative, Ave. Habib Bourguiba, Porte des Martyrs (Bab Chouhada), (tel. 20 452).

THE SAHEL

The Olive Shores

Sahel means seashore. It is the name given by the Tunisians to the olive-producing coastal area which extends from Sousse in the north to Sfax in the south. Long sandy bays, separated by little headlands, open out into the shallow sun-warmed sea. Rainfall is low, but evaporation from the sea provides enough moisture for the trees.

The Sahel is also a region with an ancient civilization. Sousse, Monastir, Mahdia, and Sfax all contain notable monuments that testify to the refinement and vigor of the Moslem dynasties. An enormous Roman amphitheater, one of the most impressive ancient remains in North Africa, dominates El Jem, Roman Thysdrus, on the plateau which stretches out to the west of the Sahel. It proves that the entire region was once prosperous, and that the olive groves, now confined to the coastal strip, extended far inland in ancient times.

Traditions inherited from the Moors of Andalusia have kept the quality of craftsmanship high. The farmers live in sturdy stone houses, cultivating their olive trees, bent and twisted by the wind and seeming to express all the hardships of creation. Strings of huge beach hotels in the seaside towns have transformed the Sahel into an international tourist area, with the usual blessings and evils. Among the latter are the children begging round the theater of El Jem.

Exploring the Sahel

Route GP1 continues south of Hammamet to Sousse (43 km., 27 miles) through olive groves to Bou Ficha on the low-lying coast bordered by salt marshes. 9 km. (5½ miles) beyond Bou Ficha, above the village of Aïn Er-rahma, are the ruins of ancient Aphrodisium, with a triumphal arch. A fortress is perched on top of the hill, from which the view extends over the plain of Enfida (Enfidaville), where the Eighth Army's spectacular advance across North Africa in World War II ended. Enfida's small museum displays some Roman mosaics.

Takrouna, perched on a rock, is reached from Enfida by following MC133 right (west) 5 km. (3 miles) and then taking a track for a further 1 km. (½ mile). Its white houses with their arched roofs are built right out to the edge of the mountain spur. According to legend, the village was founded by a Moroccan soldier of fortune and for a long time was a hideout for outlaws. Today, the villagers cultivate olive trees, but rather than settle in the plain around the wells they prefer to carry water laboriously uphill to their houses, not wanting to waste good fertile earth. Takrouna produces esparto grass mats and is famed for its honey.

South of Enfida, GP1 skirts the marshy area of the sebkhet (salt lake) of Halk el Menzel till the 8 km. (5 miles) branch left (east) to Hergla. Though on the coast, this is an agricultural village, renowned for weaving *scroutins,* alfalfa filters used in oil presses.

From Hergla a scenic coastal road between the sea and a smaller sebkhet passes Chott Mariem on the way to Port El Kantaoui, which claims to be Africa's most prominent garden harbor. It is certainly harmoniously integrated—miracles can still happen even in modern coastal developments—contending with Skanès for first place as a beach resort, and also as Tunisia's film capital (after the filming of *Pyrates,* Polanski's turkey). Well-kept gardens surround hotels, villas, and apartment blocks in derivations from Andalusian and Arab styles. A credible reproduction of a traditional souk abuts on a fine beach with a marina for 300 boats. The 18-hole golf course extends to the olive groves and orchards that stretch all the 6 km. (4 miles) south to Sousse. The center of the fruit industry is Hammam Sousse, a town of some 10,000 inhabitants on GP1.

Sousse

With almost 300,000 inhabitants, Sousse is the third largest city in Tunisia. The agricultural products of the Sahel and the salt of the sebkhets are exported from its harbor. The modern town, busy and lively, extends in part along a lovely sandy beach bordered with modern hotels.

Sousse stands on the site of the Phoenician Hadrumetum, a thriving trading post two centuries before the founding of Carthage. Around 800 B.C., Hadrumetum was a bartering point and a stop on the route from Tyre to Spain. Hannibal used its port during his campaign against Scipio at the end of the Second Punic War. Under the Roman Empire the town was inhabited by colonists whose wealth came from the fertile hinterland. In the 9th century, the Aghlabids rebuilt the port and restored the ruins left behind by battles between the Arabs and the Byzantines. The Normans from Sicily captured it in the 12th century and turned it into a base for their operations. Later, in the 16th century, Sousse was coveted by Spain. Finally, during the Tunisian Campaign of 1942–43 the Allies bombed the port, which was being used by the Germans, and caused serious damage to the residential quarter. Since the war the modern town has been rebuilt, and the medina carefully restored.

There are several gates in the wall surrounding the medina, but the most convenient entrance is by a large opening made by bombs in 1943 on the

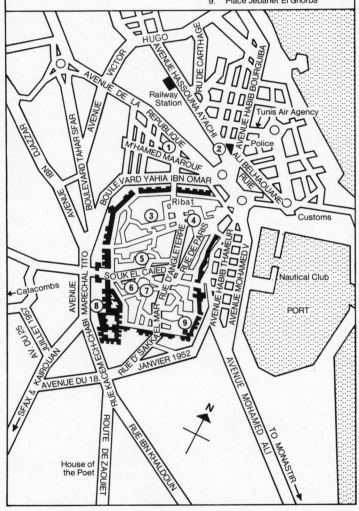

SOUSSE

1. Post Office
2. Tourist Information
3. Zakak Mosque
4. Great Mosque
5. Hanafite Mosque
6. The Souk
7. La Sofra
8. Museum of La Kasbah
9. Place Jebanet El Ghorba

northeast side, near the Place Farhat Hached, where cars can be parked. As soon as you enter you see the Great Mosque and the fortified monastery, or ribat.

As a rule, the Great Mosque can be visited only in the morning. The courtyard is surrounded by galleries with squat pillars supporting very tall arches. A wide staircase gives access to the upper part of the mosque, built in the 9th century and later used as a fortress. Remodeled during the 17th century and restored in 1965, it now has a gallery on the side of the courtyard adjacent to the prayer hall, distinguished by its more ornate style from the other sides of the courtyard. Similarly, inside the prayer hall, slender bays of a more graceful design stand side by side with those of the original construction. The minbar with its luxuriant filigree woodwork contrasts with the more sober style of the mosque as a whole.

The ribat is one of those fortified monasteries built by military brotherhoods during the first centuries of Islam to defend their conquered territory. This one was built in the 8th and 9th centuries, largely of columns and stones from ancient ruins. Within the fortified walls is a courtyard with arcades. A double staircase leads to the upper story and also to a low vaulted room, lit only by arrow-slits, where the soldier-monks prayed. Their cells opened onto the wide balcony on the upper floor. Three of the cells have been transformed into a small museum exhibiting glass from Kairouan, Fatimid ceramics and coins.

More stairs lead up to the top story of the fortress. A wall-walk connects the towers, which have projecting positions from which the defenders could crossfire, completely covering the wall in between. In one corner stands the *nador* or watchtower, from the top of which you can see the town, the kasbah, the harbor, and the surrounding countryside.

In front of the ribat, the Rue d'Angleterre runs south. Follow it, and on the right you will come to the most picturesque alleyways in the souks. In Rue Tazerka, the Zakkak zaouïa has an elegant minaret. More or less in the middle of the medina is the Kalaout el Koubba, a small building—now a café—whose architecture recalls that of a marabout. Take Rue El Mar and Rue El Majira, and you will come to the small mosque of Bou Fatata (9th century) and the fortified gate of Bab el Khabli, in the southern sector of the walls surrounding the kasbah.

The kasbah is easily reached by car along a modern boulevard. The high citadel, dominated by a large watchtower, has been transformed in part into an important archeological museum laid out around a patio and set in a garden (open 9–2, closed Mondays). On the floor and walls of the patio there are Roman mosaics from Sousse and the surrounding region. Most of the subjects illustrate the comfortable existence of the Romans who lived in the Sahel during the 2nd and 3rd centuries A.D. Pavements depict fruit, vegetables, fish, and birds. Other mosaics show the luxury and the entertainments of the time: a peacock fans its tail and struts in a garden, animals fight in an amphitheater, racehorses frisk about. There are many early Christian mosaics from the catacombs in Sousse, a unique representation of a lion devouring his Christian victim. There is also a series of terracotta plaques depicting Old Testament stories.

Room VIII at the far side of the patio has mosaics depicting pleasures and gods. Facing the entrance a "triumph of Neptune" is remarkable for the quality of its workmanship. Another triumph is that of Bacchus in a chariot drawn by four tigers. A 3rd-century hunt on the banks of the Nile betrays Hellenistic influence; and a veritable gallery of the fish found in the Mediterranean. These unusual works are placed beside mosaics whose subject are more common—cupids in a garden, Orpheus charming the animals, Apollo and the Muses, the toilet of Venus, and the inevitable Jupiter kidnapping Ganymede.

Other rooms contain Punic, Roman, and Byzantine funeral objects. One of them contains stelae and pottery from the Tophet of Sousse, with a notice explaining the Punic custom of child sacrifice. The rites were no different from those at Carthage, and the sepulchers are similar: the six archeological levels identified at Sousse have disclosed tombs which show a development comparable to that at Carthage, and their chronological arrangement follows the evolution of the symbol of Tanit through the centuries. There is, however, an important difference between the Tophets of Sousse and Carthage. Here, sacrifices went on long after the Roman conquest, for the sixth level corresponds to the 2nd century A.D., though by that time animals replaced children in the sacrificial rites.

At the far end of the garden are two Roman rooms. A huge lion was both a symbol of social triumph and the trademark of a shipowner. Mosaics of the months of the year form an illustrated calendar of rural work and festivals. In an adjoining room there are fragments of frescos with figures of Nereids. A mosaic representing a hunting scene staged in an amphitheater shows a servant bearing on a tray the fees of the hunter-actors. Finally, there is the complete mosaic floor of a *triclinium* (dining room), resplendent with dozens of remarkable animals which pranced beneath the feet of the diners.

The entrance to the catacombs of Sousse (open 9–12, 3–6, closed Monday) is near the road which turns from Bab el Gharbi, the western gate in the medina walls. On request, attendants from the kasbah museum will take you through galleries of the Bon Pasteur Catacomb nearly 5 km. (some 3 miles) in total length, lined with pagan and, above all, Christian tombs totaling some 6,000 graves. There are three series of catacombs and more than 15,000 tombs all damaged by water seepage and cave-ins. With the most interesting objects now in the kasbah, the catacombs are of relatively little interest.

Monastir

MC28 follows the coast fairly closely southeast from Sousse through olive groves and past another small sebkhet to the palms of the Dkhila oasis, renowned for its *lagmi* (palm wine). The large hotels in lovely gardens strung along the fine beach of Skanès rival those of El Kantaoui, so far avoiding over-development. Guards stand sentry before the richly decorated neo-Arabic palace where former President Bourguiba is now confined, comfortably enough, to judge by the luxuriant park. The airport inland near salt flats is a little close, but there is not much traffic except charter flights at weekends. The coastal road passes numerous marabouts, one of them on a deserted islet, before entering Monastir (25 km., 16 miles) on the southern promontory of the Gulf of Hammamet.

Punic Rous Penna became Roman Ruspina from which in 47 B.C. Caesar launched his African campaign against Sextus Pompeius, son of the great Pompey. A Byzantine fortress to the end of the 7th century, it then formed part of a chain of fortified monasteries, ribat, that spread Islam through the province of Africa, thus anticipating the Christian knightly orders of the Crusades. After the decline of Kairouan in the 11th century, Monastir assumed the role of holy city and center of pilgrimage. Conquered by the Turks from the Spaniards, the fortresses continued to guard the coast. Since independence, President Bourguiba has made his birthplace the showcase of Tunisia.

The most important of the original Aghlabid ribats, enlarged in the 9th and 11th centuries, still dominates the town from the esplanade beyond the coastal boulevard. On this vast square, encircled by the restored 8th-century battlements, the dual military and religious purpose of the ribat scorns decorative ornaments and relies on its powerful austerity.

Thick walls, with almost no windows, surround an interior courtyard with tiers of cells opening off. The prayer hall with strong pillars houses a Museum of Islamic Arts, containing some very fine illuminated manuscripts in rich bindings, Arabic papyri, reed pens and inkwells used by calligraphers, jewels, coins, and fabrics, from the Ommiad to the Turkish periods. A long ramp leads up from the courtyard to a walkway on top of the wall. Note the variations in the way the stones are laid in the wall, the finest masonry being also the oldest. There is a good view from the top of the watchtower. A smaller courtyard was reserved for the women and opens into a tiny prayer room. Sound and Light performances in summer are very impressive.

The 9th-century Great Mosque adjoining the ribat is likewise grandly severe in a minor key. The columns in the prayer hall are, as so often, taken from earlier places of worship, as shown by the Roman and Byzantine capitals. Near the Great Mosque is the small Saïda Mosque and also the foundations of another ribat whose plan with round towers can easily be made out.

At the other end of the square, two graceful symmetrical cupolas resting on delicate pillars contrast with the severe architecture of the ribat. Behind them is a cemetery containing the tombs of pious people who wished to be buried near a place made holy by religious fervor and military virtue. The Bourguiba family mausoleum was built here in 1963, and the former chief of state has chosen it as his final resting place. Together with the adjoining Bourguiba Mosque, this is as splendid an example of the revival of traditional Moslem architecture as the mausoleum and mosque of Mohammed V in Rabat. A large courtyard paved with marble and surrounded by arcades is separated by 19 carved teak doors from a vast prayer hall with 86 rose-colored columns. A large chandelier hangs in front of the golden mihrab framed by onyx colonnettes and decorated at the top with blue and gold mosaics. The teak minbar was carved by craftsmen from Kairouan and Skanès.

Some crenellated walls with square towers remain from the 18th-century fortifications of the medina, where the Chraga quarter has been restored in the traditional style, with craftshops, cafes, and restaurants. O.N.A.T. offers a particularly choice range of local products. In the Rue Trabelsia, off central Place du 3 Août, the former president was born on August 3rd, 1903. His paternal home is now a National History Museum.

In the Avenue Farhat Hached is a large Congress Center, as Monastir has entered the 20th century with a university campus, film studios, and a stadium seating 20,000. Subway tunnels below the coastal boulevard connect the town to the fine beach, which extends from the luxury holiday complex on Cap Monastir north to the pleasant fishing port at the other end of the waterfront. The spacious, uncrowded town above the sea sprinkled with islets forms a Mediterranean setting at its best.

Farther offshore, 18 km. (11 miles) away, lie the Kuriate Islands, flat and deserted, except for the largest one where a few fishermen live.

Mahdia

South from Monastir, MC82 follows a low-lying coast stretching out into sandbars. In the shallow water women wash sheepskins which are then carried on the backs of donkeys to primitive tanneries and spinning mills. Camels amble in procession toward a nearby market.

Lamta, 12 km. (7 miles) from Monastir, stands on the site of Leptis Minor, which has not yet been excavated. In front of the scattered houses wool hangs out to dry, and olive trees cover the low shoreline down to the edge of a sandy beach. After Lamta the road veers away from the sea, and passes through Sayada and then through Ksar Hellal, a town of farmers and weavers of wool and cotton, where the women wear pretty shawls with black or red fringe.

Moknine, 20 km. (12 miles) from Monastir and 25 km. (16 miles) from Mahdia, is a large settlement on the edge of a barren salt deposit, the Moknine Sebkhet, surrounded on all sides by vast olive groves. The town has several oil crushers, and for centuries families of Jewish silversmiths have made very fine silver jewelry there. A small museum in a disused mosque, away from the main street, contains textiles, embroideries, and jewelry as well as agricultural implements and articles for everyday use.

From Moknine to Mahdia the road runs through olive groves squeezed in between the sea and the sebkha. At Bekalta, 15 km. (9 miles) from Mahdia, a sign points toward the ruins of Tapsus, 5 km. (3 miles) inland. The track is passable by car, but little is left of the town made famous by Caesar's victory over Juba and the followers of Pompey. Before arriving at Mahdia, the road passes fields of rich crops surrounded by hedges of prickly pear. Here the old olive trees grow in close-set rows, unlike the widely-spaced rows of modern plantations, which are designed to make the most of what little rainfall there is.

Mahdia stands on a fairly high promontory, and was thus easy to defend. The Phoenicians and later the Romans made it into a strategic base. But it is to the Arabs that Mahdia owes its glory, for in 916 the first Fatimid leader, Obeid Allah—called *al-Mahdi* ("he who is guided right," or "the deliverer")—built a fort there that faced toward Egypt, the object of his desires. Mahdia, named after him, had to endure religious revolts and peasant uprisings which the Fatimids crushed, sometimes under the very walls of their fortified city. Finally in 968, assisted by his general Jouher, the Fatimid El Muizz ed Din fulfilled his dynasty's great ambition by becoming Caliph in Cairo. At the end of the 10th century Mahdia was attacked and destroyed by a Christian fleet; during the 12th century, the Normans from Sicily took their turn and ruled the town for a few years. Conquerors from Barbary turned Mahdia into a base, and the Spaniards dismantled it in the 16th century, but soon afterwards the Ottoman Turks refortified the town.

A fish-canning industry has been established among the pretty houses with brightly colored *moucharabieh,* wooden window-lattices, strung out along the quay. On the headland, a powerful bastion protects the entrance to the old town. Under it runs a vaulted gallery, the Skifa Kahla, or dark porch. For access to the upper terrace of the fortress (the only part open to the public), ask at the town hall nearby.

Mosque and Kasbah

The Great Mosque is less than a hundred feet from the Skifa Kahla.
It is a venerable building, erected by Obeid Allah, altered several times
and well restored. A porch of great simplicity leads into a courtyard surrounded by harmonious arcades. The prayer hall is very bare, and carpeted
with rush mats. The severity of this building contrasts with the shimmering tiles and fanciful minarets of later mosques.

At the very tip of the headland stands the restored kasbah, built at the
end of the 16th century. A long arched passage leads to an inner courtyard.
About 5 km. (3 miles) northeast of the lighthouse that stands on the point
of the headland, the wreckage and cargo of a Greek galley were discovered
in 1907; the remains are now in the Bardo Museum.

In the cliff and around the kasbah, sections of ruined wall point to the
Roman occupations. Between the kasbah and the Great Mosque ancient
stones stand guard above what was once the Roman Military harbor.

From Mahdia MC82 follows the sea south for a while and then turns
inland through an area of plantations irrigated by numerous *dalou* wells
worked by animals. These wells, common throughout the Maghreb, consist of two masonry weights at either end of a transverse beam; one of the
weights is attached to a pulley whose cord is pulled by a camel or a donkey.
As the animal walks away, a goatskin full of water is drawn up. A man
on the surface tips it over with a rope, and the water flows out through
a tube fixed to the goatskin. The animal then turns back, and the goatskin
sinks back into the well.

Ksour Essaf, 12 km. (7½ miles) south of Mahdia, is a town of 15,000
inhabitants. Pretty carved architraves decorate the facades of the houses
and mosques. MC87 turns right (east) to El-Jem; MC82 continues along
the coast to Chebba, above a beach sheltered by the cape of Ras Kapoudia,
with a little port overlooked by an old medieval tower. MC82 then passes
through the green hills around Jebeniana for the last 67 km. (42 miles)
south to Sfax.

El-Jem stands on a plateau whose ancient fertility is gradually being
restored. No ancient site in Tunisia is more impressive than Thysdrus,
which can also be reached directly from Sousse on GP1. But from either
approach toward the olive groves of the plain, the ruins of the enormous
amphitheater of El-Jem rise up overwhelmingly.

El-Jem, Ancient Thysdrus

El-Jem, a small town of 10,000 people, occupies part of the site of what
was during the 3rd century A.D. one of the richest cities in the Roman province of Africa. Thysdrus drew its wealth from agriculture, especially from
the cultivation of olives. Just how important it was is shown by its huge
amphitheater, almost as large as the Colosseum in Rome, whose massive-
ness crushes the village around it. It was built at the beginning of the 3rd
century, though no precise dates are known. The immense oval structure
measures 148 MX 122 meters (526 MX 406 feet), which compares with
a maximum diameter for the Colosseum of 187 meters (604 feet) and for
the arena at Nîmes of 133 meters (443 feet). Over the centuries its stone
has mellowed to a golden yellow. The three tiers of superimposed arches
rise to a height of 36 meters (120 feet), but the decoration of attached columns is fairly crude.

At the end of the 17th century or the beginning of the 18th, a tax collector got permission from the bey to use artillery to dislodge some rebellious taxpayers holed up in the amphitheater. The resulting breach in the wall disturbed the balance of thrusts that held the fabric together, and if repairs had not been undertaken the whole vast tottering structure would have collapsed. Now, although the tiers of seats which once held 30,000 spectators have nearly all disappeared, and although the walls have been only partially—and badly—restored, the building still thrusts its enormous silhouette up into the sky. (A further problem is that, as the arena was proof against scorpions, many of the stones from the amphitheater were taken away and set into the walls of neighboring buildings.) Under the floor of the arena there are two galleries in the form of a cross, their extremities partially blocked, which have given rise to a number of theories. It *is* known, however, that in the middle of one of the now-open passageways stood a statute of Marcus Aurelius. When the gladiators left their dressing rooms, they filed out and passed, dividing left and right around the statue, before ascending to the arena to fight. Here Gordian was proclaimed emperor at the age of eighty in A.D. 238, but whether the Berber heroine Kahena made her last stand against the Arab invaders in the amphitheater is somewhat doubtful.

Recent excavations have uncovered a wealthy area of the town just outside El-Jem, by the side of the road to Sfax. Large villas with beautiful pavements, some with interior gardens watered from underground cisterns, were built around colonnaded courtyards. The atrium, bedrooms, and living rooms of the Roman colonists have mosaic floors that illustrate their religious attitudes, their taste for good food and drink, their sports, their entertainments, and even their amorous exploits (expressed either by allusion or literally—as in a house at the far side of the excavated area, in line with the entrance). A small museum protects the finest mosaics.

On the other side of the road to Sfax, a trail crosses over the railroad tracks and leads to the badly damaged ruins of an amphitheater older and smaller than the giant one at El-Jem. Some villas have been located or uncovered here and there on the steppe around the modern town.

Sfax

Sfax is 64 km. (40 miles) south from El-Jem. GP1 crosses the El-Jem Sebkhet which begins 12 km. (7½ miles) south of the town. In this plain without drainage the waters of the autumn rains stagnate on ground made sterile by its high salt content. Immediately after the railroad tracks, there is a trail to the left leading to Rougga, ancient Baraus, where enormous cisterns once gathered the water which today is wasted in the sebkhet. After Rougga, the road enters a region of olive groves. You may come across children holding out flowers to passing travelers as in this part of the Sahel the land can be used to grow flowers.

The Sfax region is famous for its plantations. The old olive trees are clustered together near the town, while in the newer groves they stand far apart in straight rows that cover dozens of kilometers. If you are interested in seeing these plantations, take route MC81 which leaves Sfax in the direction of Sidi Amor Bou Hadjela; at Bogat el Beïda you look down from a rise some 100 meters (350 feet) high at the plantations spread out over the plain. Not far from there, at Cheridi, is an even more extensive view.

Sfax, the second largest city in Tunisia, has 375,000 inhabitants. The port's activity is largely based on the export of phosphates brought from Metlaoui by train. Sfax also exports salt and agricultural products, primarily olive oil. The fishing port harbors about a thousand vessels of all types from the simplest fishing bark to the large boats of the sponge fishermen. Octopus is fished along the coast and off the Kerkennah Islands. A special fishing technique is made possible by the great difference between high and low tide (on average, 2 meters, or 6½ feet), which means that fish traps in the form of poles interwoven with reeds can be placed on the beaches in the shallow waters. The southern part of the city has an artificial beach. The town hall in the modern city contains a little museum where you can see statuettes and mosaics from Thaenae and Ancholla.

The old town still retains a few traces of the period during the 9th century when it was used as a port by the Aghlabids. The medina, a vast rectangular area, is surrounded by a mighty wall with massive towers entered through a handsome triple-arched gate, Bab Diwan, near which cars can be parked. It dates in part from the 9th century, when the religious fervor and the economic and political power of the Aghlabids were at their height. The three-storied minaret with its powerful silhouette recalls that of the mosque at Kairouan, but here the severity of early Moslem architecture is tempered by sculpture that has a certain grace.

Next to the Great Mosque are the street of the jewelers and the street of the dyers. In Place Barberousse there is a pretty 18th-century house that is worth seeing. Parallel to the Rue de la Grande Mosquée, the Rue du Bey, a lively thoroughfare, leads back to Bab Diwan where you can see several patrician houses with carved doors and windows decorated with wrought iron. Other traditional houses line the nearby streets, for instance Rue de la Driba.

The Sfax Museum is located in the front of the City Hall on the ground floor (open summer 9–12, 3–6; winter 9–12, 2:30–4). In Room 1 to the left are several mosaics in charming primitive style as well as a classical representation of the Muses. In the left foyer is a galaxy of marine animals and shells and opposite on the right a huge mosaic from Taparura. In Room II are early Christian remains from the 4th-century Basilica at Skhira. Especially note Daniel and the two lions—one of the best early Christian works in Tunisia. Also mosaic covers of tombs and a rare 4th-century fresco fragment.

At 5 Rue Sidi Ali Nouri, near the intersection of Rue du Bey and Rue de la Driba, is Dar Djellouli, an elegant palace built in the 18th century. The palace is also signposted in Rue du Bey. It houses a folk museum. A square courtyard inside the palace has walls covered with tiles, carved doors, windows decorated with carved stucco, and a pretty loggia on the upper story. The exhibits include heavy embroidered wedding outfits, men's silk costumes, carved wood, craftsmen's tools, and alembics for the distillation of flowers. Among the jewels are diadems made of gold coins, and wide necklaces like breastplates. Notice the size of the earrings: they were held in place by a piece that went behind the ear, their weight supported by a thread passed over the head and hidden in the hair. A display devoted to domestic economy shows how food was prepared, and still is prepared today in many Tunisian households. Large jars hold supplies stored up during the autumn to last until the following spring.

The Kerkennah Islands

The archipelago of long sandy strips shaded by palm groves rises above the water. The port, Sidi Youssef, is about 20 km. (12 miles) from Sfax—a mere halfhour by ferry boat. The two main islands are Gharbi and Chergui. From the port, MC204 crosses both over a connecting causeway, built on Roman foundations, for a distance of 35 km. (22 miles). The fine sand of the beaches forms bars a long way out into the shallow sea, which is ideal for floating and splashing about. The offshore oil rigs are luckily too far out to spoil the skyline. The local flat-bottomed boats, dhow-rigged with a backward sloping mast, are designed to negotiate the shallows without running aground.

Despite the fertility of the soil which produces an abundance of fruit and vegetables, the main occupation of the 15,000 islanders is the cultivation of the even more fertile sea, staked out in strips. At one end of the palisades of palm stalks is placed a kind of gigantic lobster pot into which bream, mullet, seabass, and sole swim on their own or are driven by palm fronds. Octopus is caught by dropping hollowed-out white stones to which the suckered arms readily attach.

The inhabitants of the Kerkennah Islands have held on to their traditions, but the presence of tourists eager for a show has changed the mood. Upon request, the islanders will perform circumcisions and weddings. They even organize shows on the mainland, and perform wedding celebrations on request with the same participants. But there still remain the orchards and vineyards growing in the shade of palm trees, the elegance of a few old houses, the tranquillity and the brilliant sunsets, and the charm of the small fishing port of El Attaïa on the northeast shore of the island of Chergui. The fishing boat in which Bourguiba escaped from the French to Libya is surrounded by a rather incongruous building on the headland beyond.

PRACTICAL INFORMATION FOR THE SAHEL

WHEN TO GO. The Sahel is pleasant at all seasons, except during the heavy rains of fall. Summer is perfectly bearable. The wind from the sea may blow in great gusts from time to time but this doesn't last long; and abundant evaporation from the sea may cause a mist which hides the sun for a while. Winter is mild and sunny. Springtime is the best season of all, with nature in full bloom, and very pleasant temperatures.

Regional Music and Popular Arts, April. Regional Theater Festival, June. Birthday of the President of the Republic, 2 weeks beginning 3 August. Opposite the Marabout Sidi Mansour, Light and Sound show at the ribat, Monastir. Aoussou Festival, beginning with a parade of floats on July 15, Sousse. Music and Popular Art Festival, July through August, Mahdia and June and August in Sfax. Arous el Bahr Festival in July, Kerkennah Islands.

GETTING ABOUT. By Train. The airconditioned trains Tunis-Sousse-Sfax (3½ hrs) are comfortable on a narrow-gauge line; the same can be said for the continuation Sfax to Gafsa and Tozeur.

By Bus. Several bus lines serve the towns and villages of the Sahel; Sousse and Sfax are linked to the major towns of Tunisia. The bus station in Tunis is 74 Ave. de Carthage.

By Car. Some distances—Tunis-Sousse, 140 km. (97 miles); Sousse-Sfax, 130 km. (81 miles); Sfax-Gabès, 138 km. (86 miles), Sfax-Gafsa, 235 km. (146 miles).

By Plane. The international airport at Skanès-Monastir is used mainly by charter services, but there are a number of direct scheduled flights in season.

Group Taxis. These run several times a day between Tunis, Sousse, and Sfax, from the gare routière, 72 Ave. Farhat Hached and from Garage Soudan, 4 Rue Soudan. There is also a service to Sousse only from Garage Ellouh, 37 Rue El Jazira. At Sousse there are frequent departures from Place Bab Jedid.

By Ferry. Twice daily Sfax-Kerkennah Islands in winter, 3 in high season, more on weekends.

HOTELS AND RESTAURANTS
(Area code 03)

Sousse (Beach) Hotels

The hotels on the sea corniche along the beach to the north are mainly patronized by charter groups and large package tours and are not recommended for individual travelers.

Luxury

Orient Palace (42 888 or 43 010). 265 rooms. This only deluxe hotel in Sousse has 3 restaurants, an open-air and a covered pool, fitness room, sauna, massage, jacuzzi, and baby-sitting services.

Expensive

Chems El Hana (tel. 28 190/92). 250 rooms. Covered pool. The new and most luxurious flagship of this chain on a mediocre and rather crowded beach. Connected by an 8-floor passage to El Hana (see below).

El Hana (tel. 25 818). 140 rooms. 3 restaurants, large pool, tennis.

El Hana Beach (tel. 26 900). 620 rooms, but only 13 bungalows on the beach; also a rare indoor pool.

El Ksar (tel. 41 822). 260 rooms. Large pool and terraces, but closed in by the adjacent Tour Khalef (see below).

Hill Diar (tel. 41 811). 116 airconditioned rooms, 76 bungalows. Well-managed and popular with English tour operators.

Justinia (tel. 26 382). 130 rooms. No private beach; closest to town.

Marabout (tel. 26 245). 208 rooms. Pleasant restaurant; pool, terrace, and good beach.

Marhaba (tel. 42 170), 290 rooms, and **Marhaba Club** (tel. 40 091), 205 rooms. Huge vacation complex redeemed only by its 29 acres of beautiful gardens directly on the sea.

Marhaba Beach (tel. 40 112 or 40 688). 250 rooms, heated pool, nightclub, restaurants. This is a comfortable and well-kept hotel.

Samara (tel. 23 699). 117 apartments. Set back from the sea, but large pool, and the use of the Riadh's beach. Suitable for groups of 3 to 4.

Tour Khalef (tel. 41 844). 575 rooms. On the sea with acres of marble halls in mock Moorish. Cavernous and crowded diningrooms, but good pool and disco.

Moderate

Alyssa (tel. 40 713). 265 rooms in bungalows, 90 in central block. On beach.

Jawhara (tel. 25 611). 185 rooms, 40 bungalows. With bowling alleys.
Karawan (tel. 25 388). 120 rooms. On Corniche with no private beach but small pool.
Riadh (tel. 24 828). 68 rooms in bungalows. No pool; open summer only.
Shéhérazade (tel. 41 412). 208 rooms. Fine pool in patio.

Sousse (Town) Hotels

Expensive

Aparthotel Nejma (tel. 26 811). 100 airconditioned studios in the Abou Nawas chain. Pool and garden on the seafront.
Phoenix (tel. 24 288). 60 airconditioned rooms in new block.
Samara (tel. 23 699). 300 units, pool, and restaurant.

Moderate

Aparthotel Fares (tel. 27 800). 90 rooms. Central.
Hadrumete (tel. 26 292). 35 airconditioned rooms. Near the port; pool.
Okba (tel. 25 522). 50 apartments.
Sofra (tel. 41 657). 30 apartments.

Restaurants

La Caleche (E), 6 Rue Remada (tel. 26 489). Seafood and local specialties by candlelight.
Le Gourmet (E), 3 Rue Amilcar (tel. 20 751).
Le Lido (E), Ave. Mohammed V (tel. 22 329).
Le Pacha (E), Route de la Carniche (tel. 20 258).
Le Bonheur (M), Place Farhat Pacha.
Le Malouf (M), Place Farhat Pacha.
Le Marmite (M), Rue Remada.
Le Sportif (I), Ave. Bourguiba, as good as any of the nearby dearer places.

Entertainment

In the hotels, as well as outside, shows are based on stereotyped folklore performances and discos. *Atlantic* (M), and *Top Kapi* (M), Ave. Bourguiba. At the northern exit is *Le Douar,* an entertainment center with a restaurant, nightclub, and a show in a large garden. Farther north, away from the road in an olive grove, is the *Bedouine Ranch* (M), with tents, camels, and yet more folklore.

HOTELS AND RESTAURANTS FOR THE SAHEL REGION

Chott Mariem. (Area code 03.) *Tennis Beach* (M), tel. 48 063. 175 rooms. New formula emphasizing sports; exceptional for Tunisia, predominantly female personnel.

El Jem. (Area code 03.) *Relais Julius* (I), tel. 90 044. 15 rooms. On the main square.

Kerkennah Islands. (Area code 04.) On **Chergui Island:** *Farhat* (M), tel. 81 236. 154 rooms in several blocks with pool; best on Sidi Frey beach, though the beach is rather rocky. *Grand Hotel* (M), 81 266. 112 rooms. On Sidi Frey beach; pool. *Cercina* (I), tel. 81 228. 4 rooms, 35 huts. *Residence Club* (I), tel. 81 221. 180 huts. Pool. Inexpensive hotels are very rustic and open in the summer only.
At **Remla,** 9 km. (5 miles) from port: *El Jazira* (I), tel. 81 058. 25 rooms. Good fresh fish.

Mahdia. (Area code 03.) *Club Cap Mahdia* (M), tel. 80 300. 250 bungalows in this resort with pool and nightclub. *El Mahdi* (M), tel. 81 300. 130 rooms, 35 bungalows. Remote location on splendid beach; pool. *Sables d'Or* (I), tel. 81 137. 80 rooms, 68 bungalows. German favorite.

In town: *Grand Hotel* (I), tel. 80 039. 35 rooms, 10 with showers.

Monastir. (Area code 03.) *Regency* (L), tel. 60 033. 190 rooms. Together with *Marina* (E), tel. 62 066, 250 apartments, in outstanding vacation complex round the 400-berth marina on Cap Monastir. Beach, pool, tennis, cinema, nightclub, boutiques, and restaurants.

Esplanade (E), tel. 61 147. 130 rooms. Next to the Ribat fortress. Private beach across the Corniche; pool. *Hibab* (E), tel. 62 944. 150 rooms. This apartment-hotel has a pool and sports facilities. *Sidi Mansour* (E), tel. 61 311. 130 airconditioned rooms. Convenient to Congress Hall in town; pool on terrace overlooking sea. *Yasmine* (I), tel. 62 511. 16 rooms.

Restaurants. *La Chraga* (E), in that quarter. *El Ferik* (E), both on Rte. de la Corniche. *Le Central* (E), *Le Chandeliert* (E), *La Plage* (E), and *Le Sindbad* (E), in the port. *Le Bonheur* (E), and *Le Rempart* (E), both on Ave. Bourguiba. *La Marina* (M) and *La Pizzeria* (M), in the port.

Nightclubs. *Borj El Kalb* (E), Rte. de la Corniche. *El Kahlia* (E), Rte. de la Corniche.

Sports. The Hippodrome (Racecourse) puts horses and qualified personnel at the disposal of tourists. An 18-hole golf course was opened in 1987.

Port El Kantaoui (Sousse Nord). (Area code 03.) 8 km. (5 miles) north, one of Tunisia's smartest beach resorts. 18-hole golf course, lovely beach, spacious gardens, marina, playgrounds for children, and riding. Every hotel has a large pool, tennis, restaurants, bars, and discos.

Diar El Andalous (L), tel. 41 855. 282 rooms, 18 suites, on 3 floors. 3 restaurants; nightclub; indoor pool. *Marhaba Palace* (L), tel. 43 633 or 40 200. Built like a palace, this new imposing hotel of pink marble has 250 plush rooms, restaurants, and indoor and outdoor pools. In the garden is the *Club Alhambra* (E), tel. 40 900. 200 apartments and studios in the traditional architecture. Both in the Abou Nawas chain. *Hannibal Palace* (L), tel. 41 577. 242 rooms, 8 suites.

Green Park Hotel (E), tel. 43 277. Newly constructed, this elegantly appointed hotel has 110 rooms, restaurants, indoor and outdoor pools, and fitness facilities. Operated by the Iberotel chain.

Hasdrubal Palace (E), tel. 41 944. 200 comfortable rooms, but service is slow; heated indoor and outdoor pools. *El Kanta* (E), tel. 40 466. 255 rooms, 2 suites. *Les Maisons de la Mer* (E), tel. 41 799. 750 airconditioned apartments on the marina.

Abou Sofiane (M), tel. 42 844. 175 rooms. *Bulla Regia* (M), tel. 43 924. 52 rooms. Teaching hotel with closely supervised service. *Club Salima* (M), tel. 40 080. 300 rooms in vacation village. *Open Club* (M), tel. 48 005. 160 rooms, nightclub, and pool. *Tergio* (M), tel. 48 488. 430 huts, pool, and sports facilities.

El Kantaoui (I), tel. 42 011. 325 huts in vacation village.

Restaurants. *Beach Club* (E), *Des Emirs* (E), *L'Escale* (E), *Yacht Club* (E), *Pizzeria Ezzitouna* (M).

Sfax. (Area code 04.) *Sfax Center* (L), tel. 25 700. Opened 1987. 115 rooms, 8 suites. *Novotel Syphax* (E), tel. 43 333. 127 airconditioned rooms in the quiet Public Gardens on Rte. Soukra. *Le Colisée* (M), tel. 27 801. 63 rooms. Pool. *Mabrouk* (M), tel. 29 833. 40 rooms. Central. *Mondial* (M), tel. 26 620. 42 rooms. *Les Oliviers* (M), tel. 25 188. 50 rooms; pool. Best bet in this price range. *Thyna* (M), tel. 25 266.

Alexander (I), tel. 21 911. 30 rooms.

Restaurant. *Le Corail* (E), Rue Habib Maazoun (tel. 27 301). Excellent seafood.

Skanès. (Area code 03.) An outstanding beach resort under threat of overdevelopment. *Kuriat Palace* (L), tel. 60 855. 200 rooms, 19 suites. 4 restaurants; Moorish cafe; disco, hammam, mini souk. *Abou Nawas Sunrise Club* (E), tel. 27 144. 213

bungalows in large park. *Club Robinson* (E), tel. 31 055. 314 rooms. Part of the German chain. *El Hana* (E), tel. 62 256. 255 rooms. *Jockey Club* (E), tel. 61 833. 200 rooms, 15 suites. In large palm grove extending to beach. *Skanès Palace* (E), tel. 61 350. 120 rooms, 30 bungalows in spacious grounds. *Tropicana Club* (E), tel. 60 554. 155 rooms.

Club Méditerranée (M), tel. 31 887. 500 comfortable bungalows. *Houda* (M), tel. 25 340. 175 rooms. *Les Palmiers* (M), tel. 61 151. 69 rooms in bungalows. Close to the Presidential Palace; pool. *Marina* (M), tel. 62 066. 110 comfortable rooms in this apartment-hotel. *Residence Chems* (M), tel. 33 350. 600 airconditioned bungalows. *Rivage* (M), tel. 30 122. 35 rooms, 124 bungalows. *Ruspina* (M), tel. 61 360. 180 rooms. Most expensive in this class. *Sahara Beach* (M), tel. 61 088. 1,050 small rooms in 3 blocks. Mass tourism rampant; furthest north on Sousse road. *Sangho Farah* (M), tel. 33 140. 162 rooms. *Tanit* (M), tel. 62 522. 76 rooms, 176 bungalows.

Restaurants. *La Falaise* (E), also nightclub. *Les Flamants Roses* (E), entertainment center.

EXCURSIONS. The hotels and tour operators in the main resorts offer many day and half-day trips—to Kairouan, Monastir and El-Jem, the oases of Gabès and Matmata, Tunis and Carthage and a two-day excursion to Tozeur and Nefta. Minisafaris are offered in season with an overnight stop at Kebila, visiting the Tuareg market at Douz and various oases en route. For those not going south to Jerba, a visit to the Kerkennah Islands gives a good idea of the dreamt-of desert isle—only one hour by ferry from Sfax.

SHOPPING. In the souks and medinas of Sousse and Sfax you can bargain over a wide choice of craft goods from the Sahel—Bedouin rugs from El-Jem, embroideries from the Kerkennah Islands, beaten copper from Sfax, silver jewelry from Moknine. The Sunday market in Sousse is strong on local handicrafts. The better items are available at fixed prices, at the O.N.A.T. shops near the Mosque Habib Bourguiba, Monastir, and Rue H. Tej, Magasin 8, Sfax.

USEFUL ADDRESSES. Tourist Information. Monastir: Office National du Tourisme, Quartier Chraga (tel. 61 960). Skanes airport tourism office (tel. 61 205). **Port El Kantaoui,** Syndicat d'Initiative (tel. 31 799). **Sfax:** Syndicat d'Initiative, Place de l'Indépendence (tel. 24 606). **Sousse:** Office National du Tourisme, 1 Ave. Habib Bourguiba (tel. 25 157); Syndicat d'Initiative, Place Farhat Hached (tel. 22 331).

Group Taxis. Sfax: Rue Belouane. **Sousse:** Pl. Farhat Hached (for the north), and Blvd. Mohammed Ali (for the south).

Car Hire. Monastir: Africar, Ave. Bourguiba (tel. 61 381); Avis, Airport Skanès (tel. 61 314). **Sfax:** Africar, Ave. Hedi Chaker (tel 22 287); Avis, Rue Tahar Sfar (tel. 24 605). **Sousse:** Africar, Ave. Khaled Ibn Walid (tel. 20 509); Avis, Blvd. de la Corniche (tel. 20 901); Hertz, Ave. Bourguiba (tel. 21 428).

THE GREAT SOUTH

Lotus Land Discovered

In the smallest of the Maghreb countries, the oases can be visited in the greatest comfort, along GP3 connecting Gafsa, Tozeur and Nefta where vacation dreams materialize below rustling palms, once the columns of Land Rovers packed with tourists have roared off. The desert of endless sand dunes round Kebili is easily reached on GP16 from Gabès. But for sandy beaches, palm trees and warm seas, and if you are seeking rest rather than activity, comfort rather than discovery, then it would be hard to beat the Island of Jerba.

Nor is the desolation of the Lunar landscapes missing. The Matmata hills, south of Gabès, retain a savage and unspoiled beauty; here the Berbers live in underground houses. South of Medenine, in the region of Tataouine, other tribes live in villages perched high on rocky escarpments at the edge of the desert. Clefts below the villages are painstakingly irrigated; the people's existence is precarious, and the men often leave home to find jobs elsewhere to support their families.

Only Land Rovers should attempt the trails between Kebali and Medenine or Tataouine. And though the tourist offices claim that the crossing of the infamous Chott el Jerid between Tozeur and Kebili presents no difficulty from May to September when the corrugated salt crust is hard and dry, it may be nerve-racking as GP16 is often covered with sand. To say that the heat might not suit everyone would be a wicked understatement, but in cooler weather this is strictly a one-way trip—to the bottom of the treacherous quagmire.

For any visit to the Sahara it is essential to consult the tourist offices at Douz, Gabès or Tozeur. It might save a lot of trouble to stick to organized tours, though even these are fairly strenuous, often starting at unearthly hours. However, with a specially equipped car, a real adventure is within your reach. Once you have all the necessary permits you can head into the desert on the pistes beyond the terminus of GP19 at Remada.

Discovering the Tunisian South

GP15 from Kasserine, GP3 from Kairouan, and GP14 from Sfax meet at Gafsa, the first turning southeast to the coast at Gabès, the second continuing southwest into the desert to Tozeur, Nefta and El Oued across the Algerian border. GP1 more or less follows the coast from Sfax to Gabès, then turns inland to Medenine, where MC108 leads north to Jerba, GP19 via Tataouine to Remada, while GP1 continues east to rejoin the sea at the Libyan border.

Gafsa and Region

Gafsa is the most northerly oasis. Arriving from the north, about 10 km. (6 miles) from the town a blanket of green, due to underground springs, begins to spread on the desert-like steppe. The palm grove serves as a garden for this not very remarkable town of 60,000 inhabitants, the administrative capital of the southwest.

The 15th-century kasbah, skillfully restored after bombardment in World War II, now houses the law-courts. There is a dramatic view of the fort from the gardens below where hot springs flow.

At the end of the main street are two Roman pools, deep basins filled with limpid water from the hot springs. Children dive to retrieve, at a depth of 4 meters (13 feet), coins thrown by tourists. Pestering is pernicious. A house with an arch in front of it overlooks the pools; this is the exhibit and sales center for carpets. By walking down the vaulted passage and turning to the left you reach the Great Mosque, which has a mihrab decorated with attractive light-blue tiles. From the minaret there is a fine view of the town, the palm grove, which is crisscrossed by good trails, the desert countryside, and the jebels. At the craft center on the boulevard near the kasbah, girls work on tapestry looms.

The oasis, which can be explored by car, is planted with a hundred thousand palm trees, whose dates have little commercial value, and with fruit trees which are its real wealth. Near Lalla in the direction of Gabès, 2 km. (just over a mile) from the railroad station of Gafsa, there is a small but colorful oasis.

GP3 follows the railway southeast through barren rocks to Metlaoui. The railway then keeps close to the Oued Seldja before coming to an end at Redeyef, while MC201 makes a wide sweep north via the phosphate mines in the very mineral landscape of Moularès. South of Redeyef, the Jebel Alima caves contain flint tools and small shells, proof of the existence of a prehistoric culture which archeologists have labelled Capsian (from Capsa, the Roman name for Gafsa).

MC201 roughs it west to Tamerza, despite a hotel little spoilt by tourists. Another mountain oasis is Midès, originally a Roman settlement, 5 km. (3 miles) northwest from Tamerza on the Algerian border. GP16 leads more comfortably south from Tamerza to Chebika at the mouth of a narrow pass through which a stream cascades. It is an island of coolness and greenery in a harsh land, where the original mud-brick village, hardly distinguishable from the rock around it, has been deserted for a modernized neighboring community.

On GP3 3 km. (2 miles) south of Metlaoui, take the piste right to the impressive gorges of the Oued Seldja. The trail ends in front of a narrow cleft in a reddish cliff, and the rest of the excursion is done on foot. Going up the stream between rocky walls, you reach a natural amphitheater. Upstream, the gorge narrows and the cliffs rise 200 meters (650 feet). The railway crosses this apocalyptic landscape.

Tozeur

GP3 runs through several *chotts* (saline depressions) before reaching the immense Chott el Jerid, once part of the Mediterranean. Its cracked surface glittering with mineral salts stretches over nearly 100 km. (62 miles), and many caravans, led astray by its mirages, have been lost in its uncharted wastes. Tozeur, with its 15,000 inhabitants and 250,000 palm trees, is not a mirage, but can be explored by car, donkey or on foot. Beyond the reddish-brown houses with their original brickwork, under the date-palms, small streams crisscross and merge to form little pools where kneeling women do their washing.

Tozeur is the capital of the Jerid, the palm country. Around the little square, the center of the settlement, the facades of the houses are decorated with bricks moulded in relief and forming geometric patterns, a speciality of the Jerid oases and best seen in the Sidi Abid Mosque, the reconstructed Zaouïa Sidi Mouldi, and the Great Mosque at Bled el Hader, dating from 1030, its minaret resting on Roman foundations, the only vestige of antique Tusuros. Nearby is the 1282 Marabout of Ibn Chabbat. 200 springs irrigate more than 1,000 hectares (about 4 square miles). Yet compared to the Moroccan ksour it is frankly disappointing.

The Belevedere is just 3 km. (2 miles) along GP3 to Nefta. A pretty palm grove dominated by a rock rising over the oued. By no means a must, though it was favorite of the poet Aboul Kacem Chebbi (1909–34), who brought about a renaissance of Tunisian poetry. He is buried here in the oasis, beneath a palm tree in a patio.

The Paradise is a somewhat neglected garden at the other side of the town. At the entrance is an enormous jujube tree which was planted by a holy man, Sidi Bou Ali, whose shrine stands nearby. If there are indeed any of the advertized 3,000 rosebushes, they are cleverly hidden among a variety of trees and plants, among which the yellow hibiscus are the most striking. Plums are picked in June, grapes gathered in July, and strawberries in February. Nor is the African Zoo much to write home about. A few caged lions, hyenas, jackals and plenty of vipers. The keeper cheers the visitors by joking tiredly that their venom is not dangerous . . . just occasionally fatal.

Nefta

Between Tozeur and Nefta, GP3 draws a black line across the softly undulating desert. To the left lies the endless brownish crust of the great salt lake. Nefta welcomes you with an avenue of eucalyptus. At the crossroads, the road to the right leads to the Sahara Palace hotel overlooking the Corbeille, and the road to the left leads to the settlement and oasis. 150 warm springs water some 300,000 palm trees, including 70,000 deglas that bear particularly fine dates. Nefta is also a holy oasis, with nearly a hundred shrines.

At the entrance to Nefta, near a waterfall, the oasis café is a departure point for walks or camel rides to the shrine of Sidi Bou Alil, a Sufi mystic.

The famous Corbeille is north of the town; a hundred springs flowing from the sides of the basin, dotted with the white domes of shrines, to form a sheet of green water at the bottom. A path leads steeply down to the fish-filled river. Near the café a zaouïa stands near the tombs of the Moslem mystics Sidi Ibrahim and his son. The top of the minaret affords the best view of the Corbeille, the oasis and the desert.

If the salt crust is dry and hard, May to September, you can cross the Chott el Jerid from Kriz to Kebili, only 90 km. (56 miles) from Tozeur by this direct route. Besides the thrill of adventure, the crossing of the Chott offers a regional specialty—the mirage. In the afternoon, the air heated by the burning salt distorts the landscape, and islands and palm groves appear where there is nothing but desert waste. Mirages can also be seen from the edges of the salt lake.

Gabès, Oasis by the Sea

Encompassing the two ancient villages of Jara and Menzel, ringed by chemical complexes, the featureless modern town of Gabès sprawls between the oasis, the steppe and the sea. An ideal position largely ruined by air pollution and even more by sea pollution from the Oued Gabès discharging its slime just beyond the small artificial harbor, while a smaller oued adds its filth halfway along the splendid beach. Alas, the greenish water, pleasantly warm, is only inviting when the wind blows from the right quarter; the sea may rise 2½ m. (8 feet), or more when there is a wind. In the market of the medieval Jara quarter, salt fish, dried octopus and a great variety of articles are displayed on the ground, and everyone squats down to bargain. Behind the square, whose arcades include a few Roman pillars, are the craftsmen: basket weavers, salt merchants, smiths, and many others.

Already in Roman times, Pliny wrote glowingly of the site of the colony of Tacapae, at the head of the Gulf of Syrtis, "where palm, olive and fig trees live in mutual shade." The very beautiful oasis of Gabès is unique in that it extends right out to the coast. It can be visited by horse-drawn carriage (agree on price beforehand) or by car (take the road towards Sfax and turn left for Chenini, opposite the Agip service station, though the road itself is not well-signposted). A large shady avenue leads into the oasis. At Chenini an arrow points the way to the waterfall—though note that the waterfall can sometimes dry up—and in any case children will offer to accompany you. Behind the cafe there are shady paths bordered by irrigation canals. The road passes in front of the waterfall and leads to an oued dammed by Roman masonry that forms a sleepy pool of green water. A track branching off to the left at the shrine of Sidi Ali Bahloul goes through the Berber village of El Maïta and ends on a plateau of bare earth, where you must get out to take a look back at the oued of Gabès and the palm grove. A path leads down to the oued, where a heart-shaped body of water is held back by a Roman dam. This is the starting-point for a pleasant 20-minute stroll. A laurel-shaded path winding among gardens follows the river. Cut into the right bank are many cave-dwellings, while upstream, the valley widens out and the shallow water trills over a bed of pebbles. At the source the scenery becomes less attractive.

Kebili and the Nefzaoua Oases

GP16 west to El Hamma and Kebili runs through flat desert country with occasional mountains outlined against the sky. El Hamma is an oasis fed by hot springs famed for their curative qualities since Roman times. The Chott el Fejaj is visible from the Tomb of Rabbi Sidi Jusef, goal of Jewish pilgrims in December. The desert of pebbles and rocks gives way to salt desert, the Chott, or to sand desert. From the ridge of Khanguet Mansoura a string of oases stretches out among the sand dunes, centered on Kebili, whose low white houses shelter Berbers and Blacks from the Sudan. (Kebili was for centuries a slave market.) The 800,000 palm trees are owned by semi-nomadic Nefzaoua tribes, who leave in springtime to graze their camels, returning to the oasis for the harvest.

MC206 to Douz, 27 km. (17 miles) south, passable for cars but some-times blocked by sand-drifts, offers many picturesque sights: children, white or black, playing in Roman pools, women dressed in colored robes carrying water jugs held on their backs by a strap that runs across the forehead; camels drinking greedily as they are given a bath; Tuareg Bedou-ins standing motionless around the water holes; caravans strung out across the empty plain. Jemma is a palm grove irrigated by an artesian well, while Douz, in the sand dunes, is a village built of stone blocks and mud. Chil-dren climb among the eucalyptus trees during siesta time. Palm trees top the dunes at the southern edge of the village.

The Chott el Jerid road passes through small oases until it reaches the salt deposits. If you feel adventurous, continue across the Chott toward Tozeur. After 7 km. (4 miles) you reach Telmine, a charming oasis which includes the remains of a Roman outpost. Tombar, 3 km. (2 miles) farther on, still boasts a few gardens. Here an effort has been made to provide water for the young palm trees by means of earthen dikes. On leaving Tombar the desert begins, sometimes sand, sometimes salt. Here and there, clumps of palms still cling to the tops of the dunes.

There are signs of life again between El Goléa, 8 km. (5 miles) from Tombar, and Fatnassa, on a spur 10 km. (6 miles) long which extends like a peninsula into the Chott. The vegetation is sparse and stunted, but the inhabitants, mostly black, are tall and handsome. At the far end of the peninsula, the piste again enters the Chott. The sparkling salt crackles under your tires like powdery snow. On either side of the track, there are many traces in the soft sand of skidmarks and places where cars have got stuck. The hot air plays tricks with the landscape: dunes become houses and scraggy tufts become palm trees. The far side of the Chott, at the oasis of Kriz, lies 50 km. (30 miles) away, and Tozeur is only 10 km. (6 miles) farther, but drivers run a serious risk of getting stuck in this desert region.

The El Faouar road is passable only if the weather is dry and you have equipment for digging your car out of the sand. It is wise to arrange for a local guide to accompany you. The piste follows the eastern edge of the Chott, south of Kebili. You pass on the left the track to Bechelli, bordered by telephone poles, and soon you are rolling along on a sparkling salt crust, with the mirages ahead reflecting blue water and islands. Blidet, 20 km. (12 miles) away, is surrounded by high white dunes which are very photo-

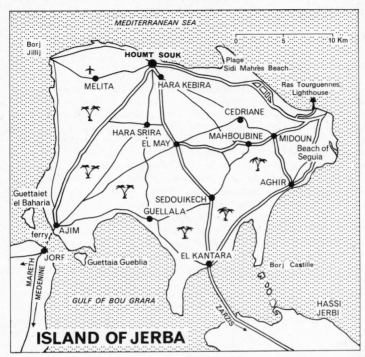

genic. From there on the piste becomes less clear and often consists only of the tracks left by other cars; sometimes the sand has obliterated them and that is why you need a guide. There is also the constant danger of getting stuck in the sand. If you are sure of your equipment, you can drive on toward Touiba and El Faouar, 30 km. (19 miles) south of Blidet in a beautiful dune landscape. From there a track, still difficult to negotiate, will take you back to Douz (a distance of 40 km., 25 miles) via Sabria and Zaafrane. If caution keeps you from attempting the trek to El Faouar, you could turn off shortly after leaving Blidet down a track to the left leading to Zarsine, a palm grove inhabited by hospitable Blacks. Your arrival will be treated as a great event by all the children and you will see an oasis in its natural state.

The crossing of the Chott el Fejaj is the most difficult of the excursions listed, only by Land Rover and even then you must find out the state of the trails before setting off. Leave Kebili by the motor road leading to Seftimi, a small village with an oasis 15 km. (9 miles) away. Mirages—some very strange—appear before you in the Chott el Fejaj. MC103 winds upward between the mountains of Hachichina on the right and Sif el Laham on the left. On the far side of the Chott, 40 km. (25 miles) away, lies Bir Oum Ali and, soon after, the Gabès-Gafsa highway. Between El Guettar and Gafsa, visit the charming oasis and above all see its oued.

Matmata and Medenine

A mere 40 km. (25 miles) south of Gabès, by MC107 across a plain traversed by many oueds, brings you to the Matmata hills. The first surprise is the hamlet of Tijma, from which a track to the left leads to the village of Hadege, a neighbor of Matmata.

The road winds through bare and wild hills. The new Matmata, which faces the old town, consists of featureless houses surrounded by greenery; the old village of Matmata lies on the other side of the valley, almost hidden in irregular terrain. The approximately 3,000 inhabitants do not have homes above ground, but some ghorfas have been dolled up for tourists; cars and camels are parked in front of apparently nothing. Instead of squares and streets, there is only a lunar landscape, dotted with small craters from which rise wisps of smoke; these are round holes, some 10 meters (33 feet) in diameter and 7 or 8 meters (20 to 25 feet) deep, with hollowed-out rooms opening off the vertical face inside. It was here that Harrison Ford ("Indiana Jones") first came to popular attention in the movie *Star Wars*. The desert and Matmata caves proved the ideal landscape for the movie.

The Arab invasions drove these Berbers underground, and the climate of the interior kept them there. For these extraordinary dwellings are cool during even the most scorching summers. At Matmata you can visit these original homes, where steps or earthen ramps lead down to an open courtyard, off which lie small habitable rooms, storerooms and even chicken houses.

Wells and springs are non-existent. Only cisterns provide water for these underground houses, whose occupants cultivate the slopes of the surrounding craters and the terraced bottoms of the ravines. In the depths, sheltered from the intense heat of summer, women go about their household tasks, spin wool without a spinning wheel in a most primitive way, or weave blankets on their ancestral looms. The rooms are closed off by thick doors made of palm wood. But ever fewer troglodytes persist in living in such craters in the midst of these almost inaccessible hills, at Toujane, Hadege, Temezret, etc. Three marhalas provide food—by all means—and lodgings, but only for the hardy.

From Matmata unpaved MC104 suitable for Land Rovers only crosses east a magnificent mountainous landscape dotted with white marabouts and former Foreign Legion forts to Toujane (27 km., 16 miles). At Toujane the Berbers have moved above ground; the village clings to the side of the mountain like a beehive, houses seeming to be piled on one another. From here the piste descends to meet the Gabès-Medenine road (70 km., 43 miles), affording great views of olive groves to the sea.

After Gabès, GP1 to Jerba crosses a monotonous region before reaching Medenine, once endowed with a whole district of ghorfas—windowless, vaulted cells, built one on top of another, where semi-nomads stored their crops. The largest accumulation of these strange anthills is at Metameur, 6 km. (4 miles) before Medenine. A short trail leads up to the village, perched on a hill. Dangerous mud stairways without hand-holds lead from one level to the next; sometimes even these are missing and you have to climb perilously on stones projecting from the walls. These weird constructions are sometimes four stories high. Today they are used only for storage, but witness what man is capable of devising when he has no building materials.

Jerba

From Medenine two roads lead to the island of Jerba. The shorter, MC108 to the ferry at Jorf, passes within 500 meters (550 yards) of the

Roman ruins of Gighti, above the gulf of Bou Grara: they consist of a paved forum, the podium of a temple with steps leading up to it, and the remains of public buildings and baths. Near the ruins is the charming fishing village of Bou Grara, at the foot of a sandy cliff.

The other road goes through Zarzis, a coastal resort situated in a grove of olive trees planted in widely spaced rows, then continues along the El Kantara causeway, resting on Roman and perhaps Phoenician foundations, 7 km. (4 miles) long.

The island of Jerba appears like a mirage shimmering above the water. Whether or not Ulysses, when he landed on the Isle of the Lotus Eaters 3,000 years ago, tasted here the lotus of forgetfulness, it is certain that the softness of the air scented with oranges, lemons, and pomegranates, the blue of the sky, and the hot sands have properties comparable to those of the sacred flower. The inhabitants of Jerba are the first to benefit. Their nonchalance, even at work, and their serene faces set a contagious example for the harried tourist. Through the centuries, this island oasis was invaded many times by Phoenicians, Greeks, Romans, Moors, Normans from Sicily, and Spaniards. The Turks occupied it in the 16th century. Today it is invaded by tourists of every nationality.

The surface of the island, 514 square kilometers, with a maximum length and width of about 29 km. (18 miles), and a coastline of 125 km. (78 miles), is covered with palm trees and, in the center, with gardens. The native Berbers, outnumbered in season by the hotel personnel from other regions, belong mostly to the austere Kharijite sect, considered heretical by other Moslems. A few Jews are left in the villages of Hara Srira and Hara Kebira, as the majority returned to Israel, whence their ancestors had come either at the time of the Babylonian Captivity in 590 B.C. or, more likely, after the destruction of the Temple in A.D. 70. The Jews of Jerba have retained their individuality, though they have adopted some features of Arab costume. The women rarely allow themselves to be seen; the men wear wide pants gathered at the knee by a black crepe ribbon, a sign of mourning in memory of the Diaspora. This distinguishes them from the rest of the population.

Houmt Souk and the Beaches

The 6,500 inhabitants of Houmt Souk, the island capital, live on tourism and sponge fishing. Their brilliantly white houses in the shape of beehives are called *menzels*. The mosques with domes and squat minarets show Turkish influence. One, with two phallic minarets above the cupolas, is even called Jami-et-Turuk (The Mosque of the Turks). In the souk merchants sell wool and silk fabrics, jewelry and leather goods made on the island. The port teems with large lateen-rigged boats dating from another age. The 13th-century Aragonese fortress was enlarged during the Spanish occupation in 1560, but captured in the same year by the Turkish pirate Dragut, whose Tower of Skulls stood until 1848, when the awesome remains of the massacred Spanish garrison were buried in the Christian cemetery behind the Lotos Hotel. Dragut further strengthened the castle, and for long after it served lesser pirates as a stronghold. Restorations in the early 1970s have brought to light Roman columns and capitals. The Museum of Folk Arts and Crafts (closed on Wednesday) in the Zaouïa of Sidi Zitouni displays costumes, jewelry, and everyday articles which were collected from all over the island before outside influences had altered the traditional culture.

The beach of Sidi Mahrès, to the east of Houmt Souk, is dotted with modern hotels. 20 km. (12½ miles) from Houmt Souk you come to the lighthouse of Tourguennes, pointing the way to the beaches of Seguia and Aghir, with more hotels as well as the building complexes of the Club Méditerranée and the Association Tunisienne de Tourisme et Jeunesse. Seemingly rising straight from the shallow sea, a rectangular fortress, the Borj Castille, is a reminder of the many Spanish conquerors who have passed through Jerba in the course of the centuries—Loria, Montaner, Navarro, and Emperor Charles V's admirals. On the other inland side of the road the largely unexcavated ruins of Roman Meninx with its catacombs are scattered among the olive groves.

At Guellala, 7 km. (4½ miles) from El Kantara, a colony of potters produce in their primitive workshops articles that are crude but quite stylish, including fairly good imitations of Roman oil lamps. Ajim, 11 km. (7 miles) from blue-and-white Guellala is the terminus of the Jorf ferry. The villagers fish for sponges, diving to depths of 10 to 15 meters (30 to 50 feet).

The western shore of the island is less attractive than the others, though there is a lovely beach at Sidi Jemour, half way along the coastal road to Borj Jillij. An alternative is inland MC116 to Houmt Souk (21 km., or 13 miles) passing palm groves, farms and *menzels* with immaculate domes. After Houmt Souk, continue on to Borj Jillij on the northwest tip of the island, either by the Melita road, or by a coastal track that winds among palm groves through an area that is little frequented. At Borj Jillij there is a small harbor with fish traps made of palm leaves, and, if you are lucky, flocks of pink flamingos.

In the interior of the island, menzels stand in olive groves or in gardens irrigated by wells. The formerly exclusively Jewish villages of Hara Kebira, 2 km. (about a mile) from Houmt Souk by the MC117, and Hara Srira, 8 km. (5 miles) away, contain now a majority of Moslem inhabitants, but still only one mosque to nine synagogues. Half a mile out in the olive groves stands one of the most famous and, according to local tradition, oldest Jewish sanctuaries in the world, the *Ghriba,* signifying stranger, after the mysterious female who appeared after a stone had fallen from heaven to mark the site and who helped the builders with miracles. Though generally believed to have been founded by the first arrivals from the Babylonian captivity in the 6th century B.C., the beautifully tiled building, where the ancient guardian opens the tabernacle enshrining yellowed parchment scrolls of the Torah wound round silver rolls, dates only from 1920. The pilgrims congregating each Jewish Passover from as far away as the U.S., are accommodated in the hostelry opposite.

Farther along the same road, El May has a curious mosque whose windowless walls are supported by flying buttresses. There are other pleasant excursions to be made to neighboring villages—to Midoun, with its lively main square, to Sedouikech, where the women wear high conical straw hats reminiscent of ancient Greece, to Cedriane and to Mahboubine with its white menzels set among rich gardens.

A Tour of the Ksour

If you are the adventurous type and don't mind punishment to your backside and the car's inside on some excruciating 100 km. (60 miles), go from Medenine to Tataouine, not on GP19 due south, but turn west to Beni Khedache, then southeast, past several ksour cut into the soft rock of the cliffs or perched on the hillsides, Ksar Jouama, Hadada and Ghomrassen. As you cross these desert regions you will understand the near impossibility of wringing a living from such arid land. Most of the men seek work either in Tunis or in Europe, sending money home.

Leaving Medenine, the MC113 toward Beni Khedache crosses a plain, then climbs up into an eroded jebel. 27 km. (17 miles) from Medenine, on the left, a short road leads to Ksar Jouama, whose ghorfas are visible from a great distance. 15 km. (9 miles) north of Beni Khedache (a modern village built near some cave dwellings) is a small oasis dominated by ghorfas.

Heading south from Beni Khedache toward Ghomrassen on the MC207, after 11 km. (about 7 miles) over a bumpy plateau, a track 4 km. (2½ miles) long leads off to your left to Ksar Kherachefa, whose extraordinary fortified walls, high above the desolate desert landscape, enclose a cluster of ghorfas. Ksar Hadada has been converted into a hotel. The village of Ghomrassen, 6 km. (nearly 4 miles) farther on, lies in part underground, and is encircled by rocky cliffs. An asphalt road 22 km. (about 14 miles) long links the cave-dwellers' villages to Tataouine.

All but the most intrepid should content themselves with an excursion to the last two—and after all one ksar is very much like another—from Tataouine, which can be reached quite painlessly, barring a sandstorm, over 50 paved kilometers (31 miles). Tataouine, with its Monday market, is of little interest but it is close to three easily accessible Berber villages in a harsh and grandiose landscape.

Chenini, 20 km. (12 miles) west, clings like an eagle's nest to the slopes of a rocky hill, housing in its grottos about 1,500 Berbers. Stone walls protect the mouths of their caves. The twisting path to the top affords glimpses into courtyards and cave dwellings, and the summit is crowned with ruinous stone constructions reminiscent of a medieval castle. Further down a stark white mosque of great antiquity, a center for pilgrimages, commands the view over the barren waste to Tataouine. Chenini must at one time have been a great fortress, dominating the valley, one of the gateways from the Sahara to the plains of the south of Tunisia. A whole string of these ksour extends across the mountains of the south, largely founded in Roman times as the *limes Tripolitanus,* a line of forts to contain the nomads of the desert and to prevent them from devastating the fertile coast.

Guermessa, 22 km. (14 miles), can be reached from the Chenini road. The mouths of cave dwellings appear on several hills, one of which is crowned by a tower-shaped outcrop. A roadway paved with large stones leads up to the lower slopes. Douirat, 30 km. (19 miles) southwest (right) of GP19, is somewhat less spectacular.

Toward the Sahara

A few miles south of Tataouine are the almost deserted ruins of the Ksar Beni Barka, whose inhabitants have literally gone to ground. They have dug themselves new homes in the neighboring plain. GP19 to Remada presents no difficulties; between Remada and the military camp at Borj Bourguiba west, the piste crosses a rocky desert traversed by oueds.

South of Remada GP19 is open only to cars which meet the Sahara requirements; a front-wheel-drive car with sandtires, preferably a Land

Rover, shovels to dig out the car, and—unless you are traveling in convoy—a guide.

The even more adventurous MC101 is often obliterated by sand. But unless there are special reasons, and it is difficult to think of any, it is unlikely that anyone would choose to follow the Libyan border south along its bleak 296 km. (185 miles) through Bir Zar and Mechiguig and across the last dunes of the Great Eastern Erg to the eucalyptus, sham-pepper and palm trees of Borj El Khadra on the borders of Tunisia, Algeria and Libya, even if a greenish-blue lake offers a boat ride in the middle of the desert. 13 km. (8 miles) south is Ghadames . . . but that is Libya. An easier border crossing is Dehibat, cave-dwellings below an ancient ksar among violet table-mountains, a mere 50 km. (31 miles) on MC112 southeast of Remada.

PRACTICAL INFORMATION FOR
THE GREAT SOUTH

WHEN TO GO. Jerba and the coast are pleasant all year round and though the sea is uninviting in winter, many hotels feature heated pools. The oases of Tozeur and Nefta are very hot in summer, and few would enjoy an excursion to Kebili and Douz during the hottest season. Don't go south of Remada between June and September. A hot, desiccating wind blows in the south during the month of August although the worst sandstorms occur March through May.

Festivals. March: Berber Festival, Tatouine. **April:** El Jezz (Sheep shearing), Medenine; **May/June:** Regional Music and Popular Arts, Gabès and Gafsa. Purebreed horse show, Meknessy. **June:** Festival of the Ksour, Ghoumrassen, Tatouine. **July:** Regional Poetry, Sidi Bouzid; Horsemanship festival, Medenine; Sidi Ahmed Zarrouk Celebration, Gafsa. **July/August:** Ulysses Festival, Jerba; Sponge Festival, Zarzis. **November:** Popular Song, Gafsa; Sahara Festival, Douz. **December,** Oasis Festival, Tozeur. Sahara Festival, Douz.

GETTING ABOUT. By Plane. Tunis-Jerba, flights lasting 45 minutes, all year round. Jerba (Melita Airport) is equipped for international charters, and there are several scheduled services a week from European destinations in season. Tunis-Air offices in Jerba at Houmt Souk. Tozeur's airport, on the edge of the Sahara, is 40 minutes' flight from Tunis.

By Train. One line links Sfax via Gafsa and Metlaoui in about 6 hours; a branch goes from Metlaoui to Redeyef, which can also be reached from Kasserine. The main line links Sfax and Gabès in 2h. 30; none by any means fast.

By Car. Some distances—Tunis–Gafsa, 360 km. (224 miles); Tunis–Gabès, 390 km. (242 miles); Gafsa–Tozeur, 90 km. (56 miles); Gafsa–Gabès, 150 km. (93 miles); Gabès–Kebili, 115 km. (71 miles); Gabès–Medenine, 76 km. (47 miles); Gabès–Jerba (Houmt Souk) by ferry from Jorf, 145 km. (90 miles); Gabès–Jerba (Houmt Souk) by the causeway, 190 km. (118 miles); Medenine–Tatouine, 50 km. (31 miles); Tatouine–Remada, 81 km. (50 miles); Tataouine–Borj–Khadra, 377 km. (235 miles).

Car Hire. The main agencies have representatives in Jerba, Gabès and Zarzis.

By Bus. The southern towns of Tunisia are connected with the rest of the country by regular bus lines. Bus stations in Tunis, 74 Ave. de Carthage; in Gafsa, Pl.

Bourguiba; in Gabès, Rue Dziri and Blvd. Farhat Hached; in Houmt Souk Société Al Djazira. *Note:* The Tunis–Tripoli bus goes through Gabès and Medenine.

Group Taxis. Fairly numerous from Tunis; gare routière for Gabès and Gafsa, for the former also Garage Ayachi, Bab Souika; for Jerba Garage Ayachi and Garage Soudan, 6 Rue Soudan. Services between the southern towns infrequent.

Ferries. Besides the causeway, ferries from Jorf connect Jerba with the mainland, a picturesque journey, especially at sunset, of about 20 minutes. There is also a service between Gabès and Jerba which shortens greatly communications between the two centers.

HOTELS AND RESTAURANTS

Douz. (Area code 05.) *Mahari* (E), tel. 95 149. New luxurious hotel in the middle of the desert with 100 rooms, pool, nightclub, and all comforts; operated by Iberotel chain. *Marhala* (I), tel. 95 315. 20 showers to 50 rooms. *Les Roses des Sables* (I), tel. 95 336. 45 fairly comfortable rooms. *Saharien* (I), tel. 95 339. 110 rooms, 53 showers.

Gabès. (Area code 05.) *Chems* (M), tel. 70 547. 275 rooms, only a few facing the sea in this noisy, package-tour bungalow complex. Pool, aquatic bar, on the beach; food could be better; camel riding. *Oasis* (M), tel. 70 381. 82 airconditioned rooms. No pool, but quieter. Both are affected by air and sea pollution.

In town: *Nejib* (M), tel. 71 686. 56 rooms, 4 suites. *Tacapes* (M), tel. 70 700. 25 rooms with bath or shower; restaurant. *Atlantique* (I), tel. 70 034. 48 rooms. *Chela* (I), tel. 70 442. 50 bungalows. Pool, but at town fringe, far from sea.

Restaurants. *El Mazar* (E). *Casino Plage* (M), seafood. *L'Oasis* (I).

Gafsa. (Area code 06.) *Jugurtha Palace* (E), tel. 21 300. 78 airconditioned rooms. 3 km. (2 miles) from the town at the foot of a bare jebel. With garden, tennis, and large pool. *Maamoun* (E), tel. 22 740 or 22 501. 46 airconditioned rooms; completely renovated. Central; pool. *Gafsa* (M), tel. 22 676. 338 rooms. *La République* (I), tel. 21 807. 20 rooms.

Kebili. (Area code 05.) *Borj des Autruches* (M), tel. 90 233. 60 rooms.

Ksar Hadada. *Gorfa* inn (I). 26 converted rooms (even some duplex ghorfas with private bath) for an exotic night.

Ksar Ouled Dabbab. 9 km. (5 miles) south of Tataouine. *Ghorfa* inn (I). 45 cells converted into primitive accommodations. Communal sanitation a health hazard. Terrace overlooking the valley of the oued.

Mareth. (Area code 05.) *Relais du Golf* (I), tel. 36 135. 14 rooms.

Matmata. (Area code 05.) *Matmata Hotel* (M), tel. 30 006. 32 rooms. *Marhala* (I), tel. 30 015. 140 beds. Run by the Tunisian Touring Club. *Relais des Berbères* (I), tel. 30 024. 80 beds, least comfortable. *Sidi Driss* (I). tel. 30 005. 130 beds. These cave dwellings connected by tunnels are only for those who must try everything. They are very primitive—mostly 8-bedded dormitories, candlelight and communal plumbing—but certainly original.

Medenine. (Area code 05.) *Agil* (M), tel. 40 151. 14 airconditioned rooms. *Sahara* (I), tel. 40 007. 20 rooms. In town, if your car breaks down.

Restaurant. *Sahara* (M).

Nefta. (Area code 06.) *Sahara Palace* (L), tel. 57 046. 100 airconditioned rooms, 9 suites. Above the oasis, with attractive decor, admirable view, and excellent service. Olympic size pool; hairdresser, disco, etc. *Marhala* (I), tel. 57 027. 35 rooms, 8 showers. Run by the Tunisian Touring Club; lots of local color. *Mirage* (I), tel. 57 041. 26 rooms. Near the viewing point for the oasis. *Les Nomades* (I), tel. 57 052. Tent village.

Restaurant. *Des Sources* (M), in the palm grove.

Sidi Bouzid. (Area code 06.) *El Horchani* (I), tel. 30 855. 20 rooms.

Tamerza. (Area code 06.) *Les Cascades* (I), tel. 45 365. 50 rooms, communal showers.

Tataouine. (Area code 05.) *Les Gazelles* (M), tel. 60 009. 23 airconditioned rooms.

Tozeur. (Area code 06.) *Continental* (E), tel. 50 411. 150 rooms. Large pool. *El Hafsi* (E), tel. 50 966. 62 rooms. Restaurant, nightclub, and pool. *Ras El Ain* (E), tel. 50 811. 60 rooms. This new hotel has a restaurant, pool, sports facilities, and nightclub. *Club Méditerranée* (M). In airconditioned building; pool. *Oasis* (M), tel. 50 522. 55 airconditioned rooms. Built around pool; gardens. *Sunos* (M), tel. 57 533. 125 rooms. Operated by the French chain of Caravan Serail, this new hotel has 2 restaurants, large pool, sports facilities and nightclub. *El Jerid* (I), tel. 50 488. 50 rooms. Pool.

Restaurant. *Le Petit Prince* (M).

Zarzis. (Area Code 05.) All these hotels are geared to the needs of groups, to the neglect of the independent traveler. *Sangho Club* (M), tel. 80 124. 194 airconditioned rooms in central block, and 222 bungalows. *Oamarit* (M), tel. 80 770. 422 bungalows in a vacation village. *Zarzis* (M), tel. 80 160. 225 rooms, 3 airconditioned suites; warm thermal pool. *Zephir* (M), tel. 81 026. 200 rooms. *Zita* (M), tel. 80 246. 600 rooms in large bungalows. Good pool.

HOTELS AND RESTAURANTS FOR JERBA ISLAND
(Area code 05)

None of the large hotels which stand in their own gardens along the beaches of Sidi Mahres and D'Ahgir on the east coast is (L) but the (E)'s are up to the expected standard. This is not always the case in the lower categories, where food, maintenance and service vary unpredictably from one season to another. Two distinct architectural styles predominate: the large block with balconies to each room, and the bungalow type, sometimes of the pretty local variation of *menzels* (irregular conglomerations of dazzling white cubes topped with cupolas and flat roofs and centered around flowering patios).

All the hotels offer swimming pools, nautical sports, tennis, horse and camel riding; discos and folkloric evenings.

Deluxe

Hasdrubel (L), tel. 57 730. Scheduled to open in mid-1990, this 215-room hotel boasts 2 restaurants, covered and outdoor pools, fitness room, and nightclub.

Expensive

Abou Nawas (tel. 57 022). 225 rooms, 9 suites in a vaguely T-shaped block between a lovely beach and a palm grove. Spacious rooms but patchy service.

El Menzel (tel. 57 070). 140 rooms. Public rooms in a central building and 10 pavilions, each with 14 rooms built around a courtyard on two levels with a treacherous staircase between and a bath below; also a secluded terrace for private sunbathing. Beach rocky but a well-sited pool. Restaurant specialty is *pâté de poisson chaud*. For long Jerba's best.

Palm Beach (tel. 57 350). 200 rooms. Two restaurants, nightclub, thermal pool.

Ulysse Palace (tel. 57 422). 126 rooms. Large block and closest to Houmt Souk. Recently refurbished, this hotel now has a very chic appearance, with large pool and pleasant gardens.

Moderate

El Bousten (tel. 57 200). 183 rooms. Huge airconditioned building. Recent criticisms of the hotel have ranged from the condition of the napkins to the state of the pool.

Jerba Holidays (tel. 57 807). With 300 beds in 4 buildings, this new holiday village features a restaurant, pool, sports facilities, and nightclub.

Robinson Club (tel. 57 805). Slated to open mid-1990, this new holiday village contains 608 beds in bungalows on the beach with watersports facilities.

Les Sirènes (tel. 57 266). 122 rooms. Long low building with many rooms facing the sea. Good beach; large arcaded terrace surrounds the thermal pool.

Inexpensive

El Jazira (tel. 57 300). 120 rooms, most in bungalows. Thermal pool.

Medina (tel. 57 233). 193 rooms, 117 with bath, remainder with shower. Excellent beach, mini-pool.

Meninx (tel. 57 051). 160 rooms. Arranged in several blocks with bungalows in the grounds. Well-maintained and spacious foyer, plus pleasant bar/nightclub. Congested dining room.

Club Tanit (tel. 57 132). 300 rooms, **Sidi Slim** (tel. 57 023), 161 bungalows, and **Yati** (tel. 57 016), 36 rooms, are on the Midoun beach to the south; closed in winter.

Houmt Souk. *Arischa* (I), tel. 50 384. 35 rooms. *Dar Faiza* (I), tel. 50 083. 24 rooms. *Hajji* (I), tel. 50 630. 50 rooms, some airconditioned. *Nozha* (I), tel 50 381. 30 rooms. *Sinbad* (I), tel. 50 047. 23 rooms.

Dar Jerba. Among the spacious hotel grounds on the northeast coast, the Dar Jerba is a monument to mass tourism boasting everything from cinemas and casinos to congress halls, hotels and summer camps. With accommodations for 2,400, it is Tunisia's largest tourist complex.

To explore the complex you might hire one of the canopied bicyclettes. The complex consists of four separate hotels, the *Dahlia, Nardjess, Zahra* and *Yasmina,* each with its own reception staff and foyer, and with a central block housing essential services (tel. 57 191.) Rooms are of three classes and distinctions there are aplenty. All huddled in the central courts, the standard rooms, not airconditioned, are uncomfortably small and stifling. Only slightly better, though with airconditioning and a ceiling dome, are the semi-luxe, boasting vaulted roofs and a special door for room service so that your less affluent neighbors won't feel resentment. And towering above all are the 13 luxe duplex apartments, dubiously luxurious with downstairs baths and upstairs beds and a terrace from which to observe the life of your inferiors; yet rightly the official classification denies the luxury label. Tucked away is the *Hôtel des Enfants,* where 87 vociferous small ones can spend a vacation exploring their holiday megalopolis.

Now to the essential services—a large and very crowded standard-class diningroom above a charming coffee shop where only the luxe can dine at no extra cost. A Congress Hall, a Tunisian restaurant (luxe only), so many shops that you need never see the natives for your souvenirs, and Turkish baths and *cafés maures* for relaxation. The casino is a great domed chamber built above a reflecting pool, and last, high above the sea, the *Pacha Restaurant* for the luxe—all chic and white and tiles and stainless steel with cupolas which open to the sky. In the midst of all is the main swimming pool with several others scattered about, including one Olympic size. And beyond, near the entrance, is the radio station—three programs and news on the hour in four languages—and a bar for the drivers of the cars which can be rented to explore the nearby palm groves.

There are two *Club Méditerranée* villages on the island. *Jerba la Douce* (E), tel. 57 129, open all the year, offers luxurious accommodation in 330 bungalows; huge pool near the beach. All sporting facilities and good evening entertainment; everything for elegant communal living.

Open in summer only, *Jerba la Fidèle* (M), tel. 57 028, is much simpler; 400 *paillotes*, round thatched huts with the roof of palm fronds, for a rustic outdoor holiday; good food and an excellent beach. Varied evening entertainment.

Restaurants. Eating out is restricted by the long intervals between the buses connecting the beach hotels with Houmt Souk; the line stops rather early. Taxis are expensive.

Haroun (E), good seafood in the port. *De l'Ile* (M). Among the disco-restaurants along the coastal road, *Boomerang* (M) and *Minaret Club* (M) near the Tourgeness lighthouse hardly differ from the hotel-grown variety.

EXCURSIONS. Jerba is the ideal base for exploring the south of Tunisia. Excursions by Land Rover: day trips to Tataouine, Chenini and the ghorfa country; to Gabès, Matmata and Toujane; two-day trips to Gabès, Kebili and Douz with the night spent at Douz and also to Tozeur and Nefta with the night spent at Tozeur. The regimentation of these trips is severe. For example, you would arrive at the oasis at dusk and visit it before dinner, which in turn is followed by a display of native dancing. You breakfast at seven and digest it by going for a ride on a camel, after which you immediately leave. Moreover, though only eight passengers can fit comfortably into a Land Rover, some travel agents sometimes cram in as many as eleven—which makes a terrible day. A longer excursion to the south includes three days camping in the desert and plenty of camel riding.

The Club Méditerranée offers two unique expeditions to its members from May to October.

One, the aptly-named Light of Islam trip, is a bus journey the length of the country taking in Gabès, Matmata, Tozeur, Tunis and the holy city of Kairouan. The trip lasts eight days and accommodations are in hotels.

The second trip, the very much more rugged Nomad's Land, delves deep into the Sahara. A Land Rover takes you south from Jerba through Berber villages to the western Erg, where a three-day camel ride, sleeping in tents at night, awaits you. This trip also lasts eight days.

SHOPPING. The hotel shops as well as the O.N.A.T. shops, Blvd. Farhat Hached, Gabès, and in Houmt Souk are well stocked with rugs, embroidered articles, Saharan costumes, etc.

In the south, especially at Tozeur but also at Douz, you will be offered gazelle skins (it is against the law to hunt them).

At Nefta in the café overlooking the Corbeille there is a wide choice of sand roses. Big sponges are sold at the ferry landing Ajim on Jerba.

The souks of Houmt Souk are worth a visit; antique dealers there display "Bedouin dressing tables" (small pieces of furniture with mirrors and drawers), marriage chests and sandalwood sea-chests. The Société des Arts et Antiquités offers for sale, in addition to the items already mentioned, turtle shells, oil lamps from the 1880s, flintlocks, etc. (you have to bargain).

For English-language papers, books, etc., *El Kitab*, off the souk at Houmt Souk, 2 days late, magazines more.

Interesting Markets. On Jerba, in Houmt Souk Monday and Thursday; in Midoun, Friday. In Tataouine, Thursday. In Douz, Thursday.

TOURIST OFFICES. Douz: Office National du Tourisme and Syndicat d'Initiative, Rue Farhat Hached (tel. 90 930). **Gabès:** O.N.T.T. and Syndicat d'Initiative, Place de la Libération (tel. 70 254). **Gafsa:** O.N.T.T., Place des Piscines (tel. 21 664). **Jerba:** O.N.T.T., Houmt Souk (tel. 50 016); Syndicat d'Initiative, Midoun (tel. 57 320). **Nefta:** Ave. Habib Bourguiba (tel. 57 184). **Tozeur:** O.N.T.T., Ave. Aboul Kacem Chebbi (tel. 50 503); Syndicat d'Initiative, Place Ibn Chaabat (tel. 50 034). **Zarzis:** O.N.T.T., Route des Hotels (tel. 80 445).

For permission to travel with a private car south of Remada apply to the Office National du Tourisme, 1 Ave. Mohammed V in Tunis (tel. 341 077).

VOCABULARY

This vocabulary is divided into two parts. In the first we list useful phrases in French, since this is the foreign language universally understood in the Maghreb, and one which the visitor is more likely to be able to use than Arabic. The second section is a glossary of the Arab or Berber words that appear in the text.

Miscellaneous

English	French
Good morning	Bonjour
Good evening	Bonsoir
Good night	Bonne nuit
Goodbye	Au revoir
How are you?	Comment allez-vous?
Mr	Monsieur
Mrs—Miss	Madame—Mademoiselle
Thank you	Merci
Pardon me	Pardon
Do you understand?	Comprenez-vous?
Do you speak English/French?	Parlez-vous anglais/français?
Bring me	Apportez-moi
No, thanks	Non, Merci
Very well	Très bien
How much?	Combien?
It is too expensive	C'est trop cher
Today	Aujourd'hui
Tomorrow	Demain
Yesterday	Hier
Morning	Le matin
Noon	A midi
Afternoon	L'après-midi
Night	La nuit
Here—There	Ici—Là
Hot	Chaud
Cold	Froid
Heavy	Lourd
Light	Léger
Long	Long
Short	Court
Red	Rouge
Blue	Bleu
Black	Noir
White	Blanc
Green	Vert

In Hotels and Restaurants

Bring me my luggage	Apportez-moi mes bagages
Bathroom	Salle de bain

English	French
Waiter	Garçon
Breakfast	Petit déjeuner
Lunch—Dinner	Déjeuner—Dîner
Meat	Viande
Fish	Poisson
Egg	Oeuf
Water	Eau
Ice	Glace
Wine	Vin
Salt—Pepper	Sel—Poivre
Prepare the bill for me	Préparez-moi l'addition

In the Street

Taxi	Taxi
Take me to the hotel	Conduisez-moi à l'hôtel
Wait for me here	Attendez-moi ici
Stop	Arrêtez
Look out	Attention
Right	Droite
Left	Gauche
Straight ahead	Tout droit

Numbers

One	Un
Two	Deux
Three	Trois
Four	Quatre
Five	Cinq
Six	Six
Seven	Sept
Eight	Huit
Nine	Neuf
Ten	Dix
A hundred	Cent
A thousand	Mille

GLOSSARY OF ARAB AND BERBER WORDS

Abd-el- . . . or Abdel	Arabic name: servant of . . . (used in connection with one of God's 99 adjectives; e.g. Abd-el-Krim = Servant-of-the-Generous).
Adel (plural: adoul)	notary, lawyer
Aguedal or agdal	sheet of water, ornamental tank
Aguelmane	mountain lake
Aïd	holy day
Aïn	source
Aït	children of = a tribe: Aït Ourir, etc.
Akbar	elder
Allah	God
Amogdul	safe anchorage
Arba	four or Wednesday (Souk-el-Arba = market of the-fourth day)
Atai benaana	mint tea
Azrou	rock

Bab	monumental gate
Babouche(s)	Moroccan slipper(s)
Balek	attention
Bali	ancient (Fez-el-Bali = Old Fez)
Baraka	divine protection
Ben	son of . . . (Yusuf-ben-Tashfin = Joseph, son of Tashfin)
Beni	sons of = a tribe
Bled	countryside
Bordj	high-lying small fort
Bstila (or Pastilla)	stuffed pancake (kind of savory *millefeuille*)
Caftan	sophisticated cassock-like woman's dress, usually close-fitting and often superbly embroidered
Caïd	high official, mayor of a township
Charia	Avenue
Chleuh	High Atlas and Sous Valley Berber
Chott	salt flat
Choukhara	Moroccan leather holdall, worn over the shoulder
Couscous	semolina
Dahir	law, order in council
Daïet or dayat	mountain lake
Dar	castle
Diffa	tribal banquet
For words beginning "Dj" see under "J"	
Douar	small village
Erg	desert of sand dunes
Fondouk	caravanserai
Foum	narrow pass, gorge
Ghorfa	vaulted storage chamber
Guelta	watering place for nomads
Had	one or Sunday
Hadj	epithet given to people who accomplished their pilgrimage to Mecca
Haik	tentlike white garment worn by Moslem women
Halqah	council of 12 clerics
Hammam	bathing establishment
Hammada	stony desert
Harira	soup
Horm	place of asylum
Ibn	son of
Ifri	abyss, pit
Imam	religious leader
Imi	defile
Inch'Allah	if God wills
Jamaâ (Jemaâ, Djamaâ)	assembly (mostly for prayers, hence mosque); Friday
Jebel (Jbel, Djebel)	mountain
Jedid (Jdid, Djedid)	new (Fez-Jedid = the newer part of Old Fez)
Jellaba	men's garment, shapeless, with sleeves and hood; often homespun and striped
Jenina (Djenina)	garden
Jenoun (Djenoun)	spirit, gremlin

Kab el ghzal	Gazelle horn (almond crescent)
Kasbah	citadel (in the north): fortified house or granary (in the south)
Kebir	great
Kesrah	Moroccan bread
Khatib	prayer leader
Khemis	five or Thursday (Souk-el-Khemis = Thursday market)
Kissaria	commercial center in the medina
Kouba	small, whitewashed mausoleum of a saintly man
Ksar (plural: ksour)	fortified village
Lalla	title of a woman of noble birth
Litham	what most Europeans and Americans call a 'Yashmak'; a form of double veil
Maasra	oil press
Maghrib or Maghreb	where the sun sets, i.e. Northwest Africa (nowadays used to denote Tunisia, Algeria and Morocco)
Maghzen	government, administration
Mahakma	Moslem courthouse
Mechoui	mutton cooked over embers
Mechouar	royal enclosure
Medersa (Medresa, Medrassa)	Moslem law and theological college
Medina	medieval part of a city
Mehari—meharist	buff-colored, fast dromedary used by the Blue Men— trooper of the Camel Corps
Mellah	Jewish quarter of the medina
Mezyan	very good
Mihrab	alcove-type recess in a mosque, indicating direction of Mecca
Mokkadem	government agent
Moukkala	heavily-encrusted Moroccan rifle
Moulay	sovereign
Moussem	pilgrimage followed by festivities
Oued	river
Ouled	tribe (e.g. Ouled Teima)
Pasha	title of person of high rank
Reg	rocky desert plain
Riad	patio or palace garden
Ribat	fortified monastery or gathering before a holy war
Salaam	peace, used as greeting
Sebkhet (Sebkha)	saltwater marsh
Sebt	seven or Saturday
Seghir	small
Sheik	chieftain
Shoukran	thank you
Skala	fortification facing the sea
Souk or suk	trading-place (in a medina): market day (in small country towns)
Tajin (plural: touajen)	meat dish cooked slowly in sauce
Taleb (plural: tolba)	student in medersa
Tarboosh	red fez
Tizi	high mountain pass

Tleta	three or Tuesday
Tnine	two or Monday
Touareg	desert nomads of Berber origin (the Blue People or Touaregs)
Vizier	minister, governor
Zalagh	goat
Zankat (or Zenkat)	street
Zaouïa	seat of a religious fraternity
Zellig	Moorish decorative tile
Zitoun	olive grove

INDEX

In this Index **H** indicates Hotels & other accommodations,
R indicates Restaurants

GENERAL INFORMATION

Auto rental, 9–10
Auto travel, 9–10

Calendars, 2–3
Camping and caravanning, 8
Climate, 1–2
Clothing, 4
Costs, 1
Credit cards, 6
Currency and exchange, 1, 5–6
Customs, 5, 10–11

Drinks, 8
Driving hints, 10

Exchange rates, 1

Food and drink, 52–59

Health certificates, 5
History of North Africa, 24–51
Holidays, 2–3
Hotels, 6–7

Information sources, 3–4
Introduction to the Maghreb, 12–23

Language, 6

Medical services, 8
Medicines and toiletries, 4
Money, 5
Mosques, 9
Museums and archeological sites, 9

Packing and clothing, 4
Passports & visas, 4–5
Photography, 9

Religious festivals, 2
Road conditions, 10

Shopping, 9

Theft, 9
Time, 6
Tipping, 8
Tours, 3–4
Travel agents, 3–4
Travel documents, 4–5

Vacation villages, 7–8
Visas, 5

MOROCCO

Practical Information

Air travel
  in Morocco, 79
  to Morocco, 73, 74
Auto itinerary, 71
Auto rental, 81
Auto travel
  in Morocco, 80–81
  to Morocco, 74

Beaches, 77
Bus travel
  in Morocco, 79
  to Morocco, 73

Car routes, 79–80
Climate, 70–71
Costs, 70

Geographical

ALGERIA

Practical Information

Geographical

TUNISIA

Practical Information

Geographical

Fodor's Travel Guides

U.S. Guides

Alaska
Arizona
Boston
California
Cape Cod
The Carolinas & the
  Georgia Coast
The Chesapeake
  Region
Chicago
Colorado
Disney World & the
  Orlando Area

Florida
Hawaii
The Jersey Shore
Las Vegas
Los Angeles
Maui
Miami & the Keys
New England
New Mexico
New Orleans
New York City
New York City
  (Pocket Guide)

New York State
Pacific North Coast
Philadelphia
The Rockies
San Diego
San Francisco
San Francisco
  (Pocket Guide)
The South
Texas
USA
The Upper Great
  Lakes Region

Virgin Islands
Virginia & Maryland
Waikiki
Washington, D.C.

Foreign Guides

Acapulco
Amsterdam
Australia
Austria
The Bahamas
The Bahamas
  (Pocket Guide)
Baja & the Pacific
  Coast Resorts
Barbados
Belgium &
  Luxembourg
Bermuda
Brazil
Budget Europe
Canada
Canada's Atlantic
  Provinces
Cancun, Cozumel,
  Yucatan Peninsula
Caribbean
Central America
China

Eastern Europe
Egypt
Europe
Europe's Great
  Cities
France
Germany
Great Britain
Greece
The Himalayan
  Countries
Holland
Hong Kong
India
Ireland
Israel
Italy
Italy's Great Cities
Jamaica
Japan
Kenya, Tanzania,
  Seychelles
Korea

Lisbon
London
London Companion
London
  (Pocket Guide)
Madrid & Barcelona
Mexico
Mexico City
Montreal &
  Quebec City
Morocco
Munich
New Zealand
Paris
Paris (Pocket Guide)
Portugal
Puerto Rico
  (Pocket Guide)
Rio de Janeiro
Rome
Saint Martin/
  Sint Maarten
Scandinavia

Scandinavian Cities
Scotland
Singapore
South America
South Pacific
Southeast Asia
Soviet Union
Spain
Sweden
Switzerland
Sydney
Thailand
Tokyo
Toronto
Turkey
Vienna
Yugoslavia

Special-Interest Guides

Bed & Breakfast
  Guide to the Mid-
  Atlantic States

Bed & Breakfast
  Guide to New
  England
Cruises & Ports
  of Call

A Shopper's Guide
  to London
Health & Fitness
  Vacations
Shopping in Europe

Skiing in North
  America
Sunday in New York
Touring Europe